the Unofficial Guide® to Hawaii

1st Edition

Also available from IDG Books Worldwide:

the Unofficial Guide® to Hawaii

1st Edition

Lance Tominaga

Every effort has been made to ensure the accuracy of information through-out this book. Bear in mind, however, that prices, schedules, etc., are constantly changing. Readers should always verify information before making final plans.

IDG Books Worldwide, Inc.
An International Data Group Company
919 E. Hillsdale Blvd., Suite 400
Foster City, CA 94404

Copyright © 2000 by Lance Tominaga
1st edition

Produced by Menasha Ridge Press

MACMILLAN is a registered trademark of Macmillan General Reference USA, Inc., a wholly owned subsidiary of IDG Books Worldwide, Inc.

UNOFFICIAL GUIDE is a registered trademark of Macmillan General Reference USA, Inc., a wholly owned subsidiary of IDG Books Worldwide, Inc.

ISBN   0-02-863073-4
ISSN   1521-494X

Manufactured in the United States of America

10 9 8 7 6 5 4 3 2 1

Contents

List of Maps

Acknowledgments

I extend a big *mahalo* to Wendy Wakabayashi, Paul Philpott, Robert Mabesa, and Maureen Tominaga for their assistance in the research of this book. And many thanks to Bob Sehlinger, Rachel Pearce Anderson, Steve Jones, Christi Stanforth, Annie Long, Holly Cross, Jenny Tice, and Jeff Goodwin, the pros who managed to transform all this effort into a book.

About Our Authors

Lance Tominaga is the former editor of *ALOHA Magazine*, which for 21 years brought the best of Hawaii into homes and offices throughout the United States, Canada, and other parts of the world. In his ten years with the publication, he spent time on every major Hawaiian island and wrote features on everything from a charming little art community on the Big Island to Mister "Tiny Bubbles" himself, Don Ho. In the process, he gained an immeasurable appreciation for the beauty and uniqueness of the Islands' lands and cultures. At the same time, as a lifelong resident of the Islands (on the island of Oahu, to be exact), he knows full well the price of living in paradise and has always been forthright in passing on Hawaii travel–related advice.

Betty Fullard-Leo wrote our dining chapter and has been sampling Hawaii restaurants ever since she arrived in the Islands in 1962. After graduating from the University of Hawaii's school of journalism in 1980, she worked as associate editor of *Aloha Magazine* and *RSVP* magazine for more than six years; she then edited *Pacific Art & Travel* magazine before turning to full-time freelance writing in 1990. She writes regularly about food for *Hawaii Magazine* and also contributes articles about Hawaii destinations, attractions, activities, restaurants, culture, and lifestyle to numerous publications, including *Los Angeles Times, Westways AAA,* and *Spirit of Aloha* magazine.

the Unofficial Guide® to Hawaii

1st Edition

Introduction

The Pearls (and Perils) of Paradise

Hawaii. No sooner does the word roll off your tongue than you're swept away, far away, to visions of an idyllic tropical Eden: Tall, swaying palm trees lining crescent-shaped white-sand beaches. Shimmering waterfalls nestled deep within misty, evergreen valleys. Spectacular sunsets, with the sky lit in brilliant shades of orange, red, purple, and gold. Lovely hula maidens dancing with graceful precision. Handsome beach boys taking on monstrous ocean waves.

Rest assured, you are not alone. Every day, thousands of people dream about the Hawaiian Islands, whether it is from behind a work-cluttered desk at a Fortune 500 company or from behind the wheel of a checkered taxi cab. There is, even in today's shrinking world, a special magic about this one-of-a-kind destination.

But is it *truly* magic? Or merely an illusion?

Strip away the veil of Hawaii's natural beauty and you'll find many of the same problems that burden most other modern-day locales. Here you'll find a struggling economy, crime, overpopulation, and other tough community issues. For the visitor, there are the added pitfalls of steep hotel rates, unfamiliar language use and customs, unscrupulous "tourist traps," and an overwhelming number of available activities and attractions with too little time to enjoy them all.

We tell you this up front because, as the old adage goes, to be forewarned is to be forearmed. And that's what this guidebook is all about. We're here to present the true Hawaii to you so you can enjoy its many pearls while avoiding the perils.

The good news is, with a little *kokua* (help), every problem frequently encountered by visitors can be overcome. In this guide, we'll tell you how to find the best deals on hotel rooms, with accommodations to fit every budget. We'll provide insights on local customs and protocol and teach you enough Hawaiian words and phrases to make you feel like a *kama'aina* (longtime or native-born Hawaii resident). We'll separate the attractions, activities, and restaurants that are well worth your time from the businesses that are simply out to get their slice of the tourism pie. And yes, we'll even suggest a few itineraries, and give you all the information you need to customize your own!

Along the way, we'll answer questions we get all the time from prospective visitors to Hawaii, such as:

- When is the best time to go?
- Which islands should we visit?
- Where are the best beaches?
- What hiking trails are recommended for young families?
- Who are Hawaii's "must-see" entertainers?
- How did these wonderful places get their names?

For the first-time visitor, we understand that the desire to experience Hawaii comes with several natural apprehensions and uncertainties. No matter where you're coming from, after all, a Hawaiian vacation isn't cheap. You want to make the most of your time in the Islands. You want to be able to fit into and immerse yourself in the local culture. You want to be at the right places at the right times, taking in the very best Hawaii has to offer. This book will help you do these things.

For those of you who have been to the Aloha State before, perhaps even many times over, this book will help you uncover many new gems of information. Like everything else these days, the Hawaiian landscape is always changing, constantly evolving. There is always something new to be discovered in paradise, and within these pages are insights on the very latest—and future—developments.

So mix your favorite tropical drink, plop down on the sofa, and start your Hawaiian adventure on the right foot—by reading *The Unofficial Guide to Hawaii*. You'll discover that, yes, Hawaii can be everything you've dreamed of. As for separating the magic from illusion, well, just leave that to us.

From us to you, *E komo mai!* Welcome!

About This Guide

As you might expect, there have been many guidebooks written about the Hawaiian Islands over the years. Some are pictorial in nature, providing beautiful images of the Aloha State and little else. Others include a tedious stream of information yet offer virtually nothing in the way of practical and useful advice. And most unfortunate of all, the typical Hawaii guide-book merely echoes the public relations slants of groups like the Hawaii Visitors & Convention Bureau, with enough "spin" to inspire a Samoan fire-knife dance routine. This book strives to be different.

Our goal at *Unofficial Guides* is to be more prescriptive than descriptive, going the extra mile to help you, the reader, make the most informed decisions possible. For example, it's simple enough to tell you that the Bishop Museum is open daily from 9 a.m. to 5 p.m., but when is the best time to go? How much walking is involved, how are the exhibits displayed, and will they keep the kids interested? And most important of all, is the museum really worth the price of admission?

Trust us. There are so many different things to do and see in Hawaii, and on different islands, that you could never possibly experience everything in one visit. We don't recommend that you even attempt such an undertaking; one of the main reasons to go to the Islands, after all, is to relax and enjoy some leisurely beach time! Instead, read this guide, which is specially designed to give you all the information you need—in a concise, easy-to-read format—to plan the optimal Hawaiian experience.

Included in this book is information on all the "little things" (which aren't so little when you discover the need for them) that other guides typically overlook: parking recommendations, accessibility to rest rooms, driving distances, avoiding traffic jams, and so on. Enough minor inconveniences can add up to a major vacation letdown, and this guide aims to eliminate all of that.

The Unofficial Guide to Hawaii is written with the first-time visitor in mind, understanding all the concerns and anxieties of planning that first Hawaiian vacation. "Can I leave the coat and tie at home?" "Should I visit the *Arizona* Memorial?" "Are the natives friendly to tourists?" These are perfectly natural questions to ask, and you'll find the answers within these pages.

Finally, in writing this guide, one of our goals was to effectively capture—and then convey—the myriad colors and flavors of the Hawaiian Islands. In other words, we promise you'll have some fun along the way!

How *Unofficial Guides* Are Different

From the very beginning, the people behind *Unofficial Guides* have worked diligently to deliver honest, straight-up reviews of major destinations and U.S. cities. For this book, for example, the authors themselves carefully researched every bit of information, filling short stacks of notebooks and compiling enough data to fill an oversized file cabinet.

Special care was taken to conduct evaluations from the visitor's point of view. In other words, while the Maui Ocean Center solicits oohs and aahs for its 750,000-gallon open ocean tank, we spent time going over the layout of the facility and made notes on the amount of time needed to visit the center, the locations of rest rooms and snack shops, and the overall friendliness of the staff.

Our philosophy on our research and evaluation process boils down to this: If it matters to you, then it matters to us. We try to cover all the bases.

Special Features

The *Unofficial Guide* includes the following special features:

- Insightful introductions to each of Hawaii's eight main islands, highlighting the unique character and features each possesses.
- A retracing of Hawaii's fascinating history, from its early settlers and the Kamehameha dynasty to statehood and today's political climate.
- A thorough presentation on local customs and protocol. Just because you're a visitor, after all, doesn't mean you can't fit right in with the local culture.
- Information to settle once and for all the questions—either vital or just plain interesting—many visitors have about the Islands. For example, where on Kauai was Elvis Presley's movie *Blue Hawaii* filmed? Is it really bad luck to take home lava rocks from Hawaii Volcanoes National Park? Is the *humuhumunukunukuapuaʻa* really Hawaii's official state fish? We'll separate fact from fiction.
- A walk-through (or is it a ride-through?) of the best transportation options in the state, including Oahu's marvelous public bus system.
- Direct, no-holds-barred opinions on the best and worst of Hawaii, including accommodations, restaurants, attractions, shows, shops, and more.
- Top recommendations for lesser-known attractions and activities— local "secrets" that should be included on every visitor's itinerary.
- User-friendly ratings on Hawaii's top attractions, with the interests of children a top priority. (One of the worst things to hear in any vacation, after all, is "Mommy, I'm bored!")
- Suggested itineraries tailor-made for different types of Hawaii visitors, including young families, honeymooners, elderly couples, and visitors with disabilities.
- A helpful guide to the state's best golf courses—and how you can secure the best possible tee times!

COMMENTS AND SUGGESTIONS FROM READERS

As always, we welcome your suggestions and comments about all our *Unofficial Guides,* including this book. And should you spot any mistakes in this volume, we would appreciate hearing from you. Over the years, we've come to recognize that some of the best ideas we find for our books come from our readers.

How to Write the Author:

Lance Tominaga
The Unofficial Guide to Hawaii
P.O. Box 43673
Birmingham, AL 35243

When you write, be sure to put your return address on your letter as well as on the envelope—sometimes envelopes and letters get separated. And remember, our work takes us out of the office for long periods of time, so forgive us if our response is delayed.

Reader Survey

At the back of this guide you'll find a short reader questionnaire that will help you express your satisfaction/dissatisfaction with both this book and your visit to the Hawaiian Islands. This survey will also help us make improvements to future editions of this guide. Please clip out the survey along the dotted lines and mail it to the above address.

HOW INFORMATION IS ORGANIZED: BY SUBJECT AND BY GEOGRAPHIC ZONES

To give you speedy access to information about the very best Hawaii has to offer, we've organized material in several formats.

Hotels   With so many Island hotels available and seeking your business, choosing the right one for you can be an imposing proposition. We simplify the process through easy-to-read charts, maps, and rating and ranking systems. Included here is all the pertinent information you would want and need to know: room size, cleanliness, service, amenities, cost, accessibility to the beach, and so on. Also included is information on Hawaii's best condos and bed-and-breakfast units.

Restaurants   One of the highlights of a Hawaiian vacation is sampling some of the innovative cuisines served on every island. The menu of great dining options—ranging from simple local plate lunches to extravagant gourmet adventures—is vast and far-reaching. We include detailed information on the best restaurants in the state.

Entertainment and Nightlife   Most visitors to the Islands try to take in a couple of shows or nightspots during their stay. This is especially true of visitors to Oahu, where world-famous Waikiki is home to several ongoing engagements. Whether you enjoy a particular show or not will depend on what kind of show you are expecting. We've done all the homework for you so there won't be any unfortunate surprises. Also, we profile the best nightclubs and lounges and include fair warnings on the seedier side of Hawaii's nightlife (yes, such a side does exist).

Golf   Golf is a major draw for many Island visitors; in fact, the island of Lanai is primarily known as a resort island with two award-winning championship courses. Thus, we've included profiles detailing all the vital stats of the state's top courses, from the tee to the 19th hole. Again, the emphasis is on features that differentiate one course from another, allowing you to decide which golf experience is just right for you.

Geographic Zones   For added convenience, we've divided Hawaii into geographic zones. Say you're interested in staying somewhere in Kapalua on the island of Maui, but aren't sure where it is. We'll note for you that Kapalua is in Zone 9, which represents West Maui, and all other Zone 9 resorts, hotels, attractions, and restaurants will be in that vicinity. Of course, helpful maps of each zone are provided.

Zone 1: Waikiki	Zone 9: West Maui
Zone 2: Greater Honolulu	Zone 10: Upcountry Maui
Zone 3: Windward Oahu	and Beyond
Zone 4: The North Shore	Zone 11: Kona
Zone 5: Leeward Oahu	Zone 12: Hilo and Volcano
Zone 6: Central Oahu	Zone 13: Kauai
Zone 7: Central Maui	Zone 14: Molokai
Zone 8: South Maui	Zone 15: Lanai

Please note that the islands of **Niihau** and **Kahoolawe**, while considered links in Hawaii's main island chain, are not given zone designations. Niihau is a family-owned island and is (with few exceptions) inaccessible to visitors, while Kahoolawe, once used for target practice by the U.S. military, is uninhabited and generally off-limits.

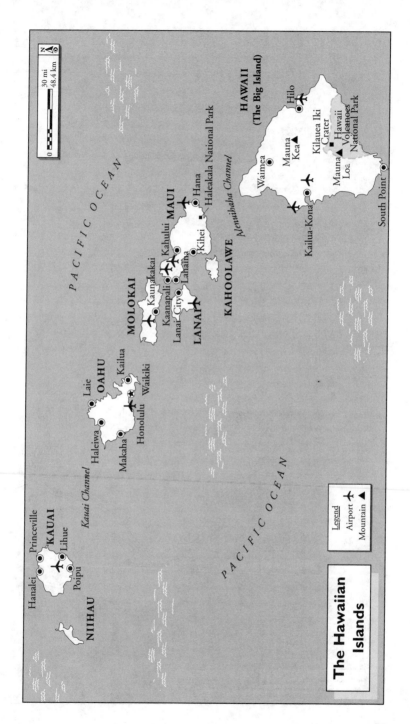

The Hawaiian Islands

Legend
✈ Airport
▲ Mountain

0 — 30 mi
0 — 48.4 km

KAUAI
- Hanalei
- Princeville
- Lihue
- Poipu

Kauai Channel

NIIHAU

OAHU
- Laie
- Kailua
- Haleiwa
- Makaha
- Honolulu
- Waikiki

MOLOKAI
- Kaunakakai

MAUI
- Kahului
- Kaanapali
- Lahaina
- Kihei
- Hana
- Haleakala National Park

LANAI
- Lanai City

KAHOOLAWE

Alenuihaha Channel

PACIFIC OCEAN

HAWAII
(The Big Island)
- Waimea
- Hilo
- Kailua-Kona
- South Point
- Mauna Kea ▲
- Mauna Loa ▲
- Kilauea Iki Crater
- Hawaii Volcanoes National Park

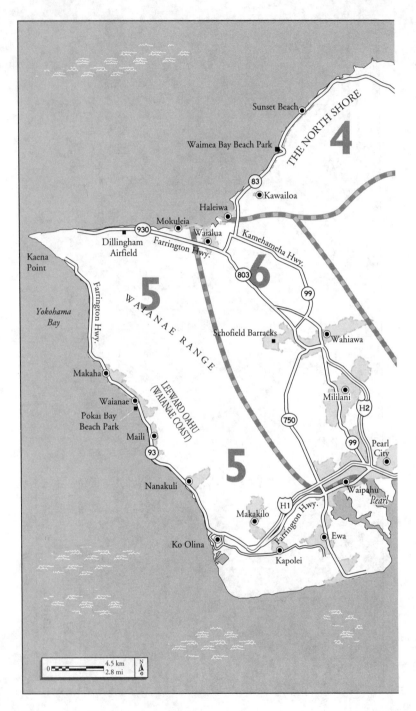

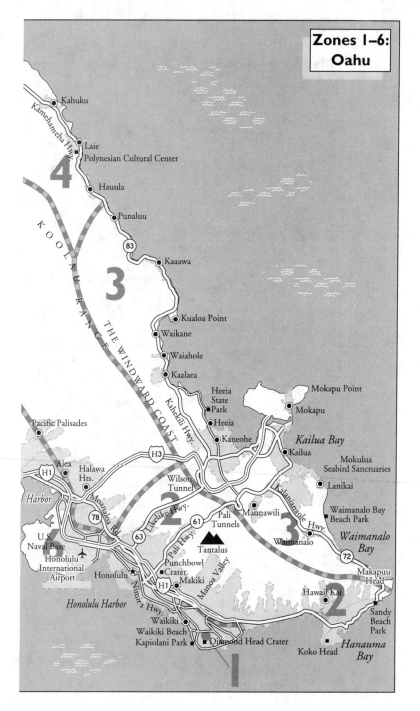

Zones 1–6:
Oahu

Kahuku

Kamehameha Hwy.

Laie
Polynesian Cultural Center

4

Hauula

Punaluu

83

K O O L A U   R A N G E

T H E   W I N D W A R D   C O A S T

3

Kaaawa

Kualoa Point

Waikane

Waiahole

Kaalaea

Kahekili Hwy.

Heeia
State
Park

Heeia

Mokapu Point

Mokapu

Kaneohe

Kailua Bay

Pacific Palisades

H3

Kailua

Mokulua
Seabird Sanctuaries

Aiea

H1

Halawa
Hts.

Wilson
Tunnel

2

Lanikai

Harbor

Moanalua Rd.

78

63

Likelike Hwy.

61

Pali Hwy.

Pali
Tunnels

Maunawili

Kalanianaole Hwy.

Waimanalo Bay
Beach Park

Waimanalo Bay

U.S.
Naval Base

Tantalus

3

Waimanalo

72

Honolulu
International
Airport

Punchbowl
Crater

Makiki

Manoa Valley

Makapuu
Head

Honolulu

H1

Nimitz Hwy.

Hawaii Kai

Honolulu Harbor

Waikiki

Waikiki Beach

Kapiolani Park

Diamond Head Crater

Koko Head

2

Sandy
Beach
Park

Hanauma
Bay

1

9

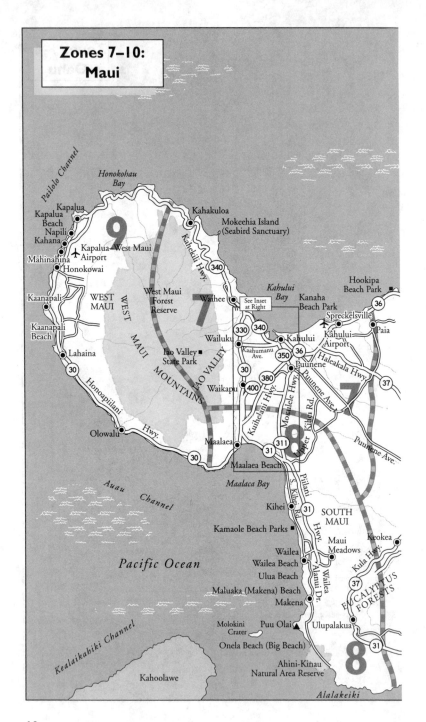

Zones 7–10:
Maui

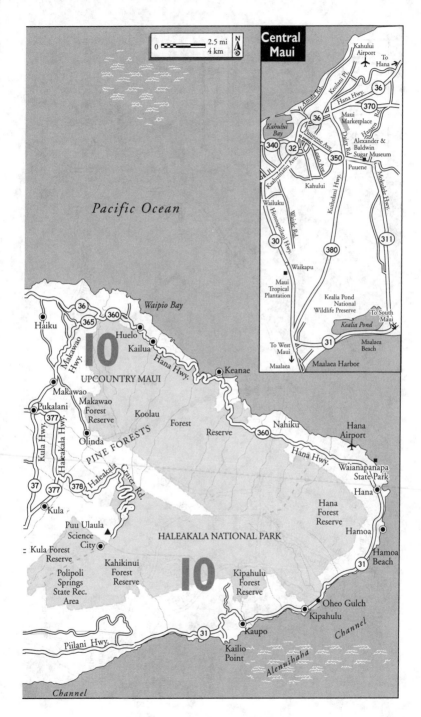

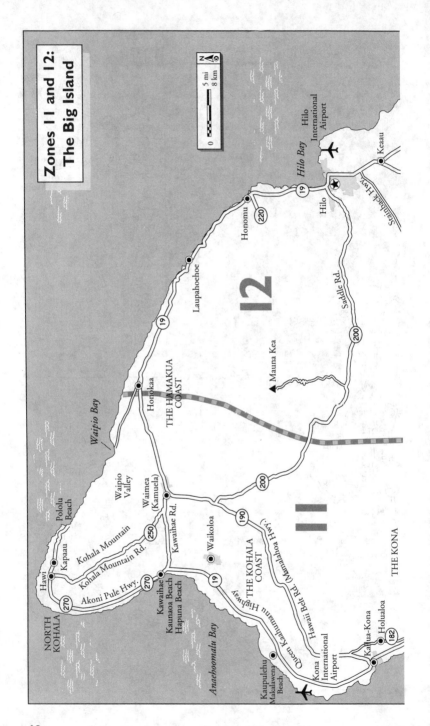

Zones 11 and 12:
The Big Island

12

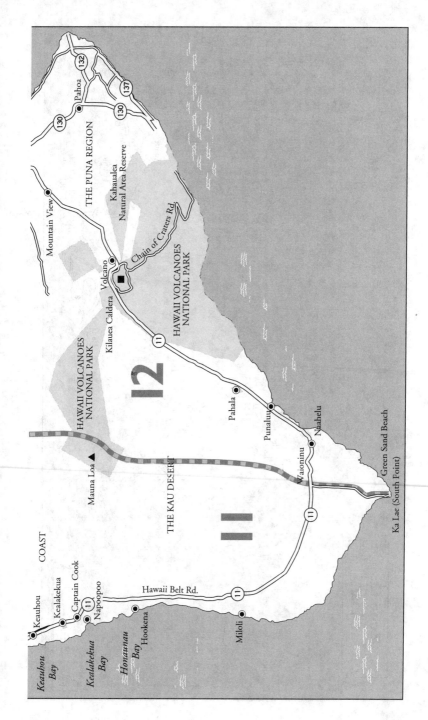

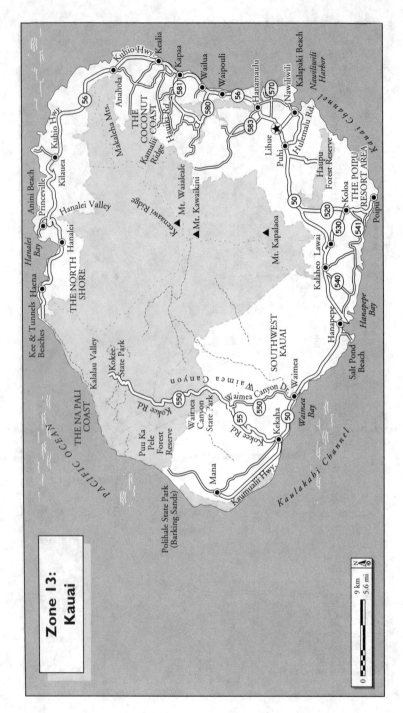

Zone 13:
Kauai

THE NORTH SHORE

THE COCONUT COAST

SOUTHWEST KAUAI

THE POIPU RESORT AREA

THE NA PALI COAST

PACIFIC OCEAN

Kee & Tunnels Beaches
Haena Beaches
Hanalei Bay
Princeville
Anini Beach
Kilauea
Kuhio Hwy.
Kalalau Valley
Hanalei Valley
Makaleha Mts.
Anahola
Kealia
Kapaa
Wailua
Waipouli
Kamalii Coast Ridge
Haiku Rd.
Hanamaulu
Kalapaki Beach
Nawiliwili Harbor
Nawiliwili
Lihue
Puhi
Hulemalu Rd.
Haupu Forest Reserve
Koloa
Poipu
Kalaheo
Lawai
Hanapepe
Hanapepe Bay
Salt Pond Beach
Waimea
Waimea Bay
Kekaha
Mana
Polihale State Park (Barking Sands)
Puu Ka Pele Forest Reserve
Waimea Canyon State Park
Kokee State Park
Kokee Rd.
Waimea Canyon Dr.
Waimea Canyon
Keeaawi Ridge
Mt. Waialeale
Mt. Kawaikini
Mt. Kapalaoa

Kanai Channel
Kaulakahi Channel

56
55
50
520
530
540
541
550
570
580
581
583

N
9 km
5.6 mi

14

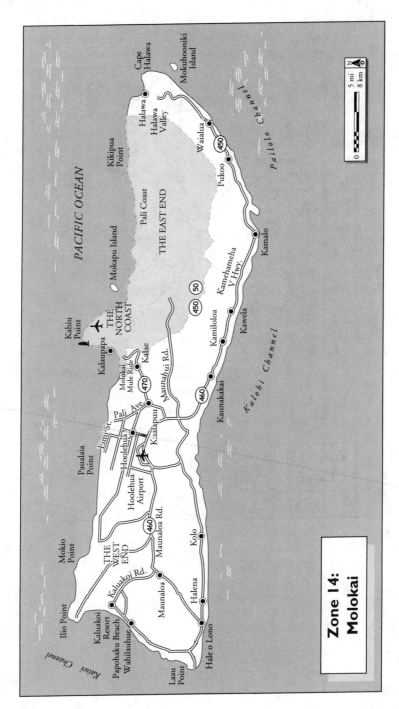

Zone 14:
Molokai

Kauai Channel

Ilio Point

Mokio Point

PACIFIC OCEAN

Kahiu Point

Kikipua Point

Cape Halawa

Mokuhooniki Island

Kalaupapa

THE NORTH COAST

Mokapu Island

Pali Coast

Halawa

Halawa Valley

Kaluakoi Resort

Papohaku Beach

Wahilauhue

Kaluakoi Rd.

THE WEST END

Molokai Mule Ride

Kalae

Maunahui Rd.

THE EAST END

Waialua

450

Pailolo Channel

Maunaloa

460

Maunaloa Rd.

Limi St.

Pali Ave.

Hoolehua

Kualapuu

470

Pukoo

Kolo

Hoolehua Airport

Kaunakakai

460

Kamiloloa

50

450

Kamehameha V Hwy.

Kawela

Kamalo

Halena

Hale o Lono

Laau Point

Paualaia Point

Kalohi Channel

N

0   5 mi
    8 km

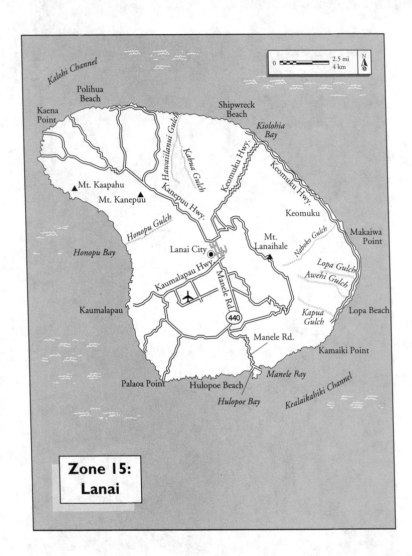

Zone 15:
Lanai

Part One

Getting Acquainted with Hawaii

About the Aloha State

While Hawaii is a huge draw as a vacation locale—the state welcomes more than 6 million visitors annually, about six times its total population—it is practically a mere speck in terms of geographic size, with a total area of 10,932 square miles. (By comparison, California is roughly 15 times the size of Hawaii; the Aloha State is closest in size to Massachusetts). Hawaii is the most isolated population center in the world, located 2,390 miles from California, 3,850 miles from Japan, 4,900 miles from China, and 5,280 miles from the Philippines.

Hawaii ranks 41st in the United States in terms of population (1.2 million residents). Young people (age 18 and under) make up more than a quarter of the state's residents, while senior citizens comprise about 14% of the population.

Hawaii is very unique among the rest of the U.S. states. Hawaii is the only state, for example, with two official languages: English and Hawaiian. It is also the only state to have once been a kingdom, ruled by native royalty Hawaiians called *ali'i*.

As a vacation experience, Hawaii compares favorably with other tropical destinations, providing gorgeous weather (the average daily temperature is a balmy 80° F), spectacular scenery, sand and surf, outdoor activities, visitor attractions, entertainment, nightlife, and the like. What's more, U.S. travelers never have to worry about foreign languages, passports, customs inspections, and currency exchanges.

The only amenity that Hawaii lacks and other popular vacation spots offer is legalized casino gaming. Gambling in any form, in fact, is illegal in the Islands. Every year, it seems, pro-gambling enthusiasts—many who see gaming as a potential savior for the state's sluggish economy—lobby for some sort of legalized wagering. Thus far, however, state lawmakers have been able to resist the idea.

The Islands and Their Zones

OAHU: THE GATHERING PLACE

Oahu Facts
Flower: 'Ilima
Color: Yellow
State Capital, County Seat: Honolulu
Area: 608 square miles
Length: 44 miles
Width: 30 miles
Population: 836,231
Highest Point: Ka'ala Peak (4,003 feet)
Coastline: 112 miles

Ironically, an island famous for offering so much for so many is now criticized for something it supposedly does *not* have.

Cynics dismiss Oahu as overdeveloped, overpopulated, and overcommercialized. Hawaii's main island, they add, lacks the natural environs that its visitors seek and expect. While the criticism isn't entirely unwarranted, it is also, appropriately enough, somewhat of an overstatement.

True, Oahu doesn't have anything to match the spectacular pyrotechnics of the Big Island's Kilauea Volcano. Nor does it boast a scenic getaway quite like Hana on Maui, or a romantic setting as alluring as the Fern Grotto on Kauai. If stunning natural scenery is everything to you, you would probably prefer any of these islands (and also Molokai and Lanai) over Oahu.

But to quote a popular American radio personality, here's the rest of the story: No other island in the state—or in the world, for that matter—offers so many things to do and see. On Oahu, there are five-star resorts and a million-star skyline. Big waves and "Tiny Bubbles." Kitsch and Cartier. A "Pearl" Harbor and "Diamond" Head. The Punchbowl and the Pro Bowl. There's a simple reason why 80% of the state's population calls Oahu home: This is where the action is.

And we'll let you in on a little secret: Oahu has its share of natural beauty, and then some. (For beach lovers, for example, the island has more than 50 miles of sandy shoreline.) All you have to do is get out there and enjoy them.

Too many visitors, unfortunately, think that an Oahu vacation begins and ends in Waikiki. In recent years, marketing and advertising execs have tried to sell the complete Oahu experience, using slogans such as "The Beach Is Just the Beginning" and, more recently, "Where Aloha Begins."

While Waikiki is indeed a one-of-a-kind playground, we highly recommend taking the time to explore other parts of the island as well.

Let's take a tour of the island of Oahu, "The Gathering Place."

Zone 1: Waikiki

Without question, Waikiki is one of the world's most famous vacation locales. Each day, nearly 100,000 residents and visitors work, sleep, and play within its 1.5-square-mile boundaries. At **Waikiki Beach,** swimmers frolic in crystal blue waters, newbie surfers test their skills on friendly waves, and sunbathers bask lazily under the warm Hawaiian sun. On the sidewalks along **Kalakaua Avenue**—Waikiki's main thoroughfare—shoppers search for everything from tacky souvenirs to the latest in designer wear. And at night, Waikiki comes alive with a wide range of dinner shows, dance clubs, street performances, and other entertainment options.

Sizing up the Waikiki of today, it's hard to believe it was once a mosquito-infested area full of gushing springs and rivers. ("Waikiki," in fact, translates to "spouting water.") Even in the early 1900s, during the infancy years of tourism, returning swimmers, wary of centipedes and scorpions, had to shake out their towels before sitting down!

In ancient times, Waikiki was actually a much larger area, encompassing the neighboring valleys of Manoa and Palolo. In the early 1400s, a high-ranking chief named Kalamakua designed an irrigation system to take advantage of the area's rich water resources. Taro patches were planted and fishponds were built, and by the middle of that century, Waikiki was established as the governmental seat of Oahu.

In 1795, the great warrior Kamehameha conquered Oahu, leading a vast fleet of war canoes from the Big Island that landed right on Waikiki Beach. It is said that after his triumphant battle, Kamehameha used Papaʻenaʻena Heiau—located on the slopes of Diamond Head—to offer sacrifices to his gods. Papaʻenaʻena was one of at least eight major *heiau* (Hawaiian temples or places of worship) constructed in Waikiki.

In later years, in the mid- to late 1800s, Waikiki served as a welcome retreat for ruling *aliʻi*, who enjoyed leisurely escapes filled with lavish parties, swimming, canoe races, and moonlight horseback rides. (By this time, the governmental seat had shifted to Honolulu, where foreign trade ships could find safe harbor.) Among the *aliʻi* who maintained homes in Waikiki were King Kamehameha IV, King Kamehameha V, King Lunalilo, King Kalakaua, and Queen Liliʻuokalani. And while their homes were fairly modest wooden cottages, Princess Kaʻiulani's estate, Ainahau, was a stunning Victorian-style mansion frequented by strutting peacocks.

The first hotel in Waikiki—the Moana—opened in 1901. Now affectionately known as "The First Lady of Waikiki," it was then the tallest building in all the Hawaiian Islands—a whopping six stories high! One woman who stayed at the Moana in 1908 wrote home to her mother, "The Moana is the most wonderful place in the world, but it's too expensive." She was paying $37.50 a month.

Today, much of Waikiki's history is alive and well. The Moana, for example, is looking exceptionally good for a grand "old lady," and one of the most pleasant afternoons you can have on the island is a leisurely spot of tea near the hotel's famous banyan tree.

Also a Waikiki fixture, of course, is perhaps Hawaii's most famous landmark: **Diamond Head Crater.** The crater was named "Diamond Head" in the early 1800s, after a group of British sailors claimed to see diamonds glittering everywhere along the crater. (*Note:* You can put away the picks and chisels. The "diamonds" were actually mere calcite crystals.) Its original name was Lae'ahi, meaning "brow of the 'ahi," and if you take a good look at its shape, you will note the resemblance! Not only is Diamond Head a scenic icon, it also offers a great hike full of panoramic views from its summit.

At the foot of Diamond Head lies **Kapi'olani Park,** a 170-acre playground that extends about a half-mile inland from the ocean. The brainchild of King Kalakaua, Hawaii's famed "Merrie Monarch," the park was officially dedicated on June 11, 1877—Kamehameha Day—and was named for Kalakaua's beloved queen. In those days, the park was home to wild peacocks, ponds of colorful goldfish, and all types of tropical foliage, including banyans, ironwoods, palms, and hibiscus. Then the most popular activity at the park was horse racing, and Kalakaua himself viewed many such races from the comforts of his private box—front and center of the action, naturally.

Today, Kapi'olani Park hosts soccer and softball games, musical concerts, cultural festivals, and a daily influx of joggers, picnickers, and kite-flyers. It encompasses the 42-acre **Honolulu Zoo** and **Waikiki Shell,** an outdoor venue for musical concerts. If you enjoy leisurely walks packed with scenery, a sunset stroll along the park is highly recommended.

Adjacent to the park is **Waikiki Beach** itself, perhaps the world's most famous stretch of coastline. More than 30,000 visitors and residents flock to Waikiki Beach every day. The beach is actually a two-mile string of several smaller beaches, but the three S's—sand, surf, and sun—are glorious throughout. Waikiki Beach isn't as crowded as one might think, so you'll have plenty of room to soak up the sun and make a splash.

While at the beach, visit the **Duke Kahanamoku Statue,** a striking bronze creation honoring Hawaii's greatest sports hero. Duke Kahanamoku was a record-setting swimmer (he captured gold medals in the 1912 and 1920 Summer Olympics) who broke the 100-meter freestyle world record in 1911 by more than four seconds. Kahanamoku's time was reported to the Amateur Athletic Union in New York, and the reply was a harsh "Unacceptable. No one swims this fast. Hawaiian judges are alerted to use stopwatches, not alarm clocks!" In later years, Kahanamoku traveled around the world, putting on surfing exhibitions and helping to popularize the sport. He died on January 22, 1968, at the age of 77. More than 10,000 people attended his funeral on Waikiki Beach, every one of them bringing a flower lei that was placed in the water. His ashes were scattered into the sea he dearly loved as the people on the beach serenaded him with the Hawaiian farewell song, "Aloha 'Oe."

A short distance from the statue are the fabled **Wizard Stones,** four large rocks situated a short stroll away from the Moana. According to legend, four Tahitian priests—Kapaemahu, Kahaloa, Kinohi, and Kapuni—traveled to Oahu and took shelter at a place called Ulukou, now occupied by the Moana Surfrider. These Tahitians lived with the ruling chief of the time and spent much of their stay healing the sick. Before returning home, they selected four stones, placed their hands on them and, the story goes, endowed them with healing powers. While the stones are today secured and identified by plaques, in previous years many unsuspecting visitors sat on the rocks, and many Hawaiians believe that whatever *mana* (power) had resided in the stones has now been lost.

On the *mauka* (toward the mountain) side of Waikiki, the **Ala Wai Canal** is another good spot for a late-afternoon stroll. On most afternoons after 5 p.m., you'll see teams of canoe paddlers racing up and down the waterway, practicing for the next big competition. The canal itself was built in the 1920s to drain Waikiki of its swamps and rivers, effectively paving the way for more hotels to be constructed. *Advisory:* Although the water may look inviting from a distance, it is not suitable for swimming. Stick to the beaches!

Finally, if you have an evening free yet don't feel like doing anything ambitious, **Kalakaua Avenue** is a great place for people-watching. Have a seat and catch the parade of passersby, including visitors from every corner of the globe. On most nights you'll encounter a smattering of hokey street entertainers. Some people view them as welcome distractions, while others feel they merely add to the unnecessary cluttering of Waikiki. (Let us know what *you* think!)

Waikiki has many of the same problems faced by other major resort areas of the world. Prostitution, for example, continues to be a visible presence in Waikiki "after dark." One police officer noted that the most frequently asked question he receives from visitors is, "Is prostitution legal here?" It's not.

As a whole, however, Waikiki is a very safe area. As tourism remains the dominant industry in Hawaii's economy, state officials are sensitive to crimes against visitors. As a result, the Honolulu Police Department maintains a strong and reassuring presence in Waikiki. In addition, a citizens group calling themselves the "Aloha Patrol" prowls the streets at night, assisting visitors and keeping an eye out for trouble. Wearing mostly shorts, T-shirts, and how-do-you-do smiles, they aren't exactly the Guardian Angels, but in Hawaii they're a perfect fit.

One final word (for now) about Waikiki: Many *kama'aina* (locals) have told us they avoid the area because of the crowds, traffic (especially in the late afternoon–early evening), and "touristy" atmosphere. In other words, in Waikiki it is almost as though Hawaiian residents are on *your* turf. To truly experience the local lifestyle, you'll have to venture out of Waikiki.

Zone 2: Greater Honolulu

Hawaii's official state capital, Honolulu, is the undisputed hub of the state's political, business, and cultural arenas. Kamehameha III officially proclaimed Honolulu as his kingdom's capital city in 1850.

Technically, the city and county of Honolulu encompasses the entire island of Oahu and extends 1,400 miles northwest up the island chain to Kure Atoll. For our purposes, however, Honolulu includes this main section of Oahu.

Heading into town from Waikiki via Ala Moana Boulevard, you'll immediately come across two attractive options as you pass Atkinson Drive: Ala Moana Beach Park on the left, a popular weekend spot for locals, and the massive Ala Moana Center on the right, one of the world's largest outdoor shopping malls. If shopping is one of your favorite vacation activities, this is your best bet. (See Part Eight, "Shopping in Paradise.")

Plan to spend at least a few hours in Honolulu's downtown area, where you'll encounter a wealth of historical landmarks and cultural treasures. (Because most of the attractions here are in one area, we recommend busing it into town and hoofing it by foot.) A good place to start is **'Iolani Palace,** the only royal palace on American soil. Completed in 1882 during the eventful reign of King Kalakaua, the palace has served in several capacities during its existence: the royal residence of Kalakaua and his sister and successor, Queen Lili'uokalani; a prison for Lili'uokalani; the capitol for Hawaii's provisional, territorial, and state governments; and even a setting for the long-running television series *Hawaii Five-0*. Today, 'Iolani Palace is available for public tours five days a week. (More detailed information on the palace and other visitor attractions mentioned in this part is provided in Part Ten, "Hawaii's Attractions.")

Heading in the *makai* direction (toward the ocean), a simple walk across King Street will bring you face to face with the regal-looking **King Kamehameha Statue,** which fronts the old Judiciary Building. The bronze statue, depicting Hawaii's greatest king holding a spear in his left hand and his right arm outstretched in a warm gesture of welcome, is one of the most photographed attractions on the island. The statue is at its photogenic best in June, during the annual King Kamehameha Day Celebration, when it is draped with more than 20 colorful flower leis, some measuring as long as 18 feet. Different flowers from the various Hawaiian islands are used, and it takes from six to ten people to carry each lei to the statue!

Another walk across the street (this time Punchbowl Street, going in the Diamond Head direction) continues your journey through old Honolulu. The **Mission Houses Museum** is comprised of the original buildings that served as the home and headquarters of American Protestant missionaries in the 1800s. The museum is run by the Hawaiian Mission Children's Society, an organization made up of descendants of the missionaries.

Next to the museum is **Kawaiaha'o Church,** known as the "Westminster Abbey of the Pacific." This handsome coral block structure was built by more than a thousand natives in the late 1830s and dedicated in 1842. The land and materials for the church were donated by King Kamehameha III. It is one of the last few remaining churches in the Islands to offer services in the Hawaiian language.

Returning *mauka* (toward the mountain) beyond 'Iolani Palace, you'll arrive at the **State Capitol Building,** a marvelously designed structure that combines elements of Hawaii's volcanic and oceanic beginnings. This is where the state legislature convenes for political wheeling and dealing, and sessions are open to the public. Farther *mauka,* as you cross Beretania Street, you'll see **Washington Place,** a gracious white mansion that has been the official residence of Hawaii's governor since 1921. It was formerly the home of Queen Lili'uokalani and her husband, John Owen Dominis.

From Washington Place, it's a brisk 15-minute walk in the Diamond Head direction to the **Honolulu Academy of Arts,** which houses an impressive collection of Asian and Pacific art, as well as American and European works. A five-minute walk *makai* from the academy leads you to the **Neal Blaisdell Center,** a major venue for concerts, sporting events, and trade shows.

If you're not an art aficionado and can pass on the Academy of Arts, head in the *'ewa* direction (toward the leeward side of the island), where Honolulu's business district is the closest Hawaii comes to a "concrete jungle," with a gathering of modern-day business towers overshadowing smaller, historic buildings. But even here, you'll typically see more men dressed in aloha shirts than business suits.

Continue in the *'ewa* direction and you'll notice the buildings seem to get older with each passing block. This is **Chinatown,** Hawaii's largest historic district (it was placed on the National Register of Historic Places in 1973).

Chinatown itself is an intriguing story: In April 1886, a small kitchen fire blazed out of control, spread to other buildings, and raged for three days before consuming eight Chinatown blocks and leaving 7,000 Chinese and 350 Hawaiians homeless. Slowly, Chinatown's homes and businesses were rebuilt. In January 1900, however, local Board of Health officials decided to set sanitary fires in Chinatown to combat the bubonic plague, which had been discovered a month earlier. Forty-one fires were set and contained with no problem, but the forty-second turned into a horrific disaster when the wind suddenly shifted. The resulting holocaust set Chinatown ablaze, raging out of control for 17 days and leaving 4,000 residents homeless.

That Chinatown was again rebuilt is testimony to the perseverance and spirit of Hawaii's immigrant population. Today, Chinatown is rejuvenated, brimming with historic sites, gift boutiques, ethnic restaurants, herb shops, and art galleries. At the cusp of Chinatown is the **Hawaii Theatre,** itself a historical treasure. Opened in 1922 and acclaimed as "The Pride of the Pacific," the theater was once the venue for Island entertainment, hosting operas, musicals, silent films, and vaudeville acts.

In the decades that followed, however, the theater became an after-thought as newer and bigger venues were built. With a wrecking ball destined as its final act, the theater closed its doors in 1984. It took a determined group of community leaders to raise the $30 million it needed to totally renovate and repair the theater. In May 1996, with much fanfare, the Hawaii Theatre finally reopened its doors. Today, the 1,400-seat theater is the setting for many events—concerts, films, dance performances, music festivals, and so on—and is available for guided tours each month.

Just a short walk from Chinatown is another section of downtown Honolulu worth a visit: **Honolulu Harbor.** Until Pearl Harbor was made navigable in the early 1900s, Honolulu Harbor was the only protected body of water of its size in Hawaii. (Appropriately enough, "Honolulu" translates to "protected bay.") In 1794, the English ship *Butterworth,* led by Captain William Brown, became the first foreign vessel to enter the harbor. Brown dubbed the harbor "Fair Haven."

The centerpiece of the harbor remains the ten-story **Aloha Tower,** the tallest building in Honolulu when it opened in 1926. From the 1930s to the 1950s, steamships carrying dreamy-eyed visitors to the Islands radioed their ETAs to harbor masters at the tower. And as luxury liners such as Matson's *Lurline* and SS *Monterey* pulled into port, a festive celebration—"Boat Days"—would take place, welcoming *malihini* (visitors) with Hawaiian music, hula, and, of course, sweet-smelling flower leis. Today, the tower is the star attraction at the Aloha Tower Marketplace, a retail-restaurant complex. Its tenth-floor observation deck provides sweeping views of Oahu's southern coastline.

At neighboring Pier 7, on the Diamond Head side of Aloha Tower Marketplace, is the **Hawaii Maritime Center,** a museum that traces Hawaii's maritime history through 50 intriguing displays. The chief highlights here include the *Falls of Clyde,* the last four-masted rigged vessel in the world, and the historic Polynesian voyaging canoe *Hokule'a.*

On the outskirts of downtown Honolulu are several neighborhood areas worth noting. They vary in terms of topography, ambience, and visual appeal, but they all have their own unique charms and offerings.

For most visitors, a drive into **Kalihi** means a visit to the **Bishop Museum,** which boasts the world's largest collection of Hawaiian and Pacific artifacts. The museum is named after Bernice Pauahi Bishop, a princess and last in the line of the Kamehameha family. Kalihi is also a good place to find local-style food, including the calorie-laden (but delicious) plate lunch. This area is said to be the home of the fire goddess Pele's sister, Kapo, and Pele's mother, Haumea.

Just a few minutes from downtown Honolulu is **Nu'uanu Valley,** a definite recommendation for your Oahu itinerary. It was here in Nu'uanu (its name translates to "cool height") where the infamous battle of 1795 took place, with Kamehameha I and his army driving their Oahu counterparts up the *pali* (cliff, precipice). More than 300 Oahu warriors either were driven off the cliffs or jumped to their deaths rather than having to surrender, depending on which account you choose to believe. Today, the **Pali Lookout** is one of the island's most visited attractions, as evidenced by the parking lot full of tour buses. TheBus (Oahu's public bus system) does not include the lookout as one of its stops, but an early-morning sojourn—it's about a 20-minute drive from Waikiki—will reward you with striking views of the windward side of the island. Bring a jacket or sweater—it is windy here! Also in this tranquil valley are several great hiking trails as well as a couple of historic attractions, the **Queen Emma Summer Palace** and **Royal Mausoleum.**

From Nu'uanu, a drive in the Diamond Head direction will lead you to **Punchbowl** and **Tantalus.** Known by ancient Hawaiians as Puowaina ("the hill for placing"), **Punchbowl Crater** was formerly used as a site of human sacrifices. One legend recalls a time when Oahu's ruler, Kakei, gained an important victory over his enemies on the island of Kauai. He even took Kauai's women as his captives. While celebrating at Punchbowl, however, the volcano erupted, and the spirits of the defeated Kauaians could be seen dancing over the lava. Frightened, Kakei returned the women to Kauai, and the volcanic activity ceased. The volcano has not erupted since.

Today, the 114-acre crater is the site of the **National Memorial Cemetery of the Pacific,** the final resting place for more than 40,000 American men and women who served their country during battle. Among those buried here is Ellison Onizuka, the American astronaut and Island son who perished in the 1986 space shuttle *Challenger* disaster. This solemn setting also provides dramatic views of Waikiki, Honolulu, and Pearl Harbor.

The 2,013-foot **Mount Tantalus,** meanwhile, is reached via Round Top Road, an appropriate name given the circular path you take on the way to the top. It's a pleasant drive, with many switchbacks and hairpin turns, and your reward is a magnificent view of Honolulu. (Better yet, if you're the active type, rent a bike and use your pedal power to reach the top!) Get there in time for sunset.

Nestled partially within the Koʻolau Mountains, misty **Manoa Valley** is about a 15-minute drive from Waikiki and is renowned for its rolling emerald hills, gorgeous waterfalls, and vibrant rainbows. Manoa is also where you'll find the campus of the **University of Hawaii–Manoa,** the state's largest university (enrollment: 20,000). Locals say that on days of UH sporting events, a rainbow spotted over Manoa Valley means a sure victory for the home team, the Rainbows. Manoa was a favorite retreat for several notable *aliʻi,* including Kamehameha I, Kamehameha III, and Queen Liliʻuokalani. Queen Kaʻahumanu, the favorite wife of Kamehameha I, maintained a home in the uppermost reaches of the valley.

Just minutes from Manoa Valley is **Kaimuki,** a pleasant neighborhood that has reinvented itself over the years from a drab, sleepy-eyed town to an active community offering a variety of family-run restaurants and specialty shops. And above and beyond Kaimuki are the upscale residential areas **Kahala** and **Hawaii Kai.**

Finally, at the gateway to windward Oahu is **Koko Head,** where urban sprawl phases into raw, natural splendor. The unquestioned highlight here is **Hanauma Bay,** renowned as one of the premier snorkeling spots in the world. It is so popular, in fact, that it hosts as many as 3,000 visitors a day. A great spot for novice snorkelers, Hanauma Bay is full of colorful reef fish that would literally eat right out of your hand. Feeding the fish, however, led to several concerns, including water pollution, damage to the coral reefs, and an overpopulation of fish. One aquatic biologist explained that a typical marine sanctuary the size of Hanauma Bay carries between 1,000 and 2,000 pounds of fish per acre. Hanauma Bay, he said, is inhabited by more than 3,000 pounds of fish.

In November 1999, the state banned fish-feeding at Hanauma Bay. Construction is underway for a $10 million renovation project, which will be completed in fall 2000 and will include a visitor center.

Zone 3: Windward Oahu

Continuing east from Koko Head affords you a breezy, scenic drive that cuts north along Oahu's southeastern coastline. To your right you will spot

Makapu'u Beach Park and the crashing waves beyond. The beach is renowned as a bodysurfing spot.

Note also a pair of offshore islands: the smaller island (11 acres) is **Kaohikaipu Island,** while the larger one (67 acres) is **Manana,** more commonly known as **Rabbit Island.** In the late 1800s, its owner, John Cummins, used the island to raise European hares, and a small population of these rabbits still resides there. (Ironically, with a little imagination, you'll see that the island looks like the head of a rabbit with its ears laid back!) Manana was designated a seabird sanctuary in 1970 and today supports one of the largest colonies of seabirds—primarily wedge-tailed shearwaters, sooty terns, and brown noddies—in the state.

Meanwhile, to your left is the entrance to **Sea Life Park,** a favorite stop for kids and lovers of marine life. While better known as a visitor attraction featuring dolphins, sea lions, penguins, and the world's only known "wholphin" (half-whale, half-dolphin), the park also serves as a center for wildlife rehabilitation. In the spring of 1998, for example, an abandoned baby melon-headed whale was found off the Kona Coast of the Big Island. Starving and dehydrated, the mammal was transported to Sea Life Park, where expert caregivers nursed it to health.

Continuing north, you'll be treated to one of Oahu's most breathtaking sights: the majestic **Ko'olau** mountain range. An ancient "King's Highway" once ran through this area, a man-made path used to deliver messages to and from this side of the island.

Very few drives are as pleasant as the one through **Waimanalo** (potable water), a picturesque locale favored for its camping and beaches. Taro, breadfruit, mountain apple, and coconut were among the fruits grown and harvested in early Hawaii, and even today tranquil country living is still the rule. There is a sizable military presence here, thanks to President Woodrow Wilson's 1917 decree that some 1,500 acres of Waimanalo land be turned over to the military. Bellows Field is named after Second Lieutenant F. B. Bellows, who was killed in an airplane accident. World War II trivia experts know that the first Japanese prisoner of war was captured in Waimanalo, right on Bellows Beach. He was captured after his two-man submarine struck a reef at Waimanalo Bay (his shipmate had drowned).

With some 60,000 residents, **Kailua** is the second largest town in the state, and it is blessed with a beautiful beach and bay, stunning natural vistas, and a strong sense of community. Its name translates to "two seas," and indeed much of the town's unique character is influenced by the surrounding saltwater and freshwater. **Kailua Beach** annually ranks as one of the state's best beaches and is famous as a world-class windsurfing spot (here, onshore trade winds blow nearly all the time). Robbie Naish, the most dominant champion in the history of the sport with numerous world titles, was born and raised in Kailua and still resides here. Kailua Bay, meanwhile, is a favorite haven among kayakers and canoe paddlers.

Nearby, **Lanikai** is still a relatively ignored destination among Oahu visitors, even though it lays claim to having "America's best beach." (It was given that designation in 1996 by a marine researcher in Maryland.) Here the sand and water are as pristine as any you'll encounter. Rent a kayak and paddle out to the **Mokulua Islets,** sister islets located three-fourths of a mile offshore. Moku Nui, the larger islet to the left as you view them from shore, is accessible to kayakers and swimmers, although you must stay within the boundaries of the beach and picnicking areas. The smaller islet, Moku Iki, is strictly off-limits.

Kailua's neighbor, **Kaneʻohe,** offers several worthwhile stops, including the **Byodo-In Temple** at the **Valley of the Temples Memorial Park, Senator Fong's Plantation and Gardens,** and the biggest shopping center on this side of the island, **Windward Mall.**

Continuing in toward the North Shore, you'll come to **Kaʻaʻawa,** home to one of the better-kept secrets on Oahu. **Kualoa Ranch** bills itself as "the ultimate Hawaiian adventure," and while this is typical tourist hyperbole, it's not too far off the mark, either. Activities offered here include horseback riding, helicopter tours, scuba diving, all-terrain vehicles (ATVs), Jet-Skiing, a garden tour, a shooting range, and more. Kualoa's Secret Island, a private island accessible by shuttle across an 800-year-old fishpond, is a special treat offering guests a wide variety of beach activities.

Located about 600 yards off of Kualoa Beach Park is another offshore island: **Mokoliʻi,** commonly referred to as Chinaman's Hat because of its distinctive triangular shape. According to legend, the goddess Hiʻiaka—Pele's sister—slew the giant lizard Mokoliʻi with a bolt of lightning and threw its tail into the ocean, forming the islet. Another fable says Mokoliʻi was captured by a Hawaiian hero named Kaulu, thrown into the air, and shattered to pieces when it crashed into the sea. Today, during low tide you can roll up your pants and wade your way to the island, which features secluded coves, a picture-perfect beach, and stunning views of the windward coastline.

Laʻie is where you'll find the **Polynesian Cultural Center,** one of the state's premier visitor attractions. Replicating the villages and cultures of seven different Polynesian nations on its 42 acres, PCC is a unique story in itself. Most of its employees are students at the neighboring Brigham Young University–Hawaii, which started the center in 1963. Qualified students from Polynesia may earn full scholarships at BYUH by working at PCC. The students can work no more than 20 hours per week, and those hours are worked around their class schedules. Slightly less than one-third of the university's student enrollment of 2,000 is employed at PCC.

Zone 4: The North Shore

The contrasts between Waikiki and Oahu's North Shore are dramatic, to say the least: Gone are the sweet-smelling scents of coconut oil and suntan lotion, replaced by the breathe-it-in aroma of fresh salt air. Gone is the jungle of towering hotels and condominiums, replaced by the raw beauty of Mother Nature at her finest. And gone are the docile, user-friendly ocean waves, replaced by gigantic swells that have helped the north shore gain notoriety as the "Aspen of surfing."

Each winter, the world's top professional and amateur surfers gather here, frequenting renowned surf spots like **Sunset Beach, Ali'i Beach,** and **'Ehukai Beach** ("home" of the world-famous Banzai Pipeline). The annual Triple Crown of Surfing—a trio of major surf competitions featuring the surfing elite—takes place from mid-November to mid-December.

The heart of Oahu's North Shore is **Hale'iwa,** a funky, thriving town with surf shops, trendy art galleries, mom-and-pop shops, and other small businesses lining its main street. On warm days, drop by Matsumoto General Store and order their famous shave ice, a frosty concoction—it comes in a rainbow of flavors and colors—to help you beat the heat.

Finally, **Waimea Valley Adventure Park** is a lush 1,800-acre cultural park with more than 6,000 plant species, including several rare and endangered indigenous species. (It is rated as one of the top ten botanical gardens in the world.) The park features preserved archaeological sites and cultural demonstrations including hula, arts and crafts, and Hawaiian games. A full menu of recreational activities is also available.

Zone 5: Leeward Oahu

In general, the western side of Oahu doesn't offer a whole lot for tourists. It lacks the "must-see" attractions you'll find on other parts of the island. The lifestyle here is very down-to-earth, very laid back, and very local. But that doesn't mean leeward Oahu isn't worth more than a passing look. Make sure you have enough film for your camera, because here you'll find some of the most spectacular, unspoiled vistas in Hawaii.

Ka'ena Point, a popular fishing spot for locals, is the westernmost point on Oahu. You can't reach it by car. It's best to load up on water, sunscreen, and some snacks, and hoof it on foot (it's about a 90-minute walk, following a dirt road, from the end of Yokohama Bay). There are fantastic coastal views all along the way. Ka'ena "points" toward the island of Kauai.

Ancient Hawaiians believed Ka'ena Point to be the spot where human souls departed from Earth—the good souls to the right, the less virtuous to the left. The departure point is said to be the huge white stone located right on the shoreline.

Yokohama Bay, formerly known as Keawa'ula ("the red harbor"), is a favorite playground for bodysurfers. It received its name at the turn of the century, when the old Oahu Railroad train between 'Ewa and Hale'iwa made stops here to drop off Japanese fishermen.

Heading east (back toward Honolulu), you'll arrive at **Makaha,** site of a popular longboard contest, a yearly surf meet emphasizing the surfing style favored in the 1950s and 1960s. While the North Shore garners most of the world's attention, true surfing insiders know that Makaha has been one of Hawaii's most fertile surf spots since ancient times. Here you'll find some of the finest surfers in the state, from young prodigies to legendary old-timers.

Past Makaha and the town of Nanakuli is **Wai'anae,** which has historically been a place generally ignored by visitors. However, this may soon change. Recently, community leaders have talked about boosting Wai'anae's economic potential through cultural tourism, recognizing visitors' desire to learn about Hawaii's unique culture. One realization of these discussions is the Na Hana Lima Store, a cooperative of a dozen Wai'anae-area artisans located at Wai'anae Mall Shopping Center. The store includes Hawaiian jewelry, sculptures, woodwork, kapa, prints, pottery, and other items.

When you pass through **Kapolei,** ambitiously nicknamed Oahu's "Second City," think of the area as a work in progress. The master plan, mapped in the 1980s and initiated in the early 1990s, called for an alternate major city to congested Honolulu. You know what they say about best-laid plans . . .

Still, Kapolei is growing, slowly but surely. It currently boasts the state's largest movie theater complex (16 screens), is earmarked for a proposed University of Hawaii–West Oahu campus, and is scheduled to unveil a $27 million sports complex in the year 2000. Kapolei also features one of Hawaii's newest attractions, the $14 million, 29-acre **Hawaiian Waters Adventure Park,** a water theme park geared for young families.

Nearby is **Ko 'Olina,** a lavish resort area featuring the **'Ihilani Resort & Spa** and the popular **Paradise Cove Lu'au.**

In Waipahu, a former sugar plantation town, the most celebrated attraction is **Hawaii's Plantation Village,** a three-acre park spotlighting the cultures and lifestyles of Hawaii's plantation families. It took nearly 20 years to construct the village, as architects painstakingly rebuilt original structures using old blueprints, photographs, and oral histories. During the process, more than 4,000 authentic artifacts—clothes, furniture, kitchen appliances, and more—were donated to the village.

Zone 6: Central Oahu

Nestled comfortably between the Wai'anae and Ko'olau mountain ranges is a section of the island rich in beauty and history. It is here you'll find the most popular visitor attraction in the state, the **USS *Arizona* Memorial** at Pearl Harbor.

Pearl Harbor was once called Wai Momi, meaning "Waters of Pearl," for the flourishing beds of oysters that were found in the bay. In early Hawaii, the area was a popular fishing and diving spot, as Hawaiians believed Wai Momi fell under the divine protection of a shark goddess.

The United States gained exclusive rights to Pearl Harbor in 1887, and dredging of the bay began in 1902. Six years later, the U.S. Congress officially designated the harbor as a naval base. The first U.S. warship to cross the channel at Pearl Harbor was the USS *California* in 1911.

At 7:45 a.m. Sunday morning, December 7, 1941, Japanese war planes descended upon Oahu, targeting military facilities at Kane'ohe Naval Air Station, Pearl Harbor, Schofield Barracks, 'Ewa Marine Corps Air Station, and airfields at the Hickam and Bellows bases. Pearl Harbor, the headquarters for U.S. military activities in the Pacific region, was hit the hardest. A 1,760-pound bomb struck the USS *Arizona,* sinking the vessel and entombing 1,000 crew members.

In all, 2,403 Americans were killed, including 68 civilians, and another 1,178 were injured; 188 aircraft were destroyed, and another 159 damaged. The Japanese attack, of course, launched the United States into World War II.

Today, the USS *Arizona* Memorial, operated by the National Park Service in cooperation with the U.S. Navy, welcomes nearly 1.5 million visitors annually.

A short walk from the memorial's visitor center is the **USS *Bowfin.*** This historic World War II submarine—credited with 44 ship sinkings in nine patrols—was launched exactly one year after the Pearl Harbor attack and was nicknamed "The Pearl Harbor Avenger." The *Bowfin* has been open to the public since 1981 and includes a museum, a mini-theater, and outdoor exhibits.

Completing the triumvirate of historic attractions at Pearl Harbor is the famed ***Battleship Missouri,*** "Mighty Mo," which opened with much fanfare in January 1999 as a memorial and museum. The 887-foot, 58,000-ton Iowa-class battleship is an appropriate "bookend" at the harbor. As the USS *Arizona* symbolized the beginning of America's involvement in the war, the *Missouri* represents its ending: On September 2, 1945, on the deck of the *Missouri,* Japan officially surrendered to the U.S.-led Allied forces. The *Missouri* served in World War II, the Korean War, and the Gulf War and was the first battleship to circumnavigate the world (it accomplished that feat in 1986).

'Ewa of Pearl Harbor, approximately a five-minute drive away, is the 50,000-seat **Aloha Stadium,** site of major sporting events (including the annual NFL Pro Bowl) and concerts. The stadium's parking lot is also the site of the Aloha Flea Market, a bustling swap meet where you can find some good knickknacks at bargain prices.

A place that few visitors know about but definitely worth a visit is **Moanalua Gardens,** located just off the H-1 Freeway. This tranquil haven, dotted with shady, umbrella-shaped monkeypod trees, is ideal for picnicking. Each July, Moanalua Gardens hosts the Prince Lot Hula Festival, a one-day hula celebration honoring Lot Kamehameha, the last of the Kamehameha kings.

Traveling inland on the H-2 Freeway will bring you to the tranquil community of **Wahiawa,** a sleepy community that has its own version of healing stones. The stones are located on California Street, resting on a simple altar inside a concrete shelter. The stones, the story goes, were once two sisters visiting from Kauai. Unlike the Wizard Stones in Waikiki, they are still believed to contain healing powers.

Slightly north of Wahiawa is the **Dole Pineapple Plantation.** Although pineapple no longer reigns as a dominant industry in the Islands, the plantation still resides within fields of pineapple. It was here that, at the beginning of the 20th century, Hawaii's pineapple industry got started. Today, the plantation includes colorful displays and exhibits about the history of the prickly fruit in the Islands, as well as a fascinating garden with 21 varieties of pineapples from locales around the globe. In 1998, the plantation welcomed an odd but successful addition to lure visitors: the Pineapple Garden Maze, a two-acre maze with a path of 1.7 miles. The maze is recognized by the *Guinness Book of World Records* as the world's largest maze.

MAUI: THE VALLEY ISLE

Maui Facts
Flower: Lokelani
Color: Pink
County Seat: Wailuku
Area: 729 square miles
Length: 48 miles
Width: 26 miles
Population: 108,400
Highest Point: Haleakala (10,023 feet)
Coastline: 120 miles

Local residents are fond of saying *"Maui no ka 'oi"*—"Maui is the best." We've been hearing that for years, but today more and more visitors are discovering it's more than just a catchphrase.

Is Maui, the second largest island in the state (729 square miles), truly *"no ka 'oi?"* Well, it depends.

Certainly, Maui is a hot locale these days, and we're not referring to the weather. More than 2 million visitors come to the island each year, and in 1997 readers of *Condé Nast Traveler* voted Maui as the best island in the world. We can understand why. More than any other Hawaiian island, the Valley Isle provides an enviable blend of modern-day sophistication and wide-open natural splendor. Here you can be as active or laid-back as you like. Wisely, the island has recently marketed itself as a fabulous family destination, and it is. Only Oahu offers more family-oriented activities and attractions.

Here's a look at Maui, "The Valley Isle."

Zone 7: Central Maui

Maui somewhat resembles a sculpted bust, with the "head"—the island's western side—facing the south. Our tour then begins near Maui's "neck," at **Kahului,** the island's center of business activity. A bay, a port, and Maui's largest shopping mall and main airport all fall within Kahului's boundaries; so does the **Maui Arts & Cultural Center (MACC).**

Kahului is primarily frequented by locals, and there aren't many attractions here for visitors. However, call the MACC or check the local newspapers and visitor publications for an updated schedule for special events at the center. If you're lucky, you'll be able to catch a concert at the MACC's 1,200-seat Castle Theater; entertainers who have performed here include Tony Bennett, Harry Belafonte, the Doobie Brothers, Carlos Santana, and Pearl Jam.

Next to Kahului is **Wailuku,** Maui's capital. Laid back and less hectic than Kahului, Wailuku offers several worthy points of interest, including the **Bailey House Museum,** formerly the missionary home of Reverend Edward Bailey and his family. Built in 1837, this historic complex houses an intriguing collection of Hawaiian artifacts and missionary-era memorabilia.

Wailuku is also the home of the 20,000-seat **War Memorial Stadium,** site of the Hula Bowl, an annual college all-star football game spotlighting the talents of the nation's top senior players. Formerly held on Oahu, the Hula Bowl has been a popular addition to the Valley Isle, and recently there have been discussions about expanding the stadium's seating capacity.

Heading west, it's a ten-minute scenic drive to **'Iao Valley State Park,** a photogenic valley carved from the West Maui Mountains. The centerpiece here is the **'Iao Needle,** a volcanic spire rising 1,200 feet from its base. Also in 'Iao Valley is **Kepaniwai Park,** an outdoor museum highlighting Maui's cultural heritage, and the **Hawaii Nature Center,** which offers environment-themed classes and guided hikes especially designed for children. The center also features an interactive arcade with some 30 hands-on exhibits focusing on Hawaii's natural history.

Zone 8: South Maui

At the tip of Maui's "chin" is a small waterfront community hugging the coast between the island's scenic sea cliffs and central valley. This is **Ma'alaea,** home to a peaceful boat harbor and surfing area known as Ma'alaea Rights.

At Ma'alaea, you'll find one of Maui's newest attractions, the **Maui Ocean Center.** While it doesn't offer dolphin shows, sea lion acts, and other marine-themed entertainment, the center does have a state-of-the-art 600,000-gallon aquarium housing hundreds of fascinating ocean creatures, including rays, sea turtles, reef fish, and even a tiger shark. The highlight here is the aquarium's transparent tunnel—located at the center of the tank—which provides a 240° view. You can literally look up and see schools of fish gliding above you!

Driving in the southern direction, you'll pass through **Kihei,** a thriving community with a wide mix of small hotels and condominiums, shops, restaurants, and businesses. Kihei is a good nightspot (a rarity on the Neighbor Islands), offering nightclubs, sports bars, karaoke, and other entertainment venues.

Just south of Kihei is the master-planned resort of **Wailea** ("water of Lea," goddess of canoes), a 1,500-acre oasis of luxurious hotels and condos, fine restaurants and shops, 54 holes of championship golf, and five of Hawaii's finest crescent beaches. In ancient lore, a mysterious bird-man named Manupae arrived at Paeahu, a land area where Wailea is today, in search of a mate. He met and fell in love with a lovely young woman named Kahaea o Kama'ole. Kahaea's father, a wealthy and powerful man on the island, did not approve of Manupae and banished him and Kahaea from the area. The young lovers fled to the high slopes of Haleakala Volcano, near a cinder cone called Pu'u Makua, and had a daughter. They named her Lelehune ("fine rain, spray"), after the refreshing mountain mists that breathed life to Maui's dry, thirsty lowlands. Today, the *lelehune* mists still kiss the pristine shores of Wailea, a gentle reminder of enduring love in the Islands.

Immediately following Wailea is another resort area, **Makena.** Its name translates to "abundance," and indeed the 1,800-acre resort remains mostly rugged, untamed natural beauty, along with two championship golf courses and the luxurious Maui Prince Hotel.

Zone 9: West Maui

It's an easy and pleasant 40-minute drive from Kahului Airport to West Maui, a magnet of visitor activity. Highway 30 includes several marked scenic points providing sweeping ocean views, so be prepared to make a stop or two along the way.

West Maui is where you'll find **Lahaina,** the most colorful and bustling town on the island. There is a great sense of history here—in fact, the entire town is designated a National Historic Landmark—and much of Lahaina's storied past continues to flavor the area today.

In the 18th century, Maui's high chief, Kahekili, declared Lahaina as his capital. He favored the area for its perfect weather, lush thickets of banana and breadfruit trees, and prime location (tucked comfortably between the West Maui Mountains and the Pacific Ocean).

Lahaina was the focal point of Hawaii's whaling industry in the mid–19th century; at the height of the whaling era, more than a hundred whaling ships lay anchor at the town's harbor. Along with the whaling ships, of course, came hundreds of pleasure-seeking sailors who turned Lahaina upside-down with their wild cavorting. A town prison was built in 1852 to contain the worst offenders.

The sailors were frequent antagonists to the disapproving Christian missionaries who lived in Lahaina. It was a constant battle between the two factions. Once, in 1825, a mob of British sailors threatened to kill William Richards, one of the first missionaries to settle on Maui, and set his house on fire unless a law forbidding prostitution and the sale of alcohol was repealed. Two years later, Richards's home was struck by a cannon from a visiting whaler. Wrote one missionary in 1837, "As a mass, the seamen are sunk in vice."

Today, a stroll through Lahaina includes many historical points of interest. At the **Baldwin Home Museum,** for example, take a guided tour of the fully restored home of the Reverend Dwight Baldwin, a prominent Protestant missionary in the 19th century, and gain insights into the triumphs and tribulations of Hawaii's missionaries. At Lahaina Harbor rests the 93-foot **Brig *Carthaginian II,*** a maritime museum featuring whaling displays along with an informative video. And nearby is **Hale Pa'ahao,** the old prison itself (appropriately enough, it's located on Prison Street), where hundreds of whaling-era sailors took "shelter" for the night, mostly for public drunkenness.

In Lahaina, the fun still heats up when the sun goes down, although not quite to the excesses of its bawdy past. Music, dancing, and trendy restaurants make this the place to be for visitors in search of nightlife. Among the well-known eateries here are Planet Hollywood and the Hard Rock Cafe, both on Front Street, the town's main street.

Front Street is the site of "Friday Night Is Art Night," a weekly celebration of Maui art featuring street entertainment and art demonstrations at participating galleries. Each Halloween night, Front Street hosts Maui's biggest and wildest costume parade, Hawaii's version of Mardi Gras. And the nearby Lahaina Civic Center is the site of the Maui Invitational, a made-for-TV college basketball tournament spotlighting some of the top NCAA schools in the U.S. (The event is televised on the ESPN cable network.)

A short drive up from Lahaina is the resort community of **Ka'anapali** ("cliffs of Ka'ana"), once a fertile playground for Hawaiian *ali'i.* A nice selection of accommodations, two championship golf courses, a three-mile beach, and an open-air shopping complex highlight an exploration of Ka'anapali. The shopping center, Whalers Village, features the **Whale Center of the Pacific**—a distinct museum spotlighting the life and history of Hawaii's state mammal, the humpback whale.

You can also reach Ka'anapali from Lahaina via the **Lahaina-Ka'anapali & Pacific Railroad,** better known as the "Sugar Cane Train." In the heyday of Maui's sugarcane era, plantations used privately owned railroad lines to transport their crops. The "Sugar Cane Train" represents the last of these railroads. It's a plodding but scenic half-hour round trip, and the conductor provides narration and entertainment throughout the excursion.

Beyond Ka'anapali, at Maui's northwest end, lies **Kapalua,** a picturesque resort community blessed with five exquisite bays. (Although Kapalua literally translates to "two borders," the preferred interpretation is the more poetic "arms embracing the sea.") Two luxury hotels—the Ritz-Carlton and the Kapalua and Kapalua Bay Hotel—as well as condominiums, three championship golf courses, two tennis complexes, and a multitude of fine shops and restaurants comprise Kapalua resort. Kapalua also hosts several major exclusive events each year, including the Mercedes Championships (an official PGA Tour event), Celebration of the Arts, Kapalua Wine and Food Symposium, and the Earth Maui Nature Summit. For hiking enthusiasts, the Kapalua Nature Society offers guests exclusive hikes into the West Maui Mountains.

Also, located three miles off of Maui's west side is **Molokini,** a tiny islet (actually a tuff cone) renowned for its pristine diving and snorkeling conditions. Measuring 18.6 acres and rising 165 feet above the ocean's surface, the crescent-shaped islet draws hundreds of visitors daily. Molokini was designated a Marine Life Conservation District in 1997.

Zone 10: Upcountry Maui and Beyond

Heading in the northeast direction from Kahului Airport on Highway 36 takes you to **Pa'ia,** a breezy former plantation town that is now famous for its **Ho'okipa Beach,** otherwise known as "the Aspen of windsurfing." Each year, Ho'okipa's superb wind and wave conditions draw the world's top windsurfers. It is quite a sight to see these ocean daredevils take on these perfect waves, riding their sleek boards with rainbow-colored "wings."

From Paʻia, head inland and start your way to the cooler elevations of upcountry Maui. The pleasant drive up the flanks of **Haleakala,** a dormant volcano and perhaps the island's top attraction, leads you to **Makawao,** a rustic *paniolo* (cowboy) town dotted with old wooden buildings, hitching posts, and other vestiges of the Wild West. Makawao also boasts an array of art galleries, restaurants, and the **Hui Noʻeau Visual Arts Center,** a charming art haven offering ongoing classes and special exhibits.

Farther upcountry is **Kula,** a scenic community known for its thriving flower and vegetable farms (Kula is renowned for its sweet onions), followed by **ʻUlupalakua Ranch.** The star attraction at this 20,000-acre ranch, believe it or not, is a winery. Drop by the tasting room at Tedeschi Vineyards and sample its famous pineapple wines. In the mid–19th century, ʻUlupalakua Ranch was a bustling sugar plantation; today, it serves as a cattle ranch.

From Kula you can take a road leading to **Haleakala National Park.** The park hosts more than half a million visitors per year and provides perhaps the most dramatic spectacle on the island.

Haleakala, a dormant volcano rising more than 10,000 feet above sea level, translates to "House of the Sun." According to Hawaiian legend, it was at Haleakala that the demi-god Maui captured the sun with his magic lasso. He convinced the sun to slow down in its travels, effectively lengthening the days and giving his mother Hina more time to dry her tapa cloths. Today, a Haleakala sunrise rates as one of the most awe-inspiring experiences on earth. Mark Twain called it "the sublimest spectacle I have ever witnessed."

Physically, Haleakala Crater actually resembles the face of the moon. In 1972, in fact, astronauts preparing for their *Apollo 16* mission spent a day hiking here. Haleakala is one of only two places in the world—the Big Island is the other—where you'll find the exotic silversword, an odd-looking plant with silvery leaves and yellow and violet florets (it flowers from June through October).

Park rangers offer free hiking excursions and informative lectures on topics ranging from Haleakala's geological history to the Hawaiian culture.

Taking a different route from Paʻia starts you on the long road to **Hana,** an arduous but rewarding two-and-a-half-hour drive that includes 56 one-lane bridges and 617 twists and turns (about 12 curves per mile!). Patience is the key here, and it helps that the drive is accompanied by some of Maui's most spectacular sights: crashing surf, steep green hills, gushing waterfalls, and flowers and fruits of every kind.

Hana itself, while covering the entire eastern portion of the island, is basically a small community of about a thousand residents. The lifestyle here is slow and unpretentious, and the locals here wouldn't want it any other way. Highlights include the **Hana Cultural Center** (a tiny museum retelling the history of the area), **Hana Coast Gallery, Hana Gardenland,** and the **Hasegawa General Store** (a popular family-run store crammed with wares of all kinds). A single resort hotel, a few condos, and some bed-and-breakfasts are among the available accommodations.

Ten miles south of the town of Hana is **Kipahulu,** where the gravesite of Charles Lindbergh is located. The famed American aviator—in 1927, he became the first person to fly solo across the Atlantic Ocean—visited Kipahulu in the 1950s and fell in love with the area and with the Valley Isle. "I love Maui so much, I would rather live one day in Maui than one month in New York," a cancer-stricken Lindbergh confided to his doctors. The "Lone Eagle" spent the final eight days of his life in a guest cottage just outside of Hana. He died on August 26, 1974, at the age of 72.

While there are no signs pointing the way to the site—Kipahulu residents take great care not to turn it into an unwieldy tourist attraction—Lindbergh's grave lies near the Palapala Ho'omau Congregational Church, beneath a mound of *'ili'ili* stones and a block of Vermont granite.

Offering a sizable menu of accommodations, restaurants, attractions, activities, shopping options, and cultural and sporting events, Maui could almost be considered a mini-Oahu. But the Valley Isle remains much less congested, and much more green. Maui and Oahu can both lay claim to having the best of both worlds. Oahu, by far, offers more visitor attractions. Maui, meanwhile, offers more natural wonders such as Haleakala, 'Iao Valley, and Hana.

Maui *no ka 'oi?* It really depends on what your own whims and desires are. But we like it.

HAWAII: THE BIG ISLAND

Hawaii Facts
Flower: Red lehua
Color: Red
County Seat: Hilo
Area: 4,028 square miles
Length: 93 miles
Width: 76 miles
Population: 137,531
Highest Point: Mauna Kea (13,796 feet)
Coastline: 266 miles

The youngest of the major Hawaiian islands, the island of Hawaii—popularly known as the "Big Island"—is also the biggest, encompassing 4,028 square miles. The Big Island, in fact, is twice the size of all other Hawaiian islands combined!

The island of Hawaii was formed by five volcanoes, two of which remain active: Mauna Loa and Kilauea (the other three are Mauna Kea, Kohala, and Hualalai). It is here that the fire goddess Pele is said to have made her home, digging into the mountaintop at Kilauea and creating a fiery pit, where she continues to reside. Lava has been flowing from Kilauea's southeastern rifts since 1983, seeping across Chain of Craters Road and spilling into the waiting sea. Pele's liquid fire has added an estimated 500 acres of land to the island in the last dozen or so years.

The Big Island is full of "big" superlatives: **Kilauea Volcano** is the state's top (and literally the hottest) visitor attraction. **Mauna Kea,** measured at 33,476 feet from the ocean floor, is the world's tallest mountain. The island boasts the world's largest anthurium and orchid flower industries and is one of the largest producers of macadamia nuts. Parker Ranch in Waimea is one of the world's largest privately owned cattle ranches. The Big Island is the home of the world's most prestigious hula festival and triathlon event. And of the 13 climatic regions on Earth, the Big Island has all but the 2 most extreme: the Arctic and Saharan.

In this case, bigger *is* better. There is a lot to like about the Big Island, offering a full menu of outdoor activities, top-flight accommodations and restaurants, cultural events, and more. The island is also steeped in history and legends and was the birthplace of Hawaii's greatest king, Kamehameha I.

Here, the easiest way to plan your vacation itinerary is to take a Big Island map and draw a vertical line right down the middle of the island. Locals refer to the left half of the island as the "Kona" side, while the right half is the "Hilo" side. Both sides of the island are well worth a visit, and unless you're willing to pay high prices for specialized van or limousine tours, renting a car is a must.

Here's an overview of Hawaii, the Big Island.

Zone 11: Kona

The hub of visitor activity on the Big Island is on the Kona side, particularly at the breezy seaside village of **Kailua-Kona.** American humorist Mark Twain, who fell in love with the Hawaiian Islands during his very first visit in March 1866, once described Kailua-Kona as "the sleepiest, quietest, Sundayest-looking place you can imagine."

We doubt Twain would approve of the area today, with its mini-jungle of hotels, condominiums, restaurants, and shops, and a steady parade of visitors walking or driving along Ali'i Drive, Kailua-Kona's mini-version of Kalakaua Avenue in Waikiki. (Then again, who knows? If Twain were alive today, perhaps he would put on his brightest aloha shirt and join in all the revelry!)

On the northern end of Ali'i Drive is **Hulihe'e Palace,** a gray, two-story structure that was built in 1838 for Governor John Adams Kuakini. The palace later became a favorite retreat for several Hawaiian *ali'i,* including King Kalakaua. Today the palace serves as a living museum, offering visitors a captivating glimpse of royal life in the 19th century.

Across the street from the palace is another historic landmark: **Moku'aikaua Church,** the first Christian church built in Hawaii. Constructed of koa and ohia wood, rocks, and coral, the church is listed on the National Register of Historic Places. Hymns and the benediction are still offered in the Hawaiian language during Sunday services.

Big-game fishing is the biggest draw in Kailua-Kona, with fishing experts and novices alike boarding charter boats in search of Pacific blue marlin, yellowfin tuna (*'ahi*), mahi-mahi, *'ulua,* swordfish, and other fish from the deep. The waters off the Kona coast are considered among the best sport-fishing spots in the world. Each summer, Kailua-Kona hosts the Hawaiian International Billfish Tournament, a prestigious fishing event luring the world's top anglers. The largest fish ever caught during the event was a 1,166-pound marlin in 1993.

While we're on the subject of major sporting events, Kailua-Kona is the site of the annual Ironman Triathlon World Championship. Held each October, this grueling test of endurance—competitors must complete a 2.4-mile swim, a 112-mile bike ride, and a full 26.2-mile marathon—attracts hundreds of top triathletes from around the globe.

A short five-mile drive from Kailua-Kona takes you to **Holualoa,** a sleepy town resting 1,400 feet above sea level on the slopes of Mount Hualalai. Art lovers in particular will appreciate the area's main strip of local art galleries (along Mamalahoa Highway). Scenic views overlooking Kailua-Kona and the ocean beyond add to Holualoa's attractions.

South of Kailua-Kona is **Kealakekua Bay,** a state marine conservation district. It is here that a 27-foot-tall white monument marks the spot of Captain Cook's death in 1779. The British sea captain and 4 of his men were killed in a skirmish with natives (4 Hawaiian chiefs and 13 commoners were also killed in the battle). Access to the monument is best via kayak or boat. If you want to go by foot, it's about a one-and-a-half-mile hike down the trail leading to the monument.

Farther south, 22 miles from Kailua-Kona, is **Pu'uhonua O Honaunau National Historical Park.** In ancient Hawaii, this site was a place of refuge, where violators of *kapu* (taboos) could escape certain death for their crimes. The Hawaiians of old strongly enforced their laws, believing that sins left unpunished would incur the wrath of their gods in the form of earthquakes, tidal waves, famines, and volcanic eruptions. They pursued violators relentlessly, and death was the immediate sentence.

However, if a *kapu* breaker managed to reach a *pu'uhonua*—a place of refuge—he would be able to seek absolution from a *kahuna,* or priest, and offer to serve penance. The violator would then be completely forgiven and allowed to return to his home.

Pu'uhonua O Honaunau is the best preserved and most renowned of all of Hawaii's places of refuge. More than 400,000 visitors visit this 180-acre site each year, breathing in the area's deep history and viewing the park's tall wooden *ki'i,* or statues. Each summer, the park hosts a cultural festival offering Hawaiian arts and crafts, *lau hala* weaving demonstrations, Hawaiian games, hula performances, food tastings, and more.

Traveling all the way down the coast not only leads you to the southernmost part of the island; **Ka Lae** (also known as South Point) is also the southernmost tip in the United States.

Heading north from Kailua-Kona brings you to the island's sunny **Kohala Coast,** a wide-open playground marked by luxury resorts, hiking trails, and white-sand beaches. Historical points of interest are also prevalent here. The area has several ancient fishponds, which early-day Hawaiians used to raise food for their kings and queens. The fish would be wrapped in ti leaves and delivered by servants to their *ali'i* in Kailua-Kona. Parts of this "King's Trail" are still visible from the coast.

Inland from the Kohala Coast, at the foot of Mauna Kea, is lovely **Waimea** (also called Kamuela), a peaceful cowtown where the *paniolo* lifestyle still thrives and the panorama is brushed with rolling emerald hills and lush pastures.

Waimea's chief occupant, **Parker Ranch,** is one of the largest cattle ranches in the United States. Established in 1847 by John Palmer Parker, an American sailor and husband to Kipikane, the granddaughter of Kamehameha I, the ranch is the setting for several community events, including a major rodeo held every Fourth of July. The nearby Parker Ranch Visitor Center and Museum spotlights the history of the ranch as well as six generations of the Parker family. Tours are given at Pu'u'opelu and a replica of Mana, the Parker family homes.

Nearby is **Kawaihae,** where **Pu'ukohola Heiau,** a magnificent stone temple honoring the war god Kuka'ilimoku, stands as a powerful reminder of the island's *mana* (spiritual power). The *heiau* was built around 1791 under the command of Kamehameha I. Visits to Pu'ukohola Heiau, named a National Historic Site in 1972, originate at the visitor center, where a park ranger shares the history of the *heiau* and two neighboring sites, Mailekini and Hale O Kapuni (Hale O Kapuni is underwater and is not visible).

North Kohala, the peninsula that forms the northernmost tip of the Big Island, is the birthplace of Kamehameha. He was born just west of the **Mo'okini Luakini Heiau,** Hawaii's first National Historic Landmark. The stones used for the construction of the *heiau* were supposedly passed hand to hand for nine miles from the coastline.

In Kapaʻau, pose for a picture in front of the gilt and bronze **Kamehameha Statue,** which fronts the town's civic center. This is the *original* Kamehameha statue; sculpted in 1880 by an American sculptor working in Europe, the statue was lost at sea somewhere off the Falkland Islands. It was later recovered and sent to Kapaʻau after a replica had been built and shipped to Honolulu.

Heading east from Kapaʻau, toward Hilo, is **Waipiʻo Valley,** a gorgeous setting carpeted with taro patches and framed by dramatic 2,000-foot cliffs and waterfalls. Once a favorite retreat of Hawaiian royalty, the valley is accessible via four-wheel-drive vehicle or by foot.

Continuing on toward Hilo, you'll pass by 13,796-foot **Mauna Kea** (33,476 feet when measured from the ocean floor), a dormant volcano that is often carpeted with snow during the winter months, providing suitable conditions for skiing enthusiasts. This is the home of the **Mauna Kea Observatory,** where leading astronomers from around the world study the heavens using the most technologically advanced telescopes on earth.

Zone 12: Hilo and Volcano

Hilo, on the eastern side of the Big Island, is the island's county seat and largest city—population: 47,639—yet it still has all the charm and ambience of an old-fashioned small town. Most years, Hilo ranks as the wettest city in the United States, and the result is as green and lush a locale as you'll find in the Islands.

In old Hawaii, Hilo was a bustling center of trade activity. The activity only heightened with the arrival of Westerners, as Hilo Bay, with its wide expanses, gave foreign vessels safe harbor. In August 1881, however, a lava flow from neighboring Mauna Loa Volcano cut a path straight toward Hilo, threatening to consume the growing town. On August 9, Kamehameha IV's half-sister, Princess Ruth Keʻelikolani—an imposing figure herself at six feet tall and 400-plus pounds—arrived from Honolulu and, standing at the edge of the lava flow, prayed and presented offerings of *ʻohelo* berries, tobacco, flowers, red silk, and brandy to the goddess Pele.

The princess's bookkeeper, Oliver Kawailahaole Stillman, later wrote: "Early the next morning, all of us went to the lava flow, and we couldn't believe our eyes. The flow had stopped right there."

Hilo was not as fortunate when it came to tsunamis. On the morning of April 1, 1946, the Hawaiian Islands were struck by devastating tidal waves, the result of an Alaskan earthquake. Hilo was the hardest hit, and nearly a hundred residents lost their lives.

Even today, inspiring accounts from the disaster readily reveal Hilo's unyielding perseverance: Using a long rope, one Hawaiian man tied one end around his body and the other to a banyan tree, then leaped into the raging Waiola River to rescue a pair of youths. Another man, spotting a young Japanese boy being sucked down the same river, rushed to grab him by the hair and pulled him to safety; to his surprise, he discovered a smaller boy, dripping wet and still clinging hard to his older brother's legs. An 84-year-old boilermaker, Fred Naylor, witnessed a young girl stumbling onto Kamehameha Avenue during the chaos. He managed to grab her and push her to a safe spot, but a wave caught him and slammed him against a building. Naylor was the first tsunami victim to be identified.

Just 14 years later, in 1960, another tsunami struck Hilo, killing 61 residents. The *Honolulu Star-Bulletin* reported the next day: "The devastation is unimaginable. It's as if the whole bayfront had been swept of its buildings like a child destroys a toy village."

Today, Hilo has completely recovered, and longtime residents say the city has never looked better. An exploration of the area should include a stop in downtown Hilo, where residents and visitors mingle in shops, restaurants, and the twice-weekly farmer's market.

Next to the public library along Waianuenue Street rests the ancient **Naha Stone.** According to legend, whoever could move this three-ton rectangular-shaped boulder would be crowned the greatest king of Hawaii. Those who tried and failed, however, would be put to death!

Other recommended stops in Hilo include the 20-acre **Nani Mau Gardens,** the **Lyman Mission House and Museum, Big Island Candies,** and the new **Pacific Tsunami Museum.**

Downtown Hilo is the site of the prestigious **Merrie Monarch Festival,** a weeklong celebration of the native Hawaiian dance. A parade, street party, and hula demonstrations are some of the preliminary highlights. During the final three nights, the finest *halau* from Hawaii and even the mainland compete for honors in both traditional and contemporary hula categories. Be aware: Tickets for the festival sell out months in advance, so make sure you call ahead of time for ticket availability.

It's a 45-minute drive from Hilo to **Volcano,** a burgeoning art community just outside **Hawaii Volcanoes National Park.** Here you'll find a terrific art center offering the works of the island's finest artists as well as the **Volcano Winery,** selling unique wines, including passion fruit Chablis.

Finally, of course, there is Hawaii Volcanoes National Park, the top visitor attraction in the state. But first drop by the visitor center, located on the northern rim of Kilauea Caldera (about a quarter-mile from the park's entrance), and get acquainted with the ins and outs of **Kilauea,** the world's most active volcano. A number of volcano-themed exhibits are on display here, including a 20-minute film showing past eruptions. Inside the park is another education-oriented center, the **Thomas A. Jaggar Museum,** showing videos of eruptions, geological displays, and working seismic equipment.

While you can see a lot of the park on foot, with several self-guided hiking trails (of varying lengths, most of them fairly easy) at your disposal, consider getting a "bird's-eye view" of Kilauea via a helicopter tour. Viewing conditions depend on the weather as well as the day's lava activity. Call 985-6000 for recorded updates. The park is open 24 hours daily.

As we mentioned before, there is a lot to like about the island of Hawaii. There are plenty of unique opportunities here. Don't believe us? Well, ask yourself this question: Where else can you ski, sunbathe, and then view a lava-spouting volcano all on the same day?

ZONE 13: KAUAI, THE GARDEN ISLE

Kauai Facts

Flower: Mokihana
Color: Purple
County Seat: Lihu'e
Area: 549 square miles
Length: 33 miles
Width: 25 miles
Population: 54,200
Highest Point: Kawaikiki Peak (5,243 feet)
Coastline: 90 miles

Of all the Hawaiian islands, none has endured as much hardship over the past couple of decades as Kauai. Devastated by two major hurricanes in a ten-year span—'Iwa in 1982 and 'Iniki in 1992—it seemed at times as though the island might never fully recover. Homes were damaged. Crops were destroyed. Tourists stopped coming. Businesses closed. And for a short time, an island famous for its natural beauty was littered with toppled trees, fallen streetlight poles, and tons of scattered debris.

That, however, was then. Today, a quick tour of Kauai will show majestic sea cliffs, verdant valleys, tranquil lagoons, shimmering waterfalls, sun-kissed beaches, and shady coconut groves.

Let the record show: "The Garden Isle" is once again in full bloom, as beautiful as it's ever been.

That's good news not only for Kauai's 54,000 residents but also for the many longtime visitors who reserve a special place in their hearts for the island. With its obvious wealth of natural beauty—it served as a scenic backdrop for Hollywood films like *South Pacific, Blue Hawaii, Donovan's Reef, Raiders of the Lost Ark,* and *Jurassic Park*—Kauai might be as close as you can get to heaven on Earth.

Geographically, Kauai is situated at the northwestern end of the Hawaiian archipelago, some 70 miles from Oahu. It is the oldest of the major islands, rising from the sea floor, scientists say, millions of years ago. It was also, many believe, the first Hawaiian island to be populated.

Kauai lays claim to several other key moments in Hawaiian history. It was at Waimea Bay, on the southwestern part of the island, where the first non-Polynesian—British Captain James Cook—first stepped on Hawaiian soil. Also, Kauai is the only island to have fended off Kamehameha I's fearsome military advances; the Big Island chief's two invasion attempts—in 1796 and 1809—failed miserably, the first due to poor weather conditions and the second because of disease. Kauai's high chief, Kaumuali'i, peacefully ceded his kingdom to Kamehameha in 1810.

Perhaps most intriguing of all, Kauai is said to be the home of the Menehune, a legendary race of small people (similar to the leprechauns of Ireland) who worked only at night, tirelessly building fishponds, roads, temples, and other important structures. Each project had to be completed in a single night or it would be left unfinished. The Menehune were the epitome of low-cost labor, accepting as payment for their deeds a single shrimp per worker. That the Menehune worked only at night was with good cause: If they were exposed to sunlight, they supposedly turned into stone. Hence, many boulders you see on the island may be referred to as petrified Menehune.

An exploration of Kauai leads you to a wealth of natural, historical, and cultural gems. A good starting point is **Lihu'e,** located on the southeastern part of the island. A drive along Rice Street takes you to the **Kauai Museum,** where the island's history is retold through a nice mix of artifacts, artworks, photographs, and other exhibit items. Also in Lihu'e is the island's major seaport, **Nawiliwili Harbor;** the **'Alekoko Fish Pond** (also known as the Menehune Fish Pond) is believed to be one example of the Menehunes' workmanship.

Just south of Lihu'e is the **Grove Farm Homestead,** a marvelous complex that encompasses a museum, washhouse, teahouse, and other mementos of Hawaii's plantation era. This former plantation site was built in 1864 by George Wilcox, whose parents were among the first American Christian missionaries to the Islands.

Continuing past the Grove Farm Homestead leads you to the resort area known as **Po'ipu,** a sun-drenched playground featuring one of Hawaii's best beaches. Po'ipu suffered major damage during Hurricane 'Iniki, and painful reminders come in the form of a few empty lots that dot the area. Among the scenic highlights here is **Spouting Horn,** an ancient lava tube where the rushing surf shoots through a narrow opening, causing seawater to explode 50 feet into the air.

In nearby Koloa, next to the Po'ipu Shopping Village, the **Moir Gardens** at **Kiahuna Plantation** is a 35-acre botanical garden characterized by lagoons, lily ponds, flowers, and trees. In all, nearly 4,000 different botanical varieties may be found here.

Continuing in the leeward (west) direction, stop in Lawa'i and visit the **National Tropical Botanical Garden,** an exotic 186-acre Eden that maintains the largest collection of tropical flora in the world. Here you'll view heliconia, anthuriums, plumeria, ginger, orchids, and other flora. Neighboring **Allerton Garden,** also managed by the National Tropical Botanical Garden, is a stunning collection of flora set amid waterfalls, gazebos, and a bamboo jungle.

Next is the ancient **Salt Ponds,** located near the small town of Hanapepe. Here, during spring and summer, traditional salt makers still fill these muddy ponds with seawater, then let the sun do its work, evaporating the water until only clusters of salt crystals remain. A scenic overlook into Hanapepe Valley makes this a worthwhile side trip.

Farther leeward, at the mouth of the Waimea River, are the rocky remains of **Fort Elizabeth,** which was built in 1816 by Anton Schaeffer (with the unwitting help of Kauai chief Kaumuali'i) in an unsuccessful attempt to claim Kauai for the Russian crown.

In the town of Waimea stands a statue of Captain James Cook, who first set foot on Hawaiian soil here on January 20, 1778. And then there is 3,567-foot **Waimea Canyon,** a breathtaking 15-mile gorge characterized by waterfalls and a deep valley covered in green. Mark Twain was so inspired by Waimea Canyon that he dubbed it "the Grand Canyon of the Pacific."

Just north of Waimea is the **Barking Sands Missile Range.** Check in at the gate and head to **Barking Sands Beach,** so named because of the unique "barking" sounds the sand makes as you hoof it on the beach.

Driving up from Waimea, you'll come to the remote town of **Koke'e** ("to bend or wind"). Here, a good stop for history buffs is the **Koke'e Natural History Museum,** which features a collection of nostalgic photographs, maps, petroglyph rubbings, and displays of endemic plants and animals. In old Hawaii, Koke'e was revered by natives as a sanctuary for their gods; its previous name was Wao Akua, or "mountains of the gods." Today, Koke'e is a favorite spot for camping and hiking, offering 45 miles of picturesque trails. (See Part Seven, "Exercise and Recreation.")

Many scenic marvels may be discovered by heading north of Lihu'e. Driving along Kuhio Highway on the island's eastern coast—popularly known as the "Coconut Coast"—you'll reach **Wailua State Park.** Sign up for a boat ride and cruise the Wailua River (the only navigable river in the state) to the Fern Grotto, a popular wedding spot draped dramatically with emerald ferns. The 1,092-acre park encompasses several historic landmarks, including prominent *heiau,* a birthing stone, and a navel stone.

In ancient Hawaii, high-ranking women gave birth at such stones because they believed this would ensure that their children would grow up to be powerful chiefs. The baby's umbilical cord would be placed in a cloth and hidden in the navel stone (or *piko* stone); Hawaiians were fearful that if the cord were snatched away by a rodent, the baby would grow up to be a common thief.

From Wailua River, take in the curious spectacle of the **"Sleeping Giant,"** a mountain so named because its ridge closely resembles the outline of a slumbering behemoth.

Driving past the town of Kapa'a and reaching the northern section of the island, make a stop at the **Kilauea Point National Wildlife Refuge,** home to one of the largest seabird nesting areas in the state. Also here is a 52-foot-high lighthouse, which was built in 1913 to help trade ships maneuver safely at sea. Now deactivated, the lighthouse was placed on the National Register of Historic Places in 1979. Spinner dolphins, humpback whales, sea turtles, monk seals, and about a dozen different species of seabirds can be viewed from Kilauea Point.

Beyond Kilauea is the carefully planned resort area of **Princeville,** featuring a luxury hotel and two championship golf courses.

Next is **Hanalei** ("crescent bay"), a misty valley that is said to be the birthplace of the rainbow. A Hawaiian god, Kaneloa, had thrown *kapa* sheets dyed in red, orange, yellow, blue, green, purple, and other hues into the pool at Namolokama Falls. The colors arched upward, reflecting vibrantly in the mist, and out from this dazzling veil appeared Anuenue, goddess of the rainbow.

Still, the dominant color in Hanalei is green, with patchworks of taro fields, deep-emerald hills, and a wild forest of trees and ferns. Hanalei, in fact, is the greenest section on the Garden Isle.

The final stop of our Kauai tour is our choice for the most scenic location on the island: the magnificent **Na Pali Coast.** Accessible only by foot or via boat during the calm summer and autumn months, the Na Pali—located on Kauai's northwestern coast—is a dramatic 25-mile stretch of wind- and wave-worn cliffs rising majestically from the sea. This remote section of the island provides some terrific (and challenging) hiking trails, including the 11-mile Kalalau Trail, which begins at Ke'e Beach.

If sheer natural beauty is what you're after, we wouldn't hesitate to recommend Kauai. Twain himself noted, "No other land could so longingly and so beseechingly haunt me, sleeping and waking, through half a lifetime, as that one has done."

Using another criterion, however, new visitor attractions and family activities on Kauai are rather sparse. We imagine this is true for two reasons: One, Hurricane 'Iniki stalled or even halted plans for future developments and attractions, and two, Kauai is the Garden Isle, not Disney World. The *true* attraction on Kauai will always be its unparalleled beauty. It is likely that honeymooners and couples seeking that special romantic getaway will enjoy a Garden Isle stay the most.

ZONE 14: MOLOKAI, THE FRIENDLY ISLE

Molokai Facts
Flower: White kukui blossom
Color: Green
County Seat: Kaunakakai
Area: 260 square miles
Length: 38 miles
Width: 10 miles
Population: 6,717
Highest Point: Kamakou Peak (4,961 feet)
Coastline: 88 miles

The island of Molokai is marketed as "The Most Hawaiian Island," and there is ample evidence to back up the claim. Other than Niihau, for example, Molokai has the greatest percentage of native Hawaiians in the Hawaiian Islands. Technically a part of Maui County, Molokai is the least-developed of Hawaii's main islands and serves as the most visual reminder of old Hawaii.

In those early days, Molokai was known as Molokai Pule O'o, or "Molokai of the Potent Prayers." Formed by two now-dormant volcanoes—Maunaloa on the west and Kamakou on the east—the island was home to *kahuna* (priests) who were revered for their spiritual strength and mystical abilities. Because of this, Molokai was largely spared from the bloody battles waged among chiefs of other islands.

Today, for better or worse, Molokai has been spared from something else: development. Here, you won't find a single traffic light. Nor will you come across a shopping mall, a nightclub, or even a McDonalds. Perhaps most telling, you won't find a single elevator on Molokai—there's no need for one, as no structure on the island is taller than a palm tree.

This doesn't mean Molokai is bare of activities and attractions. There are several enticing visitor offerings here, including the world-famous **Molokai**

Mule Ride down to historic **Kalaupapa.** But with each plan for a new development, special care is taken not to disturb the simple, unpretentious lifestyle embraced by the island's 6,700 residents.

Most visitors headquarter themselves at **Kaluako'i**—Molokai's principal resort area—on the western side of the island. The 103-room Kaluako'i Hotel and Golf Club, the island's biggest hotel, sits near **Papohaku Beach,** Hawaii's largest white-sand beach (it's three miles long). Also here is the island's only 18-hole golf course, where the par-4 Hole 10, a dogleg that hugs the ocean, recalls the famous finishing hole at Pebble Beach.

Hopping in a rental car and heading inland, you'll come to **Molokai Ranch** in Maunaloa, site of an annual rodeo and town celebration. (Molokai Ranch, with 53,000 acres, is the island's largest landowner.) The ranch's Outfitters Center is the starting point for several exhilarating adventures, including your chance to make like an old-time *paniolo* (cowboy) and learn traditional rodeo events such as barrel racing and pole bending.

Horseback riding is another worthwhile activity here, as expert guides lead you to a variety of scenic highlights, including Kalaupapa Peninsula and the world's highest sea cliffs. Other options at the ranch include mountain biking, kayaking, and cultural hikes.

A recent addition to the ranch is Paniolo Camp, made up of 40 one-unit and two-unit tents mounted on wooden platforms. The hillside camp boasts breathtaking ocean views and includes three daily meals.

On the slopes of Maunaloa is **Ka'ana,** where tradition says Laka, the goddess of the hula, created the native Hawaiian dance and set forth to teach it to natives throughout the Hawaiian Islands. In celebration of this event, the **Molokai Ka Hula Piko** is held each May at Papohaku Beach Park. The day-long festival features hula performances, Hawaiian music, food, and local arts and crafts.

Continuing your drive east, make a stop at the **Molokai Museum & Cultural Center** in Kala'e, at the center of the island. The museum is actually a restored sugar mill that was established by Rudolph Wilhelm Meyer, an engineer and surveyor who arrived on Molokai in 1851 and married a Hawaiian chiefess. Guided tours and cultural programs are among the highlights at this museum.

Heading south along Highway 450 takes you to **Kaunakakai,** a charming town not unlike what you'd find in a Hollywood Western. This is Molokai's version of "downtown," its main street lined with family-run businesses such as Kanemitsu Bakery, where you can pick up its famous Molokai bread. The Mitchell Pau'ole Center, meanwhile, is the site of softball games, art bazaars, chicken roasts, and other community events.

Beyond Kaunakakai is the island's tallest mountain, **Kamakou** (4,961 feet), home to a natural wonderland of native trees and birds. The

Kamakou Preserve is managed by the Nature Conservancy on Molokai.

Farther north is the **'Ili'ili'opae Heiau,** another historic site. More than 700 years old and measuring 320 by 120 feet, this is one of the largest preserved *heiau* in the state. According to legend, this *heiau* was built by Menehune (a legendary race of small people) out of stones taken from Wailau Valley on Molokai's northern coast. You can reach the *heiau* through the Molokai Horse and Wagon Ride, which departs from Mapulehu on the island's eastern side.

Molokai's northern coast is the setting of some of the most awe-inspiring views on Earth. Sign up for a cruise and sail along the coastline, taking in the majestic sight of the world's highest sea cliffs, which tower 3,300 feet above the crashing surf.

The best-known area of the island is **Kalaupapa,** where people stricken with Hansen's disease (leprosy) were banished in the 19th century. (They were literally pushed from a boat into the waters off the peninsula and had to swim to shore.) It is here where Father Damien de Veuster, a Belgian priest, arrived in 1873 and embraced these outcasts. He immediately requested a permanent assignment at the colony. "The sick are arriving by the boatloads," he wrote to his superiors. "They die in droves."

Damien spent the next 16 years caring for his congregation. He washed their sores and changed their dressings. He sought medicine, food, shelter, and clothing for them. It was an exhausting and arduous labor of love, and Damien was for much of the time alone in his efforts. Any contributions by visiting doctors were left on a fence post to avoid physical contact with the patients. By the end of the 1870s, approximately 1,000 people were exiled to Kalaupapa.

On April 15, 1889, Damien himself succumbed to Hansen's disease. He was 49.

Today, a visit to Molokai wouldn't be complete without a tour of Kalaupapa, now a National Historical Park where about 60 patients still reside. (Hansen's disease is now controlled by modern medicine and is no longer considered a public threat.) The popular **Molokai Mule Ride** leads guests to Kalaupapa via sure-footed mules. The ride down the 26-switchback trail is lengthy—it takes about an hour and a half to reach Kalaupapa—but the fabulous views of Molokai's northern coast make it a pleasurable experience the entire way. Upon arriving at Kalaupapa, the group connects with Damien Tours for a guided excursion to the peninsula's historic sites, including the recently restored **Saint Philomena Church** (built by Damien).

If riding a mule doesn't sound like a "kick" to you, you can also reach Kalaupapa by foot or fly in from the airport via Damien Tours. Take note, however: Kalaupapa is a restricted area, and visitors are not permitted to go exploring on their own.

All in all, a Molokai vacation isn't for everyone. There are few activities geared toward young children, for example, and parents might be hard-pressed to keep the little ones occupied. Certainly, if your idea of a great vacation includes big-city sights and a cavalcade of commercial attractions, this island isn't for you. But if unspoiled natural beauty and a quiet lifestyle appeal to you most, Molokai is a worthwhile visit.

ZONE 15: LANAI, THE PINEAPPLE ISLAND

Lanai Facts
Flower: Kaunaoa *Color:* Orange *County Seat:* Lanai City *Area:* 141 square miles *Length:* 18 miles *Width:* 13 miles *Population:* 2,800 *Highest Point:* Lanaihale (3,366 feet) *Coastline:* 47 miles

From pineapples to par-fours: That sums up the remarkable transformation the island of Lanai has undergone in recent years.

The smallest of Hawaii's six accessible islands—and, like Molokai, a part of Maui County—Lanai was once home to the world's largest pineapple plantation. Today, however, the island—a scenic Eden blessed with lush fern forests, Norfolk pines, and coconut palms—caters to weary vacationers seeking peaceful surroundings, luxurious accommodations, and resort activities such as snorkeling and golf. While Lanai once boasted more than 19,000 acres of the sweet and juicy fruit, less than 200 acres of pineapple remain on the island today.

Consequently, while Lanai's official nickname remains "The Pineapple Island," marketing execs have cast it aside in favor of a more romantic image: "Hawaii's Most Secluded Island."

It hasn't been a painless transition, as some local residents—many of whom grew up working in the pineapple fields—have struggled to embrace the island's shift from agriculture to tourism. In the end, however, considering the dark clouds that hovered over Lanai's pineapple industry, the island's owner—Castle & Cooke—likely had no choice but to find an alternative means to fuel the economy.

An old Hawaiian tale explains how agriculture was first introduced on Lanai: In ancient times, the island was ruled by evil spirits, or *ka polo*. According to the fable, it took a clever young man named Kaulula'au, exiled from Maui by his father, to rid the island of these spirits. He made the *ka polo* flee to the neighboring island of Kahoolawe, but not before tricking them into helping him plant breadfruit and taro crops on Lanai, making the island inhabitable for future residents.

History notes that one of the first attempts at establishing an agricultural industry on Lanai was made by the Mormons, who settled on the island in the 1850s after receiving a lease from an Oahu chief. Those attempts, however, were thwarted by insects and droughts. In 1904, an American businessman named Charles Gay began purchasing various parcels on Lanai, and four years later he owned the entire island. Gay sold the island in 1922 to James Dole, who quickly moved to turn his $1.1 million investment into the pineapple capital of the world. For the next six decades, pineapple reigned as king on Lanai—it even had its own "crown"!

In the 1980s, however, it became apparent that Lanai could no longer compete with foreign pineapple growers, whose production costs were much lower. In 1987, a California investor named David Murdock bought a controlling interest in Castle & Cooke, the corporation that owns 98% of the island (it had previously purchased Dole's pineapple operations and renamed it Dole Pineapple Company). Murdock's vision for Lanai was as a flourishing resort destination.

The first of two luxury hotels on Lanai, the **Lodge at Ko'ele,** opened its doors in April 1990. A year later, the **Manele Bay Hotel** made its debut. The resorts are as distinct in appearance as in location: The Lodge at Ko'ele is reminiscent of a stately English manor and is located upcountry at the center of the island, while the Manele Bay Hotel overlooks beautiful Hulopo'e Bay and was designed with classic Hawaiian and Mediterranean influences. The two properties are understated rather than gaudy, and they blend in well with the natural beauty of the island.

In sync with the resort theme, golf is the sport of choice on Lanai. Two 18-hole championship courses are available here: **The Experience at Ko'ele** was designed by golf superstar Greg Norman and noted course architect Ted Robinson. The newer **Challenge at Manele,** meanwhile, was designed by the legendary "Golden Bear" himself, Jack Nicklaus. Both courses have garnered awards from publications such as *Golf Digest.*

Other activities on Lanai include swimming, snorkeling, horseback riding, whale-watching, fishing, lawn bowling, croquet, clay shooting, and hunting (in season).

Lanai even has its own version of Stonehenge. Set on a Kanepu'u, a mountain ridge near the center of the island, lies a mysterious collection of strewn boulders and red lava cliffs. This is the **Garden of the Gods.** Some say this is the dwelling place for the spirits of ancient Hawaiian warriors. Go during sunrise or sunset, when the low light casts eerie shadows in the area, and judge for yourself.

A drive up Munro Trail leads to the summit of 3,366-foot **Lanaihale,** the highest point on the island. On clear days, you'll have sweeping views of the islands of Maui, Molokai, Kahoolawe, and the Big Island. Many historians believe that Lanaihale served as a command post for high-ranking chiefs—from this vantage point, they could monitor canoe comings and goings in the kingdom's sea lanes.

For ocean enthusiasts, Lanai is regarded as a five-star locale among divers. *Skin Diver Magazine* rated **Cathedrals,** two large underwater caves near the island's pristine **Hulopo'e Bay,** as Hawaii's top diving spot. This spot evidently got its name because of the sunlight gleaming through the caves as through a church's stained glass windows. (*Note:* The Cathedrals is for experienced divers only.) On the opposite end of the island is **Shipwreck Beach,** which features a gorgeous shoreline and the remains of the *Helena Pt. Townsend,* a World War II liberty ship impaled on the reef.

History lovers will appreciate Lanai, which has more than 300 petroglyphs scattered on the island and several significant historic sites. Among them is **Kaunolu,** a former summer retreat for King Kamehameha I, located at the southern flank of the island. Here you'll encounter petroglyphs, the ruins of an ancient *heiau,* and a 60-foot-high sea cliff known as "Kahekili's Leap." Hawaiian warriors of yesteryear tested their courage and strength by leaping into the ocean below, clearing a sizable rock outcrop in the process.

A drive into Lanai City, where the majority of the island's 2,800 residents live, is also in order. Referring to this place as a "city" is a bit of a stretch for this tiny but proud community, although you'll find a nice collection of shops, eateries, and galleries here. This is a good opportunity to "talk story" with the locals and learn more about the island's unique history. A recent addition to Lanai City is the **Kaupe Culture and Heritage Center,** a museum displaying Hawaiian artifacts and pineapple-related memorabilia.

Overall, Lanai is a good bet for anyone looking to get away from it all. Children, however, might grow restless here in a hurry. If you're after rest and solitude *and* some big-city excitement, a few days on Lanai coupled with a stay on Oahu, Maui, or the Big Island might be the way to go.

Niihau and Kahoolawe

There are two other islands in the Hawaiian chain that, although usually inaccessible to visitors, are worth a mention.

Located 17 miles across the Kaulakahi Channel from Kauai's western shores is the island of Niihau. Only between 150 and 200 people reside on this privately owned 70-square-mile island, the only island where Hawaiian is the primary language. Cattle ranching is Niihau's chief industry, along with helicopter tours, hunting safaris, and shell jewelry.

Hawaiians believe that Niihau was the original home of Pele, the fire goddess.

To visit Niihau, you need to obtain permission from the Robinson family, the island's owners, by faxing a written request to (808) 338-1463. Or you can take a helicopter tour of the island from Kauai.

There is a military presence on Niihau, at the island's westernmost point: the U.S. Navy's Pacific Missile Range. An agreement between the Navy and the Hawaii State Preservation Office permitting missile tests from the island has been the center of recent controversy.

For 50 years, Kahoolawe, the smallest of Hawaii's eight major islands (45 square miles) and located eight miles west of Maui, was used by the U.S. Navy as a practice bombing site. That ended in 1990, when President George Bush put a halt to the bombing. The U.S. federal government will formally return Kahoolawe to the state in 2003.

Efforts are still under way to completely clear the island of military debris. Ordnance crews have discovered unexploded 2,000-pound bombs in the area.

As with Niihau, permission is needed to visit Kahoolawe. For information on three- or five-day visits to the island, call (808) 956-7068.

A Brief History

Scientists believe the Hawaiian Islands were formed millions of years ago, each rising from a single "hot spot" on the floor of the Pacific Ocean. The islands were barren, without any form of life, until seeds carried by the wind or ocean currents took root in the land and began to grow. Slowly but surely, birds and insects found their way to these islands, further paving the way for human inhabitants.

It was during the third or fourth century that seafaring explorers from the Marquesas Islands discovered Hawaii and took residence along the coastlines and in valleys where freshwater was plentiful. They introduced to the Islands dogs, pigs, chickens, and a variety of plants, including taro, coconut, breadfruit, banana, sweet potato, and sugarcane. A second wave of

Polynesian seafarers, this time from Tahiti, arrived some 500 years later.

The early Hawaiians embraced a simple lifestyle, living off the land and sea. Much of their time was spent farming and fishing. Taro was a chief food source: Its root was pounded and mixed with water to make poi, the paste-like starch that is today a staple at every Hawaiian luau. Ahead of their time in understanding nature's ecosystem, the early Hawaiians built and maintained large fishponds to ensure that their supply of fish was kept in abundance. Back then, a typical *hale* (house) was a wooden frame covered with *pili* grass.

The Hawaiians lived under a strict caste system, and high-ranking *ali'i* (chiefs, rulers) wielded their power fully by imposing many *kapu* (laws, prohibitions) on the natives. In some cases, to even cross the shadow of a powerful *ali'i* could bring certain death. This was a system that brought much bickering among the people, adding to the hostilities among chiefs eager to gain more territory under their rule.

Still, the Hawaiians thrived. It is estimated that by the time Captain Cook arrived in the Islands in 1778, about 400,000 natives were living on Hawaii's eight main islands: Oahu, the island of Hawaii, Maui, Kauai, Molokai, Lanai, Niihau, and Kahoolawe.

Captain Cook's Arrival

On January 21, 1778, Captain James Cook, commander of Britain's HMS *Resolution* and HMS *Discovery,* became the first non-Polynesian to set foot on Hawaiian soil, landing at Waimea on the west coast of Kauai. Cook and his crew spent five days on Kauai before a short visit to Niihau, where they received salt and yams in exchange for goats, pigs, and various seeds.

Cook's second contact with the Hawaiians occurred a year later, this time at Kealakekua on the Big Island. As fate would have it, his arrival coincided with the Hawaiians' annual *makahiki* celebration, a four-month festival honoring Lono, the god of peace, agriculture, and fertility. (Today, this event is celebrated statewide as the Aloha Festivals.) The Hawaiians, seeing these strange vessels heading for shore, thought it was Lono himself returning to the island. Thus, Cook and his men were treated to perhaps the greatest welcome in Hawaii's history: the natives greeted the ships by the thousands, via surfboards and canoes, from the water and from the shore. Cook later wrote: "I have nowhere in this sea seen such a number of people assembled in one place; besides those in the canoes, all the shore of the bay was covered with people, and hundreds were swimming about the ship like shoals of fish."

After the *makahiki* had ended, however, the Hawaiians were no longer quite so hospitable. A scuffle broke out after the Hawaiians began taking objects from the ships, and more than 200 warriors attacked Cook's landing party. Five British marines were killed, including Cook himself. The captain's body was cut to pieces, burned, and distributed among the chiefs, although some parts were later returned. What was left of Cook's body was buried at Kealakekua Bay.

The Kamehameha Dynasty

One Big Island warrior who took great interest in the foreigners was Kamehameha. He had been wounded by a gun during the scuffle, and he realized that any chief who possessed these powerful weapons would have a decided advantage during battles.

Kamehameha set out to conquer all the Hawaiian islands and bring them under his rule. He secured Maui and Lanai in 1790, then conquered Maui again after losing it for a short time. He had his chief rival on the Big Island killed to claim sole leadership over the island. Then he conquered Molokai and Oahu. Finally, all the islands were under Kamehameha's domain with the exception of Kauai. Two invasion attempts, in 1796 and 1809, failed miserably. In 1810, Kauai's chief peacefully surrendered his island (and the neighboring island of Niihau) to his persistent rival. The entire Hawaiian kingdom was finally unified under one ruler: King Kamemahaha I.

Under Kamehameha's reign, trade with the Europeans increased. The foreigners particularly valued Hawaii's sandalwood, and Kamehameha allowed the exportation of the precious wood until the supply was exhausted.

Kamehameha succumbed to a lengthy illness in 1819 in an area now known as Kailua-Kona on the Big Island. His bones were hidden at a secret location somewhere along the Kona Coast. Historians estimate he was in his early 60s when he died.

His successor, his son Liholiho (Kamehameha II), had a short but eventful reign. Ka'ahumanu, the favorite of Kamehameha's numerous wives, made herself the joint ruler, or queen regent, of the Hawaiian kingdom, and almost immediately abolished the despised *kapu* system. She did so by persuading the new king to sit down with her at a feast (it was *kapu* for men and women to eat together). Seeing that the gods did not punish the guilty parties, the natives' faith in their system crumbled. Ka'ahumanu and Liholiho declared that all idols and *heiau* should be destroyed.

Without their idols and places of worship, the Hawaiians experienced a gaping spiritual vacuum. Again, however, fate intervened. In 1820, 14 American missionaries from New England arrived aboard the brig *Thaddeus*. They preached in Honolulu and in Kona for what was supposed to be a one-year trial period. They never left.

Liholiho and his queen, Kamamalu, died of the measles in 1924 in London, England, where they had journeyed in hopes of meeting King George IV. Liholiho's successor was his younger brother, Kauikeaouli (Kamehameha

III), Kamehameha I's last surviving son. Kaʻahumanu, meanwhile, embraced the Christian way and announced a new system of laws based on the missionaries' teachings.

The missionaries' impact on Hawaii cannot be overstated. They built churches and schools throughout the Islands and condemned the natives for their manner of dress. Hula, regarded by the missionaries as lewd, was banned. Christianity became the new religion in Hawaii. The chiefs were converted first, and the commoners followed suit.

Kauikeaouli took full control of the Hawaiian kingdom in 1825. By then, a new industry had replaced the exhausted sandalwood trade: whaling. From the mid-1820s through the 1850s, when whale blubber was replaced by oil as a source for light, the whaling industry was the kingdom's economic savior, and Honolulu on Oahu and Lahaina on Maui became two of the most vital ports in the Pacific.

Kauikeaouli's 29-year reign was marked by several landmark events. The first came in 1843, when the Hawaiian kingdom fell to British control for a brief period. Kauikeaouli had been forced to surrender his authority after receiving threats from a British commander named George Paulet. At Kawaiahaʻo Church in Honolulu, Kauikeaouli declared, *"Ua mau ke ea o ka ʻaina i ka pono"* ("The life of the land is perpetuated in righteousness"). This declaration now serves as Hawaii's official state motto. The king's authority was returned to him after British officials reversed Paulet's actions.

More significantly, in 1848 Kauikeaouli issued the Great Mahele, which divided Hawaii's land ownership among the monarchy, government, and common people. For the first time, the working class could own land. Just two years later, foreigners were also allowed to own land, and forty years after the Great Mahele was decreed, two-thirds of all government lands belonged to foreigners.

By this time, the introduction of foreign diseases (including smallpox), against which native Hawaiians had no immunity, was taking a terrible toll. At the beginning of Kauikeaouli's reign, the native Hawaiian population had already dwindled to 150,000, less than half of the population at the time of Cook's arrival. By the end of his reign, that figure would drop to 70,000.

Sugar was fast emerging as the new lifeblood of the Island economy, and Kauikeaouli knew he had to find more laborers to work in the plantations. With the native population in steep decline, he turned to contract workers from foreign countries—the Chinese arrived first, in 1852, as 293 laborers began working on the plantations for $3 a month. The Chinese were followed by the Japanese, Portuguese, Filipinos, Koreans, Puerto Ricans, Germans, Russians, and Spaniards. By the turn of the century, Polynesians were no longer the majority of Hawaii's population.

Kauikeaouli died in 1854, and his nephew Alexander Liholiho (Kamehameha I's grandson) ascended the throne as Kamehameha IV. He reigned for eight years before dying of an asthmatic attack at the age of 29. His brother, Lot (Kamehameha V), served as king from 1863 to 1872, and upon his death William Lunalilo was elected his successor. (Lot's cousin, the Princess Bernice Pauahi, had been next in line to take the throne, but adamantly refused.) Lunalilo's reign was short-lived, however: He died after only a year as king.

The Merrie Monarch

David Kalakaua was elected to succeed Lunalilo, and his tenure as Hawaii's king proved to be as colorful as the man himself. Known as the "Merrie Monarch" for his passion for Hawaiian music and dance, Kalakaua moved to restore the culture and pride of his people. Under his reign, hula was once again performed in public. He oversaw the construction of 'Iolani Palace, an extravagant American Florentine masterpiece that became his home. With a fondness for fun, he also took a trip around the world, hosted gala balls, and presented local horse races.

In his first year on the throne, Kalakaua became the first reigning monarch to visit the United States, traveling to Washington, D.C., to meet with President Ulysses S. Grant and the U.S. Congress. Of his visit, the *New York Herald* reported, "[Kalakaua] is no common king, but one to whom we can give our allegiance with a clean conscience for we believe him to be a good man who has the happiness of his nation at heart. Long live King Kalakaua, and long may he reign."

The trip was a resounding success for both parties: Kalakaua returned home with a highly desirable reciprocity treaty giving Hawaii "favored nation" status and eliminating any tariffs on sugar. For the U.S., the treaty further solidified U.S.-Hawaiian ties.

While recognizing the benefits of a strong relationship with America, Kalakaua fought to maintain Hawaii's independence. The stronger the sugar industry grew, however, the more power shifted from the king to influential businessmen. In 1887, an armed insurrection by a *haole* (foreign) political group forced Kalakaua to accept a new constitution that severely diminished his authority. The king's remaining years weren't happy ones, as he was relegated to a figurehead role in the kingdom's government. His health failing, he traveled to California in 1891 to receive treatment. He died that year in a San Francisco hotel suite.

End of the Monarchy

Kalakaua's successor, his sister Lili'uokalani, was determined to restore the Hawaiian monarchy as the Islands' rightful power. But at this point, the queen was severely outmatched. In January 1893, pro-annexation forces struck. John B. Stevens, the U.S. Minister in Hawaii, ordered American marines from the visiting USS *Boston* to occupy strategic points in Honolulu. It was a daring move that did not receive official authorization from the powers in Washington, but it worked: The next day, a new government led by Sanford B. Dole was in place. Lili'uokalani was forced to abdicate her throne.

President Grover Cleveland was dismayed by the action, calling it "an act of war against a peaceful nation." His attempts at reinstating Lili'uokalani as Hawaii's ruler, however, were resisted by members of Congress. In 1894, the new government, the Republic of Hawaii, named Dole as its first president.

In January 1895, a group of royalists led by Robert Wilcox attempted a coup. The battle lasted for two weeks, with skirmishes erupting at Diamond Head Crater and in Manoa Valley, Punchbowl, and other sites on Oahu. Ultimately, the coup was unsuccessful, and the government arrested the royalists and even Lili'uokalani, charging them with treason. Despite her denials, the queen was sentenced to five years of hard labor and a $5,000 fine. While she never served that sentence, she was imprisoned at 'Iolani Palace—her own home—for the better part of the year.

In 1898, members of the republic got what they had wanted all along: Hawaii was annexed to the United States. Two years later, it became an official U.S. territory.

World War II and Statehood

The ensuing four decades were marked by the birth of Hawaii's fledgling tourist industry as well as the dominance of the agricultural industry (primarily sugar and pineapple). Then came December 7, 1941, the day Japanese war planes bombed Pearl Harbor. With the attack, the United States was thrown into World War II, and Island residents, eager to prove their worth, did what they could to support the American effort. In Waikiki, hotels were closed to visitors, then reopened to accommodate servicemen. The famed "Pink Palace," the Royal Hawaiian Hotel, turned into an R&R center for military officers on leave. Barbed wire was strung all along the beach.

In the years following the war, Hawaii found itself in a decidedly friendlier battle, this one waged in the political arena. The battle was won, and on March 12, 1959, the U.S. House of Representatives voted 323-89 in favor of granting statehood to Hawaii. The *Honolulu Advertiser* reported, "A phone call from Governor Quinn in Washington today is expected to set off the biggest winging in Island history to celebrate Statehood Day. The Governor will ring Hawaii the minute the House passes the statehood bill. Since the bill has already passed in the Senate, this will mean that Hawaii is in. He will alert the military and the Civil Defense Agency and the 52 air raid sirens on Oahu will start screaming out the news with a five-minute take-cover blast (45 seconds upbeat, 15 seconds downbeat). Every church bell in town will begin pealing. Every ship in harbor will blow her whistle. Most folks will do a little shouting on their own, and, of course, there's nothing to stop you from hula-ing in the streets if you want to."

The announcement was indeed met with quite a celebration. Shops closed for the day. Car horns sounded and people danced in the streets. At one elementary school, more than a thousand young boys and girls paraded about, stopping only to solemnly recite the "Pledge of Allegiance." Five months later, on August 21, President Dwight Eisenhower made it official, signing the proclamation welcoming Hawaii as the 50th state in the union.

In 1999, Hawaii celebrated its 40th year of statehood. During this time span, the Islands continued to develop—some say "overdevelop"—as a tourist destination. (In the boom years of tourism in the 1970s, the joke going around was that the new state bird was the crane.) In recent years, however, the state's tourism industry has slumped, primarily due to the economic downturn in Asia (the industry had come to rely heavily on Asian visitors). Now and then, there's talk of diversifying Hawaii's economy, but it is likely that tourism will always be its driving force.

In the political arena, there is a growing movement within native Hawaiian groups to achieve some degree of sovereignty for its people. As things currently stand, however, these organizations have yet to achieve consensus on how—and to what level—this goal may be achieved.

Hawaii's Diverse Population

One of the underrated pleasures of Hawaii is the diversity of its people. In the 50th state, no ethnic group comprises the majority of the state's population. The breakdown is as follows:

Caucasian 23.3%	Hawaiian 0.8%
Japanese 20.0%	Samoan 0.5%
Filipino 10.4%	Puerto Rican 0.4%
Chinese 4.6%	Mixed race 37% (about half of
Black 1.8%	this amount represent part-
Korean 1.4%	Hawaiians)

Each ethnic group has, to some degree, made an indelible mark on the Island culture, contributing its native foods, arts, music, and customs to Hawaii's melting pot community.

The Chinese were the first immigrants to arrive. More than 200 workers from southeastern China came to the Islands in 1852 after signing five-year contracts to work in the local sugar plantations. These laborers were provided food, clothing, shelter, and a salary of $3 a month. Most of the Chinese lived near Honolulu Harbor on Oahu and Lahaina on Maui. It was in Honolulu where Dr. Sun Yat-sen, regarded as the father of modern China, founded the Hsing Chung Hui, a revolutionary group that played an integral role in China's revolutionary movement against foreign powers. Over the years, the Chinese have made major contributions to the local community. Today, many locals celebrate each Chinese New Year with the customary fireworks and traditional dances. You can find superb Chinese eateries on all the islands, particularly in the Chinatown area of downtown Honolulu, and wonderful examples of Chinese art are on display at the Honolulu Academy of Arts.

The first official group of Japanese immigrants arrived in 1868 to work on the plantations. Although the conditions at these plantations were often miserable, more Japanese made their way to what they referred to as Tenjiku, or "Heavenly Place." By the start of the 20th century, there were more than 60,000 Japanese laborers and dependents in Hawaii. Like all immigrants, the Japanese faced racial prejudices. These prejudices intensified greatly after Japan's attack on Pearl Harbor on December 7, 1941. Many local Japanese-Americans were placed into internment camps on the U.S. mainland, and many more lost their family-run businesses, even though not a single case of Japanese-American treason or sabotage occurred during the war. Today, Japanese-Americans enjoy a major presence in Hawaii, and most locals have embraced Japanese customs, including removing footwear before entering a home. Sushi, sashimi, mochi, and miso soup are favorite delicacies among locals, and Japanese festivals frequently dot the Hawaiian cultural calendar.

In 1903, the first Koreans arrived in Hawaii to work on the plantations. Ambitious and hardworking, Koreans today have the highest education and income level per capita of any ethnic group in the Islands. Korean cuisine is extremely popular among Hawaiian residents, and you'll find Korean restaurants in nearly every town. Try beef kal-bi (marinated beef) with rice and spicy kim chee (pickled vegetables).

A small group of 15 Filipino laborers began working on Island plantations in 1906; by the middle of the century, that number had swelled to 125,000. Every summer, the Filipina Fiesta festivals (held at various sites throughout the state) celebrate the colorful traditions and customs of the Filipino culture. Delicacies such as chicken adobo and lumpia are favorite items on any local menu.

The Samoans are among the newer ethnic groups to Hawaii, arriving from American Samoa shortly after the end of the First World War. Most settled in the Mormon community in La'ie on Oahu. They've made many contributions to the Islands, including the celebrated fire-knife dance that highlights most Polynesian luaus. American Samoa is one of seven Polynesian nations spotlighted at the Polynesian Cultural Center in La'ie. Local

Samoans have also made their mark in the world of football: In the 1990s, Jesse Sapolu (San Francisco 49ers), Mark Tuinei (Dallas Cowboys), and Ma'a Tanuvasa (Denver Broncos) all played significant roles in helping their teams win Super Bowl championships.

Unfortunately, even in Hawaii, certain ethnic prejudices and stereotypes do exist. Hawaiians are often perceived as lazy, Japanese are regarded as greedy land-buyers, Chinese are thought of as tightwads, and so forth. Caucasians are also the target of ethnic slurs; that situation had existed even before American businessmen caused the overthrow of the Hawaiian monarchy in 1891, and it's unlikely things will change anytime soon. The word *haole,* once used to describe any foreign visitor, now commonly refers to anyone of Caucasian descent. The word is used freely by the locals, and most of the time it's not meant in a derogatory way. If you are Caucasian and hear the word directed at you, our advice is to ignore it and smile.

Hawaii Naturally

Showing wisdom centuries ahead of their time, ancient Hawaiians handled their precious natural resources with great care. To prevent waste, for instance, they found practical uses for each part of certain native plants, from flower to stem to root. Periodic *kapu* (restrictions) were placed on certain birds whose feathers were used to make brightly colored cloaks. Man-made fishponds were used to raise fish for food, and Hawaiians took special care to never take more than they needed.

Today, unfortunately, Hawaii has the dubious reputation of being the "endangered species capital" of the United States. More than 75% of the state's native birds are extinct or threatened, and more than 250 Hawaiian species of plants and animals are on the endangered list. This is largely due to the introduction of alien wildlife, which has often resulted in disaster. Mongooses, for instance, were imported by sugar growers to rid their plantations of rats. It was an epic blunder, as the mongooses hunt during the day, while rats are active at night. The mongooses, instead, largely fed on native birds and their eggs.

Only two mammals are considered to be indigenous to Hawaii. One is the Hawaiian monk seal, which is rarely seen (hence the name "monk"). If by rare chance you find one resting on a beach, do not go near it, as it is against federal law to disturb this protected species. Instead, you can view Hawaiian monk seals at the Waikiki Aquarium on Oahu. Hawaii's other indigenous mammal is the hoary bat.

Hawaii's wildlife species are unique attractions in their own right and certainly add to the natural beauty of the Islands. The Aloha State remains a special place for nature lovers, encompassing 21 of the earth's 22 climatic zones. Hawaii features no fewer than 88 ecosystems, ranging from snowy mountaintops, rain forests, wetlands, and deserts to sea cliffs, beaches, and, of course, volcanoes.

Over the years, Hawaii's natural environment has evolved to a point where native and introduced species share an uneasy coexistence. Many animals here are what you might typically find on the U.S. mainland, including wild cats, pigs, sheep, goats, centipedes, roaches, and mongooses. There are no snakes in Hawaii, except for the occasional illegal pets that turn up in someone's backyard.

Here's a look at some of Hawaii's plants, birds, and marine life.

PLANTS

Most of the flora we commonly associate with Hawaii—including plumeria, hibiscus, guava, and pineapples—are actually introduced species. You won't have to search long and hard to find most of the Hawaiian plants and trees listed below. Many, in fact, can be viewed right on the property of your hotel. The most convenient way to see many of these species, however, is at one of Hawaii's many botanical gardens.

Recommended Botanical Gardens	
Oahu	Foster Botanical Garden (808) 522-7066
Maui	Maui Tropical Plantation (808) 244-7643
The Big Island	Amy B. H. Greenwell Ethnobotanical Garden (808) 323-3318
	Hawaii Tropical Botanical Garden (808) 964-5233
	Nani Mau Gardens (808) 959-3541
Kauai	Allerton Gardens (808) 332-7361
	Limahuli Garden (808) 826-1053

'a'ali'i *(Dodonaea)*   Native hardwood shrubs with sticky branch tips, narrow leaves, small flowers, and yellow, red, or brownish fruit. Fruit clusters are often used in lei making. In ancient times, the leaves were boiled and used to relieve rash, itch, asthma, and insomnia.

'awa *(Piper methysticum)*   Also called kava. Introduced to Hawaii by early-day seafarers, 'awa—a shrub characterized by green jointed stems and heart-shaped leaves—was once reserved only for royalty. The shrub's roots and leaves were ingredients in a narcotic drink that helped cure insomnia, anxiety, coughs, and aching muscles. Hawaiians wrapped the leaves around their heads to alleviate headaches. It's quite rare today; your best bet for viewing 'awa is at a private or public garden.

hala *(Pandanus tectorius)*   Pandanus trees are found primarily in coastal regions. You'll find these popular trees—marked with propped-up roots and elongated leaves—at most Hawaiian beaches (Waikiki is an exception). *Lau hala* ("leaf of the hala") is used to make mats and other woven items. The seeds and flowers were used by early-day Hawaiians to help purge the body. The roots were beaten and used in a tonic.

hau *(Hibiscus tiliaceus)*   Lowland tree that either is native to Hawaii or was introduced to the Islands early on by Polynesian settlers. It is generally found along the coasts and waterways of all Hawaiian islands. The hibiscus-like flowers, each with five petals, are a bright yellow in the morning, then change colors as the day progresses, winding up a dark pinkish orange by nightfall. Its buds and bark were used in a drink to purge the body. The bark by itself was used to ease childbirth and reduce fever.

'ilima *(Sida,* especially *S. fallax)*   Native shrub bearing yellow, orange, or dull red flowers. A member of the hibiscus family, the 'ilima was once Hawaii's national flower; today, it is the official flower of the island of Oahu. The flowers last only a day before withering and are so delicate that it takes about 500 flowers to make a single lei. The 'ilima is no longer common. In old Hawaii, its flowers were often used in a preparation to purge the body, and the leaf shoots and root bark were used to relieve asthma.

kalo *(Colocasia esculenta)*   Taro. Although most varieties of kalo need to be cooked before being eaten, a few varieties were edible raw and were used as a laxative. The kalo is an excellent example of how Hawaiians found uses for their vegetation: Leaves were used to help heal skin infections; the stems helped reduce swellings and the pain of stings and insect bites; the raw corm is said to have been used to stop bleeding; and the raw juice was used to lower fever. Hawaiians also used the outer skin for plant fertilizer and scrapings for animal feed. Above all, taro roots are used in making poi, a nourishing staple in the Hawaiian diet and a menu fixture at luaus.

ki *(Cordyline fruticosa)*   Ti plant. Part of the lily family. Its distinctive large green (or sometimes reddish purple) leaves are commonplace in the Islands. Leaves were dipped in cool water and used as a compress to reduce fever. They were also wrapped around heated stones and used as a "hot pack" for aching backs. The flower of the ki plant was used to treat asthma, and the root was used as an ingredient for an intoxicant. Today, ki is most commonly used in making *laulau,* a traditional delicacy of fish or pork wrapped in ti leaves. The leaves are also used in traditional Hawaiian blessing ceremonies to ward off evil spirits.

kiawe *(Prosopis pallida)*   Algaroba tree, originally from Peru. A Catholic priest planted a single seed in Honolulu in 1828, and today there are thousands of kiawe trees throughout the state. It has tiny leaves and long, slender branches. It is a source of fuel, lumber, and charcoal.

koa *(Acadia koa)*   Considered one of Hawaii's most highly regarded natural resources. The wood from this native tree is highly prized (and pricey) for making finely crafted tables, bowls, picture frames, and even ukuleles. In ancient Hawaii, koa symbolized wealth and well-being. Koa trees today are found only in upland areas on Kauai, the Big Island, Maui, and Oahu.

kukui *(Aleurites moluccana)*   Candlenut tree, found on all Hawaiian islands, especially in rural lowlands and lower mountain slopes. The official state tree of Hawaii. Its greenish white clustered flowers bloom year-round. In ancient Hawaii, the oil of dried kukui nuts served as a source of light. The leaves were used as a poultice to treat swellings and bruises. The green nuts were used to seal cuts and punctures, while mashed roasted nuts were used as a salve for sores.

limu   "Limu" is a general name for all types of underwater plants. Hawaiians had many uses for limu, including as a treatment for heartburn and body ailments. Certain seaweeds are used today as recipe ingredients by many of Hawaii's top chefs.

mamaki *(Pipturus* spp.)   Small native tree distinguished by broad, white-backed leaves and white mulberry-like fruit. The fruit was often used as a laxative, and the roots were used to dull the pain of childbirth. The bark was pounded to form a type of fiber valued in tapa making.

milo *(Thespesia populnea)*   A stately tree with yellow hibiscus-like flowers and glossy, heart-shaped leaves. It is found along Hawaiian coastlines and lowland areas. Often confused with its relative, the hau tree, but the leaves of the milo tree are darker and shinier; also, it does not grow in rambling tangles like the hau tree does. The wood is used to make calabashes.

mokihana *(Pelea anisata)*   A native tree found only on the island of Kauai. Belonging to the citrus family, the tree is known for its cube-shaped, anise-scented fruit, which used as a laxative.

naupaka *(Scaevola)*   Native shrubs found in mountain areas and near coastlines. The flowers, white or light-colored, have a unique shape: They look like only half of a flower. The leaves of the naupaka were used to heal lacerations, and the bark was used to treat skin lesions and diarrhea.

'ohelo *(Vaccinium reticulatum)* Native shrub belonging to the cranberry family, bearing edible red or yellow berries. The shoots, leaves, and berries were sometimes used in a drink to alleviate severe stomach ailments.

ohia lehua *(Metrosideros polymorpha)* Hawaii's most abundant native tree. Lehua blossoms are the official flower of the Big Island of Hawaii. Hawaiians scraped the bark to produce a liquid that eased the pain of childbirth. The leaf bud was used as a kind of tea tonic.

'olena *(Curcuma domestica)* A type of ginger plant. The bulbs were ground, added to other herbs, and then inhaled to soothe ear, nose, and throat discomfort. The plant was widely used as a spice in foods and as a dye to color cloth and tapa.

'ulu *(Artocarpus altilis)* Breadfruit tree, distinguished by one- to three-foot-long glossy leaves and heavy globular fruits (each may weigh up to several pounds). It is found on all islands, especially in rural areas or in Hawaiian communities. Its milky sap was used to heal ulcers, skin diseases, scratches, cuts, and boils.

wauke *(Broussonetia papyrifera)* Paper mulberry. The bark was used to make a tough form of tapa used for clothing. Also, its shoots were chewed to cure various body ailments, and the sap served as a mild laxative.

BIRDS

The easiest way to get an eyeful of Hawaii's native birds is to visit the Honolulu Zoo on Oahu or the Pana'ewa Rainforest Zoo in Hilo on the island of Hawaii. A more adventurous option is to book a guided tour with Michael Walther, an author and respected authority on Hawaiian native birds. His company, Oahu Nature Tours, can be reached at (800) 861-6018 or (808) 924-2473, or on the Internet at www.OahuNatureTours.com.

If you prefer to bird-watch on your own, the best places to spot forest birds are the Ko'olau Ridge Trails, the Wai'anae Range Trails, and the Lyon Arboretum on Oahu; Haleakala National Park, Hosmer Grove, Hana Forest Reserve, and 'Iao Valley State Park on Maui; Hawaii Volcanoes National Park, Mauna Kea, and Hualalai on the Big Island; and Koke'e State Park on Kauai.

The best time for forest bird observation is from November to May. Bring rain gear and warm clothes, as most forests are at high-elevation areas and are cold and damp.

'amakihi *(Hemignathus virens)* Types of 'amakihi are found on Oahu,

Maui, Kauai, and the Big Island. Generally, the males are yellowish green in color (darker above), while females are duller. They have a slightly decurved, grayish bill. The common ʻamakihi is mostly found in native forests in higher elevations, perched on leafy branches of forest trees. The ʻamakihi is one of the more common native forest birds. In old Hawaii, the feathers of the ʻamakihi were used for feather capes.

ʻapapane *(Himatione sanguinea)*   A Hawaiian honeycreeper found on all main islands, although rare on Lanai and declining on Oahu. Reaching a length of slightly more than five inches, the ʻapapane is marked by crimson on its breast and upper body, and black wings and tail. Its slightly decurved bill and legs are black. Its feathers were used by ancient Hawaiians for featherwork.

ʻelepaio *(Chasiempis sandwichensis)*   The ʻelepaio is common in native forests on Kauai and the Big Island and is sometimes seen in the mountains and forest valleys on Oahu. All species have white wing markings and tail spots and a cocked-tail posture. They have dark bills and legs. The Kauai ʻelepaio are gray-brown above and pale below, with gray and black splotches on its breast. On the Big Island, ʻelepaio in the wet forests are brown above, pale below, and have chestnut flank streaks. Dry forest species are similar but paler, with a whitish head and throat. On Oahu, the species are rich brown above and pale below, with streaks on their flanks. Hawaiians believed the ʻelepaio to be the goddess of canoe makers.

ʻiʻiwi *(Vestiaria coccinea)*   A Hawaiian honeycreeper fairly common on the islands of Hawaii, Kauai, and Maui in native forests above the 2,000-foot elevation mark. The ʻiʻiwi, however, is extremely rare on Oahu and Molokai. Growing to a length of about five and a half inches, this attractive bird is bright vermilion with a long, curved pinkish bill. The wings are black with a white patch. Its feathers were once used extensively for featherwork.

ʻomaʻo *(Myadestes obscurus)*   Also known as the Hawaiian thrush. Found only on the island of Hawaii, the ʻomaʻo is found in windward native forests in high-elevation areas. The body is colored dark gray-brown above and a much paler gray below; it has a dark bill and legs and is characterized by its slurred, flute-like voice.

REEF AND SHORE FISH

Most of the marine life in Hawaii are native fishes, with the notable exception of the snapper fish, which were imported from Tahiti as game fish. Following are introductions to some of the more common fish you'll encounter during a snorkeling or scuba-diving adventure in the Islands. If you prefer viewing these colorful fish without having to get wet, head to the Waikiki Aquarium and Sea Life Park on Oahu, and the Maui Ocean Center on Maui (see Part Ten, "Hawaii's Attractions").

humuhumunukunukuapua'a *(Rhinecanthus rectangulus)* Triggerfish. Hawaii's unofficial state fish. The body is a light brown (shading to white below) and has an oblique black band extending from the eye and broadening to the rest of the body. Also has gold and blue lines. Grows to a length of about ten inches. Literally translated, *humuhumu* means "with a snout like a pig."

kala *(Naso unicornis)* Bluespine unicornfish. A tapering bony horn in front of its eyes is the distinguishing physical characteristic of this algae-nibbling fish. The body is a light olive to yellowish gray in color, with blue markings at its fins.

kihikihi *(Zanclus cornutus)* Moorish idol. A brilliantly colored fish with black bands alternating with yellow. Possesses a long dorsal fin. Feeds on sponges and algae.

mamo *(Abudefduf abdominalis)* Sergeant fish. Very abundant in calm shallow waters. Its body is a light blue-green in color, with five blackish vertical stripes. Feeds mainly on zooplankton and algae.

manini *(Acanthurus triostegus)* Convict tang. Very common shore fish in the Islands. Greenish white, with six narrow black vertical bars.

palani *(Acanthurus dussumieri)* Surgeonfish. Yellowish brown, the palani has irregular blue stripes on its body and a yellow spot behind and adjacent to its eyes. It can grow up to 18 inches in length. Like all surgeonfish, the palani is able to slash other fish (or unsuspecting humans) with its caudal spines by a quick side-sweep of the tail, so handle with care. Also possesses a strong odor.

ta'ape *(Lutjanus kasmira)* Bluestripe snapper. A colorful fish with a yellow body and four narrow bright blue stripes. Rarely exceeds a foot in length.

Part Two

Planning Your Visit to Hawaii

The Best Time to Go

Ask any Island tourism official, "When is the best time for me to visit Hawaii?" and the reply will almost always be an enthusiastic "Anytime!" And for the most part, it's true. With sunny skies and ideal temperatures practically year-round, weather is rarely a concern. But there are a couple of factors to consider in deciding when to make your Hawaii trip.

First, there is the matter of hotel prices. In typical supply-and-demand fashion, "high" season—when room rates are at their highest—runs from December through March (not coincidentally, when the weather where *you* live is likely at its worst). During this time, the average hotel room rate in Hawaii is $146–151.

In terms of hotel prices, then, a better time to visit the Islands would be during low season, which falls from September through November and the months of April and May. The average hotel room rate during this time dips to $130–144. The average rate during the summer, the most popular travel period for families, falls somewhere in between.

The second consideration deals with your personal expectations. Ask yourself this question: "What do I most want to see or experience in Hawaii?" If whale-watching is at the top of your "must-do" list, for example, make sure your visit falls between mid-December and mid-May. Or if you want to see the world's finest hula dancers competing in the art form's most prestigious event, you'd book your vacation for late March or early April (when the Merrie Monarch Festival is held in Hilo on the Big Island).

At *ALOHA Magazine,* one of the questions we received most from mainland readers was, "What are the dates for the Aloha Festivals?" Indeed, many visitors plan their Hawaii trips to coincide with this all-Island festival, the biggest annual celebration in the state. Aloha Festivals takes place September through October, with each main Hawaiian island having its own nine- or ten-day celebration. *Tip:* The Aloha Festivals committee actually schedules festival dates years in advance, so if you're planning to visit the Islands in 2003 and want to attend the Aloha Festivals, just give them a call at (808) 545-1771.

For a complete guide to annual festivals, cultural celebrations, sporting events, and more, contact the Hawaii Convention & Visitors Bureau at 2270 Kalakana Avenue, 8th Floor, Honolulu, HI 96815; (800) GO-HAWAII; www.gohawaii.com.

The Weather Report

If Hawaii's climate were submitted to a psychiatric exam, the results would read like this: "Very pleasant, with a sunny disposition and only a few stormy moments. Extremely stable, with lows never too low and highs never too high."

For most of the year, temperatures range from the mid-70s to the mid-80s. The mercury can dip into the 60s during the winter months (December through March) and creeps into the mid-90s in the summer.

The rainy season is December through February but usually amounts to nothing more than passing showers. The amount of annual precipitation can vary greatly, however: While Waikiki averages only 25 inches of rain per year, for instance, just five miles away, Manoa Valley receives an average of 158 inches of rain. Mount Wai'ale'ale on Kauai is one of the wettest spots on Earth, with more than 400 inches of rainfall annually. Hilo on the island of Hawaii, meanwhile, is the wettest city in the United States, averaging 128 inches of precipitation per year.

The average humidity level in the state ranges from 56% to 72%.

"Trade winds" usually blow in from the northeast and were named after the steady breezes that helped merchant ships reach the Islands.

"*Mauka* showers" mean heavier rainfall in the mountain slopes and valleys.

In general, there is a 3.5° drop in temperature for every 1,000-foot rise in elevation above sea level. This helps explain how, during winters on the Big Island, you can sunbathe on a sun-kissed beach in the morning, then go skiing on the powdery slopes of Mauna Kea in the afternoon!

Gathering Information before You Leave

What your grumpy old science teacher used to say still rings true: Knowledge *is* power. To get the most out of your visit to Hawaii, learn everything you can about the Aloha State. Request free guides and brochures from the Hawaii Visitors & Convention Bureau. Read books and magazines on Hawaiiana. Ask friends and relatives who have been to Hawaii for their tips and suggestions. Request free brochures and visitor publications. Log on to the Internet. In other words, use every source of information at your disposal. You'll enjoy Hawaii a lot more if you already feel like a seasoned *kama'aina!*

Here are some sources to help get you started:

TOURISM BUREAUS AND TRAVEL ORGANIZATIONS

Hawaii Visitors & Convention Bureau
2270 Kalakaua Avenue, 8th Floor
Honolulu, HI 96815
(808) 923-1811 or (800) GO-HAWAII
www.gohawaii.com

Request a free copy of *The Islands of Aloha,* the official visitors guide of the Hawaii Visitors & Convention Bureau. This magazine-sized guide provides some good information on things to see and do in Hawaii.

Oahu Visitors Bureau
733 Bishop Street, Suite 1872
Honolulu, HI 96813
(808) 524-0722 or (877) 525-OAHU
www.visit-oahu.com, www.gohawaii.com

Big Island Visitors Bureau (Hilo)
250 Keawe Street
Hilo, HI 96720
(808) 961-5797 or (800) 648-2441
www.bigisland.org, www.gohawaii.com

Big Island Visitors Bureau (Kona)
75-5719-W Ali'i Drive
Kailua-Kona, HI 96740
(808) 329-7787 or (800) 648-2441
www.bigisland.org, www.gohawaii.com

Maui Visitors Bureau (includes Molokai and Lanai)
1727 Wili Pa Loop
Wailuku, HI 96793
(808) 244-3530 or (800) 525-MAUI
www.visitmaui.com, www.gohawaii.com

Call or write for a free copy of *Maui, The Magic Isles,* the official travel planner of the Maui Visitors Bureau. This colorful travel planner highlights the islands of Maui, Molokai, and Lanai.

Kauai Visitors Bureau
4334 Rice Street, Suite 101
Lihu'e, HI 96766
(808) 245-3971 or (800) 262-1400
www.kauaivisitorsbureau.org, www.gohawaii.com

Molokai Visitors Association
P.O. Box 960
Kaunakakai, HI 96748
(808) 553-3876 or (800) 800-6367
www.molokai-hawaii.com, www.gohawaii.com

Destination Lanai
P.O. Box 700
Lanai City, HI 96763
(808) 565-7600 or (800) 947-4774
www.aloha.net/~dlanai/lanaitour.html, www.gohawaii.com

Hawaii Attractions Association
615 Pi'ikoi Street, Suite 1812
Honolulu, HI 96814
(808) 596-7733
www.HawaiiAttractions.com

INTERNET WEB SITES

E-Hawaii . . . Everything Hawaii (www.e-hawaii.com/main.cfm)   A breezy Web site that has a little bit of everything: political articles, beach and surf information, a restaurant listing, links to other Hawaii-related Web sites, a celebrities section, local-style jokes—even Hawaiian astrology! You can even download a Hawaii scenic screensaver and send free electronic postcards.

Hawaii Visitors & Convention Bureau (www.gohawaii.com)   The official Web site of the Hawaii Visitors & Convention Bureau. This site includes basic information on the six main Hawaiian islands, as well as a large calendar of events section; information on accommodations, attractions, outdoor activities, and dining; and a helpful "student" section filled with information geared for student reports. Information-wise, the site isn't as thorough as it could be, as emphasis is placed squarely on HVCB members. Lots of links to member sites are included.

Hawaii for Visitors (www.gohawaii.about.com.)   Full of good information on the main Hawaiian islands, plus golf, flowers, history, hula, luaus, weather, music, recipes, volcanoes, and more. Also included are a chat room, a photo section, a "book of the week," and a day-by-day travel-ogue of a 16-day trip to the Islands. The site is easy to navigate.

Hawaii Main Index (www.808.com)   A thorough catalog of Hawaii-related Web sites, listed by island, city, and subject category. Headings include each of the six main Hawaiian islands, weather information, news, and event listings.

Hawaii's Visitors Guides (www.aloha.com/~hvguides/)   A very simple site with information on dining, shopping, sight-seeing, entertainment, culture, and beaches. Money-saving coupons and island maps are also featured.

Planet Hawaii (www.planet-hawaii.com/production/shock/ph/)   A unique travel directory with links to local news organizations, a chat room, an on-line marketplace, University of Hawaii sports, screensavers, and a "Web Cam" tour of the Islands. Useful information on accommodations, activities, tours, and transportation is also provided.

RECOMMENDED MAGAZINES

Hawaii Magazine   A bimonthly magazine published by Fancy Publica-tions in California. Featured are articles on Hawaii's people, culture, arts, history, foods, and more. Available at most newsstands. Or call (800) 365-4421 for subscription information.

Honolulu Magazine   A monthly city magazine published by Honolulu Publishing. Featured are stories on Hawaii politics, issues, personalities, sports, history, and arts. Call (808) 524-7400 for subscription information.

RECOMMENDED GUIDES

Check your local bookstore or library for these worthwhile reads. When possible, we've included the phone numbers of the publishers so you can contact them directly if necessary.

Camping Hawaii, by Richard McMahon, published by University of Hawaii Press (call (808) 956-8255). 1997. A thorough, authoritative guide to 120 campgrounds in the Aloha State.

Great Outdoor Adventures of Hawaii, by Rick Carroll, published by Foghorn Press. 1991. A helpful guide to some of Hawaii's best outdoor activities.

Hawaiian Heritage Plants, by Angela Kay Kepler, published by Fernglen Press. 1998. Thorough presentation of Hawaii's native plants. Full-color photos complement insightful and skillfully written text.

Hawaiian Hiking Trails, by Craig Chisolm, published by Fernglen Press. 1999. Informative and detailed look at 50 of the best hiking trails on Hawaii's six major islands.

Hawaii's Best Beaches, by John R. K. Clark, published by University of Hawaii Press (call (808) 956-8255). 1999. A guide to 50 of Hawaii's best beaches.

Hawaii's Best Golf, by George Fuller, published by Island Heritage Publishing (call (808) 487-7299). 1999. Hawaii's best golf courses are profiled. The text is more descriptive than detailed. Breathtaking full-color photography.

Hawaii's Birds, published by the Hawaii Audubon Society (call (808) 528-1432). 1993. A full-color guide providing detailed information about native and introduced birds in Hawaii.

Shore Fishes of Hawaii, by John E. Randall, published by University of Hawaii Press (call (808) 956-8255). 1996. Detailed guide on Hawaii's marine life. Ideal for snorkelers and scuba divers. Loaded with full-color pictures.

Surfer's Guide to Hawaii, by Greg Ambrose, published by Bess Press (call (808) 734-7159). 1991. Exhaustive guide to Hawaii's favorite surf spots.

Trees of Hawaii, by Angela Kay Kepler, published by University of Hawaii Press (call (808) 956-8255). 1990. A colorful and informative look at native and introduced trees in the Hawaiian Islands.

Visiting One Island versus Multiple Islands

The fact that Hawaii is made up of six main inhabitable islands poses a unique problem for the first-time visitor: When planning your trip, one of the first decisions you need to make is whether to visit one, two, or even three or more islands. Since you're investing much time and money into your vacation, the temptation is to see as much of the Aloha State as you can, and it's not uncommon for first-time visitors to have ambitious visions of island-hopping from one end of the Hawaiian chain to the other.

Our advice? Remember that while two may be company, three (or more) is a definite crowd!

The major drawback to visiting more than one island is the time involved. Unless you opt for a cruise, you'll have to pack, check out of one hotel, drive to the airport, return your rental car, check into the airport, wait for the plane, board the plane, spend at least 25 minutes in flight, deboard, get your luggage, pick up another rental car, drive to another hotel, register your room, and unpack. Each check-in/check-out and rental pick-up/drop-off won't likely take more than a few minutes, but it all adds up. You can expect to lose up to half a day of vacation time moving from one island to another.

There are two more considerations: A round-trip inter-island ticket for visitors is about $190 per person if you book on your own. And although you usually won't have trouble finding a flight—combined, Aloha Airlines, Island Air, and Hawaiian Airlines make more than 400 daily flights—many inter-island flights require a stopover—usually to Honolulu—adding up to another 30–60 minutes of travel time. Most Kahului (Maui) to Lihu'e (Kauai) and all Kona (Big Island) to Lihu'e flights, for example, currently require a stopover.

A cheaper option for island-hopping from Maui to Lanai is the Lahaina-Lanai Passenger Shuttle, a ferry ride which makes five round trips daily between the two islands. The fare is $25 each way for adults and $20 for children aged 11 and under. The trip is scenic and pleasant and takes only from 45 minutes to an hour (which is still twice the length of time of a Kahului-Lanai flight on Island Air). See "Getting There" later in this part and Part Five, "Getting around Hawaii," for more transportation information.

Speaking of trips via boat, American Hawaii Cruises makes weekly trips visiting several major islands. There are pros and cons here, as well. A cruise affords convenience, as you only have to check in and unpack once. Also, in this instance, the transportation itself is a huge part of the overall experience. However, the time you'll have to explore each island is very limited, and you won't fully gain an appreciation for the uniqueness and special flavor each island provides. See our section on Hawaii cruises on pages 76–88.

Another argument against island-hopping is that you can save money by staying for a longer length of time on a single island. Some of the major hotels, for example, offer a free night's stay when you book between four and six consecutive nights at their property. And many of the money-saving or value-added packages offered by the hotels require a minimum stay of at least four nights. You lose out on these possibilities if you pursue a commando raid approach to your Island vacation.

A third disadvantage is a matter of both practicality and aesthetics. Each Hawaiian island, like an expensive bottle of fine wine, is meant to be admired, savored, and experienced. It's not something you gulp down in one swallow. By trying to see too much within a short length of time, you'll miss out on some of the subtleties that makes each island unique and, as a consequence, you won't be getting the most out of your visit. Also, keep in mind that many of Hawaii's top attractions—including the Polynesian Cultural Center on Oahu, Hawaii Volcanoes National Park on the Big Island, and visiting Hana on Maui—are practically all-day excursions.

Finally, remember that in Hawaii, people enjoy a slower pace. No one's in a hurry. It's one of the therapeutic benefits of being on "Hawaiian time," and it would be a shame if you spent all your time packing and unpacking, hurrying to get to your next destination.

You'll need at least five days to a week to fully enjoy Oahu, and we recommend allotting that many days if you plan to visit Maui or the Big Island as well. If your trip goes beyond a week, however, go ahead and visit two islands. This is especially true for first-time and infrequent visitors planning a ten-day to two-week vacation. (Frequent visitors to Hawaii often start out by visiting one island per trip, eventually settling on their favorite as an annual vacation destination.)

The three islands that have the most to offer, in our view, are Oahu, Maui, and the island of Hawaii (the Big Island). We advise spending a week on any of these islands, then hopping over to another island (including Kauai, Molokai, and Lanai) for another few days. Mix and match according to your whim and fancy: Combine the big-city trappings of Honolulu on Oahu with the sheer natural beauty of Hanalei on Kauai; supplement your big-game fishing adventure on the Big Island with a historical trail ride on Molokai.

For families with two or more generations in the traveling party, a two-island itinerary provides a better likelihood of fulfilling that always elusive goal of satisfying everyone. While Grandma and Grandpa might enjoy the many tropical botanical gardens on Kauai, for example, the young ones would undoubtedly have more fun visiting the more kiddie-oriented attractions on Oahu.

Visiting more than one island gives you a more complete sampling of Hawaii's many flavors. At the same time, trying to visit three or more islands is, we feel, too ambitious and too time-consuming, and it will ultimately water down your overall Hawaiian adventure.

The bottom line: If you have just a week to spend, spend it on Oahu, Maui, or the Big Island—the islands that offer the most attractions and activities. If you have more than a week, visiting two islands will help you make the most of your Hawaiian experience.

Hawaii by Cruise Ship

If you've never visited Hawaii and are interested in sampling two or more of the islands, a cruise is an excellent option. You'll avoid changing hotels and save all the wasted time involved in island-hopping by plane. The journey from island to island aboard a cruise ship is an absolute pleasure and you'll only have to unpack once.

On the negative side, cruises afford only about 6–10 hours on most islands, but that's more than enough time to determine whether the island is someplace you might enjoy visiting again. You can sign up for shore excursions offered by the cruise line or strike out on your own on foot, by taxi, or in a rental car. Of the various options, we prefer the rental car. It's less expensive than the excursions and provides maximum freedom and flexibility. You can visit the same sights offered by the excursions (if you wish) without the inevitable regimentation of traveling with a big group in a bus or passenger van. Rental car arrangements can be made onboard through the cruise director or in advance by you or your travel agent.

With the exception of the Big Island and Oahu, you can see a surprising amount of a given island in one day by rental car. If you cruise out of Honolulu, arriving a day or so early will give you the extra time needed to more thoroughly enjoy Oahu. Because many cruise itineraries call at two different ports on the Big Island, you'll actually have two days there to explore in your rental car. Understand, however, that while a cruise is the best way to sample two or more of the islands, it cannot provide that depth of experience that comes with actually staying on the island. In your brief exposure, you'll be able to sense the flavor of the island and catch the major sights, but you will not have sufficient time to really connect with the local population or to apprehend the island's extensive cultural and natural diversity. But, hey, that's the difference between sampling from a buffet and savoring a single dish. Sacrificing intimacy for variety is not a bad trade-off for first-time visitors.

Meals are likewise a trade-off. The good news is that meals are included in the price of your cruise, while the bad news is that you won't have much of a chance to try restaurants on shore. Fortunately, the cruise lines that visit Hawaii serve excellent food and offer many of the special, local dishes that you would find in better restaurants throughout the islands.

If you book an outside cabin on a cruise ship, you won't have to worry about being assigned a hotel room with a bad view: The ocean will be right outside your window. But even if you economize and go for a windowless inside cabin, a chaise lounge on deck and a perfect view await you whenever you desire.

If you love the beach and the sun, the ship will allow plenty of opportunity both onboard and ashore to swim and work on your tan. At Nawiliwili, Kauai, you can be on the beach within five minutes of setting foot onshore, and it doesn't take much longer at Kahului, Maui, to reach the white-sand beach of H. A. Baldwin Park. At the ports of Hilo and Kona on the Big Island, the better beaches (usually black volcanic sand) are most easily accessed by rental car. On Oahu, it's a fairly good haul by cab from the cruise passenger terminal to the beach at Waikiki, but not so long that you'd need a rental car. If you're really passionate about the beach, your best bet is to schedule a couple of beach days before or after your cruise.

All the cruise lines that visit Hawaiian ports offer shore excursions. Excursions that require special equipment or guides, like the helicopter tour of Kauai, the bike descent of Haleakala on Maui, and deep-sea fishing from Kona on the Big Island, as well as kayak, snorkeling, and diving excursions on any of the islands, are most easily accomplished through the ship's shore excursion program. For excursions that consist of general sightseeing, you're better off renting a car and seeing the same sights on your own. Not only will you avoid the regimentation; you will also save money. Finding your way around the islands (except Oahu) is a snap. In fact, it's hard to get lost.

Although several cruise lines offer itineraries that include one or more of the Hawaiian Islands, only American Hawaii Cruises and its sister United States Lines specialize exclusively in Hawaiian cruises, offering the best and most comprehensive introduction to the people, history, culture, and natural environment of the Islands. Cruises on American Hawaii are four or seven days in duration; United States Lines cruises last seven days. Four days, in our opinion, is too short for a Hawaiian cruise. We recommend the seven-day itinerary departing Honolulu (Oahu) and making ports of call on the islands of Kauai, Maui, and Hawaii (the Big Island) before returning to Honolulu. All seven-day cruises also include one complete day at sea. Pre- or post-cruise stays on Oahu or Maui are available. For longer cruises originating from or ending at North American ports (Vancouver (BC), Los Angeles, San Francisco, Ensenada (Mexico)), try Princess or Holland American Cruise Lines.

UNITED STATES LINES

Contact Info: 1380 Port of New Orleans Place, Robin St. Wharf, New Orleans, LA 70130-1890; (877) 330-6600; fax (504) 585-0694; www.unitedstateslines.com

Type of Ship: Modern, classic oceanliner

Type of Cruise: Destination- and family-oriented, casual and all-American

Comments   United States Lines is a new line owned by the same company that owns American Hawaii Cruises and the Delta Queen Steamboat Company. The line will commence operations in December 2000 with a single ship, the 1,214-passenger *Patriot,* formerly Holland American's *Nieuw Amsterdam.* Once the *Patriot* comes on line, American Hawaii's present liner, the *Independence,* will be repositioned and initiate its seven-day cruises from Kahului, Maui. The *Patriot* will offer a slightly more upscale product than the *Independence.* Two additional 1,900 passenger ships, currently under construction in Mississippi, are scheduled to join the United States Lines fleet in winter 2003 and 2004. They will be the largest U.S. cruise ships ever built, and the first large cruise vessels built in the United States in more than 40 years.

AMERICAN HAWAII CRUISES

Contact Info: 1380 Port of New Orleans Place, Robin St. Wharf, New Orleans, LA 70130-1890; (800) 765-7000; fax (504) 585-0694; www.cruisehawaii.com

Type of Ship: Modern, classic oceanliner

Type of Cruise: Destination- and family-oriented, casual and all-American

Cruise Line's Strengths: Destination, friendly staff, kids' program, shore excursions, theme cruises

Cruise Line's Shortcomings: Lack of amenities in cabins, small bathrooms

Fellow Passengers: Families with children during summer; honeymooners, seniors, and retired couples year-round. Most are experienced travelers; 40% have visited Hawaii before, and 60% have been on a cruise. The average age is 50+; 20% of the passengers are age 70+. The median household income is $40,000+. More than a third are celebrating a special event, usually an anniversary.

Recommended For: Families, particularly those with children; first- and second-time visitors to Hawaii; honeymooning couples; seniors and others who want the most convenient way to see the Islands; those looking for a cultural experience and a slower pace. New, shorter cruise segments are designed to attract first-timers, younger travelers, and newlyweds.

Not Recommended For: Sophisticated travelers who prefer luxury, gourmet cuisine, and individual travel. Singles looking for companionship or those looking for 24-hour entertainment, gambling, and discos.

Cruise Areas and Seasons: Four islands/five ports, Hawaii, year-round.

The Line

Following two multi-million-dollar renovations of its ship by Chicago-based American Classic Voyages Company (the parent company of Delta Queen Steamboat Company, which acquired American Hawaii Cruises in July 1993), American Hawaii Cruises has turned a liability—its aging ship—into an asset, by celebrating its distinguished history, stressing the appeal of traditional cruising, and focusing strongly on the Hawaiian aspect of its name.

Sailing into challenges is nothing new for AHC. Created specifically to cruise in Hawaiian waters at a time when U.S. flag operations had all but disappeared, it took an act of Congress (the Jones Act) to get AHC's SS *Independence* (in 1979) and SS *Constitution* (in 1982) recommissioned as American flag vessels. (The Jones Act required that ships cruising solely between U.S. ports must be American-flag vessels, owned by U.S. citizens, built and refurbished in the United States, and staffed with an American crew. AHC's vessels are the only oceangoing cruise ships sailing under the American flag today.) In 1988, under new ownership, health and fitness centers were added, along with other innovations meant to attract a younger audience. These include more active, sports-oriented shore excursions, a stronger Hawaiian content to the cruises, and a strong environmental commitment, particularly for protecting the whales that migrate from Alaska to breed in the warm Hawaiian waters in winter. Whale-watching cruises accompanied by experts are offered.

The Fleet	Built/Renovated	Tonnage	Passengers
Independence	1951/'94/'97	30,090	1,021

Style   Informal, family-oriented cruises focused on the destination in a warm and congenial atmosphere meant to reflect the traditional aloha spirit of Hawaii with a friendly, if not highly polished, crew. By the second day, you are likely to be wearing a muumuu or Hawaiian shirt. The Hawaiian experience begins with "Saturday Sail Away" festivities featuring native floral arrangements displayed throughout the ship, crew members dressed in traditional Hawaiian attire, and traditional island chants and drums to send cruisers on their way.

On boarding, passengers receive a lei, the traditional necklace of fresh flowers, to welcome them. During the cruise, the emphasis is on experiencing the Hawaiian culture, with Hawaiian activities, entertainment, educational programs, and Hawaiian regional specialties in the dining room. The atmosphere is casual and so is the dress; there's never a need for a tuxedo, and only once—the Captain's Party—will you need a tie.

Life on board goes at a slower pace than on typical mainstream ships on Caribbean and Mexican itineraries. There are no really late nights—most people are in bed by midnight if not before, and the food, activities, and entertainment are geared toward passengers 35 years and up. At the same time, American Hawaii welcomes kids with its seasonal children's program, which keeps them happy and well occupied, and it celebrates honeymooning couples and about-to-be-newlyweds with its "Weddings in Paradise" package.

Distinctive Features   A cultural display created by the Bishop Museum in Honolulu to stimulate passengers' interest in and knowledge of Hawaii. A *kumu,* a storyteller and teacher of traditions, on every cruise to enhance passengers' knowledge and enjoyment of Hawaiian culture and lore. Children's rates on most shore excursions.

Rates   Port charges are additional.

Special Fares and Discounts   Passengers may extend pre- and postcruise on any of the four major islands for $85–340 per person per night.

Third/Fourth Passenger: $780.

Children's Fare: Ages 17 and under, sharing cabin with two full-fare passengers, sail free through the year 2000.

Standby Fares: Occasionally, there are special rates for Hawaii residents.

Single Supplement: 160% for all categories except suites, which are 200%. A few cabins in two inside deluxe categories are available as singles for $100 additional.

Packages   Air/Sea: Yes. Other packages include golf, special occasion, honeymoon, anniversary. The "Romance in Paradise" package includes the services of a minister or judge, a lei and *haku* (floral hairpiece) for the bride, a lei or boutonniere for the groom, a chilled bottle of champagne, two dozen 5-by-7 photos in a keepsake album, live music by Hawaiian musicians, and a wedding cake for up to ten. Cost is $595. A wedding reception may be arranged for an additional fee. Weddings are performed on board; only one wedding is scheduled per day, three per cruise. Times for ceremonies are given at the time of the booking. Contact AHC for information on documentation required. Any length hotel stays pre- or post-cruise can be combined with three-day, four-day, or seven-day cruises.

Past Passengers   Holokai Hui (meaning Seafarer's Club) is the past passenger club and provides special benefits, including free cabin upgrades, separate check-in, an on-board party, and other features. Passengers are eligible after their second cruise with AHC.

The Last Word   The very factors that helped AHC develop its strong niche—American-built/flag vessels with required American crew (along with the inherent high costs)—are also those that have hampered the line's development. The Jones Act requires that ships cruising solely between U.S. ports be built in the United States. Added to this, gambling—a big money-maker for cruise ships—is forbidden (that's the law of Hawaii). Nor is there duty-free shopping; even on the ship, state sales tax is collected on gift shop purchases.

AHC's cruises have broad appeal and could be enjoyed by almost anyone visiting Hawaii, offering the most comfortable way to visit the Islands and enjoy some of the local flavor.

American Hawaii Standard Features

Officers   American.

Staff   Dining, Cabin, Cruise, and Entertainment/American.

Dining Facilities   Two dining rooms with two seatings/three meals. Breakfast, lunch buffet daily, tea on deck on one afternoon. Cookies, ice cream, popcorn around the clock.

Special Diets   Accommodated with advance notice.

Room Service   24 hours with a limited menu through Bell Station, reached by phone. Cabin attendants are on duty 7:30–11:30 a.m. and 12–2 and 5–9 p.m. and cannot be reached by phone during these times.

Dress Code   Casual; tie and jacket for captain's gala requested.

Cabin Amenities   Direct cellular telephone service, bathrooms with showers, mirrored vanity. No televisions.

Electrical Outlets   110 AC; shaver and hair dryer outlets in cabins.

Wheelchair Access   Two cabins.

Recreation and Entertainment   Nightclub, show lounge; three bars, lounges; television screens in top deck bar; movie theater.

Sports and Fitness   Two freshwater outside swimming pools, Ping-Pong, fitness center, shuffleboard.

Spa and Beauty   Beauty/barber shop, massage.

Other Facilities   Boutique, hospital, launderettes/coin-operated machines; conference facilities with audiovisuals.

Children's Facilities   Youth center; children's program June–August, enhanced during holidays; children's rates for shore excursions.

Theme Cruises   Whale-watching, Big Band, Aloha Festivals.

Smoking   No smoking allowed in public rooms. Smoking permitted in cabins and outside decks.

AHC Suggested Tipping   Per person, per day: cabin steward, $3.50; waiter, $3.50; busboy, $1.75. 15 percent added to bar bills.

Credit Cards   For cruise payment and on-board charges, American Express, Visa, MasterCard, Discover.

The Ship

Independence	
Quality Rating: 4	*Speed:* 17 knots
Value Rating: C	*Maximum Passengers:* 1,021
Registry: United States	*Crew:* 317
Length: 682 feet	*Passenger Decks:* 9
Beam: 89 feet	*Elevators:* 4
Cabins: 446	*Space Ratio:* 37
Draft: 26.5 feet	

Following $57 million in renovations, the *Independence* made her first voyage in November 1994, sporting a new logo on her smokestack that looks even more Hawaiian than the familiar red hibiscus used since the line began. The extensive renovations were aimed at creating a more authentic Hawaiian ambience in the decor. Even the rooms and decks were renamed using authentic Hawaiian names. Other major improvements included upgrading the air conditioning, electrical, and pollution control systems, plus structural repairs and replacements. Another $13 million worth of enhancements, particularly for safety, were added in 1997.

The most dramatic changes were in the elegant Kama'aina Lounge and other public areas on the Kama'aina Deck, where, on both sides of the room, 40 feet of windows were added to open up the space with an indoor-outdoor "lanai" environment, creating a more inviting ambience and giving passengers better views of the islands and sea.

A large open area that now houses Bishop Museum exhibits is splendid, as are the updated showroom and the lounge. The Hawaiian lanai effect extends to the aft section, part of which is shaded by canopies. The warmly decorated public rooms display artwork by local artists.

Because the ship originally was designed for three classes of passengers—making some public areas difficult to reach—better access and passenger flow were the primary objectives of the renovations. A grand stairway was added to the pool area aft to connect the ship's three main decks: Kama'aina, Ohana, and the Sun Deck. An additional aft stairway allows access to the pool area from the cabins on the lower decks. New corridor carpeting with images of dolphins and whales swimming toward the bow is also meant to help passengers orient themselves within the ship.

To make way for new deluxe suites in the former sports deck solarium and on the boat and main decks, the fitness center and conference center were relocated. Handicapped-accessible suites were also created, and all cabins were renovated and redecorated.

Cabins The cabins are very comfortable and storage space more than ample. Concealed compartments and beds as well as foldout tables are some of the features—created by the ship's original designer, Henry Dreyfuss—that have been retained.

The decor uses brightly colored Hawaiian fabrics from the 1940s and 1950s, with traditional Hawaiian patterns in the bedspreads. Although the bathrooms were renovated, they are still smaller than those in comparable-size cabins on newer ships, and the fixtures are still of the 1950s vintage. All cabins have baths with showers and a mirrored cabinet, except for three top suites on the boat deck that also have tubs; most have a mirrored vanity.

All cabins are equipped with a cellular telephone service that takes advantage of Hawaii's extensive cellular telephone network and enables passengers to phone directly to the U.S. mainland at considerably less cost than normally is the case on cruise ships. You will find instructions in your cabin that explain the system and costs. There are two types of rates: in port at the dock, and at sea or anchored offshore. You will be charged for all calls, including credit card and operator-assisted calls. Sample rates at the dock to the continental United States: $2 for first minute, $0.75 each additional minute. At sea, all calls: $3 for first minute, $2 each additional minute.

Room service is available through the Bell Station (like the bell captain's desk in a hotel), reachable by phone 24 hours a day for beverages, light snacks, and ice. (You might get a recorded message asking you to leave a message.) Cabin attendants are on duty 7:30–11:30 a.m., 12–2 p.m., and 5–9 p.m.; they are available for all cleaning services, towels, and turndowns; delivery of *Tradewinds,* the daily schedule; and general maintenance.

As the cruise line's brochure explains, the ships' original layout for three classes results now in 52 different cabin configurations, which AHC has grouped into 13 different fare categories. The cabins are pictured and described in AHC's easy-to-use brochure. The bed configurations vary— queen, twins that convert to double, lower and upper Pullman-style berths, or single lower sofabed. The *Independence's* six new solarium suites added on the bridge deck are some of the largest, each with 300 square feet, and have high ceilings, skylights, and windows that open. Two cabins designed for the disabled are located on the Aloha Deck.

Specifications   240 cabins inside, 206 outside; 37 suites. Standard dimensions are 85–242 square feet. 90 with twin; 126 double/queen; 136 upper and lowers; 24 singles.

Dining   Over the years, American Hawaii's cuisine has gotten mixed reviews—from poor to excellent—but of late, the line has been getting high marks on both quality and variety. To give passengers a taste of the Islands, menus include a selection of Pacific Rim and Hawaiian regional cuisine along with traditional favorites. Local ingredients—fresh fish, fruit, vegetables, and herbs—are used to ensure authenticity. In addition, a variety of familiar items boast a new spin, such as Maui mango pasta and roasted rack of lamb with Molokai herbs.

A typical dinner menu includes choices from two appetizers, two soups, two salads, six entrees (with at least one fish, one pasta, and one vegetarian selection), three desserts, plus a selection of ice creams and sherbets. California and French wines are featured and range from $16 to $42.

One notable improvement has been the expansion and redesign of the buffet on the Ohana Deck (upper deck), where breakfast and lunch offer a wide selection of dishes. The buffet has Hawaiian-style indoor-outdoor cooking, and seating areas extend to the swimming pool area, partially shaded by canopies.

Ice cream and sherbet treats are a long-standing tradition. *Pu'uwai,* meaning "healthy heart," is a low-fat, low-cholesterol program available in the dining room. Daily, a Hawaiian cocktail specialty, such as a Blue Hawaiian or Mai Tai, is featured for $4.75; in the afternoon a self-service popcorn machine provides a snack.

To accommodate passengers who are off the ship during the regular meal hours, the ship has extended lunch service from 2:30 to 4:30 p.m., with hot dogs and hamburgers available at the buffet. Coffee and tea, juice, and sodas are available 24 hours a day in the Ohana Buffet.

Service   The young American crew is friendly, courteous, energetic, high spirited, and attentive. Both men and women serve as cabin and dining room attendants and are given high marks for efficiency. Particularly noteworthy are the waitresses in the dining room and on the pool deck.

Facilities and Entertainment   Evening entertainment is family-oriented, with local Hawaiian entertainers as standard fare. The Hoi Hoi Showplace on the Kama'aina Deck is the show lounge where performers celebrate Hawaiian traditions with island entertainment, and the Ray Kennedy Entertainers perform three Broadway-style shows weekly. Next door, the Hapa Haole Bar re-creates the "tourist" Hawaii of the 1930s and 1940s. "Concerts on the Pacific" by headliner vocalists is a nightly feature in the Kama'aina Lounge.

The ship's orchestra is also very good, with a range from Elvis to traditional Hawaiian music that passengers seem to enjoy thoroughly. On a recent cruise, many passengers seemed to enjoy dancing but had limited opportunities to do so. AHC adds gentlemen hosts to dance with the unaccompanied women on the ship during Big Band cruises.

At the stern, the Constitution Lounge, a semicircular bar/lounge, is one of the most pleasant areas on the ship, offering passengers a 180° view of Hawaii's beautiful scenery. In the evening, the lounge is the venue for low-key entertainment.

Two large television screens are located in the poolside Surfrider Bar on the sun deck. There are no televisions in the cabins, and the ship has no casinos because gambling is prohibited in Hawaii. The movie theater shows current films as many as four or five times daily. Selections and times are listed in the daily program.

Activities and Diversions   The *kumu,* a teacher of Hawaiian traditions, is on board for every cruise and is an integral part of the passengers' Hawaiian experience. She (or he) brings the spirit of aloha and talks about island history, music, craft, cultural tradition, lore, and mythology, meeting with passengers at different times throughout the day and evening, choosing appropriate shipboard settings to enhance and illustrate her stories. She teaches native Hawaiian words, the meaning of the hula dance, and how to play ancient island games, blow conch shells, make leis and other crafts, and play the ukulele. The *kumu*'s study has been added by the main lounge on the Kama'aina Deck.

Exhibits created by the renowned Bishop Museum also enable passengers to learn about Hawaii through displays of ancient Hawaiian games, arts and crafts, traditional garments, and natural artifacts, as well as three-dimensional interactive exhibits on the wildlife and natural history of Hawaii. During whale-watching months, from January through March, seminars on nature and wildlife by experts from the Pacific Whale Foundation are offered on board.

In addition, the daily program includes games, line dancing, and unusual activities like instruction in making fabric hibiscus flowers or shell hair combs and earrings and weaving palm fronds. The ship has a conference center.

Sports and Fitness   Since the ship is in port every day but one, and so many of the shore excursions are sports-oriented, shipboard sports are limited. The ship has two small swimming pools that were given a much-needed renovation during dry dock in 1997. The ship also has a small fitness room with a few exercise machines, but no daily fitness programs other than an early-morning walk and stretching program. The open deck space is generous.

On shore, passengers can arrange to go biking, hiking, deep-sea fishing, horseback riding, kayaking on the Huleia River (where *Raiders of the Lost Ark* was filmed), sailing, swimming, snorkeling, and diving (novices and certified). The newest golf package provides for play on four islands at some of Hawaii's leading courses.

Spa and Beauty   The beauty salon is small; prices are moderate. The massage schedule fills quickly; you should sign up early to schedule an appointment.

Children's Facilities   A supervised children's program is available during the summer months and holidays, with organized games, talent shows, crafts sessions, special parties, and other activities for children in two groups: the Keiki (Kids) program for ages 5–12, and the Hui O Kau Wela Nalu (Summer Surf Club) for teens, ages 13–17. The ship has an on-board youth recreation center and a full-time recreation coordinator. There are also special kids' rates on most shore excursions.

Shore Excursions   American Hawaii shore excursions are some of the best of any cruise line and offer enough choices to suit everyone in the family. The ships are in port every morning of the cruise except one.

To help you make your selection, you will find a shore excursion book with color photos, descriptions, and prices in your cabin. A colorful, graphic display center on board shows the 55 or so options currently available. They include beach picnics, submarine and helicopter rides, tropical gardens, tours of a macadamia nut farm or working ranch or plantation, the Polynesian Cultural Center, nature parks, craft shops, and local feasts and festivals. You can go biking, hiking, kayaking, and snorkeling, and see whales, birds, volcanoes, rain forests, and more. Golfers should inquire about the line's golf package. Prices range from $50 to $145. Shore excursions cannot be purchased in advance of the cruise.

Particularly noteworthy are those excursions that enable passengers with a sense of adventure to enjoy the less explored areas of Hawaii and experience the state's many natural attractions. You can join a raft exploration of the Na Pali Coast, fly over the 5,000-foot-high rim of Mount Waialeale in a helicopter, ride horseback along Hawaii's spectacular ocean bluffs, or take part in a kayak trip down the Huleia River in the heart of the Huleia National Wildlife Refuge, site of the opening scenes from the film *Raiders of the Lost Ark.*

On Hilo, the Hawaii Volcanoes National Park is the big attraction; the Old Hawaii: Hilo 100 Years Ago Tour is a quieter, gentler look at Hawaii. The Kauai highlight is a helicopter flight, subject to weather conditions.

Note: Schedule the Haleakala Crater helicopter flight for morning; afternoons are often cloudy and windy, and aircraft cannot fly.

If shore excursions fill up, you can find one on your own; several companies provide them. You could also read up on the islands in advance, rent a car on each island (your ship will make arrangements), and explore on your own.

Theme Cruises   American Hawaii offers theme cruises almost year-round; inquire from AHC for the exact dates. Whale-watching cruises are traditionally from January through March, the height of the season when humpback whales are in warm Hawaiian waters with their young. For 1999, the cruises will be accompanied by marine naturalists from the Pacific Whale Foundation of Maui, a nonprofit educational organization, who will give seminars about the breeding, feeding, and migration habits of these endangered giants. Optional small-boat excursions to the Hawaiian Islands Humpback Whale National Marine Sanctuary will bring passengers closer to the whales (under federal whale-protection regulations). Early-bird savings are available.

Big Band cruises, featuring music of the 1940s and headliner entertainers, are offered throughout the year. Aloha Festival sailings, mid-September through mid-October, coincide with Aloha Month, the annual fall festival celebrated throughout the Islands. Started in 1946 by the Jaycees as Aloha Week, it has become an annual tradition on all the Islands to highlight Hawaii's rich cultural heritage. Passengers enjoy special presentations on Hawaiian history, art, music, and dance by distinguished local hula schools, storytellers, and artists, who share their expertise and rich talents. These guest performers, known in Hawaii as "living treasures," dedicate their lives to the preservation of Hawaiian heritage. In port, passengers can attend colorful parades and street celebrations.

Postscript

When the Delta Queen Steamboat Company acquired American Hawaii, it made a commitment to do whatever it took to make its ship first class and the cruise the most authentic way to see the Islands and experience their culture. To that end, they have invested large sums in the ship to restore and improve it. Even so, this is not a new ship. Don't expect a fancy, two-level showroom or a state-of-the-art health spa. Rather, it remains typical of the oceanliners built during its time, when dining rooms and theaters were located on lower decks and bathrooms were small. The ship should be enjoyed as a classic.

The ship is comfortable, with a quiet dining room and spacious open decks. It offers a great introduction to the Hawaiian Islands and the easiest, most unhurried way to island-hop, especially for first-time Hawaii visitors who want to see as much of the Islands as possible in a week. With the three- and four-day cruises, it's easy to have your cake and eat it too by combining a cruise with a hotel stay in a week's holiday.

It also provides a good sample of cruising for first-timers—you only unpack once—and there's ample time in port for those who worry about seasickness, claustrophobia, or boredom. The first day of the cruise is at sea—a welcome amenity for those who have traveled long distances and are likely to have jet lag.

For old Hawaii hands, the cruise is a new way to see the Islands. For experienced cruisers, it's a pleasant cruise and comprehensive visit to the 50th state. But if you are looking for excitement, 24-hour entertainment, gambling, discos, fitness activities, and gourmet cuisine, this is not the cruise for you.

One passenger reports being particularly impressed with the staff's handling of her partially nonambulatory husband. She told us:

> *While not wheelchair-bound, my husband was too weak to walk long hallways and gangways or to board the ship. I merely had to phone from the cabin, and, almost instantly, a crew member arrived to push him wherever we needed to go, including to leave the ship. The same was true when we reboarded in port. They were extremely helpful.*

Tips and Suggestions for Specialized Travelers

Singles

Best Island to Visit: Oahu

Other Recommended Island: Maui

Things to See and Do: Gain insights into Hawaii's history at the Bishop Museum, Hawaii Maritime Center, and Damien Museum. Hike to the top of world-famous Diamond Head Crater. People-watch on Kalakaua Avenue, Waikiki's main street. Make new friends at a nightclub in Waikiki or Honolulu. On Maui, enjoy the lively atmosphere in Lahaina, where the most of the island's after-dark action takes place.

Comments   Quite simply, Oahu has the most things to do and places to see and will keep your itinerary filled from beginning to end. If you're hoping to make new friends and enjoy some socializing during your trip, Oahu is also your best bet, as it's the one island that offers a sizable menu of nightlife activities.

Couples and Honeymooners

Best Island to Visit: Kauai

Other Recommended Islands: Oahu, Maui, Big Island

Things to See and Do: Stay on Kauai's north side in Princeville, which provides gorgeous views of idyllic Hanalei Bay. Take a leisurely boat ride up the Wailua River to the Fern Grotto, another favorite romantic spot. On Oahu, have dinner at Bali-by-the-Sea, Michel's at the Colony Surf, the Hau Tree Lanai, or La Mer (all wonderfully romantic, and all located in Waikiki). Enjoy a sunset walk on the beach, or take a sunset dinner cruise. On Maui, make the early-morning drive to Haleakala to take in the spectacular sunrise, then stroll hand in hand on Wailea Beach, named the "Best Beach in America" in 1999. On the Big Island, hike the trails at Hawaii Volcanoes National Park.

Comments   Kauai is an easy choice for Hawaii's most romantic island, offering a blissful combination of postcard-like scenery and uncrowded settings. For on-the-go couples who want to enjoy a lot of outdoor activities, Oahu, Maui, and the Big Island are also recommended islands.

Families

Best Island to Visit: Oahu

Other Recommended Islands: Maui

Things to See and Do: Take in family attractions such as Sea Life Park, the Honolulu Zoo, Waikiki Aquarium, Atlantis Submarines, Waimea Valley Adventure Park, and Bishop Museum. Enjoy some sun, surf, and sand at Waikiki Beach and Ala Moana Beach Park, two of the most popular and swimmable beaches in Hawaii. Let the kids make new friends at a supervised children's program (the one at the Hilton Hawaiian Village is outstanding), while Mom and Dad get to enjoy some time for themselves. On Maui, visit the Maui Ocean Center, Hawaii Nature Center, and Whalers Village Museum, all family-oriented attractions designed to educate as well as entertain.

Comments   In recent years, thanks to the addition of unique attractions such as the Maui Ocean Center, the island of Maui has attempted to reinvent itself as a tremendous family destination. We feel it's getting there, and fast. But the best island to avoid the dreaded "Mommy, I'm bored!" scenario remains Oahu, which offers many family-oriented attractions and activities right in Waikiki, and even more in Honolulu and the rest of the island.

Seniors

Best Island to Visit: Oahu

Other Recommended Islands: Big Island, Kauai

Things to See and Do: Visit Oahu's historical attractions, including the Bishop Museum, 'Iolani Palace, Aloha Tower, Hawaii Maritime Center, and the Mission Houses Museum. Enjoy healthy exercise walks along Waikiki Beach and Kapi'olani Park. Learn to string a lei, dance a hula, and play the ukulele. For couples, should the Islands bring out the romantics in you, arrange to renew your wedding vows on the beach at sunset!

Comments   Many of the best visitor attractions in the Islands offer discounts for seniors. (Very few golf courses, on the other hand, offer senior discounts.)

Visitors with Disabilities

Best Island to Visit: Oahu

Other Recommended Islands: Maui, Big Island

Things to See and Do: Take in a concert, film, or dance performance at the historic Hawaii Theatre in Honolulu, which provides special seating areas for the disabled. Visit popular attractions such as 'Iolani Palace, Sea Life Park, Polynesian Cultural Center, Honolulu Zoo, Hawaii's Plantation Village, and Mission Houses Museum on Oahu; Haleakala National Park, Maui Tropical Plantation, and Maui Ocean

Center on Maui; Hawaii Volcanoes National Park, Pana'ewa Rainforest Zoo, Nani Mau Gardens, and Pu'uhonua O Honaunau on the Big Island; and the Kauai Museum, Fern Grotto, and Kilauea Point National Wildlife Refuge on Kauai—all of which can accommodate disabled visitors.

Comments   The *Aloha Guide to Accessibility,* published by the Commission on Persons with Disabilities, provides detailed information on accessibility features of Island hotels, attractions, beaches, parks, theaters, shopping centers, transportation services, and medical and support services. Write to the commission at 919 Ala Moana Blvd., Room 101, Honolulu, HI 96814, or call (808) 586-8121. General information is free. Rates for individual informational packets: Beaches & Parks, $3; Theaters & Auditoriums, $3; Shopping Centers, $3; Visitor Attractions, $3; Hotels, $5. The entire set may be purchased for $15. Also, the Hawaii Centers for Independent Living has a Web site that provides useful information for the disabled. Log on to www.assistguide.com for more information.

A WORD TO BUSINESS TRAVELERS

Despite its reputation as one of the world's most popular tropical playgrounds, Hawaii is, in fact, a hotbed for major business deals and transactions, particularly those with international roots. Situated in the middle of the Pacific Ocean, the Aloha State is the only place in the world where you can conduct business with major financial centers in New York, Japan, China, and Hawaii all in the same business day.

Although it is business before pleasure, 99% of all business travelers in the Islands do manage to squeeze in some time for fun in the sun. It's simply a matter of budgeting your time wisely. On your first night in your hotel room, armed with a bevy of free visitor publications (and this book, of course), plan a complete day-by-day itinerary for your trip. If you have enough time, the possibilities are endless!

The Hawaii Convention Center

Perhaps you won't be alone on your business trip to the Hawaiians Islands. Maybe it'll be you and a few hundred—or thousand!—of your closest colleagues in your field. More and more, local marketers and visitor industry officials are trying to lure major conventions to the Islands.

Located on the outskirts of Waikiki on the island of Oahu, the Hawaii Convention Center was unveiled in the summer of 1998. The facility boasts 100,000 square feet of meeting space (including two presentation rooms), 200,000 square feet of exhibit space, a 36,000-square-foot ballroom, a 35,000-square-foot registration/lobby area, and an 800-stall parking garage.

Masterfully designed by the award-winning architectural firm of Wimberly Allison Tong and Goo, the four-story center combines high-tech wizardry with an appreciated Hawaiian "sense of place." The ground floor houses the lobby area and exhibit hall; the second floor is reserved exclusively for parking; the third level features the meeting rooms; and the fourth (top) floor houses the grand ballroom and rooftop garden terrace. The airy structure is enhanced by a glass wall.

Some high-tech features at the center include fiber-optic cable throughout, providing speedy and state-of-the-art communication; a press room providing capability for global links to any nation in the world; a built-in six-station interpretation room, allowing the translator to view the speaker through a video monitor with maximum privacy; a meeting room capable of hosting 400 computers working simultaneously; a large video display screen; and an auditorium equipped with a built-in projection room and concert sound quality—ideal for a multi-media presentation.

For more information on the Hawaii Convention Center, call the Hawaii Visitors & Convention Bureau at (808) 923-1811 or visit the center's Web site at www.hvcb.org/hconv.

Approximately 30,000 hotel rooms and condominium units are located within a one-mile radius of the center. The nearest hotel is the Ala Moana Hotel, directly across the street. And a handful of local eateries are within easy walking distance of the center, but we recommend hoofing it to nearby Ala Moana Shopping Center, which offers dozens of restaurants and fast-food fare, as well as Hawaii's best shopping experience.

Recommendations for Travelers with Special Interests

Art Aficionados

Best Island to Visit: Oahu

Other Recommended Islands: Maui

Things to See and Do: The Honolulu Academy of Arts and the Contemporary Museum, both in Honolulu, are the state's two best art museums. Maui has a thriving art community, with many galleries in Lahaina, and also at the Maui Arts & Cultural Center and Hui No'eau Visual Arts Center.

Fine Dining Connoisseurs

Best Island to Visit: Oahu

Other Recommended Islands: Big Island, Maui, Lanai

Things to See and Do: There are superb fine dining establishments on every island except for Molokai. The greatest concentration of the best restaurants, however, are in Honolulu and Waikiki on Oahu. Many of Hawaii's top chefs—including Sam Choy, Jean-Marie Josselin, and Alan Wong—first gained notoriety on the Neighbor Islands but now have restaurants on Oahu as well. Be sure to treat your palate to a Hawaii regional cuisine dinner, which features fresh ingredients produced or grown in the Islands. (See Part Eleven, "Dining in Hawaii.")

History Lovers

Best Island to Visit: Oahu

Other Recommended Islands: Maui

Things to See and Do: Again, the greatest concentration of historical attractions is in downtown Honolulu, where the 'Iolani Palace, State Capitol Building, Kamehameha Statue, Mission Houses Museum, Kawaiaha'o Church, and Hawaii State Library are within easy walking distance of each other. Along with the palace, the best place to visit is the Bishop Museum, a ten-minute drive from downtown Honolulu.

Sports Fanatics

Best Island to Visit: Oahu

Other Recommended Islands: Maui, Big Island

Things to See and Do: Football fans have a lot to cheer about on Oahu, which hosts the NFL Pro Bowl (held the week following the Super Bowl) and a Christmas Day doubleheader featuring two NCAA post-season bowl games. In December, the University of Hawaii hosts the prestigious Rainbow Classic, an eight-team collegiate basketball tournament. Other major Oahu sporting events include the Honolulu Marathon and Sony Open (golf). Maui, meanwhile, hosts the annual Hula Bowl (a college football all-star game), Maui Invitational (a college basketball tournament televised on ESPN), Mercedes Open (golf), and Maui Marathon.

Getting There

Until someone decides to construct a 2,500-mile highway connecting Hawaii to the continental U.S., your ticket to paradise will likely be stamped with "United," "Delta," "Continental," or some other major airline.

Dress for comfort. It's about a five-hour flight from the West Coast to Honolulu. From New York, the in-flight duration is about 11 hours.

While the majority of U.S. mainland–to-Hawaii flights touch down in Honolulu, there are some flights that fly directly to the Neighbor Islands: United Airlines has daily flights from Los Angeles and San Francisco to Kona on the Big Island and Kahului on Maui, and from Los Angeles to Lihu'e on Kauai. Delta Airlines offers twice-daily flights into Kahului from Los Angeles, while American Airlines schedules one daily direct flight from Los Angeles to Kahului. In addition, Hawaiian Airlines offers four flights weekly between Seattle and Kahului.

All schedules are subject to change. Call the selected toll-free numbers below for updated information.

The Honolulu International Airport (HNL) on Oahu is one of the 20 busiest U.S. airports, with more than 24 million passenger arrivals and departures annually. Airports serving the Neighbor Islands include the Keahole Airport in Kona and Hilo Airport in Hilo on the Big Island; Kahului Airport and Kapalua Airport on Maui; Lihu'e Airport on Kauai; Molokai Airport on Molokai; and Lanai Airport on Lanai.

Booking your vacation through a travel agent saves you both time and money, as he or she can combine bulk rates for airfares, lodgings, and car rentals into one tidy, simplified package. If you decide to make the arrangements on your own, however, here are some tips, suggestions, and advisories on finding a good deal on airfares:

- The major airlines offer the most departures, while the smaller airlines have fewer flights but cheaper fares. Taken as a group, low-cost carriers have a good safety record, about equal to that of the major carriers.
- To get the lowest possible fare, be prepared to be flexible in your travel plans. The best deals are usually limited to travel on certain

Airlines	
Air Canada..	(800) 776-3000
Air New Zealand	(800) 262-1234
American Airlines	(800) 433-7300
British Airways...................................	(800) 247-9297
Continental Airlines............................	(800) 523-3273
Delta Airlines......................................	(800) 221-1212
Hawaiian Airlines	(800) 367-5320
Northwest Airlines..............................	(800) 225-2525
TWA..	(800) 221-2000
United Airlines	(800) 241-6522

days of the week or even particular hours of the day. After receiving a price quote, ask the reservations agent if you might be able to save more money by leaving a day earlier or later, or by taking a different flight on that day.

- The best bargains usually sell out early, so book your flight as far ahead as possible. At the same time, some airlines provide more discounted seats later. In this instance, you can try calling just before the advance purchase deadline.

- After you purchase your ticket, check back with the airline at least once before the scheduled departure to check the current fares. Since fares frequently change, the airline might refund the difference if the fares go down.

- If your travel itinerary falls into a busy flight period, book your reservations early. Flights during holidays, for example, may sell out weeks or months ahead of time. Never book a stand-by flight or "open-return" ticket if you need to fly during this busy period.

- Many discount fares are nonrefundable. If you want to change flights or dates on your discounted booking, you may have to pay the difference in fares if your discounted fare is not available on your new flight.

- Your airline ticket should show the flight number, departure date and time, and status of your reservation for each flight of your itinerary. If the status box says "OK," that means your reservations are confirmed.

- Remember that a "direct" flight isn't as direct it seems—"direct" in this case means making at least one stop, but not changing planes ("non-stop" means making no stops between the departure and arrival point). Try to avoid connecting flights, which require a change of plane. Be sure to ask about your exact routing.

- Always bring a photo I.D. when you fly, and make sure the name on your airline ticket matches that on the I.D.

- Check in early to minimize the likelihood of being "bumped" from your flight (airlines routinely oversell their flights). When airlines bump passengers, they usually start with the people who checked in last. Also, airline personnel are required by law to ask for volunteers willing to be bumped before they begin selecting passengers to bump. If you are being bumped against your will, make sure the gate agents ask for volunteers first.

FIGHTING JET LAG

Circadian desynchronization, better known as jet lag, is a fact of life after flying across several time zones to Hawaii. Jet lag is *not* a state of mind. It is an actual condition that has physical and mental ramifications. There are several books available about jet lag and how to combat it. We recommend *Jet Smart* by Diana Fairechild, a former flight attendant whose 21 years of experience included numerous stops to the Hawaiian Islands.

Here are some practical tips for combatting jet lag:

- Book a hotel room with a deep bathtub (not just a shower). Not only can a warm bath replenish moisture lost during your flight, it also relaxes your nervous system.
- Do not drink alcohol on the plane. Alcohol can sharply intensify jet lag. Similarly, avoid carbonated drinks such as soda. Instead, drink lots of water to prevent dehydration.
- During your flight, remove your shoes and don slippers to improve the circulation of your feet. Flex your feet, ankles, and legs frequently, and take short walks around the cabin.
- Get some sleep during your flight.
- Adjust your watch to Hawaii Standard Time as soon as you board the plane. This will better prepare you mentally as you adjust to Hawaiian time.
- Eat a light meal on your flight, and avoid rich or exotic foods on the first two days of your trip. This will help your body focus on adjusting to your surroundings rather than digesting strange new foods.
- Get acclimated to Hawaii's time zone as soon as possible (which means going to bed later than you're used to on the first night, even though you may feel extremely tired).
- Finally, as tempting as it may be, don't try to do too much on the day or night of your arrival. Get some rest early. Establish a routine that is in sync with the local time.

What to Pack (and Not to Pack)

Ready to pack? Casual resort wear should be the attire of choice for your Hawaii visit: shorts, T-shirts, jeans, tank tops, sundresses, sneakers, slippers, and so forth. Also, bring along a visor or cap and some sunscreen to protect you from the sun's rays.

If you plan to visit high-elevation spots such as Mauna Kea on the Big Island or Haleakala on Maui, pack a sweater, coat, scarf, and other winter-weather items. Also, there are very few gourmet restaurants that require dinner jackets for gentlemen. See Part Eleven, "Dining in Hawaii," for exceptions.

The State Department of Agriculture maintains strict regulations on plants and animals entering Hawaii. The importation of uninspected flora and fauna can have a negative impact on Hawaii's fragile ecosystem. (You can imagine, for instance, what the unwanted introduction of snakes could do in the Islands!) Conversely, keep in mind that the U.S. Department of Agriculture restricts the movement of fruits, plants, and other items from Hawaii to the U.S. mainland to prevent the spread of fruit flies and other pests.

For inquiries, call the Plant Quarantine Branch at (808) 586-0844 or the Animal Quarantine Branch at (808) 483-7171.

Saying "I Do"

Boasting some of the most beautiful natural settings in the world, Hawaii *inspires* romance. One California woman reminisced to us how she met her husband-to-be while relaxing at the pool of her Waikiki hotel. Their first date was an evening sail along the Waikiki coastline, and their first kiss happened on the beach at sunset. Two years later, the couple returned to the Islands—and the beach—to exchange "I dos."

Getting hitched was a simple event in old Hawaii, with marriage ceremonies reserved for only high-ranking *ali'i*. The first Christian marriage took place in 1822, two years after the arrival of the American missionaries. For a time, it was illegal for non-Christian marriages to be held in the Islands.

Today, more than 10,000 out-of-state couples are wed in Hawaii, "tying the knot" at locales ranging from secluded beaches and evergreen valleys to historic churches and private oceanfront estates.

Of course, to be married in the Aloha State, you'll need a valid marriage license. You can obtain one at the State Department of Health, Marriage License Office, 1250 Punchbowl Street, Honolulu, HI 96813. On the Neighbor Islands, you can get a license from a marriage license agent (ask your hotel concierge or wedding coordinator to direct you to the nearest agent). Both bride and groom must be present when the license is issued. The license is valid statewide and is good for 30 days. The fee is $50 in cash.

The Marriage License Office is open from Monday to Friday from 8 a.m. to 4 p.m. (closed on holidays).

Both the bride and groom must be at least 18 years of age in order to be married without parental consent. Also, if either partner has been married before, he or she is required to provide the date, county, and state (or country) in which the divorce was finalized for each previous marriage. The names of each partner's parents and places of birth must also be provided.

A free "Getting Married" pamphlet is available from the state of Hawaii's Marriage License Office. Write to the address above or call them at (808) 586-4544. In addition, the Hawaii Visitors & Convention Bureau has a sizable listing of available wedding coordinators and planners on all islands. Log on to their Web site at www.gohawaii.com.

Part Three

Lodging

Deciding Where to Stay

Since your hotel, condominium, or bed-and-breakfast will likely be your "home away from home" throughout your stay, it's no stretch to think that choosing the right accommodations can be vital to your Island vacation experience.

We all have stories of dream vacations–turned-nightmares after being stuck in hotels with slummy room conditions, poor service, and back-alley views. Thankfully, if you're like us, you've also enjoyed hotels that are so beautiful and offer such attentive service and magnificent views that it was only with great reluctance that we turned in our room keys.

In Hawaii, you have a choice of more than 70,000 rooms and suites—from budget to ultra-deluxe—on the six main islands. You'll find most of the major names here—Hilton, Sheraton, Hyatt, Ritz-Carlton, and Four Seasons—as well as lesser-known entities and locally owned chains such as Aston or Outrigger Hotels. The vast majority of these hotel rooms are either beachfront or just a few minutes away by foot.

The hotels that made it into our ratings all provide good to superb room accommodations. The rooms, in general, are tastefully appointed, spacious, and accented with enough Hawaiian touches to remind you of where you are. As far as the views go, they range from outstanding (several Waikiki hotels, for example, provide breathtaking views of the beach and/or Diamond Head) to average. One thing to watch out for is a hotel's definition of "ocean-view," which can sometimes mean being able to see a patch of blue peeking out between competitor properties.

Overall, we were very impressed at the service level maintained by the hotels we visited. We found that the hotel staffs here take their "aloha spirit" seriously and even take special courses so they can better share Hawaii's culture and history with their guests. Female staff members are usually clad in attractive muumuus, while the men are attired in tasteful aloha shirts. The service is exceptionally friendly and courteous, from the parking valets and hotel managers to the registration clerks and housekeeping personnel.

The chief factors you should consider in selecting a hotel—and the factors we used in evaluating them—are location, service, amenities, views, and, of course, price and value.

Some special considerations: While Waikiki on the island of Oahu remains the mecca for most visitors to Hawaii, it isn't for everyone. If you're seeking a quiet and secluded getaway with little traffic, for example, you probably won't enjoy Waikiki. Instead, check out the 'Ihilani Resort and Spa on Oahu's Leeward Coast or the Turtle Bay Hilton on the North Shore. However, if you want to stay in an area offering lots of nightlife and providing attractions, shopping, fine dining, and entertainment, Waikiki is your best bet. Waikiki is also the place to be for convention travelers, as more than 30,000 hotel rooms are located within a one-mile radius of the Hawaii Convention Center.

The resort areas of Wailea, Makena, Ka'anapali, and Kapalua top our Maui recommendations. The Kona side of the island of Hawaii is where most visitors stay, and our favorite hotels are located along the Kohala Coast. The prime resort areas on Kauai include Po'ipu, Princeville, and Hanalei. Molokai only has one major hotel (Kaluako'i Resort), while Lanai offers two (The Lodge at Ko'ele and the Manele Bay Hotel).

Getting a Good Deal on a Room

In Hawaii, there are a number of factors that determine a hotel's room rate: consumer demand, location, season, availability, type of view, grade of room, and the proximity to beaches, shopping centers, and even entertainment venues.

According to the Hawaii Visitors & Convention Bureau, Hawaii room rates are highest from December through March. During this time, the average hotel room rate in Hawaii is $146–151. The low season—when the average room rate falls to $130–144—runs from September through November and the months of April and May.

Many of these hotels provide the ultimate in luxury accommodations and services and rank among the top tropical resorts in the world. The bad news, naturally, is that you will likely have to pay dearly to stay in them, with nightly rates of $250 and up.

The good news, from the visitor's point of view, is this: Mired in an economic slump, the state is relying on tourism more than ever, and hotels are constantly coming up with money-saving deals and extra value vacation packages to entice more visitors. One travel expert called Hawaii "by far the best value of any leisure destination on the planet, because if you look back 10 years, airfares and hotel prices haven't gone up even close to what's proportionate to the cost of living." Contrast this with the U.S. mainland, where a booming economy has translated to a heavier demand for vacation travel and, consequently, increases in room rates.

The Asian market also plays a role in the pricing of Hawaii hotel rooms. To make up for the recent drop in Asian visitors, for example, many local hotels have become less restrictive and more aggressive in attracting visitors from the West. "It's not obvious, and certainly no hotel dropped their rates 50%," offered one insider. "But, for example, you may be able to get an oceanfront room at a good deal, whereas in the past you could only get a garden-view room at a good deal."

The state's dependency on tourism is unlikely to change anytime soon. A 1999 report issued by the World Travel & Tourism Council noted that Hawaii's visitor industry provides a quarter of the state's Gross State Product, a quarter of the state's tax revenue, and one-third of the jobs over a wide range of occupations. The prevailing opinion among state officials is that, if anything, Hawaii's reliance on tourism will only increase in the near future. This can only benefit you, the visitor.

Your travel agent should be able to help you find the best possible deals, but you can also do some digging on your own. Searching for a good deal on a hotel room can be a painstaking process, but the results can be rewarding if you can spare the time.

WHERE THE DEALS ARE

Corporate Rates

Many hotels provide discounted corporate rates (up to 20% off regular rack rates). Check with the hotel of your choice and ask for their corporate rates. Some hotels may ask for a written request on company letterhead, but others will guarantee you the rate whether you work for a major company or not. The screening process isn't usually rigorous.

Preferred Rates

A preferred rate is a discount offer designed to entice a specific class of traveler. Most are offered exclusively through a travel agent. Keep in mind, however, that preferred rates and corporate rates involve only your hotel accommodations. When you add your discounted room rate to your airline fare and car rental fees, the total cost will likely still exceed the price of a complete travel package offered by travel agents and tour operators.

Travel Clubs

The largest hotel discounts in Hawaii are usually available through half-price hotel programs, or travel clubs. These programs work with participating hotels to provide the consumer with room discounts up to 50% off the rack rate.

These discounts, however, come with certain restrictions. They are generally applicable on a space available basis, which usually means you can book a room at the discounted rate when the hotel expects its occupancy rate to fall below 80%. There are also blackout periods when the discounted rate is not made available. Still other discounts may be applicable only on certain days of the week.

Most of these travel clubs or half-price programs charge an annual fee, usually from $25 to $50, and sometimes up to $125. (Therefore, unless you plan to travel several times a year, this might not be the best option for you.) When you join, you are given a membership card and a directory listing of participating hotels and other establishments. The more established programs offer members over 1,000 hotels to choose from in the U.S. but, in most cases, only about 100 in Hawaii.

While these discount programs do have their merit, they often force you to plan your trip around the various restrictions, thus limiting your travel options. Also, not all hotels offer a true 50% discount, and many that do usually base their discount on an exaggerated rack rate that is ridiculously high. For example, a hotel may apply the discount to a superior room rate, even though the room you wind up with is a standard accommodation.

These discounted rooms are not commissionable to travel agents, meaning you'll likely have to make all the calls and reservations on your own.

Each of the following programs lists between 50 and 120 lodgings on Hawaii's six main islands:

Encore (800) 638-0930
Entertainment Publications (800) 285-5525
International Travel Card (800) 342-0558
Quest (800) 638-9819

A cautionary note: There are a lot of gimmicks out there, remarked one travel insider. You might uncover a true gem of a bargain through a travel club. However, the general rule is that, nine times out of ten, if it sounds too good to be true, it usually is. The Federal Trade Commission advises:

- Always be wary of "great deals" and low-priced offers. Few legitimate businesses are able to provide products and services substantially below the market value.

- Don't be pressured into accepting a deal on the spot. A good offer today should be a good offer tomorrow. A legitimate business won't expect you to make snap decisions.
- Ask detailed questions. Find out what the total cost covers and what it doesn't. Inquire whether there are any additional charges. Ask about cancellation policies and refunds.
- Get all the information in writing before you agree to purchase a travel package. And when you do receive the written information, read it carefully to make sure it accurately reflects what you were told over the phone.
- Do not send money by messenger or overnight mail. You have to question any company or agent that asks you to send them money immediately. Additionally, do not provide your credit card number or bank information over the phone unless you are familiar with the company.

Tour Wholesalers and Operators

Tour wholesalers and operators do business by purchasing blocks of rooms from hotels at a low, negotiated rate. Then they resell the rooms for profit to travel agents, tour packagers, or sometimes directly to the public. While most have a provision for returning unsold rooms to the hotels, they are usually reluctant to do so because their relationship with the hotels is based on volume. If they return unsold rooms, the partnering hotel might not be willing to make rooms available to them the next time. This is potentially good news for you, as wholesalers will sometimes offer rooms at bargain prices—anywhere from 15 to 50% off the rack rate—to avoid returning unsold rooms to the hotel.

The wholesalers generally prefer that you reserve these packages through your travel agent. By going directly to a wholesaler, you'd be undercutting your travel agent's commissions, which are his or her primary means of income.

Some tour wholesalers offering travel packages to Hawaii include:

All About Hawaii (800) 274-8687
Classic Custom Vacations (800) 221-3949
Creative Leisure International (800) 426-6367
Globetrotters/MTI Vacations (800) 635-1333
Pleasant Hawaiian Holidays (800) 2-HAWAII

Newspaper Travel Sections

One convenient and effective way of finding a good room deal or travel package is by scouring the Sunday travel sections of major U.S. newspapers like the *Los Angeles Times*. Said one travel wholesaler, "Almost always, our best deals are found in the travel sections. It's a very good place to look." The Sunday travel section in the *Honolulu Advertiser* is geared more for Hawaii residents seeking weekend escapes to the Neighbor Islands.

Travel Agents

Booking a hotel room or travel package through a travel agent is easy and convenient. A good travel agent should be able to interpret value for you. If you find a deal that seems too good to be true, take it to a travel agent, who sifts through hundreds of travel deals as part of his or her line of work.

Travel agents often work with wholesalers who offer special packages in conjunction with certain airlines (such as American, Delta, and TWA). They are usually easy to book; however, they are also usually more expensive than a package offered by a high-volume wholesaler.

To help your travel agent find the best deal for you, decide in advance which island (or islands) you want to visit and in which area of the island you wish to stay. If possible, choose a specific hotel in advance. (The hotel profiles later in this part will help you select a hotel.)

Travel Packages

The benefits of buying a travel package to Hawaii are many: Most save you money, provide value, and eliminate the time-consuming process of finding separate deals for airlines, hotel rooms, car rentals, and so forth. Because these packages are largely put together by tour operators who get bulk rates from hotels, airlines, and car rentals, the end result for you should be a cheaper rate than if you yourself bought these components separately. These packages can be exceptional values.

It doesn't always work that way, however. Some sellers will cash in on these savings and pass none of them on to the buyer. Worse, some packages are loaded with extras that cost the seller very little, yet still inflate the package price.

When choosing a travel package, find one that includes features and amenities you are certain to use (after all, you'll be paying for them). Also, find out what it would cost if you booked each component—airfare, lodging, car rental, etc.—separately and on your own. The package cost should be less than the "a la carte" price.

OTHER MONEY-SAVING SUGGESTIONS

Many hotels offer package deals that include value-added amenities, such as free use of a rental car, food and beverage credits, rounds of golf, and special gifts. Some hotels offer a free extra night if you book a room for a certain number of nights (usually from four to seven). Most, however, do not include airline fares.

Use every money-saving option at your disposal: If you're a member of the American Automobile Association (AAA) or Association of American Retired People (AARP), for example, there are a handful of discounts available to you.

Hotels located away from the beach are generally much cheaper, so if you can do without having the sand and surf right at your doorstep, we recommend exploring this option. Also, ocean-view rooms are priced higher than mountain- or garden-view rooms.

Another suggestion is to book your room early. Giving the hotel as much advance notice as possible increases your chances of reserving a room at the best possible rate.

For families with young children, inquire whether the kids can stay in your room free of charge. Or consider booking a one-bedroom suite that includes a sofa with a pullout bed.

Internet users should log on to Hawaii hotel Web sites (provided elsewhere in this part) to find special deals and package offerings. *Note:* Many of these deals come with restrictions and black-out dates.

Finally, most hotels offer what's known as *kama'aina* rates, or special discounts for Hawaiian residents. (You'll likely need a Hawaii state I.D. or driver's license to qualify.) If there's any chance you feel you might be eligible for this discount, by all means ask. You have nothing to lose.

If You Make Your Own Reservation

Should you decide to go bargain hunting on your own, here are some helpful considerations. Always call the specific hotel rather than the hotel chain's national toll-free number. The reservationist you deal with by calling the 800 number may not be aware of special deals offered locally.

Remember that quoted room rates aren't written in stone. Don't be shy about inquiring about lower rates, especially during the low season. More often than not, hotel managers would prefer filling rooms at discounted prices than having them be totally unoccupied. Inquire about specials before asking about corporate rates.

Some Final Words of Wisdom

One experienced tour wholesaler noted that the typical traveler today searches for two things: value and time-saving convenience. "They don't want to hassle with looking through 50,000 brochures and making a hundred phone calls," she said. We agree, and for that reason we think booking your Hawaiian vacation through a travel agent is the best way to go.

This will save you time and money and will enable you to find the best value for your dollar. (The best values, you'll find, are rarely the cheapest packages.)

Lodging Alternatives: Condominiums and Bed-and-Breakfasts

Below is a list of some of the best condominium and bed-and-breakfast offerings in Hawaii. In addition, here are a number of agencies that can help you find a condo or bed-and-breakfast to best suit your needs and budget.

CONDOMINIUMS

One major advantage of staying at a condominium instead of a hotel is added space: While standard rooms at most hotels are a cozy fit, condo units are usually larger, from 700–800 square feet for a one-bedroom unit to 2,000 square feet for a two-bedroom unit, making this a good option for families. The convenience of having a full kitchen is another benefit, and you'll be able to save money by enjoying home-cooked meals instead of eating out (or ordering room service) three times a day.

Booking through a condo rep is advised, especially for first-timers. A condo rep is like a professional matchmaker, helping you find the condo that best suits your needs and desires. Just tell the agent your preferences on location, unit size, price range, amenities, ambience, and the number in your party, and you'll be given a list of properties that meet your criteria. Some operations, like the Hawaii Condo Exchange, can also provide extra services including car rental and lei greetings.

Terms and policies differ according to the condo rep. A deposit is usually required, payable by a major credit card. Reservations should be booked at least three months in advance, although last-minute bookings are possible. Condo unit prices can range as low as $45 and as high as $300 per night, depending on the type of accommodation, location, and dates of stay. All lodging is subject to an 11% tax (7% room tax plus 4% state tax).

Condo Reps and Reservations (Statewide)

Hawaii Condo Exchange
(800) 442-0404 or
(323) 436-0300
www.hawaiicondoexchange.com

Hawaiian Condo Resorts, Inc.
(800) 487-4505 or
(808) 949-4505
www.hawaiicondo.com

Condominiums

Aston Hotels & Resorts
(808) 931-1400 or
(800) 92-ASTON
www.aston-hotels.com
Properties on Oahu, Maui,
the Big Island, and Kauai

Castle Resorts & Hotels
1150 South King Street
Honolulu, HI 96814
(808) 591-2235 or
(800) 367-5004
www.castle-group.com
Properties on Maui, the Big
Island, Kauai, and Molokai

Kapalua Villas
500 Office Road
Kapalua, HI 96761
(808) 669-8088 or
(800) 545-0018
www.kapaluavillas.com
Properties on Maui

Marc Resorts Hawaii
(808) 922-9700 or
(800) 436-1304
www.marcresorts.com
Properties on Oahu, Maui, the
Big Island, Kauai, and Molokai

Outrigger
(800) 688-7444
www.outrigger.com
Properties on Oahu, Maui,
the Big Island, and Kauai

Turtle Bay Condos
P.O. Box 248
Kahuku, HI 96731
(808) 293-2800 or
(888) 266-3690
www.turtlebaycondos.com
Zone 4: Oahu's North Shore

BED-AND-BREAKFASTS

For some travelers, staying at a five-star hotel is an integral part of the entire vacation experience. They enjoy the services, amenities, and on-site facilities that the Ritz-Carltons, Hiltons, and Sheratons provide. For those who can do without the posh luxuries and resort accommodations, however, a bed-and-breakfast may provide a more satisfying and memorable Island experience.

In some parts of the U.S. mainland, the term "bed-and-breakfast" can mean a refurbished mansion with several guest rooms maintained by a professional staff. In Hawaii, however, a bed-and-breakfast means a guest room or adjoining studio at someone's residence. Bed-and-breakfast owners here abide by the following regulations: The owner must reside on the property, the bed-and-breakfast can have no more than two units to rent out, and, likely for liability purposes, the owner is not allowed to cook for any of his or her guests.

The major advantage of choosing a bed-and-breakfast over a hotel or even a condominium is the personalized service you receive. The typical bed-and-breakfast guest, says one veteran of the business, is weary of grand but largely impersonal hotels. They're not the type to sit around a swimming pool and work on their tans; instead, they have a keen interest in the history and culture of the island they're visiting and feel there's a lot of knowledge to be gained from their host or hostess, each of whom has a strong knowledge of their home island.

Another benefit involves cost. Most bed-and-breakfasts provide a partial or full kitchen for your use; thus, you save money by not having to eat out all the time. You're also welcome to enjoy a picnic lunch and even enjoy an outdoor barbecue (grills and small pavilions are often on the premises). Also, many host families provide their guests with discount coupons on things to see and do.

There are three types of bed-and-breakfast accommodations in Hawaii: studios, family cottages, and guest rooms. Most prevalent are the studios, which provide either tea kitchens or full kitchens.

There are more than 700 bed-and-breakfast operations in the state, spread evenly among Oahu, Maui, the Big Island, and Kauai (with fewer numbers on Molokai and Lanai). While you can contact each bed-and-breakfast directly, a better way to go is through a reservations service (there is no difference in price whether you call a bed-and-breakfast directly or seek it through a service). Reservations services inspect each property personally and provide personalized assistance in finding a bed-and-breakfast that best suits your likes and dislikes. "We're very careful with who we put where," said one agent. "It's very customized."

Generally, bed-and-breakfasts require a minimum stay of three nights, although there are a few on the Big Island and in Hana on Maui who will make an occasional exception. "Keep in mind, you're going into a person's private home," said the agent. "They have a right to get to know who's coming in. They don't want people calling and saying, 'Hi, my boyfriend and I just want to come over and sleep tonight.' We get a lot of that locally, and we just have to tell them no."

Reservations should be booked at least two and a half to three months in advance. When you call, have the following information ready: specific dates, places, type of unit desired, the number of people in your party, the price range you wish to pay, and any special needs or desires you may have. The reservations agent will call you back (usually within 15 minutes to an hour) with a description of available host homes that fit your needs.

Terms and policies vary by reservations service. At All Islands Bed & Breakfast, a 20% deposit is required to hold a reservation. Personal checks, Visa, MasterCard, American Express, and Discover cards are accepted. There is a 3% fee on deposits. Deposits are refundable (minus a $25 service fee) if you cancel your reservation at least two weeks prior to your arrival date. The balance is paid directly to the host family in cash or traveler's checks. You will receive a confirmation letter shortly after your deposit is received, followed by a welcome letter, map, and brochure.

Prices range from $55 to $300 per night. A room in a private home averages between $55 and $75 a night for two people and usually includes a continental breakfast (juice, coffee, and pastries). A studio (with private entrances, private baths, and tea kitchens) range from $65 to $85 per night. And a cottage (separate and apart from the main house) averages from $75 to $95 per night for two people. All lodging is subject to an 11% tax (7% room tax plus 4% state tax).

Most reservations services can also provide assistance with car rentals and inter-island airfares.

Bed-and-Breakfast Reservations (Statewide)

All Islands Bed & Breakfast
(800) 542-0344 or (808) 263-2342
www.home.hawaii.rr.com/allislands

Bed & Breakfast Hawaii
(800) 733-1632 or (808) 822-7771
www.bandb-hawaii.com

Bed & Breakfast Honolulu
(877) 866-5402 or (808) 595-7533
www.aloha-bnb.com

Hawaii's Best Bed & Breakfasts
(800) 262-9912 or (808) 885-4550
www.bestbnb.com

Bed-and-Breakfasts

Akamai Bed & Breakfast
Zone 3: Windward Oahu
172 Ku'umele Pl.
Kailua, HI 96734
(808) 261-2227 or (800) 642-5366
www.planet-hawaii.com/aka-maibnb/

Ali'i Bed & Breakfast
Zone 3: Windward Oahu
237 Awakea Rd.
Kailua, HI 96734
(808) 262-9545 or (800) 262-9545

Aloha Country Inn
Zone 13: Kauai
505 Kamalu Rd.
Kapa'a, HI 96746
(808) 822-0166 or (800) 634-5115
www.aloha.net/~wery

Aloha Lani Inn
Zone 9: West Maui
13 Kauaula St.
Lahaina, HI 96761
(808) 661-8040 or (800) 572-5642
www.maui-net/~tony/

Alohilani Bed & Breakfast
Zone 13: Kauai
1470 Wana'ao Rd.
Kapa'a, HI 96746
(808) 823-0128 or (800) 533-9316
www.hawaiian.net/~alohila/

Blue Horizons B&B
Zone 9: West Maui
3894 Mahinahina St.
Lahaina, HI 96761
(808) 669-1965 or (800) 669-1948
www.maui.net/~chips

Carson's Volcano Cottages
Zone 12: Hilo and Volcano
P.O. Box 503
Volcano, HI 96785
(808) 967-7683 or (800) 845-5282
www.carsonscottage.com

A Dragonfly Ranch:
  Tropical Fantasy Lodging
Zone 11: Kona
P.O. Box 675
Honaunau-Kona, HI 96726
(808) 328-2159 or (800) 487-2159
www.dragonflyranch.com

Dreams Come True
Zone 15: Lanai
P.O. Box 525
Lanai City, HI 96763
(808) 565-6961 or
(800) 566-6961
www.go-native.com/Inns

Hale 'Ohia Cottages
Zone 12: Hilo and Volcano
P.O. Box 758, Volcano, HI 96785
(808) 967-7986 or
(800) 455-3803
www.haleohia.com

A Hawaiian Getaway
Zone 14: Molokai
P.O. Box 788
Kaunakakai, HI 96748
(808) 553-9803 or
(800) 274-9303

Inn by the Sea
Zone 3: Windward Oahu
963 Aalapapa Dr.
Kailua, HI 96734
(808) 261-2644 or
(800) 773-0260

Ka Hale Mala B&B
Zone 14: Molokai
P.O. Box 1582
Kaunakakai, HI 96748
(808) 553-9009
www.molokai-aloha.com/
kahalemala

Kamalo Plantation B&B
Zone 14: Molokai
HC01 Box 300
Kaunakakai, HI 96748
(808) 558-8236
www.molokai.com/kamalo

Kula Hula Inn
Zone 10: Upcountry Maui
  and Beyond
112 Ho'opalua Dr.
Makawao, HI 96768
(808) 572-9351 or
(888) 485-2466
www.maui.net/~kulahula

Lokahi Lodge
Zone 12: Hilo and Volcano
P.O. Box 998
Volcano, HI 96785
(808) 967-7244 or
(800) 457-6924
www.volcano-hawaii.com

Mahina Kai Bed & Breakfast
Zone 13: Kauai
P.O. Box 699
Anahola, HI 96703
(808) 822-9451 or
(800) 337-1134
www.vantage21st.com/mahina/
mahina.html

Pillows in Paradise
Zone 3: Windward Oahu
336 Awakea Rd.
Kailua, HI 96734
(808) 263-7917
www.isstb.com/pillows

Po'ipu Bed & Breakfast Inn
Zone 13: Kauai
2720 Ho'onani Rd.
Po'ipu, HI 96756
(808) 742-1146 or
(800) 227-6478
www.poipu.net

Shipman House Bed & Breakfast
Zone 12: Hilo and Volcano
131 Ka'iulani St.
Hilo, HI 96720
(808) 934-8002 or
(800) 627-8447
www.hilo-hawaii.com

Silver Cloud Ranch
Zone 10: Upcountry Maui
    and Beyond
RR II Box 201
Kula, HI 96790
(808) 878-6101 or
(800) 532-1111
www.maui.net/~slvrcld

The Lodge at Volcano
Zone 12: Hilo and Volcano
P.O. Box 998
Volcano, HI 96785
(808) 967-7244 or
(800) 736-7140
www.volcano-hawaii.com

Volcano Bed & Breakfast
Zone 12: Hilo and Volcano
P.O. Box 998
Volcano, HI 96785
(808) 967-7779 or
(800) 736-7140
www.volcano-hawaii.com

Wild Ginger Inn
Zone 12: Hilo and Volcano
100 Pu'ueo St.
Hilo, HI 96720
(808) 935-5556 or
(800) 882-1887
www.wildgingerinn.com

Hotels Rated and Ranked

Below, we've ranked more than 65 hotels and resorts in Hawaii. To find more information on a particular hotel in this table, see the profiles later in this chapter. The ratings were based on the following criteria: room quality (including cleanliness, spaciousness, state of repair, views, amenities, and overall visual appeal), value, service, and location. Ratings in this guide apply to Hawaii properties only and do not necessarily correspond to ratings awarded by the department of tourism, automobile clubs, or other travel critics. A five-star ranking doesn't necessarily mean the hotel is among the most expensive properties; nor does a low ranking indicate the hotel is among the cheapest.

What the Ratings Mean	
★★★★★	The Best of the Best
★★★★½	Excellent
★★★★	Very Good
★★★½	Good
★★★	Average
★★½	Below Average
★★	Poor

The value ratings—A to D—are a combination of the overall and room quality ratings, divided by the cost of an average guest room. They are an indication rather than a scientific formulation—a general idea of value for money. If getting a good deal means the most to you, choose a property by looking at the value rating. Otherwise, the numbers and stars are better indicators of a satisfying experience. If a wonderful property is fairly priced, it may only get a C value rating, but you still might prefer the experience to an average property with an A value rating.

Cost Indicators	
$$$$$	Above $350
$$$$	$250–$350
$$$	$150–$250
$$	$100–$150
$	Below $100

The rates used are based on the rack rate for a standard ocean-view room (or suitable equivalent) during tourism's high season, which runs from December through March. Don't be intimidated by the cost indicators. Lower and higher prices (depending on the room category) are available at each hotel.

How the Hotels Compare					
Hotel	Zone	Room Quality	Overall Quality	Value	Cost
Oahu					
Halekulani	1	A+	★★★★★	B	$$$$$
'Ihilani Resort & Spa	5	A+	★★★★★	B	$$$$$
Hawaii Prince Hotel Waikiki	1	A	★★★★½	C+	$$$$
Hilton Hawaiian Village	1	A	★★★★½	B	$$$$
Hyatt Regency Waikiki	1	A	★★★★½	B	$$$$$
Kahala Mandarin Oriental	2	A	★★★★½	C	$$$$$
Royal Hawaiian Hotel	1	A	★★★★½	C+	$$$$$
Sheraton Moana Surfrider	1	A	★★★★½	C+	$$$$$
Hawaiian Regent Hotel	1	A	★★★★	C	$$$$
'Ilikai Hotel Nikko Waikiki	1	A	★★★★	C+	$$$
Sheraton Princess Ka'iulani	1	A	★★★★	C	$$$$
Sheraton Waikiki	1	A	★★★★	C	$$$$$
W Honolulu– Diamond Head	1	A	★★★★	C	$$$$
Waikiki Parc Hotel	1	A	★★★★	B+	$$$
Ala Moana Hotel	2	B+	★★★★	B+	$$
Aston at Executive Centre Hotel	2	B+	★★★★	C	$$$
New Otani Kaimana Beach Hotel	1	B+	★★★★	C+	$$$
Royal Garden at Waikiki	1	B+	★★★★	B	$$
Turtle Bay Hilton Golf & Tennis Resort	4	B+	★★★★	B	$$$
Waikiki Joy Hotel	1	B+	★★★★	B	$$$

		Room	Overall		
How the Hotels Compare (continued)					
Hotel	Zone	Quality	Quality	Value	Cost
Waikiki Beachcomber Hotel	1	B	★★★★	C+	$$$
Doubletree Alana Waikiki Hotel	1	B+	★★★½	C	$$$
Outrigger East Hotel	1	B+	★★★½	C	$$
Outrigger Reef on the Beach	1	B+	★★★½	C	$$$$
Outrigger Waikiki on the Beach	1	B+	★★★½	B	$$$$
Radisson Waikiki Prince Kuhio	1	B+	★★★½	C	$$$
Waikiki Terrace Hotel	1	B+	★★★½	C	$$$
Hale Koa Hotel	1	B	★★★½	A	$
Pacific Beach Hotel	1	B	★★★½	C	$$$
Pagoda Hotel	2	B	★★★½	C	$$
Maui					
Four Seasons Resort Maui	8	A+	★★★★★	B	$$$$$
Ritz-Carlton, Kapalua	9	A+	★★★★★	B+	$$$$
Grand Wailea Resort Hotel & Spa	8	A+	★★★★½	C+	$$$$$
Embassy Vacation Resort	9	A	★★★★½	C+	$$$$$
Kea Lani Hotel	8	A	★★★★½	B	$$$$$
Hotel Hana-Maui	10	A	★★★★	C	$$$$$
Hyatt Regency Maui	9	A	★★★★	C+	$$$$$
Kapalua Bay Hotel	9	A	★★★★	C	$$$$$
Maui Marriott Resort	9	A	★★★★	C	$$$$
Outrigger Wailea Resort	8	A	★★★★	B	$$$$
Renaissance Wailea Beach Resort	8	A	★★★★	C	$$$$
Sheraton Maui	9	A	★★★★	C	$$$$$
Westin Maui	9	A	★★★★	C+	$$$$$

How the Hotels Compare (continued)					
Hotel	Zone	Room Quality	Overall Quality	Value	Cost
Ka'anapali Beach Hotel	9	B+	★★★★	B	$$$
Maui Prince Hotel	8	B+	★★★★	C	$$$$
Lahaina Inn	9	B	★★★★	B+	$
The Big Island					
Four Seasons Resort Hualalai	11	A+	★★★★★	C+	$$$$$
Mauna Lani Bay Hotel & Bungalows	11	A+	★★★★½	C+	$$$$$
Hapuna Beach Prince Hotel	11	A	★★★★½	C	$$$$$
Hilton Waikoloa Village	11	A	★★★★½	C	$$$$$
Kona Village Resort	11	A	★★★★½	C	$$$$$
Mauna Kea Beach Hotel	11	A	★★★★½	C	$$$$$
The Orchid at Mauna Lani	11	A	★★★★½	C	$$$$$
Aston Keauhou Beach Resort	11	B+	★★★★	C+	$$$
Hawaii Naniloa Resort	12	B+	★★★★	B	$$
Outrigger Waikoloa Beach Hotel	11	B+	★★★★	C+	$$$
Hilo Hawaiian Hotel	12	B+	★★★½	C+	$$
King Kamehameha's Kona Beach Hotel	11	B	★★★½	B+	$$$
Volcano House	12	B	★★★½	C	$$
Uncle Billy's Hilo Bay Hotel	12	B	★★★	C	$$
Uncle Billy's Kona Bay Hotel	11	B	★★★	C	$
Kauai					
Hyatt Regency Kauai Resort & Spa	13	A+	★★★★½	C+	$$$$$

How the Hotels Compare (continued)					
Hotel	Zone	Room Quality	Overall Quality	Value	Cost
Princeville Resort	13	A	★★★★½	C	$$$$$
Hanalei Bay Resort & Suites	13	A	★★★★	C+	$$$
Kauai Marriott Resort & Beach Club	13	A	★★★★	C	$$$$$
Sheraton Kauai Resort	13	A	★★★★	C	$$$$$
Outrigger Kauai Beach Hotel	13	B+	★★★★	C	$$$
Molokai					
Kaluako'i Hotel & Golf Club	14	B	★★★½	C	$$
Lanai					
The Lodge at Ko'ele	15	A	★★★★½	C+	$$$$$
The Manele Bay Hotel	15	A	★★★★½	C+	$$$$$
Hotel Lanai	15	B	★★★½	B	$

Hotel Profiles

Presented here, in alphabetical order and categorized by island, is more information on the hotels and resorts listed in our table.

OAHU

ALA MOANA HOTEL			$$
Overall: ★★★★	Room Quality: B+	Value: B+	Zone 2

It doesn't front Waikiki Beach, but this hotel still offers one of the best locations on Oahu: A short skybridge leads you to Hawaii's largest shopping center, Ala Moana Center; the Hawaii Convention Center is a mere walk across the street; and it's a short five-minute walk to Ala Moana Beach Park, one of our favorite beaches. For nightclubbers, the hotel is home to one of the island's best nightspots, Rumours. As you might expect, vehicle traffic in this area is almost always busy, but it's nonetheless manageable. Noise was a concern when the convention center was built, but it hasn't been much of a factor. The views are a bit disappointing, as the jungle of Waikiki hotels obstructs most of Diamond Head and Waikiki Beach. (Every Fourth of July, however, the hotel provides optimal views of the huge fireworks show off Magic Island at the park.) Other than the shopping center and the beach park, the hotel's surroundings don't offer much save for some fast-food joints, local strip clubs, and Tower Records (where you'll find the best selection of Hawaiian music offerings).

SETTING & FACILITIES

Location: On the fringe of Waikiki.
Dining: Aaron's is the signature restaurant here, offering fine Continental cuisine. Other dining options include Royal Garden (Chinese) and Tsukasa (Japanese). The Plantation Cafe serves a variety of international cuisine for breakfast, lunch, and dinner.

Amenities & Services: Room service, laundry facilities (coin-operated), ice and soda machines, ATM machine, business center, sundry shop, shopping arcade, concierge, self-parking ($8 daily), valet parking, swimming pool.

ACCOMMODATIONS

Rooms: 1,169. 67 suites; 28 rooms equipped for the disabled; 800 non-smoking rooms.
All Rooms: A/C, color TV, pay movies, clock radio, mini-refrigerators, in-room safe, 2 doubles, direct dial phone system, data port, in-room coffee, hair dryer, voice mail, etc.
Some Rooms: King and 2 doubles, concierge services, in-room steam and Jacuzzi unit, iron and ironing board, yukata robes. IBM PC-compatible systems available for additional $15 per night.

Comfort & Decor: Rooms small to medium, tastefully decorated with light colors and Hawaiiana-accented artwork. Airy and bright ambience. Very clean and well maintained.

RATES, RESERVATIONS, & RESTRICTIONS

Family Plan: Children age 17 and under stay free when sharing room with parents and using existing bedding. Each additional adult is $25 a night. Maximum of 4 people per room (maximum of 2 per room in Kona Tower). $25-per-night charge for rollaway beds. Cribs available free of charge.
Deposit: To guarantee reservation, a deposit of 1 night's room rate is required within 10 days of confirmation. Cancellations within 72 hours prior to arrival will result in forfeit of deposit.
Credit Cards: All major credit cards accepted.
Check-In/Out: 3 p.m./Noon. Early check-in possible if the room is available.
Contact: 410 Atkinson Dr. Honolulu, HI 96814
(800) 367-6025 or (808) 955-4811
Fax: (808) 944-6839
www.alamoanahotel.com

ASTON AT THE EXECUTIVE CENTRE HOTEL $$$

| Overall: ★★★★ | Room Quality: B+ | Value: C | Zone 2 |

Stylish and comfortable, this all-suite hotel is geared toward the business traveler who spends most of his or her time in Honolulu's business district. The service staff is friendly and professional, and the swimming pool and fitness center are welcome diversions after a long day of meetings. However, don't expect anything resembling a resort atmosphere. While the area is populated by an intriguing mix of people by day—from smartly clad professionals and college students to senior citizens gathering to "talk story"—the streets are nearly deserted at night and are not safe for walking. If you're here strictly on business, this hotel is a good bet. Otherwise, stick to Waikiki.

SETTING & FACILITIES

Location: In the heart of the downtown business district.
Dining: The New Eagle Cafe serves a full menu of local-style favorites. It is closed on weekends.

Amenities & Services: Swimming pool, fitness center, parking facilities ($6 per day), laundry and dry cleaning service.

ACCOMMODATIONS

Rooms: 116. All suites.
All Rooms: A/C, color TV, phone, partial kitchen, etc.
Some Rooms: Full kitchen, washer and dryer, fax machines.
Comfort & Decor: Well-appointed,

spacious suites. Some rooms have fax machines (be sure to request a room with one if you feel you'll need it). The decor is elegant but subdued. Floor-to-ceiling windows provide superb views of downtown Honolulu.

RATES, RESERVATIONS, & RESTRICTIONS

Family Plan: Children age 18 and under stay free with parents.
Deposit: $400 (cash or credit card). Cancellation notice must be provided at least 72 hours prior to arrival.
Credit Cards: Visa, MC, AmEx, Discover, Diners.
Check-In/Out: 3 p.m./Noon. Early

check-in and late departure available on request (no guarantees).
Contact: 1088 Bishop St.
Honolulu, HI 96813
(800) 321-2558 or (808) 539-3000
Fax: (808) 523-1088
www.aston-hotels.com

DOUBLETREE ALANA WAIKIKI HOTEL $$$

| Overall: ★★★½ | Room Quality: B+ | Value: C | Zone 1 |

The hotel's Web site claims that the property is just "steps" away from the beach and Ala Moana Shopping Center, but it doesn't tell you how many steps. The truth is, it's about a 15-minute walk to either destination. Still, what this property lacks in location, it makes up for in enthusiasm and hospitality. The service here is friendly and efficient, and there's a certain level of charm and comfort here that you might not find in the larger hotels. Part of the charm, we suppose, includes the famous Doubletree Cookie, a tasty (and filling) baked treat given to all hotel guests as a special welcome. The views are so-so: most of Diamond Head is obscured by other hotel properties.

SETTING & FACILITIES

Location: On the fringe of Waikiki.
Dining: Padovani's Bistro & Wine Bar, one of Oahu's newest fine dining establishments, serves superb Italian cuisine.
Amenities & Services: Room ser-

vice, valet parking ($10 per day), dry cleaning and laundry service, 24-hour business center, fitness center, swimming pool.

ACCOMMODATIONS

Rooms: 313. Includes 25 suites and penthouse suite. Non-smoking rooms available.
All Rooms: A/C, private lanai, TV, mini-cooler, in-room safe, coffeemaker, hair dryer, iron and ironing board, etc.

Some Rooms: Living room with sofa-bed.
Comfort & Decor: Very spacious, tastefully appointed. Hawaiian-themed artwork adorns the walls. Plush sofas and chairs.

RATES, RESERVATIONS, & RESTRICTIONS

Deposit: Credit card guarantee with 1-night deposit.
Credit Cards: All major credit cards accepted.
Check-In/Out: 3 p.m./Noon. Early check-in/late check-out available by request.

Contact: 1956 Ala Moana Blvd. Honolulu, HI 96815
(800) 367-6070 or (808) 941-7275
Fax: (808) 949-0996
www.alana-doubletree.com

HALE KOA HOTEL	Rates vary according to rank

Overall: ★★★½	Room Quality: B	Value: A	Zone 1

The Hale Koa, originally built by U.S. servicemen and -women from their own funds, today operates on a self-sustaining basis. Guests at the hotel have to be active or retired military personnel, current or retired Department of Defense civilian employees, U.S. Reserve and National Guard members, or their dependents or sponsored guest. If you qualify, by all means consider the Hale Koa as a place to stay. The service is excellent, the atmosphere is decidedly "R&R," and the cost is much more reasonable than at most Waikiki properties. This is a popular site for weddings, especially among local families with military ties. Even if you're not eligible to stay here, you're welcome (encouraged, really) to sign up for the Hale Koa's weekly festivities, including a twice-weekly luau (Monday and Thursday, $29.50 for adults/$17.95 for children under age 12) and magic show (each Tuesday, $19.95 for adults/$10.50 for children under age 12).

SETTING & FACILITIES

Location: In Waikiki, near Fort DeRussy Beach.
Dining: The Hale Koa Room offers a palate-pleasing selection of Continental favorites, while the more informal Koko Cafe serves a variety of appetiz-ers, salads, pasta dishes, entrées, sandwiches, and burgers.
Amenities & Services: Swimming pools, beach facilities, barbershop, beauty salon, fitness center, safety deposit boxes (at front desk).

ACCOMMODATIONS

Rooms: 817. Includes 53 rooms equipped for the disabled. Non-smoking rooms available on request.
All Rooms: A/C, cable TV, phone, lanai, hair dryer, etc.
Comfort & Decor: Rooms small to medium, nice tropical-themed decor with floral bedspreads and artwork. Nothing fancy, but very serviceable and pleasant overall.

RATES, RESERVATIONS, & RESTRICTIONS

Deposit: 1-night deposit required. Cancellation notice must be given 30 days prior to arrival.
Credit Cards: All major credit cards accepted.
Check-In/Out: 3 p.m./Noon. Early check-in and late check-out available on request (no guarantees).
Contact: 2055 Kalia Rd.
Honolulu, HI 96815
(800) 367-6027 or (808) 955-0555
Fax: (808) 955-9429
reservations@halekoa.com
www.halekoa.com

HALEKULANI			$$$$$
Overall: ★★★★★	Room Quality: A+	Value: B	Zone 1

The Halekulani is the only hotel in Hawaii to receive the American Automobile Association's prestigious Five Diamond Award for both hotel and restaurant categories. We found the hotel to be more than worthy of both honors. Although the hotel is within easy walking distance of the hustle and bustle of Kalakaua Avenue, its ambience is exceptionally peaceful and elegant. No experience exemplifies this more than sunset cocktails at *House without a Key*, a near-religious experience created by an enchanting hula performance by a former Miss Hawaii, soothing Hawaiian music, and a dazzling view of the sunset. The service here is impeccable and includes personalized registration in your hotel room. Another highlight here is the view, which includes postcard-like vistas of Diamond Head and Waikiki

Beach. A weekly manager's reception serves complimentary heavy *pupus* (hors d'oeuvres). Geared more toward well-to-do couples than large families, the hotel has gained a loyal following: We've met elderly couples who say they've been coming to the Halekulani nearly every year without fail.

SETTING & FACILITIES

Location: On Waikiki Beach.
Dining: The Halekulani has several notable fine dining establishments, including the AAA Five Diamond Award–winning La Mer, which serves Neoclassic French cuisine. Orchids serves breakfast, lunch, and dinner.

Amenities & Services: Fresh fruit bowl and chocolates on arrival, complimentary morning newspaper, valet parking, fitness center, business center, heated swimming pool.

ACCOMMODATIONS

Rooms: 456. Includes 44 suites, 16 rooms for the disabled. Non-smoking rooms available.
All Rooms: A/C, lanai, 3 telephones, cable TV, mini-refrigerator, clock radio, etc.
Some Rooms: 2 bedrooms.

Comfort & Decor: Spacious, stylishly appointed decor with light colors and tasteful furnishings. High ceilings. Plenty of drawer space. Large balconies include table, 2 chairs, and an adjustable folding chair.

RATES, RESERVATIONS, & RESTRICTIONS

Family Plan: Children age 17 and under stay free in room with parents; $40 per night for extra bed.
Deposit: Credit card guarantees reservation with 1-night deposit within 14 days of confirmation. Cancellation notice must be given at least 72 hours prior to arrival.
Credit Cards: All major credit cards accepted.

Check-In/Out: 3 p.m./Noon. Hospitality room available for early arrivals and late departures. Early check-ins and late check-outs based on availability.
Contact: 2199 Kalia Rd.
Honolulu, HI 96815
(800) 367-2343 or (808) 923-2311
Fax: (808) 926-8004
www.halekulani.com

HAWAII PRINCE HOTEL WAIKIKI			$$$$
Overall: ★★★★½	Room Quality: A	Value: C+	Zone 1

An upscale property offering exceptional service and every kind of amenity. Ala Moana Center, Ala Moana Beach Park, and the Hawaii Convention Center are all within easy walking distance. The hotel's proximity to the convention center plus its impressive business facilities and services make this a favorite among business travelers. All 521 hotel rooms provide great views of the Ala Wai Yacht Harbor. The expansive Italian marble lobby lets you know right away this isn't your local Motel 6. The fifth floor is a favorite hangout, with a swimming pool, sundeck, and terraces that are ideal for cocktails and sunsets. If you're looking for a tee time, be aware that the Hawaii Prince Golf Club, one of Oahu's best courses, isn't anywhere near the hotel (it's a 40-minute drive away on the 'Ewa side of Oahu). Preferred tee times and limited shuttle service are available for hotel guests.

SETTING & FACILITIES

Location: On the outskirts of Waikiki at the Ala Wai Yacht Harbor.
Dining: Two restaurants of note are the Prince Court, which features Hawaii regional cuisine, and Hakone,

specializing in exquisite Japanese fare.
Amenities & Services: Hot towels upon check-in, valet parking, business facilities, fitness center, daily newspaper.

ACCOMMODATIONS

Rooms: 521. Includes 57 suites; 10 rooms for the disabled. Non-smoking rooms available.
All Rooms: A/C, cable TV with pay movies, phone, mini-refrigerator, in-room safe, hair dryer, robes, etc.
Some Rooms: Extra BR and bath.

Comfort & Decor: Very spacious, with lavish decor and floor-to-ceiling windows that can partially open. Well-lit, with bright, warm colors. Floral-themed artworks adorn walls.

RATES, RESERVATIONS, & RESTRICTIONS

Family Plan: Children age 17 and under stay free if staying with parents and using existing bedding. Maximum occupancy is 3 adults or 2 adults/2 children per room. $40 per night for extra adult.
Deposit: 1-night deposit due 14 days within booking. Cancellation notice must be given 72 hours prior to arrival for refund.

Credit Cards: Visa, MC, AmEx, Diners.
Check-In/Out: 2 p.m./Noon. Early check-in and late check-out available on request.
Contact: 100 Holomoana St. Honolulu, HI 96815
(800) 321-6248 or (808) 956-1111
Fax: (808) 946-0811
www.princehawaii.com

HAWAIIAN REGENT HOTEL			$$$$
Overall: ★★★★	Room Quality: A	Value: C	Zone 1

Although it's one of Hawaii's larger hotels, we like the Hawaiian Regent because it has been able to maintain a level of intimacy usually found in smaller hotels. The hospitality here is warm and friendly. Another definite plus is the hotel's family-friendly location: Kuhio Beach Park (part of Waikiki Beach) is just a walk across the street (the ocean views from the hotel are stupendous), the Damien Museum is next door, and Kapi'olani Park and the Honolulu Zoo are also nearby. One of Waikiki's more popular nightspots, Eurasia, is located on the first floor of the hotel's Kalakaua Tower. Or, if you're not the dancing type, you can enjoy Hawaiian entertainment provided nightly at the Lobby Bar.

SETTING & FACILITIES

Location: Across the street from Waikiki Beach, 1 block from Honolulu Zoo.

Dining: The hotel's signature restaurant, Acqua, serves MediterranNeoPacific cuisine, which combines the exotic flavors of the Mediterranean and the Pacific Rim.

Amenities & Services: Room service, laundry, parking, business center, fitness center.

ACCOMMODATIONS

Rooms: 1,346. Includes 6 suites; 4 non-smoking floors; 18 ADA-approved rooms.

All Rooms: A/C, TV, phone, in-room safe, refrigerator, lanai, etc. Hair dryer and coffeemaker available on request.

Some Rooms: More space, upgraded amenities.

Comfort & Decor: Tastefully appointed, medium-sized rooms, Island-accented furnishings and decor.

RATES, RESERVATIONS, & RESTRICTIONS

Family Plan: Children age 17 and under stay free when sharing room with parents and using existing bedding.

Deposit: Credit card guarantee (except for Diners Card) or 1-night deposit within 10 days of booking to guarantee reservation.

Credit Cards: Visa, MC, AmEx, JCB, Discover, Diners.

Check-In/Out: 3 p.m./Noon. Early check-in and late check-out available on request.

Contact: 2552 Kalakaua Ave. Honolulu, HI 96815
(800) 367-5370 or (808) 922-6611
Fax: (808) 921-5222
hwnrgnt@aloha.net
www.hawaiianregent.com

HILTON HAWAIIAN VILLAGE			$$$$
Overall: ★★★★½	Room Quality: A	Value: B	Zone 1

Hawaii's largest hotel. Epitomizes the term "self-contained resort." Terrific for young families, offering one of Hawaii's best year-round children's programs (including excursions to nearby attractions such as the Honolulu Zoo and Waikiki Aquarium). Also a popular choice among business travelers. Regular activities here include cultural demonstrations (such as lei making, hula, and ukulele lessons), torchlighting ceremonies, and property tours. Every Friday evening at 6:15 p.m., the hotel holds its free King's Jubilee & Fireworks show, featuring a precision rifle drill team, Hawaiian musical entertainment, and a fireworks show. The HHV also has five bars (with nightly entertainment provided), more than 100 shops and services, and activities ranging from undersea submarine rides to wildlife tours (the property is home to penguins, tropical birds, waterfowl, turtles, and fish). Expect crowds here, as the Hilton is a popular choice among large tour groups. The hotel rooms are currently housed in four separate towers:

Tapa, Rainbow, Diamond Head, and upscale Ali'i. Construction began in August 1999 on a new 453-room, 25-story Kalia Tower, located at the corner of Kalia Road and the entrance to the hotel, where the property's geodesic dome once stood. Among the planned facilities will be a health and wellness spa, an interactive Hawaiian cultural center, and four floors of retail space. Completion is scheduled for May 2001.

SETTING & FACILITIES

Location: Fronting Duke Kahanamoku Beach (part of Waikiki Beach) near the gateway to Waikiki.

Dining: Of the 6 restaurants located here, 2 stand out as among the finest on Oahu: Bali-by-the-Sea, an oceanfront restaurant serving innovative cuisine with an Island accent; and Golden Dragon, perhaps the best Chinese restaurant in the state, serving Can-

tonese and Szechuan specialties.

Amenities & Services: 3 outdoor swimming pools, valet parking, parking garage, travel services, laundry and dry cleaning, wedding chapel, physicians on call, beauty- and barbershops, post office and express mail pickup and delivery, meeting and banquet space, business services, children's program, florist.

ACCOMMODATIONS

Rooms: 2,545. Includes 363 suites; 526 non-smoking rooms; 75 rooms for the disabled.

All Rooms: A/C, cable TV with pay movies, phone, in-room safe, refreshment center, etc.

Some Rooms: Evening hors d'oeuvres, concierge service, robes,

sparkling water, in-room fax, upgraded bathroom amenities, valet laundry service.

Comfort & Decor: Best described as "comfortably elegant." Moderate space, well-lit, airy, attractive Hawaiian decor. Wicker furnishings and floral-themed bedspreads.

RATES, RESERVATIONS, & RESTRICTIONS

Family Plan: No charge for children under the age of 18 when staying with parents and using existing bedding.

Deposit: A 1-night deposit due within 10 days after confirmation. Cancellation notice must be given 72 hours prior to arrival for refund.

Credit Cards: All major credit cards accepted.

Check-In/Out: 2 p.m./11 a.m. Early check-in and late departure available (confirmed upon arrival).

Contact: 2005 Kalia Rd. Honolulu, HI 96815 (800) 445-8667 or (808) 949-4321 Fax: (808) 947-7898 www.hawaiianvillage.hilton.com

HYATT REGENCY WAIKIKI			$$$$$
Overall: ★★★★½	Room Quality: A+	Value: B	Zone 1

Located in the center of all the action in Waikiki. Everything, including the beach, is just a short walk away. The Hyatt comprises twin 40-story towers connected by an open-air Great Hall. The impressive lobby features a 10-story atrium with a man-made waterfall. The hotel has three floors of shops offering jewelry, apparel, and gifts. Free entertainment is provided in the lobby on the stage next to Harry's Bar. The Hyatt also has a wonderful children's program, Camp Hyatt, which provides kids ages 3–12 with fun and educational activities with an emphasis on Hawaii's history and culture. The area does get pretty noisy at night, especially with the recent influx of street entertainers.

SETTING & FACILITIES

Location: Across the street from Waikiki Beach.
Dining: A number of fine restaurants here, including unique and fun establishments such as the Texas Rock 'n' Roll Sushi Bar (country-style food with a wide range of sushi creations) and Ciao Mein (Italian and Chinese food).
Amenities & Services: Room service, valet ($12), and self-parking ($10), children's program.

ACCOMMODATIONS

Rooms: 1,230. Includes 18 suites; 193 non-smoking rooms; 24 rooms for the disabled.
All Rooms: A/C, TV, phone, lanai, refrigerator, mini-bar, hair dryer, iron and ironing board, in-room safe, coffeemaker, etc.
Some Rooms: Connecting parlor.
Comfort & Decor: Spacious, well maintained. Decor is sparse, but each room has a clean, simple elegance, with rattan furnishings and subdued colors.

RATES, RESERVATIONS, & RESTRICTIONS

Family Plan: Children age 17 and under stay free when sharing same room with parents and using existing bedding.
Deposit: 1-night deposit required 10 days within confirmation. Cancellation notice must be given 72 hours prior to arrival for refund.
Credit Cards: All major credit cards accepted.
Check-In/Out: 3 p.m./Noon. Early check-in and late check-out available on request.
Contact: 2424 Kalakaua Ave. Honolulu, HI 96815
(800) 233-1234 or (808) 923-1234
Fax: (808) 923-7839
info@hyattwaikiki.com
www.hyattwaikiki.com

'IHILANI RESORT & SPA $$$$$

Overall: ★★★★★	Room Quality: A+	Value: B	Zone 5

The 'Ihilani, which translates to "Heavenly Splendor," is a favorite of Oahu visitors seeking to escape from it all. (It's about a 40-minute drive to Waikiki from this upscale resort.) Situated on the first of four lagoon sites, the 'Ihilani overlooks one of the prettiest white-sand beaches on the island. Spend a few hours relaxing on the beach and you're sure to meet some friendly locals who cherish the beauty of the area as much as you will. The resort's full-service spa is regarded as one of the finest in the world (see Part Seven, "Exercise and Recreation"). Six state-of-the-art tennis courts and the nearby Ko 'Olina Golf Club make this a favorite site among sports-minded visitors. Celebrity Alert: During the week of the NFL Pro Bowl (usually the first week in February), the 'Ihilani hosts the players and their families, and practices are often held on a makeshift field.

SETTING & FACILITIES

Location: At the Ko 'Olina Resort in Kapolei, on the leeward side of the island.

Dining: Azul is 'Ihilani's signature restaurant, serving an extensive menu blending the flavors of the Mediterranean and Hawaii.

Amenities & Services: Twice-daily maid service, automatic turndown service, daily ice delivery, 24-hour room service, full-service health spa, tennis club, beauty salon, year-round children's program.

ACCOMMODATIONS

Rooms: 387. Includes 36 luxury suites; 120 non-smoking rooms; 14 rooms equipped for the disabled.

All Rooms: A/C, ceiling fan, color TV, in-house movie library, in-room safe, AM/FM radio with CD player, mini-bar, 3 telephones, private lanai, hair dryer, robes, etc.

Some Rooms: Whirlpool spas, walk-in closets, large-screen TVs, second bathrooms.

Comfort & Decor: Very spacious (the smallest room is 640 square feet) and exceptionally clean. Tastefully decorated with Island-themed artworks and teak furnishings. One unique amenity here is that you can turn lights on and off, adjust the room temperature (in 1° increments!), and even find out the current time anywhere around the world—right from your specially equipped phone.

RATES, RESERVATIONS, & RESTRICTIONS

Family Plan: No additional charge for children age 17 and under when sharing same room with parents and using existing bedding. Additional $35 charge for rollaway beds.

Deposit: To guarantee reservation, a 1-night deposit is required within 14 days of booking. Cancellation notice must be received at least 72 hours prior to arrival for refund.

Credit Cards: All major credit cards accepted except Discover.

Check-In/Out: 3 p.m./Noon. Early check-in available by request.

Contact: 92-1001 Olani St. Kapolei, HI 96707
(800) 626-4446 or (808) 679-0079
Fax: (808) 679-0295
reservations@ihilani.com
www.ihilani.com

'ILIKAI HOTEL NIKKO WAIKIKI			$$$
Overall: ★★★★	Room Quality: A	Value: C+	Zone 1

A *kama'aina* favorite, the 'Ilikai offers a little bit of everything for visitors, including friendly service, fine dining, beautiful harbor views and, for the kids, Ultrazone (a laser tag game). It's a short walk from the hotel to the beaches, Ala Moana Shopping Center, and the Hawaii Convention Center. About 80% of the rooms have harbor views. The 'Ilikai has one of the prettiest wedding chapels in Waikiki. Don't miss the daily torchlighting ceremony at the hotel's courtyard; held at sunset, this popular Hawaiian tradition has been observed at the 'Ilikai for more than 30 years. Trivia fans should note that the 'Ilikai is where the famous opening shot of *Hawaii Five-0* was filmed (when Jack Lord, a.k.a. Steve McGarrett, stands on the penthouse balcony). *Note:* At press time, the 'Ilikai was put up for sale; it was uncertain what changes (if any) might be forthcoming for the hotel.

SETTING & FACILITIES

Location: At the Ala Wai Yacht Harbor, Waikiki.
Dining: Sarento's Top of the "I" serves sumptuous Italian regional cuisine, while Tanaka of Tokyo West was voted one of the "10 Best Japanese Restaurants in the U.S."
Amenities & Services: 2 swimming pools, tennis services, fitness center, poolside bar, gift shops and boutiques, meeting facilities.

ACCOMMODATIONS

Rooms: 800. Includes 52 suites, 120 non-smoking rooms.
All Rooms: A/C, cable TV with pay movies, phone, in-room safe, hair dryer, coffeemaker with daily coffee and tea, etc.
Some Rooms: Lanai, full kitchen, fax capability, data port, extra phone.
Comfort & Decor: Spacious and clean. Tropical-accented furnishings, well-lit rooms.

RATES, RESERVATIONS, & RESTRICTIONS

Family Plan: No charge for children age 17 and under if staying with parents and using existing bedding. $30 per day for additional adults.
Deposit: Credit card deposit of 1 night's rate is taken at time of confirmation. Cash deposits must be received within 14 days after placing reservation.
Credit Cards: All credit cards accepted.
Check-In/Out: 3 p.m./Noon.
Contact: 1777 Ala Moana Blvd. Honolulu, HI 96815
(800) 245-4524 or (808) 949-3811
Fax: (808) 944-6373
ilikairz@lava.net
www.ilikaihotel.com

KAHALA MANDARIN ORIENTAL			$$$$$
Overall: ★★★★½	Room Quality: A	Value: C	Zone 2

Old-timers might recall this luxurious property as the Kahala Hilton. The Mandarin is an ideal option if you prefer more tranquil surroundings than what you'll experience in bustling Waikiki. Complimentary shuttle service transports you to and from a trio of major shopping destinations: Kahala Mall, Ala Moana Shopping Center, and the Royal Hawaiian Shopping Center. The Mandarin has its own reef-protected beach, exotic gardens, a waterfall, turtle ponds, and a lovely beachfront lawn. The hotel's Dolphin Lagoon, home to Atlantic bottlenose dolphins, is an especially popular attraction here.

SETTING & FACILITIES

Location: In the upscale neighborhood of Kahala, about 15 minutes from Waikiki.
Dining: The oceanfront Hoku's is the signature restaurant, serving fine international cuisine prepared with fresh Island ingredients.
Amenities & Services: Room service, laundry service, valet parking, business facilities, fitness center, children's program.

ACCOMMODATIONS

Rooms: 371. Includes 29 suites. Non-smoking and ADA-approved rooms available.
All Rooms: A/C, cable TV, CD player, clock radio, video games, 3 telephones, mini-bar, computer outlets, fax port, hair dryer, in-room safe, bathrobes, etc.
Some Rooms: Upgraded amenities.
Comfort & Decor: Spacious, luxurious, and impeccably clean. Rooms have a stylish turn-of-the-century motif. Mahogany furnishings, teak parquet floors. Warm, relaxing, and extremely comfortable.

RATES, RESERVATIONS, & RESTRICTIONS

Family Plan: Children age 17 and under stay free.
Deposit: All reservations guaranteed by credit card. Cancellation notice must be given 72 hours prior to arrival for refund.
Credit Cards: All major credit cards accepted.
Check-In/Out: 2 p.m./Noon. Early check-in and late check-out available on request.
Contact: 5000 Kahala Ave. Honolulu, HI 96816
(800) 526-6566 or (808) 739-8888
Fax: (808) 739-8800
sales@mohg.com
www.mandarin-oriental.com

NEW OTANI KAIMANA BEACH HOTEL			$$$
Overall: ★★★★	Room Quality: B+	Value: C+	Zone 1

What we like best about the Kaimana is its location. It's in Waikiki, yet comfortably removed from the traffic and noise you find in the area's main strip. Kapi'olani Park is just a walk across the street. A low-key hotel with stylish touches from the Orient, the Kaimana fronts the gorgeous—and usually less crowded—San Souci Beach. The poet Robert Louis Stevenson noted over a century ago, "If anyone desires lovely scenery, pure air, clear sea water, good food, and heavenly sunsets, I recommend him cordially to Sans Souci." We echo that sentiment. The service is friendly and efficient, and here you have all the charm you'd expect of a small hotel plus most of the services and facilities found at larger hotels.

SETTING & FACILITIES

Location: At the far Diamond Head end of Waikiki, across from Kapi'olani Park.

Dining: The oceanfront Hau Tree Lanai has one of Hawaii's most romantic settings and offers fine Continental cuisine. Miyako serves traditional Japanese fare.

Amenities & Services: Room service, laundry and dry cleaning service, valet parking ($8 per day), fitness center, business facilities.

ACCOMMODATIONS

Rooms: 124. Includes 5 suites and 3 ADA-approved rooms. All rooms permit smoking.

All Rooms: A/C, TV, VCR, lanai, refrigerator, in-room safe, hair dryer, etc. Coffeemaker available on request.

Some Rooms: Mini-bar.

Comfort & Decor: Rooms are smallish, but clean and well maintained. Light, soft pastels and contemporary Island-theme decor.

RATES, RESERVATIONS, & RESTRICTIONS

Family Plan: Children age 12 and under stay free. $20 fee for rollaway beds, $10 for cribs.

Deposit: Credit card guarantee or 1-night deposit required. Cancellation notice must be given 72 hours prior to arrival for refund.

Credit Cards: All major credit cards accepted.

Check-In/Out: 2 p.m./Noon. Hospitality room available for early arrivals and late departures.

Contact: 2863 Kalakaua Ave. Honolulu, HI 96815
(800) 421-8795 or (808) 923-1555
Fax: (808) 922-9404
kaimana@pixi.com
www.kaimana.com

OUTRIGGER EAST HOTEL			$$
Overall: ★★★½	Room Quality: B+	Value: C	Zone 1

One of Outrigger's more popular properties. If you don't require unobstructed ocean views, the Outrigger East is a good choice because it's in the center of Waikiki, and the beach is just a few minutes away on foot. Situated near the International Market Place and next to Ka'iulani Park. Has suites with kitchenettes for visitors here on extended stays. Nothing exceptional, but nothing sub-par, either.

SETTING & FACILITIES

Location: At the corner of Kuhio and Ka'iulani Avenues, 2 blocks away from the beach.

Dining: A trio of restaurants on the premises, including Pepper's Waikiki Grill & Bar (American, Southwest, and Mexican cuisine) and Chuck's Cellar (prime rib and seafood specialties).

Amenities & Services: Room service (7 a.m.–9:30 p.m.), activities desk, parking ($8 per day), coin-operated washer and dryer.

ACCOMMODATIONS

Rooms: 445. Includes 25 suites, 5 rooms for the disabled. Half the rooms are designated non-smoking.
All Rooms: A/C, cable TV, phone, refrigerator, in-room safe, coffeemaker, etc.

Some Rooms: Lanai, kitchenette.
Comfort & Decor: Rooms small to medium, tastefully adorned with Island-accented art and furnishings. Rooms recently renovated.

RATES, RESERVATIONS, & RESTRICTIONS

Family Plan: Children age 17 and under stay free if staying with parents and using existing bedding.
Deposit: Credit card guarantee or 1-night deposit required. Cancellation notice must be given 72 hours prior to arrival for refund.
Credit Cards: All major credit cards accepted.

Check-In/Out: 3 p.m./Noon. Early check-in and late check-out available on request.
Contact: 150 Ka'iulani Ave.
Honolulu, HI 96815
(800) 688-7444 or (808) 922-5353
Fax: (808) 926-4334
www.outrigger.com

OUTRIGGER REEF ON THE BEACH $$$$

Overall: ★★★½   Room Quality: B+   Value: C   Zone 1

The Outrigger Reef provides all the Island hospitality this *kama'aina* chain is known for, plus the added convenience of being right on Waikiki Beach. The atmosphere here is very informal and is great for young families (the hotel offers a nice children's activity program). The lobby area includes 15 specialty shops. The Outrigger Reef is the official hotel of the Honolulu Marathon, which takes place each December, and during the week of the event you can expect to see a lot of international runners (the majority from Japan) here.

SETTING & FACILITIES

Location: On Waikiki Beach near Fort DeRussy.
Dining: A quartet of eateries, including the popular Shorebird Beach Broiler, a lively nightspot serving burgers, sand-

wiches, and other American favorites.
Amenities & Services: Room service, activities desk, parking, coin-operated washer and dryer.

ACCOMMODATIONS

Rooms: 900. Includes 25 suites; 450 non-smoking rooms; 10 rooms for the disabled.
All Rooms: A/C, cable TV, phone, refrigerator, in-room safe, coffeemaker.

Some Rooms: Kitchenette.
Comfort & Decor: Medium-sized rooms, clean and comfortable. Cool colors, fairly well lit, simple furnishings.

RATES, RESERVATIONS, & RESTRICTIONS

Family Plan: Children age 17 and under stay free if staying with parents and using existing bedding.
Deposit: 1-night deposit or credit card guarantee. Cancellation required 72 hours prior to arrival for refund.
Credit Cards: All major credit cards accepted.

Check-In/Out: 3 p.m./Noon. Early check-in and late check-out available on request.
Contact: 2169 Kalia Rd. Honolulu, HI 96815
(800) 688-7444 or (808) 923-3111
Fax: (808) 924-4957
www.outrigger.com

OUTRIGGER WAIKIKI ON THE BEACH $$$$

Overall: ★★★½	Room Quality: B+	Value: B	Zone 1

This is considered Outrigger's flagship property, and we can understand why. A short stroll around the second-floor lobby tells you right away you're in Hawaii, with soft Hawaiian music, attractive floral-motif carpeting, handsome Island artworks, an ocean shell–shaped chandelier, and, most telling, the soothing sounds of the beach. The location is fabulous, too. Not only is the Outrigger Waikiki right on the beach, it is also next door to Waikiki's largest shopping complex, the Royal Hawaiian Shopping Center. Duke's Canoe Club, the hotel's best-known restaurant, is worth a visit just to peruse the historic photographs and other memorabilia paying tribute to Duke Kahanamoku, Hawaii's surfing legend. The Outrigger Waikiki is also the home of the popular Society of Seven show, one of Waikiki's longest-running dinner shows. The atmosphere, thankfully, remains typical of most Outrigger properties: informal, colorful, and friendly.

SETTING & FACILITIES

Location: On Waikiki Beach, next to the Royal Hawaiian Shopping Center.
Dining: Duke's Canoe Club is a Waikiki favorite, serving breakfast, lunch, and dinner.
Amenities & Services: Room service, parking, activities desk, coin-operated washer and dryer.

ACCOMMODATIONS

Rooms: 530. Includes 30 suites. Half of the rooms are designated non-smoking rooms. Rooms for the disabled are available.
All Rooms: A/C, cable TV, phone, refrigerator, in-room safe, coffeemaker.
Some Rooms: Kitchenettes.
Comfort & Decor: Medium-sized rooms, subdued colors with few adornments. Clean and nicely maintained.

RATES, RESERVATIONS, & RESTRICTIONS

Family Plan: Children age 17 and under stay free if staying with parents and using existing bedding.
Deposit: 1-night deposit or credit card guarantee. Cancellation notice must be given 72 hours prior to arrival for refund.
Credit Cards: All major credit cards accepted.

Check-In/Out: 3 p.m./Noon. Early check-in and late check-out available on request.
Contact: 2335 Kalakaua Ave. Honolulu, HI 96815
(800) 688-7444 or (808) 923-0711
Fax: (808) 921-9749
www.outrigger.com

PACIFIC BEACH HOTEL $$$

Overall: ★★★½	Room Quality: B	Value: C	Zone 1

Every Waikiki hotel tries to distinguish itself from the others in some form or fashion, and the Pacific Beach Hotel definitely makes a big splash with its three-story, 280,000-gallon oceanarium, featuring hundreds of marine life. The oceanarium is the centerpiece of the hotel's dining establishments. The PBH is a busy hotel with friendly service and a prime location. The beach is directly across the street, the Damien Museum is a block away, and both the zoo and Kapi'olani Park are just minutes away on foot.

SETTING & FACILITIES

Location: Across the street from Waikiki Beach.
Dining: The most renowned restaurant here is the Oceanarium, whose star attraction is not the food but the 280,000-gallon ocean aquarium. Shogun is a highly regarded Japanese restaurant, while Neptune's Garden serves seafood, steaks, and other Continental fare.
Amenities & Services: Swimming pool and whirlpool, parking, laundry service, travel desk, 24-hour fitness center, business facilities, meeting rooms.

ACCOMMODATIONS

Rooms: 830. Includes 10 suites; 5 floors of non-smoking rooms; 13 rooms for the disabled.
All Rooms: A/C, cable TV, balcony, phone, lanai, coffeemaker, in-room safe, mini-refrigerator, bath slippers, etc.
Some Rooms: Bathrobes, iron and ironing board, vanity kit.
Comfort & Decor: Rooms small to medium. Soft pastel colors help brighten the room. Potted plants add to the subtle tropical decor. Lanais open to scenic mountain or ocean views.

RATES, RESERVATIONS, & RESTRICTIONS

Family Plan: Children age 17 and under stay free if staying with parents and using existing bedding. Maximum of 4 people per room.
Deposit: 1-night deposit required within 14 days of confirmation. Cancellation notice must be given 72 hours prior to arrival for refund.
Credit Cards: All major credit cards accepted.

Check-In/Out: 3 p.m./Noon. Early
check-in and late check-out based on
availability.
Contact: 2490 Kalakaua Ave.
Honolulu, HI 96815

(800) 367-6060 or (808) 922-1233
Fax: (808) 923-2566
reservation@hthcorp.com
www.pacificbeachhotel.com

PAGODA HOTEL $$

Overall: ★★★½	Room Quality: B	Value: C	Zone 2

While the Pagoda offers an affordable alternative to the high-priced
Waikiki hotels, we recommend it only to visitors who have a strong desire
to avoid Waikiki yet stay where there's plenty of nightlife. And even then,
we think the Ala Moana Hotel would be a superior choice. The Pagoda
does have its positives: It's within walking distance of both the Ala Moana
Shopping Center and the Hawaii Convention Center, and you'll find a lot
of good local eateries in the surrounding area. On the other hand, the
Pagoda is also close to Ke'eaumoku Street, widely known for its wealth of
strip clubs and hostess bars. (Personally, we prefer to bump into sunscreen-
lubricated beachgoers than inebriated bar-hoppers.) The Pagoda does have
good service, and kids will likely enjoy the Pagoda Restaurant's surrounding koi pond, filled with colorful carp.

SETTING & FACILITIES

Location: In Honolulu, a few blocks
mauka from Ala Moana Shopping
Center.
Dining: The Pagoda Restaurant is a
favorite among locals, serving Island
favorites for breakfast, lunch, and dinner. The koi pond is practically a local
landmark.
Amenities & Services: Room service, laundry service, parking ($3 per
day), business facilities.

ACCOMMODATIONS

Rooms: 362. Includes 1 suite; 8 rooms
for the disabled. Non-smoking rooms
available.
All Rooms: A/C, cable TV, phone,
refrigerator, etc.
Some Rooms: Kitchen, coffeemaker.
Comfort & Decor: Spacious rooms,
very clean and well kept. Simple decor,
fairly bright atmosphere.

RATES, RESERVATIONS, & RESTRICTIONS

Family Plan: Children age 17 and
under stay free if staying with parents
and using existing bedding.
Deposit: $50 cash or credit card guar-
antee. 72-hour cancellation notice
required for refund.
Credit Cards: All major credit cards
accepted.
Check-In/Out: 3 p.m./Noon. Early
check-in and late check-out available
on request.

Contact: 1525 Rycroft St.
Honolulu, HI 96814
(800) 367-6060 or (808) 941-6611

Fax: (808) 923-2566
reservation@hthcorp.com
www.pagodahotel.com

RADISSON WAIKIKI PRINCE KUHIO			$$$
Overall: ★★★½	Room Quality: B+	Value: C	Zone 1

The Prince Kuhio is centrally located and requires only a short stroll to Waikiki Beach. The Ala Wai Canal, Honolulu Zoo, and Kapi'olani Park are also within easy walking distance. Kuhio Avenue can be just as busy as Kalakaua Avenue, and the area tends to get noisy at night. The lobby area is attractive but rather dimly lit. The hotel recently added a new fitness room and renovated its swimming pool.

SETTING & FACILITIES

Location: On Kuhio Avenue in Waikiki, 2 full blocks from the beach.
Dining: Trellises serves nightly theme buffets and Sunday brunch. Shanghai Garden serves Chinese cuisine and seafood specialties.
Amenities & Services: Room service, activities desk, parking ($8 per day), coin-operated washer and dryer, swimming pool.

ACCOMMODATIONS

Rooms: 620. Non-smoking rooms and rooms for the disabled available.
All Rooms: A/C, cable TV, phone, refrigerator, in-room safe, coffeemaker, etc.
Some Rooms: Balcony, kitchenette.
Comfort & Decor: Rooms small to medium, tastefully appointed and very clean. Floor-to-ceiling windows, Hawaiian artwork, comfortable furnishings. Rooms recently renovated.

RATES, RESERVATIONS, & RESTRICTIONS

Family Plan: Children age 17 and under stay free if staying with parents and using existing bedding.
Deposit: 1-night deposit or credit card guarantee required. 72-hour cancellation notice required for refund.
Credit Cards: All major credit cards accepted.
Check-In/Out: 3 p.m./Noon. Early check-in and late check-out available on request.
Contact: 2500 Kuhio Ave. Honolulu, HI 96815
(800) 688-7444 or (808) 922-0811
Fax: (808) 923-0330

ROYAL GARDEN AT WAIKIKI			$$
Overall: ★★★★	Room Quality: B+	Value: B	Zone 1

It's a decent walk to the beach from this property—about 20 minutes—but the Royal Garden is still a great recommendation. Everything is first-class here, from the service (which is outstanding) to the amenities. The setting is one of quiet refinement, with interiors inspired by Hawaii's natural beauty. Lush gardens surround the property's two swimming pools. The recent development of the King Kalakaua Plaza—which has Niketown, All Star Cafe, and Banana Republic—adds to the shops and attractions within easy walking distance from the hotel. A morning or late-afternoon stroll along the Ala Wai Canal, which is practically next door to the Royal Garden, makes for a pleasant activity, especially during the summer months.

SETTING & FACILITIES

Location: In Waikiki, near the King Kalakaua Plaza and the Ala Wai Canal.
Dining: Cascada serves Mediterranean and Pacific Rim cuisine, while Shizu offers Ginza-style teppanyaki and traditional Japanese delicacies.

Amenities & Services: Laundry facilities, business center, fitness center, sauna, Jacuzzi, swimming pool, soda machines. Hair dryer, iron and ironing board, and crib available upon request.

ACCOMMODATIONS

Rooms: 220. Includes 19 suites. Nonsmoking rooms and rooms for the disabled available. Inquire when placing reservation.
All Rooms: A/C, cable TV, phone, private lanai, refrigerator, coffeemaker, voice mail, wet bar, in-room safe, etc.

Some Rooms: Separate shower and Jacuzzi.
Comfort & Decor: Very spacious, exceptionally clean and luxurious. Features marble bathrooms, extra closet space, and elegant furnishings with tropical plants.

RATES, RESERVATIONS, & RESTRICTIONS

Family Plan: Children age 12 and under stay free if staying with parents and using existing bedding.
Deposit: 1-night deposit required within 10 days of confirmation. Cancellation notice must be given 72 hours prior to arrival for refund.
Credit Cards: All major credit cards accepted.

Check-In/Out: 3 p.m./Noon. Early check-in and late check-out available on request (no guarantees).
Contact: 440 Olohana St. Honolulu, HI 96815
(800) 367-5666 or (808) 943-0202
Fax: (808) 946-8777
rgsales@royalgardens.com
www.royalgardens.com

ROYAL HAWAIIAN HOTEL	$$$$$

Overall: ★★★★½	Room Quality: A	Value: C+	Zone 1

The famed "Pink Palace." Few hotels in Hawaii have a history like this property, which opened in 1927. The Royal Hawaiian has aged remarkably well and still offers great dining and shopping experiences. The hotel's design reflects a strong Moorish influence, with mission overtones supplied by cupolas resembling bell towers, and the atmosphere is deliciously reminiscent of Waikiki's golden years. The lobby area is dimly lit, but the hotel's back end opens up to a dreamlike beach setting with pure white sand and azure waters. There are a handful of shops located on the property, but you can also take the short walkway to the Royal Hawaiian Shopping Center, Waikiki's biggest shopping complex. The hotel holds a lavish luau every Monday evening ($78 for adults, $48 for children ages 5–11). Over the years, the Royal has hosted numerous celebrities and dignitaries, including U.S. President Franklin Roosevelt, Mary Pickford, Douglas Fairbanks, Shirley Temple, the Beatles, and contemporary luminaries such as Kevin Costner and Harrison Ford.

SETTING & FACILITIES

Location: Fronting Waikiki Beach, behind the Royal Hawaiian Shopping Center.

Dining: The Surf Room serves breakfast, lunch, and dinner, including its popular Friday seafood buffet and Sunday brunch.

Amenities & Services: Fresh flower lei greeting, freshly baked Hawaiian banana bread upon arrival, nightly turndown service, concierge, 24-hour fax service, morning newspaper, laundry and dry cleaning service, valet parking, nurse and physician service.

ACCOMMODATIONS

Rooms: 527. Includes 33 suites; 37 non-smoking rooms; 4 rooms with roll-in showers for wheelchair users.

All Rooms: A/C, telephone, color TV, refrigerator, in-room safe, robes, etc.

Some Rooms: Wet bar, Continental breakfast.

Comfort & Decor: Very spacious bedroom with high ceilings and chandelier. The bathroom is a little cramped, however. Decor best described as "classical elegance," with stylish furnishings and an Old World charm.

RATES, RESERVATIONS, & RESTRICTIONS

Family Plan: No charge for children age 17 and under when sharing same room as parents and using existing bedding. $25-per-night charge for rollaway beds.

Deposit: Credit card guarantee or 1-night deposit required within 10 days of booking to guarantee reservation. Cancellation notice must be provided 72 hours prior to arrival date for refunds.

Credit Cards: All major credit cards accepted.

Check-In/Out: 3 p.m./Noon. Hospitality suite available for early arrivals and late departures.

Contact: 2259 Kalakaua Ave. Honolulu, HI 96815
(800) 782-9488 or (808) 923-7311
Fax: (808) 924-7098
www.royal-hawaiian.com

SHERATON MOANA SURFRIDER $$$$$

Overall: ★★★★½	Room Quality: A	Value: C+	Zone 1

Opened in 1901, this was the very first hotel built in Waikiki. Nicknamed the "First Lady of Waikiki," the Moana has lost none of her charm. We particularly favor the second-floor balcony that overlooks Kalakaua

Avenue; here, you can sit back in a rocking chair and watch the parade of passersby. The ocean and beach views here are simply fantastic. The staff is efficient, courteous, and smartly dressed—complete with bow tie and sash. Visit the mini-museum on the second floor for a fascinating look at the golden age of both the Moana and Waikiki. Memorabilia here include historic photos, postcards, room keys, stock shares, sheet music, menus, old brochures, and more. You'll also see a sofa that once belonged to King Kalakaua, Hawaii's "Merrie Monarch." A historic centerpiece is the hotel's 75-foot-high, 150-foot-wide banyan tree, located near where the radio show *Hawaii Calls* was broadcast for 40 years. The central portion of the Moana is listed on the National Register of Historic Places. In the late 1980s, it underwent a 20-month, $50 million architectural restoration, reopening in March 1989.

SETTING & FACILITIES

Location: Fronting Waikiki Beach.
Dining: The Ship's Tavern serves contemporary cuisine; the Beachside Cafe offers breakfast, lunch, and dinner in a casual setting; and the Banyan Veranda serves breakfast, afternoon tea, cocktails, and an evening buffet.
Amenities & Services: 24-hour room service, maid service, valet service, fitness center, concierge, children's program.

ACCOMMODATIONS

Rooms: 793. Includes 44 suites; 8 ADA-approved rooms for the disabled. Non-smoking rooms available.
All Rooms: A/C, cable TV, phone, in-room safe, hair dryer, slippers, bathrobe, coffeemaker, etc.
Some Rooms: Oceanfront lanai, wet bar, refrigerator, pullout sofa.

Comfort & Decor: Rooms small to medium in size, with high ceilings, over-sized porthole windows, and great views. The design is an interesting mix of old and new, with elegant Old World furnishings and modern amenities, including video messages/check-out system.

RATES, RESERVATIONS, & RESTRICTIONS

Family Plan: Children age 17 and under stay free if staying with parents and using existing bedding. Maximum of 4 people per room.
Deposit: 1-night deposit or credit card guarantee within 10 days of placing reservation. 72-hour cancellation notice required for refund.
Credit Cards: All major credit cards accepted.

Check-In/Out: 3 p.m./Noon. Early check-in and late check-out available on request.
Contact: 2365 Kalakaua Ave. Honolulu, HI 96815
(800) 782-9488 or (808) 922-3111
Fax: (808) 923-0308
www.moana-surfrider.com

SHERATON PRINCESS KA'IULANI $$$$

Overall: ★★★★	Room Quality: A	Value: C	Zone 1

Named after Hawaii's beloved Princess Victoria Ka'iulani, the last heir to the Hawaiian throne, this hotel is situated on her garden estate, 'Ainahau, where the beautiful princess spent her childhood. While not as established as her sister Sheraton properties, the Princess Ka'iulani has carved out a niche for itself nonetheless. The 1,150 rooms are housed in three separate wings—Princess, Ka'iulani, and 'Ainahau—surrounded by lobby areas, specialty shops, and gardens. The lobby area is airy, bright, and fairly busy during the day. Original artworks and mementos from the era of Princess Ka'iulani are found throughout the hotel. Arts and crafts demonstrations are held daily, and poolside entertainment is provided nightly. The hotel does offer something the Royal Hawaiian, Sheraton Waikiki, and Moana Surfrider do not: *Creation—A Polynesian Odyssey,* a marvelous dinner show in the hotel's 'Ainahau Showroom (see the section on dinner shows in Part Six, "Entertainment and Nightlife").

SETTING & FACILITIES

Location: In Waikiki, next to the International Market Place and across the street from Waikiki Beach.
Dining: Momoyama serves Japanese specialties in a traditional setting, while Lotus Moon features an extensive menu of Chinese cuisine.
Amenities & Services: Room service, parking ($8 per day), swimming pool, Laundromat.

ACCOMMODATIONS

Rooms: 1,150. Includes 8 suites, 13 ADA-approved rooms, and 6 rooms with roll-in showers; smoking-designated areas are available.
All Rooms: A/C, cable TV, phone, mini-refrigerator, in-room safe, hair dryer, etc.
Some Rooms: Lanai.
Comfort & Decor: Spacious, very clean. Simple but pleasant Island decor reflects Island accents.

RATES, RESERVATIONS, & RESTRICTIONS

Family Plan: Children age 17 and under stay free with parents if using existing bedding. Maximum of 4 per room.
Deposit: 1-night deposit or credit card guarantee. Cancellation notice must be given by 6 p.m. on date of arrival or deposit will be forfeited.
Credit Cards: All major credit cards accepted.
Check-In/Out: 3 p.m./Noon. Early check-in and late check-out available on request (no guarantees).
Contact: 120 Ka'iulani Ave. Honolulu, HI 96815
(800) 782-9488 or (808) 922-5811
Fax: (808) 923-9912
www.princess-kaiulani.com

SHERATON WAIKIKI $$$$$

Overall: ★★★★	Room Quality: A	Value: C	Zone 1

The second-largest hotel in the state (next to the Hilton Hawaiian Village), this 30-story property more than lives up to the Sheraton name. The lobby is continuously busy, yet the staff seems to maintain their aloha spirit well. The main lobby's centerpiece is a striking collection of colorful, ocean-themed glass sculptures, from fish and sharks to sea turtles. It actually personifies the hotel as a whole: elegant, but far from stuffy. An aquarium at the entrance to the hotel is occupied by a Hawaiian green sea turtle (or *honu* in Hawaiian); this endangered species was adopted by the Sheraton Waikiki in 1996, and audio information is provided with a push of a button. The Sheraton is also one of Hawaii's top convention sites, with its entire second floor dedicated to meetings and featuring Waikiki's largest indoor ballroom (26,000 square feet). Hawaiian entertainment is provided nightly. For club-goers, the Sheraton offers Waikiki's only beachfront nightclub, the Esprit Nightclub.

SETTING & FACILITIES

Location: Fronting Waikiki Beach.
Dining: Situated on the 30th floor, the Hanohano is renowned among visitors and locals for its incredible views (it has the highest vantage point on Waikiki Beach) and award-winning Continental menu. Other restaurants include Ciao!, serving Italian cuisine; and the Ocean Terrace, which features buffets with various international themes.
Amenities & Services: On-site parking, meeting facilities, secretarial business services, nightly poolside entertainment, fitness center, travel services, daily children's program.

ACCOMMODATIONS

Rooms: 1,852. Includes 130 suites, 8 rooms for the disabled. Most rooms are non-smoking.
All Rooms: A/C, private lanai, color TV with first-run movies, clock radio, mini-bar, refrigerator, in-room safe, safety deposit box, phone, in-room video message and check-out facilities, room service, coffeemakers, etc.
Some Rooms: Full kitchen.
Comfort & Decor: High ceilings, spacious bathrooms, complete line of amenities. Stylish furnishings reflect a comfortably elegant ambience with Island-accented decor.

RATES, RESERVATIONS, & RESTRICTIONS

Family Plan: Children age 17 and under stay free with parents if using existing bedding.
Deposit: Credit card guarantee or 1-night deposit required. Cancellation notice must be given before 6 p.m. on day of arrival.

Credit Cards: All major credit cards accepted except Discover.
Check-In/Out: 3 p.m./Noon. Hospitality suite available for early arrivals and late departures.

Contact: 2255 Kalakaua Ave.
Honolulu, HI 96815
(800) 782-9488 or (808) 922-4422
Fax: (808) 923-8785
www.sheraton-waikiki.com

TURTLE BAY HILTON GOLF & TENNIS RESORT $$$

Overall: ★★★★   Room Quality: B+   Value: B   Zone 4

Situated on Oahu's North Shore, the Turtle Bay Hilton rests on a scenic peninsula that juts out into the ocean. It is far removed from the commercial atmosphere of Waikiki yet still delivers all the comforts and amenities you'd expect from a top Hilton property. The atmosphere is comfortable and relaxed, appropriate to the area's lifestyle. Hawaiian entertainment is provided at the Bay View Lounge, with dancing available on weekends. As its name implies, this is a favorite destination for avid golfers and tennis players. Other activities available here include horseback riding and snorkeling.

SETTING & FACILITIES

Location: On Oahu's North Shore, at the tip of Kuilima Point. Nearby attractions include the Polynesian Cultural Center (4 miles away) and Waimea Valley Adventure Park (5 miles away). The hotel is also located near some of the best surfing spots and beaches in the world, including the legendary Banzai Pipeline.

Dining: The Cove offers fine Continental cuisine as well as spectacular ocean views. The Palm Terrace, meanwhile, serves breakfast, lunch, and dinner daily, including theme buffets.
Amenities & Services: Room service, laundry service, parking, swimming pool and Jacuzzi, exercise room, activity desk, tennis, golf, horseback riding.

ACCOMMODATIONS

Rooms: 485. Includes 26 suites; 5 rooms for the disabled. Non-smoking rooms available.
All Rooms: A/C, cable TV, phone, refrigerator, in-room safe, coffeemaker, data port, etc.

Comfort & Decor: Very spacious, exceptionally clean and well maintained. Light tropic colors. Beautifully appointed with Hawaiian artworks, plants, and elegant furnishings.

RATES, RESERVATIONS, & RESTRICTIONS

Family Plan: Children age 17 and under stay free if staying with parents and using existing bedding.
Deposit: 1-night deposit or credit card guarantee required within 10 days of confirmation. 48-hour cancellation notice required for refund.

Credit Cards: All major credit cards accepted.
Check-In/Out: 3 p.m./11 a.m. Early check-in and late check-out available for fee ($25 for 2 p.m. check-in, $50 for 5 p.m. check-out).

Contact: 57-091 Kamehameha Hwy.
Kahuku, HI 96731
(800) 445-8667 or (808) 293-8811

Fax: (808) 293-9147
www.turtlebayresort.hilton.com

W HONOLULU–DIAMOND HEAD $$$$

Overall: ★★★★	Room Quality: A	Value: C	Zone 1

Formerly known as the Colony Surf Hotel, this small hotel is a hidden gem nestled the foot of Diamond Head. The setting here is peaceful and calm—a far cry from the non-stop action you find in the center of Waikiki. The service is very personal and friendly, about what you would expect of a hotel of this size. The views here are gorgeous no matter what room you're in, and if you decide to stay here we suggest spending at least one evening at Diamond Head Grill, one of Oahu's best new restaurants. Nothing at the hotel offers anything exciting for children, but kid-friendly attractions like the Waikiki Aquarium, Kapiʻolani Park, and the Honolulu Zoo are all within easy walking distance.

SETTING & FACILITIES

Location: At the far Diamond Head end of Waikiki.
Dining: One of Waikiki's newer fine dining restaurants, Diamond Head Grill serves New American cuisine.
Amenities & Services: Room service, laundry service, valet parking ($12 per day).

ACCOMMODATIONS

Rooms: 73
All Rooms: A/C, radio, TV, phone, refrigerator, lanai, mini-bar, coffee-maker, hair dryer, etc.
Some Rooms: 2 bedrooms.
Comfort & Decor: Very spacious and clean. Understated decor reflects casual ambience. Light, sunny colors add to the overall pleasant look of the interiors.

RATES, RESERVATIONS, & RESTRICTIONS

Deposit: Credit card guarantees reservation. 72-hour cancellation notice required for refund.
Credit Cards: All major credit cards accepted.
Check-In/Out: 3 p.m./Noon. Early check-in and late check-out okay if available.
Contact: 2885 Kuhio Ave. Honolulu, HI 96815
(888) 924-7873 or (808) 924-3111
Fax: (808) 923-2249

WAIKIKI BEACHCOMBER HOTEL $$$

Overall: ★★★★   Room Quality: B   Value: C+   Zone 1

Although not as well known as many of Waikiki's name-brand hotels, the Beachcomber has a lot going for it. On one side of the hotel is the International Market Place, where you can find bargains on all kinds of souvenirs and gifts; on the other side is a trio of big-screen movie theaters; and directly across the street is the Royal Hawaiian Shopping Center. The beach is also across the street. The small lobby area displays a large pair of saltwater aquariums as well as striking Hawaiian artworks, including paintings, portraits, and framed Hawaiian quilts. We especially like the second-floor pool deck, which directly overlooks Kalakaua Avenue. The Beachcomber is the home of two of Waikiki's finest dinner shows: *The Don Ho Show* and *The Magic of Polynesia* (see the section on dinner shows in Part Six, "Entertainment and Nightlife").

SETTING & FACILITIES

Location: In the heart of Waikiki, on the *mauka* side of Kalakaua Avenue.
Dining: Hibiscus Cafe serves everything from burgers and pizzas to a wide selection of international specialties.
Amenities & Services: Maid service, parking, washer and dryer, swimming pool, ice machine.

ACCOMMODATIONS

Rooms: 500. Includes 4 suites; 7 wheelchair-accessible rooms. Nonsmoking rooms available upon request.
All Rooms: A/C, cable TV with in-room movies, lanai, refrigerator, in-room safe, phone, voice mail, coffeemaker, etc.
Some Rooms: 2 TV sets, 2 balconies, king-size bed.
Comfort & Decor: Spacious and clean. Soft tropical colors lead to a soothing and relaxing atmosphere. Decor is simple but pleasant, with Hawaiian paintings adorning the walls.

RATES, RESERVATIONS, & RESTRICTIONS

Family Plan: Children age 17 and under stay free if staying with parents and using existing bedding. Maximum of 4 people per room. $22 per night for rollaway bed.
Deposit: 1-night deposit due no later than 10 days after confirmation. Cancellation notice must be given 72 hours prior to arrival for refund.
Credit Cards: All major credit cards accepted.

Check-In/Out: 3 p.m./Noon. Additional charge for early check-in of 50% the 1-day rack rate (guarantees check-in at 10 a.m.).
Contact: 2300 Kalakaua Ave. Honolulu, HI 96815
(800) 622-4646 or (808) 922-4646
Fax: (808) 926-9973
beach@dps.net
www.waikikibeachcomber.com

WAIKIKI JOY HOTEL $$$

Overall: ★★★★	Room Quality: B+	Value: B	Zone I

One of Waikiki's best boutique hotels. Its location allows you to be near the center of all the action in Waikiki, and the beach is just minutes away on foot. The Italian marble–accented open-air lobby symbolizes the property's style and elegance. Music lovers will appreciate the impressive stereo system in each guest room (it sure beats the static-filled sounds that come from the usual alarm clock radios). Every guest receives a free hour at the property's G. S. Studio, a karaoke center with 15 private rooms and more than 4,000 songs to select from. (We tried it, and it's terrific fun for people of all ages!)

SETTING & FACILITIES

Location: In the center of Waikiki, a block *mauka* of Kalakaua Avenue.
Dining: Cappucinos Cafe offers a wide range of favorites for lunch and dinner.
Amenities & Services: Laundry service (valet and self-serve), valet parking.

ACCOMMODATIONS

Rooms: 94. Includes 47 suites; I room with roll-in shower and 2 wheelchair-accessible rooms. Non-smoking rooms available on request.
All Rooms: A/C, stereo entertainment center, cable TV, phone, Jacuzzi, mini-refrigerator, hair dryer, modem hookup, voice mail, I hour free karaoke, etc.
Some Rooms: Full kitchen.
Comfort & Decor: Spacious, ultra-luxurious, and exceptionally clean. Rooms have their own marble entries, a state-of-the-art entertainment system with Bose speakers, and private Jacuzzis.

RATES, RESERVATIONS, & RESTRICTIONS

Family Plan: Children age 17 and under stay free if staying with parents and using existing bedding.
Deposit: $100 cash if no credit card provided; prepay entire stay at registration. Or 1–2 nights' deposit with credit card, depending on length of stay. 72-hour cancellation notice required for refund.
Credit Cards: All major credit cards accepted.
Check-In/Out: 3 p.m./Noon. Early check-in and late check-out available on request (no guarantees).
Contact: 320 Lewers St. Honolulu, HI 96815
(800) 922-7866 or (808) 923-2300
Fax: (808) 924-4010
www.aston-hotels.com

WAIKIKI PARC HOTEL $$$

Overall: ★★★★	Room Quality: A	Value: B+	Zone I

Some refer to this hotel as simply a more affordable version of its AAA Five Diamond Award–winning sister property, the neighboring Halekulani.

But the Waikiki Parc has a certain charm of its own. Its location isn't visually appealing—it's crammed in among its neighboring properties—but it has some practical advantages, like being within the immediate vicinity of the Royal Hawaiian Shopping Center. It's also about 100 yards from the beach. If you want to be where the action is in Waikiki and don't require fabulous amenities or undisturbed ocean views, the Waikiki Parc might be for you.

SETTING & FACILITIES

Location: In Waikiki, across from the Halekulani Hotel.
Dining: The Parc Cafe's sumptuous buffets are popular with visitors and locals alike. The elegant Kacho serves traditional Japanese fare.
Amenities & Services: Room service, laundry service, parking, concierge desk, business facilities.

ACCOMMODATIONS

Rooms: 298. Includes 3 floors of non-smoking-designated rooms; 1 room equipped for the disabled.
All Rooms: A/C, cable TV, 2 phones, mini-refrigerators, in-room safe, hair dryer, etc. Hot pots available upon request.
Some Rooms: Lanais.

Comfort & Decor: Spacious and impeccably maintained. Color scheme is soft shades of white with accents of Pacific blue. Ceramic tile floors with plush inlaid carpeting, shutters, tinted glass lanai doors, and custom rattan furnishings.

RATES, RESERVATIONS, & RESTRICTIONS

Family Plan: Children age 14 and under stay free if staying with parents and using existing bedding. Maximum of 3 people per room.
Deposit: Credit card guarantee or 1-night deposit due within 14 days of booking. Cancellation notice must be given 72 hours prior to arrival for refund.
Credit Cards: All major credit cards accepted.

Check-In/Out: 3 p.m./Noon. Early check-in and late check-out available on request (may be charged, depending on length).
Contact: 2233 Helumoa Rd. Honolulu, HI 96815
(800) 422-0450 or (808) 921-7272
Fax: (808) 931-6638
www.waikikiparc.com

WAIKIKI TERRACE HOTEL			$$$

Overall: ★★★½	Room Quality: B+	Value: C	Zone 1

This is an attractive and affordable hotel whose lone drawback is its location. It's three long blocks to the beach, and the only worthwhile visits in the immediate vicinity are Fort DeRussy and the King Kalakaua Plaza shopping/restaurant complex. Still, there's much to like about the Waikiki Terrace, which recently renovated all 242 of its guest rooms and suites. The service is friendly and enthusiastic, and the atmosphere is very comfortable. Overall, a good-value hotel.

SETTING & FACILITIES

Location: At the gateway to Waikiki, next to Fort DeRussy.
Dining: The Eastern Garden serves breakfast, lunch, and dinner.

Amenities & Services: Room service, laundry and dry cleaning, swimming pool, Jacuzzi, business center, fitness center, parking ($8 per day).

ACCOMMODATIONS

Rooms: 242. Includes 2 suites; 7 ADA-approved rooms. Non-smoking rooms available.
All Rooms: A/C, cable TV, mini-refrigerator, lanai, phone, in-room safe, hot pot, hair dryer, etc.

Some Rooms: Separate sleeping quarters, extra bathroom.
Comfort & Decor: Medium-sized rooms, clean and comfortable. Soft colors with subtle Island accents and decor.

RATES, RESERVATIONS, & RESTRICTIONS

Family Plan: Children age 17 and under stay free with parents.
Deposit: Credit card guarantee or 1-night cash deposit due 14 days after booking. Prepay entire stay plus $50 deposit at registration. 72-hour cancellation notice required for refund.
Credit Cards: All major credit cards accepted.

Check-In/Out: 3 p.m./Noon. Early check-in and late check-out available on request.
Contact: 2045 Kalakaua Ave. Honolulu, HI 96815
(800) 367-5004 or (808) 955-6000
Fax: (808) 943-8555
www.castle-group.com

MAUI

EMBASSY VACATION RESORT			$$$$$
Overall: ★★★★½	Room Quality: A	Value: C+	Zone 9

Opened in 1988, this was the first Hawaii property to offer all-suite accommodations. Ninety percent of the suites provide stunning ocean views (you can also see the neighboring islands of Molokai and Lanai). A variety of Island-flavored art adorns the resort's lobby. A popular feature here is the 42-foot water slide, which plops you straight into a one-acre swimming pool. The young ones can participate in Beach Buddies, the resort's year-round children's program (ages 4–10), which includes lei making, beachcombing, coconut weaving, and other activities. A challenging miniature golf course is also on the premises, although serious golfers may prefer taking on the championship courses located elsewhere at the Ka'anapali Resort.

SETTING & FACILITIES

Location: On Ka'anapali Beach.
Dining: The North Beach Grille serves steaks, seafood, chicken, and other American favorites.

Amenities & Services: Room service, laundry and housekeeping service, workout room, parking, children's day care, etc.

ACCOMMODATIONS

Rooms: 413. All suites. 12 ADA-approved rooms. Most rooms are designated non-smoking.
All Rooms: A/C, cable TV, VCR, phone, microwave, mini-refrigerator, in-room safe, hair dryer, etc.
Comfort & Decor: Extremely spa-cious (over 800 square feet), with separate living room area. An oversized soaking tub, separate shower, walk-in closets, dual marble vanities, and 35-inch-screen TV are among the luxuries. Elegant and stylish, with a cool tropical appeal, cheerful and airy.

RATES, RESERVATIONS, & RESTRICTIONS

Family Plan: Children age 17 and under stay free if staying with parents and using existing bedding.
Deposit: 1-night deposit due within 10 days of booking. Cancellation notice must be given 72 hours prior to arrival for refund.
Credit Cards: All major credit cards accepted.
Check-In/Out: 4 p.m./11 a.m. Early check-in and late check-out available on request. Hospitality suite available for early arrivals and late departures.
Contact: 104 Ka'anapali Shores Pl. Lahaina, HI 96761
(800) 669-3155 or (808) 661-2000
Fax: (808) 667-5821
embassy@maui.net
www.embassy-maui.com

FOUR SEASONS RESORT MAUI $$$$$

Overall: ★★★★★	Room Quality: A+	Value: B	Zone 8

Condé Nast Traveler magazine named the Four Seasons the "Top Tropical Resort in the World" in 1993, and this luxurious resort continues to rate highly among travel experts. (The resort garnered the AAA Five Diamond Award in 1999.) The breezy open lobby is testament to the resort's Island-accented architectural design, which also includes specially commissioned reproductions of early Hawaiian furniture as well as paintings, sculptures, and other Hawaii-inspired artworks. On-site features include a children's program, health club, game room, and salon. The service is highly professional and courteous. To top everything off, the Four Seasons is located at Wailea Resort, which offers three championship golf courses and the 11-court Wailea Tennis Center (known as "Wimbledon West"). Overall, the Four Seasons has to rate as one of the best resorts (if not *the best*) on Maui.

SETTING & FACILITIES

Location: At Wailea Resort.
Dining: Season's showcases contemporary American cuisine with locally grown produce and fresh Island seafood.

Amenities & Services: 24-hour room service, full laundry service, workout facilities, business center, children's program, game room.

ACCOMMODATIONS

Rooms: 380. Includes 75 suites. ADA-approved and non-smoking rooms available.
All Rooms: A/C, cable TV, VCR, lanai, in-room safe, mini-bar, hair dryer, data port, robes.
Some Rooms: Fax machines, extra bedroom.

Comfort & Decor: Very spacious, exceptionally clean and well maintained. Soft white and gentle sunset hues. Deep-cushioned rattan and wicker furnishings. Large bathroom includes marble counter and dual vanities. Elegant Island-themed artwork adds to the warm atmosphere.

RATES, RESERVATIONS, & RESTRICTIONS

Family Plan: Children age 17 and under stay free if staying with parents and using existing bedding.
Deposit: 1-night deposit due within 7 days of booking. Cancellation notice must be given 14 hours prior to arrival January 3–April 30; 7 days prior May 1–December 18.
Credit Cards: All major credit cards accepted.

Check-In/Out: 3 p.m./Noon. Early check-in and late check-out available on request.
Contact: 3900 Wailea Alanui Wailea, HI 96753
(800) 334-6284 or (808) 874-8000
Fax: (808) 874-6449
resmaui@fourseasons.com
www.fourseasons.com

GRAND WAILEA RESORT HOTEL & SPA $$$$$

Overall: ★★★★½	Room Quality: A+	Value: C+	Zone 8

Even if you don't intend to stay here, this $600 million ultra-luxury resort is well worth a visit. There are six major design themes—flowers, water, trees, sound, light, and art—and all are on full display throughout the 40-acre property. (For example, there is more than $30 million in artworks adorning the resort's public areas.) Among the unique features here are Camp Grande, a 20,000-square-foot children's facility; the 50,000-square-foot Spa Grande; a breathtaking wedding chapel (complete with stained glass windows); and a 2,000-foot-long river pool that includes valleys, water slides, waterfalls, caves, grottos, whitewater rapids, a Jacuzzi, a sauna, and the world's only "water elevator," which lifts guests from the lower-level pool to the higher-level pool. No doubt, the resort is aptly named: Everything here is "grand"—perhaps too grand. While there are many visitors who will love this place, other travelers might find it too large, intimidating, and lacking in intimacy. It's simply a matter of what you're looking for in a resort.

SETTING & FACILITIES

Location: At Wailea Resort.
Dining: Kincha serves Japanese cuisine in a traditional setting. Bistro Molokini offers fine Italian fare, and the Humuhumunukunukuapua'a specializes in (you guessed it) fresh seafood.

Amenities & Services: Room service, full-service spa and fitness center, 3 championship golf courses, squash/racquetball court, parking, children's program, swimming pool.

ACCOMMODATIONS

Rooms: 761. Includes 51 suites; 10 rooms for disabled. Non-smoking rooms available.
All Rooms: A/C, cable TV, lanai, in-room safe, honor bar, coffeemaker, hair dryer, robes, slippers, etc.

Some Rooms: Larger accommodations, extra baths.
Comfort & Decor: Very spacious, ultra-luxurious, with opulent furnishings and decor. Warm colors, high ceilings add to the elegant setting.

RATES, RESERVATIONS, & RESTRICTIONS

Family Plan: Children age 17 and under stay free with parents if using existing bedding. Maximum 4 per room.
Deposit: 2-night deposit required within 14 days of booking (or reservation will be automatically canceled). Cancellation notice must be given 72 hours prior to arrival for refund (14 days' notice for suites).
Credit Cards: All major credit cards

accepted.
Check-In/Out: 3 p.m./Noon. Early check-in and late check-out available on request.
Contact: 3850 Wailea Alanui Dr. Wailea, HI 96753
(800) 888-6100 or (808) 875-1234
Fax: (808) 874-2411
info@grandwailea.com
www.grandwailea.com

HOTEL HANA-MAUI			$$$$$
Overall: ★★★★	Room Quality: A	Value: C	Zone 10

What this cozy small hotel lacks (including TV and air-conditioning), it makes up for in charm, location, and friendly and attentive service. Hana sits on 66 acres of abundant flora, tropical trees, and landscaped gardens, and the panoramic ocean and mountain views are simply heavenly. As remote as most resorts get, this is a wonderful place for couples and honeymooners. A weekly luau is held on the beach, with hotel employees providing the entertainment. Available outdoor activities are plentiful and include horseback riding, hiking, snorkeling, bike riding, and historical tours. A wellness center offers everything from massages to yoga. The hotel has hosted numerous celebrities, including Hillary and Chelsea Clinton and Caroline Kennedy.

SETTING & FACILITIES

Location: In Hana, on the eastern end of the island.
Dining: The hotel's dining room serves Continental cuisine.

Amenities & Services: Room service (breakfast only), laundry service, parking, wellness center, etc.

ACCOMMODATIONS

Rooms: 93. Includes 7 suites. Non-smoking suite available.
All Rooms: Wet bar, lanai, coffee- and tea-maker, etc.
Some Rooms: Jacuzzis.

Comfort & Decor: Rooms small to medium, mostly clean, comfortable atmosphere. Bleached hardwood floors, wicker and bamboo furnishings, handmade quilts, and private patios.

RATES, RESERVATIONS, & RESTRICTIONS

Family Plan: Children age 12 and under stay free if staying with parents and using existing bedding.
Deposit: 1-night deposit required. Cancellation notice must be given 72 hours prior to arrival for refund.
Credit Cards: All major credit cards accepted.

Check-In/Out: 3 p.m./Noon. Early check-in and late check-out available on request.
Contact: P.O. Box 9
Hana, HI 96713
(800) 321-4262 or (808) 248-8211
Fax: (808) 248-7202

HYATT REGENCY MAUI $$$$$

Overall: ★★★★	Room Quality: A	Value: C+	Zone 9

At first glance, it's easy to stamp the Hyatt Maui as a typical Hyatt hotel. By digging a little deeper, however, you'll uncover some features here that are as unique as they are marvelous. Its nightly "Tour of the Stars" program, for example, gives guests a guided tour of the Hawaiian skies and allows them to peer through a state-of-the-art, computer-controlled 16-inch reflector telescope. There is also an insightful wildlife tour that brings visitors face to face with penguins, swans, parrots, macaws, flamingos, and koi. You can also take a guided tour of the property's gardens (it's about a two-mile walk) or simply browse through the hotel's $2 million art collection. All in all, this is a property we wouldn't hesitate to recommend, as it offers something for travelers of all ages and interests. In 1996, the property underwent a $16 million renovation of all its guest rooms.

SETTING & FACILITIES

Location: On Ka'anapali Beach.
Dining: The romantic Swan Court features Continental cuisine with a Pacific Rim flair, Spats Trattoria serves Italian fare in an intimate setting, and Cascades Grille & Sushi Bar offers fresh seafood, steak, and other favorites.

Amenities & Services: Fitness center, tennis, golf, outdoor dinner theater, activities desk, children's program, shops, meeting and convention facilities, rooftop astronomy program, etc.

ACCOMMODATIONS

Rooms: 815. Includes 32 suites; 4 rooms for the disabled. Non-smoking rooms available.
All Rooms: A/C, cable TV, phone, honor bar, in-room safe, hair dryer, robes, coffeemaker, etc.

Some Rooms: Living room, dining area, wet bar, refrigerator.
Comfort & Decor: Spacious, clean. Warm earth and mauve Asian/Pacific tones reflect stylish elegance. Comfortable furnishings, attractive wall hangings.

RATES, RESERVATIONS, & RESTRICTIONS

Family Plan: Children age 17 and under stay free with parents if using existing bedding. Maximum 4 per room.
Deposit: 2-night deposit due within 14 days after booking. Cancellation notice must be provided 72 hours prior to arrival for refund.
Credit Cards: All major credit cards accepted.
Check-In/Out: 3 p.m./Noon. Early check-in and late check-out based on availability.
Contact: 200 Nohea Dr.
Lahaina, HI 96761
(800) 233-1234 or (808) 661-1234
Fax: (808) 667-4497
www.hyatt.com

KA'ANAPALI BEACH HOTEL			$$$
Overall: ★★★★	Room Quality: B+	Value: B	Zone 9

Located on one of the widest stretches of Ka'anapali Beach, the Ka'anapali Beach Hotel is widely accepted as Hawaii's "most Hawaiian" hotel. The management and staff here pride themselves on their aloha spirit, and the smiles and friendliness of the staff are downright contagious. Modern amenities aside, everything here is reminiscent of the Islands' romantic plantation era. Four separate wings form a semicircle around a ten-acre courtyard. A variety of Hawaiiana activities—including hula lessons, lei making, *lau hala* weaving, and *ti leaf* skirt making—are held daily, and employees provide Hawaiian entertainment three days a week. *Travel & Leisure* recently ranked this hotel tops for "best value" in Hawaii. For visitors seeking a hotel that places a strong emphasis on Hawaiian hospitality, look no further.

SETTING & FACILITIES

Location: On Ka'anapali Beach.
Dining: The Tiki Terrace Restaurant serves Continental and Island cuisine.

Amenities & Services: Laundry service, parking, children's program, etc.

ACCOMMODATIONS

Rooms: 430. Includes 15 suites. Non-smoking rooms and rooms for the disabled available on request.
All Rooms: A/C, cable TV, phone, in-room safe, refrigerator, coffeemaker.
Some Rooms: More space, upgraded amenities.

Comfort & Decor: Spacious, clean, and nicely maintained. Tropical green and golden sand hues accentuate the Hawaiian setting, along with Hawaiian quilt-designed bedspreads, light tropical furniture, and local artwork.

RATES, RESERVATIONS, & RESTRICTIONS

Family Plan: Children age 17 and under stay free if staying with parents and using existing bedding.
Deposit: 1- or 2-night deposit due 10 days after booking. Cancellation notice must be given 3–7 days prior to arrival.
Credit Cards: All major credit cards accepted.

Check-In/Out: 3 p.m./Noon. Early check-in and late check-out available on request.
Contact: 2525 Ka'anapali Pkwy. Lahaina, HI 96761
(800) 262-8450 or (808) 661-0011
Fax: (808) 667-5978
www.kaanapalibeachhotel.com

KAPALUA BAY HOTEL $$$$$

Overall: ★★★★	Room Quality: A	Value: C	Zone 9

The Kapalua Bay Hotel isn't as highly regarded as its neighbor, the Ritz-Carlton, Kapalua, but it likely deserves to be. This is a world-class facility fronting one of Maui's finest beaches. The hotel exudes an understated elegance that blends perfectly with its natural surroundings. Piano and Hawaiian music are provided nightly at the Lehua Lounge, located below the lobby area. The Kapalua Shops, a mini-mall of some 20 boutiques, is on the premises, and golf aficionados have a choice of three championship golf courses, one of which hosts the prestigious PGA Mercedes Open in January.

SETTING & FACILITIES

Location: Fronting Kapalua Bay in West Maui.
Dining: The Bay Club serves seafood specialties for lunch and dinner. The less formal Gardenia Court offers tasty international fare, including a popular

Friday night seafood buffet and Sunday brunch.
Amenities & Services: Room service, laundry service, daily maid service, tennis courts, children's program, shops, etc.

ACCOMMODATIONS

Rooms: 194. Includes 3 suites; 1 floor designated for non-smoking rooms; 6 rooms for the hearing impaired; 8 wheelchair-accessible rooms.
All Rooms: A/C, cable TV, in-room safe, mini-bar, lanai, 3 phones, hair dryer, etc.
Some Rooms: Washer and dryer, Jacuzzi, second bedroom.
Comfort & Decor: Spacious, over-sized rooms with natural colors and marble accents. Large private lanai.

RATES, RESERVATIONS, & RESTRICTIONS

Family Plan: Children age 17 and under stay free if staying with parents and using existing bedding.
Deposit: 1-night credit card guarantee (5-night deposit during the Christmas holidays). Cancellation notice must be given 72 hours prior to arrival for refund.
Credit Cards: All major credit cards accepted except Discover.
Check-In/Out: 3 p.m./Noon. Early check-in and late check-out available on request.
Contact: One Bay Dr.
Kapalua, HI 96761
(800) 367-8000 or (808) 669-5656
Fax: (808) 669-4690
www.kapaluabayhotel.com

KEA LANI HOTEL, SUITES & VILLAS			$$$$$
Overall: ★★★★½	Room Quality: A	Value: B	Zone 8

This is simply a gorgeous all-suite hotel that features an extensive menu of in-room amenities, including a complete home entertainment system. The hotel's open-air, Mediterranean-style architecture evokes a quaint village feel. Children ages 5–12 can participate in Keiki Lani, the hotel's year-round children's program, which features hula and lei making lessons and swimming. The hotel has two marvelous swimming lagoons that are con-nected by a 140-foot water slide and swim-up beverage bar. One of the more unique features on the property is the Organic Garden, which fea-tures more than 150 varieties of produce, including 18 varieties of rare exotic fruits. (These garden items are utilized in the hotel's restaurants; inquire about a guided garden tour.) Readers of *Condé Nast Traveler* voted the Kea Lani one of the top five resorts in the Pacific region.

SETTING & FACILITIES

Location: At Wailea Resort.
Dining: Nick's Fishmarket Maui is one of the island's favorite seafood restau-rants. Caffe Ciao serves Italian cuisine in a garden setting.
Amenities & Services: Spa and fit-ness center, 3 swimming pools, tennis, golf, children's program, indoor/out-door meeting and conference space, etc.

ACCOMMODATIONS

Rooms: 450. All suites. Includes 37 oceanfront villas; 201 non-smoking suites; 11 suites for the disabled.
All Rooms: A/C, cable TV, stereo entertainment center (with CD player, VCR, and laser disc player), private lanai, phone, etc.
Some Rooms: Private pool, gourmet kitchen, sun deck, BBQ grill, extra BR.

Comfort & Decor: Very spacious, with separate bedroom and living room, exceptionally clean. Soft tropical colors provide cheerful ambience. Luxurious furnishings with Island-themed artworks. Large European marble bathroom and soaking tub and twin pedestal sinks.

RATES, RESERVATIONS, & RESTRICTIONS

Deposit: 2-night deposit due within 14 days after booking. Cancellation notice must be given 72 hours prior to arrival for refund.
Credit Cards: All major credit cards accepted.
Check-In/Out: 4 p.m./Noon. Early check-in and late check-out available on request.
Contact: 4100 Wailea Alanui Wailea, HI 96753
(800) 882-4100 or (808) 875-4100
Fax: (808) 875-1200
www.kealani.com

LAHAINA INN $

Overall: ★★★★	Room Quality: B	Value: B+	Zone 9

Proof that good things can come in small packages. Rick Ralston, founder and owner of the popular Crazy Shirts stores, is also a collector of fine antiques and other nostalgic things. It was Ralston who lovingly restored the dozen rooms of his historic inn; pieces from his personal collection furnish each individually decorated room. Because of the value of the furnishings, children under the age of 15 are not allowed at this inn. A complimentary Continental breakfast is served at the end of the hall every morning. The inn's close proximity to Front Street is a "good news, bad news" situation: It's good to be close to the action (Lahaina is the most bustling town on this side of the island), but it also tends to get pretty noisy. Also, keep in mind that there are no television sets at the inn. Our guess is, the people who will most appreciate this type of setting are the type of folks who won't miss the boob tube for a second.

SETTING & FACILITIES

Location: In the heart of Lahaina.
Dining: David Paul's Lahaina Grill, one of the best restaurants on Maui, serves New American cuisine.
Amenities & Services: Parking ($5 per day).

ACCOMMODATIONS

Rooms: 12. Includes 3 suites. All are non-smoking rooms (smoking permitted on lanais).
All Rooms: A/C, ceiling fans, daily Continental breakfast, etc.
Some Rooms: Lanai, full bath and shower, king-size bed.
Comfort & Decor: Rooms are smallish, but well maintained and clean. Antique furnishings include restored brass and wood beds, period wall decorations, and wood armoires. Dimly lit.

RATES, RESERVATIONS, & RESTRICTIONS

Deposit: 1-night deposit required. Cancellation notice must be given 10 days prior to arrival for refund.
Credit Cards: All major credit cards accepted except Discover.
Check-In/Out: 3 p.m./11 a.m. Late check-out (until noon) on request.

Contact: 127 Lahainaluna Rd.
Lahaina, HI 96761
(800) 669-3444 or (808) 661-0577
Fax: (808) 667-9480
inntown@lahainainn.com
www.lahainainn.com

MAUI MARRIOTT RESORT $$$$

Overall: ★★★★	Room Quality: A	Value: C	Zone 9

This is a full-service resort with a casual, family-oriented atmosphere and friendly service. Waterfalls, koi ponds, and tall coconut palms adorn the attractive grounds. A year-round children's program is available, as are Hawaiian craft lessons and the full menu of recreational sports and activities. The Marriott also has one of the island's best luaus (held nightly on the beach). A mini-mall with 20 shops is located on the premises.

SETTING & FACILITIES

Location: On Ka'anapali Beach.
Dining: The Moana Terrace serves American fare for breakfast and dinner. Nikko offers traditional Japanese cuisine.
Amenities & Services: Room service (until 10 p.m.), valet and self-parking ($7 per day), nightly luau (except Monday), 2 swimming pools, 2 Jacuzzis, fitness center, coin-operated laundry service, etc.

ACCOMMODATIONS

Rooms: 720. Includes 19 suites; 14 rooms for the disabled. Non-smoking rooms available.
All Rooms: A/C, cable TV, lanai, phone, refrigerator, in-room safe, coffeemaker.
Some Rooms: Sofa sleeper, larger lanai, separate dressing area.
Comfort & Decor: Spacious rooms adorned with tasteful furnishings and Island artwork. Soft pastel colors add to overall pleasant ambience.

RATES, RESERVATIONS, & RESTRICTIONS

Family Plan: Children age 17 and under stay free if staying with parents and using existing bedding. Maximum of 2 adults/2 children per room.
Deposit: Credit card guarantee. Cancellation notice must be given 72 hours prior to arrival for refund.
Credit Cards: All major credit cards accepted.

Check-In/Out: 3 p.m./Noon. Early check-in and late check-out available on request (no guarantees).
Contact: 100 Nohea Kai Dr.
Lahaina, HI 96761
(800) 763-1333 or (808) 667-1200
Fax: (808) 667-8300
www.marriott.com/marriott/HNMHI

MAUI PRINCE HOTEL $$$$

| Overall: ★★★★ | Room Quality: B+ | Value: C | Zone 8 |

Situated on the cool slopes of Mount Haleakala and fronting lovely Maluaka Beach, this 1,800-acre resort is an isolated haven south of the Wailea Resort. The picturesque grounds offer a lovely courtyard with a colorful koi pond and waterfall, all of which adds to the resort's tranquil, understated atmosphere. All rooms have views of the ocean as well as the neighboring islands of Molokai, Lanai, and Kahoolawe. (The mountain views aren't shabby, either: Haleakala provides a breathtaking backdrop.) The service level here is impeccable. Snorkeling and scuba diving are among the outdoor activities available; there are six tennis courts at the nearby Makena Tennis Club, and two championship golf courses. A hula show is presented at the oceanfront Molokini Lounge.

SETTING & FACILITIES

Location: In Makena in south Maui.
Dining: The Prince Court features Continental and Island cuisine, while Hakone offers traditional Japanese fare and a sushi bar.

Amenities & Services: Room service, welcome baskets upon arrival, laundry service, fitness center, parking, children's program, etc.

ACCOMMODATIONS

Rooms: 300. Includes 57 suites; 5–10 rooms for the disabled. Non-smoking rooms available.
All Rooms: A/C, cable TV, lanai, in-room safe, phone, hair dryer, iron and ironing board, bottled water, coffee-

maker, etc.
Some Rooms: Second bedroom.
Comfort & Decor: Spacious and clean, simple decor with creamy pastel tones, Island-themed artworks, in a modern, casual setting.

RATES, RESERVATIONS, & RESTRICTIONS

Family Plan: Children age 12 and under stay free if staying with parents and using existing bedding. $40 charge per extra person.
Deposit: 1-night deposit required. Cancellation notice must be given 72 hours prior to arrival for refund.
Credit Cards: All major credit card accepted.

Check-In/Out: 3 p.m./Noon. Early check-in and late check-out available on request.
Contact: 5400 Makena Alanui Kihei, HI 96753
(800) 321-6248 or (808) 874-1111
Fax: (808) 879-8763
www.princehawaii.com

OUTRIGGER WAILEA RESORT $$$$

Overall: ★★★★	Room Quality: A	Value: B	Zone 8

Although it was opened as the Maui Inter-Continental Resort and for a short time known as the Aston Wailea Resort, Outrigger took over operations of this oceanfront resort in early 1999. We were impressed with the level of service and friendly hospitality. The resort's predominately low-rise building design is a comfortable fit on 22 oceanfront acres. Lei-making classes and craft demonstrations are offered regularly, and Hawaiian entertainment is provided nightly. Arcade games, billiards, darts, and air hockey are among the diversions offered at Pa'ani, a game bar. A shuttle provides transportation to the Maui Ocean Center, one of the island's newer visitor attractions. Overall, the Outrigger Wailea is a pleasant gem suitable for families and couples alike.

SETTING & FACILITIES

Location: At Wailea Resort.
Dining: Lea's is well regarded for its sumptuous seafood specialties. The poolside Hula Moons features lighter fare and popular Island favorites.
Amenities & Services: Laundry service, children's program, parking, business facilities, game room, etc.

ACCOMMODATIONS

Rooms: 516. Includes 46 suites; 446 non-smoking rooms; 10 rooms for the disabled.
All Rooms: A/C, cable TV, phone, in-room safe, refrigerator, coffeemaker, hair dryer, iron and ironing board, etc.

Some Rooms: Robes.
Comfort & Decor: Very spacious, clean, well appointed, with sunny pastels, attractive tropical furnishings, artwork, and private lanai.

RATES, RESERVATIONS, & RESTRICTIONS

Family Plan: Children age 12 and under stay free if staying with parents and using existing bedding.
Deposit: 1-night deposit required. Cancellation notice must be given 72 hours prior to arrival for refund.
Credit Cards: All major credit cards accepted.

Check-In/Out: 3 p.m./11 a.m. Early check-in and late check-out available on request.
Contact: 3700 Alanui
Wailea, HI 96753
(800) 688-7444 or (808) 879-1922
Fax: (808) 874-8331
www.outrigger.com

RENAISSANCE WAILEA BEACH RESORT $$$$

| Overall: ★★★★ | Room Quality: A | Value: C | Zone 8 |

Another jewel property in Wailea. Opened in 1978 as the Stouffer Wailea Beach Resort, this 15-acre property received a dramatic facelift in 1990. The elegant main lobby is made of marble and limestone and features hand-blown Italian glass fixtures and a grand stairway. Outside, the landscape is dotted with waterfalls and tropical flora. Golfers can choose from a trio of championship courses in Wailea, and tennis action is readily available at the 11-court Wailea Tennis Center. The Renaissance also offers a recreational rarity among Hawaii resorts: half-court basketball. In terms of ambience and scenery, enjoy late-afternoon cocktails at the Sunset Terrace.

SETTING & FACILITIES

Location: At Wailea Resort.
Dining: The Palm Court features Mediterranean cuisine and buffets for dinner. Hana Gion is an intimate Japanese eatery.
Amenities & Services: Room service, laundry service, parking, fitness center, etc.

ACCOMMODATIONS

Rooms: 347. Includes 12 suites. Rooms for the disabled and non-smoking rooms available.
All Rooms: A/C, cable TV, VCR, private balcony, phone, mini-refrigerator, hair dryer, coffeemaker, etc.

Comfort & Decor: Spacious and clean, light colors and subtle tropical touches add to bright atmosphere. Island-themed furnishings and artworks.

RATES, RESERVATIONS, & RESTRICTIONS

Family Plan: Children age 17 and under stay free if staying with parents and using existing bedding.
Deposit: 1-night deposit due within 10 days of booking. 72-hour cancellation notice required for refund.

Credit Cards: All major credit cards accepted.
Check-In/Out: 3 p.m./Noon. Early check-in and late check-out available on request.

Contact: 3550 Wailea Alanui
Wailea, HI 96753
(800) 992-4532 or (808) 879-4900

Fax: (808) 874-5370
www.renaissancehotels.com

RITZ-CARLTON, KAPALUA $$$$

Overall: ★★★★★	Room Quality: A+	Value: B+	Zone 9

A perennial AAA Five Diamond Award recipient, and it's not hard to understand why. Everything here, from the service to guest rooms to dining, is impeccable. The atmosphere here is one of quiet, blissful elegance. Set on 50 acres, the Ritz features two six-story wings that contour unobtrusively to the area's rolling terrain. Public areas are enhanced by 18th- and 19th-century artworks as well as paintings and ceramics created by gifted local artists. Recently added to the property is a 19,200-square-foot pavilion, located adjacent to the hotel's entrance. The Ritz Kids program allows children to learn about Maui's culture, nature, art, and ecology. Evening entertainment is provided at the Terrace Restaurant and Lobby Lounge. Kapalua Resort has a trio of championship golf courses and ten tennis courts. The Ritz hosts several notable annual events, including the PGA Mercedes Championships (January), Celebration of the Arts (April), Kapalua Wine & Food Symposium (usually July), and the Earth Maui Nature Summit (September). The Ritz-Carlton, Kapalua, is currently the world's only Audubon Heritage Cooperative Sanctuary Resort Hotel, meaning it has met Audubon's standards for championing land conservation, wildlife protection, and cultural and natural resource preservation.

SETTING & FACILITIES

Location: At Kapalua Resort in West Maui.
Dining: The stately Anuenue Room features Hawaiian-Provençal cuisine, focusing on fresh Island flavors. The Terrace Restaurant serves a popular buffet for breakfast and fresh local seafood for dinner. Also serves a Friday night seafood buffet and Sunday night Italian buffet. There is also a trendy sushi bar located near the lobby.
Amenities & Services: 24-hour room service, twice-daily maid service, laundry service, fitness center, spa treatments, multi-level swimming pool, hydrotherapy pools, business facilities, children's program, golf, tennis, ocean activities, etc.

ACCOMMODATIONS

Rooms: 548. Includes 58 suites. ADA-approved rooms and non-smoking rooms available.
All Rooms: A/C, cable TV with pay movies, 3 phones, lanai, in-room safe, honor bar, hair dryer, data port, bathrobes, etc.
Some Rooms: Personal concierge service, complimentary food and beverages.

Comfort & Decor: Oversized rooms, exceptionally clean and well maintained. Warm colors and tropical-inspired furnishings with Hawaiian artworks. Large private lanai (80% of all guest rooms have ocean views).

RATES, RESERVATIONS, & RESTRICTIONS

Deposit: No policy given. Cancel reservations 7 days prior to scheduled arrival for refund.
Credit Cards: All major credit cards accepted.
Check-In/Out: 3 p.m./Noon. Early check-in and late check-out available on request (no guarantees).
Contact: One Ritz-Carlton Dr. Kapalua, HI 96761
(800) 241-3333 or (808) 669-6200
Fax: (808) 669-2028
www.ritzcarlton.com

SHERATON MAUI			$$$$$
Overall: ★★★★	Room Quality: A	Value: C	Zone 9

After an extensive renovation, the Sheraton Maui, a very attractive full-service resort set on 23 acres, is back in business. Its elevated ground lobby opens to a wide panorama of the Pacific Ocean and a spectacular 147-foot-long ocean-front swimming lagoon (one of the resort's recently added amenities). The resort is built along the side of Black Rock, a striking natural rock formation. Children ages 5–12 can participate in the complimentary Keiki Aloha Club (available during the summer), which includes lei-making and hula lessons, beach activities, and field trips to historic sites. Locals regard Black Rock as one of the best snorkeling areas on Maui.

SETTING & FACILITIES

Location: On Ka'anapali Beach.
Dining: The Coral Reef serves seafood specialties. Teppan Yaki Dan offers a blend of European and Pacific cuisines (chefs prepare meals while you watch).

Amenities & Services: Swimming pool, room service, laundry facilities, parking ($5 per day), fitness center, spa, children's program (summer), etc.

ACCOMMODATIONS

Rooms: 510. Includes 46 suites; 15 rooms for the disabled. Non-smoking rooms available.
All Rooms: A/C, cable TV, phone, in-room safe, mini-refrigerator, coffeemaker, iron and ironing board, hair dryer, etc.

Some Rooms: Microwave, second TV, parlor.
Comfort & Decor: Spacious, clean, well maintained. Custom bedspreads and tropical furnishings. Hawaiian artworks adorn wall. Large lanai.

RATES, RESERVATIONS, & RESTRICTIONS

Family Plan: Children age 17 and under stay free if staying with parents and using existing bedding.
Deposit: 1-night deposit due 10 days after booking. Cancellation notice must be given 72 hours prior to arrival for refund.
Credit Cards: All major credit cards accepted.

Check-In/Out: 3 p.m./Noon. Early check-in and late check-out available on request.
Contact: 2605 Ka'anapali Pkwy. Lahaina, HI 96761
(800) 782-9488 or (808) 661-0031
Fax: (808) 661-0458
www.sheraton-maui.com

WESTIN MAUI	$$$$$

Overall: ★★★★	Room Quality: A	Value: C+	Zone 9

Elegant resort with Asian influences and works of art found throughout the property. The most notable physical feature here is the resort's 87,000-square-foot aquatic playground. There are five pools in all, three joined together by a pair of water slides, and two divided by a swim-through grotto with twin waterfalls and a hidden Jacuzzi. One of the pools is designated "adults only" and features a swim-up bar. The Westin Kids Club provides supervised fun and games for the *keiki*. Island-style entertainment is provided nightly. For night owls, a side benefit of staying in Ka'anapali is that it's just a five-minute drive away from Lahaina, where most of West Maui's after-dark action takes place.

SETTING & FACILITIES

Location: On Ka'anapali Beach.
Dining: The Villa specializes in fresh seafood selections as well as Hawaii regional cuisine. Sen Ju features traditional Japanese delicacies.

Amenities & Services: Room service, laundry/valet service, parking, business center, health club, children's program, etc.

ACCOMMODATIONS

Rooms: 713. Includes 28 suites; 14 rooms for the disabled. Non-smoking rooms available.
All Rooms: A/C, cable TV, phone, balcony, mini-bar, in-room safe, coffeemaker, iron and ironing board, hair dryer, etc.

Some Rooms: Sofabed in living room, upgraded amenities.
Comfort & Decor: Spacious and clean rooms. Light colors, comfortable furnishings, mostly modern setting. The ambience is elegant without being stuffy.

RATES, RESERVATIONS, & RESTRICTIONS

Family Plan: Children age 17 and under stay free if staying with parents and using existing bedding. Maximum of 4 guests per room.
Deposit: 2-night deposit due within 15 days after booking. 72-hour cancellation notice required for refund.
Credit Cards: All major credit cards accepted.

Check-In/Out: 3 p.m./Noon. Early check-in and late check-out on availability.
Contact: 2365 Ka'anapali Pkwy. Lahaina, HI 96761
(800) 937-8461 or (808) 667-2525
Fax: (808) 661-5831
www.westin.com

THE BIG ISLAND

ASTON KEAUHOU BEACH RESORT $$$

Overall: ★★★★	Room Quality: B+	Value: C+	Zone 11

This ten-acre oceanfront property reopened in March 1999 after an extensive $15 million renovation to its guest rooms and public areas. It remains a favorite for *kama'aina* visiting from the other islands. We feel visitors will like this place too, especially since local chef Sam Choy now oversees the property's food and beverage operations. (The popular Choy hosts his own cooking show on local TV.) The resort also features several prominent historic Hawaiian sites, including several *heiau* and a replica of King Kalakaua's private vacation cottage. Children are welcome to explore several on-site tidal pools, while adults can enjoy snorkeling, scuba diving, or tennis on one of six courts. Sam Choy's Beach Club offers live music and dancing nightly.

SETTING & FACILITIES

Location: Oceanfront near Kahalu'u Bay in Kailua-Kona.
Dining: Sam Choy's Keauhou features Island-inspired cuisine by one of the state's most famous chefs.

Amenities & Services: Daily maid service, fitness center, activities and travel desks, parking, swimming pool, sundry shop, etc.

ACCOMMODATIONS

Rooms: 311. Includes 6 suites; 4 floors with non-smoking rooms; 14 rooms for the disabled.
All Rooms: A/C, cable TV, private lanai, clock radio, phone, etc. Crib, hair dryer, iron and ironing board, refrigera-

tor available on request.
Some Rooms: Ceiling fans, bathtub.
Comfort & Decor: Spacious, very clean, with earthy tones, Hawaiian-style decor, and attractive wicker furnishings.

RATES, RESERVATIONS, & RESTRICTIONS

Family Plan: Children age 17 and under stay free if staying with parents and using existing bedding.
Deposit: 1-night deposit due 10 days after booking. Cancellation notice must be given 72 hours prior to arrival for refund.
Credit Cards: All major credit cards accepted.

Check-In/Out: 3 p.m./Noon. Early check-in and late check-out based on availability.
Contact: 75-7540 Ali'i Dr.
Kailua-Kona, HI 96740
(800) 922-7866 or (808) 322-3441
Fax: (808) 322-3117
www.aston-hotels.com

FOUR SEASONS RESORT HUALALAI $$$$$

Overall: ★★★★★	Room Quality: A+	Value: C+	Zone 11

One of the Big Island's newest resorts, this is less a hotel than a hideaway. Sitting on a dramatic landscape formed by 19th-century eruptions from Hualalai Volcano, this AAA Five Diamond property features 36 low-rise ocean-view bungalows strategically organized to ensure quiet and privacy. Hawaiian artworks—some dating back to the 18th century—are displayed throughout the resort. Located below the lobby is one of our favorite features at Hualalai: the Ka'upulehu Cultural Center, which presents Hawaii's culture and history through artworks, exhibits, video and audio recordings, and hands-on educational programs (ask the host at the center for an updated schedule). Enjoy snorkeling in the King's Pond, a 2.5-million-gallon black lava anchialine pool inspired by the traditional fishponds of old Hawaii. The pond was sculpted from an ancient lava flow and is fed by natural artesian springs as well as water from the sea. More than 3,500 tropical fish are said to inhabit the pond.

SETTING & FACILITIES

Location: At Ka'upulehu on the Kohala Coast.
Dining: Pahu i'a serves international and local specialties.
Amenities & Services: Valet and laundry service, self-serve washer and dryer, valet and self-parking, concierge service, Hawaiian Cultural Center, golf, tennis, 3 swimming pools, children's program, etc.

ACCOMMODATIONS

Rooms: 243. Includes 16 suites; 14 rooms for the disabled. Most rooms are designated non-smoking.
All Rooms: A/C, color TV, refrigerated private bar, phone, lanai, in-room safe, walk-in closets, fax line, etc.
Comfort & Decor: Very spacious, with walk-in closets, large bathroom with oversized tub and separate shower. Bathroom windows look into a private garden. Room decor set in natural, earthy tones with a stylish tropical motif.

RATES, RESERVATIONS, & RESTRICTIONS

Deposit: 1-night deposit due 7 days after booking. Cancellation notice must be given 14 days prior to arrival Jan. 3–April 30, and 7 days prior to arrival May 1–Dec. 18. Special deposit policy in effect during the Christmas holidays.
Credit Cards: All major credit cards accepted.

Check-In/Out: 3 p.m./Noon. Early check-in and late check-out available on request.
Contact: P.O. Box 1269 Kailua-Kona, HI 96745
(888) 340-5662 or (808) 325-8000
Fax: (800) 325-8100
www.fourseasons.com

HAPUNA BEACH PRINCE HOTEL $$$$$

Overall: ★★★★½	Room Quality: A	Value: C	Zone 11

Opened in 1994, the Hapuna Beach Prince Hotel is located next to its sister property, the Mauna Kea Beach Hotel. The layout of the property includes a large number of suites inter-mixed with guest rooms in single-loaded buildings so that every room and suite has ocean and coastal views. Built with a contemporary Hawaiian-style design, the hotel includes an open foyer and lobby that provide a sweeping view of Hapuna Beach, regarded as one of the best beaches in Hawaii. The fourth level of the hotel includes an indoor recreation area equipped with pool tables, table tennis, shuffleboard, foosball, board games, and a fully stocked bar (guests must be at least 21 years of age). Ocean activities include swimming, snorkeling, scuba diving, sailing, and whale-watching (in season). Each Friday, the hotel holds "Paniolo Night," a country hoedown with food and live entertainment ($60 per adult, $30 for children ages 5–12).

SETTING & FACILITIES

Location: On the Big Island's Kohala Coast.
Dining: Coast Grille specializes in fresh Island seafood. Hakone serves traditional Japanese fare. The Ocean Terrace offers a wide menu of breakfast selections, including an extensive buffet.
Amenities & Services: Freshwater pool, Jacuzzi, welcome amenities, golf, water sports, beauty salon, game room, business services, etc.

ACCOMMODATIONS

Rooms: 350. Includes 36 luxury suites; 2 floors designated for non-smoking; 10 rooms for the disabled.
All Rooms: A/C, cable TV, phone, lanai, etc.
Some Rooms: Sitting rooms, upgraded amenities.

Comfort & Decor: Spacious, attractive, and very clean. All rooms have ocean views. Soft tropical colors, Island-accented furnishings and artwork.

RATES, RESERVATIONS, & RESTRICTIONS

Family Plan: Children age 17 and under stay free if staying with parents and using existing bedding. Maximum 2 adults/2 children or 3 adults per room.
Deposit: 1-night deposit due 15 days after booking. Cancellation notice must be given 14 days prior to arrival for refund.
Credit Cards: All major credit cards accepted except Discover.
Check-In/Out: 3 p.m./Noon. Early check-in and late check-out available on request.
Contact: 62-100 Kauna'oa Dr. Kohala Coast, HI 96743
(800) 882-6060 or (808) 880-1111
Fax: (808) 880-3200
www.hapunabeachprincehotel.com

HAWAII NANILOA RESORT $$

Overall: ★★★★	Room Quality: B+	Value: B	Zone 12

At first glance, this bayside hotel doesn't look like much. The exterior is rather drab and unattractive, and even the bay isn't picturesque compared to other Island vistas. The lobby, on the other hand, is airy and adorned in pleasant pastels. What we like best about the Naniloa is its attentive service and a surprisingly large menu of facilities. We never imagined, for example, that the Naniloa has an excellent fitness center and spa featuring exercise equipment, an oceanfront aerobics studio, whirlpool, sauna, and steam room (body massages are also available). The swimming pool is large and inviting. All in all, the Naniloa is a good-value hotel that certainly rivals the neighboring Hilo Hawaiian Hotel as the premier Hilo resort. The hotel is also the official headquarters of the Merrie Monarch Festival, the world's most prestigious hula competition.

SETTING & FACILITIES

Location: Fronting Hilo Bay.
Dining: Continental fare is served at the Sandalwood Room, while Ting Hao Seafood Restaurant offers sumptuous Chinese cuisine.
Amenities & Services: Courtesy airport transfer service, laundry service, gift and sundry shop, ice machine, safety deposit box (at front desk), etc.

ACCOMMODATIONS

Rooms: 325. Includes 20 suites; 3 floors with non-smoking rooms; 1 floor for the disabled.
All Rooms: A/C, cable TV with pay movies, phones, etc.
Some Rooms: Kitchen.
Comfort & Decor: Rooms small to medium, mostly clean, with attractive Island decor and tasteful furnishings.

RATES, RESERVATIONS, & RESTRICTIONS

Family Plan: Children age 12 and under stay free if staying with parents and using existing bedding.
Deposit: 1-night deposit due within 10 days of confirmation. Cancellation notice must be given 72 hours prior to arrival for refund.
Credit Cards: All major credit cards accepted except Discover.

Check-In/Out: 3 p.m./Noon. Early check-in and late check-out available on request.
Contact: 93 Banyan Dr.
Hilo, HI 96720
(800) 367-5360 or (808) 969-3333
Fax: (808) 969-3333
www.planet-hawaii/sand/naniloa

HILO HAWAIIAN HOTEL $$

Overall: ★★★½	Room Quality: B+	Value: C+	Zone 12

The Hilo Hawaiian doesn't qualify as a luxury resort, but it still rates as one of the best hotels in Hilo. Its sloping arc design blends well with its surroundings, including Hilo Bay. Built in 1974 and renovated in 1992, the hotel has attractive rooms, a friendly staff, and a popular seafood buffet (it's even a favorite among locals), but nothing really stands out as extraordinary. This is a good choice for travelers who plan to spend most of their time exploring the island and want a comfortable, clean, and affordable place to stay.

SETTING & FACILITIES

Location: At Hilo Bay.
Dining: Queen's Court serves nightly seafood buffets.

Amenities & Services: Free parking, Laundromat.

ACCOMMODATIONS

Rooms: 286. Includes 18 suites; 7 wheelchair-accessible rooms. Half the rooms are designated non-smoking.
All Rooms: A/C, cable TV, refrigerator, phone, etc. Hair dryers and iron/ironing board available upon request.

Some Rooms: Lanai, coffee, tea, miso soup.
Comfort & Decor: Spacious, mostly clean and well maintained. Simple furnishings with a few Island-inspired artworks. Dim lighting.

RATES, RESERVATIONS, & RESTRICTIONS

Family Plan: Children age 17 and under stay free if staying with parents and using existing bedding.
Deposit: 1-night deposit or credit card guarantee within 10 days after booking. 72-hour cancellation notice required for refund.

Credit Cards: All major credit cards accepted.
Check-In/Out: 3 p.m./Noon. Early check-in and late check-out available on request.

Contact: 71 Banyan Dr.
Hilo, HI 96720
(800) 367-5004 or (808) 935-9361

Fax: (808) 961-9642
www.castle-group.com

HILTON WAIKOLOA VILLAGE $$$$$

| Overall: ★★★★½ | Room Quality: A | Value: C | Zone 11 |

Think of this 62-acre resort as an Island-style Disneyland, complete with
boat rides, lush tropical gardens, and encounters with some exotic-but-
friendly creatures (in this case, Atlantic bottlenose dolphins). The Hilton
Waikoloa consists of three separate towers surrounding a beautiful five-
acre lagoon, where the dolphins live and play. You can explore the hotel
via canal boats or Swiss trams or by hoofing it on the mile-long museum
walkway, which is adorned with a multi-million-dollar collection of Asian
and Pacific art. A daily lottery determines which lucky guests can get into
the water and pet the dolphins, learning about these ocean mammals
from a marine specialist. Another property that epitomizes the term "self-
contained resort," the Hilton Waikoloa has something for everyone:
restaurants, beach activities, shops, health spa, children's programs, luaus,
entertainment, golf, tennis, etc. Families with children, in particular, will
love this resort.

SETTING & FACILITIES

Location: In Waikoloa.
Dining: The Palm Terrace offers a wide
range of international specialties. Donatoni's serves fine Italian cuisine. Imari
features traditional Japanese fare. And
the Kamuela Provision Company
serves steak and seafood.
Amenities & Services: Room service, laundry service, valet parking,
business center, health spa, children's
program, Dolphin Encounter program,
etc.

ACCOMMODATIONS

Rooms: 1,241. Includes 57 suites.
Rooms for the disabled and non-
smoking rooms available.
All Rooms: A/C, cable TV, lanai,
phone, honor bar, refrigerator, coffeemaker, in-room safe, hair dryer, iron
and ironing board, etc.
Some Rooms: Second bedroom,
upgraded amenities.
Comfort & Decor: Spacious (standard rooms are 530 square feet), clean,
bright atmosphere. Elegant furnishings
and tasteful Hawaiian artworks.

RATES, RESERVATIONS, & RESTRICTIONS

Family Plan: Children age 17 and
under stay free if staying with parents
and using existing bedding.
Deposit: 1- or 2-night deposit due at
least 10 days before arrival. Cancellation notice must be given 72 hours
prior to arrival for refund.

Credit Cards: All major credit cards accepted.
Check-In/Out: 3 p.m./Noon. Early check-in and late check-out available on request (no guarantees).
Contact: 425 Waikoloa Beach Dr.

Waikoloa, HI 96738
(800) 445-8667 or (808) 886-1234
Fax: (808) 886-2900
waikoloa_rooms@hilton.com
www.hilton.com/hawaii/waikoloa

KING KAMEHAMEHA'S KONA BEACH HOTEL $$$

Overall: ★★★½	Room Quality: B	Value: B+	Zone 11

We've all heard of hotels that claim to treat their guests like royalty. Well, the King Kamehameha's Kona Beach Hotel sits next to a historic grounds once occupied *by* royalty! In old Hawaii, high-ranking *ali'i* used this site as a summer retreat. Kamehameha the Great himself, in fact, made this the final site for his royal residence nearly two centuries ago. The focal point of this historic area is the Ahu'ena *heiau,* which dates back to the 15th century and was used for human sacrifices. One of the hotel's major pluses is its central location, as it is within easy walking distance to restaurants, shops, and a small but lovely white-sand beach. The hotel is also popular among *kama'aina* visiting from other islands.

SETTING & FACILITIES

Location: In the heart of Kailua-Kona.
Dining: The Kona Beach Restaurant serves breakfast and dinner buffets, and its popular Sunday champagne brunch.

Amenities & Services: Free parking, room service, laundry facilities, swimming pool, Jacuzzi, tennis, etc.

ACCOMMODATIONS

Rooms: 457. Includes 12 suites; 10 rooms for the disabled. Non-smoking rooms available.
All Rooms: A/C, cable TV, mini-refrigerator, phone, in-room safe, coffee-maker, etc. Hair dryer, iron/ironing

board available upon request.
Some Rooms: Refrigerator, pay movies.
Comfort & Decor: Medium-sized rooms, clean. Subdued colors with simple furnishings and Hawaiian artworks.

RATES, RESERVATIONS, & RESTRICTIONS

Deposit: Credit card guarantee or 1-night deposit required. Cancellation notice must be given 72 hours prior to arrival for refund.
Credit Cards: All major credit cards accepted.
Check-In/Out: 3 p.m./Noon. Early

check-in and late check-out (up to 1 p.m.) available on request.
Contact: 75-5660 Palani Rd.
Kailua-Kona, HI 96740
(800) 367-6060 or (808) 329-2911
Fax: (808) 923-2566
www.pacificbeachhotel.com

KONA VILLAGE RESORT $$$$$

Overall: ★★★★½	Room Quality: A	Value: C	Zone 11

The ultimate escape. Receives our vote as the most unique resort in Hawaii. Each "room" is actually a thatched-roof bungalow that comes with king-sized beds, a mini-refrigerator, a lanai, and a few other choice amenities. However, there are no TV sets, radios, phones, or air-conditioning. In this case, we think it's addition by subtraction. Upon your arrival, you're greeted with a fresh flower lei and a cool glass of the resort's secret rum punch. Then you're set for a truly fabulous experience that you won't find anywhere else in the Islands. Beach activities, tennis, and a weekly luau are among the recreational options here. *Note:* There are no locks on the doors of the bungalows, as the resort is isolated from the rest of the world by a vast lava field, and only guests and staff members are allowed past the entry gate. We haven't heard of any thefts, but if the idea of no locks makes you squeamish, we suggest you leave your valuables at home.

SETTING & FACILITIES

Location: In Ka'upulehu, 14 miles north of Kailua-Kona.
Dining: Hale Moana serves a wide variety of international and American favorites, while the more formal Hale Samoa specializes in Pacific Rim cuisine.
Amenities & Services: Fitness center, beach facilities, tennis, transportation to and from airport, etc.

ACCOMMODATIONS

Rooms: 125 hales. 8 rooms for the disabled. Smoking permitted in all hales.
All Rooms: Ceiling fan, lanai, mini-refrigerator, hair dryer, in-room safe, coffeemaker, etc. No A/C, TV, or phone.
Some Rooms: Private whirlpool spa.

Comfort & Decor: Spacious, with high ceilings; furnishings have a distinct tropical motif. Ambience colored in rich earth tones and tasteful Island-themed art.

RATES, RESERVATIONS, & RESTRICTIONS

Family Plan: Children age 5 and under stay free.
Deposit: 2-night deposit due within 3 weeks of booking. Cancellation notice must be given 14 days prior to arrival for refund (60 days for the Easter holiday, 90 days for the Christmas holiday).
Credit Cards: All major credit cards accepted except Discover.

Check-In/Out: 3 p.m./Noon. Hospitality room available for early arrivals and late departures.
Contact: P.O. Box 1299 Kailua-Kona, HI 96745
(800) 367-5290 or (808) 325-5555
Fax: (808) 325-5124
kvr@aloha.net
www.konavillage.com

MAUNA KEA BEACH HOTEL $$$$$

| Overall: ★★★★½ | Room Quality: A | Value: C | Zone 11 |

The "Grand Dame" of the Kohala Coast. While it's one of the older resorts on the Big Island—it opened in 1965—the Mauna Kea remains a perennial favorite. (We've met some older guests who've been coming here every year since their honeymoon!) We love the hotel's open-air architectural design, which adds to the ambience of complete serenity and luxurious comfort. Longtime patrons were concerned when the hotel closed for renovations in 1994, but it reopened in late 1995 and has lost little of its familiar charm and graciousness. The hotel doesn't neglect visitors with a thirst for sport: Golfers have their choice of the Mauna Kea Golf Course or the Hapuna Golf Course (both are award winners), while tennis players can serve and volley at the oceanside Tennis Park, which features 13 Plexipave courts. The Mauna Kea even has its own stables, located 12 miles from the hotel, offering scenic trail rides across Parker Ranch uplands. For fans of the culinary arts, the hotel hosts the annual Winter Wine Escape, a three-day food and wine extravaganza held in November.

SETTING & FACILITIES

Location: On the Big Island's Kohala Coast.
Dining: The Batik features classical Provence-inspired European cuisine. The Pavilion offers Italian and Pacific Rim cuisine. The Terrace/Copper Bar serves steaks and fresh seafood.
Amenities & Services: Swimming pool, Jacuzzi, fitness center, maid service, golf, tennis, horseback riding, meeting facilities, beauty salon, children's program, etc.

ACCOMMODATIONS

Rooms: 310. Includes 10 suites; 10 rooms for the disabled. No non-smoking rooms are designated.
All Rooms: A/C, cable TV, VCR, private lanai, phone, clock radio, coffeemaker, etc.
Some Rooms: 2 full baths, sitting room, 2 TVs.
Comfort & Decor: Very spacious, exceptionally clean. Classy tropical adornments include rattan furnishings. Original watercolors are among the Island-themed artworks.

RATES, RESERVATIONS, & RESTRICTIONS

Deposit: 1-night deposit due within 15 days after booking. Cancellation notice must be given 14 days prior to arrival.
Credit Cards: All major credit cards accepted except Discover.
Check-In/Out: 3 p.m./Noon. Early check-in and late check-out available on request (no guarantees).
Contact: 62-100 Mauna Kea Beach Dr. Kohala Coast, HI 96743
(800) 882-6060 or (808) 882-7222
Fax: (808) 882-5700
mkrres@maunakeabeachhotel.com
www.maunakeabeachhotel.com

MAUNA LANI BAY HOTEL & BUNGALOWS $$$$$

Overall: ★★★★½	Room Quality: A+	Value: C+	Zone 11

A perennial AAA Five Diamond Award winner, the Mauna Lani is one of our favorite resorts in Hawaii. The service is friendly and impeccable, and the ambience is a masterful blend of sophisticated luxury and Island-style hospitality. The hotel's main structure directly faces the ocean and has an atrium-style design with resplendent waterfalls, ponds, trees, and flora. Golf, tennis, and water sports are among the outdoor diversions available here, and kids ages 5–12 can participate in Camp Mauna Lani, which offers lei making, hula dancing, history tours, and other activities. The resort hosts the annual Cuisines of the Sun, a summer food festival spotlighting the cuisines of sunny regions from around the world. In a nod to energy conservation, the Mauna Lani in 1998 became the first hotel in the state to be powered by commercial-scale solar electric energy. If you hit a giant lottery someday, you might consider a stay at one of the resort's five world-class bungalows, each a 4,000-square-foot hideaway with two bedrooms, a private swimming pool, a whirlpool spa, and 24-hour butler service. (Nightly rates are $4,000 for an ocean-view bungalow and $4,550 for an oceanfront bungalow.)

SETTING & FACILITIES

Location: On Big Island's Kohala Coast.

Dining: The signature restaurant is CanoeHouse, serving Pacific Rim cuisine. The poolside Ocean Grill features salads, gourmet pizza, and fresh seafood selections.

Amenities & Services: 24-hour room service, twice-daily maid service, laundry and dry cleaning service, concierge service, meeting and banquet facilities, secretarial assistance, golf, tennis, spa, children's program, etc.

ACCOMMODATIONS

Rooms: 350. Includes 5 exclusive bungalows, 10 suites, 28 villas; 12 rooms for the disabled. Non-smoking rooms available.

All Rooms: A/C, cable TV, VCR, phones, private lanai, honor bar, in-room safe, refrigerator, clock radio, hair dryer, ceiling fan, flashlight, umbrella, robes, slippers, etc.

Some Rooms: Bungalows have private swimming pool, 24-hour butler service, whirlpool spa.

Comfort & Decor: Very spacious, well kept, and clean. Rooms reflect a tropical theme, with tasteful Island decor and furnishings. Cool tones of white and beige. Large private lanai (more than 90% of the rooms have ocean views).

RATES, RESERVATIONS, & RESTRICTIONS

Family Plan: Children age 12 and under stay free with parents if using existing bedding. Maximum of 2 adults/2 children or 3 adults per room.
Deposit: 2-night deposit required to guarantee reservation. Cancellation notice must be given 72 hours prior to arrival for refund (14 days for villas).
Credit Cards: All major credit cards accepted.

Check-In/Out: 3 p.m./Noon. Early check-in and late check-out available on request.
Contact: 68-1400 Mauna Lani Dr. Kohala Coast, HI 96743
(800) 367-2323 or (808) 885-6622
Fax: (808) 885-1484
reservations@maunalani.com
www.maunalani.com

THE ORCHID AT MAUNA LANI $$$$$

Overall: ★★★★½	Room Quality: A	Value: C	Zone 11

The first incarnation of this hotel was the epitome of luxury and opulence. Unfortunately, it lacked the Hawaiian ambience most visitors expect when they arrive in the Islands. Now under the auspices of ITT Sheraton, the Orchid has been enhanced to give it a more Hawaiian "sense of place" yet still deliver a first-class experience. Exquisite Hawaiian quilts and original artworks adorn the walls, and attractive crystal chandeliers hang overhead. Koa is used prominently, from elevator walls to stairway banisters. Other physical features at this U-shaped hotel (divided into two six-story wings) include a 10,000-square-foot swimming pool, a pretty stretch of beach, and scenic jogging and walking trails. Children ages 5–12 can enjoy activities and make new friends at the Keiki Aloha Program, while adults can sign up for a massage or body treatment at the resort's Centre for Well-Being.

SETTING & FACILITIES

Location: On the Kohala Coast.
Dining: The Grill offers fresh seafood specialties, while The Orchid Court serves California cuisine and American favorites. Brown's Beach House serves Island fare with a "California twist."

Amenities & Services: Room service, twice-daily maid service, spa and fitness center, business facilities, concierge desk, swimming pool, golf, tennis, child care, daily newspaper, etc.

ACCOMMODATIONS

Rooms: 539. Including 100 suites; 5 rooms and 1 suite for the disabled. Non-smoking rooms available on designated floors.
All Rooms: A/C, cable TV, lanai, 3 phones, honor bar, robes, etc.
Some Rooms: Living room, extra

bath, pullout sofa.
Comfort & Decor: Very spacious and clean. Large Italian marble bathrooms, Hawaiian-accented decor with neutral tones and handcrafted quilts, private lanai.

RATES, RESERVATIONS, & RESTRICTIONS

Family Plan: Children age 17 and under stay free if staying with parents and using existing bedding.
Deposit: Credit card guarantee only. Cancellation notice must be given 7 days prior to arrival.
Credit Cards: All major credit cards accepted.

Check-In/Out: 3 p.m./Noon. Early check-in and late check-out (up to 2 p.m.) available on request.
Contact: One N. Kaniku Dr. Kohala Coast, HI 96743
(800) 782-9488 or (808) 885-2000
Fax: (808) 885-8886
www.orchid-maunalani.com

OUTRIGGER WAIKOLOA BEACH HOTEL $$$

Overall: ★★★★	Room Quality: B+	Value: C	Zone 11

Formerly the Royal Waikoloan, the resort closed for renovations in mid-1999 and reopened in the fall as the Outrigger Waikoloa Beach Resort. The reconstructed 15-acre property has a new open-air lobby, porte cochere, restaurant, lounge, and meeting rooms. The lobby overlooks the resort's pool and gardens, and cultural sites and an ancient Hawaiian fish-pond add a sense of relevance and history. The King's Shops, one of the better shopping spots in the area, is just across the road, and golfers can play one (or all) of three nearby courses in Waikoloa. In all, this is a good-value hotel, and we expect even bigger and better things now that it's under Outrigger ownership.

SETTING & FACILITIES

Location: 'Anaeho'omalu Bay, on the Big Island's Kohala Coast. 'Anaeho'omalu Bay, a crescent-shaped white-sand beach, is considered an excellent site for snorkelers and scuba divers.

Dining: Hawaii Calls serves breakfast, lunch, and dinner, and offers American cuisine as well as Island favorites.
Amenities & Services: Room service, laundry service, swimming pool, business center, spa and fitness center, tennis, golf, children's program, etc.

ACCOMMODATIONS

Rooms: 523. Includes 21 suites; 11 rooms for the disabled. Non-smoking rooms available.
All Rooms: A/C, cable TV with pay movies, phone, lanai, in-room safe, coffeemaker, hair dryer, refrigerator,

iron and ironing board, robes, etc.
Some Rooms: Oversized rooms, concierge service.
Comfort & Decor: Well appointed, spacious, clean. Elegant rattan furnishings, Island artworks add to tropical flavor.

RATES, RESERVATIONS, & RESTRICTIONS

Family Plan: Children age 17 and under stay free if staying with parents and using existing bedding.
Deposit: 2-night deposit required.

Cancellation notice must be given 72 hours prior to arrival for refund.
Credit Cards: All major credit cards accepted.

Check-In/Out: 3 p.m./Noon. Early check-in and late check-out available on request.
Contact: 69-275 Waikoloa Beach Dr.

Waikoloa, HI 96738
(800) 688-7444 or (808) 886-6789
Fax: (808) 886-7852
www.outrigger.com

UNCLE BILLY'S HILO BAY HOTEL $$

Overall: ★★★	Room Quality: B	Value: C	Zone 12

Sandwiched between the Hilo Hawaiian Hotel and Hawaii Naniloa Resort, this funky bayside property is a good option if you're on a tight budget. The lobby is wonderfully tacky, carrying a thatched longhouse theme. (A sign posted by the registration desk dispenses this advice in the event of a tsunami: "1. Stay calm. 2. Pay hotel bill. 3. Run like hell.") The Hilo offers little in the way of amenities and extra comforts, and we weren't fond of the creaky elevators and narrow hallways, but it does have its own unique charm. More important, the service is friendly, and the hotel offers a convenient, central location in Hilo.

SETTING & FACILITIES

Location: Fronting Hilo Bay.
Dining: Uncle Billy's Restaurant serves American and Island favorites.

Amenities & Services: Parking, laundry facilities.

ACCOMMODATIONS

Rooms: 143. Rooms for the disabled and non-smoking rooms available.
All Rooms: A/C, cable TV, refrigerator, phone, lanai, etc.

Some Rooms: Kitchenette.
Comfort & Decor: Rooms small to medium, sparse amenities and decor, but clean and comfortable. Dimly lit.

RATES, RESERVATIONS, & RESTRICTIONS

Family Plan: Children age 17 and under stay free if staying with parents and using existing bedding.
Deposit: 1-night deposit required. Security deposit of $50 at check-in. Cancellation notice must be given 72 hours prior to arrival for refund.
Credit Cards: All major credit cards accepted.

Check-In/Out: 3 p.m./Noon. Early check-in and late check-out available on request. Check with front desk.
Contact: 87 Banyan Dr.
Hilo, HI 96720
(800) 367-5102 or (808) 935-0861
Fax: (808) 935-7903
resv@unclebilly.com
www.unclebilly.com

UNCLE BILLY'S KONA BAY HOTEL $

Overall: ★★★	Room Quality: B	Value: C	Zone 11

The Kona version of Uncle Billy's Hilo property. The staff is exceptionally friendly and full of the aloha spirit that visitors have come to expect. The hotel features a central courtyard and garden containing a cafe, swimming pool, and bar. Again, this is a good recommendation if you're on a limited budget. If you've got the green to spend on a more upscale resort, however, we recommend going that route.

SETTING & FACILITIES

Location: In the heart of Kailua-Kona.
Dining: Kimo's Family Buffet features breakfast and lunch buffets, offering American, Oriental, and Pacific Rim specialties.
Amenities & Services: Free parking, laundry facilities, business facilities, etc.

ACCOMMODATIONS

Rooms: 143. Includes 5 rooms for the disabled. All rooms permit smoking.
All Rooms: A/C, cable TV, lanai, phone, mini-refrigerator, etc.
Some Rooms: Kitchenette, bath amenities.
Comfort & Decor: Medium-sized rooms, clean and well maintained. Modest decor with simple furnishings and cool ocean colors.

RATES, RESERVATIONS, & RESTRICTIONS

Family Plan: Children age 17 and under stay free if staying with parents and using existing bedding.
Deposit: 1-night deposit required within 7 days of booking. Security deposit of $50 at check-in. Cancellation notice must be given 72 hours prior to arrival for refund.
Credit Cards: All major credit cards accepted.
Check-In/Out: 3 p.m./Noon. Early check-in and late check-out available on request.
Contact: 75-5739 Ali'i Dr. Kailua-Kona, HI 96740
(800) 367-5102 or (808) 329-1393
Fax: (808) 935-7903
resv@unclebilly.com
www.unclebilly.com

VOLCANO HOUSE $$

Overall: ★★★½	Room Quality: B	Value: C	Zone 12

This is, as far as we know, the only hotel situated in a U.S. national park. Perched on the edge of Kilauea Volcano and overlooking its caldera, this quaint hotel is a good place to stay if you plan on spending a lot of time at Hawaii Volcanoes National Park (the hotel is located directly across from the park's visitor center). The reception area features a warm fireplace to comfort you during the chilly nights, and the walls are peppered with nostalgic photographs and paintings of Hawaiian royalty. Be advised that the hotel's lone restaurant fills fast with tourists during the lunch hour.

SETTING & FACILITIES

Location: Inside Hawaii Volcanoes National Park.
Dining: The Ka Ohelo Dining Room specializes in prime rib and other American favorites. Also features breakfast and lunch buffets.
Amenities & Services: Parking, snack shop.

ACCOMMODATIONS

Rooms: 42. Includes 1 wheelchair-accessible room. All rooms permit smoking.
All Rooms: Portable heater, bed, and bath. (No TV.)
Comfort & Decor: Clean, spacious, with koa furnishings, Hawaiian comforters, and tasteful decor.

RATES, RESERVATIONS, & RESTRICTIONS

Family Plan: Children age 12 and under stay free if staying with parents and using existing bedding.
Deposit: 1-night deposit due within 15 days of booking. Cancellation notice must be given 72 hours prior to arrival for refund.
Credit Cards: All major credit cards accepted.
Check-In/Out: 3 p.m./Noon. Early check-in and late check-out available on request.
Contact: P.O. Box 53
Hawaii Volcanoes National Park, HI 96718
(808) 967-7321
Fax: (808) 967-8429

KAUAI

HANALEI BAY RESORT & SUITES $$$

Overall: ★★★★	Room Quality: A	Value: C+	Zone 13

This sprawling 22-acre resort is renowned for its breathtaking ocean views and a sparkling white-sand beach. Carved into a lovely hillside and featuring lush tropical landscaping, the resort offers lots of privacy and solitude, making it ideal for couples. On the other hand, children might find the resort a bit too uneventful. There are eight tennis courts on the premises, and a pair of world-class golf courses are located next to the resort.

SETTING & FACILITIES

Location: In the Princeville Resort area on the island's north shore.
Dining: The Bali Hai Restaurant serves Pacific Rim cuisine.
Amenities & Services: Free parking, coin-operated laundry facilities, dry cleaning service, 2 swimming pools, Jacuzzi, 8 tennis courts, etc.

ACCOMMODATIONS

Rooms: 250. Includes 50 suites; 2 rooms for disabled. Smoking permitted on lanais.
All Rooms: A/C, cable TV, lanai, phone, refrigerator, in-room safe, coffeemaker, etc.

Some Rooms: Full kitchens, washer and dryer, separate bedroom and bath.
Comfort & Decor: Spacious and clean. Tastefully appointed with Island-themed art and furnishings. Cool, tropical colors.

RATES, RESERVATIONS, & RESTRICTIONS

Deposit: 1-night deposit or credit card guarantee due within 10 days after booking. Cancellation notice must be given 72 hours prior to arrival for refund.
Credit Cards: All major credit cards accepted.
Check-In/Out: 3 p.m./Noon. No early

check-ins granted. Hospitality room available.
Contact: 5380 Honoiki Rd.
Hanalei, HI 96722
(800) 367-5004 or (808) 826-6522
Fax: (808) 826-6680
www.castle-group.com

HYATT REGENCY KAUAI RESORT & SPA $$$$$

Overall: ★★★★½	Room Quality: A+	Value: C+	Zone 13

Perhaps Kauai's finest resort, the Hyatt Regency Kauai offers an atmosphere reminiscent of the 1920s and 1930s, Hawaii's golden age. The open-air settings are dressed with brilliant tropical flowers, koa wood furnishings, and handsome Italian marble. In terms of amenities and services, the Hyatt pulled out all the stops here. One of the splashier centerpieces is a huge playground of saltwater lagoons and freshwater pools, which come complete with the obligatory water slides. Among the highlights are cultural activities, a children's program, a luxurious health spa, great dining, and nightly entertainment. Of course, it doesn't hurt that Po'ipu is a marvelous resort destination with a world-class beach.

SETTING & FACILITIES

Location: Fronting Keoneloa Bay in Po'ipu.
Dining: Tidepools features Pacific Rim specialties, while Dondero's serves fine Italian cuisine.

Amenities & Services: Room service, parking, laundry service, business center, spa, beauty salon, children's program, etc.

ACCOMMODATIONS

Rooms: 602. Includes 37 suites. 26 rooms for the disabled. Non-smoking rooms available.
All Rooms: A/C, cable TV, lanai,

phone, coffeemaker, iron and ironing board, hair dryer, etc.
Some Rooms: Kitchen, daily Continental breakfast and snacks.

Comfort & Decor: Very spacious (standard rooms are 600 square feet), exceptionally clean and well maintained. Elegant yet comfortable ambience, with handsome wood furnishings and Hawaiian-themed art.

RATES, RESERVATIONS, & RESTRICTIONS

Family Plan: Children age 17 and under stay free if staying with parents and using existing bedding.
Deposit: 2-night deposit due within 14 days after booking. Cancellation notice must be given 72 hours prior to arrival for refund.
Credit Cards: All major credit cards accepted.

Check-In/Out: 3 p.m./Noon. Early check-in and late check-out available on request.
Contact: 1571 Po'ipu Rd.
Koloa, HI 96756
(800) 554-9288 or (808) 742-1234
Fax: (808) 742-1557
www.hyatt.com

KAUAI MARRIOTT RESORT & BEACH CLUB $$$$$

| Overall: ★★★★ | Room Quality: A | Value: C | Zone 13 |

This fabulously situated resort has toned down the glitz and glamour enjoyed by its former incarnation—as the Westin Kauai—but is still a world-class destination offering excellent service and a sizable menu of amenities. Tranquil lagoons and inland waterways are traversed via mahogany launches, while horse-drawn carriages provide a leisurely exploration of the resort grounds. Golfers are advised to play a round at one of the resort's two championship courses, both designed by Jack Nicklaus. Also, Kalapaki Beach is an excellent locale for swimming, making the Kauai Marriott a good choice for families.

SETTING & FACILITIES

Location: Fronting Kalapaki Beach.
Dining: Duke's Canoe Club serves steak, fish, and seafood specialties. The poolside Kukui's Restaurant & Bar features Pacific Rim cuisine.

Amenities & Services: Room service, coin-operated laundry facilities, free parking, valet service, business center, golf, tennis, free airport transportation, fitness spa, etc.

ACCOMMODATIONS

Rooms: 356. Includes 252 suites. 10 rooms for the disabled. Non-smoking rooms available.
All Rooms: A/C, cable TV, phone, mini-bar, in-room safe, coffeemaker, hair dryer, iron and ironing board, etc.

Some Rooms: Kitchenette, microwave.
Comfort & Decor: Rooms are small to medium, clean, and pleasant, with subtle tropical decor and artworks.

RATES, RESERVATIONS, & RESTRICTIONS

Family Plan: Children age 17 and under stay free if staying with parents and using existing bedding.
Deposit: 1-night deposit due within 10 days of booking. Cancellation notice must be given 72 hours prior to arrival for refund.
Credit Cards: All major credit cards accepted.

Check-In/Out: 4 p.m./Noon. Early check-in (from 2 p.m.) and late check-out (until 2 p.m.) available on request.
Contact: Kalapaki Beach
Lihu'e, HI 96766
(800) 220-2925 or (808) 245-5050
Fax: (808) 245-2993
www.marriotthotels.com/LIHHI

OUTRIGGER KAUAI BEACH HOTEL $$$

Overall: ★★★★	Room Quality: B+	Value: C	Zone 13

Just a few minutes away from Lihu'e Airport, this 25-acre Outrigger property provides everything most visitors would want of a great hotel, with one notable exception: a great beach. (The ocean conditions here are considered unsafe for most of the year.) However, the hotel does offer a fabulous swimming pool. The Outrigger's open-air design promotes a relaxing and refreshing atmosphere, and its central location makes the property a good starting point to any Kauai adventure. The hotel offers four tennis courts, two of which are lit for night play. For golfers, the adjacent Wailua Golf Course is considered by many locals to be the best municipal course in Hawaii.

SETTING & FACILITIES

Location: In Lihu'e, just minutes from the Lihu'e Airport.
Dining: The Hale Kipa Terrace serves breakfast, lunch, and dinner, featuring American favorites.
Amenities & Services: Room service, free parking, business center, children's program, etc.

ACCOMMODATIONS

Rooms: 341. Includes 3 suites. 12 rooms for the disabled. One-third of the rooms are designated non-smoking.
All Rooms: A/C, cable TV, lanai, phone, voice mail, mini-refrigerator, in-room safe, coffeemaker, etc.
Some Rooms: Separate parlor, upgraded amenities.
Comfort & Decor: Spacious and clean (recently renovated), with rattan furnishings, quilted bedspreads, and Island artworks.

RATES, RESERVATIONS, & RESTRICTIONS

Family Plan: Children age 17 and under stay free if staying with parents and using existing bedding.
Deposit: 1-night deposit or credit card guarantee due within 10 days after booking. Cancellation notice must be given 72 hours prior to arrival for refund.

Credit Cards: All major credit cards accepted.
Check-In/Out: 3 p.m./Noon. Early check-in and late check-out granted based on availability. Hospitality room available.

Contact: 4331 Kauai Beach Dr. Lihu'e, HI 96766
(800) 688-7444 or (808) 245-1955
Fax: (808) 246-9085
okb@outrigger.com
www.outrigger.com

PRINCEVILLE RESORT $$$$$

| Overall: ★★★★½ | Room Quality: A | Value: C | Zone 13 |

Another AAA Five Diamond Award recipient, Princeville is ultra-luxurious and overlooks scenic Hanalei Bay. Glittering chandeliers, fountains, and Greek statues adorn the lobby, setting a standard of quality matched only by the resort's professional service and complete menu of services and amenities. Everything's here: shopping, dining, a swimming pool, nightly Hawaiian entertainment, etc. It's a place where people come to be pampered—Princeville also has a terrific spa—and, perhaps most of all, to get in a round or two: The resort's Prince Course is considered by many enlightened experts to be the best golf experience in the Islands.

SETTING & FACILITIES

Location: At Princeville on the island's north shore.
Dining: La Cascata serves fine Italian cuisine.
Amenities & Services: 24-hour room service, laundry service, concierge desk, valet service, health and fitness center, swimming pool, business center, etc.

ACCOMMODATIONS

Rooms: 252. Includes 51 suites. 7 rooms for the disabled. 7 of the resort's 11 floors are designated for non-smoking rooms.
All Rooms: A/C, cable TV, phone, honor bar, safe, oversized bath, hair dryer, iron and ironing board, robes.
Some Rooms: Lanai, second TV, fax machine.
Comfort & Decor: Very spacious, exceptionally clean, with custom-designed furnishings and original artworks. Shower window provides wonderful scenic views (for you, not passersby; windows can fog with a click of a switch).

RATES, RESERVATIONS, & RESTRICTIONS

Family Plan: Children age 17 and under stay free if staying with parents and using existing bedding. Cot available for $60.
Deposit: 1-night deposit required. Cancellation notice must be given 72 hours prior to arrival for refund.
Credit Cards: All major credit cards accepted.
Check-In/Out: 3 p.m./Noon. Early check-in and late check-out available on request.

Contact: 5520 Kahaku Rd.
Princeville, HI 96722
(800) 782-9488 or (808) 826-9644

Fax: (808) 826-1166
www.princeville.com

SHERATON KAUAI RESORT $$$$$

| Overall: ★★★★ | Room Quality: A | Value: C | Zone 13 |

A $40 million renovation project, completed in late 1997, has essentially
created a new Sheraton Kauai, one that blends beautifully with its beachfront surroundings. Half of the resort embraces the wonderful Po'ipu
Beach, while the other half seems to explode in tropical colors painted with
ginger, anthurium, heliconia, and bamboo. No building is taller than a
fully-grown coconut tree, which certainly adds to the sense of seclusion and
solitude that is celebrated at this 20-acre resort. The 413 rooms are housed
in a trio of four-story buildings, each identified according to the major
views (Ocean, Beach, and Garden). As you'd expect of a Sheraton property,
all the amenities are here, including a children's program, swimming pools,
a fitness center, and a full complement of beach activities.

SETTING & FACILITIES

Location: Fronting Po'ipu Beach.
Dining: Shells serves a variety of
international cuisine for breakfast,
lunch, and dinner. Naniwa is a fine dining Japanese restaurant.

Amenities & Services: Room service (breakfast and dinner only), free
parking, fitness center, laundry facilities,
tennis, business facilities, children's
program.

ACCOMMODATIONS

Rooms: 413. Includes 14 suites. 12
rooms for the disabled. Smoking is permitted on lanais only.
All Rooms: A/C, cable TV, radio, video
games, refrigerator, in-room safe, hair
dryer, iron and ironing board, data port,
robes, etc.

Some Rooms: Larger space, fresh
flowers.
Comfort & Decor: Spacious and
clean. Warm earth tones and handsome
wood furnishings lend casually elegant
ambience.

RATES, RESERVATIONS, & RESTRICTIONS

Family Plan: Children age 17 and
under stay free if staying with parents
and using existing bedding. Children
age 12 and under eat free in dining
rooms when accompanied by an adult.
Deposit: 1-night deposit due within
10 days of booking. Cancellation notice

must be given 72 hours prior to arrival
for refund.
Credit Cards: All major credit cards
accepted.
Check-In/Out: 3 p.m./Noon. Early
check-in and late check-out available
on request. Hospitality room available.

Contact: 2440 Hoʻonani Rd.   Fax: (808) 742-9777
Koloa, HI 96756   www.sheraton-kauai.com
(800) 782-9488 or (808) 742-1661

MOLOKAI

KALUAKOʻI HOTEL & GOLF CLUB $$

Overall: ★★★½	Room Quality: B	Value: C	Zone 14

Molokai's only full-service resort. Situated near a nice stretch of white-sand beach, but distant from most of the island's best visitor attractions. The hotel itself isn't much to look at, but the service is very friendly, and the atmosphere reflects the simple and comfortable lifestyle enjoyed by Molokai residents. Beach activities and tennis are among the recreational diversions available, but golf reigns as the activity of choice here: The Kaluakoʻi Golf Course provides challenging play and spectacular scenery, especially the five holes that hug the Pacific Ocean.

SETTING & FACILITIES

Location: At Kepuhi Beach on Molokai's west end.
Dining: The Ohia Lodge serves American fare.

Amenities & Services: Free parking, coin-operated laundry facilities, baby-sitting service, travel desk, meeting facilities, golf, etc.

ACCOMMODATIONS

Rooms: 103. Includes 6 rooms for the disabled. 24 non-smoking rooms.
All Rooms: Ceiling fan (no A/C), cable TV, VCR, phone, mini-refrigerator, etc.
Some Rooms: Kitchenette.

Comfort & Decor: Spacious rooms, clean and comfortable. High ceilings with ceiling fan. Fading tropical colors and rattan furnishings showing a little wear and tear.

RATES, RESERVATIONS, & RESTRICTIONS

Family Plan: Children age 12 and under stay free if staying with parents and using existing bedding. $15 for roll-away bed, $8 for crib.
Deposit: Credit card guarantee or 1-night deposit due within 15 days after booking. 72-hour cancellation notice required for refund.
Credit Cards: All major credit cards accepted.

Check-In/Out: 3 p.m./Noon. Early check-in and late check-out available on request.
Contact: P.O. Box 1977
Kepuhi Beach, HI 96770
(888) 552-2550 or (808) 552-2555
Fax: (808) 552-2821
kaluakoi@juno.com
www.kaluakoi.com

LANAI

HOTEL LANAI $

| Overall: ★★★½ | Room Quality: B | Value: B | Zone 15 |

Originally opened in 1923 as a lodging for visiting executives of the Dole Pineapple Company, the Hotel Lanai has always attracted a following, and even more so since Henry Clay Richardson and his family took the management reigns in 1996. This is your alternative if you can't afford to stay at The Lodge at Ko'ele or Manele Bay Hotel, and it isn't a bad one, either. The rooms are comfortable, the service is exceptionally friendly, and you'll even gain a better appreciation for the island's lifestyle by being closer to the town's residents. Richardson doubles as the chef of Henry Clay's Rotisserie, the hotel's restaurant.

SETTING & FACILITIES

Location: In Lanai City.
Dining: Henry Clay's Rotisserie serves a hearty selection of split-roasted meats, seafood, pasta, gourmet pizzas, and more.
Amenities & Services: Free parking. No room service or laundry service.

ACCOMMODATIONS

Rooms: 11. All are non-smoking.
All Rooms: Ceiling fans, phone.
Some Rooms: TV, bathtub.
Comfort & Decor: Medium-sized rooms with pine hardwood floors, ceiling fans, custom quilts, and original photographs depicting the island's plantation days.

RATES, RESERVATIONS, & RESTRICTIONS

Family Plan: Children age 8 and under stay free if staying with parents and using existing bedding.
Deposit: Pay 50% deposit of total stay in advance upon booking. Cancellation notice must be given 14 days prior to arrival for refund. Cancellations are charged a $10 processing fee.
Credit Cards: Visa, MC, AmEx.
Check-In/Out: 1 p.m./11 a.m. Early check-in and late check-out available on request.
Contact: P.O. Box 520
Lanai City, HI 96763
(800) 795-7211 or (808) 565-7211
Fax: (808) 565-6450
hotellanai@aloha.net
www.onlanai.com

THE LODGE AT KOʻELE $$$$$

Overall: ★★★★½   Room Quality: A   Value: C+   Zone 15

Earns high scores for its uniqueness. Nestled on the island's central high-lands, the Lodge is reminiscent of a stately New England estate, complete with manicured lawns, cozy fireplaces, and afternoon tea. Paintings, sculp-tures, and artifacts collected from around the world adorn the resort's interi-ors, while the outside grounds offer pathways that meander through flower gardens, past an English conservatory, and to an inviting swimming pool. The atmosphere is decidedly calm and relaxed, providing a welcome (if momentary) escape from your everyday world. You'll want to get *some* exer-cise, of course, and the Lodge doesn't disappoint here, either: Work up some sweat at the new fitness center, explore the countryside on a mountain bike, play tennis, or enjoy a round at one of Lanai's two award-winning champi-onship courses. A unique offering at the Lodge (and the neighboring Manele Bay Hotel) is the Visiting Artist Program, where guests get to meet and min-gle with internationally renowned authors, chefs, and entertainers.

SETTING & FACILITIES

Location: Upcountry, on the island's central highlands.
Dining: The award-winning Formal Dining Room showcases the sumptu-ous flavors of the Pacific Rim.
Amenities & Services: Room ser-vice, concierge, laundry service, fitness center, swimming pool, golf, etc.

ACCOMMODATIONS

Rooms: 102. Includes 14 suites. 2 rooms for the disabled. The Lodge is a non-smoking facility.
All Rooms: Ceiling fans, cable TV, VCR, phone, private lanai, mini-bar, in-room safe, robes, slippers, etc.
Some Rooms: Fireplaces, larger space, upgraded amenities.
Comfort & Decor: Very spacious, luxurious and exceptionally clean. Hand-carved poster beds, quiet ceiling fans, and oil paintings by local artists.

RATES, RESERVATIONS, & RESTRICTIONS

Family Plan: Children age 15 and under stay free if staying with parents and using existing bedding. Maximum of 4 guests per room (2 adults/2 chil-dren). $40 charge per extra guest.
Deposit: 2-night deposit due within 14 days of booking. Cancellation notice must be given 14 days prior to arrival for refund.
Credit Cards: All major credit cards accepted except Discover.
Check-In/Out: 3 p.m./Noon. Hospi-tality rooms available.
Contact: P.O. Box 310
Lanai City, HI 96763
(800) 321-4666 or (808) 565-7300
Fax: (808) 565-4561
reservations@lanai-resorts.com
www.lanai-resorts.com

THE MANELE BAY HOTEL $$$$$

| Overall: ★★★★½ | Room Quality: A | Value: C+ | Zone 15 |

A stark contrast to its sister property, the Lodge at Koʻele. Perched atop windswept red-lava cliffs, the Manele overlooks Lanaiʻs magnificent coastline and sports a more "resort" ambience. The Manele features a blend of Mediterranean and Hawaiian designs: Its public areas are adorned with pricey Oriental artifacts, local artworks, and spectacular wall murals painted by the renowned John Wullbrandt. Various tropical gardens add color to the resortʻs lush landscapes but still fall short of the commanding views of the Pacific Ocean. Itʻs just a short stroll to Hulopoʻe Beach, one of the best beaches in the U.S. The waters here are considered prime snorkeling and scuba-diving spots. Fabulous golf awaits you at the Experience at Koʻele or the Challenge at Manele. Or try your hand at target shooting at the nearby Lanai Pines Sporting Clays, the best sporting clays facility in the state. Like the Lodge, the Manele delivers a memorable and thoroughly invigorating experience.

SETTING & FACILITIES

Location: At Hulopoʻe Bay.
Dining: The ʻIhilani Restaurant serves fine Hawaii regional cuisine.
Amenities & Services: Room service, valet and self-parking, spa, golf, tennis, concierge service, childrenʻs program, etc.

ACCOMMODATIONS

Rooms: 250. Includes 13 suites. 6 rooms for the disabled. Non-smoking rooms available.
All Rooms: A/C, cable TV, VCR, phone, radio, in-room safe, lanai, mini-bar, hair dryer, sitting area, tub and shower, etc.

Some Rooms: Butler service.
Comfort & Decor: Spacious, comfortable with refined furnishings, floral-themed decor and accessories collected from around the world.

RATES, RESERVATIONS, & RESTRICTIONS

Family Plan: Children age 15 and under stay free if staying with parents and using existing bedding. Maximum of 4 per room (2 adults/2 children).
Deposit: 2-night deposit due within 14 days of booking. Cancellation notice must be given 14 days prior to arrival for refund.
Credit Cards: All major credit cards accepted except Discover.

Check-In/Out: 3 p.m./Noon. Early check-in and late check-out available on request (no guarantees).
Contact: P.O. Box 310
Lanai City, HI 96763
(800) 321-4666 or (808) 565-7700
Fax: (808) 565-2483
reservations@lanai-resorts.com
www.lanai-resorts.com

Part Four

Aloha! Welcome to Hawaii!

When You Arrive

While Hawaii's streets and highways can have tongue-twisting names like "Kalaniana'ole," "Mamalahoa," and "Honoapi'ilani," finding your way through the state's major airports is, thankfully, a much more user-friendly experience! The Honolulu International Airport, while one of the nation's busiest airports (it is a literal gateway between East and West), is simple to navigate, with gates assigned numbers and baggage claim areas assigned letters in the alphabet. TV monitors with the latest arrival and departure information are available throughout the premises. The airports on the Neighbor Islands, meanwhile, are much smaller—and it's a snap to find your way around them!

Arriving in Hawaii is an experience for the senses. Just as your ears tell you you're in Las Vegas as soon as you disembark your plane at the airport (the "clink-clink-clink" of the slot machines is the giveaway), your nose immediately lets you know you're in Hawaii thanks to the sweet fragrances emitted from nearby lei stands. You will also likely feel the higher humidity and the gentle trade winds. (Don't be disappointed when you aren't instantly bombarded by postcard-like scenes of Oahu, however. That will have to come later.)

Upon arriving, make sure you remember your baggage claim assignment from the flight crew, then proceed into the airport terminal and follow the clearly marked signs directing you to the baggage claim area, which is located on the street level. (*Note:* Make sure you have your baggage claim numbers ready, as airport checkers are fairly strict about inspecting them before allowing you to proceed outside.) The wait before retrieving your luggage can be as short as a few minutes or as long as half an hour.

Also in the baggage claim area are helpful information agents who can direct you to nearby car rental agencies, taxis, and shuttle vans to Waikiki.

While some of the major airlines (United, Delta, and American) fly directly to Maui, the Big Island, and Kauai, most flights to the Neighbor Islands include a short layover in Honolulu. Here's a quick look at the Neighbor Island airports:

Maui has a trio of airports. The main airport is the Kahului Airport, located at the center of the island. Car rentals and taxi service are available at this full-service facility. The Kapalua Airport, located at the west end of the island, is a commuter airport servicing only inter-island flights. Car rentals are available here. The Hana Airport, meanwhile, is basically a landing strip servicing residents and visitors of this lovely but remote destination tucked away on the island's eastern coast.

The Big Island has two major airports. The Keahole-Kona International Airport is a full-service airport located on the Kona side of the island, while the Hilo Airport (also called General Lyman Field) serves the eastern side of the island. Both facilities house car rental agencies.

The Lihu'e Airport is the principal airport on Kauai. A smaller airport, at Princeville, services private planes, helicopters, and the commuter airline Aloha Island Air.

The airports on Molokai and Lanai are small but very efficient and convenient.

TRANSPORTATION OPTIONS FROM THE AIRPORTS

Oahu

Honolulu International Airport   Five car rental agencies—Avis, Budget, Dollar, Hertz, and National—have customer service desks in the baggage claim area (located at street level) except for baggage claim D. Other car rental agencies are located within the vicinity of the airport and have courtesy phones inside the baggage claim area. See the section on car rentals for more detailed information.

If you don't want to rent a car, the next-best option is the Airport-Waikiki Express. From the baggage claim area, head outside and look for any ticket agent wearing a blue aloha shirt. He or she will direct you to the nearest pickup point. The cost is $8 per person for a one-way fare and $13 per person for a round trip (cash only). The 18-seat, air-conditioned shuttle—colored red, white, and blue, and clearly marked "Airport-Waikiki Express"—arrives approximately every half-hour and operates around the clock. Call (808) 566-7340 for more information.

Another convenient option is a taxi. SIDA Cabs are available just outside the baggage claim area. Look for a dispatcher wearing a mustard-colored shirt. The fare from the airport to Waikiki ranges from $20 to $23, not including tips.

A final option is catching the city bus to Waikiki. The cost is $1 per adult (have exact change ready). Look for the #19 and #20 buses marked "Waikiki Beach & Hotels." The bus stops—two at the main terminal and one at the inter-island terminal—are located on the second level (departures). Buses arrive approximately every 20 minutes during the day; in the evening, only the #19 bus serves the airport. Call (808) 848-5555 for more information. Think of TheBus as your "last resort" option: It'll take at least half an hour to reach your hotel, depending on traffic conditions, and the last thing you'd want after a long flight is to be stuck in a stop-and-go bus. Another minus: You are allowed only one piece of luggage, which must measure no more than 24" x 18" x 12" and must be able to fit under your seat or on your lap.

Maui

Kahului Airport   You'll find all the major car rental agencies—Alamo, Avis, Budget, Dollar, Hertz, and National—just outside the main terminal (turn right as you leave the baggage area). A few other car rentals—including Thrifty, Regency, and Word of Mouth—have a courtesy phone set up at the airport's Information Board along the wall inside the baggage claim area.

For taxi service, Maui Airport Taxi has a dispatcher inside the baggage claim area. Or just walk directly across the street and hail one of the cabs lined up at the curb.

There are several shuttles ready to take you where you need to go. Use the Information Board courtesy phone mentioned above to contact the Airport Shuttle or Speedy Shuttle. The wait is usually between 5 and 15 minutes, and costs vary depending on the destination. The Airport Shuttle, as an example, charges $22 for two passengers bound for Wailea and $32 for transportation to Ka'anapali. To reserve a shuttle in advance, call the Airport Shuttle at 661-6667 or Speedy Shuttle at (808) 875-8070.

TransHawaiian (call (808) 877-7308) also provides transportation to the resort area of Ka'anapali from 9 a.m. to 4 p.m. daily, with a final run between 6:30 and 7 p.m. Look for the customer service desk marked "Airport Hotel Shuttle" in the baggage claim area next to the Information Board (directly across from carousel #4). Shuttles depart every half-hour. The cost is $13 per person.

Kapalua Airport   For car rentals, use the courtesy phone at the baggage claim area for a free shuttle van pickup, which will take you directly to the car rental counters. Taxis are located curbside near the baggage claim area, as are pre-arranged pickups from various hotels and resorts.

The Big Island

Keahole-Kona International Airport   The car rental counters for Avis, Alamo, Budget, Dollar, Hertz, National, and Thrifty are all located across the street from the main terminal (directly across from the Onizuka Space Center). The walk takes only about a couple of minutes.

Taxis are another option here. The cabs are parked across the street from the baggage claim area. There is no public transportation service available from the airport.

Pre-arranged pickups from various hotels are available. Be sure to let your hotel know your arrival time well ahead of schedule. Otherwise, you can call for a pickup at the airport's Information Booth, located just outside the baggage claim area.

Hilo International Airport   Car rental pickups for Alamo, Avis, Budget, Dollar, Hertz, and National are conveniently located directly across the street from the airport's restaurant, near the main gates. Taxi cabs are available curbside near the baggage claim area. As in Kona, there is no public transportation service available at the airport.

The only shuttle that services the airport is for guests at the Hawaii Naniloa Resort, and even this is based on availability. Visitors booked at the Naniloa should call (800) 442-5845 or check with a customer service agent at the Visitors Information Desk near the baggage claim area.

Kauai

Lihu'e Airport   Car rental pickups are conveniently located directly across the street from the airport's restaurant, near the main gates. A slew of taxi cabs are available curbside near the baggage claim area. There is no public transportation service available at the airport.

Taxis are the only other transportation option available to general visitors. Cabs are lined up curbside directly outside the baggage claim area. If there are no cabs available, use the dispatch phone located by the Visitors Information Desk to summon a cab immediately.

Visitors booked at the Kauai Marriott can take advantage of a free shuttle. At the Visitors Information Desk, phone the hotel and request a pick-up. Allow about ten minutes for the shuttle to arrive.

Molokai

Molokai Airport   Budget and Dollar are the only two car rental agencies at the Molokai Airport. Their customer service desks are located inside the baggage claim area.

Two cab companies service the airport: Kukui Tours (call (808) 552-2282) and Molokai Off-Road (call (808) 553-3369). Neither has a courtesy phone. Check outside the baggage claim area to spot either taxi van. If none are on the premises, call either cab for a pickup. Expect a wait of 15–20 minutes.

Lanai

Lanai Airport   Dollar Rent-A-Car is the lone car rental agency on Lanai. Upon arrival, walk to the reception desk and pick up the red courtesy phone. A van will pick you up and transport you to Dollar's pickup location, about three miles away.

A convenient way to get around the island is via the Lanai Resort's shuttles. The $10-per-person charge includes round-trip airport transportation and all shuttles between the island's two resorts, The Lodge at Koʻele and the Manele Bay Hotel. The shuttle vans are located right outside the airport's baggage claim area.

Things the Natives Already Know

LOCAL CUSTOMS AND PROTOCOL

Hawaii is as unique as it is beautiful, blending the traditions and customs of many different cultures. Certainly, it's a good idea to get acquainted with these local customs (when in Rome, after all . . .). Consider the following customs unique to Hawaii:

- While English is Hawaii's primary language, you're bound to also hear some Hawaiian, Japanese, Chinese, Korean, Filipino, and Samoan, all languages that help make up the melting pot of cultures in the Islands. You'll also hear pidgin English, a dialect that originated during Hawaii's plantation era, as laborers sought a common form of verbal communication. For some examples of pidgin words and what they mean, see pages 194–195.

- In terms of directional terminology, you'll rarely encounter the usual "north, south, east, and west." Instead, locals use *mauka* (toward the mountains) and *makai* (toward the sea). Additionally, on Oahu, going in the *ʻewa* direction means heading west and going in the Diamond Head direction means heading east. Above all, to avoid an embarrassing situation, know the difference between the words *kane* (man) and *wahine* (woman), particularly if you need to use rest rooms marked by Hawaiian words!

- Do this: Close your middle three fingers of either hand while keeping your thumb and pinky finger fully extended. Now shake that hand a few times in the air. You've just done the "shaka" sign, a local hand gesture expressing acknowledgment, goodwill, or appreciation. Say you're on the crowded H-1 freeway in the middle of the afternoon, and you allow a driver to cut into your lane. If the driver sticks his hand out and waves you the shaka sign, it's the same as *Mahalo!* or "Thank you!"

■ Thank God it's Friday? In Hawaii, it's "thank God it's *Aloha* Friday," when Island residents dress a bit more casually, donning aloha shirts and muumuu in celebration of their unique culture and lifestyle. Incidentally, the first aloha shirt was sold in the mid-1930s in Honolulu. Boys during the time had been wearing similar-type shirts (but made from Japanese-print fabric), and the idea caught on with local manufacturers. The origin of the first muumuu dates back to the mid-1800s.

■ If you're invited to a *kama'aina's* home, remember that it is customary at most Island residences to remove your shoes or flip-flops before entering the house.

■ Locals of all generations and ethnicities generally maintain a deep reverence for the *'aina,* or land. Respect for the environment is a must. Also, on the Big Island of Hawaii, the practice of taking home pieces of lava rock is not only frowned upon but is also considered bad luck. We've heard many accounts from distressed U.S. mainland residents who have experienced illness, accidents, and other bouts of misfortune after ignoring this local advice.

■ Above all, keep in mind that locals often go by "Hawaiian time," which means life goes on at a more leisurely pace. This is true particularly on the Neighbor Islands. Residents late for appointments might use the excuse, "Sorry, I'm on Hawaiian time." This, of course, is perfect for you, the visitor. Relax. Take it easy. Enjoy paradise. You're now on Hawaiian time!

The Lei Tradition

One of the most colorful—and famous—traditions in Hawaii is the custom of bestowing a flower lei on someone, usually a family member, friend, or special guest. This act can signify a warm welcome, farewell, or congratulations, and is usually followed by a warm hug and friendly peck on the cheek. A lei greeting remains perhaps Hawaii's most tangible expression of aloha, and locals shower loved ones with leis of all types at graduations, anniversaries, birthdays, and other special celebrations.

The tradition of lei giving is believed to have originated with Hawaii's earliest settlers, who brought over flowering plants to be used, in part, for adornment. Early Hawaiians often offered leis to their gods during sacred ceremonies. Today, leis are also draped over the statues or images of important people in Hawaiian history. (Each June, for example, the King Kamehameha Day Celebration kicks off with a colorful lei-draping ceremony at the King Kamehameha Statue in downtown Honolulu.)

It was writer-poet Don Blanding who initiated Lei Day, a colorful annual celebration held each May 1. (The first May Day was celebrated on May 1, 1928.) The biggest Lei Day event is held at Kapi'olani Park in Waikiki, where the most exquisite floral creations by the state's top lei makers are put on display and judged in several different categories.

Fresh flower leis are available throughout Hawaii, including at every major airport. You'll find leis adorned with all kinds of flowers, including plumeria, ginger, vanda orchids, pakalana, 'ilima, and carnations. Also, many high-quality lei stands are concentrated around the 1000 block of Maunakea Street in the Chinatown area of downtown Honolulu. Costs range from $3 for a simple crown tuberose lei to $40 for an intricately crafted rope pikake lei.

Like clothing, new styles and fashions for leis are frequently introduced. One of the most popular new leis is the Cristina lei, an expertly sewn garland made of purple dendrobium orchids (it sells for $25–$30). It's interesting to note that the plumeria lei, the most popular lei among visitors, is no longer as plentiful as it was in past years. Once fixtures in local backyards, plumeria trees have been declining in popularity among Island residents. Once sold for $2, a plumeria lei today can cost as much as $7.

Most leis last only a day, with the more hardy leis lasting up to three days if you store them in the fridge after every use. If you want to bring home a lei as a lasting souvenir, consider a non-flower lei. Many attractive leis are made of leaves, seashells, *kukui* nuts, and even paper ornaments. At local graduation ceremonies, it's not unusual to find a proud graduate draped with leis of all types, including some unique and contemporary creations fashioned out of candy bars, dollar bills, and even boxes of instant noodles!

Check your hotel concierge for available lei-making classes at your hotel.

A TIP ABOUT TIPPING

Many service workers in Hawaii, like their counterparts at every other major vacation destination, depend heavily on tips to fill out their total salary. While the smart traveler finds ways to cut costs during a vacation or business trip, try not to skimp on the tips. (Consider also that the cost of living in Hawaii is among the highest in the United States.)

At the airport, a porter (if you decide to use one) is generally tipped a dollar or two per bag. Taxi drivers, meanwhile, usually receive a 15% tip of the total fare plus 25¢ per bag or parcel.

At the hotel, it is customary to tip the bellhop $5 for transporting your luggage to and from your room, and a few dollars for the valet parking attendant. Also, leave a dollar or two each day for the housekeeping service.

For dining, the tip is typically 15 to 20% of the bill at fine dining establishments, and 15% at other restaurants.

STATE HOLIDAYS

In addition to all U.S. federal holidays, Island residents celebrate a trio of official state holidays.

Kuhio Day (March 26)

This holiday honors Prince Jonah Kuhio Kalaniana'ole (1871–1922), the last influential member of Hawaii's royal family. Born on the island of Kauai to Chief David Kahalepouli Pi'ikoi and Victoria Kinoiki Kekaulike II, the handsome statesman—some called him the "Cupid Prince"— served as a delegate to the U.S. Congress, defeating political rival Robert W. Wilcox in a 1902 election.

King Kamehameha Day (June 11)

Revered as Hawaii's greatest king, Kamehameha conquered the Hawaiian islands and united them under one rule. An imposing figure—some witnesses reported him to be as tall as eight feet—the Big Island–born king ruled with wisdom and cunning, strength and courage. He died in May 1819—he was believed to be in his early 60s—and his bones were hidden at a secret location on the Kona coast.

It was Kamehameha's grandson, Lot (Kamehameha V), who declared June 11 to be a public holiday: "By Authority, We, Kamehameha V, by the Grace of God, of the Hawaiian Islands, do hereby proclaim, that it is Our will and pleasure that the eleventh day of June of each year be hereafter observed as a Public Holiday in memory of Our Grandfather and Predecessor, Kamehameha I, the founder of the Hawaiian Kingdom." Today, Islanders celebrate the life of Kamehameha with a variety of festivities, including lei-draping ceremonies, parades, and *ho'olaule'a* (public celebrations).

Admission Day (Third Friday in August)

On August 21, 1959, U.S. President Dwight D. Eisenhower signed the proclamation welcoming Hawaii as the 50th state of the union. The act culminated a long and often emotional campaign for statehood that originated over a century earlier: In November 1852, at a reception for

President-elect Franklin Pierce, a toast was raised to "the Sandwich Isles—may they soon be added to the galaxy of the States."

An intriguing side note is that many Island residents expected Hawaii to be named the 49th state of the Union. The fact that Hawaii had served the country so well during World War II had convinced many that it was sure to become the next U.S. state. Instead, of course, that distinction went to Alaska in 1958. Today, "Hawaii—49th State" memorabilia—ranging from record labels to buttons—are highly prized by collectors.

Note: While not an official state holiday, Lei Day (May 1) has become a traditional day of celebration, paying homage to the Hawaiian culture through a variety of concerts and school activities. Many residents wear their favorite floral lei on this colorful and festive day.

SAYING IT IN HAWAIIAN

Although there are only 13 letters in the Hawaiian alphabet (the 5 vowels and the consonants h, k, l, m, n, p, w, and the glottal stop '), learning the native language requires practice and patience.

Here are some general rules of thumb for you to remember:

- Vowels are pronounced as follows: *a* as "ah," as in "lava"; *e* as "ay," as in "hay"; *i* as "ee," as in "fee"; *o* as "oh," as in "low"; and *u* as "oo," as in "moon".

- All consonants are pronounced as in English except for *w*, which is usually pronounced as *v* when it follows an *i* or *e*. Example: 'Ewa Beach is pronounced as "Eva" Beach. When following an *u* or *o*, it is pronounced as *w*. When it is the first letter in the word or follows an *a*, there is no designated rule, so the pronunciation follows custom.

- Some vowels are diphthongized, forming single sounds. Examples: *ai* as in "Waikiki," *au* as in *"mauka,"* *ei* as in "lei," *oi* as in "poi," *ou* as an *"kou,"* and *ao* as in *"haole."*

- The glottal stop, or *'okina*, is a backward apostrophe that keeps similar words from being confused. For instance, *pau* means "finished," while a *pa'u* is a "skirt or sarong worn by women horseback riders." A short pause is required after a glottal stop. Hence, *pau* is pronounced as "pow," while *pa'u* is pronounced as "pah-oo."

- A macron, or *kahako*, designates a long vowel. A macron is marked as a line directly over the vowel. Long vowels last longer than a regular vowel.

- Every Hawaiian syllable ends with a vowel. Thus, every Hawaiian word ends with a vowel.

- If a word contains no macrons, the accent usually falls on the next-to-last syllable. Examples: a-LO-ha, ma-HA-lo, ma-li-HI-ni, and 'o-HA-na.

There are a number of helpful Hawaiian language resources available, including books and cassettes that let you study at home at your convenience. The most recognized Hawaiian language book is the *Hawaiian Dictionary*, originally published in 1957 by noted authorities Mary Kawena Pukui and Samuel H. Elbert.

Commonly Used Hawaiian Words and Phrases

'aina   Land, earth

aloha   Love, kindness, or goodwill. Can be used as a greeting or farewell

E komo mai   Welcome!

hale   House

hana hou   Do again, repeat, or encore

haole   Formerly any foreigner, now primarily refers to anyone of Caucasian ancestry

holoholo   To go out for a walk, ride, or other pleasurable activity

ho'olaule'a   A big party or celebration

ho'oponopono   To correct or right a situation

ikaika   Strong, powerful

'ilima   A native shrub bearing bright yellow, orange, greenish, or dull red flowers; frequently used for leis

kahuna   Priest, minister, expert

kala   Money

kama'aina   Native-born or longtime Island resident

kanaka   Person, individual

kane   Male, husband, man

kapu   Taboo

keiki   Child

kohola   Humpback whale

kokua   Help, assistance, cooperation

kolohe   Mischievous, naughty; a rascal

kupuna   Grandparent

ku'uipo   My sweetheart

lanai   Porch, veranda

lua   Toilet, bathroom

lu'au   A native Hawaiian feast

luna   Foreman, boss, leader

Commonly Used Hawaiian Words and Phrases (continued)

mahalo   Thank you

makahiki   Four-month ancient Hawaiian festival with sports and religious activities; during the *makahiki* season, war was forbidden

makai   Toward the ocean; used in giving directions

malihini   Newcomer or visitor

mana   Spiritual power

mauka   Inland, toward the mountain; used in giving directions

Me ke aloha pumehana   With warm regards

mele   Song, chant

Menehune   Legendary small people who worked at night, building fishponds, roads, and temples; according to legend, if the work was not completed in one night, it was left unfinished

muumuu   Loose-fitting Hawaiian gown, usually with a floral print

'ohana   Family

'ono   Delicious

pau   Finished, done

pupu   Hors d'oeuvre, appetizer

tutu   Grandmother

wahine   Female, wife, woman

Local Slang (Pidgin)

Here are some of the more commonly used pidgin English words and phrases you're likely to hear during your Island stay. The pros and cons of pidgin English are often the subject of debate among local educators and cultural experts: Some say that the practice should not be encouraged because it is not an acceptable manner of speech in the business arena, while others insist that pidgin is a treasured cultural asset that should not be looked down upon. In truth, it's not uncommon for a *kama'aina* to speak perfect English in an office setting, then return home and speak pidgin to his or her family.

an' den?   So? And then?

any kine   Anything

bolo head   Bald

braddah   Brother or friend

brah   Short for "braddahp"

bumbye Do it later
bummahs! That's unfortunate!
fo' real? Really?
garans Guaranteed
geev' um! Go for it!
how you figgah? How do you think that happened?
howzit! How are you?
latahs See you later
li'dat Like that
minahs Minor; no problem; don't worry about it
mo' bettah Better
no shame Don't be shy or embarrassed!
'nuff already! That's enough!
shaka Greetings; good job; thank you
small keed time Childhood
soah? Does it hurt?
talk story Converse, talk, or gossip
t'anks, eh? Thank you
whatevahs Whatever
who dat? Who is that?
yeah, no? That's right!

IMPORTANT PHONE NUMBERS

Here's a list of phone numbers that may come in handy during your stay. For inter-island calls, you must use the area code (808) before the number.

All Islands

Police, Fire, Ambulance: 911
Directory Assistance: 1411

Oahu

Weather Forecast: 973-4380, 973-4381
Marine Conditions: 973-4382
Time of Day: 983-3211
Honolulu International Airport: 836-6413
Honolulu Physicians Exchange: 524-2575
Hawaii Dental Association Hotline: 593-7956
Information and Complaint: 523-4385
Office of Consumer Protection: 586-2630
Better Business Bureau: 536-6956

Maui

(Note: Maui County also includes Molokai and Lanai)
Weather Forecast: 877-5111
Marine Conditions: 877-3477
Time of Day: 242-0212 (Maui), 553-9211 (Molokai), 565-9211 (Lanai)
Kahului Airport: 872-3803, 872-3893
Kapalua Airport: 669-0623
Hana Airport: 248-8208
Molokai Airport: 567-6140
Kalaupapa Airport: 567-6331
Lanai Airport: 565-6757
Office of Consumer Protection: 984-8244

The Big Island

Weather Forecast: 961-5582, 935-8555 (Hilo)
Marine Conditions: 935-9883
Time of Day: 961-0212
Volcano Eruption Information: 985-6000
Keahole-Kona International Airport: 329-3423
Hilo International Airport: 934-5801
Office of Consumer Protection: 974-6230

Kauai

Weather Forecast: 245-6001
Marine Conditions: 245-3564
Time of Day: 245-0212
Lihu'e Airport: 246-1400

NEWSPAPERS

The local newspapers are another handy resource in helping you make the most of your Island visit. The dailies include the *Honolulu Advertiser* and *Honolulu Star-Bulletin* on Oahu; the *Hawaii Tribute-Herald* and *West Hawaii Today* on the island of Hawaii; the *Maui News* on Maui; and the *Garden Island* on Kauai.

The most complete source for updated entertainment news and listings is the *Honolulu Advertiser*'s "TGIF" section, which comes out each Friday.

TELEVISION

You can learn more about available attractions and activities in Hawaii via the TV. In-room televisions at most hotels include a visitor channel, with cheerful narrators taking you on a highlight-filled tour of the island you're visiting. The information tends to come at a slower pace, and it's not as detailed as what a good visitor publication would provide. If you have some time to kill, however, it can serve as an entertaining introduction to some of the sights and sounds you'll encounter in the Islands.

Practical Safety Tips

On the whole, Hawaii is a safe place to visit. Honolulu, in fact, was rated by *Money* magazine as the safest large U.S. city (based on an analysis of crime statistics provided by the Federal Bureau of Investigation). In 1996, Hawaii had the 39th highest violent crime rate in the U.S. (based on number of violent crimes per 100,000 people).

Still, crime does exist. Here you'll find (and we hope you'll avoid) the usual pitfalls of a major U.S. city, including drug- and gang-related misdeeds. But using the following suggestions as well as common sense should help you enjoy a safe and incident-free stay in the Islands:

- Carry only enough cash or traveler's checks with you for the day's activities.
- Never leave your luggage or travel bags unattended.
- Never display large amounts of cash during transactions (take special caution when you withdraw cash from any automated teller machine).
- Walk in groups whenever possible.
- Avoid shortcuts through poorly lit areas, alleys, or vacant lots.
- Beware of pickpockets, especially in crowds. If you are bumped or crowded, check your pocket immediately.
- Carry your purse close to your body, with a firm grip on the latch.
- Carry your wallet in a front pocket rather than a rear pocket.
- Avoid waiting alone at a bus stop if you can wait with people at a nearby stop.
- Never leave money or other valuables unattended in your rental car (vehicle break-ins have been on the rise in Hawaii).
- If your vehicle is bumped from behind, do not stop on any desolate roadway or shoulder; instead, proceed to the nearest public area and call 911 for police assistance.
- Do not carry your hotel room key. It is better to leave it with the front desk.

Part Five

Getting around Hawaii

There are no commuter trains or subway systems in Hawaii, although talk of a high-tech monorail system on Oahu surfaces every now and then (several years ago, the city council narrowly voted down a proposal that called for a monorail system connecting leeward Oahu and downtown Honolulu). Still, there are a number of transportation options in the state to help you get where you want to go, particularly on Oahu, the only island with a major municipal bus system.

Before choosing your primary mode of transportation in the Islands, carefully weigh the following considerations: convenience, flexibility, time, and cost. For example, catching a taxi from Waikiki to, say, the *Arizona* Memorial may be the fastest and most convenient option, but it will also set you back about $25. On the other hand, catching the city bus is the cheapest way to go, but the travel time is longer and you won't have the flexibility of making impromptu side trips.

Each option has its advantages and disadvantages, and it's not a bad idea to use a combination of choices. This chapter provides information on everything you need to know about getting around in the Aloha State, from car rentals, taxis, buses, and shuttles to inter-island flights and ferry boats.

Car Rentals

By far, renting a car provides the greatest flexibility and mobility among your transportation options. And there's nothing quite like cruising a Hawaiian island in a shiny convertible, taking in the sights in open-air comfort. Car rentals are available on all islands, and the cost is reasonable—usually about $30 per day for an economy car. Even better, most major car rental firms offer special rates, often included in money-saving travel packages with airfare and accommodations. Check with your travel agent or call the car rental agencies for details.

On the islands of Maui, Hawaii, Kauai, and Molokai—where the activities and attractions are usually spread out by fair distances—renting a car is a must. You could get by without a car on Oahu, which has a very efficient municipal bus system, but we'd recommend going the car rental route because it will save you time and provide you with the most flexibility. If you're staying on Lanai, you can enjoy shuttle transportation to most of the island's attractions, so renting a car shouldn't be a priority.

All the major car rental agencies are located at the airports, and many have reservations desks at various hotels and resorts. On Maui, besides Kahului Airport and the hotels, many rental agencies are found at the Ka'anapali Transportation Center (30-1 Halawai Drive), a five-minute drive from the Kapalua Airport in West Maui (complimentary shuttle service from the airport to the center is provided). To save you time and the need to lug your baggage around, it's a good idea for one person to pick up the rental car while the rest of the traveling party retrieves the luggage and waits outside the baggage claim area.

Most car rental agencies have a sizable selection of vehicles, ranging from economy cars and luxury sedans to four-wheel-drive roadsters. In other words, if you've ever fantasized about donning a bright aloha shirt and driving a red Ferrari in Hawaii (a la Tom Selleck on *Magnum P.I.*), you *can* make it happen!

If necessary, you can rent a car when you arrive. Courtesy phones connecting you to the rental agencies are on hand at the airport (near the baggage claim area), and free transportation is provided to their nearby offices. However, it is far better to place your reservations at least a week in advance. Rental rates are based on the number of cars available, so they constantly fluctuate. The earlier you place your reservations, the better. (Since you don't have to pay up front, you can always recheck rates after you've made your reservations.)

There are several add-on costs besides the rental fee: Car rentals on all islands are subject to a $2-per-day road tax and a nominal vehicle license tax (24¢–45¢ a day on Oahu and 17¢–45¢ per day on the Neighbor Islands). In addition, transactions that take place at any airport are subject to an airport concession fee of 10% of the rental fee per day on Oahu and 7.5% on the Neighbor Islands. Optional insurance rates vary by car rental agency; if you use a major credit card to pay for the rental, check to see if it already provides insurance coverage.

Then there is the matter of gasoline prices, which on Hawaii are exorbitant. Gas on Oahu often exceeds $1.40 per gallon (regular unleaded, self-service), which is about 50% more than the average price on the U.S. mainland. In addition, gas prices on the Neighbor Islands are generally 15% higher than on Oahu.

Be sure to use any discounts you're entitled to, including benefits from credit cards, frequent-flyer clubs, and AAA or AARP memberships. Also, log on to agency Web sites (provided below) for special money-saving offers (some offer as much as 20% off their regular rental rates).

Alamo Rent-A-Car

Toll-free Reservations: (800) 327-9633
Web Site: www.goalamo.com
Oahu:
 Honolulu International Airport: (808) 833-4585
 'Ilikai Hotel Nikko Waikiki: (808) 947-6112
Maui:
 Kahului Airport: (808) 871-6235
 Ka'anapali Transportation Center (30-1 Halawai Dr.): (808) 661-7181
Big Island:
 Keahole-Kona International Airport: (808) 329-8896
 Hilo International Airport: (808) 961-3343
Kauai:
 Lihu'e Airport: (808) 246-0645

Avis Rent-A-Car

Toll-free Reservations: (800) 331-1212
Web Site: www.avis.com
Oahu:
 Honolulu International Airport: (808) 834-5536
 Hilton Hawaiian Village: (808) 973-2624
 Outrigger East Hotel: (808) 971-3700
 Sheraton Waikiki Hotel: (808) 922-4422
Maui:
 Kahului Airport: (808) 871-7575
 Ka'anapali: (808) 661-4588
 Renaissance Wailea Beach Resort: (808) 879-7601
 Ritz-Carlton Kapalua: (808) 669-5046
Big Island:
 Keahole-Kona International Airport: (808) 327-3000
 Hilo International Airport: (808) 935-1290
 Hilton Waikoloa Village: (808) 886-2821
Kauai:
 Lihu'e Airport: (808) 245-3512
 Princeville Airport: (808) 826-9773
 Hyatt Regency Kauai: (808) 742-1627

Budget Rent-A-Car

Toll-free Reservations: (800) 777-0169
Web Site: www.budgetrentacar.com

Oahu:

Honolulu International Airport: (808) 836-1700
Hyatt Regency Waikiki: (808) 921-5808

Maui:

Kahului Airport: (808) 871-8811
Kaʻanapali: (808) 661-8721

Big Island:

Keahole-Kona International Airport: (808) 329-8511
Hilo International Airport: (808) 935-6878

Kauai:

Lihuʻe Airport: (808) 245-1901

Molokai:

Molokai Airport: (808) 567-6877

Dollar Rent-A-Car

Toll-free Reservations: (800) 367-7006
Web Site: www.dollarcar.com

Oahu:

Honolulu International Airport: (808) 831-2330
Hawaiian Regent Hotel: (808) 952-4264
Hale Koa Hotel: (808) 952-4264
Waikiki: (808) 952-4242

Maui:

Kahului Airport: (808) 877-2731
Hana: (808) 248-8237
Kaʻanapali Transportation Center: (808) 667-2651

Big Island:

Keahole-Kona International Airport: (808) 329-2744
Hilo International Airport: (808) 961-6059

Kauai:

Lihuʻe Airport: (808) 245-3651

Molokai:

Molokai Airport: (808) 567-6156

Lanai:

Lanai Airport: (808) 565-7227

Harper Car & Truck Rentals

Toll-free Reservations: (800) 852-9993
Web Site: www.harpershawaii.com

Big Island:
Kona: (808) 329-6688
Hilo: (808) 969-1478

Hertz Rent-A-Car

Toll-free Reservations: (800) 654-3011
Web Site: www.hertz.com
Oahu:
Honolulu International Airport: (808) 831-3500
Hyatt Regency Waikiki: (808) 971-3535
Maui:
Kahului Airport: (808) 877-5167
2580 Keka'a Dr.: (808) 661-7735
Westin Maui: (808) 667-5381
Maui Marriott: (808) 667-1966
Big Island:
Keahole-Kona International Airport: (808) 329-3566
Hilo International Airport: (808) 935-2896
Kauai:
Lihu'e Airport: (808) 245-3356
Kauai Marriott Resort: (808) 246-0027

National Car Rental

Toll-free Reservations: (800) CAR-RENT
Web Site: www.nationalcar.com/index.html
Oahu:
Honolulu International Airport: (808) 831-3800
Kahala Mandarin Oriental: (808) 733-2309
Maui:
Kahului Airport: (808) 871-8851
Ka'anapali Transportation Center: (808) 667-9737
Big Island:
Keahole-Kona International Airport: (808) 329-1674
Hilo International Airport: (808) 935-0891
Kauai:
Lihu'e Airport: (808) 245-5636

DRIVE TIMES

Here are some estimated drive times from popular resort areas to specific points of interest. The estimations are given for non–rush hour periods.

Drive Times

Oahu
From Central Waikiki to: Time to Travel

Ala Moana Shopping Center..7 minutes
Aloha Tower Marketplace..15 minutes
Arizona Memorial ....30 minutes
Bishop Museum..20 minutes
Chinatown Honolulu...15 minutes
Haleʻiwa...1 hour
Hanauma Bay ....30 minutes
Honolulu International Airport ....25 minutes
Polynesian Cultural Center...1 hour 15 minutes
Sea Life Park ....40 minutes
University of Hawaii-Manoa..15 minutes
Waimea Falls Park ....1 hour

Maui
From Kahului Airport to: Time to Travel

Haleakala National Park...1 hour 45 minutes
Hana...2 hours 30 minutes
Kaʻanapali ....50 minutes
Kapalua...1 hour
Kihei...25 minutes
Lahaina...45 minutes
Makena...40 minutes
Wailea ....35 minutes
Wailuku ....10 minutes

Big Island
From Kona to: Time to Travel

Hilo ....2 hours 15 minutes
Volcano..2 hours 30 minutes
Waimea (Kamuela)..50 minutes

From Hilo to: Time to Travel

Volcano...45 minutes
Waimea (Kamuela) ....1 hour 15 minutes

Drive Times (continued)

Kauai

From Lihu'e to:	Time to Travel
Kilauea	50 minutes
Koke'e	1 hour 30 minutes
Po'ipu	30 minutes
Princeville	1 hour
Waimea Canyon	1 hour 15 minutes

Molokai

From Molokai Airport to:	Time to Travel
Halawa Valley	2 hours
Kaunakakai	15 minutes
Kepuhi Beach	25 minutes
Mapulehu	35 minutes
Maunaloa	15 minutes
Papohaku Beach	30 minutes

Lanai

From Lanai Airport to:	Time to Travel
Garden of the Gods	45 minutes
Hulopo'e and Manele Bays	25 minutes
Lanai City	5 minutes
Munro Trail	15 minutes
Shipwreck Beach	35 minutes

TRAFFIC ADVISORY

If you decide to explore the island of Oahu by car, keep in mind one thing: Oahu is said to have more cars per capita than anywhere else in the United States, and the number of registered vehicles on the road on the island has doubled in the past 20 years. The times to avoid the freeways and major highways—Nimitz Highway in particular—are 6:30–8:30 a.m. and 3:30–6 p.m. on weekdays. The morning traffic can get especially brutal during late August through early September (when most local students begin the school year). The traffic also gets fairly busy during the downtown Honolulu area during the lunch hour. Vehicular traffic in and leading into Waikiki can get very congested during weeknights—and doubly so on weekends. During all other times, the freeways, highways, and roads are usually quite friendly to drivers, especially on Sundays.

You won't have to worry about major traffic jams on any of the Neighbor Islands. Traffic officials on Maui, the Big Island, and Kauai all say the busiest times are 6:30–8:30 a.m. and 3:30–5:30 p.m., when residents are commuting to and from work. Traffic can also get fairly congested in Kapa'a on Kauai during the lunch hour. All in all, the traffic on these islands is nowhere near as bad as the bumper-to-bumper jams you might see on Oahu.

You'll have no problem at all traversing the roads on Molokai and Lanai, where the residents' idea of traffic congestion is a three-car backup.

The road system in Hawaii is efficient and fairly simple, with posted signs (white lettering against dark green background) providing directions throughout your drive. And considering the number of vehicles in the state, particularly on Oahu, Hawaii's paved highways and streets are in very good condition. Potholes and bumps are few and far between, although there are some rough spots along the H-1 Freeway (eastbound) near the 'Aiea exit and on Kamehameha Highway on Oahu's windward and North Shore areas.

Don't use this as an excuse to drive like Mario Andretti, however. In recent years, the Honolulu Police Department has placed a stronger emphasis on traffic enforcement. In the first half of 1999, HPD officers issued 21,244 speeding tickets on Oahu—a 44% increase from the same period in 1998. HPD has identified the H-1 Freeway, Pali Highway, and the Kalaniana'ole Highway on Oahu as the problem areas, so be especially careful while driving on these roads.

PARKING

First, the good news: Finding a parking spot isn't a problem for most areas on Oahu. And better news: Parking is even easier to find on the Neighbor Islands. In Waikiki and downtown Honolulu, however, it's a different story.

Parking rates can get ridiculous in Honolulu's main business district, where available parking garages charge as much as $3 per half-hour. Two affordable parking structures: The Ali'i Place lot at Alakea and Hotel Streets (enter off of Alakea) charges 50¢ per half-hour for the first 2 hours and $1 per each following half-hour. On weekends and evenings, the rate is only 25¢ per half-hour, with a $2 maximum. The Chinatown Gateway Plaza lot at King and Bethel Streets (enter off of Bethel) also charges 50¢ per half-hour for the first 2 hours and $1 per each additional half-hour.

In the downtown area near 'Iolani Palace, your best bet is finding metered parking alongside Punchbowl Street (the rate is $1 an hour, with a 2-hour limit). There is no metered parking available on King Street, the area's main street.

You can also try to find a metered parking spot alongside Bethel, Merchant, and Nu'uanu Streets near Chinatown. The best time to find an empty space in downtown is during the mid-morning and mid-afternoon.

If you're catching a show at the Hawaii Theatre in downtown, we recommend parking at the Liberty House lot at King and Bethel (enter off Bethel Street). It's a flat rate of $3 anytime after 4 p.m.

In Waikiki, the best option is to leave the car in your hotel parking garage and explore the area on foot. If you're driving into Waikiki, however, the best parking option is the multi-level IMAX garage located on Seaside Avenue (look to the right immediately after turning left from Kalakaua Avenue). This parking garage is centrally located and has the most affordable rate (a flat fee of $6 for all-day parking). In the Honolulu Zoo and Kapi'olani Park area, parking becomes much easier to find. Metered stalls there cost only a quarter per hour, with a four-hour limit at Kapi'olani Park and a three-hour limit at the zoo.

On the Neighbor Islands, finding an available parking space can be tough in Lahaina on Maui, which is always congested with pedestrians and cruising cars. The best option here is to park at the Lahaina Center (enter from either Papalaua or Waine'e Street). If you purchase any item from one of the shops—even a single postcard—they'll validate your parking for up to four hours.

Currently there are no parking meters on any of the Neighbor Islands except near a few public office buildings. (The downtown Hilo area had meters—a nickel per half-hour, a dime for a full hour—but recently discontinued them. The time limit of two hours, however, remains in effect.)

All the parking lots we've seen are fairly well lit, and the fact that the lots are almost always filled to near capacity (particularly the ones in Waikiki) lessens the chance of an unwanted encounter. *One important precaution:* Do not leave valuables in your car, and do not let anyone see you putting your possessions into the car's trunk. Car thefts and break-ins have been on the rise.

Public Transportation

USING THEBUS ON OAHU

If you prefer a less expensive way to get from here to there on Oahu, TheBus is a good option. The City and County of Honolulu has one of the most efficient municipal bus systems in the United States (it was named "America's Best Transit System" by the American Public Transit Association in 1994 and 1995). Each day, the city's fleet of buses collectively transports 260,000 passengers and travels 60,000 miles, equal to two and a half trips around the world!

The advantages of riding TheBus go beyond cost. This is an excellent opportunity to mingle with the locals (and chances are, you'll want their help in figuring out which stop you need to get off on). Strike up a conversation and, hopefully, enjoy a generous sampling of Hawaii's aloha spirit. During non–rush hour traffic, the buses are usually uncrowded and the ride is quite pleasant.

A one-way fare on TheBus is $1 for adults and 50¢ for students (ages six through high school). You can request a free transfer pass, which entitles you to a second boarding on a bus where routes intersect. Stopovers or picking up a bus again in a continuous direction is not permitted, and there is a time limit to the transfer. Be sure to ask for the transfer when you pay your fare.

If you plan on using TheBus frequently during your stay, we recommend purchasing a $10 visitor pass, which allows you unlimited rides for four days. There is also a $25 monthly pass ($12.50 for students). These passes are available at all ABC stores in Waikiki.

As this book went to press, the Honolulu City Council was seriously mulling over a proposal that would increase one-way bus fares to $1.50 per adult. The measure is likely to pass.

For bus route information, call (808) 848-5555 between 5:30 a.m. and 10 p.m. daily. Be sure you have a pencil and paper handy, and be ready to provide the following information: your current location, your desired destination, and the time of day you need to arrive at that destination.

Also, recorded route information from Waikiki to some of Oahu's most popular visitor attractions is available by calling (808) 296-1818, entering code number 8287, and then following the directions. If you want to take the bus to the Polynesian Cultural Center, for example, press option "13" and listen to the recording, which will instruct you to board any *'ewa*-bound bus numbered 8, 19, 20, 47, or 58, ride to Ala Moana Shopping Center, then transfer to the #55 bus, which will take you to the PCC. It's that simple.

For more information, call the customer service office at (808) 848-4500. TheBus also has an informative Web site at www.thebus.org.

Abbreviated List of Bus Numbers and Their Destinations
Note: Routes and numbers are subject to change.
3   Kaimuki/Pearl Harbor
4   Nuʻuanu/Punahou
6   Pauoa/Woodlawn (University of Hawaii)
8   Waikiki/Ala Moana
19   Waikiki/Airport & Hickam
20   Airport/Halawa Gate
47   Waipahu
48   Honolulu/Waikele & ʻEwa Mill
52C   Wahiawa/Circle Island
55C   Kaneʻohe/Circle Island

Abbreviated List of Bus Numbers and Their Destinations (cont.)
57　Kailua/Waimanalo/Sea Life Park
58　Hawaii Kai/Sea Life Park
88A　North Shore Express

RIDING THE WAIKIKI TROLLEY

A fun and thoroughly pleasant way to get around Waikiki and Honolulu is riding the Waikiki Trolley, operated by Enoa Tours. The trolley's Red Line covers all of Waikiki and Honolulu, stopping at the Honolulu Zoo, Waikiki Aquarium, Bishop Museum, Chinatown, Aloha Tower, and 'Iolani Palace (26 stops in all). The Blue Line traces Oahu's scenic southern coast, including stops at Hanauma Bay and Sea Life Park (11 stops in all). And the Yellow Line takes passengers on a shopping and dining excursion, with dropoff/pickup points at Ala Moana Center, Ward Warehouse, Ward Centre, Duty Free Shoppers, and other locales (20 stops in all).

Four-day passes are available at the following rates: $30 per adult ($10 per child ages 4–11) for unlimited rides on either the Red & Yellow or Blue & Yellow routes, and $42 ($12 per child) for unlimited rides on all three routes. For a one-day pass, the cost is $18 per adult ($8 per child) for either the Red & Yellow or Blue & Yellow routes, and $30 ($10 per child) for all three routes. Passes may be purchased at all major hotel tour desks or from customer service representatives at selected stops.

The Waikiki Trolley operates daily from 8:30 a.m. to 11 p.m. Red Line trolleys arrive/depart at their appointed stops every 20 minutes; Blue Line trolleys every 60 minutes; and Yellow Line trolleys every 10 to 30 minutes. All routes originate from the Royal Hawaiian Shopping Center depot in Waikiki (located on Royal Hawaiian Avenue).

Enoa Tours also operates several tours via trolleys and air-conditioned vans to popular visitor attractions such as the *Arizona* Memorial and Polynesian Cultural Center.

Call (808) 596-2199 or (800) 824-8804 for more information.

TAXIS

While taxis come in handy in a pinch, they will also pinch your wallet. Thus, we recommend using a taxi only for emergencies or as a final option. A fare from the Honolulu International Airport to Waikiki will be from $18 to $25, depending on which end of Waikiki your hotel is located. Typically, meters begin at $2, with 25¢ added for each eighth of a mile. A few taxi companies provide sight-seeing excursions at a fixed rate.

Taxi Companies

Oahu
Aloha State Taxi: (808) 484-0202 or (808) 847-3566
Americabs: (808) 591-8830
Charley's Taxi & Tours: (808) 531-1333
City Taxi: (808) 524-2121
Royal Taxi & Tours: (808) 944-5513
SIDA Taxi: (808) 836-0011
TheCab: (808) 422-2222

Maui
AB Taxi: (808) 667-7575
Alanui Cab: (808) 874-4895
Ali'i Cab: (808) 661-3688
Caroline's Taxi: (808) 572-9915
Central Maui Taxi: (808) 244-7278
Classy Taxi: (808) 661-3044
Kahului Taxi Service: (808) 877-5681
Kihei Taxi: (808) 879-3000
La Bella Taxi: (808) 242-8011
Royal Sedan & Taxi Service: (808) 874-6900
Wailea Taxi & Tours: (808) 874-5000
Yellow Cab of Maui: (808) 877-7000

Big Island
A-1 Bob's Taxi: (808) 963-5470
Ace One Taxi: (808) 935-8303
Aloha Taxi: (808) 325-5448
Alpha Star Taxi: (808) 885-4771
C&C Taxi: (808) 329-0008
D&E Taxi: (808) 329-4279
Hilo Harry's Taxi: (808) 935-7091
Kona Airport Taxi: (808) 329-7779
Laura's Taxi: (808) 326-5466
Marina Taxi: (808) 329-2481
Paradise Taxi: (808) 329-1234
Percy's Taxi: (808) 969-7060

Kauai
Ace Kauai Taxi: (808) 639-4310
Akiko's Taxi: (808) 822-7588

Taxi Companies (continued)

City Cab: (808) 245-3227
Po'ipu Taxi: (808) 639-2044

Molokai
Molokai Off-Road Tours & Taxi: (808) 553-3369
Kukui Tours & Limousines: (808) 552-2282

Lanai
There are no full-time taxi companies on the island of Lanai.
Dollar Rent-A-Car, however, does provide taxi service on a
driver-available basis. Call (808) 565-7227.

RESORT AND SHOPPING SHUTTLES

Another option you have is hopping aboard a shuttle that takes visitors to specific destinations. The shuttles are usually air-conditioned vans or buses, and the cost is very nominal; some are even free of charge. The following are some of the most widely used shuttle services in the Islands. Ask your hotel concierge for any new shuttle services that may be available from your hotel.

Oahu

TransHawaiian operates a daily shuttle between Waikiki and the Ala Moana Shopping Center, one of the largest outdoor shopping malls in the world. The shuttle schedule is 9:30 a.m.–9:30 p.m. Monday–Saturday, and 10 a.m.–7:30 p.m. on Sunday. Round-trip fares are $4 for adults ($2 for children ages 3–10), while one-way fares are $2 ($1 for children). Pickup/dropoff points in Waikiki include the Outrigger Islander Hotel, Waikiki Police Station, Hawaiian Waikiki Beach Hotel, Outrigger West, Duty Free Shoppers, and the Hilton Hawaiian Village. Call (808) 955-9517.

A trolley service between Waikiki and the Aloha Tower Marketplace is available daily from 9:15 a.m. (departing the Hilton Hawaiian Village) to 9 p.m. (departing the marketplace). Pickup/dropoff points in Waikiki include the Hilton, Outrigger Islander Hotel, the Duke Kahanamoku Statue, Honolulu Zoo, Waikiki Aquarium, Outrigger Prince Kuhio, Outrigger West, Outrigger Waikiki Surf, and Waikiki Parkside. The one-way fare is $2 for adults and $1 for children. Call (808) 528-5700.

Maui

Operated by TransHawaiian, the West Maui Shopping Express provides transportation from Kapalua and Ka'anapali resorts to Whalers Village, Wharf Cinema Center, Hilo Hattie, Lahaina Mall, and Napili Plaza. The trolley runs daily from 8 a.m. to 9:40 p.m. One-way fares are $1 per passenger, while round-trip fares are $2. Call (808) 877-7308.

TransHawaiian also runs a shuttle that takes visitors from Wailea- and Makena-area hotels to the Maui Ocean Center and Whalers Village. The daily shuttle service runs from 8:30 a.m. to 11:20 p.m. One-way fares are $7 (the Wailea-to–Whalers Village route is $15), while round-trip fares are $14 ($30 for Wailea-to–Whalers Village transportation). Call (808) 877-7308.

Free shuttles offer visitors transportation within the island's Wailea Resort, with stops at the Renaissance Wailea Beach Resort, Grand Wailea Resort, Four Seasons Resort Wailea, Outrigger Wailea Resort, and the area's golf courses and (upon request) tennis facilities. The shuttle operates daily from 6:30 a.m., with the final dropoff at 8:30 p.m. Call (808) 879-2828.

In Ka'anapali, a free shuttle transports guests between the Whalers Village Shopping Center and hotels within the resort area. The service is provided daily from 9 a.m. to 11 p.m. Call (808) 669-3177.

Guests staying at Kapalua Resort can take advantage of a free shuttle that stops at the major hotels, golf courses, tennis facilities, and shops in the area. The daily service runs from 6 a.m. to 11 p.m. Call (808) 669-3177.

The Big Island

In the Hilo area, the Hele-On Bus can get you to where you want to go. Fares can range from 75¢ to $6, depending on the length of the route. Several bus pass options are available. Call (808) 961-8744.

Lanai

Guests staying at either the Lodge at Ko'ele or Manele Bay Hotel on Lanai can enjoy shuttle service between the hotels and the airport. Other shuttles transport guests to the island's two championship golf courses: the Experience at Ko'ele and the Challenge at Manele. The charge is $10 per person, and the fare is good for the entire length of stay. Call (808) 565-7600.

PEOPLE WITH SPECIAL NEEDS

On the island of Oahu, curb-to-curb transportation service is provided by the City and County of Honolulu via the Handi-Van (call (808) 456-5555 for reservations, (808) 454-5050 for customer service). A sister company to TheBus, the Handi-Van transports some 2,000 passengers daily, taking them wherever they need to go on Oahu.

Free passes may be picked up at the state's Department of Transportation Services (call (808) 523-4083), located at 711 Kapi'olani Boulevard on the second floor. The office hours are 8 a.m.–4:30 p.m. Monday–Friday. It is highly advisable that you write to the above address and request an application form about six weeks in advance of your arrival.

The van service is available from 5:30 a.m. to 11:00 p.m. Fares are $1.50.

In addition, it should be pointed out that all city buses in Honolulu are equipped with elevator lifts to service the disabled.

There are no major public transportation systems on the Neighbor Islands, so special services for disabled travelers are few. However, the state of Hawaii has published a helpful guide, titled *Aloha Guide to Accessibility*, for travelers with disabilities. Call the Commission on Persons with Disabilities at (808) 586-8121 or write to them at 919 Ala Moana Boulevard, Honolulu, HI 96814. You can visit their Web site at www.hawaii.gov/health/cpd_indx.htm.

INTER-ISLAND FLIGHTS

So you're staying on more than one Hawaiian island? Good for you! Island-hopping is easy, convenient, and affordable. Inter-island flights are provided by two major local carriers: Aloha Airlines and Hawaiian Airlines. Both fly to and from Honolulu on Oahu; Kona and Hilo on the Big Island of Hawaii; Kahului on Maui; Lihu'e on Kauai; and Molokai and Lanai. In addition, Aloha has a sister airline, Island Air, which flies to the smaller airports, including Kapalua and Hana on Maui, and Kalaupapa on Molokai.

Aloha Airlines makes more than 300 daily inter-island flights, while Hawaiian Airlines offers more than 140. Both offer first-class seating, but the flights are so short—a Honolulu-Hilo flight is 50 minutes, while a Honolulu-Lihu'e flight takes only half an hour—that you won't get to enjoy it for very long.

Passengers are allowed one carry-on bag or item that weighs no more than 20 pounds and is 8" × 14" × 22" or smaller. Bag size "testers" are available at the check-in counters and gates. Boogie boards, coolers with ice, skateboards, and strollers are among the items not allowed into the cabin.

Booking a round-trip inter-island flight isn't cheap. Aloha's rate is $143.50, while Hawaiian Air's is as high as $186. A better deal for you would be to purchase a book of six one-way coupons, available in Hawaii at airport ticket counters or at the airline counters at Sears. These coupons are convenient and will save you money. Hawaiian Airlines sells their coupon books for $351, which comes out to an average of $58.50 per ticket. (The average ticket price if you booked directly through Hawaiian Air, without the coupon, would be $93.) Also, consider that a round-trip flight for two on Hawaiian could set you back $372, which is already higher than the cost of the book of six coupons. Aloha Airlines sells their coupon books for $315, an average of $52.50. All coupons are transferable, so you can always sell any extra coupons to fellow travelers looking for a deal.

When booking your inter-island flight, ask for any special deals that may be offered. Or check Aloha's and Hawaiian's Web sites (provided below).

Aloha Airlines

Toll-free: (800) 554-4833
Oahu: (808) 484-1111
Maui: (808) 244-9071
Big Island: (808) 935-5771
Kauai: (808) 245-3691
Web site: www.alohaair.com

Island Air

Toll-free: (800) 652-6541
Molokai (ticket counter): (808) 567-6115
Lanai (ticket counter): (808) 565-6744

Hawaiian Airlines

Toll-free: (800) 367-5320
Oahu: (808) 838-1555
Maui: (808) 871-6132
Big Island: (808) 326-5615
Kauai: (808) 245-1813
Molokai: (808) 553-3644
Lanai: (808) 565-7281
Web site: www.hawaiianair.com

THE LAHAINA-LANAI FERRY

Thus far we've mentioned travel by land and by air, and we'll close with an excursion by sea: Visitors to Maui and Lanai can take advantage of Expeditions' Lahaina-Lanai Passenger Shuttle, which makes five round-trips daily between the two islands.

Departure times from Lahaina Harbor on Maui are 6:45 and 9:15 a.m. and 12:45, 3:15, and 5:45 p.m. Departure times from Lanai are 8 and 10:30 a.m. and 2, 4:30, and 6:45 p.m. The fare is $25 each way for adults, $20 for children age 11 and under. Each trip takes between 45 and 55 minutes. If you're prone to motion sickness, take your Dramamine ahead of time, as the ride can get bumpy on occasion. Call (808) 661-3756.

Part Six

Entertainment and Nightlife

Performing Arts

Here's a little secret about Hawaii: While better known for its sun-dappled beaches and magnificent volcanoes, the Aloha State also offers world-class symphony performances and some of the most enjoyable theater productions you'll find anywhere.

Several theater productions are based on original works by gifted local playwrights such as Lisa Matsumoto, who takes traditional children's tales and turns them into imaginative—and hilarious—"local-style" fables. **Kumu Kahua Theatre** presents insightful and often poignant looks at the local lifestyle at its downtown Honolulu theater.

Major Concert and Performing Arts Venues	
Aloha Stadium	(808) 486-9300
Hawaii Theatre Center	(808) 528-0506
Maui Arts & Cultural Center (Maui)	(808) 242-7469
Neal Blaisdell Center Arena	(808) 591-2211
Neal Blaisdell Concert Hall	(808) 591-2211
Waikiki Shell	(808) 924-8939

Hawaii Nightlife

The nightlife scene in Hawaii is best summarized this way: If you're on Oahu, you have a wide range of options (particularly in Waikiki and Honolulu), but on the Neighbor Islands, your after-dark options are much more limited.

On Oahu, your after-dark options are nearly endless and include dinner shows, nightclubs, lounges, and even a full menu of adult entertainment. Even here, however, the entertainment scene isn't what it once was. In the 1960s and 1970s, Waikiki was a mecca for local performers such as Don Ho, who entertained SRO audiences with happy sing-alongs and touristy favorites. Today, although Ho still delights audiences—he currently performs at the Waikiki Beach Hotel—the state's slumping economy has had a trickle-down effect even in Waikiki, where dinner shows are struggling to survive.

The dinner shows in Waikiki largely cater to visitors. If you see local people at a Society of Seven show, for example, you'll find that they're usually in the company of visiting friends, family members, or business clients. Generally, most locals tend to avoid Waikiki, although hangouts like **Duke's Restaurant & Barefoot Bar**—where favorite local musicians like Henry Kapono perform—are notable exceptions.

The dance club scene on Oahu, especially considering the big-city atmosphere of Honolulu and Waikiki, is average at best. **Rumours** at the Ala Moana Hotel and the **Wave Waikiki** enjoy a faithful local following and are worth a visit. Don't be intimidated by the locals. Like you, they're there to have a good time. This could be a good opportunity, in fact, to "talk story" with them and get better acquainted with the local lifestyle.

If you're staying on any of the Neighbor Islands, you're simply out of luck. A handful of nightclubs do exist, but generally the natives here draw their shades quite early. The notable exception is the bustling town of Lahaina on Maui, where **Front Street** hosts a constant parade of passersby—mostly visitors—and hot spots like the **Hard Rock Cafe**, **Planet Hollywood**, and the **World Cafe** draw young adults like bees to honey.

SHOW TIME IN PARADISE

In terms of sheer numbers, Hawaii doesn't exactly overwhelm visitors with dinner shows and other ongoing evening entertainment. This is unfortunate, because the Islands are full of gifted musicians and singers, from veterans like Don Ho and the Society of Seven to more recent talents like Keali'i Reichel, Willie K, Amy Gilliom, B. B. Shawn, and Na Leo Pilimehana.

The good news, however, is this: The shows that *are* available are all entertaining, of high quality, and (in our view, at least) thoroughly enjoyable. Each show is unique, from Las Vegas–style glitz to simpler, local-style cabarets.

As you'd expect, most of the shows are located right in the heart of Waikiki on the island of Oahu. *Tip:* Check the weekly visitor publications for coupons offering discounts or free gifts. Also, most shows have discounted rates for Hawaiian residents, so try to get a local friend to take you (show tickets can be purchased under his or her name).

THE DINNER SHOWS

Oahu

Creation—A Polynesian Odyssey

Location: 120 Ka'iulani Ave., 'Ainahau Showroom, Sheraton Princess Ka'iulani Hotel, Waikiki

Phone: (808) 931-4660

Show Times: 2 shows nightly, 5:45 and 8:30 p.m. Dinner seating at 5:15 and 8 p.m.; cocktail seating at 6 and 8:30 p.m.

Length: 90 minutes

Cost: $105 per adult ($72 per child age 5–12) for the premium dinner; $62 per adult ($34.50 per child) for the standard dinner, first show; $55 per adult ($30.75 per child) for the second show; and $32 per adult ($21 per child) for the cocktail show.

Discounts: Discount coupons available inside "Best of Oahu" booklets (available throughout Waikiki). Guests staying at the hotel also enjoy a discounted rate.

Type of Seating: Guests are seated on long tables facing the stage. First come, first served.

Menu: An all-you-can-eat buffet. Items include prime rib, shoyu chicken, chow mein noodles with vegetables and char siu, beef curry stew, mahi-mahi, fresh salad, fruits. Desserts include cakes and ice cream. The premium dinner package is a sit-down dinner featuring lobster tail, a tenderloin steak, salad, starch, dessert, and two drinks.

Vegetarian Alternative: Salads are available at the buffet.

Beverages: Mai Tai, draft beer, soft drinks, and juice.

Description and Comments   One of the newest shows in Waikiki—it debuted in October 1998—*Creation* replaced the showroom's *Spectacular Polynesian Revue*, which enjoyed a ten-year run. *Creation* is more high-tech, with state-of-the-art sound and light systems, special effects, and staging, yet has been able to maintain a high level of cultural authenticity that many visitors seek.

The show traces the exploits of Polynesian voyagers and their journey through history. There is plenty of humor and romance, and stirring segments relive Hawaii's colorful "boat days" in the 1930s and 1940s, its statehood celebration (1959), and the impact of the rock-and-roll era in the Islands. Among the show's most popular highlights is a spectacular Samoan fire-knife dance (always a favorite among the visitors). The proceedings are narrated by a lavishly costumed storyteller.

Smartly produced and evenly paced, *Creation* is a good bet for young families. It is an entertaining way to learn about Hawaii's culture and legends and provides a continuous treat for the senses.

The Don Ho Show

Location: 2300 Kalakaua Ave., Hoku Hale Showroom, Waikiki Beach-comber Hotel, Waikiki

Phone: (808) 923-3981

Web Site: www.donho.com

Show Time: 1 show Sunday–Thursday, 7 p.m. (dark Friday and Saturday)

Length: 90 minutes

Cost: $52 per adult ($26 per child ages 6–12) for the dinner show; $32 per adult ($16 per child) for the cocktail show.

Discounts: None.

Type of Seating: Table seating.

Menu: A sit-down dinner of chicken, prime rib, mashed potatoes, salad, and dessert.

Vegetarian Alternative: Varies nightly.

Beverages: Tropical drinks, wine, beer, soft drinks, juice, tea, coffee.

Description and Comments   Even in the twilight of his career, Don Ho still knows how to throw a party. The local legend, born Donald Tai Loy Ho on August 13, 1930, remains a popular fixture on the Island entertainment scene, serenading old and new fans alike with favorite hits like "Tiny Bubbles," "Pearly Shells," "Blue Hawaii," and "I'll Remember You." (If you think Ho is passé, consider that alternative bands such as Green Day, Porno for Pyros, Foo Fighters, and the Mighty Mighty Bosstones have all attended his show in recent years.) The sleepy-eyed Ho sits behind his organ on stage, fronting his veteran band, and presides over a delightful show featuring sing-alongs, lots of jokes, audience participation, and guest performers.

A simple format? Yes. But it works. Ho himself admits he's never had a great singing voice, but his skillful interaction with his audience—most of them silver-haired grandmas and grandpas—is a wonder to behold.

A special treat is a guest performance by Hoku Ho, Don's teenage daughter. She is a gifted vocalist with great poise and presence ("When she sings better than her daddy, what are you going to do?" the proud dad likes to say.) Expect great things from Hoku, whose name, appropriately enough, translates to "star."

Also, you'll get a chance to meet the senior Ho before *and* after the show for picture-taking and autographs.

The bottom line? If you're expecting a high-budget, Las Vegas–style extravaganza, don't bother. Also, young children might get bored with the playful banter that goes on between songs. However, if you've never seen Ho perform and want to relive Hawaii's golden years of music, this is the show to see. And while Ho insists the word "retirement" isn't in his vocabulary, remember that he's nearing 70. See him soon before he does decide to call it a career.

Magic of Polynesia

Location: 2300 Kalakaua Ave., Waikiki Beachcomber Hotel, Waikiki

Phone: (808) 971-4321

Show Times: 2 shows nightly, 6:30 and 8:45 p.m. Dinner seating at 5 p.m.; cocktail seating at 6 and 8 p.m.

Length: 75 minutes

Cost: $129 per adult ($89 per child age 4–12) for deluxe dinner; $64 per adult ($44 per child) for the standard dinner; and $35 per adult ($25 per child) for the cocktail show.

Discounts: Entertainment Book coupons offer 20% off for the cocktail show.

Type of Seating: Table seating. Smaller tables seat 10; larger tables are set in rows and seat up to 40. First come, first served. A seat toward the back will give you a better view of the entire show.

Menu: Sit-down dinner of roast beef, chicken, rice, steamed vegetables. Cake is served for dessert.

Vegetarian Alternative: Usually steamed noodles with vegetables. Request in advance.

Beverages: Tropical drinks, wine, beer, soft drinks, juice, coffee.

Description and Comments The "magic" of the Islands takes on a new meaning at this spectacular show, which was formerly housed at the Hilton Hawaiian Village. The new show takes full advantage of the new $9 million showroom, which includes two "volcanoes" and waterfalls.

The star of the show is John Hirokawa, a local product who once apprenticed under David Copperfield. Youthful, handsome, and engaging, Hirokawa has a natural show biz flair to go along with his superb illusionist skills.

The illusions themselves are masterful, and many have a distinct Polynesian theme: At one point in the show, Hirokawa brings a Hawaiian warrior helmet to life! He also levitates a woman on a fountain of water, makes amazing disappearances and reappearances, and even "shrinks" right before your eyes! The climax of the show (as with most magic shows) is an act of death-defying drama: Hirokawa must free himself before a torch burns through a rope securing a giant slab of spikes. Unless he *really* wants to be different, you know Hirokawa will somehow survive the ordeal. But the effect is there, and you'll leave the show wondering, "How did he do that?"

Included in the show are some touches of Polynesia, including a Samoan fire-knife dance and Polynesian dancers. Thankfully, rather than just being thrown in the show for the sake of adding culture, they blend in nicely with Hirokawa's act.

This is another show that caters to families, and children as well as adults would enjoy it from start to finish. Hirokawa has established himself as one of Hawaii's top entertainers, and he delivers a solid and consistent performance night after night. An excellent show, recommended especially for anyone with an appreciation for the art of illusions.

The Society of Seven

Location: 2335 Kalakaua Ave., Main Outrigger Showroom, Outrigger Waikiki Hotel, Waikiki

Phone: (808) 922-6408

Web Site: www.angelfire.com/hi/societyofseven

Show Times: 1 show on Monday, 8:30 p.m.; 2 shows Tuesday–Saturday, 6:30 and 8:30 p.m. (dark Sunday).

Length: 80 minutes

Cost: $55 per adult ($39.50 per student age 13–20; $36 per child age 12 and under) for the Sunset Dinner package; $49.50 per adult ($35.50 per student, $32 per child) for the Ali'i Buffet (6:30 p.m. show only); $59 per adult ($44 per student, $40.50 per child) for the Pikake Buffet (8:30 p.m. show only); and $32 per adult ($19.50 per student, $16 per child) for the cocktail package.

Discounts: None.

Type of Seating: Cabaret-style table seating.

Menu: Buffet includes meats, fish, chicken, rice, salad bar, and dessert. Sit-down dinner includes a choice of prime rib, chicken or fish, and starch, vegetables, and dessert.

Vegetarian Alternative: Pasta is available.

Beverages: Tropical drinks, beer, wine, mixed drinks, soft drinks, juice, coffee.

Description and Comments Like Don Ho, the Society of Seven are seasoned veterans on the Island entertainment scene, with 30 years in the business. Their lineup has evolved over the years, but they remain as popular as ever. Readers of *Honolulu Magazine*, in fact, voted their show the best in Waikiki.

The group's current lineup consists of Tony Ruivivar, Bert Sagum, Gary Bautista, Randy Abellar, Hoku Low, Roy Guerzo, and Wayne Wakai.

Expect a little bit of everything at an S.O.S. show: comedy, Broadway tunes, musical skits and impressions, oldies and contemporary hits, and lots of audience participation. Slick showmen, the S.O.S. can have you laughing hysterically one minute and mesmerized by their vocal skills the next. Each member of the septet has his own special talent—from Sagum's comedy antics to Low's falsetto stylings—and it all comes together masterfully in this 80-minute production.

Fast-paced and masterfully produced, the S.O.S. show is a worthwhile experience, and suitable for entertainment-seekers of all ages.

YES! International Revue

Location: Polynesian Palace Showroom, 227 Lewers St., Outrigger Reef Towers Hotel, Waikiki

Phone: (808) 923-7469

Show Times: 6 and 8:30 p.m. Tuesday–Sunday (dark Monday). Dinner seating at 5 p.m.; cocktail seating at 6 and 8 p.m.

Length: 85 minutes

Cost: $49.50 per adult ($32 per student age 13–20; $18 per child age 5–12) for the dinner show; $32 per adult ($16 per student, $12.50 per child) for the cocktail shows.

Discounts: None.

Type of Seating: Table seating. Tables are a bit too close together, obviously in an attempt to fit in as many patrons as possible.

Menu: Filet mignon, mahi-mahi, mashed potatoes, steamed vegetables, salad, roll, and dessert.

Vegetarian Alternative: Pasta or salad.

Beverages: Tropical drinks, mixed drinks, beer, wine, soft drinks, juice, coffee.

Description and Comments It'd be tempting to call *YES!* a mini-version of *Cirque du Soleil*, but that wouldn't be entirely fair. Sal Murillo's inspiring production has a life of its own, with a handful of unique acts that range from nostalgic doo-wops to living sculptures.

The show's premier act (and the crowd favorite) is Los Mayas, a trio of performers that display amazing feats of balance and strength through living body "sculptures" in silent slow motion. Remy Farfan, Sachenka Pacheco, and Mario Vargas form various configurations with their gold-painted bodies. This is simply one of those "see it to believe it" performances.

Another act, Anatoli and Irina, blend modern dance and gymnastics while using an oversized quadrilateral "cube." Their youthful son, Vladik, is a sure show-stopper, with his champion juggling and tumbling skills. (He was the gold medal winner in the 1997 International Juggling Association Competition.) Comedian Joe Monti provides the evening's laughs, while never once uttering a single word! And the *YES!* dancers provide visual segues between acts, delighting the audience with hula and Hollywood-style flair.

Our favorite act, however, was DisGuyz, a local quintet featuring a cappella harmonies. The members of DisGuyz are all young men, recently graduated from high school, and their enthusiasm and energy drive the show. Their vocal talents are excellent, as evidenced in songs like "Under the Boardwalk," "In the Still of the Night," "I Believe I Can Fly," and even a Beach Boys medley.

This is a marvelous show for families. No one will be bored. If you're looking for something unique and want to treat the kids to a real "ooh and ahh" experience, we say yes to *YES!*.

Maui

Warren & Annabelle's

Location: 900 Front Street, Lahaina

Phone: (808) 667-6244

Show Times: 2 shows Monday–Saturday, 6:45 and 8:15 p.m.

Length: 60 minutes

Cost: $36. Guests must be 21 or older. Special *pupus* (hors d'oeuvres) packages are available: $69 includes show, dessert, coffee, and 2 drinks; $75 includes show, appetizer platter, 2 drinks; and $86 includes show, appetizer platter, dessert, 2 drinks, and coffee. Prices include tax and tip.

Discounts: Coupons offering a 20% discount off the show are periodically available. They're stapled on show rack cards available at hotel lobbies, visitor attractions, the airport, and other visitor-oriented locations. Discount does not apply to any of the package offerings.

Type of Seating: Table seating for *pupus* and cocktails. Then you enter an intimate 78-seat theater (stadium seating). First come, first served.

Menu: Unless you order a *pupus* package, everything is a la carte. You can order from a *pupus* menu that includes spicy crab cakes, coconut-battered shrimp, chicken satay, and crab-stuffed mushrooms. An appetizer medley of all of the above is also available. Desserts include chocolate truffle cake, rum cake, white chocolate raspberry cheesecake, crème brûlée, deep-dish apple pie, and New York–style cheesecake.

Vegetarian Alternative: Request in advance.

Beverages: Tropical drinks, specialty drinks, beer, wine, soft drinks, juice, coffee.

Description and Comments   Hawaii's newest show (it debuted in April 1999), *Warren & Annabelle's* is a welcome addition to bustling Front Street in Lahaina. Warren Gibson performs an assortment of amazing sleight-of-hand tricks in an intimate, 78-seat theater. One of the premier close-up magicians in Southern California, Gibson and his wife Lisa relocated to Maui in 1997 and fulfilled his dream of opening his own magic nightclub.

The tricks are innovative and very well presented, and while it's not nearly as high-budget as you'll find at the *Magic of Polynesia* show on Oahu, the results are just as effective.

Before the start of the show, patrons are treated to an amusing diversion, where "Annabelle," the theater's "invisible ghost," sits at the piano and takes musical requests.

AFTER-DINNER ALTERNATIVES

For those who can't work up the energy to dance up a storm or mingle among noisy crowds, there are plenty of after-dinner alternatives that feature pretty settings, a pleasant atmosphere, and usually some good Hawaiian musical entertainment. These bars and lounges provide a nice way to enjoy a nightcap and unwind after an active day.

Here's a list of bars and lounges we recommend for after-dinner relaxation, fun, and entertainment. Most are located at Hawaii's finer hotels and resorts, so you can enjoy a nightcap at your leisure, then head up to your room when you want to call it a night.

Oahu

Banyan Veranda, Sheraton Moana Surfrider: (808) 922-3111

Duke's Canoe Club, Outrigger Waikiki: (808) 922-2268

Hibiscus Cafe, Waikiki Beachcomber Hotel: (808) 922-4646

House without a Key, Halekulani Hotel: (808) 923-2311

Lobby Bar, Hawaiian Regent Hotel: (808) 922-6611

Lobby Lounge, Kahala Mandarin-Oriental: (808) 739-8888

Mahina Lounge, Ala Moana Hotel: (808) 955-4811

Mai Tai Bar, Royal Hawaiian Hotel: (808) 923-7311

Moose McGillyCuddy's Pub & Café, 310 Lewers St., Waikiki: (808) 923-0751

Paddles Bar, 'Ilikai Hotel-Nikko Waikiki: (808) 949-3811

Paradise Lounge, Hilton Hawaiian Village: (808) 949-4321

Pikake Lounge, Sheraton Princess Ka'iulani Hotel: (808) 922-5811

Shell Bar, Hilton Hawaiian Village: (808) 949-4321

Tropics Bar, Hilton Hawaiian Village: (808) 949-4321

Maui

Anuenue Lounge, Ritz-Carlton-Kapalua: (808) 669-6200

Botero's Gallery Bar, Grand Wailea Resort Hotel & Spa: (808) 875-1234

Game in the Bar, Grand Wailea Resort Hotel & Spa: (808) 875-1234

Hula Moons, Outrigger Wailea Resort: (808) 879-1922

Lehua Lounge, Kapalua Bay Hotel: (808) 669-5656

Lobby Lounge, Four Seasons Resort Maui: (808) 874-8000

Polo Beach Grille & Bar, Kea Lani Hotel: (808) 875-4100

Reef's Edge Lounge, Sheraton Maui: (808) 661-0031

Weeping Banyan, Hyatt Regency Waikiki: (808) 661-1234

The Big Island

Billfish Bar, King Kamehameha's Kona Beach Hotel: (808) 329-3111

Honu Bar, Mauna Lani Bay Hotel and Bungalows: (808) 885-6622

Polo Bar and Paniolo Lounge, The Orchid at Mauna Lani: (808) 885-2000

Reef Lounge, Mauna Kea Beach Hotel: (808) 882-7222

The Second Floor, Hilton Waikoloa Village: (808) 886-1234

Kauai

Captain's Bar, Hyatt Regency Kauai Resort & Spa: (808) 742-1234

Duke's Canoe Club, Kauai Marriott Resort & Beach Club: (808) 245-5050

The Living Room, Princeville Resort: (808) 826-9644

The Point, Sheraton Kauai Resort: (808) 742-1661

Whaler's Brew Pub, 3132 Ninini Pt., Lihu'e: (808) 245-2000

ADULT ENTERTAINMENT

For better or worse, hostess bars and strip clubs have long been a fixture of Hawaii's nightlife. A quick scan of the sports sections of Honolulu's two major daily newspapers revealed nearly 20 adult-oriented advertisements—from XXX video stores and "massage" parlors to hostess bars and strip joints—a telling indicator of how the business of selling sex has proliferated in recent years.

By far, most of these establishments are based on Oahu and seem to be concentrated in certain areas of Honolulu. Local authorities periodically check in on these places to make sure the "action" doesn't proceed beyond what the laws and regulations allow, but, in truth, their efforts are akin to putting out a fire with a water pistol.

If you visit a hostess bar or strip club, just remember a few precautions. Never openly display the amount of cash you carry, try to travel in groups, and don't consume alcohol to the point of losing your good judgment. The hostesses (mostly young to middle-aged Oriental women) may be pretty and quite charming, but remember that their job is to separate you from your hard-earned cash. After buying them drinks (always of the non-alcoholic variety) at $10 or $20 a pop, well, by the end of the evening you might be wondering how your cash disappeared so quickly!

Most of the more popular establishments are located in the heart of Honolulu, along Kapiʻolani Boulevard and Keʻeaumoku Street (a few minutes' drive from Waikiki and a short walk from Ala Moana Shopping Center). Area to avoid: Hotel Street in downtown Honolulu. The few remaining adult-oriented establishments there are run-down and unfriendly and cater more to locals.

DANCE CLUBS AND OTHER NIGHTSPOTS

Night owls with a lust for a party atmosphere have plenty to hoot about on the island of Oahu, and there are a couple of hip hot spots on Maui. But the rest of the islands tend to draw their shades rather early. Here's a listing of the top nightclubs in the Aloha State. Ask your hotel concierge for more recommendations. (*Note:* The legal drinking age in Hawaii is 21. Entertainment schedules and formats are subject to change.)

Oahu

BREW MOON

Hip Island dining spot featuring eclectic decor and beer brewed on-site.
Who Goes There: 20–45 crowd; office workers, college kids, book browsers, and professionals

1200 Ala Moana Blvd., Honolulu (at Ward Centre); (808) 593-0088
Greater Honolulu Zone 2

Cover: None
Minimum: None
Mixed drinks: $4–5
Wine: $4.50 and up
Beer: $3.25–5.50
Dress: Anything from aloha shirts to casual business attire
Specials: "Zero Gravity Hour" offers $2 beers, $3 wine, and half-priced appetizers, including their addictive Beer Crackers, tasty Fire-Roasted Ribs, and hefty Heavy Metal Nacho platter; 4–7 p.m. daily
Food available: Jambalaya, chicken curry, herb-crusted sirloin, burgers, shakes, and daily fish specials

Hours: Monday–Wednesday, 11 a.m.–1 p.m.; Thursday–Saturday, 11 a.m.–2 a.m.; Sunday, 2 p.m.–midnight

What goes on: One of Honolulu's newest venues where customers can people-watch, mingle, and listen to music ranging from Top 40 hits to reggae beats or from blues to jazz. Occasionally, live contemporary Hawaiian and jazz entertainment is performed each Wednesday (9 p.m.–midnight) and Sunday (5–8 p.m.).

Setting & atmosphere: This brewery boasts spectacular views of Waikiki Honolulu. The dining room features art deco furniture and a menu that will satisfy even the most finicky eater. For more information on their beers or other locations, check their Internet site at www.brewmoon.com.

If you go: Try going at "Zero Gravity Hour" to partake of their half-priced Lunar Sampler—five 4-oz. servings of Brew Moon beer—or any of their other award-winning beers.

THE CELLAR

No-frills bar and dance venue
Who Goes There: 18–30; 20-somethings, people-watchers, visitors, and curfew-breakers

205 Lewers St., Waikiki Imperial Hotel; (808) 923-9952
Waikiki Zone 1

Cover: $5
Minimum: None
Mixed drinks: $3.75 and up
Wine: $3.50
Beer: $3.50

Dress: Casual
Specials: $1.50 drink specials are
   offered throughout the night
Food available: None

Hours: Wednesday, Friday, and Saturday, 8 p.m.– 4 a.m.; Tuesday, Thursday, and Sunday, 9 p.m.– 4 a.m.; closed on Mondays

What goes on: A variety of entertainment and dance themes, including Top 40 hits, hip-hop, R&B music, and a male dance revue every Wednesday, Friday, and Saturday, 8–10 p.m. Dancing nightly.

Setting & atmosphere: Watch your step as you walk down the stairwell that leads to the main dance floor. When you reach the main room, what you'll find is everything you expect a bar to be: dark, smoke-filled, and packed with people dancing the night away. The club features two bars, a couple of pool tables, and a lounge for those who want to get away from the crowd and converse. What the club lacks in decor, it makes up for with its nightly drink specials and come-as-you-are attitude.

If you go: Call ahead to find out what the evening's theme is. If the all-male revue isn't for you, you may want to check out Ladies Night on Wednesdays.

DON HO'S GRILL

Nostalgic, casual pier-side hangout
Who Goes There: 21–55; visiting families, beach boys, and music lovers

1 Aloha Tower Dr. (Aloha Tower Marketplace), Honolulu; (808) 528-0807
Greater Honolulu Zone 2

Cover: None
Minimum: None
Mixed drinks: $4.25–5.50
Wine: $4 and up
Beer: $2 and up
Dress: Board shorts, sandals,
   khakis, and the obligatory

aloha shirt
Specials: Happy Hour daily,
   4:30– 6:30 p.m.; half-priced
   appetizers and $2 draft beers
Food available: Seared 'ahi, calamari,
   pizzas, sandwiches, and salads

Hours: Monday–Wednesday, Sunday, 10:30 a.m.–11 p.m.; Thursday–Saturday, 10:30 a.m.– 2 a.m.

What goes on: Live Hawaiian entertainment daily. Sunday–Wednesday, 6 – 8:30 p.m.; Thursday–Saturday, 9 p.m.–closing.

Setting & atmosphere: Rattan chairs and large, picnic cloth–covered tables fill this restaurant named after Mr. Tiny Bubbles himself, Don Ho. This family-oriented bar boasts one of the best views of Honolulu Harbor and is decorated with photographs and memorabilia from Ho's heyday. It isn't a mini-museum by any means, but rather a combination of old and new Hawaii.

If you go: Set aside time to explore the pier, ascend the Aloha Tower's observation deck, and learn about Hawaii's Boat Day history.

ESPRIT LOUNGE

Live music nightclub and hotel lounge
Who Goes There: 18–45; locals, hotel guests, professionals, and live music fans

2255 Kalakaua Ave. (Sheraton Waikiki Hotel), Waikiki; (808) 922-4422
Waikiki Zone 1

Cover: None	Dress: Casual
Minimum: 2 drinks	Specials: None
Mixed drinks: $5.25 – 5.50	Food available: Pizzas, sandwiches,
Wine: $5.25/glass	hot wings, and nachos
Beer: $3.50 – 3.75	

Hours: Sunday–Thursday, 4 p.m.–12:30 a.m.; Friday–Saturday, 4 p.m.–1:30 a.m.

What goes on: This is a popular and stylish nightspot where the entertainment ranges from energetic live shows with local bands to dancing (R&B, Top 40). Entertainment is featured 8:30 p.m.–12:30 a.m. Tuesday–Thursday, and 8:30 p.m.–1:30 a.m. Friday and Saturday.

Setting & atmosphere: The club's neon marquee sign, which reads "Dancing Nightly," stands out like a sore thumb in the hotel's Alice in Wonderland–like lobby. Venture inside and you'll find a dark, candle-lit room connected to the hotel's beach bar/lounge. The venue's fully stocked bar is like an island separating the two distinct club areas. On the left of the entrance you'll find cocktail tables and shimmering lights hanging over a small dance floor next to the main stage, where music lovers and the like can sing and twist the night away. On the right you'll find, where the carpet ends, a more relaxed, open-air beach bar lounge area.

If you go: Go early to catch the live musical acts. Since the bar closes early by nightclub standards, you may miss the musical act and feel rushed to finish your drinks if you arrive late.

EURASIA

Upscale sports bar and nightclub
Who Goes There: 25–45; suits, tourists, and dance lovers

2552 Kalakaua Ave. (Hawaiian Regent Hotel), Waikiki; (808) 922-6611
Waikiki Zone 1

Cover: $5 for those over 21 and $10 for those 18–20
Minimum: None
Mixed drinks: $4.75 and up
Wine: $5.25/glass
Beer: $3.50

Dress: Anything goes except hats, caps, and sportswear
Specials: Local Island radio stations broadcast live from the venue on Fridays and Saturdays; no cover before 10 p.m.
Food available: None

Hours: Every day, 4 p.m.–4 a.m.

What goes on: Dancing nightly, 9 p.m.–4 a.m., featuring a variety of DJ-spinned music.

Setting & atmosphere: This hotel nightspot is charming, with its post-modern cocktail tables and dark stucco walls. And, frankly, Eurasia is definitely more nightclub than sports bar. On any given night this club draws in a crowd, whether it be for salsa dancing lessons on Thursdays or for its Original College Night on Wednesdays. But sports lovers shouldn't be discouraged. There are enough televisions strewn throughout the club, showcasing live sporting events, and enough nightly drink specials to satisfy even the biggest sports nut.

If you go: Call ahead to find out what the drink specials of the night are. And try to get there early to witness the sunset over Waikiki.

FUSION WAIKIKI

An alternative club for an alternative lifestyle
Who Goes There: 18–28; club kids, night owls, retro geeks, and cool-kid wannabes

2260 Kuhio Ave., 3rd floor, Waikiki; (808) 924-2422
Waikiki Zone 1

Cover: $5 Friday and Saturday, free the rest of the week
Minimum: None
Mixed drinks: $3 and up
Wine: $3 and up
Beer: $3 and up
Dress: Come with what you have on, as long as it isn't ragged, tattered, or torn

Specials: Dance to 1970s and 1980s tunes during Retro Night on Thursdays or groove to alternative tunes of the 1980s during Mod Society (held every other Thursday); kids age 18 and over get their chance to shine, too, on Kids Club Night on Sundays
Food available: None

Hours: Monday–Thursday, 9 p.m.–4 a.m.; Friday–Saturday, 8 p.m.–4 a.m.; Sunday, 10 p.m.–4 a.m.

What goes on: Dancing nightly. Occasional live entertainment and club circuit parties. Friday and Saturday nights are reserved for the club's weekly male review show.

Setting & atmosphere: One of Hawaii's better-known alternative clubs is pretty low-key. Located above a rib restaurant and next to a pizza place, the only way you know it's there is by the discreet banner that hangs alongside the stairway that leads up to the spot. After ascending a couple of floors, you'll find a small venue with dark walls decorated with green stars, a small dance floor, and a crowd your mother warned you about. But that's where this club gets its energy, spunk, and character—from patrons who don't care where you come from, what you do, or where you have to be.

If you go: Be prepared to stay late, because the serious booty shaking doesn't begin until after midnight.

HARD ROCK CAFE

Internationally known music-themed restaurant
Who Goes There: 18–50; tourists, music lovers, and the occasional rock star

1837 Kapi'olani Blvd., Waikiki; (808) 955-7383
Waikiki Zone 1

Cover: None
Minimum: None
Mixed drinks: $4 and up
Wine: $3.50 and up
Beer: $3.50–4
Dress: Casual

Specials: None
Food available: Hard Rock Cafe's famous pig sandwiches, pot roast, grilled fajitas, burgers, and barbecue chicken

Hours: Dining: 11:30 a.m.–11 p.m. daily; Bar: Sunday–Saturday, 11:30 a.m.–12:30 a.m.; Friday, 11:30 a.m.–1:30 a.m.

What goes on: Live entertainment (ranging from rock and roll to R&B) each Friday, 11 p.m.–1 a.m. Occasionally, major-label recording artists will make special appearances.

Setting & atmosphere: Diners are surrounded by some of the rock-and-roll memorabilia that makes the Hard Rock Cafe a worldwide attraction and keeps visitors from all walks of life coming. Guests can gawk at items such as Eddie Van Halen's guitar, a bust of Mick Jaggar, or the outfit worn by No Doubt's Gwen Steffani. If that isn't enough, there's a 1949 Cadillac hanging over the bar and a tribute to Elvis one can peruse before entering the bathrooms.

If you go: This is a popular spot for celebrity memorabilia seekers and rock-and-roll lovers, so if you're coming to eat, prepare to wait—sometimes up to an hour. If you can, get a table outside the restaurant; besides getting away from the conversation-killing decibel levels in the main room, dining amid tiki torches and being exposed to the Island's cool trade winds makes this venue stand out from the rest.

NASHVILLE WAIKIKI

Authentic Waikiki watering hole
Who Goes There: 21–30; college cowpokes, country bumpkins, and the occasional curious visitor

2330 Kuhio Ave., Waikiki; (808) 926-7911
Waikiki Zone 1

Cover: None
Minimum: None
Mixed drinks: $3–5.75
Wine: $3.25/glass
Beer: $3 and up
Dress: From blue jeans to shorts, from boots to sandals; shirts and footwear are required, but 10-gallon hats are optional
Specials: Nightly line-dancing lessons offered 7–9 p.m.
Food available: Basic bar fare (chips and popcorn)

Hours: Every day, 4 p.m.–4 a.m.

What goes on: Music provided by Hawaii's top country disc jockeys nightly. Pool tournaments held on Sundays and Tuesdays; dart tournaments held on Wednesdays.

Setting & atmosphere: Midwest meets West in this Waikiki venue. Because it's sandwiched in between two hotels, you can easily miss the staircase leading to this golden nugget in Waikiki. Run your fingers across the brick wall and pass the wagon wheel in the doorway and you'll enter the only country-and-western bar in Waikiki. This Island corral has all the fixings—bullhorns, saddles, copper paneling, drink specials that would satisfy any cowboy, and a dance floor large enough for the whole posse to two-step on.

If you go: If line dancing doesn't do it for you, try grabbing drinks during Vegas Night on Wednesdays.

OCEAN CLUB

Chic downtown nightclub and discotheque
Who Goes There: 23–35; urbanites, downtown suits, dancing queens, and singles

500 Ala Moana Blvd. (Restaurant Row); (808) 526-9888
Greater Honolulu Zone 2

Cover: Monday–Thursday, $4 after 8 p.m.; Friday, $5 after 8 p.m.; Saturday, $5 after 9 p.m.
Minimum: None
Mixed drinks: $1.75 and up
Wine: $3.75 and up
Beer: $3.25–3.75
Dress: Gap and Banana Republic fare; men must wear collared shirts; hats and athletic wear prohibited

Specials: $2 for most drinks during Ladies Night on Tuesdays and Paddlers Night on Thursdays; Thursdays, win cash for wearing the best aloha outfit
Food available: More on the elegant side, with generous servings of calamari, spring rolls, crab dip, and teriyaki steak; for the less adventurous, chicken wings and nachos are available

Hours: Tuesday–Thursday, 4:30 p.m.–2 a.m.; Friday, 4:30 p.m.–3 a.m.; Saturday, 6 p.m.–3 a.m.; closed Sundays and Mondays; available for private parties

What goes on: Live, local musicians perform on a sporadic basis. Other than that, dancing Tuesday–Thursday nights to the tunes of Top 40 hits, R&B, hip-hop, and urban beats.

Setting & atmosphere: This trendy spot features two loaded bars, a kitchen that pumps out high-end *pupus* or appetizers, and an outdoor lounge perfect for unwinding after a long day. As soon as the sun sets, the crowd rolls in like ants, and on a good night, you'll be lucky to find a place to stand. Come to this club and expect the music to be loud, the drinks cheap, and the crowd young and hip.

If you go: It seems like everyone and their brother comes out to this downtown club, which in turn causes the line to snake quite a bit. So, if you aren't connected, be prepared to wait. Also, don't go to celebrate your 21st birthday. Only club-goers 23 and over are allowed.

RUMOURS

Oldies disco and nightclub
Who Goes There: 18–45; tourists, suits, and private party-goers

410 Atkinson Dr. (Ala Moana Hotel), Honolulu; (808) 955-4811
Greater Honolulu Zone 2

Cover: $5 on Sunday, Tuesday, Friday, and Saturday; free before 9 p.m. daily and on Wednesday
Minimum: 2 drinks
Mixed drinks: $3.75 and up
Wine: $3.75 and up
Beer: $3.75 and up
Dress: Anything goes except beach wear, tank tops, and slippers

Specials: Free *pupus* daily 5–8 p.m.; dance to the music of the 1960s and 1970s during the club's Big Chill Night on Fridays
Food available: Nachos, potato wedges, steak strips, veggie platters, pizzas, burgers, wontons, and cheesecake slices

Hours: Tuesday–Thursday, 5 p.m.–midnight; Friday and Saturday, 5 p.m.–4 a.m.; Sunday, 5 p.m.–9 p.m.; closed Monday, but available for private parties

What goes on: A different theme every night, from ballroom dancing and country music to Top 40 mixes and Latin dancing.

Setting & atmosphere: Waiters/waitresses decked out in formal black-and-white attire will take your cocktail order with a smile. You'll wait seated in rust-colored, old-style lounge chairs, which are peppered throughout this two-story club, and, as you sit patiently awaiting the arrival of your order, you'll examine the cages, stone pillars, and a huge television screen that flank the dance floor. The only thing that detracts from this exquisite club is the 1980s video game tables that are set up and operational at the back of the room. *Sans* game machines, this is how a lounge should look.

If you go: Bring your dancing shoes and be prepared to strut your stuff. People will be watching.

SCRUPLES BEACH CLUB

Waikiki beach bar that's not near a beach
Who Goes There: 18–25; tourists, people-watchers, and the occasional superstar

2310 Kuhio Ave., Waikiki; (808) 923-9530
Waikiki Zone 1

Cover: $5 for those 21 and over, $15 for those 18–20
Minimum: 2 drinks
Mixed drinks: $4.75 and up
Wine: $4.75 and up

Beer: $4.75 and up
Dress: Jeans, skirts, trousers, and shorts; no athletic wear
Specials: None
Food available: None

Hours: Every day, 8 p.m.–4 a.m.

What goes on: Dancing to Top 40, alternative, and reggae beats.

Setting & atmosphere: This club is so tacky that it's cool—from the bamboo paneled walls to the plastic palm leaves that hang from the club's pillars. There isn't much in the way of food or views—unusual for a beach bar—but what you do get is a lit dance floor, all-night rug cutting, and a bikini contest every Thursday night at midnight.

If you go: Take the time to peruse Scruples Beach Club's Wall of Fame. Some celebrities that have passed through include Robert DeNiro, Jim Carrey, and Jean-Claude Van Damme.

WAVE WAIKIKI

Alternative nightclub and rare alternative live music venue
Who Goes There: 18–28; college kids, eccentric folk, jocks, skirts, and alterna-lovers

1877 Kalakaua Ave., Waikiki; (808) 941-0424
Waikiki Zone 1

Cover: $5 after 10 p.m. daily, none before 10 p.m.
Minimum: 2 drinks
Mixed drinks: $5
Wine: $4–5
Beer: $4–5

Dress: Slacker garb and Generation-X gear is the norm
Specials: Each week boasts a different drink special; happy hour 9–10 p.m. and 1–4 a.m.
Food available: None

Hours: Every day, 9 p.m.–4 a.m.

What goes on: Live entertainment (various themes, including classic and alternative rock) and DJs nightly 9 p.m.–4 a.m. Live bands are featured Wednesday–Friday, and Thursday is Ladies Night.

Setting & atmosphere: This two-story hot spot is one of the few Honolulu clubs that still hosts live alternative bands. A large, wooden dance floor fronts the Wave's big-screen TV and performance stage. Adornments are meager, and there aren't any tables on the main floor, so if you're not dancing you're standing against the club's carpeted walls. If you get bored with the music you could always amuse yourself with the arcade machines located at the back of the club.

If you go: Take a cab, as parking is scarce and what is available is pricey. Also, if you can't stand the heat generated by all the dancing maniacs in the main room, kick back in the air-conditioned, second-floor lounge, which features a full-service bar and is also a great place to perch yourself while watching the band or crowd perform.

Maui

HAPA'S BREW HAUS

Locals-meet-tourists Neighbor Island hangout
Who Goes There: 21–35; celebrities, water lovers, and visitors

41 E. Lipoa St., Suite 4A, Kihei; (808) 879-9001
South Maui Zone 8

Cover: $5	Dress: Come as you are
Minimum: None	Specials: Ladies Night every
Mixed drinks: $4–6	Thursday
Wine: $5–7	Food available: Pizzas, burgers, and
Beer: $4	sandwiches

Hours: Every day, 4 p.m.–2 a.m.

What goes on: Nightly entertainment featuring a variety of live bands, dancing, bikini contests, and comedy acts. Call for an updated schedule.

Setting & atmosphere: This bar on the Valley Isle is a hot spot, and entrance lines are usually long. A great place to mingle, socialize with friends, or grab a relaxing drink at the bar.

If you go: Go before 8:30 p.m. and get in for free.

MAUI BREWS

10,000-square-foot eatery and club situated in an old whaling town
Who Goes There: 18–35; postgrads, whale-watchers, slackers, suits, beach boys and girls

900 Front St., Lahaina; (808) 667-7794
West Maui Zone 9

Cover: None
Minimum: None
Mixed drinks: $3.25–6
Wine: $3.25–6
Beer: $3.25 and up

Dress: A little on the nicer/neater
  side; casual garb acceptable, but
  no swimwear or tank tops
Food available: Pizza, pasta, steak,
  and sandwiches

Hours: Every day, 11:30 a.m.–2 a.m.

What goes on: One of the only games in town, this club hits all of its musical bases, with hip-hop on Tuesday; salsa on Wednesday; local entertainment on Thursday; disco on Friday and Saturday; and an open mike night on Sundays. Maui Brews Night Club is open 9 p.m.–2 a.m. The restaurant itself is open 11:30 a.m.–2 a.m. daily.

Setting & atmosphere: This venue features dining and dancing in an Island bistro setting. The thatched-roof bar features a complete drink list and offers more than 30 beers from around the world.

If you go: Call ahead for dinner. Reservations for Maui Brews are not required but are politely suggested.

Part Seven

Exercise and Recreation

The Beach Experience

While your hotel swimming pool can be an alluring and convenient option, our advice is to head for the beach! The Hawaiian Islands have more than 180 miles of sandy shoreline with some of the finest beaches in the world. In 1999, in fact, noted geologist Stephen Leatherman of Florida International University named Wailea Beach on Maui as the best beach in the United States. Leatherman, dubbed "Dr. Beach" for his expert studies on beaches throughout the globe, bases his beach evaluations on four basic criteria: physical environment (including air, sand, and water quality), amenities, water safety conditions, and aesthetics.

Four of the top five beaches on Leatherman's 1999 list are in Hawaii: **Wailea, Kauna'oa** on the Big Island (ranked second), **Hanalei Bay** on Kauai (fourth), and **Ka'anapali** on Maui (fifth). In addition, the following beaches have topped Leatherman's ratings in previous years (each year's winning beach is not included in Leatherman's ensuing surveys): **Kapalua Beach** on Maui (1991), **Hapuna Beach** on the Big Island (1993), **Lanikai Beach** on Oahu (1996), **Hulopo'e Beach** on Lanai (1997), and **Kailua Beach** on Oahu (1998).

You'll find that Hawaii's beaches are as unique as they are beautiful, with sands colored white, black, red, gold, and even green. Generally speaking, the older the island, the more attractive its beaches. Kauai, the oldest island in the Hawaiian chain, is more eroded and therefore has more scenic beaches.

Some practical advice for sunbathers: It is possible to have *too* much fun in the sun! Prolonged exposure to the sun can be harmful to your health, and long-term effects of regular sunburn can include premature aging and skin cancer. To get a nice tan, play it safe and start off with only up to half an hour of sunbathing that first day. Then gradually increase your time under the sun. Especially avoid excessive exposure to the sun between mid-morning and mid-afternoon, when the sun's ultraviolet rays are most intense. Be sure to bring some sunscreen, especially if you are fair-skinned or freckled (using a lotion with a sun protection factor (SPF) of 30 or higher is strongly recommended). If you do get a case of sunburn, apply cold compresses or take a cool bath.

A few more things you should know:

- During periods when Hawaii experiences strong offshore winds, Portuguese man-of-wars—stinging jellyfish that drift on the ocean's surface—are frequently blown ashore. Look for posted warning signs before you enter the water. You can recognize a Portuguese man-of-war by its crested blue bubble. A sting from one can be painful and may leave a blister or welt. The pain usually subsides within 15 to 30 minutes. Just like a bee sting, however, a Portuguese man-of-war sting can cause severe reactions in victims who are allergic to the venom. If this happens, medical treatment should be sought immediately.

- A more painful experience is stepping on *wana* (pronounced "vah-nah"), Hawaiian for sea urchins. If a prickly spine punctures your skin, it can cause intense pain that might last an hour or more. Again, if severe reactions occur, seek immediate medical treatment.

- Be extra cautious whenever you visit a beach that has no lifeguards on duty. Many beaches in Hawaii are not protected by reefs or other natural barriers, which means high surf can roll directly to shore, causing strong currents and other sea conditions that can pose a danger to even expert swimmers. As a general rule, never turn your back to the sea.

- They're extremely rare, but shark attacks *do* happen. Sharks, in fact, are fairly common in Hawaiian waters, especially in murky areas (avoid harbor entrances and stream or channel mouths, especially after heavy rains). Most attacks that have occurred involve tiger sharks (if you want to view one, the Maui Ocean Center on Maui has a six-foot specimen in captivity). Again, exercise caution and use common sense. Never swim alone. If you do encounter a shark, swim to safety quickly but as calmly as possible; avoid making wild, thrashing motions that might provoke the shark. High-contrast clothing or shiny jewelry can also attract sharks.

By exercising the above precautions, you'll only increase your enjoyment of most visitors' favorite activity: spending some quality time on a fabulous Hawaiian beach. An excellent resource for information is *Hawaii's Best Beaches,* by John R. K. Clark, a 150-page book published by the University of Hawaii Press. Or try Dr. Beach's Web site at www.topbeaches.com.

Provided below are capsule looks at 35 top beaches in the Aloha State.

Hawaii's Best Beaches

Oahu: Waikiki Beach
Maui: Wailea Beach
The Big Island: Kauna'oa Beach
Kauai: Po'ipu Beach Park
Molokai: Papohaku Beach Park
Lanai: Hulopo'e Beach Park

OAHU

Ala Moana Beach Park

Zone: 2, Greater Honolulu

Location: On Ala Moana Blvd., directly across from the Ala Moana
   Shopping Center, just minutes from Waikiki.

Activities: Swimming, surfing, bodyboarding, scuba diving, fishing.

Comments This is the largest urban beach park in Honolulu, and the
most popular among local families. The beach portion of the park is a narrow half-mile stretch of white sand and a deep swimming channel. It's considered one of the most swimmable beaches in Hawaii and rates as one of
the best for children and inexperienced swimmers. Lifeguards are on duty
daily. Magic Island, a 30-acre man-made extension at the eastern end of
the park, is a popular spot for picnicking and jogging. Facilities include
softball fields, tennis courts, a lawn bowling area, food concessions, showers, rest rooms, the McCoy Pavilion, and more than 100 acres of picnic
areas. Parking is available on the long road between the park and beach,
and also at a lot near Magic Island.

Hanauma Bay Nature Preserve

Zone: 1, Waikiki

Location: At Koko Head Regional Park (7455 Kalaniana'ole Hwy.) in
   Hawaii Kai on the southeastern end of the island. Head east on the
   H-1 Fwy., which turns into Kalaniana'ole Hwy.

Activities: Swimming, snorkeling, scuba diving.

Comments Renowned as one of the world's favorite snorkeling spots,
filled with colorful reef fish. This beautiful U-shaped bay—measuring a

half-mile from shore and one-third of a mile from point to point—is ideal for novice snorkelers and swimmers. Lifeguards are on duty daily. Most visitors stay on the left end of the bay, where the beach is widest. If you're looking for less congestion, head to the west end of the beach. Facilities include rest rooms, showers, picnic areas, a snack bar, and snorkel rentals. A free educational tour of the bay is offered; inquire at the beach desk. A $1-per-vehicle fee is charged for parking, and admission is $3 for all non-residents above the age of 12. Hanauma Bay is open six days a week (closed on Tuesday) from 6 a.m. to 7 p.m. Smoking is strictly prohibited. For conservation reasons, feeding the reef fish—once a favorite pastime at the bay—is now prohibited. Go early (before 8 a.m. if possible), as security personnel turn away all incoming traffic once the parking lot is full.

Kailua Beach Park

Zone: 3, Windward Oahu

Location: 450 Kawailoa Rd. in Kailua.

Activities: Swimming, surfing, windsurfing, bodyboarding, bodysurfing, canoe paddling, kayaking, beachcombing, boating.

Comments A popular site among locals, especially Kailua residents with a deep passion for ocean activities. Named "Best Beach in America" in 1998 by Stephen Leatherman, a.k.a. "Dr. Beach." The crescent-shaped white-sand beach is more than two miles long. The waters are ideal for swimming, surfing, and sailing. This is recognized as one of the island's best windsurfing spots. Inexperienced surfers, bodyboarders, and bodysurfers should head to the northern side of the park, where the waves are smaller and gentler. Facilities here include rest rooms, showers, picnic areas. Lifeguards are on duty daily.

Ko 'Olina Lagoons

Zone: 5, Leeward Oahu

Location: Near the 'Ihilani Resort & Spa, 92-1001 Olani St.

Activities: Swimming, surfing, bodyboarding, fishing.

Comments Ko 'Olina Lagoons comprises four picturesque lagoons with lovely white-sand beaches. Although owned by the Ko 'Olina Resort, these beaches are open to the public. Very popular among young local families. Lifeguards are on duty daily. Surfing, bodyboarding, kayaking, and fishing are allowed seaward of the certified public shoreline. The four lagoons are identified by number; the First Lagoon is the one nearest to the 'Ihilani Resort.

Lanikai Beach

Zone: 3, Windward Oahu

Location: Mokulua Dr. in Lanikai.

Activities: Swimming, kayaking, canoe paddling, windsurfing, sailing.

Comments   One of Oahu's better-kept secrets. This is a splendid mile-long stretch of white-sand beach, and many locals regard it as the best beach for swimming in the state. This is also a favorite spot for kayakers, many of whom paddle out to the Mokulua Islets, twin islets located off the south end of the beach. Both islets are state seabird sanctuaries. Moku Nui, the larger islet to the left as you view them from shore, is accessible to kayakers and swimmers, although you must stay within the beach and picnicking areas. The smaller islet, Moku Iki, is off-limits. There are no public rest rooms or showers on Lanikai Beach, and no lifeguards are on duty. There are three public rights-of-way that lead to the beach from Mokulua Dr. (three others are reserved for Lanikai residents). Read the posted signs designating a public entrance.

Makapu'u Beach Park

Zone: 3, Windward Oahu

Location: 41-095 Kalaniana'ole Hwy. in Waimanalo. Located on the leeward side of Makapu'u Point, which is the easternmost point on the island.

Activities: Swimming, bodyboarding, bodysurfing, fishing.

Comments   This beach, a curved stretch of white sand about 1,000 feet long, is especially suited for bodysurfers and bodyboarders. The waters are calm during the summer but get rough during the winter months. Rest rooms and showers are on the premises. Lifeguards are on duty daily. Makapu'u Beach is off-limits to surfers.

Sandy Beach

Zone: 2, Greater Honolulu

Location: 8800 Kalaniana'ole Hwy. in Hawaii Kai.

Activities: Swimming, surfing, bodyboarding, bodysurfing, skimboarding, fishing.

Comments   Another local favorite. Great atmosphere. The 1,000-foot-long beach, lying at the base of Koko Crater, is considered one of the best shorebreak bodysurfing and bodyboarding sites in the state. Because the beach is subject to treacherous surf throughout the year, swimming is recommended only when the wave conditions are flat. Check with the lifeguards (on duty daily) before entering the water. Rest rooms, showers, and picnic areas are among the on-site facilities. Some of Oahu's best body-surfers, skimboarders, and bodyboarders strut their stuff here, and it's worth a visit just to see these ocean daredevils in action.

Sunset Beach

Zone: 4, The North Shore

Location: 59-100 Kamehameha Hwy. on the North Shore.

Activities: Swimming, surfing, bodyboarding.

Comments The beach fronting the park stretches about a mile long and is frequented mainly by locals. It's the widest beach on Oahu—over 200 feet—during the summer but narrows considerably during the winter, when the pounding surf erodes the beach. Suitable for swimming during the summer, but leave the ocean action to the experts during the winter, when the waves exceed ten feet in height. Sunset Beach is renowned as a big-wave surfing spot and is a host site to the annual Triple Crown of Surfing, a major event on the professional surfing circuit. Lifeguards on duty daily. Portable rest rooms available. Overall, this is a pleasant stop on an around-the-island drive.

Waikiki Beach

Zone: 1, Waikiki

Location: The beach fronts the entire Waikiki resort area.

Activities: Swimming, surfing, bodyboarding, snorkeling, sailing, kayaking, fishing.

Comments Probably the world's most recognized beach. A gorgeous two-mile stretch of white sand extending from the Hilton Hawaiian Village on the west end to the Elks Club near world-famous Diamond Head Crater. Great for swimming, sunbathing, surfing, and people-watching. The average water temperature at Waikiki Beach in the afternoon is a comfortable 77° Fahrenheit in March, rising to 82° in August. The highest concentration of beach users is found in the areas fronting four major hotels: the Sheraton Waikiki, Royal Hawaiian, Outrigger Waikiki, and Sheraton Moana Surfrider. However, it's fairly crowded everywhere, and there are no secluded areas. It does tend to get less congested the farther you go toward Diamond Head. Waikiki Beach actually comprises several individually named beaches, including (in order from 'Ewa to Diamond Head) Duke Kahanamoku Beach, Fort DeRussy Beach, Gray's Beach, Queen's Surf Beach, and Sans Souci Beach. San Souci Beach, which fronts the New Otani Beach Kaimana Hotel, ranks as one of our favorite spots; it's generally less crowded, and the water is especially suitable for young children. Facilities and services include rest rooms, showers, beach rentals, and surfing lessons. You can also sign up for outrigger canoe and catamaran rides from the beach. Lifeguards on duty daily. If you're not staying at a Waikiki hotel, the best place for parking is at Kapi'olani Park on the Diamond Head side of the beach.

Waimanalo Bay Beach Park

Zone: 3, Windward Oahu

Location: 41-043 Alo'ilo'i St. in Waimanalo.

Activities: Swimming, surfing, bodyboarding, bodysurfing, fishing.

Comments More than three miles long, this is one of the longest white-sand beaches on the island. The 75-acre park itself is located in the center of the beach. A favorite among local families. The waters are ideal for beginning bodysurfers and bodyboarders. Rest rooms, showers, picnic areas, and campsites are among the facilities. Lifeguards are on duty daily. *Note:* The beaches on the windward side of Oahu, including Waimanalo, are noted for being frequented by Portuguese Man-of-War, a stinging jellyfish. Check with the lifeguard before entering the water.

Waimea Bay Beach Park

Zone: 4, The North Shore

Location: 61-031 Kamehameha Hwy. in Waimea.

Activities: Swimming, surfing, bodyboarding, bodysurfing, fishing.

Comments A rugged white-sand beach measuring 1,500 feet in length. Renowned for having some of the biggest surfing waves in the world (waves can exceed 20 feet here during the winter months). We can't emphasize this enough: If you're not an experienced and expert big-wave surfer, *stay out* of the water here during the winter! On the other hand, the bay is very tame in the summer months. Lifeguards are stationed at the beach daily. At the southwest end of the beach is Jumping Rock, a natural landmark: Local daredevils climb to the top of this black-lava rock and take a plunge into the ocean 20 feet below.

MAUI

Fleming Beach Park

Zone: 9, West Maui

Location: Along Honoapi'ilani Hwy. at Honokahua Bay.

Activities: Swimming, surfing, bodyboarding, bodysurfing, snorkeling.

Comments Named after David Thomas Fleming, a former manager of Honolua Ranch, this beach park is perhaps West Maui's best spot for body-surfing and bodyboarding. The beach itself—Honokahua Beach—is about

1,500 feet long, fairly wide, and very scenic. Conditions can get hazardous during the winter months, when high surf generates strong rip currents along the entire length of the beach. Be sure to consult with a lifeguard (on duty daily) before entering the water. Facilities include rest rooms and showers.

Ka'anapali Beach

Zone: 9, West Maui

Location: Along Honoapi'ilani Hwy. in Ka'anapali, fronting the Ka'anapali Resort.

Activities: Swimming, bodysurfing, bodyboarding, snorkeling, scuba diving, windsurfing, kayaking, sailing, fishing.

Comments A beautiful beach frequented by visitors and guests staying at Ka'anapali Resort. Swimming conditions are excellent whenever the surf is low or flat. Black Rock, a volcanic cinder cone rising from the center of the beach, is a great spot for snorkeling and scuba-diving adventures. During periods of high surf, however, it's advisable to stay out of the water. A county lifeguard is on duty at the south end of the resort. Beach concessions are available at the southern end of the beach at the activity center fronting Whalers Village shopping center, and at the north end at the activity desk fronting the Aston Maui Ka'anapali Villas.

Kapalua Beach

Zone: 9, West Maui

Location: Lower Honoapi'ilani Hwy. in Kapalua.

Activities: Swimming, snorkeling, scuba diving, sailing.

Comments Although small (about 600 feet long and 100 feet wide), this is one of Maui's most beautiful beaches and is frequented by locals and visitors alike. Swimming and snorkeling are favorite activities here. Lava points protect both sides of the beach from high surf, making this a safe beach for young families. Showers and rest rooms are located at the southern point of the bay, but there are no lifeguards on duty. If you come in the late afternoon, be sure to stay for the sunset, which is often spectacular from this vantage point.

Makena State Park

Zone: 8, South Maui

Location: On South Kihei Rd. in Makena (drive south past Wailea).

Activities: Swimming, surfing, snorkeling, bodysurfing, bodyboarding, fishing.

Comments   Makena State Park has two scenic white-sand beaches: Big Beach and Little Beach. Big Beach is 3,300 feet long and is the longest undeveloped white-sand beach on the island. It's a favorite spot among experienced bodyboarders and bodysurfers. Little Beach, meanwhile, is a small cove with gentler ocean conditions, making it a good recommendation for novice wave riders. No lifeguards are on duty, and there are no public rest rooms or showers on the premises. A special note on Little Beach, where some of the views have nothing to do with the ocean: This secluded spot is considered one of Hawaii's most popular "unofficial" nude beaches, even though public nudity, by law, is prohibited.

'Ulua Beach

Zone: 8, South Maui

Location: On Wailea Alanui Rd. in Wailea, nestled between the Renaissance Wailea and Outrigger Wailea resorts.

Activities: Swimming, bodysurfing, bodyboarding, snorkeling, scuba diving, windsurfing, kayaking, sailing.

Comments   Wailea Resort has five pristine white-sand beaches: Polo, Wailea, Ulua, Mokapu, and Keawakapu. Ulua is the centermost beach and is approximately 1,000 feet long and 200 feet wide. Locals regard the reef between Ulua and Mokapu Beaches as one of the best snorkeling spots on Maui. A deeper reef, providing excellent conditions for scuba diving, is about 100 yards from the shore. Rest rooms, showers, and a small park are located inland of the beach. There are no lifeguards on duty.

Wailea Beach

Zone: 8, South Maui

Location: On Wailea Alanui Rd. in Wailea, fronting the Grand Wailea and Four Seasons resorts.

Activities: Swimming, bodysurfing, bodyboarding, snorkeling, scuba diving, windsurfing, sailing, fishing.

Comments   A picturesque, crescent-shaped beach about 1,000 feet long. Named the "Best Beach in America" by Stephen Leatherman, a.k.a. "Dr. Beach," in 1999. It's easy to see why. Delights both expected (great year-round weather) and unexpected (green sea turtles frequent the waters, as do humpback whales during the winter) abound. In addition, the relatively calm waters provide opportunities for many ocean activities. Facilities include rest rooms and showers. Beach concessions offer board rentals and instructional classes. However, there are no lifeguards on duty at any time.

THE BIG ISLAND

'Anaeho'omalu Beach

Zone: 11, Kona

Location: At the south end of 'Anaeho'omalu Bay, adjacent to the Outrigger Waikoloa Beach Hotel (formerly known as the Royal Waikoloan).

Activities: Swimming, surfing, snorkeling, scuba diving, windsurfing, kayaking

Comments A great beach frequented by visitors and locals alike. Suitable for a wide range of ocean activities. This beach is particularly favored as a windsurfing site. Novices can frolic in the waters near the shore (windsurfing rentals and lessons are available from Ocean Sports Waikoloa, a beach activities desk at the beach's north end), while expert riders enjoy the challenging wave conditions farther offshore. Rest rooms and showers are available at 'Anaeho'omalu Beach Park, located at the south end of the beach. There are no lifeguards on duty.

Green Sand Beach

Zone: 11, Kona

Location: Near Ka Lae (South Point), the southernmost point in the United States. Follow South Point Rd. to the Kaulana Boat Ramp near South Point. You need a four-wheel-drive vehicle to take the access road from the ramp from the beach. If you don't have one, park at the boat ramp and walk; the beach is about two and a half miles east of the ramp via a dirt road.

Activities: Swimming, beachcombing, fishing.

Comments An off-the-beaten-path beach recommended for active adventurers who won't mind the hike to and from the beach. Not recommended for young children. High surf is a possibility throughout the year and can pose a danger. Swim only when the water is totally calm. There are no lifeguards on duty at any time. Olivines—attractive greenish minerals made of magnesium and iron—are found in abundance here, and large gemstone-sized olivines are prized by beachcombers. This is the most famous green-sand beach in the Islands.

Hapuna Beach State Recreation Area

Zone: 11, Kona

Location: On Queen Ka'ahumanu Hwy. in South Kohala. Just look for the highway sign signaling the entrance to the park.

Activities: Swimming, surfing, bodyboarding, bodysurfing, snorkeling.

Comments   Named "Best Beach in America" in 1993 by Stephen Leatherman ("Dr. Beach"), Hapuna Beach remains highly popular with Big Island residents, especially with bodyboarders and bodysurfers. It can get fairly crowded during weekends and holidays. Measuring over a half-mile in length and more than 200 feet in width, Hapuna is one of the largest beaches on the island. Rest rooms, showers, camping shelters, and pavilions are among the facilities available here. Check with a lifeguard (on duty daily) for current ocean conditions, which are calm during the summer and less so during the winter.

Kauna'oa Beach

Zone: 11, Kona

Location: The beach fronts the Mauna Kea Beach Hotel on the island's Kohala Coast.

Activities: Swimming, surfing, bodyboarding, bodysurfing, snorkeling.

Comments   Stretching about 2,500 feet in length, this is a gorgeous white-sand beach, probably the most beautiful on the Big Island. "Dr. Beach" Stephen Leatherman rated Kauna'oa as the second-best beach in America in both 1998 and 1999. Mostly frequented by visitors, but many locals enjoy this beach as well. The water is usually calm, except during the winter, and invites ocean enthusiasts of all types, from snorkelers to bodysurfers. While there are no lifeguards, beach attendants at the Mauna Kea Beach Hotel are able to provide information on current ocean conditions. Public facilities are located at the south end of the beach and include rest rooms and showers.

Makalawena Beach

Zone: 11, Kona

Location: Four miles north of the Keahole-Kona International Airport. Access the beach by following the paved road to Mahai'ula Beach at Kekaha Kai State Park, then following the trail across Kawili Point.

Activities: Swimming, surfing, bodyboarding, bodysurfing, snorkeling, scuba diving.

Comments   This is the most isolated white-sand beach on the Kona Coast and is a great choice for a long, romantic walk along the shore. Swimming conditions are best on the beach's south end, while surfers often take on the waves on the northern side. No facilities or lifeguards are on the premises. Bring drinking water. The winter months typically bring high surf conditions, and swimmers and snorkelers are advised to stay away during these periods. *Note:* The property inland of the beach is privately owned, so stay on the beach to avoid trespassing.

Pololu Beach

Zone: 11, Kona

Location: The end of Highway 270 in North Kohala. Access is via a 15-minute hike down an ancient switchback trail from the Pololu Lookout at the end of the highway.

Activities: Swimming, surfing, bodyboarding, beachcombing, fishing.

Comments A scenic black-sand beach that provides plenty of photo opportunities. The ebony grains are actually lava fragments that have eroded over time. There are no lifeguards on duty at any time. Because this remote beach is exposed to treacherous surf throughout the year, do not swim here unless the ocean conditions are calm and flat. No rest rooms or showers are provided. This is another favored site for beachcombers, who scour the shoreline regularly after storms or prolonged periods of high surf.

KAUAI

Hanalei Bay

Zone: 13, Kauai

Location: The beach is located between Makahoa and Pu'upoa Points in Hanalei, on Kauai's north shore.

Activities: Swimming, surfing, bodyboarding, bodysurfing, snorkeling, windsurfing, sailing, fishing, canoe paddling.

Comments "Dr. Beach" rated the white-sand beach at Hanalei Bay as the fourth-best beach in the United States in 1999. Approximately two miles long and surrounded by lush mountain peaks and shimmering waterfalls, the circular bay is one of Hawaii's most enchanting settings. Favored equally by residents and visitors. A trio of beach parks are located at Hanalei Bay: Black Pot Beach Park, Wai'oli Beach Park, and Hanalei Pavilion Beach Park. Rest rooms and showers are available at each of the parks. The surf can exceed ten feet in the winter months, making Hanalei a popular site for Hawaii's best surfers. Lifeguards are stationed at Black Pot Beach Park (located at the eastern corner of the bay) and should be consulted before entering the water.

Kalapaki Beach

Zone: 13, Kauai

Location: The beach fronts the Kauai Marriott Resort on Nawiliwili Bay in Lihu'e, Kauai's capital.

Activities: Swimming, surfing, bodyboarding, bodysurfing, snorkeling, windsurfing, sailing, fishing.

Comments One of Kauai's busiest beaches, frequented by both locals and visitors. Protected by a sea cliff at one end and a sea wall at the other, Kalapaki is an enjoyable and safe playground for families with young children. Also a good training ground for novice surfers. Showers and rest rooms are provided courtesy of the Kauai Marriott. Picnic facilities are available at Nawiliwili Park, which is adjacent to Kalapaki. There are no lifeguards on duty at any time.

Keʻe Beach

Zone: 13, Kauai

Location: At Haʻena State Park, at the west end of Hwy. 56. The beach is next to the small parking lot.

Activities: Swimming, snorkeling.

Comments The patches of reef surrounding Keʻe Beach provide excellent snorkeling conditions, and this is likely the most popular snorkeling spot on Kauai's north shore. The shallow, protected lagoon is home to several species of rainbow-colored reef fish, including butterfly fish, damsel fish, convict fish, wrasses, and surgeon fish. The lagoon area is also a safe swimming spot for families with young children. There are no lifeguards stationed here. The beach is exposed to high surf during the winter.

Lumahaʻi Beach

Zone: 13, Kauai

Location: On Hwy. 56 at the foot of Lumahaʻi Valley. On the east end, park along the highway, then follow the trail down to the beach. On the west end, park in a deep grove of ironwood trees.

Activities: Swimming, surfing, bodyboarding, bodysurfing, snorkeling, windsurfing, sailing, fishing.

Comments Approximately 4,000 feet long, this beautiful strip of shoreline is best known as the setting for the movie *South Pacific*. It remains one of the most captivating, unspoiled settings in the state. Most visitors stay on the east end of the beach, where a cove provides some protection from the winds and ocean currents. Due to the lack of protective reefs, however, Lumahaʻi is extremely vulnerable to the ocean's forces, and swimming here isn't advisable except during the summer months. There are no lifeguards on duty.

Poʻipu Beach Park

Zone: 13, Kauai

Location: On Hoʻowili Rd., just off of Poʻipu Beach Rd. in Poʻipu.

Activities: Swimming, bodysurfing, bodyboarding.

Comments   Over 1,000 feet long, Poʻipu Beach is another popular playground for both locals and visitors. The eastern side of the beach fronts the park, while the western side is backed by several resorts. This is a good site for families with young children. Rest rooms, showers, and picnic tables are available, and lifeguards are on duty daily. Wave riders should avoid the area past Brennecke's, a rocky and hazardous point at the eastern end of the beach.

Polihale State Park (Barking Sands)

Zone: 13, Kauai

Location: The west end of Kaumualiʻi Hwy. in Kekaha.

Activities: Swimming, surfing, bodyboarding, windsurfing.

Comments   Measuring three miles long and 300 feet wide, this is one of Hawaii's longest and widest beaches. This is the home of the famous "Barking Sands," which are sand dunes that emit "barking" noises when stepped on. Hawaiians called sites such as this *ke one kani* (the musical sands). During the summer, a small section of reef provides beginning swimmers with a protected swimming area popularly known as "Queen's Pond." Facilities include rest rooms, showers, and a pavilion. No lifeguards are on duty.

Salt Pond Beach Park

Zone: 13, Kauai

Location: The beach is found west of Puʻolo Point in Hanapepe, near Kauai's south shore.

Activities: Swimming, surfing, bodyboarding, snorkeling, windsurfing, fishing.

Comments   One of Kauai's most popular beaches for swimming. Its friendly conditions are ideal for a wide variety of ocean endeavors, including swimming, surfing, snorkeling, and scuba diving. Stay in the lagoon area during high surf conditions, however. Salt Pond Beach is known for its production of rock salt, which occurs when seawater evaporates inside tiny, shallow ponds near the beach. Harvesting sea salt is a popular summertime activity. Rest rooms, showers, and picnic tables are available. No lifeguards are on duty at any time.

Secret Beach

Zone: 13, Kauai

Location: Between Kilauea Point and Kalihiwai Bay in Kilauea. Public access to the beach is via a dirt road that intersects Hwy. 56 just east of Kalihiwai Rd.

Activities: Swimming, surfing, bodyboarding, bodysurfing, snorkeling, windsurfing, sailing, fishing.

Comments This 3,000-foot-long white-sand beach is "secret" because it's not visible from any roads. From land, in fact, it can be viewed only from the Kilauea Point National Wildlife Refuge. Once a haven for a transient group of hippies in the early 1970s, Secret Beach is now a favorite swimming spot during the summer months. In the winter, however, high surf conditions pose a danger to swimmers. There are no public facilities or lifeguards here. *Note:* Although nude sunbathing is illegal in Hawaii, this is considered Kauai's foremost nude beach.

Shipwreck Beach

Zone: 13, Kauai

Location: The beach fronts the Hyatt Regency Kauai in Po'ipu.

Activities: Swimming, surfing, bodyboarding, bodysurfing, windsurfing, fishing.

Comments Shipwreck Beach got its name from an unidentified wooden boat that lay on the shore for many years. The remains of the boat were destroyed when Hurricane 'Iwa struck Kauai in November 1982. Unfortunately, low-lying rocks prevent this white-sand beach from being a great site for swimming, but bodysurfers and bodyboarders love this spot, especially during the summer months. The ocean bottom here drops quickly to overhead depths. Rest rooms and showers are available on the east side of the Hyatt Regency Resort. No lifeguards are on duty, but the Hyatt uses a flag system to inform guests of current ocean conditions. Red indicates that the conditions are dangerous.

Tunnels Beach

Zone: 13, Kauai

Location: At Ha'ena Point, about a half-mile east of Ha'ena Beach Park.

Activities: Swimming, surfing, bodyboarding, snorkeling, scuba diving, windsurfing, beachcombing, fishing.

Comments Located on the eastern end of Ha'ena Beach Park, Tunnels is a wide and sandy beach that provides good summer swimming. Its name refers to the "tunnels" that are found in the lagoon on the inside of Makua Reef, a popular snorkeling and scuba-diving spot. When the surf rises, Tunnels becomes one of Kauai's best surfing locales, populated by the island's best wave riders. Rest rooms and showers are available at the beach park. There are no lifeguards on duty.

MOLOKAI
Papohaku Beach Park

Zone: 14, Molokai

Location: On Kaluako'i Rd. near the Kaluako'i Resort.

Activities: Swimming, surfing, bodyboarding, bodysurfing, snorkeling.

Comments Over two miles long and 400 feet wide, Papohaku Beach is the longest beach on the Friendly Isle. Facilities at the park include rest rooms, showers, and camping sites. Because the beach is exposed to the ocean, with no reefs or points to buffer the surf, you need to be cautious here. Swimming is usually safe during the summer, but high surf conditions are liable to occur at any time of the year. No lifeguards are on duty.

LANAI

Hulopo'e Beach

Zone: 15, Lanai

Location: Adjacent to the Manele Bay Hotel. A 15-minute drive from
Lanai City.

Activities: Swimming, surfing, bodyboarding, bodysurfing, snorkeling,
fishing.

Comments While mostly known for its world-class golf courses, the tiny island of Lanai has a world-class beach as well: Hulopo'e Beach was chosen "Best Beach in America" in 1997 by Stephen Leatherman, a.k.a. "Dr. Beach." Measuring 1,500 feet long and 200 feet wide, Hulopo'e is easily the best beach for swimming on the island. Locals also cherish this place as a surfing and bodyboarding site. Hulopo'e Beach Park has rest rooms, showers, picnic areas, and a campsite (camping by permit only). If you're staying on Lanai, this is the best and most convenient beach to visit.

National and State Parks

There are 2 national parks and 52 state parks in Hawaii, encompassing more than 50,000 acres on the islands of Oahu, Maui, the Big Island, Kauai, and Molokai.

In our view, visiting **Hawaii Volcanoes National Park**—home to the world's most active volcano—is a must visit for Big Island visitors, as it is the single most spectacular attraction on the island. (Just don't expect to enjoy close-up views of current lava flows.) On Maui, **Haleakala National Park**, a great place for stargazing and watching the sun rise, also receives our enthusiastic recommendation.

As for the state parks, there are four that we feel are noteworthy and are worth making the drive for: **Hanauma Bay Underwater Park** on Oahu, **'Iao Valley State Park** on Maui, and **Koke'e State Park** and **Waimea Canyon State Park** on Kauai. Each provides fabulous settings, exceptional views, and a handful of activities for young and old. Information on all four parks is included below.

For more information on Hawaii's state parks, write to the Division of State Parks, 1151 Punchbowl St., Room 310, Honolulu, HI 96813, or call (808) 587-0300.

SAFETY TIPS AND PARK REGULATIONS

- Guard against sunburn by using sunscreen and wearing a cap. Avoid prolonged exposure to the sun.
- Drink plenty of water to avoid dehydration.
- Do not enter streams and ponds if you have an open cut or abrasion, and do not drink the water. Harmful bacteria may be present and pose a health risk.
- Do not experiment with unfamiliar plants. Some may be poisonous.
- Be wary of insects and arachnids that may pose a danger, including centipedes, scorpions, and black widow spiders.
- Never leave your valuables unattended. Do not let anyone see you storing valuables in your car.
- The consumption or possession of alcoholic beverages is strictly prohibited.
- Build fires only in provided fireplaces and grills. Portable stoves and other warming devices may be used in designated picnicking and camping areas unless otherwise prohibited.
- Do not disturb any plants or geological, historical, and archaeological features.
- Public nudity is prohibited.
- Skating and skateboards are prohibited where signs to that effect are posted.

NATIONAL PARKS

Hawaii Volcanoes National Park

Zone: 12, Hilo and Volcano

Location: About 30 miles from Hilo, traveling down Hwy. 11. Follow the road signs and turn left into the park entrance.

Phone: (808) 985-6000

Web Site: www.nps.gov/havo

Hours: Daily, 7:45 a.m.–5 p.m. The park itself is open 24 hours year-round.

Admission: $10 per vehicle. Admission is good for 7 days.

When to Go: Anytime. The best time of day to view eruption activity is after sunset.

How Much Time to Allow: At least half a day.

Description and Comments The 377-acre Hawaii Volcanoes National Park, established in 1916 by the U.S. National Park Service, is certainly one of the world's most unique visitor attractions. What other park, after all, houses an active volcano? (Kilauea Volcano has been spewing lava continuously since New Year's Day 1983.) The starting point is the visitor center, which houses a gallery of volcano exhibits and a 200-seat mini-theater showing a terrific 23-minute film about the history of Hawaii's volcanoes and their significance to the Hawaiian culture. Park rangers are on hand to answer any questions and offer suggested itineraries at the park. Taking the time here to learn all you can about the park will help you make the most out of your experience.

Next door, the Volcano Art Center offers a wide range of works by some of Hawaii's top artists, including Herb Kane, Peggy Chun, Rocky Jenson, and Dietrich Varez. A park ranger leads an optional introductory hike from the visitor center. If you're ready to venture out on your own, return to your car and head farther into the park, where you'll soon arrive at the Thomas A. Jaggar Museum. This museum features exhibits spotlighting Hawaii's volcano eruption history, current seismic activity, land formations, and even a profile of Madame Pele, Hawaii's goddess of fire. Just outside the museum are stunning views of Halemaʻumaʻu Crater—measuring 2.5 miles wide and more than 400 feet deep—inside the Kilauea Caldera. (Translated, Halemaʻumaʻu means "House of Ferns." Centuries ago, two craters existed, one filled with ferns. A terrible eruption caused the two fire pits to merge.)

From the museum, you can drive to any and all public trails in the park. Devastation Trail is a short (less than a mile) hike on a paved path that shows the havoc caused by lava flows. Farther up Crater Rim Drive is the Thurston Lava Tube, a pleasant nature walk that includes a trek through a large lava tube. It's a half-hour drive (about 20 miles) to the end of Chain of Craters Road, which hugs the ocean coastline. At the end of the road, you'll see billowing steam clouds rising at a distance, the result of molten lava pouring into the sea. A short, 300-yard hike on a rocky and uneven trail is marked by cones. A longer, more strenuous seven-mile hike is also available but is not recommended. Other notes: Overnight camping is available via free permit (stays are limited to seven days per year), but collecting lava rocks or plants from the park is strictly *kapu* (prohibited). Overall, be respectful of the surroundings, which native Hawaiians regard as sacred to their culture.

Haleakala National Park

Location: The park extends from the 10,023-foot summit of Haleakala down to the southeast flank of the mountain and to the Kipahulu coastline near Hana. The summit area is accessible from Kahului via roads 37, 377, and 378. The park's Kipahulu area, at the east end of the island between Hana and Kaupo, can be reached via Hwy. 36. Driving times are about 3–4 hours each way.

Phone: (808) 572-9306

Web Site: www.nps.gov/hale

Hours: Park Ranger Headquarters open daily, 7:30 a.m.–4 p.m. The visitor center is open daily, sunrise–3 p.m. (Overnight camping is permitted. The Hosmer Grove Campground in the summit area, located just inside the park's entrance, can be used without a permit; all other camping areas require permits.)

Admission: $10 per vehicle. The entrance fee is good for 7 days.

When to Go: Anytime. Haleakala is renowned as a setting for dramatic sunrises and sunsets, although most people come for the sunrise. Be sure to arrive at least 30 minutes before either event.

How Much Time to Allow: Up to half a day, depending on whether you hike or take part in one of the park's programs.

Description and Comments Once considered part of Hawaii Volcanoes National Park, Haleakala ("House of the Sun")—a dormant volcano—was redesignated as a separate entity in 1961. The park consists of nearly 29,000 acres, most of it wilderness. This is a fabulous place for stargazing. In the summit area, begin at the park's headquarters and the Haleakala Visitor Center, which houses a variety of cultural and natural history exhibits. Rangers are on duty to answer your questions and can be a tremendous help in making the most out of your visit. In the Kipahulu area, start at the Kipahulu Ranger Station/Visitor Center. Each facility has a nice selection of books, maps, postcards, and other souvenirs for sale. The summit area is the origin of two hiking trails: The four-mile Sliding Sands Trail begins at the visitor center parking lot and descends 2,500 feet to the valley floor. (The return trip is much more difficult due to the steep grade; allow twice the time to hike out as you take to hike in.) The longer Halemau'u Trail, meanwhile, starts at the parking lot 3.5 miles above the park headquarters. At Kipahulu, meanwhile, all trails begin at the ranger station/visitor center.

Touring Tips Check the park's bulletin board for a schedule of daily programs and guided hikes. Obey all posted warning signs. Because the weather at the summit of Haleakala is unpredictable—temperatures usually range from 40° to 65° Fahrenheit but can dip below freezing at any time, with the wind chill factor—it's advisable to wear lightweight, layered clothing. Sturdy and comfortable shoes are a must. There are no restaurants or gas stations at the park. Due to the high elevation and reduced oxygen at the park, anyone with heart or respiratory conditions is advised to check with their doctor before visiting here.

STATE PARKS

Oahu

'Aiea Bay State Recreation Area

Zone: 6, Central Oahu

Location: Off Kamehameha Hwy. at McGrew Loop near Aloha Stadium.

Comments Good picnicking site offering views of Pearl Harbor and the *Arizona* Memorial.

Diamond Head State Monument

Zone: 1, Waikiki

Location: Off Diamond Head Rd. between Makapu'u and 18th Avenues.

Comments Diamond Head Crater is designated a National Natural Landmark. Picnicking is available on the crater floor. A moderate 0.7-mile hike to the summit rewards you with sweeping views of Honolulu and the ocean.

Hanauma Bay State Underwater Park

Zone: 2, Greater Honolulu

Location: Hanauma Bay Beach Park, off Kalaniana'ole Hwy.

Comments One of Hawaii's most famous snorkeling and swimming sites. A City & Country beach park adjoins the area.

He'eia State Park

Zone: 3, Windward Oahu

Location: 46-465 Kamehameha Hwy. at Kealohi Point in He'eia.

Comments Provides beautiful views of Kane'ohe Bay, Mokoli'i islet (better known as Chinaman's Hat), and the majestic Ko'olau Mountain Range. Adjacent to the park is the ancient He'eia fishpond. A party hall is available for rent on weekends.

Ka'ena Point State Park

Zone: 5, Leeward Oahu

Location: The end of Farrington Hwy. in Makua.

Comments A 778-acre park located in West Oahu. Picnicking and shore fishing are among the popular activities here. Swimming is possible only during completely calm sea conditions. You can also view Kaneana, a large sea cave that is the legendary home of a shark-man. No drinking water. Frequented mainly by local area residents.

Kahana Valley State Park

Zone: 3, Windward Oahu

Location: 52-222 Kamehameha Hwy. in Kahana.

Comments   A wide range of beach activities are available at this wild-land valley, as well as picnicking and picking fruit. A 1.25-mile hiking trail is located nearby. In early Hawaii, the valley served as a thriving setting for local agriculture.

Kaka'ako Waterfront Park

Zone: 2, Greater Honolulu

Location: End of Ahui or Ohe Streets off Ala Moana Blvd. in Honolulu.

Comments   A 35-acre waterfront park located in downtown Honolulu, favored by locals who come here during lunch breaks and *pau hana* (after work) gatherings. A waterfront promenade, an amphitheater, and picnic areas highlight this scenic park.

Pu'u 'Ualaka'a State Wayside

Zone: 2, Greater Honolulu

Location: On Round Top Dr., off Makiki St. in Honolulu.

Comments   A great picnic setting for families, providing sweeping views of Honolulu. Rarely crowded. Nearby is the trailhead for the one-mile 'Ualaka'a Loop Trail.

Sacred Falls State Park

Zone: 3, Windward Oahu

Location: On Kamehameha Hwy., 1 mile south of Hau'ula town.

Comments   Also known as Kaliuwa'a Falls. Tradition says this was the home of Kamapua'a, the legendary pig god. Good area for picnicking. A half-hour hike to the falls along Kalanui Stream is a favorite among hikers. *Note:* As this book went to press, the hiking trail has been closed indefinitely due to a tragic May 1999 landslide that killed eight visiting hikers.

Sand Island State Recreation Area

Zone: 2, Greater Honolulu

Location: End of Sand Island Access Rd., off Nimitz Hwy.

Comments Pleasant 14-acre park offering picnicking, camping, shore fishing, a small sandy beach, and nice views of Honolulu Harbor. No swimming permitted. Mostly frequented by locals.

Waʻahila Ridge State Recreation Area

Zone: 2, Greater Honolulu

Location: End of Ruth Pl., via Peter St. off Waiʻalae Ave. at St. Louis Heights in Honolulu.

Comments A tranquil 50-acre park good for picnicking and hiking. Provides attractive views of Manoa and Palolo Valleys.

Maui

ʻIao Valley State Park

Zone: 7, Central Maui

Location: End of ʻIao Valley Rd. (Hwy. 32) in ʻIao Valley.

Comments The centerpiece here is undoubtedly ʻIao Needle, a scenic marvel that rises 1,200 feet from the valley floor. A nice rest stop offering pretty scenery and lots of photo opportunities.

Makena State Park

Zone: 8, South Maui

Location: South of Wailea, beyond the end of Wailea Alanui Rd.

Comments Scenic 164-acre beach park offering swimming (during calm ocean conditions), bodysurfing, bodyboarding, and other beach-related activities. No drinking water.

Polipoli Spring State Recreational Area

Zone: 10, Upcountry Maui and Beyond

Location: At the 6,200-foot elevation level in the Kula Rainforest Reserve.

Comments A four-wheel-drive vehicle is recommended for reaching this ten-acre site. Forest area with nice views of Central and West Maui. Camping and lodging available.

Puaʻa Kaʻa State Wayside

Zone: 10, Upcountry Maui and Beyond

Location: Hana Hwy., 38 miles east of Kahului Airport.

Comments   Serene spot for picnicking, laced with pretty waterfalls and pools. No drinking water available.

Wai'anapanapa State Park

Zone: 10, Upcountry Maui and Beyond

Location: End of Wai'anapanapa Rd., off Hana Hwy. in Hana.

Comments   Remote area offering camping, fishing, and family hikes. This is especially a good spot for picnicking and swimming (when ocean conditions are calm). Features here include a native forest, a cave, a *heiau,* and a small black-sand beach.

The Big Island
'Akaka Falls State Park

Zone: 12, Hilo and Volcano

Location: End of 'Akaka Falls Rd. (Hwy. 220) in Hilo.

Comments   Picnic facilities highlight this scenic site in Hilo. Take a walk through the tropical vegetation to scenic points overlooking Akaka Falls.

Kalopa State Recreation Area

Zone: 11, Kona

Location: End of Kalopa Rd., 3 miles inland from Mamalahoa Hwy.

Comments   A scenic 100-acre setting situated in a large forest reserve. Favorite activities here include picnics, camping, and nature hikes, including an easy 0.7-mile loop trail.

Kohala Historical Sites State Monument

Zone: 11, Kona

Location: On a coastal dirt road off Akoni Pule Hwy. in Kohala.

Comments   This is the reputed birth site of Kamehameha I, regarded as Hawaii's greatest king. Also the setting for Mo'okini Heiau, one of old Hawaii's most notable sacrificial temples.

Wailoa River State Recreation Area

Zone: 12, Hilo and Volcano

Location: At the banks of the Wailoa River in downtown Hilo.

Comments   Home to the state's shortest river. A great place for relaxing, picnicking, walking, and fishing. Cultural exhibits are on display at the park's Wailoa Center.

Wailuku River State Park

Zone: 11, Kona

Location: Off Waianuenue Ave. in Hilo.

Comments At 32 miles in length, Wailuku River is Hawaii's second-longest river. This 16-acre park is the home of Rainbow Falls, named for the brilliant rainbows that form through a misty waterfall. Boiling Pots, a series of pools that appear to "boil" after frequent rains, is nearby. The cave beneath the waterfall is said to be the home of Hina, mother of the demigod Maui.

Kauai

Ha'ena State Park

Zone: 13, Kauai

Location: End of Kuhio Hwy. in Ha'ena.

Comments Beach activities are available at this wild-land park, but they take a back seat to the views of Kauai's spectacular Na Pali Coast. Here you can also view ancient sea caves, said to have been formed by the volcano goddess Pele as she searched for a new home.

Koke'e State Park

Zone: 13, Kauai

Location: On Koke'e Rd., 15 miles north of Kekaha. Adjoins Waimea
    Canyon State Park.

Comments Picnicking, camping, and hiking are favorite activities at this renowned 4,345-acre park, which boasts sweeping views of Kalalau Valley.

Polihale State Park

Zone: 13, Kauai

Location: End of dirt road from Mana Village off Kaumuali'i Hwy.
    (Hwy. 50).

Comments Popular site among locals, known for its sandy beach and spectacular sunsets. Swimming is a suitable activity during the summer months. Picnic areas available.

Wailua River State Park

Zone: 13, Kauai

Location: Along banks of Wailua River off Kuhio Hwy. in Wailua.

Comments   Historic 1,092-acre site set within a river valley. Picnicking and river fishing are possible, as are scenic boat tours (there is an admission charge) to the Fern Grotto. *Heiau,* places of refuge, and birthstones are among the sacred landmarks found here.

Waimea Canyon State Park

Zone: 13, Kauai

Location: On Koke'e Rd., about 11 miles north of Kekaha. Adjoins Koke'e State Park.

Comments   The rim of this 1,866-acre park overlooks spectacular Waimea Canyon, one of Hawaii's most breathtaking scenic wonders. Picnicking and hiking are among the activities here.

Molokai
Pala'au State Park

Zone: 14, Molokai

Location: End of Kalae Hwy. in Pala'au.

Comments   This 230-acre park overlooks historic Kalaupapa, the place where people stricken with Hansen's disease (leprosy) were once banished. Picnicking and camping are available. A short trail leads to a phallic stone reputed to enhance fertility among native women.

Great Activities in Paradise

Two things visitors do a *lot* of in Hawaii are relaxing on the beach and eating. (And rightfully so!) Therefore, unless you want to return home with an expanded waist size to go along with your expanded luggage, we advise you to head out, enjoy Hawaii's great outdoors, and get some exercise! The good news is that there is plenty to do here, from hiking to the top of Diamond Head to trying your hand at surfing (trust us, you can do it!).

Below is a listing of recreational activities available to you in the Islands. There's something for everyone here, and some options are more physically strenuous than others. (Golf is so popular here that it merits its own section, found later in this chapter.) Many of these activities may be arranged for you at your hotel's activity desk. Once again, be sure to pick up the free visitor publications at the airport or your hotel; most contain money-saving coupons that apply to many of the following activities.

CAMPING: OUT IN THE WILD

Offering temperate weather year-round, Hawaii is well regarded among veteran campers. There are more than 120 official campsites and campgrounds on the six main islands, with sites ranging from sandy beaches and open mountain terrain to lush green valleys and thick rain forests. For many visitors, Hawaii presents the ideal camping environment for families; there are no dangerous animals, snakes, or poisonous contact plants to worry about.

Nearly every cabin and campsite in Hawaii falls under the auspices of a county, state, or federal agency—and they all require camping permits. It's a good idea to book ahead as far as possible, because camping is a popular pastime here among locals as well as visitors (especially during holiday weekends).

Above all else, plan ahead and come well prepared. Here are some helpful tips you should know before you arrive:

- Unless you plan to stay inside a cabin, tents are highly recommended. Not only will a tent protect you from insects, it can also provide shade during the day and covered shelter during the evening (when it does rain in Hawaii, it usually rains at night). If you plan to do a lot of backpacking, bring a lightweight tent; if you'll likely stay in one place, pack a heavier and roomier tent.
- You could get by with a comfortable blanket, especially on the beach or other low-altitude areas, but we recommend bringing along a sleeping bag. It'll provide added comfort, and you can always leave it unzipped and let it double as a thin mattress.
- Bring a ground pad if you plan to sleep on a hard surface.
- A propane stove will come in handy, especially since it is illegal to chop down branches from living trees or shrubs. Keep in mind, however: If you plan to do some inter-island hopping, it is illegal to transport propane, butane, or any other type of pressurized fuel container on a commercial plane.
- Bring insect repellent. The mosquitoes in Hawaii seem to love out-of-towners.
- While most campgrounds with facilities provide potable drinking water, watch for posted warning signs that tell you if the water requires treatment. Do not drink water from streams and pools, which can be contaminated by birds and wild goats. You can purify water by boiling it or using chemicals like halazone and chlorine. Our advice is to bring your own drinking water, whether it be tap water stored in gallon jugs or bottled springwater.
- As usual, bring plenty of sunscreen and be careful not to expose your body to the sun for prolonged periods of time.
- As mentioned above, there are no dangerous wild animals in Hawaii. There are the occasional goats and pigs, but if by rare chance you should encounter one, you can usually scare it away by shouting or making sudden movements. Leave these animals alone and they'll extend the same courtesy. There are no snakes, or any other dangerous reptiles, in the state.

- There are, however, insects and certain other arthropods, including centipedes, scorpions, and possibly even black widow spiders. The most common is the centipede. Using common sense (like checking your shoes or boots before you slip them on) will help prevent any unpleasant encounters.
- Hawaii, thankfully, doesn't have poison ivy or other plants that can harm you merely from contact. Certain plants, however, are poisonous if consumed. Again, a little common sense will go a long way toward ensuring your safety.
- Light campfires only where permitted.

Where to Camp

The following is a look at 20 great campsites in Hawaii. A terrific resource is *Camping Hawaii*, a 254-page book authored by local resident and camping expert Richard McMahon. More camping information is available on the official Web site of the Hawaii Visitors & Convention Bureau (www.gohawaii.com).

Oahu
Bellows Beach Park

Zone: 3, Windward Oahu

Location: Located at Bellows Air Force Station, about 2.5-miles northwest of Waimanalo. On Kalaniana'ole Hwy., turn right at the sign marking BAFS and follow the road to the park and campground.

Type of Camping: Tent camping only.

Permit Info: Applications accepted no earlier than 2 Fridays before the requested camping dates. You must apply in person at any satellite city hall on Oahu or at the Dept. of Parks and Recreation at 650 South St. in Honolulu. Call (808) 523-4525.

Time Limit: Camping permitted only on weekends and adjoining holidays. Hours: Noon Friday to 8 a.m. Monday.

Cost: Free

Comments An extremely popular campground. There are 50 campsites located in a beautiful ironwood forest. Picnic tables, rest rooms, and outdoor showers are available, and the water here is drinkable. Swimming and beachcombing are popular activities year-round.

Camp Mokule'ia

Zone: 4, The North Shore

Location: About 4 miles west of Waialua (toward the ocean) on Farrington Hwy. (Hwy. 930).

Type of Camping: Cabins, lodge, and tent camping.

Permit Info: Write to Camp Mokule'ia at 68-729 Farrington Hwy., Waialua, HI 96791, or call (808) 637-6241.

Time Limit: None

Cost: Tent camping: $7 per person per night; cabins: $125 (14 beds) or $160 (18 beds) per night; lodges: $45–50 (rooms with shared bath), $55–60 (with private bath), $90–100 (suites). Optional meal service ranges from $5 to $7 per meal.

Comments　Considered the best of four campsites situated on Mokule'ia Beach. Used primarily by groups. The area is fairly peaceful and offers the rugged beauty of the island's North Shore. Swimming and snorkeling are favorite activities, but be especially careful during the winter months, when the conditions become rough. The tent area is rather sparse when it comes to facilities, but all campers may use the facilities at the main camp section.

Kualoa Beach Park

Zone: 3, Windward Oahu

Location: In windward Oahu at Kane'ohe Bay. From Honolulu, head west on the H-1 Fwy. and take the Likelike Hwy. exit. Drive north through the tunnel, turn on Kahekili Hwy., and drive another 9 miles to the park. Campground A is at the end of the paved road (drive straight ahead onto the dirt road), while Campground B is located near a large parking lot by the ocean (follow the paved road that curves past the Campground A entrance).

Type of Camping: Tent camping only.

Permit Info: Applications accepted no earlier than 2 Fridays before the requested camping dates. For family permits for Campground A, you must apply in person at the Dept. of Parks and Recreation at 650 South St. in Honolulu. Call (808) 523-4525. Campground B permits may be obtained at the above location or at any satellite city hall on Oahu.

Time Limit: 5 nights, from Friday at 8 a.m. to Wednesday at 8 a.m.

Cost: Free

Comments　Facilities at Campground A, which is geared more toward groups, include rest rooms, showers, picnic tables, sinks, a volleyball court, and potable water. Campground B has rest rooms, showers, picnic tables, drinking water, and a public phone. Both sites offer scenic views and a tranquil atmosphere (particularly Campground B). The conditions are usually excellent for swimming and snorkeling. *Note:* Gates to the park close at 8 p.m. and reopen at 7 a.m. the following morning. Therefore, vehicles are not able to leave or enter the campgrounds during this period.

Waimanalo Beach Park

Zone: 3, Windward Oahu

Location: On Kalaniana'ole Hwy. (Hwy. 72) about 2 miles south of Waimanalo in windward Oahu.

Type of Camping: Tent and vehicle camping.

Permit Info: Applications accepted no earlier than 2 Fridays before the requested camping dates. You must apply in person at any satellite city hall on the island or at the Dept. of Parks and Recreation at 650 South St. in Honolulu. Call (808) 523-4525.

Time Limit: 5 nights, from Friday at 8 a.m. to Wednesday at 8 a.m.

Cost: Free

Comments Rest rooms, outdoor showers, picnic tables, and a public phone are among the facilities available here, and the water is drinkable (Waimanalo, interestingly, means "potable water"). Water and beach conditions here are wonderful for swimming and beachcombing. Popular visitor attractions like Sea Life Park and Hanauma Bay are just a short drive south.

Maui

Hosmer Grove

Zone: 10, Upcountry Maui and Beyond

Location: At the 6,800-foot elevation level on the slopes of Haleakala, just off Haleakala Crater Rd. Watch for the sign indicating Hosmer Grove, which is slightly less than 10 miles from the Crater Rd. turnoff.

Type of Camping: Tent and vehicle camping. Vehicles must stay within the confines of the parking lot.

Permit Info: None. The entire campground is limited to 25 people, with no more than 12 in a single group.

Time Limit: 3 nights

Cost: Free

Comments The campsite is located in an open grassy area surrounded by trees. A covered pavilion with two picnic tables and two grills is located on the campground. Rest rooms and potable water are available. Hiking is the recreational activity of choice here, and a half-mile nature trail begins at one end of the parking lot, loops around, and returns near the pavilion.

Pick up hiking trail information at the park headquarters. Bring extra blankets, because it can get cold here at night.

Holua Cabin and Campground

Zone: 10, Upcountry Maui and Beyond

Location: Inside Haleakala Crater, behind Holua Cabin on the Halemau'u Trail.

Type of Camping: Tent and cabin camping.

Permit Info: Permits are issued at the Haleakala National Park headquarters on a first-come, first-served basis on the day of use. The entire campground is limited to 25 people, with no more than 12 in a single group. Requests for cabins must be made 3 months in advance. Be sure to include alternate dates. Write to Haleakala National Park, P.O. Box 369, Makawao, HI 96768, or call (808) 572-9306.

Time Limit: 2 consecutive nights

Cost: Free for tent campers. Cabins are $40 (accommodate 1–6 people) and $80 (7–12 people) per night.

Comments Awe-inspiring views of Haleakala's crater walls are among the highlights here at the near-7,000-foot elevation level. Another treat is the presence of the protected nene goose, Hawaii's official state bird. Facilities for tent camping are sparse—only pit toilets and water—and the campground is fairly rocky. For cabin users, there are bunks with mattresses, a table, chairs, some cooking utensils, and a wood-burning stove with firewood. No bedding materials are provided, however.

Kipahulu Campground

Zone: 10, Upcountry Maui and Beyond

Location: About 10 miles past the secluded town of Hana on Hwy. 31.

Type of Camping: Tent and vehicle camping.

Permit Info: None

Time Limit: 3 nights

Cost: Free

Comments This scenic site is also known as 'Ohe'o Pools, which translates to "Gathering of Pools." As the name implies, this area of Haleakala is highlighted by a series of cascading waterfalls that form more than 20 separate pools. The campground rests on a grassy area and offers rest rooms, picnic tables, and grills. Bring your own drinking water, or collect water as far up the stream as possible (the pools near the road are heavily populated by swimmers). Swimming and hiking are the two chief activities here.

Wai'anapanapa State Park

Zone: 10, Upcountry Maui and Beyond

Location: Off Hana Hwy. on the ocean side.

Type of Camping: Tent and cabin camping.

Permit Info: Place your reservations as far in advance as possible (especially during the summer), as this is a very popular spot. Permits can be obtained at any state parks office. Write to the Maui office at Division of State Parks, P.O. Box 1049, Wailuku, Maui, HI 96793, or call (808) 984-8109.

Time Limit: 5 nights in any 30-day period

Cost: Free for tent campers. Housekeeping cabins are $45 per night, while Group cabins are $55 per night. Each cabin accommodates up to 4 people, and there is a $5-per-night charge for each additional camper (limit of 6 people for the Housekeeping cabins).

Comments Located on a grassy open field, this tranquil campground sits in a rugged coastal setting surrounded by trees. Rest rooms, outdoor showers, picnic tables, grills, and drinking water are all available for tent campers. Each cabin is furnished with a kitchen, living room, bedroom, and bathroom. Bedding, linens, towels, and cooking and eating utensils are also provided. There are several good hiking trails, but the ocean conditions usually aren't safe for swimming. Wai'anapanapa translates to "Glistening Water."

The Big Island

Kalopa State Recreation Area

Zone: 12, Hilo and Volcano

Location: At the northern end of the Hamakua coast, 7 miles from the town of Honoka'a. From Hilo, drive north on Hwy. 19 to Kalopa State Park. Turn right and follow signs to the park.

Type of Camping: Tent and cabin camping.

Permit Info: Permits can be obtained at any state parks office in the Islands. Write to the Big Island office at Division of State Parks, P.O. Box 936, Hilo, HI 96720, or call (808) 974-6200.

Time Limit: 5 nights

Cost: Free for tent campers. Cabins are $55 per night for 1–4 people. There is a charge of $5 for each additional person.

Comments Located in a deep forest of 'ohi'a trees, this well-maintained park houses a campground, picnic area, and cabin area. Campground facilities are found in a concrete-block building and include rest rooms, show-ers, picnic tables, sinks, and drinking water. The nearby picnic area features a covered pavilion with several tables. The two cabins are located up the road; each contains a pair of bunk rooms, toilets, hot showers, and sinks. Cabin users share a large dining hall with a fireplace and kitchen ameni-ties. This is a favorite locale among hikers. Free hiking brochures are some-times available in a kiosk near the trailhead.

Kilauea State Recreation Area

Zone: 12, Hilo and Volcano

Location: On Kalanikoa Rd. in Volcano, just off Hwy. 11.

Type of Camping: Cabin camping only.

Permit Info: There is only one cabin here, and it is in high demand year-round. Try to place your reservations as far in advance as possible. Per-mits can be obtained at any state parks office in the Islands. Write to the Big Island office at Division of State Parks, P.O. Box 936, Hilo, HI 96720, or call (808) 974-6200.

Time Limit: 5 nights

Cost: $45 per night for 1–4 people, $5 for each additional person.

Comments Count yourself lucky if you're able to reserve a stay at this site, comfortably nestled within a shady forest of trees and ferns. Accommo-dating up to six people, the cabin features a kitchen (including a sink, refrigerator, electric range, and utensils), dining room/living room, two bedrooms, and a bathroom with a hot shower. Towels, blankets, and linens are all provided. Hawaii Volcanoes National Park is only a half-mile away.

Mauna Loa Cabin

Zone: 12, Hilo and Volcano

Location: The eastern rim of the Mauna Loa summit crater. Exit Hawaii Volcanoes National Park to Hwy. 11, turn left (in the Kona direction), and drive to Mauna Loa Rd. Drive up the narrow road until it ends at a trailhead by a parking lot. Follow the trail 7.5 miles to Red Hill Cabin. The Mauna Loa Cabin is located 11.6 miles farther up the trail.

Type of Camping: Tent and cabin camping.

Permit Info: Permits are obtained at the Hawaii Volcanoes National Park Visitor Center and are issued on a first-come, first-served basis up to a day before your scheduled stay. There is a limit of 8 people per night per group. For more information, write to the Hawaii Volcanoes National Park, Volcano, HI 96718, or call (808) 985-6000.

Time Limit: 3 nights

Cost: Free

Comments   Used primarily by die-hard hikers. Located at the 13,250-foot elevation level, Mauna Loa Cabin rests near the edge of Mokuʻaweoweo, Mauna Loa's breathtaking caldera. The single cabin offers 12 bunk beds and spare mattresses (so additional people can sleep on the floor). There is one enclosed pit toilet situated behind the cabin. You should bring your own stove and drinking water (the water here needs to be treated before use). While tent camping is allowed here, use the cabin if at all possible; when the winds are blowing during the winter, temperatures here can dip to below freezing at night. Bring warm clothes. Keep in mind that, at this elevation level, rain, winds, and even snow are possible at any time of the year. Altitude sickness can pose another problem.

Namakani Paio Campground

Zone: 12, Hilo and Volcano

Location: Inside Hawaii Volcanoes National Park, about 5 miles west of the park entrance on Route 11.

Type of Camping: Tent, vehicle, and cabin camping.

Permit Info: None required for tent and vehicle camping. To place cabin reservations, write to the Volcano House at P.O. Box 53, Volcano, HI 96718, or call (808) 967-7321. Reservations should be made as far in advance as possible if you hope to come here during the summer and holiday periods.

Time Limit: 7 days

Cost: Free for tent and vehicle campers. Cabins are $32 per night and accommodate up to 4 people.

Comments   Located at the 4,000-foot elevation level, this scenic campsite is surrounded by towering eucalyptus trees. Tents are pitched on an open grassy field or under trees. The tent and vehicle campground section has a large pavilion with two grills and a fireplace. Picnic tables, rest rooms, sinks, and potable water are all available. There are ten cabins located adjacent to the campground, each containing a pair of single bunk beds and a double bunk bed (for a total of four persons). Toilets, sinks, and hot showers are provided in a separate building (available only to the cabin renters). Bring warm clothing, as it tends to get chilly at night. Namakani Paio is the closest campground to the Hawaii Volcanoes National Park's Kilauea Caldera, Devastation Trail, and Thurston Lava Tube.

Spencer Beach Park

Zone: 11, Kona

Location: On the Kohala Coast, south of Kawaihae. From Kailua-Kona, drive north on Hwy. 19. Look for the large sign to the park on the left-hand side after you pass the junction with Hwy. 270.

Type of Camping: Tent and vehicle camping.

Permit Info: Book your reservations early, particularly if you plan to camp here during the summer. Write to the Department of Parks and Recreation, County of Hawaii, 25 Aupuni St., Hilo, HI 96720, or call (808) 961-8311.

Time Limit: 1 week during the summer, 2 weeks during the rest of the year.

Cost: $1 per day for adults; 50¢ per day for juniors ages 13–17; free for children age 12 and under.

Comments Spencer Beach Park offers some of the best camping facilities on the Big Island, with plenty of picnic tables and a large pavilion housing rest rooms, sinks, washrooms, changing areas, and showers. The water here is drinkable. Swimming and snorkeling are among the favored ocean activities here (the ocean conditions are usually calm), and you can serve and volley to your heart's content at one of the park's tennis courts. History lovers should note that the campground is located next to Pu'ukohala Heiau, an ancient place of worship constructed by Kamehameha, Hawaii's greatest king.

Kauai

Kalalau Valley

Zone: 13, Kauai

Location: The end of Kalalau Trail, about 11 miles from the trailhead at Ke'e Beach. The valley is accessible via Kalalau Trail (not recommended for novice hikers) or a Zodiac raft that is available in the summer months. (The cost is $60 each way. Call (808) 826-9371.)

Type of Camping: Tent camping only.

Permit Info: Camping in Kalalau is restricted to 60 people per day, so try to obtain a permit as far in advance as possible. For more information, write to the Division of State Parks, 3060 'Eiwa St., Lihu'e, HI 96766, or call (808) 241-3444.

Time Limit: 5 nights

Cost: Free

Comments In his book *Camping Hawaii*, Richard McMahon calls Kalalau Valley his favorite campsite and says that not going there because it lacks facilities is like "skipping the Grand Canyon because it doesn't have an escalator." Indeed, Kalalau Valley defines the term "unspoiled beauty," boasting a magnificent white-sand beach, splendid waterfalls, and steep cliffs. The camping area stretches a half-mile behind the beach. (Camping in the valley itself is prohibited.) The only facilities here are toilets and water from nearby Ho'olea Falls. Bring your own drinking water. Swimming conditions are best during the summer months. *Note:* While illegal, public nudity is generally accepted here, primarily because of the valley's isolation. If you're offended by nudity, it's best to skip this area.

Koke'e State Park

Zone: 13, Kauai

Location: The north end of Waimea Canyon, near the end of Hwy. 55.

Type of Camping: Tent and cabin camping.

Permit Info: Permits can be obtained at any state parks office in the Islands. For more information, write to the Kauai office at Division of State Parks, 3060 'Eiwa St., Lihu'e, HI 96766, or call (808) 241-3444. For cabin reservations, write to the Koke'e Lodge at P.O. Box 819, Waimea, HI 96796, or call (808) 335-6061.

Time Limit: 5 nights

Cost: Free for tent campers. Koke'e Lodge cabins: $45 per night for the newer cabins, $35 per night for the older ones.

Comments   Located on a hillside near Koke'e Lodge, the park campground permits only tent camping. Rest rooms, showers, picnic tables, sinks, and drinking water are provided. Koke'e Lodge has a dozen cabins, each accommodating up to six people. The older cabins have a large dormitory-style room, bathroom, kitchen, and wood-burning stove; the newer cabins offer two bedrooms, a living room, kitchen, bathroom, and wood-burning stove. A restaurant at the lodge offers Continental breakfast and lunch daily. Koke'e is a hot spot for avid hikers. The 11-mile Nu'alolo-Awa'awapuhi Loop, which provides dramatic vistas of the Na Pali Coast (be sure to bring a camera), is considered one of Hawaii's best hikes. The Koke'e Museum, located adjacent to the lodge, spotlights Kauai's natural history (see Part Ten, "Hawaii's Attractions"). *Note:* Other accommodations at Koke'e State Park are available. For information, call Camp Sloggett, (808) 245-5959; Koke'e Methodist Camp, (808) 335-3429; or the Hongwanji Camp, (808) 332-9563. Rates are $40–96 per night.

Polihale Beach Park

Zone: 13, Kauai

Location: At the end of Hwy. 50 on Kauai's western shore.

Type of Camping: Tent and vehicle camping.

Permit Info: Permits can be obtained at any state parks office in the Islands. Write to the Kauai office at Division of State Parks, 3060 'Eiwa St., Lihu'e, HI 96766, or call (808) 241-3444.

Time Limit: 5 days

Cost: Free

Comments Not only is Polihale State Park one of the widest beaches in the Islands (extending more than 300 feet during the summer months), it is also the westernmost beach in the entire United States. This is another site offering lots of visual delights, including the island of Niihau. There are a trio of numbered campsites here, each providing a rest room, outdoor showers, picnic tables, grills, and drinking water. Additional facilities are available at the beach park. Swimming is usually safe in a shallow area known as Queen's Pond, but be cautious everywhere else.

Waimea Canyon State Park

Zone: 13, Kauai

Location: At the bottom of Waimea Canyon, along the Waimea River and Koai'e and Wai'alae streams. Access is via the Kukui Trail, located 7.5 miles north on Waimea Canyon Rd.

Type of Camping: Tent camping only.

Permit Info: Write to the Division of Forestry and Wildlife, 3060 'Eiwa St., Room 306, Lihu'e, HI 96766, or call (808) 241-3433.

Time Limit: 4 nights

Cost: Free

Comments Think you've seen all the beautiful scenery there is to see in Hawaii? Try gazing up the steep, eroded walls of this magnificent canyon! Waimea Canyon State Park offers five different campsites spread over a six-mile stretch of the canyon's floor. The best is Lonomea Camp, located six miles from Kukui trailhead. Lonomea has pit toilets, a picnic table, and roofed shelters. Wiliwili Camp, at the base of the trail, also has those facilities. Hipalau Camp has no toilets but offers a roofed shelter, a picnic table, and two refreshing pools fed by waterfalls. The only water available at the park is from the streams, so we recommend bringing your own water. Also, stock up on food before you arrive; there are no grocery stores in the area.

Molokai

Papohaku Beach Park

Zone: 14, Molokai

Location: Just off Kaluako'i Rd. on the island's western shore. Head west on Hwy. 460 to the turnoff to the Kaluako'i Resort; continue past the hotel along Kaluako'i Rd.

Type of Camping: Tent and vehicle camping.

Permit Info: You can pick up a permit at the Pau'ole Center Multipurpose Building in Kaunakakai. For advanced reservations and more information, write to the Maui County Parks Dept., P.O. Box 526, Kaunakakai, HI 96748, or call (808) 553-3204.

Time Limit: 3 nights

Cost: $3 per person per night.

Comments   This is a good site because it is both easily accessible and fairly isolated. There is a satisfactory number of facilities, including rest rooms, showers, picnic tables, grills, and drinking water. And if you ever get fed up with camp food, the Kaluako'i Resort is just a mile away and has a restaurant and coffee shop. One drawback is that the beach is not especially suitable for swimming, and definitely not for children. But for a pleasant overall outdoor outing, Papohaku is as good a spot as any on Molokai.

Special Note: You won't need a permit to enjoy the newest and most unique camping adventure on the island of Molokai (and perhaps in the entire state). Privately owned Molokai Ranch offers Paniolo Camp, consisting of 40 comfortable tents mounted on platforms (they call them "tent-alows"); they feature queen-size beds, solar-powered lights, ceiling fans, private bathrooms, and even a lanai. A number of ranch activities are available, from children's games and outrigger canoeing to horseback riding and nature hikes. Rates are $125–200 and include airport transportation and three daily meals. Call toll-free, (877) 726-4656.

Lanai

Hulopo'e Beach Park

Zone: 15, Lanai

Location: At the end of Manele Rd. (Hwy. 440). From Lanai City, drive south on 440; the park is about 6 miles away.

Type of Camping: Tent camping only.

Permit Info: This is the only campground on Lanai, so get your permit as far in advance as possible. It's not unusual for reservations to be filled months in advance. Write to the Lanai Company (Attn: Camping Permits), P.O. Box 310, Lanai City, HI 96763, or call (808) 565-8206.

Time Limit: 7 days

Cost: $5 per person per night. There is also a $5 permit fee.

Comments   This is one of the most lovely and pristine spots in Hawaii. There are only three campsites at Hulopo'e, and each is limited to six guests. Facilities include rest rooms, showers, picnic tables, grills, and drinking water. Hulopo'e Bay is suitable for swimming nearly year-round (except during periods of severe southern swells), and snorkeling, scuba diving, bodyboarding, and bodysurfing are also favorite ocean adventures here.

HIKING: HAPPY TRAILS

Next to getting in some quality beach time, hiking is perhaps the most popular outdoor activity in Hawaii, and for good reason. What better way to celebrate Hawaii's natural environment than to experience it up close? As you might expect, there are a number of great hiking trails in the Islands.

One of the most popular hikes is right in Waikiki, where you can climb to the top of Diamond Head—it's about a 45-minute walk—and take in 360° views of Waikiki, Honolulu, the mountains, and the Pacific Ocean. Ask your hotel concierge for a trail map, or sign up for a guided walk put on by the Clean Air Team of Hawaii (call (808) 948-3299). This narrated tour stops before ascending to the summit, but you'll have the option to continue up the trail. The hike is scheduled each Saturday at 9 a.m. Meet in front of the Honolulu Zoo entrance.

Other prime hiking spots on Oahu include **Manoa Falls,** a three-quarter-mile trail through a rain forest that ends with a refreshing dip beneath a cool waterfall; **Makapu'u Head,** a series of trails at the edge of windward Oahu that features fantastic ocean views; and **Mount Tantalus,** which invites visitors with several well-marked trails flourishing with guava, bamboo, liliko'i fruit, and other tropic vegetation.

On Maui, **Haleakala**—"The House of the Sun"—ranks as one of the state's top hiking spots. The 19-square-mile interior of the crater houses many marvelous features, including the rare silversword plant.

Experienced hikers on Kauai can retrace the footsteps of early-day Hawaiians along the **Kalalau Trail,** an 11-mile path that takes you along the island's stunning Na Pali Coast. An easier hike is available at the **Kilauea Point National Wildlife Refuge** on the north side of the island. Here, a knowledgeable guide shares the history of the area and provides information on a variety of resident wildlife.

There are a number of healthy hikes on the Big Island, several of them at Hawaii Volcanoes National Park. The five-mile **Kilauea Iki Trail,** for example, begins at the Kilauea Iki Overlook and descends to a junction at the parking lot near the Thurston Lava Tube. The path then descends farther through lush forest until it reaches the crater floor; a subsequent trail leads you directly back to the overlook. A shorter walk is the half-mile **Devastation Trail,** a guided path that cuts through a stark wasteland.

Visit any bookshop in the Islands and you'll find many helpful books about local hiking trails. For free trail maps, call the Department of Forestry and Wildlife at (808) 587-0166. In addition, there are a number of hiking tours available in Hawaii, including the very informative ecotours of Oahu offered by Oahu Nature Tours & Books (call (808) 924-2473).

If you hike in a rain forest (the Manoa Falls trail on Oahu, for example), please take the "rain" in rain forest literally. The trail will probably be wet and slippery and could be quite muddy as well. It's also likely that it will rain during your outing. Even on days when it's sunny and clear at the beach, there's still a high probability of rain in the rain forest. Our advice is to take appropriate rain gear and give yourself extra time to negotiate a trail that may well serve up very trecherous footing. Rain forest trails are not recommended for anyone unaccustomed to hiking on wet, uneven surfaces.

Above all, remember to adhere to all safety rules and use common sense. Never, for example, hike alone, and always inform someone of your hiking plans ahead of time. Be alert. As beautiful as the scenery may be, there is an element of danger involved: On May 9, 1999, eight people were killed at Sacred Falls Park after a devastating landslide. We don't mention this to scare you; it's just a tragic reminder to always think safety first.

JOGGING: BORN TO RUN?

Lace up your Reeboks and head out for a variety of superb running paths in the Islands. On Oahu, we recommend morning or late-afternoon jogs at **Kapiʻolani Park** and **Diamond Head** in Waikiki or **Ala Moana Beach Park** and **Magic Island** in Honolulu (across from the Ala Moana Shopping Center). These locales are thoroughly pleasant, invigorating, and full of the postcard-like scenery for which Hawaii is known.

On the Neighbor Islands, you won't have to venture far from your hotel to enjoy an exhilarating run. Most of the larger resorts have scenic jogging paths right on their property.

The Running Room (call (808) 737-2422) on Oahu is considered one of the best sources for running gear in Hawaii and has published *The Runner's Guide for Oahu*. Another good publication to pick up is *Hawaii Race* (call (808) 735-8924), a free magazine that covers the state's running scene.

SWIMMING: MAKE A SPLASH

Your hotel swimming pool is usually an alluring (and certainly convenient) option, especially if it's a grandiose affair like the pools at the Grand Wailea Resort on Maui and the Hilton Waikoloa Village on the Big Island. On Oahu, city officials are trying to resurrect the Waikiki Memorial Natatorium, a historic saltwater pool at Waikiki Beach that once hosted international swimming events featuring the legendary Duke Kahanamoku. That may or may not happen. Our advice? Head to the beach! Combined, the Hawaiian Islands have more than 180 miles of sandy shoreline and offer some of the finest beaches in the world!

On Oahu, the most famous beach is **Waikiki Beach,** where more than 25,000 people swim, surf, play, and rest each day of the year. Another highly recommended beach is at **Ala Moana Beach Park,** just minutes from Waikiki. Two beaches definitely worth your while on the windward side of the island (and definitely less populated) are **Kailua Beach** and **Lanikai Beach.** And don't forget **Hanauma Bay,** renowned as a premier snorkeling spot but also great for swimming.

On Maui, the most swimmable beaches are clustered along the island's west and south shores. The best are the ones at **Wailea, Ka'anapali,** and **Kapalua.**

The coastline on the island of Hawaii, meanwhile, is mostly ringed by lava flows (old and new) that have run over old beaches. There are only 19 miles of sandy shoreline here, in fact, but still there are a few beaches worth a visit: **Hapuna Beach, Kahalu'u Beach Park, 'Ohai'ula Beach,** and **Kauna'oa Beach.**

Kauai has its share of great sandy beaches, including the ones at **Po'ipu, Kalapaki,** and **Hanalei.**

Most of the beaches on Molokai are inaccessible, but one that is open to the public happens to be the best: **Papohaku Beach,** located at Kaluako'i Resort.

And last but not least, Lanai has **Hulopo'e Beach,** a small but beautiful setting that is perfect for swimming and snorkeling.

Bring sunscreen and adhere to all posted warning signs and beach regulations.

KAYAKING: DIFFERENT STROKES

This is a great way to enjoy Hawaii's ocean *and* get a good workout! For expert kayakers, we recommend a trip along Kauai's picturesque Na Pali Coast, where the waters can be treacherous but the views are fantastic. For a kayaking newbie, a better recommendation is the short, three-quarter-mile trip to the Mokulua islets off Oahu's Lanikai Beach.

Kayak Rentals
Oahu
Bob Twogood Kayaks (808) 262-5656
Go Banana Kayaks (808) 737-9514
Kailua Sailboards and Kayaks (808) 262-2555
Maui
Maui Ocean Activities (808) 667-1964
South Pacific Kayaks (808) 875-4848
Tradewind Kayaks (808) 879-2247

Kayak Rentals (continued)
The Big Island Hawaii Pack & Paddle (808) 328-8911 Kona Boy Kayaks (808) 322-3600 Ocean Safari's Kayak Tours & Rentals (808) 326-4699 **Kauai** Outfitters Kauai (808) 742-9667 Kayak Wailua (808) 822-3388

Rentals for single-person kayaks are $25–32 for a full day; the rate for tandem kayaks is about $35–40 per day. A short lesson is usually included in the price, and all kayaking equipment is transported to the beach for you.

SCUBA DIVING: TAKE A DIVE

The beauty of Hawaii, it seems, has no boundaries. While everyone marvels at the magnificent scenic views on land, a growing segment of Hawaii visitors know the visual wonders found beneath the ocean's surface. Hawaii's undersea world is an entirely different universe, one inhabited by thousands of rainbow-colored fish, gliding sea turtles, playful dolphins, intriguing coral formations, and other vibrant sea life.

Scuba diving isn't for everyone, however. You need to be a competent and confident swimmer, and many dive excursions require that you be certified by a scuba training organization such as the Professional Association of Diving Instructors (PADI), National Association of Underwater Instructors (NAUI), National Association of Scuba Diving Schools (NASDS), World Association of Scuba Instructors (WASI), or the YMCA. The requirements for qualifying as a certified Open Water Diver (the beginning level certification) include being able to swim 200 yards nonstop and tread water or float for ten minutes.

An entry-level course can be completed in as little as three days and as long as several weeks, depending on the course schedule and student needs. Classes are performance-based, which means you earn your certification when you demonstrate your mastery of the skills and knowledge required. Sessions generally involve classroom lectures, confined water training (usually in a swimming pool), and on-site training dives. If you wish to participate in Hawaiian scuba-diving tours for certified divers, save time by earning your certification before you arrive in the Islands.

For more information, including the location of available scuba training classes in your area, contact the following organizations:

PADI	(800) 729-7234	www.padi.com
NASDS	(901) 767-7265	www.nasds.com
NAUI	(800) 553-6284	www.naui.org
WASI	(801) 363-9274	www.divewasi.com

It's important to seek a high-quality instructor who thinks safety first. Ask for referrals. The worst mistake you can make is finding an instructor who passes students indiscriminately, even though they may not have gained the proper skills and knowledge. (Be wary of any instructor who tells you that knowing how to swim isn't really necessary.)

You have to be at least 12 years old to become a certified scuba diver. (Divers ages 12–14 are classified as Junior Open Water Divers and should dive with a certified adult; upon turning 15, divers are upgraded to regular Open Water Diver certification.) Also, specialized dives—including explorations of wrecks and caves and night diving—require advance training.

There are numerous dive shops on the Islands that provide professional scuba instruction. Rates range from $60 for a beachside lesson to $300 or more for full open-water instruction and certification. You pay an additional $14 for a scuba certification card. All equipment is provided.

If you're not sure whether scuba diving is for you, you can sign up for an introductory dive offered by most Hawaii dive companies. No experience or certification is required. You receive basic instruction, get fitted for scuba gear, and then enjoy a dive with the instructors. The entire experience lasts 2–4 hours, and rates hover in the $100–150 range.

There are dozens of dive companies in Hawaii, most of them on Maui, considered the best island for scuba. Selecting the best adventure for you simply involves asking the right questions: How many years of experience does the company have? What kind of boat do they use? What kind of dive activities are offered? Where do they go? How much actual time in the water will you get to spend?

Above all, choose an operator that stresses safety. Offered one Oahu dive master, "There are a lot of fly-by-night operations, and you don't want to risk your life with that."

Tour rates generally are $75–175, depending on the size of the boat, range of equipment, and number of dives. Major credit cards are accepted and will help hold your reservation. Deposits are usually required and are refundable if you cancel your booking in advance (call for cancellation policies).

Expect to spend half a day for a guided scuba adventure. A typical excursion lasts from 7 a.m. to 3 p.m. (from the time you leave your hotel to your

Hawaii Scuba-Diving Companies

Oahu
Aaron's Dive Shops (808) 262-2333
Aloha Dive Shop (808) 395-5922
Aloha Water Sports (808) 841-9191
Clark's Diving Tours (808) 923-5595
Dan's Dive Shop (808) 536-6181
Fantasea Island Divers (808) 262-2318

Maui
Divers Locker (808) 875-4703
Ed Robinson's Diving Adventures (808) 879-3584
Lahaina Divers (808) 667-7496
Maui Dive Shop (808) 879-3388 in Kihei; (808) 661-5388 in
    Lahaina
Maui Dreams Dive Co. (808) 874-5332
Tropical Divers (808) 667-7709

The Big Island
Aloha Dive Company (808) 325-5560
Body Glove Cruises (808) 326-7122
Hawaiian Divers (808) 329-5662
Jack's Diving Locker (808) 329-7585
Kona Coast Divers (808) 329-8802
Pacific Rim Divers (808) 334-1750

Kauai
Dive Kauai Scuba Center (808) 822-0452
Fathom Dive Divers (808) 742-6991
Hanalei Water Sports (808) 826-7509
North Shore Divers (808) 826-1921
Scuba Tours (808) 742-9303
Seasport Divers (808) 742-9303

return). The actual time you spend in the water will vary—the deeper water you're in, the faster you use your air supply—but usually it's between 90 minutes and 2 hours. The diver-to-guide ratio has a legal maximum of six to one.

Many operators provide hotel transportation and either snacks or lunch. Book your tour as far in advance as possible (many companies accept reservations up to a year in advance), especially during the busy summer months.

A few tips and other things you should know:

- People with certain health problems—severe asthma, for example— may be prohibited from diving.
- Whenever you are in the water, be careful where you put your hands and feet. Some marine life—such as eels, jellyfish, and scorpionfish— can bite or sting. Do not touch any animal you don't recognize.
- Sharks? Divers aren't natural prey for these ocean predators, and attacks are rare.
- Never dive alone.
- If you're attempting underwater photography for the first time, four feet is the maximum distance from which to shoot your subject. For best results, use an underwater camera with a 15mm or 20mm lens.

There are more than 250 diving sites in Hawaii, with depths ranging from 20 to 150 feet. The most popular site is **Molokini,** the crescent-shaped islet that is actually a cinder cone peeking out from the ocean's surface at 'Alalakeiki Channel (about three miles off the southwestern coast of Maui). Designated a Marine Life Conservation District in 1977, Molokini is blessed with calm waters, high visibility, and thriving ocean life, including tropical reef fish, sea turtles, and manta rays. It is considered by many divers to be one of the best dive destinations in the world.

Another favorite site on Maui is **La Perouse Pinnacle,** which sits in the middle of picturesque La Perouse Bay at the island's south end. The pinnacle rises 60 feet from the sea floor to about 10 feet below the ocean's surface. Exceptional for snorkeling as well as shallow dives, here you'll find brilliantly colored damsel fish, triggerfish, goat fish, puffers, and wrasses.

A great spot for divers of all skill levels is **Five Caves** in Makena. Lava ridges and small pinnacles provide food and shelter for angler fish, sea turtles, eels, and even white-tipped sharks. The waters here are fairly shallow, around 30–40 feet, and can be accessed from shore as well as via boat.

Another treasured site is **Cathedrals,** located off the south shore of Lanai. Here, a beautiful stained glass effect occurs when the sunlight pours through the holes in twin underwater caves. This site is for only experienced divers, however.

Other recommended dive sites include: Hanauma Bay, Shark's Cove, Three Tables, Mahi, Turtle Canyon, and Makaha Caverns on Oahu; Marty's Reef, Golden Arches, Banyan Tree Reef, and Red Hill on Maui; Honaunau Bay, Kawaihae Bay, and Kealakekua Bay on the Big Island; Oasis Reef, Fishbowl, Sheraton Caverns, Brennecke's Drop, and Ahukini Landing on Kauai; and Shark Fin Rock, Knob Hill, and Turtle Cave on Lanai.

For more sites suitable for scuba diving, see our section at the beginning of this chapter titled "The Beach Experience."

SNORKELING: EXPLORING THE UNDERSEA WORLD

While not as "deep" an experience as scuba diving, snorkeling still provides plenty of stunning underwater views for thousands of Hawaii visitors each year. Some practical snorkeling tips:

- Know how to swim. While some snorkeling spots are shallow, being able to swim is the best way to ensure your safety in the water.
- Novices should practice in shallow water.
- Always snorkel with a partner or in groups.
- Don't stray too far from shore or the boat.
- Check your snorkeling equipment carefully before entering the water.

The most famous snorkeling spot is Oahu's **Hanauma Bay,** a terrific place for novice snorkelers. Lots of friendly reef fish scamper about in this picture-perfect bay. The only drawback is that sometimes it seems the swimmers outnumber the fish.

Guided snorkeling adventures are available on every island and are priced from $35 up. See the above section on scuba diving for a list of tour operators. For more sites suitable for snorkeling, see our section at the beginning of this chapter titled "The Beach Experience." In addition, there are a number of shops that rent out snorkeling equipment, including masks, snorkels, and gear bags. Snorkel Bob's, for example, has locations on Oahu (call (808) 735-7944), Maui (call (808) 879-7449, (808) 669-9603, (808) 661-4421), the Big Island (call (808) 329-0770), and Kauai (call (808) 823-9433, (808) 742-2206).

Most snorkel and dive shops accept all major credit cards. Guided snorkeling adventures usually last half a day, and instruction for beginners is available. Snorkeling destinations are sometimes determined by the overall skill and experience levels of the group.

SURFING: CATCH A WAVE

You hear it at every Beach Boys concert: "Catch a wave, and you're sitting on top of the world!" Hawaii's official individual sport is so popular that local sportscasters often provide the next day's surf conditions before giving out the sports headlines and scores.

Hawaii offers the most consistent surf, the biggest waves, the deepest tubes, and, as a result, the largest crowds. The best surfers from all over the globe test their skills here, especially during the winter months, when Oahu's North Shore turns into the world's surfing capital. The North Shore is the home of the annual Triple Crown of Surfing, a trio of prestigious surf meets spotlighting the world's top surfing professionals taking on waves often more than ten feet high. (Novice surfers, of course, should stick to kinder and gentler waves.)

No one knows exactly when surfing originated, but many historians believe that the Polynesians were already well versed in the sport when they migrated to the Hawaiian Islands nearly 2,000 years ago. (On the Big Island, some petroglyphs depict board-riding stick figures.) Ancient Hawaiians called surfing *he'e nalu* (wave sliding), and in those days only the high-ranking chiefs enjoyed access to the best surf spots. King Kamehameha himself was said to be an avid surfer.

Today, novice surfers can still head out to Waikiki Beach and hook up with a beach boy for a quick lesson. For a more formal surfing experience, however, we recommend signing up for a lesson from expert instructors like Hans Hedemann, a former surfing champion who had a 17-year professional career in the sport. Hedemann now runs the Hans Hedemann Surf School (call (808) 924-7778), which offers lessons right on the beach at Waikiki.

Lessons take place where the waves are small—usually one to two feet—and gentle enough for beginners. The locations are also relatively crowd-free, so you can learn without worrying about embarrassing yourself in front of throngs of beachgoers. Group lessons usually include three or four students (and no more than five) per instructor. Private lessons (one-on-one instruction) and semi-private lessons (one instructor and two students) are also available. The lesson begins on the beach, where the instructor provides important tips on ocean safety. Students are then taught the basics of surfing, including paddling techniques, how to jump up and stand on the surfboard, proper foot placement, and where to shift your body weight. All surfing equipment is provided. Then the class enters the water, where the instructor will again review safety tips and surfing techniques.

From there, you apply what you learned on the beach: catching a wave, paddling forward, leaping to your board, and riding the wave to shore. The instructor will critique your techniques and help you make any necessary adjustments. Once you get the hang of riding a wave, you'll learn some basic maneuvers such as controlling your board to move in a certain direction. "Everyone's different," said Hedemann. "We try to push each individual according to how quickly he or she is progressing."

You don't need to be a fitness freak to learn how to surf; surfers come in all shapes, sizes, and ages. But you should expect to do a lot of paddling and kicking in the water, and you should know how to swim (even though you won't venture out into deep waters). Consider your own physical limitations. "If you think you can do it, you probably can," said one instructor. Hedemann said almost everyone is "up and riding" on their first lesson. We saw an eight-year-old ride a wave to shore on her very first try!

Other surfing instruction schools include Hawaiian Rush (call (808) 596-0580) and Hawaiian Watersports (call (808) 255-4352) on Oahu, and Buzzy Kerbox Surf School (call (808) 573-5728), Maui Surfing School (call (808) 875-0625), and the Nancy Emerson School of Surfing (call (808) 244-7873) on the island of Maui. Most schools have a minimum age requirement of five to seven years. Surfing instruction is available year-round.

Group rates are generally $50–60 for one-hour lessons, $65–75 for two-hour lessons, and $225–250 for all-day lessons. Private lessons are about $85–125 for one-hour lessons, $115–200 for two-hour lessons, and $425–450 for all-day lessons. Multiday and week-long rates are also available. We recommend signing up for at least a two-hour lesson, which will give you about 90 minutes of actual time in the water.

Cash, traveler's checks, and major credit cards are accepted; no advance deposit is required.

Hedemann suggests that you book a lesson at least a day in advance, although he and most surf schools will try to accommodate last-minute students. Some instruction schools, such as Hedemann's, provide transportation to and from your hotel. Bring your swimsuit, a towel, and sunscreen.

For experienced surfers able to deal with crowds, Oahu is the place to be. By far, it has the highest concentration of quality surf spots in the state. Surf conditions are good year-round (the South Shore during summer, North Shore during winter, and overlapping swells during the spring and fall). Maui has a few great surf spots near Lahaina and just past Pa'ia. Kauai has several excellent surf spots located at its northern and southern shores, and the waves are usually less populated. And the Big Island has a few good surfing areas, although many are spread far apart and are inaccessible by car.

A helpful book on the best surf spots in Hawaii is the *Surfers Guide to Hawaii* by Greg Ambrose (published by Bess Press); it includes tips, descriptions, and maps.

Here are important safety and etiquette tips for all surfers riding the Hawaiian waves:

- Check with lifeguards before you surf. They can point out the hazardous rip currents, jagged reefs, and tricky waves that you will definitely want to avoid.
- Never surf alone. Make sure someone always knows where you are in case something goes wrong.
- After a meal, wait at least an hour before venturing into the surf.
- Don't overestimate your swimming ability.
- Be considerate of other surfers. Don't drop in on someone else's wave.

- Don't surf after dark.
- Obey all posted warning signs.
- Use leg ropes for your safety (and the safety of fellow surfers).
- If you get in trouble, don't panic. Signal for help by raising one arm vertically.

WINDSURFING: RIDE THE WIND

If surfing isn't thrilling enough for you, ride the winds with a colorful sail-board. Expert windsurfers already know about **Hoʻokipa Beach** on Maui—that's the hot spot known as "the Aspen of windsurfing," where the world's top wave riders gather to take advantage of brisk winds and opti-mum waves. Kailua and Lanikai Beaches on the windward side of Oahu are gentler—and safer—for beginners. Sailboard rentals are $25–40 for a full day; Alan Cadiz's HST (call (808) 871-5423) on Maui offers two-and-a-half-hour lessons for $69.

Sailboard Rentals
Oahu
Hawaiian Watersports (808) 255-4352
Kailua Sailboards and Kayaks (808) 262-2555
North Shore Eco-Surf (808) 638-9503
Maui
Action Sports (808) 283-7913
Al West's Lesson Surf (808) 877-0090
Hoʻokipa Surf and Surf (808) 667-5566
Maui Windsurf (808) 877-4816
Windrigger Maui (808) 871-7753
Kauai
Anini Beach Windsurfing (808) 826-9463
Windsurf Kauai (808) 828-6838

BIG-GAME SPORTFISHING: REEL IN THE BIG ONE

If you've ever dreamed of landing a 1,000-pound marlin, there's no better place to make it happen than Hawaii, one of the world's renowned sport-fishing destinations.

Big-game fishing is available on all the Hawaiian islands, but if your main purpose for visiting Hawaii is to fish, then you'll want to do it on the

Kona Coast of the Big Island, which is often called the big-game fishing capital of the world. The fishing itself is just as good on the other Hawaiian islands, but Kona provides the optimal fishing environment. Its 80 miles of coastline are sheltered by Mauna Kea (the highest mountain in the state, at 13,796 feet) and Mauna Loa Volcano (the second-highest mountain, at 13,677 feet), which means there is less wind and a much calmer ocean. Additionally, the waters off Kona are deeper close to shore, and you'll be able to start fishing just a few minutes after leaving the harbor. (On other islands, such as Oahu, it usually takes a half-hour or longer to get to the fish.) A Kona charter may sail as far as ten miles out to sea but rarely goes beyond five or six miles.

There are about a hundred charter boats operating out of Kona's Honokohau Harbor, although one veteran skipper told us only about half really work hard to make a living out of the business. You can sign up for a charter at your hotel activity desk, but the chances are they will have only a few companies that they'll recommend. We suggest browsing the Internet, picking up rack cards at the airport, and looking for ads in the various activity guides. Going with a charter company that is committed to its business—and who makes these fishing excursions on an almost daily basis—can only benefit you. These are the people who know best where the fish are biting.

Most charters offer half-, three-quarter-, and full-day fishing adventures that last four, six, and eight hours, respectively. Departure time is usually 7 a.m., with half-day charters returning by noon and full-day charters returning before 4 p.m. Prices vary (see listing below), with higher rates for larger boats.

To maximize your chances of landing a big-game fish, we strongly suggest booking the full-day charter. It can take an hour or more just to catch live bait—usually aku, a type of skipjack—and when you add the time required to get to the bait, put out the fishing lines, stow the light tackle, and set up the tackle to catch bigger game, you won't have much time left on a half-day excursion for the actual fishing.

Aku aren't exactly tiny, by the way. They weigh between 2 and 20 pounds, and catching them can be a lively and enjoyable experience by itself.

Even though walk-up bookings are available, it's better to make your reservations as far in advance as possible, ensuring that you get the type of boat you want. A deposit is usually required (usually from $100 up to 50% of the charter cost) and is refundable up to 48 hours prior to the charter date. Most charter companies accept major credit cards and personal checks. Shared charters are available but require advance notice unless you book through an activity desk.

Most boats are licensed to hold six passengers, along with the captain and two deckhands. The optimum number of passengers, according to one captain, is four.

Charter boats range in size from 25 to 58 feet, with the average being around 33–35 feet. Generally speaking, the comfort level and the number of amenities are directly proportionate to the size of the boat. If you're new to sportfishing—and most clients are first-timers—we suggest signing up with a mid-sized to larger boat. This will allow you to better enjoy the experience, even if the fish aren't biting that day. The views of Kona are spectacular, and during the whale season (November through mid-May) you might even spot a humpback or two rising from the ocean's surface.

When it comes to the actual fishing, however, size doesn't matter. Offered one boat captain, "The fish don't care."

The crew provides instruction and all equipment. You must, however, bring your own food and drinks (liquor is allowed). Most boats have coolers to keep your drinks cold.

There are three types of marlin roaming Hawaiian waters: black, blue, and striped. While the chances are good that you'll encounter marlin and have them biting at your bait, the odds of actually landing one is no more than 35%. One captain said, "We'll catch a marlin about once in every three trips." With any luck, you might even catch a "grander"—a marlin weighing a thousand pounds or more. However, most captains will warn you not to have unrealistic expectations; while Kona may be the best place to land the fish of a lifetime, it's more likely any marlin you bring in will weigh in at a few hundred pounds.

If you don't have much success with marlin, well, as the saying goes, there are plenty of other fish in the sea. 'Ahi (yellow-fin tuna), ono (wahoo), mahi-mahi, and spearfish are plentiful in Hawaiian waters, and those are the primary fish (along with the marlin) you'll be trying to "hook up" with. The marlin are here in steady numbers throughout the year, except for the striped marlin, which is here only during the winter. Spearfish are also more abundant in the winter months. 'Ahi are here during the summer, while ono and mahi-mahi are year-round fish.

Most charter boats fish in two ways: trolling with lures (with the boats traveling at 7–10 knots) or live baiting. Most of the big-game fish are caught using live bait, which is another reason we favor full-day trips (generally, half-day charters use lures, while full-day adventures use live bait). One skipper cautioned, however, that conditions change all the time, and some days marlin will show a preference for lures.

You won't need the strength of an Olympic weightlifter to land a giant marlin. If you're using up to 130-pound test line, the most drag a line has is about 40 or 50 pounds, meaning the most you have to worry about pulling in is between 40 and 50 pounds, and it's usually much less than that. Basically, if you can pull 20 pounds around for a while, you can reel in a marlin. One captain said, "Anyone can do it. No one's going to catch a fish by brute force, because a 200-pound person versus a 200-pound marlin is going to

Hawaii Sportfishing Charters

Operator	Phone	Web Site
The Big Island		
Anxious Sportsfishing	326-1229	www.alohazone.com
Blue Hawaii Sportfishing	322-3210	www.konabiggamefishing.com
Ihu Nui Sportfishing	325-1513	n/a
Kona Rainbow Sportfishing	331-2847	n/a
Layla Big Game Sportfishing	329-6899	www.fishkona.com
Marlin Magic Sportfishing	325-7138	www.marlinmagic.com
Pacific Blue Charters	329-9468	www.fishkona.com
Spellbound Sportfishing	329-9498	www.holoholo.com/spellbound/
Tara Sportfishing	325-5887	n/a
Tropical Sun	325-3450	n/a
Oahu		
Ilima V Sportfishing	596-2087	n/a
Kamome Sportfishing	593-8931	n/a
Maggie Joe	591-8888	n/a
Magic Sportfishing	596-2998	www.sportfishing.com
Sea Verse	591-8840	n/a
Maui		
Absolute Sportfishing	669-1449	n/a
Carol Ann Charters	877-2181	n/a
Hinatea Sportfishing	667-7548	n/a
Islander II Sportfishing	667-6625	n/a
Rascal Charters	874-8633	n/a
Kauai		
Anini Fishing Charters	828-1285	www.superpages.GTE.net
Kai Bear Sportfishing	826-4556	www.kaibearsportfishing.com
McReynolds Fishing Charters	828-1379	www.aloha.net/~themcrs
Sportfishing Kauai	742-7013	www.fishing-kauai-hawaii.com
Molokai		
Alyce C Sportfishing	558-8377	www.worldwidefishing.com

Hawaii Sportfishing Charters (continued)

Size of Boat	Departure Point	½-, ¾-, Full-Day Rates
The Big Island		
33 ft.	Honokohau Harbor	$295/$395/$495
53 ft	Honokohau Harbor	$500/$650/$750
35 ft.	Honokohau Harbor	$400/$525/$625
35 ft.	Honokohau Harbor	$295/$375/$450
34 ft.	Honokohau Harbor	$275/$350/$425
43 ft.	Honokohau Harbor	$375/$475/$625
40 ft.	Honokohau Harbor	$350/$450/$550
41 ft.	Honokohau Harbor	$275/$425/$500
46 ft./53 ft.	Honokohau Harbor	$350/$500/$650
36 ft.	Honokohau Harbor	$350/$425/$475
Oahu		
42 ft	Kewalo Basin	$450/$500/$550
53 ft.	Kewalo Basin	$450/$500/$550
42 ft./46 ft./53 ft.	Kewalo Basin	$450/$500/$550
50 ft.	Kewalo Basin	$625
44 ft.	Kewalo Basin	$450/$500/$550
Maui		
31 ft.	Ka'anapali Beach	$500/$600/$700
33 ft.	Ma'alaea Harbor	$450/$550/$650
41 ft.	Lahaina Harbor	$120/$135/$150
36 ft.	Lahaina Harbor	$120/$135/$150
31 ft.	Ma'alaea Harbor	$95/$110/$135
Kauai		
33 ft.	Anini Beach	$435/$535/$700
38 ft./42 ft.	Nawiliwili Harbor	$550/$750/$950
30 ft.	Anini Beach	$450/$500/$600
38 ft.	Port Allen	$475/$675/$875
Molokai		
31 ft.	Kaunakakai Harbor	$300/$350/$400

lose every time if it comes to strength; they're going to use the techniques we teach them."

You do need, however, to be mentally prepared. Not all big-game fish react the same once hooked; some will fight for a long time (especially the larger blue and black marlins), while others may exhaust themselves in a matter of minutes. There's no way to predict what an individual game fish will do. One captain remembers an angler fighting a fish for more than 35 hours! In other words, while you won't have to be a powerlifter to fish for big game, you'll likely need to have a lot of stamina and staying power.

Should more than one person hook a marlin at the same time—an unlikely occurrence, but it happens on occasion—the priority is first given to the person with the biggest fish on the line. That person is placed into the boat's main seat, the one with a harness. The other fish are "fought" from the regular fishing rod holders.

Another scenario to consider is the possibility of hooking a marlin near the end of your excursion. It can take an hour or more to successfully land a marlin. Our advice? Book a full-day charter on a day relatively free from other commitments, including your flight home or to another island.

The fish that are caught usually belong to the captain and his crew, although some charters will make exceptions. The captain carries a commercial fishing license and is able to sell the fish to local fish markets. A 150-pound 'ahi, for example, can be sold at $6 a pound. The money is divided among the captain and crew. This practice is actually to your benefit, as it helps keep the costs of charters down and provides added incentive for the crew to help you find and catch the big fish. "We're not going to take you out to sea, turn on the auto pilot, and take a nap," one captain remarked.

Want to mount your big catch? Today's mounts are artificial, constructed based on the marlin's type, measurements, girth, and weight, which means they last longer and have a nicer appearance. The crew will provide a professional taxidermist with the necessary information.

You won't need a fishing license to enjoy offshore fishing, but you will need suntan lotion, a cap, and sunglasses to protect yourself from the sun. Shorts and T-shirts are the recommended attire (you'll want to keep comfortable). Bring a light jacket during the winter, when the mornings can get a bit chilly. Also, if you even suspect you might need medication or patches to prevent motion sickness, it's better to be safe than sorry.

WHALE-WATCHING

Scientists estimate that two-thirds of the entire humpback whale population in the North Pacific migrates to warmer Hawaiian waters each winter to engage in breeding, calving, and nursing activities. Few sight-seeing opportunities can match the spectacle of these magnificent leviathans breaching the Pacific Ocean's surface.

There are plenty of whale-watching excursions available throughout Hawaii; most of them are on Maui, considered the best island from which to view the humpbacks. As with every other kind of tour, however, some are better than others. We recommend that you contact several tour operators and ask them the following questions:

How long have you been conducting whale-watching tours? Experience can make a big difference between whale-watching and whale-"glimpsing." Federal law mandates that all vessels must stay at least 100 yards away from the whales. Since finding and staying with whales is a learned skill, many inexperienced operators might spend their entire time 400 or 500 yards away.

Do you specialize in whale-watching tours, or are they part of a wider menu of cruise options? Many companies are in fact snorkeling or scuba operators that add whale-watching as an activity during the winter. While this isn't necessarily a bad option, there are better opportunities out there if you are a serious enthusiast seeking a deeper whale experience.

Do you guarantee sightings? The best whale-watching tours will guarantee whale sightings on every cruise. While you don't get your money back, you receive a coupon good for another whale-watching cruise free of charge. (For this reason, it's advisable to book your tour early in your vacation, so in the event you don't see a whale on the cruise, you can try again before your trip is over.) With few exceptions, the guarantees are good forever and are even transferable.

Is there a whale expert on board to provide narration? If so, what kind of training did he/she receive? Many operators will say they have a trained naturalist on board to provide expert narration. What they don't say is that many of these naturalists are deemed "experts" after taking a course (of unspecified length) on whales, reading a book or two, and attending a couple of whale watches. Again, this isn't necessarily a negative, but expect to be fed fairly generic information.

How big is your boat, and what are its amenities? Whale-watching boats come in all sizes and offer a wide range of luxury and amenity options, including shaded areas, refreshments, cushioned seats, and private rest rooms. Find a boat to suit your needs and taste. Younger people may find cruising for whales aboard a motorized rubber raft exciting, but you probably won't want grandma and grandpa bouncing around in such a boat.

The humpback whale season is from mid-December to mid-April. According to Dan McSweeney, a respected whale researcher with more than 25 years of experience observing Hawaii's whales, the peak period for humpback migration is mid-January through mid-March, although the numbers don't make a huge difference. "You'd typically see 15–20 whales as opposed to 10–15 on a given trip," says McSweeney.

While Maui is regarded as the best island to view the humpbacks (especially the areas of Lahaina and Ka'anapali in West Maui), the Kona Coast of the island of Hawaii is a close second. Whales are frequently spotted from Oahu's North and South Shores, the Kilauea Point National Wildlife Refuge on Kauai, and the coastlines of Lanai and Molokai.

Many of the tours provide state-of-the-art hydrophones that allow passengers to hear the songs sounded by nearby whales. Experts can share their knowledge on what the songs mean and help you pick out repeated phrases for you to identify. You'll also learn about the whales' migration from Alaska, what whales eat, how they nurse their young, and other insights.

Humpback whale–watching cruises generally cost $20–60 for adults and $10–30 for children age 11 and under and are scheduled daily. Major credit cards are accepted and can be used to hold your reservation. Book your tour at least a couple of days in advance, especially during the holiday periods. Most tours last between two and three hours and provide snacks and juice. Some tours offer hotel transportation. Casual attire is recommended. Bring sunscreen.

If you bring a camera, it might be best to have a fresh roll of film ready instead of a roll nearing its end (the last thing you want to experience is missing a great whale shot while changing rolls). Use higher-speed film, such as 200 or 400, and always hold the camera as still as possible (remember, you're already on a moving boat trying to photograph a moving subject). The narrator should let you know what area to focus your camera on and when to get ready to click away.

Tip: While humpback whales are only here during part of the year, Hawaii actually has six species of whales that can be viewed year-round, including sperm whales, pilot whales, melon-headed whales, false-killer whales, and beaked whales. McSweeney is one of the few operators who offers whale-watching adventures spotlighting these lesser-known ocean mammals, conducting tours about three miles south of Kona's Honokohau Harbor three times a week.

Informative Web sites on humpback whales include www.pacific-whale.org and www.ilovewhales.com. On Maui, visit the Whalers Village Museum in Ka'anapali (see Part Ten, "Hawaii's Attractions").

Whale-Watching Cruise Operators

Maui
Maui Princess (808) 667-6165
Ocean Activities Center (808) 879-4485
Pacific Whale Foundation (808) 879-8860
Royal Hawaiian Cruises (808) 661-8787
Trilogy Excursions (808) 661-4743

The Big Island
Dan McSweeney's Whale Watching Adventures (808) 322-0028

Oahu
Royal Hawaiian Cruises (808) 848-6360

BICYCLING: PEDAL POWER

In theory, a two-wheel exploration of a Hawaiian island seems like an enticing activity, and it is on most of the Neighbor Islands. However, the island where road bikes should probably be the most welcome—traffic-filled Oahu—generally has the least adequate bikeway system for cyclists. Few roads on Oahu have designated bike lanes, and from our observations, many local drivers have yet to fully embrace the concept of "sharing" their streets and highways.

The good news is, this should soon change. The City and County of Honolulu recently formulated a master plan to implement a bikeway system that will, at a minimum, connect bicycle destinations in Waikiki and Diamond Head, the University of Hawaii and Manoa Valley, Punchbowl, downtown Honolulu, Chinatown, Aloha Tower, Kewalo Basin, Ala Moana Beach Park, and the Honolulu International Airport.

Until the project comes to fruition, pedal your way on Oahu at your own risk. Pleasant and scenic rides do exist at **Ala Moana Beach Park** in Honolulu and **Kapiʻolani Park** in Waikiki (the best time to ride is in the late afternoon; be sure to take in the sunset). For more fitness-minded cyclists, a grueling but ultimately rewarding challenge is the winding road up to the summit of 2,013-foot **Mount Tantalus** in the Honolulu area of Makiki.

The roads on the Neighbor Islands are more open and traffic-free. For road bikers, Maui has the most bike-friendly roads and lanes, and coastal treks provide stunning views of the neighboring islands of Molokai, Lanai, and Kahoolawe. A popular Maui adventure is cruising down the scenic slopes of 10,023-foot Haleakala past pasturelands, farms, and forests. (Stay on the paved road, however, as biking on hiking trails is not permitted.) There are a handful of tour companies that will take you to the top of the crater, provide you with all necessary equipment, and lead you down the mountain. Some companies also provide hotel transportation and a snack, while others offer unguided tours, letting you set your own pace.

Although it's a pain to coast down the mountain in a guided tour group where everyone has to maintain the same pace, it's probably your safest bet. There are some very deceptive grades and curves coming down the mountain that have launched even experienced bikers over the side. If you elect to go on your own, take the curves slow (slower than what your past experience suggests is a safe speed), wear a helmet, and dress in layers. The top third of the coast down is pretty chilly, while the last leg is tropical. Needless to say, you'll need a daypack or panier to store the layers you peel off.

Downhill tours are also available on Oahu, the Big Island, and Kauai.

Hawaii is a terrific place for mountain biking, offering a wide range of terrain, scenic sites, and tracks, including loops (a trail that loops around and returns close to the starting point) and out-and-backs (a trail where you return on the same path you entered).

While Oahu isn't so bike-friendly on the road, it does provide the most *off*-road adventures in the state. Head to **Waimea Valley Adventure Park,** which has more than 15 trails designated for novice and experienced mountain bikers (admission cost is $10–20, or $35–55 including bike rental). Other good trails are found in **Mililani** in central Oahu, at **Maunawili Trail** in windward Oahu, in **Pupukea** on the North Shore, and at **Kaena Point** in leeward Oahu.

The favorite venue for mountain bikers on Maui is **Polipoli State Park,** where you'll find more than ten miles of single-track that winds through thick forests of eucalyptus and redwood trees.

The Big Island offers a wide range of mountain-biking experiences: Ride through a forest at **Mauna Loa,** the crater rim of a volcano, green pastures in **North Kohala,** and more. A mountain-biking trail map is available free of charge at most bike shops on the island, or call the Big Island Visitors Bureau at (808) 329-7787.

Kauai has five single-tracks and nine dirt roads open to mountain bikes. Coastal treks here provide numerous scenic stops, and even better views are among the rewards of biking at **Koke'e State Park** and **Waimea Canyon,** known as the "Grand Canyon of the Pacific."

Molokai's rugged trails provide optimal riding conditions, from dusty coastlines to lush forest trails. **Molokai Ranch** has a superb single-track and is fast becoming a mecca for avid mountain bikers.

Bike Rental Shops

Oahu
Big Mountain Rentals (808) 926-1644
Blue Sky Rentals (808) 947-0101
Paradise Isle Rentals (808) 946-7777
Raging Isle Surf & Cycle (808) 637-7707

Maui
Haleakala Bike Co. (808) 575-9575
Extreme Sports Maui (808) 871-7954
South Maui Bicycles (808) 874-0068
Island Bikes (808) 877-7744
West Maui Bicycles (808) 661-9005

The Big Island
C&S Cycle & Surf (808) 885-5005
Da Kine Bike Shop (808) 934-9861
Hilo Bike Hub (808) 961-4452
HP Bike Works (808) 326-2453
Mauna Kea Mountain Bikes (808) 883-0130

Kauai
Kauai Cycle (808) 821-2115
Outfitters Kauai (808) 742-9667

Molokai
Molokai Bicycle (808) 553-3931

There are plenty of dirt roads on Lanai, as well as a challenging climb to the summit of **Lanaihale,** the island's highest point, at 3,370 feet.

There are a handful of bike shops on all major islands, and daily rentals generally run $20–35 for a mountain bike and $15 for a road bike.

No matter what form of biking you choose to enjoy in the Islands, remember these safety tips:

- Wear a helmet. Make sure it fits properly.
- Wear comfortable shoes and clothing.
- Secure any loose clothing or accessories that may interfere with the bike's moving parts.
- If possible, carry a first-aid kit and a cell phone in case of an emergency.

- Familiarize yourself with your bike thoroughly before riding it.
- Ride with a partner.
- Bring lots of drinking water to combat dehydration.
- Bring sunscreen. Sunglasses are also strongly recommended.
- If traveling in a group, keep at least five lengths between each rider.
- If you live in a cool climate and this is your first ride under the tropical sun, take it slow and easy until you are better acclimated to the heat and humidity.
- For road bikers, always ride with the flow of traffic. Also, be predictable. Don't do anything that would surprise drivers, such as swerving in and out of traffic.
- Don't use headphones while riding.
- Novice mountain bikers should avoid single-track trails, which are narrow and sometimes hover on the edge of dangerous cliffs and other hazardous areas. Instead, ride on the dirt roads, which allow more room for error.
- Be especially careful on the Big Island, where rough and craggy lava rocks often pose a danger.
- During rainy weather, remember that tree roots and rocks become very slippery.

On Oahu, bike racks are available on TheBus, Honolulu's municipal bus system. There is no additional charge for using the rack.

Good sources for information on biking in Hawaii include the Hawaii Bicyling League (call (808) 735-5756), which puts out a bimonthly newsletter for local biking enthusiasts. Also, local biking authority John Alford has authored a pair of books, *Mountain Biking the Hawaiian Islands* and *The Mountain Biker's Guide to Oahu.* Each book features maps and photos as well as detailed descriptions of Hawaii's best biking trails. They may be ordered through www.bikehawaii.com; the *Hawaiian Islands* book is also available at most Island bookshops.

HEALTH SPAS AND FITNESS CENTERS: GET FIT!

Treat yourself to a relaxing massage, get pampered with a soothing facial, work off the calories on a Stairmaster, and strut your stuff with an aerobics class. These are just some of the activities offered at Hawaii's health spas, the best of which are found in the top hotels and resorts.

Most hotels offer at least a fitness room where you can work up a sweat lifting weights or riding a stationary bike. Several resorts, however, have pulled out all the stops and now rate among the finest resort spa destinations in the United States.

Such facilities and services, of course, are considered luxuries rather than necessities. (For instance, you could probably survive without a seaweed body mask treatment.) Also, spa-related services aren't free, and most will massage your pocketbook quite vigorously. Non-resort guests are charged a higher fee at most spas. Profiles of the best spa resort on each island follow.

Oahu
'Ihilani Resort & Spa
Zone: 5, Leeward Oahu
Phone: (808) 679-0079
Hours: Daily, 7 a.m.–7 p.m.

Comments The 35,000-square-foot 'Ihilani Spa is the only full-service spa on Oahu and was voted the third-best spa resort in the world in 1998 by readers of *Condé Nast Traveler*. The men's and women's lounges are equipped with a steam room, sauna, Needle Shower Pavilion, Roman pool, relaxation lanai, and other amenities. Fees for hotel guests are $15 during 7–11 a.m. and 2–7 p.m. (free between 11 a.m.–2 p.m.). The fee is waived if you receive a treatment. Non–hotel guests are charged $25 (automatically added to any treatment fees). In addition, the spa's Fitness Lanai offers weight and cardiovascular workout rooms, with classes led by trained staff. The Fitness Lanai is available free of charge to hotel guests. Proper athletic footwear is required.

A program adviser is available daily during spa hours. To schedule an appointment, call the spa at the above phone number. (If you're a hotel guest, just press 53 from your hotel room phone.) Non–hotel guests need a major credit card to hold an appointment reservation. You need to cancel or reschedule any appointment for a treatment at least four hours in advance to avoid being charged 50% of the treatment fee. No-shows will be charged the full fee.

The spa won't guarantee the availability of a particular therapist, but let the program adviser know if you have a preference for a male or female therapist. Also, it's important to inform the adviser of any allergies or medical conditions you have that may require special attention.

The services and treatments offered at the 'Ihilani Spa maintain a distinctive Hawaiian touch, as the products and ingredients used at the facility come directly from Hawaii's land and sea. The spa menu includes a wide range of hydrotherapies, fitness and relaxation programs, massage treatments, aromatherapies, skin care treatments, and salon services. We counted nearly 70 types of services in all.

Individual treatments range from $15 for a brow or chin wax to $95 for an age protection facial. In addition, half- and full-day programs are available, ranging from $190 to $390.

The 'Ihilani is unique because it is one of only two places in the United States to offer authentic Thalasso therapy, an underwater full-body massage using 180 pulsating jet streams of warm seawater. Fresh seawater is pumped directly into the spa for each treatment. The massage lasts for 25 minutes and costs $55. Contact the spa for a complete list of services or log on to www.ihilani.com for more information.

Maui
Grand Wailea Resort Hotel & Spa

Zone: 8, South Maui
Phone: (808) 875-1234
Hours: Treatments, 10 a.m.– 8 p.m.; fitness/workout rooms, 6 a.m.– 8 p.m.; beauty salon, 9 a.m.–7 p.m.

Comments The Grand Wailea's Spa Grande is enormous—50,000 square feet—and is exceeded only by its reputation: In 1998, readers of *Condé Nast Traveler* voted the Grand Wailea as the top spa resort in the world.

Non–hotel guests must pay a $30 surcharge added to the first spa treatment (salon and wellness services not included). The surcharge is waived if you book two or more spa treatments on the same day. You must be at least 16 years of age to use the spa; minors may receive treatments if accompanied by a parent or guardian. Non–hotel guests need a major credit card to reserve an appointment. There is a 50% charge assessed to no-shows and cancellations made less than two hours prior to your appointment. All spa and salon services are subject to an additional 15% service charge plus tax.

Use of the cardiovascular gym, weight-training gym, and all fitness classes is complimentary for guests of the hotel. Non-guests are charged $15 a day. If you're just visiting the hotel, be aware that the spa does not have lockers and showers.

The Spa Grande has an "East Meets West" philosophy, mixing traditional Hawaiian healing techniques with the latest innovations in European, American, Indian, and Oriental spa therapies. Everything's here: massage treatments, aromatherapy, body treatments, facials, hair care, manicures, toe polishes, waxings, yoga, meditation instruction, racquetball, basketball, and more. Prices range from $15 for a nail polish change up to $220 for a one-hour "massage-in-stereo" (two therapists working on you simultaneously). One of the more unique offerings is the spa's Termé Wailea Hydrotherapy Circuit, a refreshing hour-long treatment. You begin with a quick shower, enjoy some quality time in a Roman bath, take deep pool plunges, and visit the steam room and sauna before being escorted for a personalized Loofah Scrub, a cleansing treatment that reportedly exfoliates and removes dull surface skin cells, improves circulation, and produces healthier-looking skin. The treatment continues with your choice of specialty baths—Moor Mud,

Limu/Seaweed, Aromatherapy, Tropical Enzyme, and Mineral Salt—followed by a Swiss Jet Shower. Sounds invigorating? The cost is $50 for hotel guests and $100 for non–hotel guests. Call the resort for more information or log on to www.grandwailea.com.

The Big Island
Four Seasons Resort Hualalai

Zone: 11, Kona

Phone: (808) 325-8440

Hours: Daily, 6 a.m.–8 p.m.

Comments The Hualalai Sports Club & Spa is available only to resident members and guests of the Four Seasons Resort Hualalai. Here you'll find the full range of facilities: 17 indoor/outdoor body treatment rooms, outdoor saunas and steam rooms, private outdoor garden showers, an open-air equipment gym and aerobics gym, a 25-meter outdoor Olympic-style lap pool, half-court basketball arena, Cybex strength machines, free-weight equipment, treadmills, stationary bikes, tennis courts, a volleyball court, and more. Lockers and showers are provided, and yukata robes, slippers, shorts, and T-shirts are available upon request.

The sports club offers a variety of fitness classes, including high- and low-impact aerobics and aqua-aerobics. Spa therapies include several types of massages ($90 for 50 minutes, $135–140 for 80 minutes), hydrotherapy and body treatments ($55–125 for 50 minutes), and various combination packages. Fitness diehards with money to burn can sign up for the multi-day Fitness Fantastic package ($835), which includes a fitness assessment, three personal training sessions, three 50-minute massages (you'll need them), a hike, and two golf or tennis lessons. For those who prefer to be pampered, the Hualalai Masque package ($205) includes your choice of the Seaweed or Dead Sea mud masque treatment, plus a Vichy shower massage and a 50-minute Swedish or *lomilomi* massage.

Provide at least four hours' notice if you need to cancel or reschedule your appointment to avoid being charged in full (24 hours' notice is required from December 15 to January 3). Children under the age of 14 are not allowed into the spa. When making an appointment for a spa treatment, you'll be asked to arrive 20 minutes ahead of time to shower and enjoy the sauna, steam bath, whirlpool, and a cold dip.

Kauai
Hyatt Regency Kauai

Zone: 13, Kauai

Phone: (808) 742-1234

Hours: Daily, 6 a.m.– 8 p.m.

Comments   The hotel's ANARA Spa was considered state-of-the-art when it opened in 1991, and it has kept up with the times enough to remain one of Hawaii's best spa facilities. Here you'll find no fewer than ten massage rooms that overlook private gardens, a 25-meter heated lap pool in the center of the courtyard, a Turkish steam room, a Finnish sauna, and open-air "shower gardens" carved from lava rock. Combine all this with Kauai's built-in therapeutic value and you have the makings of a very refreshing and invigorating experience.

Admission into the spa is $5 for hotel guests and $25 for non–hotel guests and includes use of the fitness center. Appointments for treatments should be booked at least a day in advance (especially for treatment packages). Non–hotel guests must reserve their bookings through a major credit card. Cancellation notice must be given at least four hours in advance; otherwise, you'll be charged in full. No one under the age of 16 is allowed in the spa at any time.

Here's a sampling of ANARA Spa services and prices: A half-hour massage is $60, an hour-long massage is $100; one-hour body treatments are $100, herbal wraps are $40; manicures are $35; and pedicures are $55. Treatment packages range from $145 (one and a half hours) to $350 (six hours). Locker rooms are available.

Call the hotel for a full menu of services or log on to their Web site at www.hyatt.com.

In addition to the health spas, there are a number of health clubs and fitness centers in the Islands. Daily rates are $10–20, and weekly rates begin at $35.

Oahu

24-Hour Fitness   (808) 971-4653 in Waikiki; (808) 973-4653 in Honolulu

The Gym   (808) 533-7111

Spa Fitness Center   (808) 949-0026

Timmy's Gym   (808) 591-9494

Maui

24-Hour Fitness   (808) 877-7474

Gold's Gym   (808) 874-2844 in Kihei; (808) 242-6851 in Wailuku; (808) 667-7474 in Lahaina

Maui Muscle Fitness   (808) 661-0844

The Big Island

Gold's Gym   (808) 334-1977

The Club   (808) 326-2582

Kauai

Kauai Athletic Club   (808) 245-5381

Kauai Gym   (808) 823-8210

Iron Hut Gym & Fitness   (808) 335-3383

Hang Gliding: Free as a Bird

Imagine soaring like a bird, gliding high above tropical rain forests, azure bays, rolling pasturelands, and other scenic wonders in paradise. Hang gliding is growing in popularity in the Islands, and you can sign up for a thorough instruction course followed by a memorable flight (in tandem with your instructor) using a traditional glider or a motor-powered glider. Hang-Gliding Maui offers a four-hour adventure from the top of Haleakala for $250, with shorter excursions (using a motorized glider) priced at $90 for a half-hour and $150 for a full hour. Other hang-gliding operators include Cloudbase Enterprises (call (808) 623-3043) on Oahu, Proflyght Maui (call (808) 878-3806) on Maui, and Birds in Paradise (call (808) 822-5309) for Kauai.

Skydiving: Take a Leap of Faith

Whether you're searching for the ultimate in aerial views or simply want a thrill to last a lifetime, try skydiving. (Hey, former U.S. President George W. Bush did it!) At Dillingham Air Field in Mokule'ia is Skydive Hawaii, an experienced company that provides skydiving experiences for novices and experts alike. The half-day experience includes training and instruction, 15 minutes of flight time to a cruising altitude of 13,000 feet, the jump (you're attached in tandem with a professional skydiver, so don't worry about having to do it alone), a 5,000-foot free fall, and six or seven minutes of gliding down to earth via parachute. The cost of $225 per person includes transportation to and from your hotel (it's $180 if you prefer to drive to Dillingham Airfield yourself).

Biplane Riding: Go for a Loop

You have to have a pretty strong stomach to enjoy a ride like this, but more than a few thrill-seekers have called it the experience of their lives. You can always ask for a simple sight-seeing excursion, but why not go for the heart-thumping aerobatic adventure, which includes a dizzying repertoire of loops, spins, rolls, and hammerheads? Stearman Biplane Rides (call (808) 637-4461) at Dillingham Airfield on Oahu offers single-passenger rides aboard a fully restored 1941-vintage open-cockpit Stearman N2S biplane. A 20-minute flight over the island's North Shore is $125, while a 40-minute tour over historic Pearl Harbor is $175. Tack on another $35 for an extra 10 minutes of aerobatic action.

Also at Dillingham Airfield is Tsunami Aviation (call (808) 677-3404), which offers exciting 10-minute ($100) and 15-minute ($150) flights with all kinds of topsy-turvy maneuvers—it'll literally turn the island upside-down for you! Tsunami Aviation features the state-of-the-art aerobatic sport biplane PITTS S2B, billed as the "Formula One racer of airplanes."

HORSEBACK RIDING: BACK IN THE SADDLE

Looking for a little horseplay? Horseback riding is always a favorite activity among visitors, and there's nothing like galloping across wide-open pasturelands or trotting through an emerald valley lined with waterfalls. The horses—often bearing catchy names like Ikaika, Po'o, and Salsa—are well trained and pretty much know the trail routine, so you won't have to worry about unexpected side trips.

There are first-class horseback riding adventures on every major island, each offering guided tours and spectacular scenic views. Rates are reasonable, ranging from $35 per person for a one-hour ride to $60–100 for a two-hour trek. The one-hour rides are recommended for first-time riders. Call for age and weight restrictions: We've found that the minimum age for riders is eight for most operators, and the maximum weight riders may carry ranges from 205 to 275.

Book your reservation at least a day in advance. Most rides are limited to between 10 and 12 people, so if you have a fairly large group, make your reservation at least a full week in advance to ensure they can accommodate you. You can secure your reservation with a major credit card, and most operators also accept payment via traveler's checks or cash. You'll be asked to call in on the morning of your ride (or leave them a phone number where you can be reached) to check on weather conditions. All riders must sign liability waivers before saddling up.

A short lesson on horsemanship and safety precautions, usually up to half an hour, is given before the tour begins (the time does not count against the length of the ride). Previous riding experience is not a requirement—first-time riders are very common—but it's important that you pay attention to the introductory lessons and obey all instructions. Said one operator on Oahu, "You're going to be responsible for controlling the horse; it's not a situation where the horse does everything on its own."

Whether you're riding a thoroughbred or quarter horse, remember that horses are largely herd-like animals, and that determines the pace of the ride. If you're a first-time rider, for example, and another rider picks up the pace to a healthy gallop, your horse is also going to trot faster because it won't want to be left behind. Therefore, for safety reasons, the group will always go at the pace of the least experienced rider. (Certain trail ride operators may offer intermediate- and advanced-level rides; inquire when calling.) Most stables use thoroughbreds and quarter horses.

Hawaii's riding trails encompass a wide range of terrain and scenic sites, including wide-open pasturelands, lush forests, and tropical orchards. Some rides include stops for a picnic lunch in the country, a juicy sampling of local fruit, or even swimming. The guide usually shares insights about the surrounding property and any historic sites (how much is shared, however,

---

Horseback Riding Adventures

Oahu
Correa Trails (808) 259-9005
Happy Trails Hawaii (808) 638-7433
Kualoa Ranch (808) 237-7321
Waimea Valley Adventure Park (808) 638-8511

Maui
Ironwood Ranch Stables (808) 669-4991
Makena Stables (808) 879-0244
Thompson Ranch (808) 878-1910

The Big Island
Mauna Kea Stables (808) 885-4288
Paniolo Riding Adventures (808) 889-5354
Waipiʻo on Horseback (808) 775-7291
Waipiʻo Ridge Stables (808) 775-1007

Kauai
Esprit de Corps Riding Academy (808) 552-2791
Princeville Ranch Stables (808) 826-6777
Silver Falls Ranch (808) 828-6718

Molokai
Molokai Ranch Outfitters Center (808) 552-2791

Lanai
Call (808) 565-7300 for information on available horseback riding
adventures.

often depends on the enthusiasm of the group). Covered shoes are mandatory, long pants are suggested, and sunscreen and a sun visor are recommended.

Finally, if you haven't ridden for a while (or ever), you can expect some pretty sore muscles even after a short ride. Our advice is pass on the sexy sounding half-day trips and opt for the shortest ride possible. If you want to ride longer, try to get in shape by riding a few times before leaving home.

Golf: Tee Time in Paradise

That Hawaii is a golfer's paradise should be a "fore"gone conclusion. A memorable experience awaits golfaholics on every Hawaiian island. While none of the courses here has the prestige of Pebble Beach or Saint Andrews, most offer a wide variety of challenges, layouts, and, of course, incredible natural scenery. Where else but in Hawaii can you play a course dotted with ancient archaeological sites and surrounded by crashing surf, then play another 18 on the side of an active volcano?

Altogether, there are some 90 golf courses in Hawaii, each falling into one of the following categories: resort, municipal, public, military, semi-private, and private. Nearly all have some degree of accessibility to you.

One expert strongly recommended against booking a round of golf through a hotel activity desk. He pointed out that most of these services likely only have two or three courses that are commissioning them; therefore, they'll try to steer you to one of these courses even though there are better options. This practice, he said, is especially rampant on Oahu. He recalls surveying many couples who returned home disappointed because they wanted to golf in Hawaii but couldn't afford to pay $200-plus per round. Nearly all had relied on their hotels for information about where to play golf.

Most hotels have a vested interest in keeping their guests on their property. They are not going to promote the competition. Thus, it's largely up to you to find the course that best suits your preferences, budget, and ability. It's an effort that will reap plenty of rewards. For instance, you'll discover

Greens Fees
Based on one 18-hole round, with or without cart:
Resort Courses: $110–180
Semi-Private: $20–135
Private: $50–100
Public: $30–135
Municipal Courses: $40–54
Military: $30–50

that some of Hawaii's municipal courses (one expert named the Wailua course on Kauai and Waiehu on Maui as particular standouts) provide fantastic golf experiences at half the cost of some resort courses.

Fortunately, there are a few helpful resources at your disposal. These include:

- The Aloha Section PGA, a group comprising more than 100 PGA-certified professionals in the state. The organization puts out an annual directory of Hawaii's golf courses. Call (808) 593-2230.

- *Island Golf,* the only free monthly golf guide aimed at Hawaii visitors. The information it provides is exceptionally reliable and well researched. Log on to their Web site at www.islandgolfreview.net or call (808) 874-8300.

- *Discover Hawaii's Best Golf,* an 86-page book authored by George Fuller, one of Hawaii's top golf writers. Published in 1999 by Island Heritage Publishing, the book provides vivid descriptions and superb images of the state's best courses. Check your local bookstore or call (808) 487-7299 for ordering information.

Tee times are usually easy to reserve, except on weekends and during the winter months, when tourism is in its high season. Oahu is probably the most difficult island for booking a tee time when the courses get crowded. Most courses allow you to request a tee time at least five days in advance.

If you're looking for a last-minute tee time, try Stand-By Golf, which books last-minute tee times at discounts for the visitor. The company makes a small margin on each booking, you get discounted rates at some of the state's best courses, and the course managers themselves are happy to fill in every empty tee-time slot. Call (888) 645-BOOK.

A helpful hint: Most golf courses in Hawaii use Bermuda grass, similar to the grass used at U.S. mainland courses in warm-weather climates. Bermuda grass is ruddy and grainy, and completely different from the grass you find in the northern U.S. states. It is generally a slower surface. Most resort courses (and newer public courses) here use a hybrid Bermuda grass that is considered by experts to be of much higher quality.

As far as attire is concerned, most courses allow shorts, while most resort courses require collared shirts. T-shirts are permitted on some courses but aren't recommended (unless you don't mind sunburn on the back of your neck). Shoes-wise, the trend for today's resort courses is toward soft-spike shoes.

Here's a look at the best golf courses in the Aloha State. (Rates and tee-time information are subject to change.) Information on PGA, LPGA, and Senior PGA Tour events held in Hawaii is provided later in this chapter.

Oahu
Zone 1: Waikiki
Ala Wai Golf Course

Established: 1931
Location: 404 Kapahulu Ave., Honolulu, HI 96815 (Located *mauka* of the Ala Wai Canal. The entrance is on the right side of Kapahulu Ave.)
Phone: (808) 296-2000
Status: Municipal, 18 holes, par 70

Tees: Men's: 6,208 yds.
Ladies': 5,095 yds.
Fees: $40 daily. Cart: $12. Accepts tee times 7 days in advance (call from 6:30 a.m.). Accepts Visa, MC.
Facilities: Driving range, pro shop, and restaurant. Club rentals available.

Comments Ranked the busiest municipal course in the United States, averaging more than 500 rounds of golf per day. Hawaii's oldest municipal course. Underwent a facelift in the late 1980s, adding a driving range lit for night play. Popular among both tourists and residents. A flat course with some hilly mounds around the greens. The Ala Wai Canal comes into play on 3 holes. Collared shirt required, no cut-offs.

Zone 2: Honolulu
Hawaii Kai Golf Course

Established: 1973
Location: 8902 Kalaniana'ole Hwy., Honolulu, HI 96825 (From Waikiki, drive east on Kalaniana'ole Hwy. The course is on the left side shortly after Sandy Beach Park.)
Phone: (808) 395-2358
Status: Public, 18 holes, par 72 (Championship course), 18 holes, par 54 (Executive course)
Tees: Championship: 6,614 yds. (Championship course) Men's: 6,222 yds. (Championship), 2,116 yds. (Executive) Ladies': 5,591 yds.

(Championship), 1,896 yds. (Executive)
Fees: Championship course: $90 weekdays, $100 weekends. Includes cart. Executive course: $37 weekdays, $42 weekends for 18 holes. $32.75 weekdays, $37.75 weekends for 9 holes. Accepts tee times 7 days in advance (call from 7 a.m.). Accepts Visa, MC, Discover.
Facilities: Driving range, putting green, pro shop, and restaurant. Club rentals available.

Comments Mostly frequented by locals. Championship course rests at the base of Koko Head Crater and includes two hidden lakes and large greens. Breezy trade winds here raise the challenge level a notch. The Executive course, a long par-3 course designed by Robert Trent Jones Sr., is ideal for beginners. Collared shirt required.

Zone 3: Windward Oahu
Kane'ohe Klipper Golf Course

Established: 1949
Location: Box 63073 MCBH, Kane'ohe, HI 96863 (Drive in the Kane'ohe direction on the H-3 Fwy. until you reach the Kane'ohe Marine Corps Air Station, where you'll receive directions to the course.)
Phone: (808) 254-2107
Status: Military, 18 holes, par 72
Tees: Championship (blue tee): 6,559 yds. Men's (white tee): 6,216 yds.

Ladies': 5,577 yds.
Fees: $8–37, depending on military rank (the higher the rank, the higher the rate). Cart: $16. Club rentals are $10–25. Accepts tee times 4 days in advance (earliest time to call is 6 a.m.). Accepts Visa, MC, Discover.
Facilities: Driving range, putting green, pro shop, snack bar, restaurant, and locker rooms.

Comments Civilians may play this course if sponsored and accompanied by a member of the U.S. military. This course layout is sometimes referred to as a "poor man's Pebble Beach" because the back nine follows a scenic stretch of beach. Fairly flat course, easy to walk. No tank tops or cut-offs.

Ko'olau Golf Club

Established: 1992
Location: 45-550 Kionaole Rd., Kane'ohe, HI 96744 (Head north on the Pali Hwy., turn left on Kamehameha Hwy., and make a left on Kionaole Rd. The entrance to the course is on the left side.)
Phone: (808) 236-4653
Status: Public, 18 holes, par 72
Tees: Tournament (black tee): 7,310 yds. Championship (gold tee): 6,797

yds. Men's (blue tee): 6,406 yds.
Ladies' (white tee): 5,102 yds.
Fees: $100 daily. Special $65 twilight rate available from 1:30 p.m. Fees include cart. Club rentals: $35. Accepts tee times up to 30 days in advance. Accepts Visa, MC, and AmEx.
Facilities: Driving range, putting green, chipping range, snack bar, and pro shop.

Comments Considered the most difficult course in the United States, even though water comes into play on only one hole. The very first hole is a 593-yard par-5. The 18th requires a tee shot over a wide ravine, with a precipitous sand trap running the length of the fairway on the right. Exceptionally scenic course and very high in demand. Collared shirts required.

Luana Hills Country Club

Established: 1994
Location: 770 Auloa Rd., Kailua, HI 96734 (Head north on the Pali Hwy. through both tunnels. After the third stoplight following the second tunnel,

turn right onto Auloa and then take an immediate left to the private road leading to the course.)
Phone: (808) 262-2139
Status: Semi-private, 18 holes, par 72

Tees: Championship (black tees): 6,595 yds. Championship (blue tees): 6,164 yds. Men's (white tees): 5,522 yds. Ladies' (yellow tees): 4,654 yds.
Fees: $80. Special $50 twilight rate available from 2 p.m. on weekdays, $70 on weekends. Includes cart. Club

rentals: $30. Accepts tee times 7 days in advance. Accepts Visa, MC.
Facilities: Driving range, putting greens, pro shop, locker rooms with showers and Jacuzzi, restaurant, and cocktail lounge.

Comments   A growing favorite among both residents and visitors. Originally opened with the ill-timed intention of selling club memberships to wealthy Japanese businessmen. The front nine is carved into the side of Mount Olomana, while the back nine—the favorite of most players—takes you through a tropical rain forest. The par-3 11th hole is a scenic masterpiece dominated by a picturesque pond.

Olomana Golf Links

Established: 1967
Location: 41-1801 Kalaniana'ole Hwy., Waimanalo, HI 96795 (Take Kalaniana'ole Hwy. to the course, about a half-hour drive from Waikiki.)
Phone: (808) 259-7926
Status: Public, 18 holes, par 71
Tees: Championship: 6,326 yds. Men's: 5,887 yds. Ladies': 5,466 yds.
Fees: $60. Includes cart. Special $13 (without cart) and $23 (with cart)

twilight rates available from 3 p.m. on weekdays, $15/$25 on weekends. Twilight cart users can only use the cart for the first 9 holes. Club rentals: $25. Senior discounts available. Accepts tee times 30 days in advance (call from 7 a.m.). Accepts Visa, MC, AmEx.
Facilities: Driving range, pro shop, and restaurant

Comments   The front nine features gentle rolling hills, while water comes into play throughout the back nine. Course offers sweeping views of the island throughout. Caddies are required if you prefer to walk the course. No tank tops or cut-offs.

Pali Golf Course

Established: 1953
Location: 45-050 Kamehameha Hwy., Kane'ohe, HI 96744 (Head north on the Pali Hwy., pass through the tunnel, and turn left on Kamehameha Hwy. Take the first left into the course.)
Phone: (808) 266-7612
Status: Municipal, 18 holes, par 72
Tees: Men's: 6,524 yds.

Ladies': 6,050 yds.
Fees: $40. Special $20 twilight rate available. Cart: $14. Club rentals: $30. Senior discounts available. Accepts tee times 7 days in advance (call from 6 a.m.). Accepts Visa, MC, AmEx, Discover.
Facilities: Putting green, restaurant, and snack bar.

Comments   Situated at the base of the scenic Ko'olau Mountains. There are a few sand traps here, but the course is still challenging due to difficult lies and some interesting dogleg holes.

Zone 4: The North Shore
Kahuku Golf Course

Established: 1937
Location: P.O. Box 417, Kahuku, HI 96731 (Drive toward the North Shore on Kamehameha Hwy., make a right turn toward the ocean from Kahuku High School.)
Phone: (808) 293-5842
Status: Municipal, 9 holes, par 35

Tees: Yardage: 2,699 yds.
Fees: $20. Club rentals: $10. No clubs are rented out after 2 p.m. Senior discounts available. No tee times accepted at any time.
Facilities: Practice area with putting green and practice bunker.

Comments   A rolling, beachside course designed by plantation architects. Good course for walking. No water hazards, few sand traps. A fun but not particularly challenging course frequented primarily by area residents.

The Links at Kuilima

Established: 1992
Location: 57-049 Kuilima Dr., Kahuku, HI 96731 (Head west on the H-1 Fwy., get on the H-2 Fwy., and stay on the right side. Take the Wahiawa exit and stay on the right. Drive on Kamehameha Hwy.; the course is about a half-hour away.)
Phone: (808) 293-8574
Status: Resort, 18 holes, par 72
Tees: Men's: 7,200 yds.

Ladies': 4,851 yds.
Fees: $120. $75 for guests staying at either the Turtle Bay Hilton or Hilton Hawaiian Village. Includes cart. Special $65 ($45 for Hilton guests) twilight rate on weekdays. Club rentals: $30. Accepts tee times 14 days in advance (call from 6 a.m.). Accepts Visa, MC, AmEx, Discover.
Facilities: Driving range, putting greens, pro shop, and snack bar.

Comments   Designed by golf legend Arnold Palmer and Ed Seay. A tough course due to strong trade winds and a good number of sand traps. While the course is near the ocean, only one hole (the 17th) provides up-close views of the surf. Several holes skirt a marine wildlife sanctuary. The back nine is more scenic then the front nine. Upon its debut, *Golf Magazine* ranked the course as one of the top ten new courses in the United States, while *Golf Digest* ranked it fourth among the best new resort courses. No tank tops or cut-offs.

Turtle Bay Country Club

Established: 1972
Location: 57-049 Kuilima Dr., Kahuku, HI 96731 (Head west on the H-1 Fwy., get on the H-2 Fwy., and

stay on the right side. Take the Wahiawa exit and stay on the right. Drive on Kamehameha Hwy.; the course is about a half-hour away.)

Phone: (808) 293-8574
Status: Resort, 9 holes, par 36
Tees: Yardage: 3,200 yds.
Fees: $50 for 18 holes (you play the course twice), $25 for 9 holes. Includes cart. Special $25 twilight rate

after 3:30 p.m. Accepts tee times 14 days in advance (call from 6 a.m.). Accepts Visa, MC, AmEx, Discover.
Facilities: Driving range, putting and chipping greens, pro shop, and snack bar.

Comments   Formerly an 18-hole course until 1992, when the Links at Kuilima opened. Still an enjoyable course to play. Features Bermuda grass greens and several water hazards. No tank tops or cut-offs.

Zone 5: Leeward Oahu
Coral Creek Golf Course

Established: 1999
Location: 91-1111 Geiger Rd., 'Ewa Beach, HI 96706 (Head west on the H-1 Fwy. to 'Ewa Beach. Take Fort Weaver Rd. and turn left on Geiger Rd.)
Phone: (808) 441-4653
Status: Public, 18 holes, par 72
Tees: Championship: Coral tees: 6,870 yds. Gold tees: 6,480 yds. Men's (blue tees): 6,025 yds.

Ladies' (red tees): 5,412 yds.
Fees: $125. Includes cart. Special $75 twilight rate available after 2:30 p.m. Club rentals: $30. Accepts tee times after the 15th of each month. Accepts Visa, MC, AmEx, JCB, and Diners Club.
Facilities: Driving range, putting green, practice area, pro shop, clubhouse, restaurant, beverage carts, and locker room with showers.

Comments   Oahu's newest course. Water comes into play on 13 holes, and 6 are lined with coral reefs and interconnected by a coral creek. The signature hole, Hole 18, is a short 381-yard par-4 that demands a precise downhill approach to an island green.

'Ewa Villages Golf Course

Established: 1996
Location: 91-1760 Park Row, 'Ewa Beach, HI 96706 (Head westbound on H-1 Fwy., take 'Ewa 5A exit onto Fort Weaver Rd. At the fourth traffic light, turn right and drive a mile on Renton Rd., then turn right on Park Row.)
Phone: (808) 681-0220
Status: Municipal, 18 holes, par 72
Tees: Men's: 6,410 yds.

Ladies': 5,731 yds.
Fees: $40. Special $20 twilight rate available (9 holes only) from 2 p.m. on weekdays and 1:30 p.m. on weekends. Cart: $14 ($7 twilight rate). Accepts tee times 3 days in advance (call (808) 296-2000). Accepts Visa, MC.
Facilities: Putting green, chipping area, clubhouse, and restaurant.

Comments   One of the island's newest municipal courses. A hilly, challenging course featuring several lakes and unique tee positionings.

Hawaii Prince Golf Club

Established: 1992
Location: 91-1200 Fort Weaver Rd., 'Ewa Beach, HI 96706 (Head westbound on H-1 Fwy., get off at Exit 5A, and make a left after the sixth traffic light into the club's parking lot.)
Phone: (808) 944-4567
Status: Resort, 27 holes, par 72
Tees: Championship (blue tees): A&B courses: 5,759 yds.; B&C courses: 6,801 yds.; C&A courses: 6,746 yds. Men's (orange tees): A&B courses: 6,237 yds.; B&C courses: 6,175 yds.; C&A courses: 6,274 yds. Ladies' (white tees): A&B courses: 5,275 yds.; B&C courses: 5,205 yds.; C&A courses: 5,300 yds.
Fees: $135. $90 for Prince Hotel guests. Special $50 twilight rate ($40 for hotel guests) after 2 p.m. on weekdays, after 2:30 p.m. on weekends. Includes cart. Club rentals: $35. Accepts tee times 14 days in advance (call from 7 a.m.). Accepts Visa, MC, AmEx.
Facilities: Driving range, putting greens, pro shop, locker rooms with showers, tennis courts, clubhouse, and restaurant.

Comments Three 9-hole courses are played in 3 18-hole combinations, providing tremendous replay value. The schedule is as follows: The C&A course combo is the all-day course; the A&B course runs 6:52–8:44 a.m.; and the B&C course runs 11:30 a.m.–1:30 p.m. A total of 89 sand bunkers and ten lakes adorn the courses. Designed by Arnold Palmer and Ed Seay. Built on land formerly used for growing sugarcane. Suitable for both novice duffers and above-average players.

Kapolei Golf Course

Established: 1995
Location: 91-701 Farrington Hwy., Kapolei, HI 96707 (Head westbound on the H-1 Fwy., take the Makaha exit, then turn left on Makakilo. At the first light, turn left on Farrington Hwy. The course is about a mile ahead on the right-hand side.)
Phone: (808) 674-2227
Status: Public, 18 holes, par 72
Tees: Gold: 7,001 yds. Championship: 6,586 yds. Men's: 6,136 yds.
Ladies': 5,490 yds.
Fees: $130 weekdays, $150 weekends and holidays. Includes cart. Special $60 twilight rate available on weekdays from 1:30 p.m. (Monday–Wednesday) and 2:30 p.m. (Thursday–Friday). Club rentals: $30. Accepts tee times 7 days in advance (call from 6:30 a.m.). Accepts Visa, MC, AmEx, Discover.
Facilities: Driving range, putting green, chipping area, practice bunker, pro shop, and restaurant.

Comments Built as a centerpiece for Oahu's ambitious "Second City" development plan in 'Ewa. A well-contoured, immaculately manicured course. Water hazards often come into play. The site of the LPGA's Hawaiian Ladies Open. Designed by noted golf architect Ted Robinson. Collared-shirts are required.

Ko 'Olina Golf Club

Established: 1990
Location: 92-120 Ali'inui Dr., 'Ewa Beach, HI 96707 (Head westbound on the H-1 Fwy.; take the Ko 'Olina exit. The exit loops around to the course.)
Phone: (808) 676-5300
Status: Resort, 18 holes, par 72
Tees: Championship: 6,867 yds. Men's: 6,480 yds. Ladies': 5,392 yds.
Fees: $145. $98 for 'Ihilani Resort guests. Includes cart. Special twilight rate ($75 for 18 holes, $45 for 9 holes) after 2:30 p.m. Club rentals: $30–40. Accepts tee times 7 days in advance (call from 6 a.m.). Accepts Visa, MC, AmEx, Discover.
Facilities: Driving range, practice area, pro shop, restaurant, and a locker room with showers, steam rooms, and Jacuzzi.

Comments Brisk winds make for challenging play. Considered one of Ted Robinson's best designs. Water hazards come into play throughout the course, including distracting waterfalls, lakes, and ponds. Greens are split-level and multi-tiered. The course's signature 18th hole—featuring a water-fall to the right of the tee area, spilling into a lake surrounding the green—was ranked as the toughest finishing hole on the LPGA Tour for 4 of the 6 years that Ko 'Olina hosted an official LPGA event. Collared shirt required.

Makaha Golf Club

Established: 1974
Location: 84-626 Makaha Valley Rd., Wai'anae, HI 96792 (Head westbound on Farrington Hwy., turn right at Makaha Valley Rd., and turn left at the fork.)
Phone: (808) 695-9544
Status: Resort, 18 holes, par 72
Tees: Championship: 7,077 yds. Men's: 6,414 yds. Ladies': 5,856 yds.
Fees: $125. $115 for visitors staying at Waikiki hotels. Includes cart. Special $85 twilight rate available after noon. Club rentals: $15. Accepts tee times 14 days in advance (call from 6 a.m.). Accepts Visa, MC, AmEx, Discover.
Facilities: Driving range, putting green, chipping area, clubhouse, and restaurant.

Comments Formerly the Sheraton Makaha Golf Club. A challenging course offering spectacular views, especially at sunset. Course overlooks the ocean; the back nine plays into a valley. Water hazards come into play often. Winds blow down the valley toward the ocean. The par-4 18th hole is one of the most challenging holes on the island, with two bunkers to the left of the fairway, water on the right, and another water hazard fronting the green. Collared shirts required; no denim. Bring a light jacket in the likely event of light precipitation (as you get closer to the valley).

Makaha Valley Country Club

Established: 1969
Location: 84-627 Makaha Valley Rd., Wai'anae, HI 96792 (Head westbound on Farrington Hwy. and turn right on Makaha Valley Rd. When the road splits, stay on the right side, which leads to the course.)
Phone: (808) 695-9578
Status: Public, 18 holes, par 72
Tees: Championship: 6,369 yds.

Men's: 6,901 yds. Ladies': 5,720 yds.
Fees: $55 weekdays, $65 weekends. Includes cart. Club rentals: $30. Accepts tee times 7 days in advance (call from 6:30 a.m.). Accepts Visa, MC, AmEx.
Facilities: Driving range, putting greens, pro shop, locker room with showers, dining room, and cocktail lounge.

Comments Provides many superb ocean views. Rolling terrain provides a bit of a challenge, but for the most part the course is forgiving, thanks in part to the large greens. The signature hole is the 204-yard, par-3 17th, with a challenging green and sand traps on both sides.

Ted Makalena Golf Course

Established: 1971
Location: 93-059 Waipio Point Access Rd., Waipahu, HI 96797 (Head westbound on the H-1 Fwy., take Exit 8B, and make a left onto Waipio Point Access Rd. at the first traffic light.)
Phone: (808) 675-6052
Status: Municipal, 18 holes, par 71
Tees: Men's: 5,976 yds. Ladies': 5,551 yds.

Fees: 18 holes: $47 with shared cart, $40 without cart. 9 holes: $23.50 with shared cart, $20 without cart. Club rentals: 20. Accepts tee times 7 days in advance (call from 6:30 a.m.). Accepts Visa, MC.
Facilities: Putting green, practice area, pro shop, clubhouse, and restaurant.

Comments Named after one of Hawaii's greatest golfers. The course is very flat and far from spectacular, but still very enjoyable to play. Water hazards come into play on six holes. Provides nice views of Pearl Harbor, especially from the signature 17th and 18th holes. Frequented mostly by locals.

Waikele Golf Club

Established: 1993
Location: 94-200 Paioa Pl., Waipahu, HI 96797 (Drive westbound on the H-1 Fwy.; get off on Exit 7. Head toward the mountain and make a right

onto Paioa Pl. The course is on the left.)
Phone: (808) 676-9000
Status: Semi-private, 18 holes, par 72
Tees: Championship: 6,663 yds.

Men's: 6,261 yds. Ladies': 5,226 yds.
Fees: $103 plus tax weekdays, $108 plus tax on weekends. Includes cart. Special $40 twilight rate (9 holes only) available from 3 p.m. Club rentals:

$30. Accepts tee times 7 days in advance (call from 6:30 a.m.). Accepts Visa, MC, AmEx.
Facilities: Driving range, puttinggreen, pro shop, and locker rooms.

Comments   A scenic course providing sweeping views of both Diamond Head in Waikiki and Pearl Harbor. Course itself features multi-tiered and contoured greens. The par-3 signature hole on 17 requires a tee shot over a water hazard and onto the green. Collared shirts required; no denim.

West Loch Golf Course

Established: 1990
Location: 91-1126 Okupe St., 'Ewa Beach, HI 96706 (Head westbound on the H-1 Fwy., get off at Exit 5A, turn left on Laulaunui St., drive to Okupe St., and turn right.)
Phone: (808) 671-2292
Status: Municipal, 18 holes, par 72
Tees: Championship: 6,335 yds. Men's: 5,811 yds. Ladies': 5,018 yds.

Fees: $47. Includes cart. Special 50% twilight rate (9 holes only) available 2–4 p.m. weekdays and 1:30–3:30 p.m. on weekends. Club rentals: $20 (credit card deposit required). Accepts tee times 7 days in advance (call from 7 a.m.). Accepts Visa, MC.
Facilities: Driving range, putting green, pro shop, and restaurant.

Comments   Sand traps and water hazards creep up frequently here. Also, be prepared for the trade winds.

Zone 6: Central Oahu
Hickam Golf Course

Established: 1966
Location: 900 Hangar Ave., Hickam AFB, HI 96853 (Take the H-1 westbound and follow the signs to Hickam Air Force Base. The sentry there will provide directions to the course.)
Phone: (808) 449-6490
Status: Military, 18 holes, par 72
Tees: Championship: 6,868 yds. Men's: 6,412 yds. Ladies': 5,675 yds.
Fees: Relative or house guest of military personnel: $27.50 with cart, $20

without cart. Civilian with military sponsor: $40.50 with cart, $32 without cart. All rates are half-price after 3:30 p.m. Accepts tee times 3 days in advance (call from 6 a.m.). Accepts Visa, MC.
Facilities: Driving range, putting green, chipping area, practice bunker, pro shop, clubhouse, restaurant, and locker rooms with showers.

Comments   One of the better military courses in the state, and one of the busiest in the United States. Lit for nighttime play. Surrounded by water. The signature hole is Hole 2, which demands a solid tee shot onto a fairway that juts out over water. Collared shirts required; no denim.

Pearl Country Club

Established: 1967
Location: 98-535 Kaonohi St., 'Aiea, HI 96701 (Head westbound on the H-1 Fwy., take Pearlridge exit, and make a right. Turn right on Kaonohi St. The entrance is on the right side of the street.)
Phone: (808) 487-3802
Status: Public, 18 holes, par 72
Tees: Championship: 6,787 yds. Men's: 6,232 yds. Ladies': 5,836 yds.

Fees: $65 weekdays, $70 weekends. Includes cart. Twilight rates: $48 2–3 p.m. and $30 after 3 p.m. Nine-hole twilight rate: $20. Club rentals: $30. Accepts tee times 60 days in advance (call from 6 a.m.). Accepts Visa, MC, AmEx.
Facilities: Driving range (lit for nighttime play), pro shop, and locker room with showers.

Comments Older, hilly course that remains popular, especially among locals. Difficult lies provide a good challenge. Overlooks Pearl Harbor and the *Arizona* Memorial. No tank tops or cut-offs.

MAUI

Zone 7: Central Maui
Waiehu Golf Course

Established: 9-hole course opened in 1933 (back nine added in 1966)
Location: P.O. Box 507, Wailuku, HI 96793 (Get on Hwy. 340 and make a right just past Waihee Park. The entrance to the course is on the right side.)
Phone: (808) 244-5934
Status: Municipal, 18 holes, par 72 (par 73 for ladies)

Tees: Men's: 6,330 yds. Ladies': 5,555 yds.
Fees: $26 weekdays, $30 weekends and holidays. Cart: $8 per person. Club rentals: $15. Accepts tee times 2 days in advance (call from 7 a.m.). Accepts Visa, MC.
Facilities: Driving range, putting green, pro shop, clubhouse, and restaurant.

Comments The only municipal course on Maui. A good deal for your buck. The front nine is relatively flat, while the back nine is hilly in spots. Features one lake and more than 40 sand bunkers. Three holes front the ocean. The signature hole, the par-5 Hole 7, plays alongside the beach.

Zone 8: South Maui
Makena Resort Golf Club

Established: 1983 (split into two separate courses in 1994)
Location: 5415 Makena Alanui, Makena, HI 96753 (From the Kahului Airport, get on Dairy Rd., head to

Mokulele Hwy., and go south. Drive past Wailea. The entrance is on the left side of the road.)
Phone: (808) 879-3344

Status: Resort, 18 holes, par 72 (for both courses)
Tees: Championship: North: 6,500 yds.; South: 6,600 yds. Men's: North: 6,100 yds.; South: 6,200 yds. Ladies': North: 5,300 yds.; South: 5,500 yds.
Fees: $95 for single player, $80 per person for 2 people. Includes cart.

Special $75 twilight rate available from 2 p.m. Club rentals: $35. Accepts tee times 3 days in advance (call from 6:30 a.m.). Accepts Visa, MC, AmEx.
Facilities: Practice range, putting green, pro shop, and locker room with showers.

Comments   Located next to the Maui Prince Hotel. Both courses here are among the state's best, with views of the ocean, Haleakala, and the islands of Molokai, Lanai, and Kahoolawe. Designed by noted golf architect Robert Trent Jones, Jr. Severe slopes and fast greens make for very challenging play on both courses. The lack of strong winds at Makena is a big plus. The South Course's 15th and 16th holes are among the most picturesque oceanfront holes in the state. The North Course is generally considered the more difficult of the two.

Wailea Golf Club

Established: 1972 (Blue), 1993 (Gold), 1995 (Emerald)
Location: 100 Wailea Golf Club Dr., Wailea, HI 96753 (Heading south on Pi'ilani Hwy., drive to the end of the road and turn right. At the stop sign, turn left on Wailea Alanui St. and follow the road to the club.)
Phone: Gold and Emerald courses: (808) 875-7450; Blue course: (808) 875-5155
Status: Resort, 18 holes, par 72 (for all 3 courses)
Tees: Championship: Gold: 7,078 yds.; Emerald: 6,825 yds.; Blue: 6,758 yds. Men's: Gold: 6,653 yds. 6,152

yds.; Emerald: 6,407 yds., 5,873 yds.; Blue: 6,152 yds. Ladies': Gold: 5,442 yds.; Emerald: 5,268 yds.; Blue: 5,291 yds.
Fees: Gold and Emerald: $120. $95 for Wailea resort guests. Blue: $110. $80 for resort guests. Includes cart. Twilight $70 rate ($60 for resort guests) available on the Blue course after noon. Club rentals: $30. Accepts tee times 5 days in advance (call from 6:30 a.m.). Accepts Visa, MC, AmEx, Discover.
Facilities: Driving range, putting greens, pro shop, and restaurant.

Comments   All three courses provide breathtaking ocean and mountain views. The Blue course, with wide, open fairways, is the easiest of the three. The course, however, does have 74 bunkers and four water hazards. The Gold course, featuring ancient lava rock walls that were in place before the course was constructed, ranked as one of *Golf Magazine's* ten best new courses in 1993. The Emerald course offers stunning views of Haleakala and the Pacific Ocean and is considered a friendlier course for high-handicap players. Its signature hole is the 18th, a 553-yard, par-5 challenge with a downhill slope and slight downwind allowing for a reachable green for advanced players. Collared shirts required.

Zone 9: West Maui
Ka'anapali Golf Courses

Established: 1962 (North), 1997 (South)
Location: Ka'anapali Resort, Lahaina, HI 96761 (Head north on Hwy. 30 to the resort area of Ka'anapali. Turn left at the first entrance of the golf course.)
Phone: (808) 661-3691
Status: Resort, 8 holes, par 71 (for both courses)
Tees: Men's: North: 6,994 yds.; South: 6,555 yds. Ladies': North: 5,417 yds.; South: 5,485 yds.
Fees: $130. $105 for resort guests.

Includes cart. Special $75 twilight rate (South course only) noon–2:30 p.m. Twilight rate (both courses) after 2:30 p.m.: $65. Repeat rounds: $42. Club rentals: $30 ($20 twilight rate). Accepts tee times 2 days in advance (call from 7 a.m.). Accepts Visa, MC, AmEx.
Facilities: Driving range, putting green, pro shop, restaurant, and locker room with showers. Club rentals available ($30).

Comments   Two excellent 18-hole courses. The 18th on the North course is one of Hawaii's toughest finishing holes, with water hazards lined up on the right side and the kidney-shaped green bordered by two treacherous bunkers on the left. The shorter South course, with more forgiving greens and wider fairways, is the likely preference for less experienced golfers. In 1964, the North course was the site of the prestigious World Cup, where Arnold Palmer and Jack Nicklaus teamed up to capture the championship for the United States. The North remains a home for golf legends, hosting the annual Ka'anapali Classic, a Senior PGA Tour event.

Kapalua Golf Club

Established: 1975 (Bay), 1980 (Village), 1991 (Plantation)
Location: 300 Kapalua Dr., Kapalua, HI 96761 (Heading north on Hwy. 30, turn left at Kapalua Dr.; the courses are on both sides of the road.)
Phone: Bay course: (808) 669-8820; Plantation course: (808) 669-8877; Village course: (808) 669-8835
Status: Resort. Bay course: 18 holes, par 72; Village course: 18 holes, par 71; Plantation course: 18 holes, par 73
Tees: Men's: Bay: 6,600 yds.; Village: 6,282 yds.; Plantation: 7,263 yds.

Ladies': Bay: 5,124 yds.; Village: 4,876 yds.; Plantation: 5,627 yds.
Fees: Bay and Village courses: $140. $100 for resort guests. Plantation course: $155. $110 for resort guests. Includes cart. Twilight special: All rates are 50% off after 2 p.m. Club rentals: $35–45. Accepts tee times 4 days in advance (call from 6 a.m.). Accepts Visa, MC, AmEx, Discover.
Facilities: Driving range, putting green, pro shop, clubhouse, and restaurants.

Comments   All three courses are among the best on Maui, providing gorgeous views at every turn. The Village course features elevated tee shots on many holes, and the 367-yard, par-4 Hole 6 is one of the most scenic in Hawaii, with stately pines lined up toward the ocean. The Bay course's Hole 5 is one of the world's most dramatic signature holes, requiring a tee shot over Oneloa Bay. The links-style Plantation course, regarded by many PGA pros as one of the top courses in the state, is the home of the PGA Tour's prestigious Mercedes Championships. No tank tops or cut-offs.

Zone 10: Upcountry Maui and Beyond
Pukalani Country Club

Established: 1970
Location: 55 Pukalani St., Pukalani, HI 96768 (From Kahului Airport, drive upcountry along Hwy. 37. The course is on the right side.)
Phone: (808) 572-1314
Status: Public, 18 holes, par 72
Tees: Championship: 6,945 yds. Men's: 6,494 yds. Ladies': 5,612 yds.

Fees: $50 before 11 a.m., $35 after 11 a.m. Cart included. Club rentals: $20. Accepts tee times 7 days in advance (call from 6:30 a.m.). Accepts Visa, MC, AmEx.
Facilities: Driving range, putting green, chipping area, practice bunker, pro shop, clubhouse, and restaurant.

Comments   Located at an elevation of 1,100 feet, you might want to bring a light jacket for the cooler (but thoroughly pleasant) playing conditions. The course is somewhat of a challenge, with fast, sloped greens, although the fairways are nice and wide. As you might expect, the course provides breathtaking views of the island.

THE BIG ISLAND
Zone 11: Kona
Discovery Harbor Golf & Country Club

Established: 1972
Location: P.O. Box 130, Na'alehu, HI 96772 (In Hilo, head west on Hwy. 11. It's a 65-mile drive from the airport. Turn left on Kamoa Rd., then turn left on Wakea Ave., where the course is located on the right side.)
Phone: (808) 929-7353
Status: Public, 18 holes, par 72

Tees: Men's: 6,410 yds. Ladies': 5,731 yds.
Fees: $28. Includes cart. Club rentals: $12. Accepts tee times 2 days in advance (call from 7:30 a.m.). Accepts Visa, MC, AmEx, Discover.
Facilities: Driving range and putting green.

Comments   Set in the midst of a golf course community. Although frequently windy, the course is fairly friendly for high-handicap players. There are no water hazards and few sand traps. Several archaeological sites are preserved here.

Hapuna Golf Course

Established: 1992
Location: 62-100 Kaunaoa Dr.,
Kohala Coast, HI 96743 (From Kona,
drive north along Hwy. 19 past
Ka'upulehu and Waikoloa until you
see the roads leading to the Hapuna
Beach Prince Hotel on the left. Drive a
bit farther; the golf course is on the
right.)
Phone: (808) 880-3000
Status: Resort, 18 holes, par 72
Tees: Tournament: 6,875 yds. Cham-
pionship: 6,534 yds. Men's: 6,029 yds.
Ladies': 5,067 yds.
Fees: $135. $85 for resort guests.
Includes cart. Special $85 twilight rate
($50 for resort guests) available after 3
p.m. Club rentals: $35. Accepts tee
times 2 days in advance (call from 7
a.m.). Accepts Visa, MC, AmEx.
Facilities: Driving range, putting
green, pro shop, clubhouse, and
restaurant.

Comments Sister course to Mauna Kea Golf Course. Links-style course
set amid ancient lava flows, natural vegetation, and spectacular scenery.
Demanding course, especially the par-4s. Water hazards come into play on
four holes. The front nine plays into the trade winds that blow in from the
summit of Mauna Kea. The 545-yard, par-5 Hole 3 is regarded as one of
the best par-5s in the state, with wide expanses, an imposing ravine, a lake,
and a series of bunkers. Another Arnold Palmer–Ed Seay collaboration.
Golfers here share the course with several endangered bird species, including the nene, Hawaii's state bird. Course provides great views from every
hole. Unquestionably one of the Big Island's best. Collared shirts required;
no denim.

Hualalai Golf Club

Established: 1996
Location: 100 Ka'upulehu Dr.,
Kaupulehu, HI 96740 (Hualalai
Resort and the golf course are just a 5-
minute drive north from the Kona
Airport.)
Phone: (808) 325-8480
Status: Private, 18 holes, par 72
Tees: Championship: 7,117 yds.
Men's: 6,632 yds. Ladies': 5,374 yds.
Fees: $145. Only Hualalai home own-
ers or guests staying at the Four Sea-
sons Resort Hualalai are eligible to
play the course. Fee includes cart and
use of the driving range. Club rentals:
$50. Accepts tee times up to 90 days
in advance. Accepts Visa, MC, AmEx,
Diners Club.
Facilities: Driving range, putting
greens, short game practice area, club-
house, snack bar, and restaurant.

Comments Designed by the "Golden Bear" himself, Jack Nicklaus, this
beautiful course features ancient lava flows and is the home of the PGA
Senior Tour's Tournament of Champions. The 172-yard, par-3 Hole 17 is
the signature hole, with an expansive green that demands pinpoint pin
placement; it doesn't help that the hole plays right alongside the crashing

waves of the ocean, a sure distraction. The golf club is the first in Hawaii to be designated an official PGA Tour facility.

Kona Country Club

Established: 1985 (Kona course), 1991 (Ali'i course)
Location: 78-7000 Ali'i Dr., Kailua-Kona, HI 96740 (From the Kona Airport, drive south on Hwy. 11, then turn down Ali'i Dr. The course is located near the end of the road.)
Phone: (808) 322-2595
Status: Resort, 18 hole, par 72 (for both courses)
Tees: Championship: Ocean course: 6,579 yds.; Mountain course: 6,671 yds. Men's: Ocean course: 6,155 yds.; Mountain course: 5,828 yds. Ladies': Ocean course: 5,499 yds.; Mountain course: 4,906 yds.
Fees: $95. Includes cart. Guests at the Kona Surf Resort get a $10 discount. Special $50 twilight rate available after 3 p.m. Club rentals: $30. Accepts tee times 3 days in advance (call from 6:45 a.m.). Accepts Visa, MC, AmEx.
Facilities: Driving range, putting green, pro shop, restaurant, and lounge.

Comments The Ocean course is a good course for golfers in need of a confidence boost. It's a friendly course with wide fairways and fairly easy greens. Much of the course, as its name implies, hugs the Pacific Ocean, with particularly gorgeous vistas from Holes 11–13. The Mountain course, meanwhile, has more hazards and tricky hillside lies. The signature 7th hole is a downhill par-4 (438 yards) that plays straight into the wind and requires a tee shot over a water hazard.

Makalei Hawaii Country Club

Established: 1992
Location: 72-3890 Hawaii Belt Rd., Kailua-Kona, HI 96740 (From the Kona Airport, drive inland on Hwy. 190 for about 6 miles. Look for the sign that designates the exit for the course.)
Phone: (808) 325-6625
Status: Semi-private, 18 holes, par 72
Tees: Championship: 7,091 yds. Men's: 6,698 yds. (blue tees), 6,161 yds. Ladies': 5,242 yds.
Fees: $110. Includes cart. Special $50 twilight rate after noon. Also, 30% discount coupons are available in *Activity Express* magazine (pick one up at the airport). Club rentals: $25 ($15 twilight rate). Accepts tee times 7 days in advance (call from 6:30 a.m.). Accepts Visa, MC, AmEx, Discover.
Facilities: Driving range, 18-hole putting course, pro shop, and restaurant.

Comments Built on a side of a hill overlooking the Pacific. A demanding course whose brisk winds make intelligent club selection a must. The 213-yard, par-3 Hole 15 is an especially scenic but treacherous hole that begins with an elevated tee shot downhill to a green bordered by water on the left. The front nine climbs up to 3,000 feet in elevation. Collared shirts required.

Mauna Kea Golf Course

Established: 1964
Location: 62-100 Mauna Kea Beach
Dr., Kohala Coast, HI 96743 (From
Kona, drive north on Hwy. 19 to the
resort and golf club entrance on the
left side.)
Phone: (808) 882-5400
Status: Resort, 18 holes, par 72
Tees: Tournament: 7,114 yds. Cham‑
pionship: 6,737 yds. Men's: 6,365 yds.

Ladies': 5,277 yds.
Fees: $175. $95 for resort guests.
Includes cart. Special $95 ($60 for
resort guests) twilight rate available
after 3 p.m. Club rentals: $36 for 18
holes, $18 for 9 holes. Accepts tee
times 2 days in advance (call from
6:45 a.m.). Accepts Visa, MC, AmEx.
Facilities: Driving range, putting
green, pro shop, and restaurant.

Comments   The first course to be designed utilizing a lava-strewn land‑
scape, this Robert Trent Jones Sr.–designed course has aged well. It's a
perennial favorite, although quite demanding. The signature hole, the 210-
yard, par-3 Hole 3, requires a tee shot over 180 yards of ocean to reach the
green. Robert Trent Jones Sr., rated this hole as one of his all-time favorites.
The course itself remains one of Hawaii's top layouts. Collared shirts
required.

Mauna Lani Resort

Established: 1981 (North), 1991 (split
into two courses, adding South)
Location: 68-1310 Mauna Lani Dr.,
Kohala Coast, HI 96743 (From Kona,
drive north on Hwy. 19 and turn left
at Mauna Lani Dr. The golf course
will be on your left.)
Phone: (808) 885-6655
Status: Resort, 18 holes, par 72 (for
both courses)
Tees: Championship: North: 6,913
yds.; South: 6,938 yds. Men's: North:
6,601 yds. (blue tees), 6,086 yds.;

South: 6,436 yds. (blue tees), 5,940
yds. Ladies': North: 5,383 yds.; South:
5,028 yds.
Fees: $185. $95 for resort guests.
Includes cart. Special $75 ($60 for
resort guests) twilight rate available
from 2:30 p.m. Club rentals: $35.
Accepts tee times 5 days in advance
(call from 6:30 a.m.). Accepts Visa,
MC, AmEx, Discover.
Facilities: Driving range, putting
green, pro shop, clubhouse, and
restaurant.

Comments   Both courses here, named after noted *kama'aina* Francis H. I'i
Brown, are spectacular in both visual appeal and play. The North course,
blessed with rolling terrain and thickets of *kiawe* trees, is the longer course
and requires more strategy off the tee. The 140-yard, par-3 Hole 17 is its
signature hole, where your tee shot carries from an elevated tee to (hope‑
fully) a green framed by black lava. The South's signature hole, the 196-
yard, par-3 Hole 15, requires a bold tee shot over crashing surf. During the
winter, the 15th often features another unique distraction: humpback
whales, which are often spotted in the deep waters. Collared shirts required.

Waikoloa Beach Course

Established: 1981
Location: 1020 Keana Pl., Waikoloa, HI 96738 (From the Kona Airport, drive north along Hwy. 19. Turn left into Waikoloa Village, then make a right on Keana Pl. after the third stop sign.)
Phone: (808) 886-6060
Status: Resort, 18 holes, par 70
Tees: Championship: 6,566 yds.

Men's: 5,958 yds. Ladies': 5,094 yds.
Fees: $125. $95 for resort guests. Includes cart. Special $65 twilight rate for all golfers available after 2 p.m. Club rentals: $35. Accepts tee times 4 days in advance (call from 6:30 a.m.). Accepts Visa, MC, AmEx, Discover.
Facilities: Driving range, putting green, pro shop, and restaurant.

Comments   A challenging course with narrow fairways framed by rugged black lava. An ancient petroglyph field borders the 6th, 7th, and 8th holes, adding a unique sense of place to the course. The 479-yard, par-4 Hole 12, meanwhile, leads you to the ocean surf. It features a dogleft fairway and green bordered on the right by the Pacific. Collared shirts required.

Waikoloa Kings' Course

Established: 1990
Location: 600 Waikoloa Beach Dr., Waikoloa, HI 96738 (From the Kona Airport, drive north along Hwy. 19. Turn left into Waikoloa Village, then make a right on Keana Pl. after the third stop sign.)
Phone: (808) 886-7888
Status: Resort, 18 holes, par 72
Tees: Championship: 7,094 yds.

Men's: 6,594 yds. Ladies': 6,010 yds.
Fees: $125. $95 for resort guests. Includes cart. Special $65 twilight rate for all golfers available after 2 p.m. Club rentals: $35. Accepts tee times 5 days in advance (call from 6:30 a.m.). Accepts Visa, MC, AmEx, Discover.
Facilities: Driving range, putting green, practice sand trap, and pro shop.

Comments   Designed by Tom Weiskopf and Jay Morrish, this links-style course was voted runner-up by *Golf Digest* as the "Best New Resort Course in America" after it opened in 1990. A challenging layout characterized by many sand bunkers and lava rock formations. Treacherous greens demand expert shot placement. The signature hole, the 293-yard, par-4 Hole 5, features a long bunker stretching along the left side of the fairway, with two large boulders posing another threat for players trying to reach the green. The course is very playable for resort golfers when played from the regular tees. Collared shirts required.

Waikoloa Village Golf Club

Established: 1972
Location: 68-1792 Melia St., Waikoloa, HI 96738 (From the Kona

Airport, drive north along Hwy. 19. Turn right onto Waikoloa Rd. and look for the golf course on the left.)

Phone: (808) 883-9621
Status: Resort, 18 holes, par 72
Tees: Championship: 6,687 yds.
Men's: 6,142 yds. Ladies': 5,558 yds.
Fees: $80. Includes cart. Special $45
twilight rate available after 1 p.m.

Club rentals: $30. Accepts tee times 3
days in advance (call from 6:30 a.m.).
Accepts Visa, MC, AmEx, Discover.
Facilities: Driving range, putting
green, pro shop, and restaurant.

Comments The oldest of the Waikoloa courses. Scenic course taking you
from ancient lava beds all the way down to raging surf. Layout features
rolling terrain, several dogleg fairways, and two lakes that come into play
on three holes. No tank tops or cut-offs.

Waimea Country Club

Established: 1994
Location: P.O. Box 2155, Kamuela,
HI 96743 (Located east of Kamuela,
on Mamalahoa Hwy.)
Phone: (808) 885-8053
Status: Semi-private, 18 holes, par 72
Tees: Championship: 6,661 yds.
Men's: 6,210 yds. Ladies': 5,673 yds.
Fees: $45. Includes cart. Special $30

twilight rate available from noon. Club
rentals: $22.50 for full round, $15 for
9 holes or twilight play. Senior discounts available. Accepts tee times 2
days in advance (call from 7:30 a.m.).
Accepts Visa, MC, AmEx.
Facilities: Driving range, putting
green, and snack shop.

Comments Built on wide-open pasturelands, but features enough tall
ironwood trees to keep you honest. There are 28 sand bunkers, and water
hazards come into play on five holes. Features large, unrelenting greens. All
in all, a good course for players of all skill levels. No dress code. Pack a
sweater, as weather conditions here are often wet and misty.

Zone 12: Hilo and Volcano
Hilo Municipal Golf Course

Established: 1951
Location: 340 Haihai St., Hilo, HI
96720 (From Hilo, head south on
Hwy. 11, past the Prince Kuhio Plaza.
Turn right on Puainako St.,
left on Kilauea Ave., then right on
Haihai St.)
Phone: (808) 959-7711
Status: Municipal, 18 holes, par 71

Tees: Championship: 6,325 yds.
Men's: 6,006 yds. Ladies': 5,034 yds.
Fees: $20 weekdays, $25 weekends.
Cart: $14.50 for 18 holes, $8 for 9
holes. Club rentals: $10. Accepts tee
times 7 days in advance (call from 7
a.m.).
Facilities: Driving range, pro shop,
and restaurant.

Comments The Big Island's only municipal course. Its layout features flat,
tree-lined fairways, with no sand traps, but plenty of water hazards in the
form of streams and lakes. A good course for average players. Mostly frequented by locals. Light rains are frequent in Hilo, so pack an umbrella.

Naniloa Country Club

Established: 1968
Location: 120 Banyan Dr., Hilo, HI 96720 (The entrance is on Banyan Dr. in Hilo.)
Phone: (808) 935-3000
Status: Public, 9 holes, par 35
Tees: Championship: 2,875 yds. Men's: 2,740 yds. Ladies': 2,525 yds.

Fees: $30 weekdays, $40 weekends. $20/$25 for guests staying at the Naniloa Resort. Cart: $7. Club rentals: $19. Accepts tee times 1 day in advance (call from 7 a.m.). Accepts Visa, MC, AmEx.
Facilities: Driving range, putting green, chipping area, and clubhouse.

Comments A short and narrow course designed for quick play. Some holes feature elevated greens and tees. Water hazards come into play on two of the nine holes. There are no bunkers, but plenty of imposing banyan trees. A hot spot among locals.

Sea Mountain Golf Course

Established: 1974
Location: P.O. Box 190, Pahala, HI 96777 (Drive south from Hilo on Hwy. 11 to the 56-mile marker. The course is on the left side.)
Phone: (808) 928-6222
Status: Resort, 18 holes, par 72
Tees: Championship: 6,492 yds. Men's: 6,106 yds. Ladies': 5,663 yds.

Fees: $40. Guests of the Sea Mountain Golf Course Colony Condominiums receive $10 discount. Includes cart. Club rentals: $15. Accepts tee times 3 days in advance (call from 7:30 a.m.). Accepts Visa, MC.
Facilities: Driving range, putting green, pro shop, and restaurant.

Comments Another course with contrasting nines: The front nine here lines a picturesque beach, while the back nine is set against a mountain. Beautiful views from everywhere on the course.

Volcano Golf & Country Club

Established: 1922 (as 9-hole course). Expanded and redesigned in 1967.
Location: P.O. Box 46, Hawaii Volcanoes National Park, HI 96718 (Driving south from Hilo, pass the Hawaii Volcanoes National Park and look for the 30-mile marker on the right. Turn right on Golf Course Rd.; the golf course is on the right.)
Phone: (808) 967-7331
Status: Public, 18 holes, par 72

Tees: Championship: 6,503 yds. Men's: 6,180 yds. Ladies': 5,514 yds.
Fees: $60. Includes shared cart. Club rentals: $16. Senior discounts available. Accepts tee times 180 days in advance (call from 7 a.m.). Accepts Visa, MC, AmEx.
Facilities: Driving range, putting green, pro shop, restaurant, and lounge.

Comments Located inside Hawaii Volcanoes National Park, this course sits next to an active volcano! (But don't worry, the lava flow is a considerable distance away and won't pose a threat.) A mostly flat course except for some rolling hills. A pond and three ditches come into play on four holes. Nearly all the tees and some of the greens are elevated. No tank tops or cut-offs.

ZONE 13: KAUAI

Kauai Lagoons Resort

Established: 1989 (both courses)
Location: 3351 Ho'olaulea Wy., Lihu'e, HI 96766 (From Lihu'e Airport, turn left on Ahukini Rd., left again on Hwy. 51, and left again at the stoplight on Kalapaki Beach. The golf course is on the right.)
Phone: (808) 241-6000
Status: Resort, 18 holes, par 72 (for both courses)
Tees: Championship: Ki'ele course: 7,070 yds.; Mokihana course: 6,960 yds. Men's: Ki'ele: 6,674 yds. (blue tees), 6,164 yds.; Mokihana: 6,578 yds. (blue tees), 6,136 yds. Ladies':

Ki'ele: 5,417 yds.; Mokihana: 5,607 yds.
Fees: $123 for Ki'ele course, $83 for Mokihana course. Includes cart. Special twilight rates ($92 for Ki'ele, $61 for Mokihana) available after noon. Guests staying at the Kauai Marriott receive $20 off rates. Club rentals: $30. Accepts tee times 30 days in advance (call from 6:30 a.m.). Accepts Visa, MC, AmEx.
Facilities: Driving range, putting and chipping greens, pro shop, locker rooms with showers, snack bar, and restaurant.

Comments   Both courses here were designed by Jack Nicklaus. The Ki'ele course is the more difficult of the two, with many tee shots needing to carry over ravines. The Ki'ele course is regarded as one of Hawaii's best and offers perhaps the best greens. *Golf Digest* ranked the course as one of the 75 best upscale courses in America. The Mokihana course, formerly known as the Ki'ele course, is more favorable to players with high handicaps. Collared shirt required; no cut-offs.

Kiahuna Golf Club

Established: 1983
Location: 2545 Kiahuna Plantation Dr., Koloa, HI 96756 (In Po'ipu, drive down Po'ipu Rd. and turn left onto Kiahuna Plantation Dr. The entrance is on the left.)
Phone: (808) 742-9595
Status: Resort, 18 holes, par 70
Tees: Championship: 6,353 yds. Men's: 5,631 yds. Ladies': 4,871 yds.
Fees: $75 before 11 a.m., $55 between

11 a.m. and 2:30 p.m. daily. Special $40 twilight rate available after 2:30 p.m. on weekdays only. Includes cart. Club rentals: $15–$30. Guests staying at selected hotels on Kauai receive 10–15% discounts. Accepts tee times 30 days in advance (call from 8 a.m.). Accepts Visa, MC, AmEx, Discover.
Facilities: Driving range, putting green, pro shop, and snack bar.

Comments   A challenging layout built around ancient Hawaiian sites. The course features narrow fairways, water hazards, and plenty of trade winds.

Designed by Robert Trent Jones, Jr. Collared shirt required.

Po'ipu Bay Resort Golf Course

Established: 1991
Location: 2250 Ainako St., Koloa, HI 96756 (In Po'ipu, follow Po'ipu Rd. to Ainako St. and make a right. The course is just past the Hyatt Regency Kauai.
Phone: (808) 742-8711
Status: Resort, 18 holes, par 72
Tees: Championship: 6,959 yds. Men's: 6,499 yds. (blue tees), 6,023 yds. Ladies': 5,241 yds.
Fees: $145 before noon, $95 after noon. Includes cart. Special $60 twilight rate available after 3 p.m. Guests staying at selected Kauai hotels are eligible for discounts. Club rentals: $40. Accepts tee times 7 days in advance (call from 6:30 a.m.). Accepts Visa, MC, AmEx.
Facilities: Driving range, putting and chipping greens, practice sand bunkers, pro shop, locker room with showers, clubhouse, and restaurant.

Comments   Water hazards come into play on 11 holes at this immaculate course; more than 80 bunkers add to the challenge. The 501-yard, par-4 Hole 16 is lined by a lake on one side of the fairway and the ultimate water hazard—the ocean—on the other. The 201-yard, par-3 Hole 17 is another spectacular setting, boasting sweeping views of Po'ipu's coastal area from the tee. This is the site of the PGA Grand Slam of Golf, a unique two-day event featuring the winners of golf's four major championships. Collared shirt required.

Princeville Resort Golf Courses

Established: 1973 (Makai), 1990 (Prince)
Location: Makai course: 4080 Leiopapa Rd., Princeville, HI 96722 (From Kuhio Hwy., turn right into the Princeville Resort. The golf course is a mile away and on the left side of the road.); Prince course: 5-3900 Kuhio Hwy., Princeville, HI 96722 (From Kuhio Hwy., drive past the Princeville Airport. The golf course is on the right side.)
Phone: Makai course: 826-3580; Prince course: 826-5000
Status: Resort. Makai course: 27 holes, par 72; Prince course: 18 holes, par 72
Tees: Championship: Makai: 3,430 yds. (Ocean), 3,456 yds. (Lakes), 3,445 yds. (Woods); Prince: 7,309 yds. Men's: Makai: 3,157 yds. (Ocean), 3,149 yds. (Lakes), 3,204 yds. (Woods); Prince: 6,960 yds. (blue tees), 6,521 yds. (men's), 6,005 yds. (gold tees) Ladies': Makai: 2,802 yds. (Ocean), 2,714 yds. (Lakes), 2,809 yds. (Woods); Prince: 5,338 yds.
Fees: Makai: $150. Guests staying at Princeville pay $87–97. Includes cart. Discounted rate of $75 after 1 p.m. $39 twilight rate (for 9 holes) available after 4 p.m. Club rentals: $32 for 18 holes, $15 for 9 holes. Prince: $155. $103 for resort guests. Includes cart and use of driving range. Special $99 rate available after noon. Club rentals: $32–42. Accepts tee times 14 days in advance (call from 7:30 a.m.). Accepts Visa, MC, AmEx.

Facilities: Makai course: Driving range, putting and chipping greens, pro shop, and snack bar; Prince course: All of the above plus more putting greens, a spa, and a restaurant.

Comments The Makai course is actually three separate 9-hole courses that combine to form three different 18-hole layouts. The Ocean course's signature hole, appropriately, requires a tee shot over a stretch of ocean. Lakes come into play on three holes on the Lakes course and one hole on the Woods course. The Scottish links-style Prince course provides a challenge with its rolling hills and multitude of ravines. Views? You can see the ocean from every tee. *Golf Digest* has rated the Prince course as Hawaii's best. Collared shirt required.

Wailua Golf Course

Established: 1920 (as 6-hole course). Expanded and redesigned in 1962.
Location: 3-5350 Kuhio Hwy., Lihu'e, HI 96746 (From Lihu'e on Kuhio Hwy., drive north to Kapa'a. The golf course is on the right side.)
Phone: (808) 245-8092
Status: Municipal, 18 holes, par 72
Tees: Championship: 6,981 yds. Men's: 6,585 yds. Ladies': 5,974 yds.

Fees: $25 weekdays, $35 weekends and holidays. 50% discount rates available after 2 p.m. Cart: $14. Club rentals: $15 with $50 deposit. Accepts tee times 7 days in advance (call from 7:30 a.m.). Accepts only traveler's checks or cash.
Facilities: Driving range, putting green, pro shops, and shower rooms.

Comments One of the best municipal courses in Hawaii, and annually regarded as one of the best in the United States. A challenging course with elevated tees. Served as the site of the 1975 and 1985 Men's Public Links Amateur Championships. No tank tops or cut-offs.

ZONE 14: MOLOKAI
Kaluako'i Golf Course

Established: 1977
Location: P.O. Box 26, Maunaloa, HI 96770 (Drive westward on Kamehameha Hwy. for 20 minutes from the airport. Turn right on Kaluako'i Rd., and take the second right to the course.)
Phone: (808) 552-2739
Status: Resort, 18 holes, par 72
Tees: Championship: 6,564 yds.

Men's: 6,187 yds. Ladies': 5,461 yds.
Fees: $80. $60 for resort guests. Includes cart. Special $43 ($35 for resort guests) twilight rate available after 2:30 p.m. Club rentals: $11. Accepts tee times 30 days in advance (call from 7:30 a.m.). Accepts Visa, MC, AmEx, Discover.
Facilities: Driving range, putting green, and pro shop.

Comments An attractive course that winds its way through Kaluako'i Resort, ascends a hillside, and descends toward the ocean shore. You could easily play two rounds with no waiting time. The signature hole is the 10th, a 387-yard, par-4 dogleg left that plays slightly uphill. The right side of the fairway runs alongside a condominium, while the left side flanks the ocean. The green is fronted by a water hazard and backed by the ocean. Designed by Ted Robinson. No tank tops or cut-offs.

ZONE 15: LANAI

The Challenge at Manele

Established: 1993
Location: P.O. Box 310, Lanai City, HI 96763 (Transportation to the course is provided via Lanai Resorts shuttle.)
Phone: (808) 565-2222
Status: Resort, 18 holes, par 72
Tees: Championship: 7,039 yds. Men's: 6,684 yds. Ladies': 5,024 yds.
Fees: $175. $125 for guests staying at the Lodge at Ko'ele, Manele Bay Hotel, or Hotel Lanai. Club rentals: $35 for full round, $20 for 9 holes. Accepts tee times 30 days in advance (call from 7:30 a.m.). Accepts Visa, MC, AmEx.
Facilities: Driving range, putting and chipping greens, locker rooms, pro shop, and restaurant.

Comments   Designed by Jack Nicklaus. Links-style course that offers great ocean views from every hole. Fairways are open, while greens are small and fast. Built on the side of a hill, the course features several changes of elevation and requires several "blind" tee and approach shots. Winds often come into play. Bring extra balls for Hole 12, a 202-yard par-3 that includes a tee shot across 200 yards of Pacific Ocean. The tee area rests at a cliff 150 feet above the crashing surf and is the picturesque spot where Bill Gates got married in 1994. Archaeological sites are among the unique features here. Collared shirts required; no denim.

The Experience at Ko'ele

Established: 1991
Location: P.O. Box 310, Lanai City, HI 96763 (Transportation to the course is provided via Lanai Resorts shuttle.)
Phone: (808) 565-4653
Status: Resort, 18 holes, par 72
Tees: Championship: 7,014 yds. Men's: 6,217 yds. Ladies': 5,424 yds.
Fees: $175. $125 for guests staying at the Lodge at Ko'ele, Manele Bay Hotel, or Hotel Lanai. Club rentals: $35 for full round, $20 for 9 holes. Accepts tee times 30 days in advance (call from 8 a.m.). Accepts Visa, MC, AmEx.
Facilities: Driving range, putting and chipping greens, executive putting course, clubhouse, and snack bar.

Comments   A magnificent course designed by golf greats Greg Norman and Ted Robinson. The front nine was carved from the side of a mountain, while the back nine is more open and flat. Water features are prominent here, with seven lakes, streams, and waterfalls. The par-4, 444-yard Hole 8 is the signature hole here, featuring a 250-foot drop from tee to fairway, with a lake bordering one side and thick shrubs and trees lining the other. Even Jack Nicklaus needed seven attempts to get the ball in play! Hole 17 is surrounded by a lake. Collared shirts required; no denim.

Spectator Sports

First, the bad news: There are no major professional sports franchises in Hawaii, and the state's relatively small population base and its immense physical distance from the continental U.S. likely means we'll never see a Honolulu Surfriders in the NFL, NBA, NHL, or Major League Baseball.

But even without a major professional franchise, the islands of Oahu, Maui, Hawaii, and Kauai all host major sporting events throughout the year. If you're a sports fanatic looking for a game to go with your beach time, here's your game plan:

FOOTBALL

The Super Bowl may be *the* game in professional football, but in Hawaii the NFL Pro Bowl promises a "super" time as well. Held the week following the Super Bowl, the Pro Bowl pits the premier players in the American Football Conference against the top stars in the National Football Conference. The game is held at the 50,000-seat Aloha Stadium on Oahu and is usually sold out weeks in advance, so inquire early for tickets (call (808) 486-9300; for credit card orders, call (808) 484-1122). Also, the NFL and several local companies team up to host a number of Pro Bowl–related festivities during the week preceding the game. So this is a good opportunity to meet (and get autographs from) your favorite football superstars.

The top senior players in *college* football, meanwhile, gather on Maui each January to perform in the annual Hula Bowl. After being held on Oahu for the first 50 years, this all-star contest has found new life on the Valley Isle, with the 20,000-seat War Memorial Stadium in Wailuku filled to capacity with rabid fans and, not coincidentally, talent scouts from every NFL team. Among the many Hula Bowl participants who went on to NFL greatness are Joe Montana, Dan Marino, Steve Young, Reggie White, Deion Sanders, Ronnie Lott, Marcus Allen, Dick Butkus, Merlin Olsen, Gayle Sayers, Fran Tarkenton and Bob Lilly. Call 947-4141.

Each Christmas Day, sports fans have a pigskin feast with college football's only postseason doubleheader. The Jeep Aloha Bowl Christmas Football Classic, held at Aloha Stadium, spotlights four elite NCAA schools. The games don't enjoy the prestige of the Rose Bowl or have any national championship implications, but the action is just as exciting. Call (808) 947-4141.

Finally, there's University of Hawaii football. The green-and-white-clad Rainbow Warriors play seven or eight home games each fall at Aloha Stadium. The first and last home games are often against big-name schools such as Michigan, Notre Dame, Southern Cal, Texas, and Cal-Berkeley. Call (808) 956-4481.

GOLF

As you might expect of a golfer's paradise, there are a handful of major golf events dotting Hawaii's annual sports calendar. Held in early January is the Mercedes Championships at Kapalua, Maui, where top PGA players vie for more than $2.5 million in prize money. Formerly known as the Tournament of Champions and held in California, the Mercedes Championships debuted in 1999, with David Duval emerging victorious from a 30-player field that included Tiger Woods, Mark O'Meara, Davis Love III, Lee Janzen, and Phil Mickelson. Call (808) 669-2440.

Formerly the Hawaiian Open, the all-new Sony Open in Hawaii draws the PGA's best to the Wai'alae Country Club in Kahala, on the island of Oahu. This January tournament kicks off the official PGA Tour season, with 144 of the world's top professionals vying for more than $2.5 million in prize money. Call (808) 523-7888.

Also in January is the MasterCard Championship, which gathers winners from the previous year's Senior PGA Tour events to the Hualalai Golf Club on the Big Island. This tournament, featuring more than $1 million in prize money, kicks off the Seniors Tour. Call (808) 325-8480.

In February, the Kapolei Golf Course on Oahu hosts the annual Sunrise Hawaiian Ladies Open, a 54-hole medal play competition featuring the top women's golfers from the U.S. and Japan. Call (808) 671-5050.

One of the final stops on the Senior PGA Tour is the EMC Ka'anapali Classic on Maui. Held in October, this event annually draws some of the game's greatest legends and old-time favorites. Call (808) 661-3691.

November brings the MasterCard PGA Grand Slam to the Po'ipu Bay Course on Kauai. This unique 36-hole, two-day event features the winners of golf's four major PGA championships (Master's, British Open, U.S. Open, and PGA Championship). Call (808) 742-1234.

SURFING AND OTHER OCEAN SPORTS

A surf meet provides a different kind of experience for sports fans. Instead of being squeezed inside a chilly stadium or arena, you're sitting on gorgeous white sand, basking under a warm, tropical sun, and enjoying some breathtaking sights (and we're not necessarily referring to the action on the waves!). It's a good chance to see Hawaii's official individual sport at its finest, and admission is always free.

A professional surf meet works like this: Competitors take to the water in four-man heats, each lasting 20 to 30 minutes. During each heat, the surfers ride as many waves as they can. A panel of five judges uses a point system similar to what you'd see in gymnastics or figure skating. Criteria include the size of the waves, length of the rides, board control, riding different parts of the wave, and using creative maneuvers such as turns and cutbacks (swinging back toward the wave).

The most prestigious surfing competition in Hawaii, if not the entire surfing world, is the Triple Crown of surfing, held in November and December. The best professional wave riders from around the world gather on Oahu's North Shore for a trio of competitions—the Ocean Pacific Pro at Ali'i Beach Park, World Cup of Surfing at Sunset Beach, and Pipe Masters at the world-famous Banzai Pipeline at 'Ehukai Beach Park. The Triple Crown helps determine the year's world champion of surfing. Each Triple Crown event involves four full days of competition—the days are determined by the most optimal surf conditions—with heats usually beginning at 8 a.m. Recently, the Triple Crown added a special longboard competition at Ali'i Beach Park. Call (808) 638-5024.

There are several other ocean-related events that make a yearly splash on Hawaii's sports calendar. The Morey World Bodyboarding Championships, for example, turns the spotlight on an international field of bodyboarders. These daring ocean athletes take on the huge winter surf each January at the Banzai Pipeline on Oahu's North Shore. Call (808) 396-2326.

A variety of windsurfing competitions, showcasing top local, national, and international wave riders, take place throughout the year on the islands of Oahu and Maui. Call Hawaii Windsurfing Championships at (808) 734-6999.

The arrival of summer brings the Outrigger Hotels Oceanfest, a colorful ocean sports festival headlined by the Hawaiian International Ocean Challenge, which features the world's top lifeguards in a variety of ocean-related competitions on Oahu. (While the popular TV show *Baywatch* is indeed filmed in Hawaii, we're talking about *real* lifeguards here!) Other Oceanfest events include kayak, paddleboarding, and canoe races, as well as the Wahine Windsurfing Classic. Call (808) 521-4322.

You won't be able to follow *all* the action of the annual Bankoh Na Wahine O Ke Kai and the Bankoh Molokai Hoe, separate 41-mile outrigger canoe races that begin on Molokai. (The women's race, the Wahine O Ke Kai, is held in late September, while the men's race takes place in early October.) But you can watch the six-member canoe teams paddle to the "finish line" on the beach in Waikiki. Both events bring outrigger canoe teams from around the globe, including Australia, Canada, Tahiti, the U.S. mainland, and Hawaii. Call (808) 325-7400.

Speaking of grueling, few events are as physically demanding as the Ironman Triathlon World Championship, held each October in Kailua-Kona on the island of Hawaii. One-third of the event takes place in the water, as the world's top triathletes embark on a 2.4-mile ocean swim followed by a 112-mile bike race and full 26.2-mile marathon! Fair warning: The weekend of the triathlon is often Kailua-Kona's busiest of the year, and certain visitor necessities, like car rentals, may be hard to come by. Call (808) 329-0063.

Also in October is the annual HydroFest, where hydroplanes—the world's fastest speedboats (reaching in excess of 200 miles per hour)—race around a 2.5-mile oval course on the waters of Pearl Harbor, Oahu. Admission is charged for this event, which is hosted by the U.S. Navy. Call (808) 473-0819.

Part Eight

Shopping in Paradise

Shopping in the Islands can be as alluring as a sun-dappled beach. In fact, it's an integral part of the vacation experience—and an enjoyable part, at that!

In Hawaii—and on the island of Oahu, in particular—you'll find nearly every major retailer and brand name. Whether you're looking for tacky-but-fun souvenirs (an "I Got Lei'd in Hawaii" T-shirt comes to mind) or the latest fashions from Paris, it's all here.

Of course, you'll find some wonderful shopping opportunities that are unique to the Islands. While short on hyperbole (you won't find stores advertising themselves as having "The World's Largest Selection of . . ."), Hawaii is long on high-quality Island-produced goods such as jams and jellies, coffees, candies, and even potato chips. Almost every island is known for having some sort of specialty item: When Oahu residents travel to the Neighbor Islands, they might return home with Kona coffee, chocolates, or mochi (a traditional Japanese confection made of flour and sugar) from the Big Island; cookies from Kauai; freshly baked breads from Molokai; or locally made potato chips from Maui. Macadamia nuts and Kona coffee, both of which are in abundant supply here, seem to be everyone's favorite take-home purchases.

Here's a tip for shopaholics wanting to see all of Hawaii's specialty products under one roof: Every August, the **Made in Hawaii Festival** features more than 300 exhibitors showcasing their products—all made or grown in the Islands—including foods, wine, fashions, *lau hala* baskets, jewelry, artworks, koa boxes, tropical scented soaps, gourmet fruit-flavored teas, plants, books, perfumes, candles, pillows, fashions, hair accessories, lotions, and more. The three-day festival takes place at the Neal Blaisdell Exhibition Hall in Honolulu. For more information, call the Hawaii Food Industry Association at (808) 533-1292.

A lasting (and admittedly pricey) memento you can bring home is Hawaiian heirloom jewelry, exquisite Victorian-style pieces with black enamel and Hawaiian designs. This form of fashion has been an Island tradition since the mid–nineteenth century. Today, these precious keepsakes are given as gifts for birthdays, anniversaries, weddings, school graduations, and other special occasions. You can find Hawaiian heirloom jewelry at finer jewelry shops on all the islands. Prices vary according to the karat, the thickness and width of the band, the world market price of gold, and the length of time it takes to engrave an individual design. A bracelet, for example, might cost anywhere from $200 for a simple pattern on an ultra-light band to $600 for a more complex design on a heavier-weight band.

If you're staying in Waikiki, you could spend many hours (and even more dollars) at popular shopping outlets such as the **Royal Hawaiian Shopping Center, King's Village,** and the **International Market Place.** However, even grander shopping adventures await outside Waikiki, at major centers like **Ala Moana** (one of the largest outdoor malls in the United States), **Ward Warehouse,** and the **Waikele Premium Outlets** (where major brands like Anne Klein and Saks Fifth Avenue offer discounts between 25% and 65% off regular prices).

The Neighbor Islands of Maui and Hawaii are fast becoming shopping meccas in their own right. Major retailers like Borders Books and Wal-Mart are popping up on these islands with increasing regularity. Also, keep in mind that most hotels and resorts offer a selection of shops and boutiques right on their property.

The sales tax in Hawaii is currently 4.167%. Most stores accept major credit cards and personal checks. And for the misguided few who still think people in Hawaii live in grass shacks (trust us, you'd be surprised), yes, American currency is the rule here!

For bookworms who can't stand being away from their favorite Borders or Barnes & Noble store, Hawaii has both: Borders Books, Music and Cafe has locations in the Ward Centre in Honolulu (call (808) 591-8995) and Waikele Shopping Center in Waipahu (call (808) 676-6699) on Oahu; in Kahului (call (808) 877-6160) on Maui; in Kona (call (808) 331-1668) and Hilo (call (808) 933-1410) on the Big Island; and in Lihu'e (call (808) 246-0862) on Kauai. Barnes & Noble Booksellers has one location, at Kahala Mall in Honolulu (call (808) 737-3323).

Following is a list of recommended retail shops and major shopping malls in Hawaii, along with information on two major swap meets on Oahu. Hours of operation are subject to change. Most malls expand their shopping hours during the holiday season.

Individual Shops

These individual shops are worth a look. Some are located at one of the shopping malls listed below. One good source for unique shops on Oahu is the *Ultimate Shopper (The Local's Handbook to the Most Unique Shopping on Oahu),* published by Bess Press.

OAHU

Animation Magic

Locations: The Ward Warehouse, Aloha Tower Marketplace

Zones: 1, Waikiki; 2, Greater Honolulu

Phone: (808) 597-8807 (Ward Warehouse), (808) 545-8666 (Aloha Tower Marketplace)

Hours: Ward Warehouse: Monday–Saturday, 10 a.m.–9 p.m.; Sunday, 10 a.m.–5 p.m. *Aloha Tower Marketplace:* Monday–Saturday, 9 a.m.–9 p.m.; Sunday, 9 a.m.–6 p.m.

Description A local favorite for kids and adults alike. Features a large selection of cartoon-related apparel, accessories, novelties, and animation art. Includes characters from Disney, Hanna Barbera, Looney Tunes, Garfield, Betty Boop, Snoopy, the Simpsons, and more. Some items have Hawaiian themes.

Big Frankie Collectibles

Location: 1210 Queen St., Suite 203, Honolulu. Located directly above Pan-ya Bakery (behind 7-Eleven) near the intersection of Ala Moana Blvd. and 'Auahi St.

Zone: 2, Greater Honolulu

Phone: (808) 589-8988

Hours: Tuesday–Friday, noon–6 p.m.; Saturday, 10 a.m.–6 p.m. or by appointment. Closed on Sunday.

Description Offers an impressive selection of nostalgic toys and hot collectibles, including items that feature *Star Wars* characters, Japanese superheroes, G.I. Joe, comic book heroes, sports superstars, pro wrestling figures, cartoon favorites, and more.

Crazy Shirts

Location: International Market Place, Waikiki (more than 20 locations throughout the state; call (808) 487-9919 for the location nearest you)

Zone: 1, Waikiki
Phone: (808) 922-4791
Hours: Daily, 8 a.m.–11:30 p.m.

Description   Hawaii's most popular T-shirt shop, featuring hundreds of colorful, local-theme designs. The International Market Place location is the company's biggest and busiest outlet.

Fujioka's Wine & Spirits
Location: 3184 Wai'alae Ave., Honolulu
Zone: 2, Greater Honolulu
Phone: (808) 739-9463
Hours: Monday–Saturday, 10 a.m.–8 p.m.; Sunday, 11 a.m.–5 p.m.

Description   Fujioka's Supermarket in Hale'iwa (on Oahu's North Shore) has long been a best-kept secret among local wine connoisseurs, offering an impressive wine list—more than 500 domestic and foreign labels—to go along with the usual grocery goodies. "Wine & Spirits" is an offshoot store whose location makes it much more convenient for wine lovers in the Honolulu area.

Harry's Music Store
Location: 3457 Wai'alae Ave., Honolulu
Zone: 2, Greater Honolulu
Phone: (808) 735-2866
Hours: Monday–Friday, 9:30 a.m.–5:30 p.m.; Saturday, 9 a.m.–5 p.m.

Description   Old Hawaiian records, sheet music, and ukuleles are among the vintage items offered at this small-but-famous shop in Kaimuki. A great stop for Hawaiian music aficionados.

Hawaiian Heirloom Jewelry Factory & Museum
Location: Royal Hawaiian Shopping Center
Zone: 1, Waikiki
Phone: (808) 924-7972
Hours: Daily, 9 a.m.–11 p.m.

Description   Exquisite Hawaiian jewelry—bracelets, pendants, rings, and more—for sale and viewing. Just behind the showroom is a mini-factory, where you can watch master craftsmen manufacture these brilliant treasures.

Hawaiian Ukulele Company

Location: Aloha Tower Marketplace
Zone: 2, Greater Honolulu
Phone: (808) 536-3228
Hours: Monday–Saturday, 9 a.m.–9 p.m.; Sunday, 9 a.m.–6 p.m.

Description This breezy shop specializes in fine, handcrafted Hawaiian ukulele instruments. Ukulele accessories (including songbooks and instruction booklets) and other Hawaiian musical instruments are also for sale.

Hilo Hattie

Location: Ala Moana Shopping Center
Zone: 2, Greater Honolulu
Phone: (808) 973-3266
Hours: Monday–Saturday, 9:30 p.m.–9 p.m.; Sunday, 10 a.m.–7 p.m.

Description Hilo Hattie has the largest selection of aloha wear, Hawaiian treats and souvenirs in Hawaii. Neighbor Island locations: in Lahaina (call (808) 667-7911) on Maui; in Kona (call (808) 329-7200) and Hilo (call (808) 961-3077) on the Big Island; and in Lihu'e (call (808) 245-4724) on Kauai.

Irene's Hawaiian Gifts

Location: Ala Moana Shopping Center
Zone: 2, Greater Honolulu
Phone: (808) 946-6818
Hours: Monday–Saturday, 9:30 p.m.–9 p.m.; Sunday, 10 a.m.–7 p.m.

Description Features a nice selection of Hawaiian gifts and souvenirs, including koa boxes, porcelain dolls, soaps, perfumes, notecards, dish towels, and do-it-yourself Hawaiian quilt kits.

The Islands Best

Location: Ala Moana Shopping Center
Zone: 2, Greater Honolulu
Phone: (808) 949-5345
Hours: Monday–Saturday, 9:30 p.m.–9 p.m.; Sunday, 10 a.m.–7 p.m.

Description A wide range of unique Hawaiian gifts and souvenirs, including soaps, crafts, stationery, and artworks.

Jelly's Music, Comics & Books

Locations: Market City Shopping Center, Pearl Kai Shopping Center

Zones: 2, Greater Honolulu; 5, Leeward Oahu

Phone: Market City, (808) 735-7676; Pearl Kai, (808) 486-5600

Hours: Market City: Monday–Saturday, 10 a.m.–10 p.m.; Sunday, 10 a.m.–7 p.m. Pearl Kai: Monday–Thursday, 10 a.m.–11 p.m.; Friday and Saturday, 10 a.m.–midnight; Sunday, 10 a.m.–2 p.m.

Description   A bargain hunter's paradise. Offers both new and used books, CDs, record albums, trading cards (sports and non-sports), comic books, and games.

Kauila Maxwell Co.

Location: Windward Mall

Zone: 3, Windward Oahu

Phone: (808) 235-8383

Hours: Monday–Saturday, 10 a.m.–9 p.m.; Sunday, 10 a.m.–5 p.m.

Description   Everything here is exclusively made in Hawaii and includes clothing, crafts, artworks, and home furnishings.

Kris Kringle's Den

Location: The Ward Warehouse, Honolulu

Zone: 2, Greater Honolulu

Phone: (808) 591-8844

Hours: Monday–Saturday, 10 a.m.–9 p.m.; Sunday, 10 a.m.–5 p.m.

Description   It's Christmas 365 days a year at this unique collectibles store featuring hundreds of ornaments, figurines, and other Yuletide-related merchandise.

Kwilts 'N Koa

Location: 1126 12th Ave., Suite 101, Honolulu

Zone: 2, Greater Honolulu

Phone: (808) 735-2300

Hours: Monday–Friday, 10 a.m.–6 p.m.; Saturday, 10 a.m.–4 p.m.

Description   A great Hawaiiana shop specializing in Hawaiian quilt–themed merchandise, including patchwork quilts, pillows, pot holders, dolls, and accessories. Also offers koa bowls, boxes, and jewelry. Quilt-making classes are held five times a week.

Magnet Five-0

Location: Aloha Tower Marketplace, Honolulu

Zone: 2, Greater Honolulu

Phone: (808) 545-1050

Hours: Monday–Saturday, 9 a.m.–9 p.m.; Sunday, 9 a.m.–6 p.m.

Description This store offers a selection of more than 3,000 different magnets, including Hawaiian-themed and seasonal items.

Montsuki

Location: 1148 Koko Head Ave., Honolulu

Zone: 2, Greater Honolulu

Phone: (808) 734-3457

Hours: Monday–Saturday, 9:30 a.m.–4 p.m.

Description This shopping gem in the heart of Kaimuki offers stylish and creative apparel fashioned from vintage silk kimonos.

Native Books & Beautiful Things

Locations: Ward Warehouse and 222 Merchant St. in downtown Honolulu

Zone: 2, Greater Honolulu

Phone: Ward Warehouse, (808) 596-8885; Merchant St., (808) 599-5511

Hours: Ward Warehouse: Monday–Saturday, 10 a.m.–9 p.m.; Sunday, 10 a.m.–5 p.m. Merchant St.: Monday–Friday, 8 a.m.–5 p.m.; Saturday, 10 a.m.–3 p.m.

Description A cooperative effort among a *hui* (club) of local artisans, this store includes Hawaii-made crafts, artworks, apparel, and more. A nice selection of Hawaiiana books rounds out this shopping gem.

Nohea Gallery

Location: Ward Warehouse (additional locations at the Sheraton Moana Surfrider Hotel in Waikiki and the Kahala Mandarin Oriental in Kahala)

Zone: 2, Greater Honolulu

Phone: (808) 596-0074

Web Site: www.noheagallery.com

Hours: Monday–Saturday, 10 a.m.–9 p.m.; Sunday, 10 a.m.–5 p.m.

Description Features Island artworks and fine crafts created by some of Hawaii's best artisans. Items include paintings, prints, ceramics, woodworks, jewelry, glassware, and more.

Quilts Hawaii

Location: 2338 S. King St., Honolulu
Zone: 2, Greater Honolulu
Phone: (808) 942-3195
Hours: Monday–Saturday, 9 a.m.–5:30 p.m.

Description This *kama'aina* shop features a sizable selection of artful Hawaiian treasures, including quilted comforters, pillowcases, infant accessories, handbags, and other gift items.

Rainbow Bow-Tique

Location: Ward Centre
Zone: 2, Greater Honolulu
Phone: (808) 591-5536
Hours: Monday–Saturday, 10 a.m.–9 p.m.; Sunday, 10 a.m.–5 p.m.

Description Officially licensed University of Hawaii Rainbows sports merchandise, including apparel (for all ages) and novelty items. There's also a Bow-Tique on the university campus (inside the 10,000-seat Stan Sheriff Special Events Center), but this location is much more convenient.

Vintage Wine Cellar

Location: 1249 Wilder Ave., Honolulu
Zone: 2, Greater Honolulu
Phone: (808) 523-9463
Hours: Daily, 10 p.m.–7 p.m.

Description *Kama'aina* wine lovers Jay and Cora Kam maintain one of Hawaii's finest collections of fine wine and spirits, with wines from all over the world. The staff is friendly and knowledgeable and can help you find the perfect wine for your special occasion.

MAUI

Hasegawa General Store

Location: Hana
Zone: 10, Upcountry Maui and Beyond
Phone: (808) 248-8231
Hours: Monday–Saturday, 7 a.m.–7 p.m.; Sunday, 8 a.m.–6 p.m.

Description Offers what you'd typically find in any general merchandise store but deserves mention because it is one of the most beloved establishments on Maui. Founded in 1910, this family-run store sells everything from canned goods and postcards to liquor and flip-flops.

Hawaiiana Arts & Crafts

Location: Cinema Wharf Center, Lahaina
Zone: 9, West Maui
Phone: (808) 661-9077
Hours: Daily, 10 a.m.–8 p.m.

Description Friendly *kama'aina* shop offering handmade arts and crafts by some of Maui's best artisans. Items include raku pottery, woodcrafts, and *lauhala* items.

Hoaloha Wood Heirlooms

Location: Ka'ahumanu Shopping Center, Kahului
Zone: 7, Central Maui
Phone: (808) 873-0461
Hours: Monday–Friday, 9:30 a.m.–9 p.m.; Saturday, 9:30 a.m.–7 p.m.;
   Sunday, 10 a.m.–5 p.m.

Description Carries a wide selection of Hawaiiana and Polynesia-themed merchandise, including koa bowls, koa jewelry and accessories, Hawaiian dolls, Hawaiian quilts, hula implements, ukuleles, original artworks, wood carvings, glass art, and more.

Honolua Store

Location: Office Rd., Kapalua Resort
Zone: 9, West Maui
Phone: (808) 669-6128
Hours: Daily, 6 a.m.–8 p.m.

Description Formerly an actual plantation grocery store, Honolua Store features a nice selection of Maui- and Kapalua-related apparel and gift items, along with grocery goods and beverages. The store also maintains a sizable selection of premium wines.

Ka Honu Gift Gallery

Location: Whalers Village, Ka'anapali
Zone: 9, West Maui
Phone: (808) 661-0173
Hours: Daily, 9 a.m.–10 p.m.

Description   Colorful shop featuring fine woodworks (including koa items), handcrafted goods, Christmas ornaments, and other unique gift items.

South Seas Trading Post

Location: 780 Front St., Lahaina

Zone: 9, West Maui

Phone: (808) 661-3168

Hours: Daily, 9 a.m.–10:30 p.m.

Description   Offers a great selection of imported arts and crafts, from Neolithic bowls from China to masks and wood carvings from New Guinea. Also features porcelains, jewelry, baskets, and other fine merchandise.

THE BIG ISLAND

Alapaki's

Location: Keauhou Shopping Center, Kailua-Kona

Zone: 11, Kona

Phone: (808) 322-2007

Hours: Monday–Saturday, 9 a.m.–6 p.m.; Sunday, 10 a.m.–5 p.m.

Description   A lava rock archway welcomes you into a 900-square-foot shop full of made-in-Hawaii paraphernalia, including ceramics, koa items, *lau hala* works, ukuleles and other Hawaiian instruments, pillows, wall hangings, stationery, and more.

Big Island Candies

Location: 585 Hinano St., Hilo

Zone: 12, Hilo and Volcano

Phone: (808) 935-8890

Hours: Daily, 8:30 a.m.–5 p.m.

Description   Locally made chocolates and candies make nice gifts. The shop also has assorted souvenirs and T-shirts. Large viewing windows separate the store from the factory, letting you see how the confections are made.

Cook's Discoveries

Location: Waimea Center, Waimea (on Hwy. 19)

Zone: 11, Kona

Phone: (808) 885-3633

Hours: Monday–Saturday, 9 a.m.–6 p.m.; Sunday, 10 a.m.–5 p.m.

Description   Set in a historic home in Waimea, this charming shop features a wide array of Hawaiiana merchandise, including aloha wear, books, art, music, language tapes, hats, stationery, Kona coffee, confections, and other gift items. One of the best shops to visit on the Big Island.

Hula Heaven

Location: Kona Inn Shopping Village, Kailua-Kona
Zone: 11, Kona
Phone: (808) 329-7885
Hours: Daily, 9 a.m.–9 p.m.

Description Terrific stop for lovers of vintage Hawaiiana. Shop includes vintage aloha shirts (in mint condition), antique hula dolls, original menu art, and other nostalgic collectibles.

Harbor Gallery

Location: Kawaihae Shopping Center, Kawaihae
Zone: 11, Kona
Phone: (808) 882-1510
Hours: Daily, 11:30 a.m.–8:30 p.m.

Description Classy store featuring a diverse collection of Island art, including koa wood products, sculptures, paintings, ceramics, jewelry, and more.

Sig Zane Designs

Location: 122 Kamehameha Ave., Hilo
Zone: 12, Hilo and Volcano
Phone: (808) 935-7077
Hours: Monday–Saturday, 9 a.m.–5 p.m.

Description Hawaiiana-themed shop that specializes in fabrics with striking Hawaiian designs. Also features dresses, T-shirts, sarongs, and a good selection of Hawaiian music.

KAUAI

Kela's Glass Gallery

Location: 4-1354 Kuhio Hwy., Kapa'a
Zone: 13, Kauai
Phone: (808) 822-4527
Hours: Monday–Friday, 10 a.m.–7 p.m.; Saturday, 10 a.m.–6 p.m.;
  Sunday, 10 a.m.–5 p.m.

Description Unique gallery specializing in fine glass art, including vases and sculptures crafted by more than 75 glass artists from around the world.

Kong Lung Co.

Location: Keneke Rd., Kilauea

Zone: 13, Kauai

Phone: (808) 828-1822

Hours: Daily, 10 a.m.–10 p.m.

Description   Set in a historic stone building, this is one of Kauai's most famous shops. Unique collectibles, housewares, jewelry, apparel, and gift items make Kong Lung a worthwhile stop if you're in the Kilauea area.

Ola's

Location: Hanalei Trader Building, Hanalei

Zone: 13, Kauai

Phone: (808) 826-6937

Hours: Daily, 10 a.m.–9:30 p.m.

Description   Jewelry, glassware, woodcrafts, soaps, and other handcrafted goods fill the shelves at this fun-to-browse shop in Hanalei.

Yellowfish Trading Company

Location: New Hanalei School Center, Hanalei

Zone: 13, Kauai

Phone: (808) 826-1227

Hours: Daily, 10 a.m.–9 p.m.

Description   Features wonderful antiques and knickknacks, from vintage aloha shirts, photographs, and posters to Hawaiian furniture and kitchenwares. A great place to browse.

MOLOKAI

Big Wind Kite Factory

Location: 120 Maunaloa Hwy. (next to the U.S. Post Office)

Zone: 14, Molokai

Phone: (808) 552-2364

Hours: Monday–Saturday, 8:30 a.m.–5 p.m.; Sunday, 10 a.m.–2 p.m.

Description   Kites of all shapes, sizes, and designs are sold here. The shop's friendly owner enjoys providing free kite-flying lessons to everyone (at an adjacent open field) with "no strings attached."

Imports Gift Shop

Location: 82 Ala Malama Ave., Kaunakakai

Zone: 14, Molokai

Phone: (808) 553-5734

Hours: Monday–Saturday, 9 a.m.–6 p.m.; Sunday, 9 a.m.–noon

Description A worthwhile visit for your one-stop shopping needs. Imports Gift Shop offers apparel, shoes, accessories, jewelry, quilts, Hawaiiana gifts, surfwear, and refreshments.

Lanai

Akamai Trading

Location: 408 Eighth St., Lanai City

Zone: 15, Lanai

Phone: (808) 565-6587

Hours: Monday–Friday, 9 a.m.–6 p.m.; Saturday, 9 a.m.–5:30 p.m.; Sunday, 9 a.m.–4:30 p.m.

Description This general merchandise store offers a good selection of souvenir T-shirts, gift items, and locally made treats (such as jams and jellies).

Gifts with Aloha

Location: Seventh St., Lanai City

Zone: 15, Lanai

Phone: (808) 565-6589

Hours: Monday–Saturday, 9:30 a.m.–5:30 p.m.

Description A delightful *kama'aina* shop in Lanai City carrying a wide range of made-in-Hawaii gift items, including casual resort wear, koa wood products, scented candles, homemade jams and jellies, books, hand-quilted pillow covers, and more.

Shopping Centers

Oahu

Ala Moana Shopping Center

Location: On Ala Moana Blvd., just 10 minutes away from Waikiki

Zone: 2, Greater Honolulu

Phone: (808) 955-9517

Web Site: www.alamoana.com

Hours: Monday–Saturday, 9:30 p.m.–9 p.m.; Sunday, 10 a.m.–7 p.m.

Number of Stores and Restaurants: More than 200

Major Stores, Unique Shops: Sears, Neiman Marcus, JC Penney, Liberty House (department store), Shirokiya (Japanese merchandise and market), Christian Dior, Celine Paris, Gucci America, Cartier, Louis Vuitton, Nine West, Waterford Wedgwood, Raphael, Guess, United Colors of Benetton, MCM, Tiffany & Co., Sharper Image, Chanel Boutique, The Museum Company, Longs Drugs, Nicole, The Nature Company, The Disney Store, Warner Bros. Store, Sweet Factory, Software Etc., The Slipper House, See's Candies, Island Logo, Splash Hawaii (swimwear), Hawaiian Island Creations (swimwear, surf goods), Kay-Bee Toys, Jeans Warehouse, Field of Dreams, Tahiti Imports, Jungle Fun (stuffed animals and arcade), Town & Country Surf Shop, Sunglass Hut International.

Comments   Hawaii's largest shopping center, and one of the largest in the United States. Free entertainment is provided daily at the center-stage area.

Aloha Tower Marketplace

Location: 1 Aloha Tower Dr.

Zone: 2, Greater Honolulu

Phone: (808) 528-5700

Web Site: www.alohatower.com

Hours: Monday–Saturday, 9 a.m.–9 p.m.; Sunday, 9 a.m.–6 p.m. Most restaurants are open later.

Number of Stores and Restaurants: About 80

Major Stores, Unique Shops: Martin & MacArthur (woodcrafts, furniture, gifts), Beyond the Beach (swimwear), Bad Ass Coffee Co., Animation Magic (cartoon-themed merchandise), Endangered Species, Don Pablo of Hawaii Smoke Shops, Flags Flying, The Footwear Hut, Hollywood USA (celebrity-themed merchandise), Magnet Five-0, Point of View.

Comments   The centerpiece of this breezy shopping complex is the historic ten-story Aloha Tower, where you can take the elevator to the top and enjoy scenic views of Honolulu.

International Market Place

Location: 2330 Kalakaua Ave.

Zone: 1, Waikiki

Phone: (808) 923-9871

Hours: Daily, 9 a.m.–11 p.m.

Number of Vendors and Eateries: About 150

Comments This outdoor maze of kiosks features a wide variety of merchandise, including jewelry, T-shirts, handbags, touristy souvenirs, and assorted knickknacks. Most of the sellers here are willing to bargain, so don't always settle for the listed price. A food court provides an international menu of eateries.

Kahala Mall

Location: 4211 Waiʻalae Ave.

Zone: 2, Greater Honolulu

Phone: (808) 732-7736

Hours: Monday–Saturday, 10 a.m.–9 p.m.

Number of Stores and Restaurants: More than 90

Major Stores, Unique Shops: Liberty House (department store), Tower Records, Barnes & Noble Booksellers, Liz Claiborne, Sunglass Hut International, Waldenbooks, Paradizzio (gifts), Longs Drugs, Starbucks Coffee, Jeans Warehouse, The Gap, Kay-Bee Toys, Mark's Hallmark Shop, The Compleat Kitchen, Following Sea (gifts, crafts), Town & Country Surf Shop, Sanrio Enterprises (kiddie toys and gifts from Japan), Contempo Casuals, Foot Locker, Banana Republic.

Comments Mostly frequented by Kahala-area residents. Includes an eight-cinema movie theater.

King's Village

Location: 131 Kaʻiulani Ave.

Zone: 1, Waikiki

Phone: (808) 944-6855

Web Site: www.kings-village.com

Hours: Daily, 9 a.m.–11 p.m.

Number of Stores and Restaurants: About 40

Major Stores, Unique Shops: Royal Peddler (collectibles, gifts), Do-Re-Mi Gift Shop, Candle Odysseys (candles, gifts), Cubby's Gifts (toys, gifts), Swim City USA (swimwear), Amy's Corner (aloha wear).

Comments A "changing of the guard" ceremony takes place every evening, 6:15–6:45 p.m. A rifle team drill performance follows the ceremony each Monday, Tuesday, Thursday, and Saturday; and a hula show follows the ceremony every Sunday, Wednesday, and Friday.

Koko Marina Center

Location: 7192 Kalanianaʻole Hwy.

Zone: 2, Greater Honolulu

Phone: (808) 395-4737

Hours: Varies according to the shops. Generally, hours of operation are Monday–Friday, 9 a.m.–8 p.m.; Saturday and Sunday, 9 a.m.–5 p.m.

Number of Stores and Restaurants: 60

Major Stores, Unique Shops: Longs Drugs, Foodland, Waldenbooks, Blockbuster Video, Loco Motion (Island wear), Ben Franklin Stores, Aloha Dive Shop.

Pearlridge Shopping Center

Location: 231 Pearlridge Center in 'Aiea

Zone: 6, Central Oahu

Phone: (808) 488-0981

Hours: Monday–Saturday, 10 a.m.–9 p.m.; Sunday, 10 a.m.–6 p.m.

Number of Stores and Restaurants: More than 170

Major Stores, Unique Shops: Sears, Circuit City, JC Penney, Toys R Us, Waldenbooks, Longs Drugs, Liberty House (department store), Esprit, Shirokiya (Japanese goods and market), Ann Taylor, Gymboree, The Nature Company, The Disney Store, Kay-Bee Toys, The Gap, Town & Country (swimwear, surfing goods), Cosmic Candy, Frederick's of Hollywood, Jeans West, Crazy Shirts, Kramer's (men's apparel), Sam Goody, Mark's Hallmark Shop, Hopaco Stationers, Casual Corner, Ross Stores, Radio Shack, The Slipper House, Kid's Foot Locker, Paradise Optical, Fun Factory (arcade).

Comments   The largest enclosed shopping center in the state. Includes separate 12-cinema and 4-cinema movie theaters. Here, Oahu's only monorail (Skycab) transports shoppers between the center's Uptown and Downtown complexes. (Unless you're burdened with a lot of shopping bags or have a special liking for monorails, you'd do just as well to save the 25¢ fare—the walk between the two complexes takes only three or four minutes.)

Royal Hawaiian Shopping Center

Location: 2201 Kalakaua Ave.

Zone: 1, Waikiki

Phone: (808) 922-0588

Hours: Daily, 9 a.m.–11 p.m.

Number of Stores and Restaurants: About 160

Major Stores, Unique Shops: Chanel, Celine, Fendi, Hermés, Hunting World, Lancel, Esprit, DKNY, Giorgio Armani, Guess, Polo, Calvin Klein, Van Cleef and Arpels, Tommy Hilfiger, ABC Stores (general goods), Harley-Davidson Motorclothes and Collectibles, Hawaiian Heirloom Jewelry Factory, Sportsnut (team sports apparel and collectibles), Royal Magnets, Watumull's (Island wear).

Comments Free entertainment is provided on a regular basis, including performances by the Royal Hawaiian Band each first Thursday and fourth Wednesday of the month (at 1 p.m.). Call for an updated entertainment schedule.

Waikele Center

Location: 94-849 Lumiaina St.

Zone: 5, Leeward Oahu

Phone: (808) 671-6977

Hours: Varies by shop

Number of Stores and Restaurants: About 25

Major Stores, Unique Shops: Borders Books & Music, CompUSA, Office-Max, The Sports Authority, K-Mart, Eagle Hardware & Garden.

Waikele Premium Outlets

Location: 94-790 Lumiaina St.

Zone: 5, Leeward Oahu

Phone: (808) 676-5656

Web Site: www.chelseagca.com

Hours: Monday–Saturday, 9 a.m.–9 p.m.; Sunday, 10 a.m.–6 p.m.

Number of Stores and Restaurants: 50

Major Stores, Unique Shops: Anne Klein, Off 5th–Saks Fifth Avenue, Guess, Bose, Nine West, Kenneth Cole, Donna Karan.

Comments An increasingly popular stop among visitors searching for upscale goods and below-bargain prices. Discounts range from 25% to 65% off regular prices.

Waikiki Town Center

Location: 2301 Kuhio Ave.

Zone: 1, Waikiki

Phone: (808) 922-2724

Hours: Daily, 10 a.m.–10 p.m.

Number of Stores and Restaurants: 40

Major Stores, Unique Shops: ABC Stores (general goods), Beyond the Beach (swimwear), Gloria's Natural Worlds, Candleland, The Leather House, Koko's Jewelry, Mina Gifts, Red Dirt Shirts, Payless Shoe-Source, Makana of Hawaii (gifts).

Comments   Formerly known as Kuhio Mall. A free 50-minute hula show takes place every Monday, Wednesday, Friday, and Saturday at 7 p.m.

Ward Centre

Location: 1200 Ala Moana Blvd.

Zone: 2, Greater Honolulu

Phone: (808) 591-8411

Hours: Monday–Saturday, 10 a.m.–9 p.m.; Sunday, 10 a.m.–5 p.m.

Number of Stores and Restaurants: About 35

Major Stores, Unique Shops: Borders Books & Music, Successories, Brookstone, Franklin Covey, Paper Roses (stationery, greeting cards, gifts), Rainbow Bow-Tique (University of Hawaii–themed apparel and gifts), Tropical Clay (ceramic art and gifts), Honolulu Chocolate Company, Kamehameha Garment Co. (Island wear), Princess Bridal/Size Me Petite (women's apparel), Island Provision Company at Vagabond House (local crafts, gifts).

Comments   The number of high-quality restaurants here—including A Pacific Cafe, Compadres Mexican Bar & Grill, Ryan's Grill, Scoozee's, Keo's Thai Cuisine, Brew Moon, and Bernard's New York Deli—makes this a superb spot for lunch or dinner.

Ward Village Shops

Location: 1116 'Auahi St.

Zone: 2, Greater Honolulu

Phone: (808) 591-8411

Hours: Monday–Saturday, 10 a.m.–9 p.m.; Sunday, 10 a.m.–5 p.m.

Number of Stores and Restaurants: About 10

Major Stores, Unique Shops: Starbucks Coffee, Roxy Quiksilver (swimwear), Crazy Shirts, Kua Aina Sandwich Shop.

Ward Warehouse

Location: 1050 Ala Moana Blvd.

Zone: 2, Greater Honolulu

Phone: (808) 591-8411

Hours: Monday–Saturday, 10 a.m.–9 p.m.; Sunday, 10 a.m.–5 p.m.

Number of Stores and Restaurants: About 75

Major Stores, Unique Shops: Native Books & Beautiful Things, Logos Bookstore, Nohea Gallery (Island artworks and gifts), Animation Magic (cartoon-themed merchandise), Other Realms (comics, games, toys), Bath & Butler (bath and home products), Town & Country Surf Shop, C. June Shoes, Craft Flair (crafts, apparel), Kris Kringle's Den (Christmas ornaments, gifts), Runners Route (athletic shoes, apparel), Thongs 'N Things (slippers, gifts), Novel-T World (T-shirts), The Liquor Collection, Out of Africa (artworks and gifts), Child's Play (toys), Villa Roma (apparel), Yes Perfume, Spencer Gifts.

Comments   The Royal Hawaiian Band performs at noon on the third Wednesday of each month at the amphitheater. Other free shows and exhibits are held periodically throughout the year.

Windward Mall

Location: 46-056 Kamehameha Hwy.

Zone: 3, Windward Oahu

Phone: (808) 235-1143

Hours: Monday–Saturday, 10 a.m.–9 p.m.; Sunday, 10 a.m.–5 p.m.

Number of Stores and Restaurants: About 90

Major Stores, Unique Shops: Sears, Liberty House (department store), Kauila Maxwell Co. (Hawaiian-made arts and apparel), Waldenbooks, Tempo Music, Spencer Gifts, Sam Goody, Software Etc., The Hobby Company, Foot Locker, Cosmic Candy, Sunglass Hut International, Seeds 'N Things, Radio Shack, Kay-Bee Toys, Mark's Hallmark Shop, Hopaco Stationers, The Disney Store, Casual Corner.

Comments   The largest shopping mall in the windward Oahu area.

MAUI

Azeka Place Shopping Center

Location: S. Kihei Rd. in Kihei. Azeka Place I is located on the ocean side of the road, Azeka Place II on the other side.

Zone: 8, South Maui

Phone: (808) 879-5000

Hours: Varies by shop

Number of Stores and Restaurants: About 50

Major Stores, Unique Shops: Crazy Shirts, Sunglass Hut International, Radio Shack, Fox Photo, Ace Hardware, Elephant Walk (gifts), Maui Dive Shop, Nanette's Jewelry.

Ka'ahumanu Center

Location: Off Ka'ahumanu Ave., a few minutes north of the Kahului Airport

Zone: 7, Central Maui

Phone: (808) 877-3369

Hours: Monday–Friday, 9:30 a.m.–9 p.m.; Saturday, 9:30 a.m.–7 p.m.;
Sunday, 10 a.m.–5 p.m.

Number of Stores and Restaurants: About 75

Major Stores, Unique Shops: Sears, Liberty House (department store), JC
Penney, Waldenbooks, Sharper Image, Kay-Bee Toys, Mark's Hallmark
Shop, Island Creation Jewelers, The Disney Store, Ben Franklin
Stores, Ben Bridge Jeweler, The Coffee Store, Foot Locker, Lady Foot
Locker, The Gap, Fox Photo, Blue Ginger (Island wear),

Comments Maui's largest mall. Includes a six-cinema movie theater. A
variety of exhibits and community events (including fairs and farmer's
markets) are held here. Call for an updated schedule.

Kapalua Shops

Location: 1000 Kapalua Dr.

Zone: 9, West Maui

Phone: (808) 669-1390 (Kapalua Designs)

Hours: Monday–Saturday, 9 a.m.–6 p.m.; Sunday, 9 a.m.–5 p.m.

Number of Stores and Restaurants: About 20

Major Stores, Unique Shops: Kapalua Designs (apparel), Kapalua Logo
Shop, Kapalua Kids, Lahaina Galleries (fine arts), Reyn's (Island wear),
McInerny (apparel), Maui Coffee Co.

Lahaina Cannery Mall

Location: 1221 Honoapi'ilani Hwy.

Zone: 9, West Maui

Phone: (808) 661-5304

Hours: Daily, 9:30 a.m.–9 p.m.

Number of Stores and Restaurants: About 40

Major Stores, Unique Shops: Longs Drugs, Hawaiian Island Gems, Foot
Locker, Waldenbooks, The Pearl Factory, Maui Dive Shop, Shades of
Hawaii, Totally Hawaiian Gift Gallery, Fox Photo, Crazy Shirts, Kite
Fantasy, Hats Galore.

Comments Formerly the site of a pineapple cannery. Free *keiki* hula shows
are scheduled each Saturday and Sunday at 1 p.m.; free hula shows offered
each Tuesday and Thursday at 7 p.m.

Lahaina Center

Location: 900 Front St.

Zone: 9, West Maui

Phone: (808) 667-9216

Hours: Varies by shop. Generally, hours are Monday–Saturday, 9 a.m.–10 p.m., and Sunday, 9 a.m.–6 p.m.

Number of Stores and Restaurants: 30

Major Stores, Unique Shops: Hilo Hattie (alohawear, gifts), ABC Stores (general goods), Banana Republic, Maui Tees Outlet (T-shirts), Local Motion (swimwear, T-shirts), Royal Hawaiian Heritage Jewelry, Wet Seal, Maui Kids & Co., Maui Brews.

Comments Free *keiki* hula shows are held each Wednesday and Friday, 2 and 6 p.m.

Maui Mall

Location: 70 E. Ka'ahumanu Ave.

Zone: 7, Central Maui

Phone: (808) 877-7559

Hours: Monday–Thursday, 9 a.m.–6 p.m.; Friday, 9 a.m.–9 p.m.; Saturday, 9 a.m.–5:30 p.m.; Sunday, 10 a.m.–4 p.m.

Number of Stores and Restaurants: About 30

Major Stores, Unique Shops: Longs Drugs, Jeans Factory, Tempo Music, Maui Natural Foods, Star Market, Crystal Dreams (collectibles, jewelry, precious stones, gifts), Imperial Jewelers.

Maui Marketplace

Location: 270 Dairy Rd.

Zone: 7, Central Maui

Phone: (808) 873-0400

Hours: Varies by shop

Number of Stores and Restaurants: About 15

Major Stores, Unique Shops: Borders Books and Music, Eagle Hardware and Garden, Nine West Outlet, OfficeMax, Samsonite Company Store, Sports Authority, Starbucks Coffee, Bugle Boy, Maui Jewelry Connection, Hawaiian Island Creations (swimwear, surf goods).

Whalers Village

Location: 2435 Ka'anapali Pkwy.

Zone: 9, West Maui

Phone: (808) 661-4567

Web Site: www.whalersvillage.com

Hours: Daily, 9:30 a.m.-10 p.m.

Number of Stores and Restaurants: 60

Major Stores, Unique Shops: Chanel Boutique, Hunting World, Gucci, Versace, Tiffany & Co., Christian Dior, Louis Vuitton, Lahaina Scrimshaw, Martin & MacArthur (woodcrafts, furniture and gifts), The Gecko Store (gecko-themed apparel and gifts), Ka Honu Gift Shop, Dolphin Galleries, Pearl Factory, Blue Ginger Designs (Island wear), Cinnamon Girl (women's apparel), Reyns (Island wear), ABC Store (general goods).

Comments Free hula performances are scheduled every Monday, Wednesday, Friday, and Saturday at 7 p.m.

Wharf Cinema Center

Location: 658 Front St.

Zone: 9, West Maui

Phone: (808) 661-8748

Hours: Daily, 9 a.m.–9:30 p.m.

Number of Stores and Restaurants: 50

Major Stores, Unique Shops: Crazy Shirts, Island Coins & Stamps, Magnet Madness, T-Shirt Factory, Tropical Artware Maui, Island Swimwear, Fun Factory (arcade).

Comments Includes a three-cinema movie theater.

THE BIG ISLAND

Keauhou Shopping Center

Location: 78-6831 Ali'i Dr.

Zone: 11, Kona

Phone: (808) 332-3000

Hours: Monday–Saturday, 9:30 a.m.–6 p.m.; Sunday, 10 a.m.–5 p.m.

Number of Stores and Restaurants: Over 40

Major Stores, Unique Shops: KTA Superstores (supermarket), Longs Drugs, Ben Franklin Stores, Ace Hardware, Bad Ass Coffee Co., Fine Arts International at Keauhou, Rocky's Pizza & BBQ.

Comments Includes a six-cinema theater. Craft demonstrations and "talk story" sessions are held each Friday from 10 a.m. to 2 p.m. in the central courtyard.

Kings' Shops

Location: Waikoloa Beach Resort

Zone: 11, Kona

Phone: (808) 886-8811

Hours: Daily, 9:30 a.m.–9:30 p.m.

Number of Stores and Restaurants: About 40

Major Stores, Unique Shops: Whalers General Store, Tiffany & Co., Sgt. Leisure, Wyland Galleries, Crazy Shirts, Endangered Species, Island Shells (gifts), Sunglass Hut, Hawaiian Island Gems.

Prince Kuhio Plaza

Location: 111 E. Puainako St. (off Hwy. 11, just south of the Hilo Airport)

Zone: 12, Hilo and Volcano

Phone: (808) 959-3555

Hours: Monday–Friday, 9:30 a.m.–9 p.m.; Saturday, 9:30 a.m.–7 p.m.; Sunday, 10 a.m.–6 p.m.

Number of Stores and Restaurants: Over 75

Major Stores, Unique Shops: Sears, Liberty House (department store), JC Penney, Hilo Hattie's (aloha wear, gifts), Waldenbooks, Blockbuster Video, Radio Shack, Longs Drugs, Software Etc., Big Island Surf Co., Tempo Music, Spencer Gifts, Sunglass Hut, Champs.

Comments The largest enclosed shopping center on the Big Island. Includes a two-cinema movie theater.

KAUAI

Ching Young Village

Location: 5300 Ka Haku Rd.

Zone: 13, Kauai

Phone: (808) 826-7222

Hours: Varies by shop. Generally, hours are about 9 a.m.–7 p.m. daily.

Number of Stores and Restaurants: 30

Major Stores, Unique Shops: Hanalei Natural Foods, Hanalei Video & Music, Kauaian Eyes, Artists Gallery of Kauai.

Coconut Marketplace

Location: 4-484 Kuhio Hwy.

Zone: 13, Kauai

Phone: (808) 822-3641

Hours: Monday–Saturday, 9 a.m.–9 p.m.; Sunday, 10 a.m.–6 p.m.

Number of Stores and Restaurants: Over 70

Major Stores, Unique Shops: Around the World in 80 Days (collectibles, gifts), Elephant Walk (gifts), Paradise Music, Island Jewels, Kini's Island Christmas, Products of Hawaii Too, Kauai Casuals (Island wear), Island Surf Shop (swimwear), The Gecko Store (Island wear), Ship Store Galleries, Tropic Casuals (Island wear).

Comments Kauai's largest shopping center. Includes a two-cinema movie theater. Free entertainment (including hula performances) daily at 5 p.m.

Kauai Village

Location: 4-831 Kuhio Hwy.

Zone: 13, Kauai

Phone: (808) 822-4904

Hours: Monday, 10 a.m.–8 p.m.; Tuesday–Saturday, 10 a.m.–9 p.m.; Sunday, 10 a.m.–6 p.m.

Number of Stores and Restaurants: 25

Major Stores, Unique Shops: Safeway, Longs Drugs, Waldenbooks, Tempo Music, Wyland Galleries, Kahn Galleries, ABC Store (general goods), Crazy Shirts, TCBY Treats, A Pacific Cafe.

Comments Also found here is the Kauai Heritage Center of Hawaiian Culture & the Arts (open Monday–Friday, 10 a.m.–6 p.m.; Saturday, 10 a.m.–5 p.m.), where you can view ancient Hawaiian artifacts and learn about the Island culture.

Kukui Grove Center

Location: 3-2600 Kaumuali'i Hwy.

Zone: 13, Kauai

Phone: (808) 245-7784

Hours: Monday–Thursday, 9:30 a.m.–5:30 p.m.; Friday, 9:30 a.m.–9 p.m.; Saturday, 9:30 a.m.–5:30 p.m.; Sunday, 10 a.m.–5 p.m.

Number of Stores and Restaurants: About 50

Major Stores, Unique Shops: Sears, Gifts of Kauai, Jeans Warehouse, Foot Locker, General Nutrition Center, Zales Jewelers, Software Etc., Hawaiian Island Creations (swimwear, surf goods, T-shirts).

Po'ipu Shopping Village

Location: 2360 Kiahuna Plantation Dr.

Zone: 13, Kauai

Phone: (808) 742-2831

Hours: Monday–Saturday, 10 a.m.–9 p.m.; Sunday, 10 a.m.–6 p.m.

Number of Stores and Restaurants: About 20

Major Stores, Unique Shops: Crazy Shirts, Whaler's General Store, Wyland Galleries, Honolua Surf Co. (swimwear, T-shirts), Elephant Walk (gifts), Sandals Etc., Sunglass Hut, Kauai Bath & Body, Hale Mana Clothing & Gifts, Tropical Shirts.

Comments Free 45-minute Polynesian hula shows are offered each Monday and Thursday at 5 p.m. Strolling musicians perform Hawaiian music each Friday and Saturday evening beginning at 7 p.m.

Swap Meets and Flea Markets

If time allows, bargain hunters on Oahu should check out one of the island's two major swap meets. Both the Aloha Flea Market and the Kam Super Swap Meet are open for business each Wednesday, Saturday, and Sunday (and some holidays) and offer an astounding variety of new and used merchandise, fresh produce, plants, and even fresh fish. Located on the grounds of Aloha Stadium, the Aloha Flea Market offers a bit more in terms of visitor-related products and gift items than the Swap Meet. The sun can be relentless at both locations, especially during the summer, so a visor, sunglasses, casual wear, and comfortable walking shoes are highly recommended.

Aloha Flea Market

Location: Aloha Stadium grounds

Phone: (808) 732-9611 or (808) 486-1529

Hours: Wednesday, Saturday, and Sunday, 6 a.m.–3 p.m.

Admission: 50¢ per person. Children under age 12 are admitted free of charge.

Kam Super Swap Meet

Location: 98-850 Moanalua Rd., formerly the site of the Kam Drive-In, next to Pearlridge Shopping Center

Phone: (808) 483-5933

Hours: From 5 a.m. on

Admission: 25¢ per person. Children under age 12 are admitted free of charge.

Part Nine

Sight-Seeing and Tours

Sight-Seeing Adventures

Whichever island you're on, you're certain to spend some time taking in the sights. Whether by land, sea, or air, the beauty of the Hawaiian Islands presents itself to you in many ways.

WALKING TOURS

While walking may not seem like much, it can make a nice change from slurping Mai Tais and slumbering on the beach all day. In fact, a brisk walk three or more times a week is said to increase cardiorespiratory endurance. In Hawaii, there are several great walking tours that will help you keep fit as well as enlighten you on the Islands' proud history.

Sponsored by the Chinese Chamber of Commerce (call (808) 533-3181), the "Chinatown Walk-A-Tour" in downtown Honolulu takes visitors on a two-hour tour of Chinatown each Tuesday at 9:30 a.m. Stops include an old Chinese meeting hall (the Chee Kung Tong Society), various eateries and open markets, herb shops, lei stands, and other interesting spots. The guide shares the history of the area and makes a few lunch recommendations. The cost is $5 per person. Meet at the Chamber of Commerce office at 42 North King Street.

Every Thursday from 9:30 a.m. to 12:30 p.m. the Mission Houses Museum hosts a walking tour of downtown Honolulu. Included are visits to the museum, Kawaiaha'o Church, the Kamehameha Statue, 'Iolani Palace, Washington Place (the Governor's Mansion), and the State Capitol. Admission is $8 for adults, $7 for senior citizens and military personnel, $6 for college students, and $4 for children ages 4–12. (Because it's a long walk, the tour is not recommended for young children.) Call (808) 531-0481.

A special note: By far the best walking tours in Hawaii were put on by Honolulu TimeWalks, featuring storyteller and historian Glen Grant. TimeWalks included the popular "Ghosts of Honolulu" tours as well as programs spotlighting Hawaii's monarchy and wartime eras. Unfortunately, Grant has discontinued his walking tours to concentrate on "The Grant Files," his popular radio program on KCCN. However, we're told that it's possible that these tours may start up again. So it's worth a try to call the TimeWalks office at (808) 943-0371. If you find that the tours have returned, by all means make sure you attend one. They're *that* good.

Exploring Downtown Honolulu

Quite frankly, while there are many different walking tours in the Islands (particularly on Oahu), only one falls under the "must-do" category: a self-guided stroll through downtown Honolulu. No other walking itinerary provides the amount of history, color, and unique insights *all* within a two-block radius.

Before embarking on this tour, here's what you should know:

What   Downtown Honolulu tour (self-guided).

Who Should Go   Recommended for all visitors except for families with children under the age of five (that is the minimum age requirement for visitors to the 'Iolani Palace, the tour's centerpiece attraction).

Best Time to Go   Tuesday–Friday. Start out in the morning, reaching downtown Honolulu by 9:30 a.m. Go between the third Wednesday in January and the end of April if you want to sit in on a state legislature session.

How Much Time to Allow   About half a day.

Best Way to Get There   By bus. From Waikiki, catch the #2 or #13 bus on Kuhio Avenue and get off at Punchbowl Street. (Play it safe and ask the bus driver to let you know where you should deboard.) You can drive into town, but parking is scarce (metered parking is available on Punchbowl) and you'll have to worry about feeding the meter every two hours.

How Much Walking Is Involved   While the sites on this tour are all within walking distance of each other, you will cover a large two-block territory. You might want to stretch your legs before starting the walk. Since you'll be making periodic stops, however, you won't have to worry about walking continuously.

What to Wear and Bring   Casual wear is recommended, and comfortable, covered shoes are a must. Bring sunscreen to protect you from the

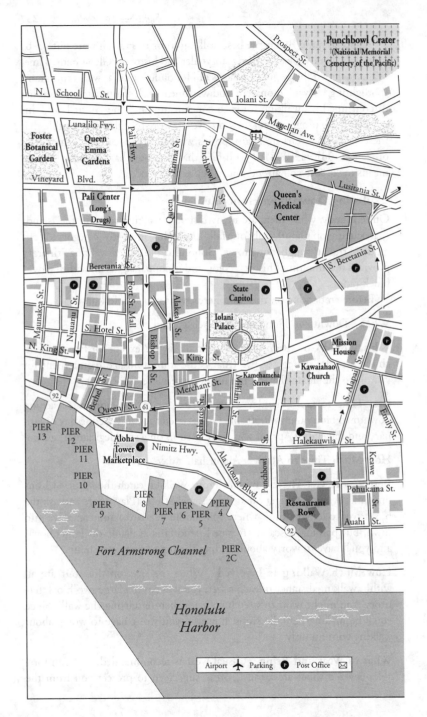

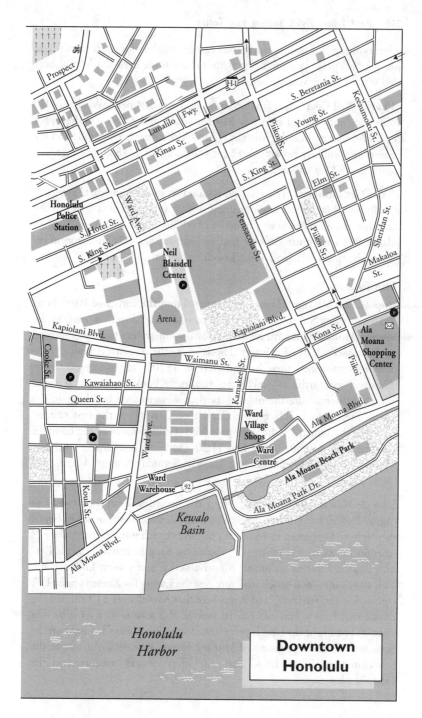

Downtown Honolulu

afternoon sun. Of course, bring your camera and/or video recorder. If you bring a backpack, you might want to include some light snacks and bottled water to keep you refreshed.

What It Will Cost   Bus fare is $1 per adult and 50¢ per child age 6–18. Admission into 'Iolani Palace is $10 for adults and $3 for children ages 5–12. Admission into the Mission Houses Museum is $6 for adults; $5 for seniors and military personnel; $3 for youths ages 13–18 and college students; and $2 for children ages 4–12.

If You Get Hungry   There are no restaurants in the immediate area, but a walk into downtown's main business district (past Richards Street in the *'ewa* direction) leads you to a bonanza of ethnic eateries. Try Yong Sing on Alakea Street for great Chinese fare, or head farther *'ewa* and drop in on one of the many fast-food and take-out restaurants.

The Tour

Stop 1: The Mission Houses Museum   From the corner of Punchbowl and South King Streets, walk in the Diamond Head direction (east) to the Mission Houses Museum, a complex of missionary-era buildings located on the *makai* side of King Street. This is where the very first American missionaries established their headquarters in 1820. The structures, which house original artifacts—including furniture, books, quilts, and other household items—are the oldest surviving Western-style buildings in the state. One of the buildings, the Coral House, is where the first printed works in the North Pacific were produced. Guided tours of the complex are scheduled at 9:30, 10:30, and 11:30 a.m., and 1, 2, and 3 p.m. The Mission Houses Museum is open Tuesday–Saturday, 9 a.m.–4 p.m. Call (808) 531-0481.

Stop 2: Kawaiaha'o Church   From the museum, head *'ewa* (west) to nearby Kawaiaha'o Church, known by many as the "Westminster Abbey of the Pacific." Dedicated in 1842, this historic church was a favorite place of worship for many Hawaiian *ali'i,* including King Lunalilo, Princess Bernice Pauahi, Princess Ka'iulani, King Kalakaua, and Queen Lili'uokalani. This handsome coral-block structure was the setting for Kamehameha IV's coronation and wedding, and it was here that Kamehameha III uttered the phrase that is now Hawaii's official motto: *"Ua mau ke ea o ka 'aina i ka pono"* ("The life of the land is perpetuated in righteousness"). Listed on the State and National Registers of Historic Places, Kawaiaha'o is one of the few churches left in Hawaii that still offers services conducted in the Hawaiian language.

Stop 3: The King Kamehameha Statue   Cross Punchbowl Street and walk on King Street until you reach the King Kamehameha Statue, one of Hawaii's most photographed attractions. The proud king is shown holding a spear in his left hand, while his right arm is outstretched in a welcoming gesture. Each June on King Kamehameha Day, the statue is draped with beautiful and colorful floral leis, some as long as 18 feet.

Stop 4: 'Iolani Palace   Walk *'ewa* to Mililani Street, then cross King Street to the 'Iolani Palace, the only royal palace on American soil. Built in 1882 in a style called American Florentine, this stately palace was the official residence of the Hawaiian kingdom's last two monarchs, King Kalakaua and Queen Lili'uokalani. It was also here that Lili'uokalani surrendered her throne under hostile pressure from American businessmen. Guided tours last about 45 minutes and are scheduled at 15-minute intervals. Pick up your tickets at 'Iolani Barracks, located on the palace grounds. The palace is open Tuesday–Saturday, 9 a.m.–2:15 p.m. Advance reservations strongly recommended. Call (808) 522-0832.

Stop 5: State Capitol Building   Behind the palace is the State Capitol Building, whose unique design pays respect to the Islands' volcanic and oceanic origins. This is the home of Hawaii's state legislature, where the political battles are just slightly less bloody than the wars of ancient Hawaii. On the *makai* side of the building is a bronze statue of Queen Lili'uokalani, Hawaii's last royal monarch. On the *mauka* side is a statue paying tribute to Father Damien, the priest who dedicated his life to ministering to Hansen's disease patients on the island of Molokai.

Stop 6: Hawaii State Library   Return to the palace and walk in the Diamond Head direction, passing by the State Archives building. The next big building you see is the Hawaii State Library. While not considered a visitors attraction, this is the state's main (and largest) library. Its "Hawaii & Pacific" section offers the state's largest collection of Hawaii-related books, periodicals, and documents. Take a pass on this if you're pressed for time. Library hours vary, but it usually opens at 9 a.m. on weekdays. Call (808) 586-3500.

Stop 7: Honolulu Hale   From the library, cross Punchbowl Street until you reach Honolulu Hale, otherwise known as City Hall. This California-Spanish-style structure, built in 1927, is especially worth a visit during the Christmas season, when the grounds are a festive wonderland of holiday-themed adornments.

From Honolulu Hale, cross South King Street and then Punchbowl to the bus stop nearest the main intersection. Catch the #2 or #13 bus back to Waikiki. (For more information on bus routes, call (808) 848-5555.)

DINNER CRUISES

For those who want to enjoy views *from* the sea, Hawaii offers several quality nightly dinner cruises, daily sunset sails, and other cruise offerings. The
scenery, especially at sunset, is mesmerizing, and we found that most of the
cruises here provide state-of-the-art facilities as well as cheerful service. On
Oahu, for example, Royal Hawaiian Cruises (call (808) 848-6360) has the
141-foot *Navatek I,* a high-tech vessel that utilizes unique SWATH (Small
Waterplane Area Twin Hull) technology to minimize the risk of motion
sickness; the ship glides above the ocean's surface while twin submarine-
like hulls ride below the waves. Rates are $70–125 for adults and $50–75
for children ages 2–11.

Also on Oahu is Paradise Cruises (call (808) 983-7827), which operates
the *Star of Honolulu,* a 232-foot, four-deck ship that offers daily cruises during the day and night. The dinner cruises are $75–199 per adult and
$36–55 per child age 3–11.

Both the *Navatek* and *Star of Honolulu* set sail from Honolulu Harbor
and take you to waters off Honolulu and Waikiki.

Cruises on the Neighbor Islands include the *Navatek II* (call (808) 873-
3475) and Windjammer Cruises (call (808) 661-8600) on Maui; Captain
Beans Cruises (call (808) 329-2955) and Body Glove Cruises (call (808)
326-7122) on the Big Island; and Captain Andy's (call (808) 335-6833)
and Holoholo Charters (call (808) 246-4656) on Kauai. Call the cruise
operators for a complete schedule of available sails, which may range from
morning excursions and whale-watching tours to sunset cruises.

Lunch and sunset meals are usually served buffet-style, with assorted
meats, starches, pasta, garden salads, fruits, and desserts. Evening cruises are
typically sit-down affairs, with a menu that includes seafood specialties
(such as Maine lobster), beef tenderloin or filet steaks, steamed rice or baked
potato, fresh garden salad, bread rolls, and dessert.

At Wailua State Park on Kauai, take a cruise of a different nature: a
leisurely boat ride along the Wailua River to the famous Fern Grotto. Smith's
Tropical Paradise offers the 90-minute cruises daily, 9 a.m.–3:30 p.m., with
rides departing every half-hour except at noon. Admission is $15.62 for
adults and $7.81 for children under age 12. Call (808) 821-6892.

HELICOPTER TOURS

Helicopter rides aren't for everyone: We've seen several gung-ho adventurers return to terra firma and immediately need to find a place to lie down.
But for those for whom motion sickness is never a problem, by all means
we recommend taking to the air aboard a chopper, which can provide the
best possible views of Hawaii.

Helicopter Operators

Oahu
Magnum Helicopters (808) 833-1133
Makani Kai Helicopters (808) 834-5813

Maui
Alex Air Helicopters (808) 877-4354
Blue Hawaiian Helicopters (808) 871-8844
Hawaii Helicopters (808) 877-3900
Sunshine Helicopters (808) 871-0722

The Big Island
Blue Hawaiian Helicopters (808) 961-5600
Hawaii Helicopters (808) 934-8438 in Hilo; (808) 329-4700
  in Kona
Mauna Kea Helicopters (808) 885-6400
Safari Helicopters (808) 969-1259

Kauai
Air-1 Inter-Island Helicopters (808) 335-5009
Bali Hai Helicopter Tours (808) 335-3166
Jack Harter Helicopters (808) 245-3774
Safari Helicopters (808) 246-0136

Schedule your tour early in your vacation; this way, if the weather doesn't cooperate on the day of your tour, you'll have an opportunity to reschedule before you depart. Try to book your reservations at least a few days in advance, as tours are often booked if you wait until the last minute (this is especially true during the Christmas holidays, Easter weekend, and spring break). You can secure your reservations with a major credit card.

Prices generally are $75 per person for a 20-minute flight, $125 for a 45-minute flight, and about $150–200 for a full-hour adventure. There are no age restrictions, but passengers weighing over 250 pounds are assessed an additional charge (usually 50%) as an extra seat will be blocked off for added comfort. Only a few operators offer transportation to and from your hotel.

This is a cost-intensive activity that should inspire some digging around on your part. Call the different operators, get a feel for each, and find the one that you're most comfortable with. "It's important that you talk directly to each operator," offered one tour company representative. "Not everyone's the same."

Keep in mind that passengers are weighed before the tour, and seats are assigned based on body weight (in order to maximize the balance of the helicopter). Generally, one of every two passengers is assigned a direct window seat. Most tours, however, use the new A-Star helicopters, which provide better viewing conditions than previous helicopters because they lack the usual partitions or bulkheads that can obstruct your view. Accommodating up to six passengers, the A-Star is comfortable and fully enclosed and has air-conditioning.

And views, of course, are what these tours are all about. Helicopter tours provide dramatic panoramas of such renowned locales as Pearl Harbor, Punchbowl, and Diamond Head on Oahu; Kilauea Volcano on the Big Island; Haleakala and the West Maui Mountains on Maui; and the rugged Na Pali coastline on Kauai. You'll get to see some spectacular hidden spots—including waterfalls, black-sand beaches, lava fields, and cinder cones—that are inaccessible by car, boat, or foot.

Each tour is fully narrated by the pilot, adding to the CD music humming in your specially equipped headset. Many pilots are certified tour guides, providing insights on each area's history, geology, and wildlife, and admirably adding an educational and cultural facet to the tour.

The pilot also operates a multicamera system within the helicopter, capturing the scenery (and sometimes you!) on tape. The video is then offered to you at the end of your journey. The cost is usually about $20.

Dress for comfort. If you plan to take photos during your tour, it's advisable to avoid wearing white attire, which can reflect off the glass windows.

Some additional words about motion sickness: It's said that nine out of every ten people experience motion sickness at one time or another in their lives. There are a number of products that may help prevent motion sickness, including Dramamine. Some people use a special patch placed behind one ear (consult your doctor before using one, as side effects are possible). Still another option is an elastic wristband that supposedly stimulates an acupuncture point on your wrist. Ginger is said to have a positive effect against motion sickness; try drinking ginger ale or snacking on ginger candy a half-hour before the flight.

MOLOKAI MULE RIDE

In today's era of high-tech attractions and show biz wizardry, it's heartwarming to see that this rugged mule ride remains a favorite among Island visitors. The Molokai Mule Ride to Kalaupapa features sure-footed mules carrying their riders down a 26-switchback trail. The 90-minute excursion includes breathtaking views of Molokai's northern coast. Kalaupapa is the historic settlement where Father Damien de Veuster ministered to patients with Hansen's disease (leprosy) from 1873 to 1889. Offered daily except for Sunday, this half-day adventure starts with the 8 a.m. check-in. The $155-per-person cost includes the tour, a picnic lunch, riding certificates, membership in the Mule Skinners of Hawaii Club, a bumper sticker, and a postcard. Call (808) 567-6088 or check out their Web site at www.-muleride.com.

SUBMARINE RIDES

The splendor of the Islands isn't limited to Hawaii's majestic mountains and towering sea cliffs, or evergreen valleys and postcard-like beaches. There is much beauty to be discovered under the ocean's surface, and you won't even have to get wet!

With Atlantis Submarines, you can explore coral reefs and get up-close views of yellow tangs, parrot fish, moray eels, and many other types of colorful sea life. Atlantis has submarine operations on three islands. On Oahu, the adventure begins at Waikiki Beach at the Hilton Hawaiian Village, where you board a shuttle boat to one of three subs: two are 48-passenger vessels, while the third can accommodate 64 guests. The undersea rides are fully narrated and air-conditioned and take you to coral reefs and two sunken ships. On Maui, shuttle boats depart from Lahaina and transport you to a 48-passenger sub that explores the ocean channel between Maui and Lanai. And in Kona on the Big Island, Atlantis's 48-passenger sub provides a memorable exploration of an 18,000-year-old, 25-acre natural coral reef.

Rates are $59–99 for adults and $39 for children. For more information, call (808) 973-9811 (Oahu), (808) 667-2224 (Maui), or (808) 329-6626 (Big Island). Or call toll-free, (800) 548-6262.

OTHER TOURING SUGGESTIONS

On Oahu, hop on the bus to Pearl Harbor and enjoy a leisurely tour of a trio of historic attractions: the *Arizona* Memorial, *Battleship Missouri,* and USS *Bowfin* Submarine Museum and Park. Or take an all-day drive around the island, stopping at whichever sites strike your fancy.

Several points of interest in Lahaina on Maui might merit a walking excursion, including the Baldwin Home Museum, Wo Hing Temple Museum, and *Brig Carthaginian.* To call it a "must" tour would be a stretch, however, and it's unlikely these attractions will have any substantial appeal for youngsters. But by all means, enjoy a leisurely stroll along bustling Front Street in Lahaina. For driving experiences, we enjoyed cruising the winding roads of upcountry Maui, taking in scenic sights and stopping at Kula Botanical Garden, a five-acre garden filled with some 1,700 varieties of tropical plants.

The Big Island is so vast, with most attractions spread far apart from each other, that even driving tours can be an exhaustive undertaking. In Hilo, a fun-for-the-family option is visiting a trio of attractions—Nani Mau Gardens, Mauna Loa (Macadamia Nuts) Visitors Center, and Pana'ewa Rainforest Zoo—that are located within minutes of each other on Highway 11. There is a lot to see on the Kona side of the island, but everything's pretty spread out. See Part Ten, "Hawaii's Attractions," for detailed information on what's available.

You can cover a lot of ground on Kauai in a day. If you're in the Po'ipu area, we suggest spending one day driving north and taking in the sights and attractions in Lihu'e, Wailua, Kapa'a, Kilauea, Hanalei, and Princeville. The next day, head in the opposite direction, stopping in Hanapepe before making your way to Waimea Canyon and Koke'e State Park. Again, most attractions are fairly spread out on the island.

TOUR COMPANIES

Looking for more assistance in planning your Hawaiian trip? One convenient option is to set up a tour through one of several local tour companies. Each offers an extensive menu of sight-seeing excursions. On Oahu, for example, you can book a half-day tour of downtown Honolulu and Pearl Harbor, take a scenic trip of windward Oahu, or even enjoy a complete circle-island itinerary. Here's a sampling of the tour companies available in the Aloha State.

Land Tours

Alpha Limousines
Oahu
(808) 955-8898
www.hawaii-limo.com

E Noa Tours
Oahu
(808) 591-2561; (800) 824-8804
www.enoa.com

Hawaii Movie Tours
Kauai
(808) 822-1192; (800) 628-8432
www.hawaiimovietour. com

Polynesian Adventure Tours
Oahu, Maui, Big Island, Kauai
(808) 833-3000 (Oahu); (808)
877-4242 (Maui); (808) 329-8008
(Big Island); (808) 246-0122
(Kauai); (800) 622-3011 (toll-free)
www.polyad.com

Roberts Hawaii
Oahu, Maui, Big Island, Kauai
(808) 523-7750 (Oahu); (808)
871-6226 (Maui); (808) 245-9101
(Kauai); (800) 767-7751 (toll-free)
www.roberts-hawaii.com

Aerial Tours

Above it All—Adventures in
Paradise
Maui
(808) 969-2000; (877) 377-7717
www.fly-hawaii.com/above/

Bali Hai Helicopter Tours
Kauai
(808) 335-3166; (800) 325-8687
www.balihai-helitour.com

Jack Harter Helicopters
Kauai
(808) 245-3774; (888) 245-2001
www.helicopters-kauai.com

Original Glider Rides
Oahu
(808) 677-3404
www.poi.net/~mrbill/glider.html

Safari Helicopters
Big Island and Kauai
(808) 329-4655 (Kona);
(808) 969-1259 (Hilo);
(808) 246-0136 (Kauai);
(800) 326-3356 (toll-free)
www.safariair.com

Soar Hawaii Sailplanes
Oahu
(808) 637-3147
www.soarhawaii.com

Will Squyres Helicopter Tours
Kauai
(808) 245-8881; (888) 245-4354
www.helicopters-hawaii.com

Sea Tours
American Hawaii Cruises
Oahu, Maui, Big Island, Kauai
(808) 538-7601; (800) 513-5022
www.cruisehawaii.com

Body Glove Cruises
Big Island
(808) 326-7122; (800) 551-8911
www.bodyglovehawaii.com

Captain Beans' Cruises
Big Island
(808) 329-2955; (800) 831-5541
www.roberts-hawaii.com/BigIsle-
CapBean.htm

Captain Zodiac
Big Island and Kauai
(808) 329-3199 (Big Island);
(808) 826-9371 (Kauai)
www.planet-hawaii.com/zodiac

Holoholo Charters
Kauai
(808) 335-0815
www.holoholo-charters.com

Paradise Cruises
Oahu
(808) 983-7827;
(800) 334-6191
www.paradisecruises.com

Royal Hawaiian Cruises
Oahu
(808) 848-6360; (800) 852-4183
www.royalhawaiiancruises.com

Trilogy Sailing Excursions
Maui
(808) 661-4743; (888) 628-4800
www.roberts-hawaii.com

Windjammer Cruises Maui
Maui
(808) 661-8600; (800) 732-4852
www.maui.net/~wjcm

Ten "Must" Things to Do in Hawaii

1. Hit the Beach   When most people think of Hawaii, a pristine beach is usually the first thing that comes to mind. Thus, getting in some beach time is practically mandatory if you're visiting the Islands, even if you don't or can't swim. (Amazingly, one survey we've seen reports that 70% of the locals in Hawaii can't swim!) Bask under the tropical sun and catch a few rays, slumber to the rolling waves that kiss the shoreline, read a book, build a sand castle, or simply take in the sights. Of the many reasons to visit Hawaii, this ranks at the top of the list.

2. Learn Hawaiian History   It's true that no matter where you travel in the United States, each place has its own unique history. But Hawaii, with its royal heritage, definitely stands out from every other state. Make it a point to gain some insights on Hawaiian history. Visit a museum (the Bishop Museum on Oahu is the biggest and best), sign up for a historical walking tour, pick up any of a number of excellent books, or just ask a knowledgeable *kama'aina*. The education you gain will make your experience here much more meaningful and memorable.

3. Acquaint Yourself with Hawaiian Culture   Visiting Hawaii and not immersing yourself in the local culture is like going to the *Rocky Horror Picture Show* and just sitting still the entire time: If you don't participate, you're definitely missing out on something! Dance a few hula steps. String a flower lei. Play a Hawaiian game. Strum a ukulele. These are just some of the cultural activities you can learn here, and everyone from Junior to Grandma is sure to have fun along the way. Many such activities are offered at your hotel (ask your concierge), and many more are available at major shopping malls, luaus, community fairs, and visitor-oriented attractions.

4. Enjoy a Plate Lunch   Okay, it won't kill you if you resist trying a local-style plate lunch (and considering the calories and fat a typical plate contains, it may kill you if you don't), but we happen to subscribe to the "When in Rome . . ." philosophy. A plate lunch usually consists of two scoops of white rice, one scoop of macaroni salad, and a meat item of your choice, including hamburger steak, roast pork, chicken *katsu* (batter-fried chicken), mushroom chicken, spare ribs, beef stew, and curry stew. (If you're particularly hungry, go for the mixed plate, which lets you choose two meat items!) The plate lunch originated during Hawaii's plantation era, when laborers of different ethnicities would share their specialty dishes with each other. Today, you'll find plate-lunch eateries at most shopping malls, or stop at one of several lunch wagons in the downtown Honolulu area of Oahu.

5. Catch a Sunset We realize we've used an exhaustive number of adjectives to describe Hawaiian sunsets, but it's best for you to see one for yourself. Even the locals don't take their sunsets for granted. Young honeymooners and romantics of all ages are especially advised to take a sunset stroll along the beach, set against a sky bathed in gold, orange, red, and lavender. There are no bad sunsets in Hawaii, but weather conditions do create better ones, especially along the Kohala Coast on the Big Island, where volcanic particles in the air often help form especially brilliant color schemes.

6. "Talk Story" with a Kamaʻaina The one book you would not want to write after your Hawaiian experience is *Everything I Know about Hawaii I Learned from My Tour Guide.* We're not knocking tour guides, but we think it's a good idea to strike up a conversation with a local every now and then. What better way to get a full flavor of the Islands? One of the best places to do this is at a major shopping center, where there is usually a nice mix of locals and visitors. More often than not, you'll find that the aloha spirit is alive and well in Hawaii, as many residents are more than happy to share their knowledge of their Island home, including providing tips on favorite restaurants, stores, shows, and more.

7. Visit the Attractions Every Hawaii itinerary should include at least a few visitor attractions. They provide the full spectrum of Island experiences and range from the pricey (such as the Polynesian Cultural Center on Oahu) to the completely free (including the *Arizona* Memorial on Oahu and Panaʻewa Rainforest Zoo on the Big Island). For detailed information on Hawaii's attractions, see Part Ten.

8. Attend a Luau The common perception is, "What's a Hawaiian vacation without a luau?" A luau is one of the most memorable experiences you can have in the Islands. A high-quality luau provides you an opportunity to learn about the Hawaiian culture, get your fill (and then some!) of local foods, and be entertained by a lively Polynesian revue. Some hotels offer luaus of their own, particularly the larger ones on the Neighbor Islands. The most popular luaus on Oahu include Paradise Cove (call (808) 842-5911) and Germaine's (call (808) 941-3338).

9. Pick Up a Souvenir Even though there are hundreds of shopping adventures available in Hawaii, you could probably get by without a full-blown shopping spree. But make sure you buy at least a few souvenirs— tacky or otherwise—to bestow on friends and relatives. Favorite items include T-shirts, caps, keychains, postcards, snow globes, calendars, playing cards, and picture frames. Other goodies to bring home include tasty local treats like chocolate-covered macadamia nuts, plain macadamia nuts, taro chips, cracked seeds, sweetbread, mochi (a Japanese confection), and, of course, pineapple.

10. Go for a Drive   Like we mentioned earlier, many visitors spend their entire vacations within the boundaries of Waikiki. Others may be perfectly content to enjoy the amenities of a self-contained resort like Wailea, Kapalua, Ka'anapali, and Princeville. To make the most of your trip, however, we suggest renting a car, getting out a map, and going exploring. Don't worry about losing your way—how lost can you get on a Pacific island?—and be prepared to stop at whatever scenic spots or points of interest strike your fancy. It's the best kind of "cruising," Island-style!

Part Ten

Hawaii's Attractions

Choosing which attractions to visit during your Island vacation is like being the proverbial mouse in a cheese factory: So much to do, so little time! This is good, of course—better to have too many options than not enough—and in Hawaii you'll find a worthy attraction to suit every age and taste.

Following is a detailed listing of Hawaii's top visitor attractions, from museums and gardens to historic sites and theme parks. Most have a nominal fee, but many others are completely free of charge. Once again, for added convenience, we've grouped the attractions by regional zones.

Hours and admission rates are subject to change. Upon arriving in the Islands, pick up some of the free visitor publications at the airport. Some attractions have coupons offering discounts on admission prices.

Oahu

ZONE 1: WAIKIKI

Damien Museum

Location: 130 Ohua Ave.

Phone: (808) 923-2690

Hours: Monday–Friday, 9 a.m.–3 p.m.

Admission: Free

When to go: Anytime

How much time to allow: 30 minutes

Author's rating: ★★½; A "must" visit for anyone with an appreciation for the life of Father Damien. The younger ones, however, will likely be bored.

Overall appeal by age group:

Pre-school	Grade School	Teens	Young Adults	Over 30	Senior Citizens
★	★	★★½	★★★	★★★	★★★

Description and comments This mini-museum houses several artifacts belonging to Father Damien de Veuster (1840–1889), the kind-hearted Belgian minister who dedicated much of his life to caring for patients stricken with Hansen's disease (leprosy) at Kalaupapa settlement on the island of Molokai. Among the displays here are some of Father Damien's possessions, including books, work tools, candlesticks, and personal letters. A 20-minute video highlights the minister's life and reflects on this poignant chapter in Hawaiian history.

Other things to do nearby The Honolulu Zoo and Kapi'olani Park are a block away, and Waikiki Beach beckons just across Kalakaua Avenue, Waikiki's main thoroughfare.

Honolulu Zoo

Location: Kapi'olani Park; the entrance is on the *makai* side of the zoo.

Phone: (808) 971-7171

Web site: www.honoluluzoo.org

Hours: Daily, 9 a.m.–4:30 p.m. Special "Moonlight Walks" are offered from 6:30 to 8:30 p.m. once a month (before the full moon). Rates are $9 for visitors age 13 and over, $7 for children age 12 and under.

Admission: $6 for visitors age 13 and over; $1 for children ages 6–12; free for children under the age of 6

When to go: Anytime

How much time to allow: 2 hours

Author's rating: ★★★; Considering the great number of visitor-oriented attractions on Oahu, we find it difficult to recommend going to a zoo, particularly one that doesn't match up to some of the larger, better-known zoos elsewhere in the U.S. But a zoo is a zoo, after all, and what child won't enjoy seeing lions, tigers, and bears? (Oh, my!)

Overall appeal by age group:

Pre-school	Grade School	Teens	Young Adults	Over 30	Senior Citizens
★★★	★★★★	★★★½	★★★½	★★★	★★★★

Description and comments Set on 42 acres at Kapi'olani Park, the Honolulu Zoo is the largest zoo in the state—and the largest within a 2,300-mile radius. It is also big on history: The land for the zoo was donated in 1876 by King David Kalakaua, Hawaii's "Merrie Monarch," and thus it is the only zoo in America originating from a king's grant. The zoo began exhibiting animals in 1914: A monkey, a bear, and a few lion cubs were among the first furry occupants. Today, the roster of wildlife has expanded to include more than 120 different species divided into four separate exhibits. The "African Savanna" includes lions, hippos, gazelles, rhinoceros, giraffes, zebras, cheetahs, chimpanzees, crocodiles, warthogs, hyenas, flamingos, tortoises, pelicans, and more. The "Tropical Rainforest" features tigers, monkeys, sun bears, gibbons, alligators, black swans, Amazon parrots, king vultures, toucans, Burmese pythons, iguanas, and the zoo's biggest (literally) attractions: Mari and Vaigai, a pair of Indian elephants. A popular spot for the kids is the "Children's Zoo," with a variety of donkeys, sheep, llamas, potbellied pigs, and common farm animals. And the "Islands of the Pacific" exhibit spotlights a few indigenous bird and reptile species. The zoo has several nice spots for picnicking, and food stands and strollers are available. Also, the Zootique gift shop carries an impressive selection of wildlife-related merchandise that stresses education as well as fun.

Touring tips Be sure to visit "Islands of the Pacific," a small but intriguing exhibit that lends some uniqueness to the zoo. This is probably your best chance to view a nene (Hawaiian goose), the official state bird of Hawaii. Also, the zoo holds special "Moonlight Tours" each month from 6:30 to 8:30 p.m. These evening programs reveal some of the nocturnal habits of the zoo's residents and include some fascinating folk tales. Admission is $9 for adults and $7 for children under the age of 12. ("Moonlight Tours" are not recommended for children under 5 years of age.) Purchase tickets in advance at the zoo's front desk.

Other things to do nearby The zoo is located at Kapi'olani Park, a great place for picnicking. The Waikiki Aquarium is within easy walking distance, as is Waikiki Beach.

IMAX Waikiki

Location: 325 Seaside Ave.

Phone: (808) 923-4629

Hours: Daily, 11:30 a.m.–9:30 p.m.

Admission: $9.75 for adults, $8 for children ages 2–11

When to go: Anytime

How much time to allow: 50 minutes

Author's rating: ★★★★; Simply a lot of fun, particularly for those who have yet to experience an IMAX presentation.

Overall appeal by age group:

Pre-school	Grade School	Teens	Young Adults	Over 30	Senior Citizens
★★½	★★★★	★★★★	★★★★	★★★★	★★★★

Description and comments To paraphrase the late Ed Sullivan, this is a really, really big show! Recently having undergone a $2 million renovation, IMAX has a new six-story screen and new projector equipment capable of showing 3-D films. A mix of 2-D and 3-D movies is shown daily. The 3-D presentations require state-of-the-art, heavy-duty eyeglasses that are handed out before the show (unlike the light paper frame glasses with cellophane lenses that were used in the past, you can't take these glasses home). Altogether, this is a memorable visual and audio experience, especially for people who have yet to take in an IMAX show.

Other things to do nearby There are lots of shopping opportunities at the nearby Royal Hawaiian Shopping Center and International Market Place.

Ultrazone Hawaii

Location: 'Ilikai Hotel Nikko Waikiki, 1777 Ala Moana Blvd.

Phone: (808) 973-9932

Web site: www.ultrazonehawaii.com

Hours: Sunday–Thursday, 10 a.m.–10 p.m.; Friday and Saturday, 10 a.m.–midnight

Admission: $17.50 per game ($26.25 for a 2-game package). Special deals and package offerings are provided daily.

When to go: Anytime

How much time to allow: 1 hour

Author's rating: ★★★½; An exciting "shoot-'em-up" activity most appropriate for teenagers.

Overall appeal by age group:

Pre-school	Grade School	Teens	Young Adults	Over 30	Senior Citizens
—	★★★★	★★★★½	★★★★	★★½	★

Description and comments Laser Tag is a futuristic shoot-'em-up adventure that lets you be right in the thick of the action (like being inside a video game). Players don electronic vests and are grouped into three teams of up to ten members each. Each team is identified by the different color—red, green, or yellow—of the flashing lights on the vests. The object is to help your team win by scoring points while defending yourself and your team's base from attack. You'll know when you've been hit because your chest pack will vibrate, emit a bright flash, and sound an alarm. Scores are kept via computer. *Note:* Another Ultrazone is located at the Pearl Highlands Center in Pearl City (phone (808) 456-7646). That location is open Monday–Thursday, 11 a.m.–10 a.m.; Friday, 11 a.m.–midnight; Saturday, 10 a.m.–midnight; and Sunday, 10 a.m.–10 p.m.

U.S. Army Museum

Location: Battery Randolph, Fort DeRussy, at the intersection of Kalia and Saratoga Rds., next to the Hale Koa Hotel; validated parking available in Fort DeRussy's Saratoga parking lot

Phone: (808) 438-2821

Hours: Tuesday–Sunday, 10 a.m.–4:30 p.m.

Admission: Donations accepted

When to go: Anytime

How much time to allow: 1 hour

Author's rating: ★★★½; This museum houses a wealth of historic military memorabilia, and you can't beat the price.

Overall appeal by age group:

Pre-school	Grade School	Teens	Young Adults	Over 30	Senior Citizens
★	★★★	★★★	★★★½	★★★½	★★★★

Description and comments Built in 1909, the Battery Randolph served as an imposing military fortress, ready to defend Waikiki from attacking battleships. (It was a part of the military's "Ring of Steel" that encircled Oahu.) However, when it outlived its usefulness, officials faced a dilemma: The structure was nearly impossible to tear down. Its walls were 22 feet thick (solid concrete) and built to withstand a direct hit from a 2,000-ton artillery shell. Any attempt to bring it down with explosives would undoubtedly cause damage in the surrounding areas of Waikiki. Thus, in 1976, the battery was transformed into the 13,500-square-foot U.S. Army Museum, a unique attraction spotlighting the history of the American army in the Pacific region.

Included here are more than 2,000 artifacts and 1,900 photographs tracing the U.S. military's presence in Hawaii. The artifacts range from small (medals and tags) to huge (a Japanese battle tank). One popular exhibit pays tribute to the 100th/442nd Regimental Combat Team, a unit made up of local Japanese men who overcame prejudice to enlist in the U.S. Army during World War II. They would become the most highly decorated unit in the war, living up to their battle cry of "Go for broke!" Another poignant exhibit is the "Gallery of Heroes," which honors Hawaii's most courageous and highly decorated war veterans. A gift shop is available on the premises.

Waikiki Aquarium

Location: 2777 Kalakaua Ave.

Phone: (808) 923-9741

Web site: www.waquarium.mic.hawaii.edu or www.makaha.mic.hawaii. edu/aquarium

Hours: Daily, 9 a.m.–5 p.m.

Admission: $7 for adults; $5 for senior citizens, military personnel, and college students; $3.50 for children ages 13–17 and people with disabilities; free for children age 12 and under.

When to go: Anytime

How much time to allow: 1 hour

Author's rating: ★★★½; Educational and insightful. A good recommendation for anyone with an interest in marine life.

Overall appeal by age group:

Pre-school	Grade School	Teens	Young Adults	Over 30	Senior Citizens
★★★	★★★★	★★★½	★★★½	★★★½	★★★½

Description and comments   The Waikiki Aquarium's history is no mere "fish story." Built in 1904, it is the third-oldest public aquarium in the United States and has distinguished itself as a living classroom for anyone interested in Hawaii's ocean life. The aquarium is one of the first aquarium facilities in the world to successfully breed mahi-mahi (also known as "dolphin fish"), and the first in the U.S. to breed the chambered nautilus. Although not very large, the facility houses more than 2,000 ocean creatures representing some 350 different species. Here you can learn about endangered species like the Hawaiian monk seal and threatened species like the Hawaiian green sea turtle. A gallery of aquariums display colorful reef fish, coral, a giant clam, jellyfish, and even the unusual-looking mahi-mahi. In addition to the live exhibits, several educational classes focusing on Hawaii's marine environment are available. Call (808) 923-9741 for an updated schedule and class fees.

Other things to do nearby   The Honolulu Zoo is within easy walking distance.

Zone 2: Greater Honolulu

Aloha Tower

Location: Aloha Tower Marketplace, Pier 9 at Honolulu Harbor

Phone: (808) 528-5700

Web site: www.alohatower.com/atm/atmtower.htm

Hours: Daily, 9 a.m.–sunset.

Admission: Free

When to go: Anytime

How much time to allow: 20 minutes

Author's rating: ★★★; One visitor gushed to a local newspaper reporter that visiting Aloha Tower "should be a 'must' on everybody's list." We won't go that far, but it is a nice little activity, especially if you have some extra time or plan to do some browsing at the marketplace.

Overall appeal by age group:

Pre-school	Grade School	Teens	Young Adults	Over 30	Senior Citizens
★	★½	★★★	★★★	★★★½	★★★½

Description and comments   Now that it's dwarfed by a series of office towers, high-rises, and other modern-day structures in downtown Honolulu, it's hard to imagine that the Aloha Tower was once the tallest building in Hawaii. But that's exactly what it was when it was built in 1926. The slender, square-shaped ten-story tower was erected as a landmark welcoming passenger ships arriving at Honolulu Harbor. Now the centerpiece of the Aloha Tower Marketplace shopping/restaurant complex, the historic tower is perhaps the most recognized man-made structure in all of the Islands, with its large clock with faces on each side, the huge letters *A-L-O-H-A,* and the 40-foot flagstaff. (You've likely seen the tower portrayed on postcards, keychains, T-shirts, and other Hawaiian souvenirs.) In 1997, the tower closed for two years, undergoing an extensive $822,000 renovation (among the additions were handicapped-accessible rest rooms, security cameras, and emergency exits). It reopened in April 1999 and is once again accessible to visitors. Take the elevator to the tenth floor and take in 360° views of Honolulu. You'll have sweeping views of the downtown area, Honolulu Harbor, and the leeward coast. Unfortunately, the views aren't what they once were decades ago.

Touring tips   Frankly, the Aloha Tower Marketplace has struggled to attract the crowds everyone hoped for when it opened in 1994. You likely won't have a long wait in line. Be sure to bring your camera or video camera.

Other things to do nearby   Many good shops are at Aloha Tower Market-place. The tower is also a very short walk away from the Hawaii Maritime Center.

Bishop Museum

Location: 1525 Bernice St.

Phone: (808) 847-3511

Web site: www.bishop.hawaii.org

Hours: Daily, 9 a.m.–5 p.m.

Admission: $14.95 for adults; $11.95 for children ages 4–12

When to go: Anytime

How much time to allow: 2½ hours

Author's rating: ★★★★½; A "must" for history lovers. While there are numerous museums in the state spotlighting Hawaii's history, this is, by far, the largest and the best.

Overall appeal by age group:

Pre-school	Grade School	Teens	Young Adults	Over 30	Senior Citizens
★★	★★★	★★★½	★★★★★	★★★★★	★★★★★

Description and comments   The Bernice Pauahi Bishop Museum boasts the world's largest collection of Hawaiian and Pacific artifacts. There are literally thousands of cultural treasures here, including ancient Hawaiian weaponry, feather cloaks, clothing, jewelry, koa bowls, photographs, illustrations, and even a re-created Hawaiian grass *hale* (house). At the entrance to the museum, you'll see the gift shop to the left (be sure to pay a visit before you leave, as the shop carries an impressive line of Hawaiian books, artwork, and souvenirs) and a small exhibit on Hawaii's political and natural histories to your right. From the ticket box office, proceed to any (and we recommend *all*) of the following: The distinguished stone building houses the bulk of the Hawaiiana artifacts. Take your time and read the descriptions of each display—the galleries here likely provide the most powerful and effective way of discovering Hawaii's rich past. The adjacent Castle Building houses visiting interactive exhibits, which are very popular among local families. Past exhibits have featured such themes as dinosaurs, insects, space exploration, forests, and oceans. The planetarium, meanwhile, educates visitors on how ancient Polynesian voyagers used the stars to navigate their arduous journeys throughout the Pacific.

Also, sports fan should take note that one of the newer attractions at the museum is the Hawaii Sports Hall of Fame, located in the Paki Building.

This insightful gallery pays tribute to Hawaii's most storied athletes, coaches, promoters, and other contributors to local sports. Among them are famed surfer/swimmer Duke Kahanamoku, Alexander J. Cartwright (the "father of baseball" lived in Hawaii for much of his life), sumo pioneer Jesse Kuhaulua, and legendary women's surfer Rell Sunn. Lei-making and craft demonstrations at the museum are held regularly.

Touring tips Guided tours of the museum's Hawaiian Hall are scheduled daily at 10 a.m. and noon. Also, a garden tour is held at 12:30 p.m. The "Journey by Starlight" program at the planetarium is conducted daily at 11:30 a.m.

Contemporary Museum

Location: 2411 Makiki Heights Dr.

Phone: (808) 526-1322

Web site: www.tcmhi.org

Hours: Tuesday–Saturday, 10 a.m.– 4 p.m.; Sunday, noon– 4 p.m.

Admission: $5 for adults; $3 for students and senior citizens; free for children under the age of 12

When to go: The museum provides free admission to all comers on the 3rd Saturday of each month.

How much time to allow: 75 minutes

Author's rating: ★★★; If you love modern art, you'll enjoy this peaceful haven. If you don't, you'd probably want to pass on this one.

Overall appeal by age group:

Pre-school	Grade School	Teens	Young Adults	Over 30	Senior Citizens
★★	★★½	★★★½	★★★½	★★★½	★★★½

Description and comments Originally built in 1925 as a residence of a wealthy socialite, the Contemporary Museum opened its doors in 1988, filling a niche for modern art aficionados. At present, the museum boasts a collection of approximately 1,300 works, representing all media and spanning from 1940 to today. Not all are on display, however; the exhibits are shown on a rotating basis. The exhibits include works by noted contemporary artists. A special highlight is a walk-in multimedia exhibit by David Hockney, inspired by Maurice Ravel's opera *L'Enfant et les Sortiliges*. Works by local artists are also on display.

You'll likely spend as much time outside the museum as you will inside: The museum's three-and-a-half-acre garden is dotted by a variety of bronze, ceramic, stainless steel, copper, and aluminum sculptures. The garden was originally created in the 1930s by a Honolulu reverend with a passion for landscape design, and it remains a blissful retreat from the hustle and bustle of downtown Honolulu. In case you're hungry, the Contemporary Café is a favorite among locals, and shoppers will want to visit the museum's gift boutique.

Other things to do nearby   Continue your drive up Mount Tantalus, where breathtaking views of Honolulu await.

Foster Botanical Garden

Location: 50 N. Vineyard Blvd.

Phone: (808) 522-7066

Hours: Daily, 9 a.m.–4 p.m.

Admission: $5 for adults; $1 for children ages 6–12

When to go: Go in the morning, when it's coolest.

How much time to allow: 1 hour

Author's rating: ★★★; A thoroughly pleasant outing.

Overall appeal by age group:

Pre-school	Grade School	Teens	Young Adults	Over 30	Senior Citizens
★★	★★½	★★★	★★★	★★★½	★★★½

Description and comments   One of Oahu's best-kept secrets is that right in downtown Honolulu lies a beautiful 14-acre oasis. Foster Botanical Garden, in fact, boasts one of the nation's largest collections of tropical plants (about 10,000 species), including many rare and endangered species. Among the highlights here are an exquisite orchid garden, several rare and endangered trees (some of which are extinct in the wild), an herb garden, and an "economic" garden, which displays plants that are used for food, fabrics, dyes, and medicine. Foster Botanical Garden was placed on the Hawaii Register of Historic Places in 1988 and was the setting for several Hollywood films and TV shows (featuring such stars as Tom Selleck and Carol Burnett).

Touring tips   Guided tours are available weekdays at 1 p.m. Call for reservations.

Hawaii Children's Discovery Center

Location: 111 Ohe St.

Phone: (808) 522-8910

Hours: Tuesday–Friday, 9 a.m.–noon; Saturday and Sunday, 10 a.m.–3 p.m.

Admission: $8 for adults; $6.75 for children ages 2–17. No strollers permitted in the exhibit area.

When to go: Anytime

How much time to allow: 2 hours

Author's rating: ★★★★; Visitors have commented that this children's museum is among the very best in the United States. While it's not exactly a Hawaiian cultural experience, the kids will love it.

Overall appeal by age group:

Pre-school	Grade School	Teens	Young Adults	Over 30	Senior Citizens
★★★★	★★★★★	★★★★	★★★½	★★★	★★★

Description and comments Originally opened in 1989 as the Hawaii Children's Museum at Dole Cannery, the $10 million Children's Discovery Center reopened in 1998 at a larger, 37,000-square-foot location. Four separate galleries—Fantastic You, Our Town, Hawaiian Rainbows, and Your Rainbow World—are featured on three floors, each with a variety of hands-on, interactive galleries designed for children. Our favorites were Fantastic You, which helps children understand their bodies and organs, and Our Town, which features a working television station that lets children take on roles as news anchors and camera technicians. A gift shop sells a variety of educational toys, games, and books. The center stresses fun as much as education. The president of HCDC once explained the center's mission this way: "The museum isn't really [there] to educate children. Instead, it's to motivate them, stimulate them, to arouse their curiosity about things, and to give them an excitement and joy about learning." Based on that criteria, from what we've seen, the new center is a resounding success.

Other things to do nearby Kaka'ako Waterfront Park is directly across the street and provides a great picnic setting.

Hawaii Maritime Center

Location: Pier 7, Honolulu Harbor

Phone: (808) 536-6373

Web site: www.bishop.hawaii.org

Hours: Daily, 8:30 a.m.–5 p.m.

Admission: $7.50 for adults; $4.50 for children ages 6–17

When to go: Anytime

How much time to allow: 75 minutes

Author's rating: ★★★; This maritime museum is among the finest of its kind in the world, but your enjoyment of it will largely depend on your interest in maritime history.

Overall appeal by age group:

Pre-school	Grade School	Teens	Young Adults	Over 30	Senior Citizens
★★	★★★	★★★	★★★½	★★★½	★★★½

Description and comments   Covered here is Hawaii's colorful ocean history, from ancient Polynesian voyagers and rowdy whalers to the legendary Waikiki beach boys and the luxury liners of the 1920s and 1930s. Take an audio tour and browse through the 50 displays, including a huge skeleton of a humpback whale (one of only two such displays in the world). The two major attractions here are the *Falls of Clyde* (built in 1817) and the historic Polynesian voyaging canoe *Hokule'a*. You can actually board the *Falls of Clyde,* which is the last four-masted, full-rigged ship in the world and is a National Historic Landmark. The *Hokule'a,* meanwhile, is a double-hulled sailing canoe that, in the 1970s and 1980s, retraced the voyages of ancient Polynesians with native Hawaiians using only the stars and ocean currents to guide them.

Other things to do nearby   The Aloha Tower Marketplace is just a few minutes away on foot.

Honolulu Academy of Arts

Location: 900 S. Beretania St.

Phone: (808) 532-8701

Web site: www.honoluluacademy.org

Hours: Tuesday–Saturday, 10 a.m.–4:30 p.m.; Sunday, 1–5 p.m.

Admission: $7 for adults; $4 for students, senior citizens, and military personnel; free for children age 12 and under

When to go: Anytime

How much time to allow: 90 minutes

Author's rating: ★★★½; The biggest and best of Hawaii's art museums.

Overall appeal by age group:

Pre-school	Grade School	Teens	Young Adults	Over 30	Senior Citizens
★½	★★½	★★★	★★★½	★★★★	★★★★

Description and comments Founded by Anna Rice Cooke, a Hawaiian-born daughter of New England missionaries, the Honolulu Academy of Arts opened in 1927 with some 4,500 donated works of art. That number has grown to more than 34,000 pieces, ranging from paintings and textiles to sculptures and prints. The academy's collection is split just about evenly between Western and Asian art. The Western art collection includes Roman, Greek, and Egyptian works that date as far back as the third millennium B.C. to American and European works of the 1990s. The academy's collection of Asian works, meanwhile, is among the most highly regarded in the country and includes paintings, sculptures, ceramics, lacquerware, and prints. Of special note is the sizable collection—more than 8,000 works in all—of Japanese wood block prints, most of which were donated by the famous American novelist James A. Michener. The collection ably represents the wood block printmaking masters in Japan in the 18th and 19th centuries. Also, the academy's collection of Chinese works includes more than a hundred paintings, some of which date back to the Ming dynasty.

Touring tips Guided tours are scheduled at 11 a.m. Tuesday–Saturday and 1:15 p.m. on Sunday. The museum is fairly large, and taking the tour will likely make your visit much more enjoyable.

Other things to do nearby Across the street is Thomas Square Park, which often hosts local arts and craft fairs.

'Iolani Palace

Location: King St. and Richards St.

Phone: (808) 522-0832

Web site: www.openstudio.hawaii.edu/iolani

Hours: Tuesday–Saturday, 9 a.m.–2:15 p.m.

Admission: $10 for adults; $3 for children ages 5–12. Children under the age of 5 are not allowed into the palace. Reservations required.

When to go: Anytime

How much time to allow: 1 hour

Author's rating: ★★★★½; "Historic" only begins to describe the 'Iolani Palace; a visit here is practically a "must." Where else in the entire United States can you visit a palace? (Caesar's Palace doesn't count!)

Overall appeal by age group:

Pre-school	Grade School	Teens	Young Adults	Over 30	Senior Citizens
—	★★½	★★★½	★★★★½	★★★★½	★★★★½

Description and comments Built in 1882, the ʻIolani Palace—the only royal palace standing on American soil—served as the royal residence of Hawaii's last two monarchs, King Kalakaua and Queen Liliʻuokalani. In its heyday, the palace hosted spectacular galas and events, including the fun-loving Kalakaua's 50th birthday jubilee. It was also, sadly, the site of much political chaos, which led to Liliʻuokalani surrendering her throne in January 1893. From that year until 1969, when the State Capitol building was completed, the palace served as the capitol of the republic, territory, and state of Hawaii. Work to restore the palace will soon begin, with financing coming from both state and private funds.

Now operated by the non-profit Friends of ʻIolani Palace, this remarkable building is open five days a week for docent-guided public tours. The inside of the palace is striking, with a large staircase serving as a magnificent centerpiece. The Throne Room, adorned in maroon and gold, was the setting for royal audiences, receptions, and even the 1895 trial of Liliʻuokalani (when she was accused by the new government of knowing about a spirited-but-futile rebellion staged by her loyal supporters). The Blue Room was the site of more informal gatherings and parties, while the Dining Room is beautifully appointed with portraits of various world leaders of the time. The second floor includes the King's Suite, the Queen's Room, two guest rooms, and the Music Room, where the royal family often gathered. It was in the front room where Liliʻuokalani was imprisoned for eight months after her trial.

A royal uproar of more recent vintage occurred in the summer of 1998, when the president of Friends of ʻIolani Palace actually sat on one of the palace's thrones for a photo session with a *LIFE* magazine photographer. Her faux pas caused some damage to the fabric. Bishop Museum officials later said that the throne's silk material was in such a deteriorated condition that any touch would cause damage. The damage was eventually repaired, but the president—a great-grandniece of King Kalakaua—was forced to resign.

Touring tips Guided tours are scheduled at 15-minute intervals, each lasting about 45 minutes. Pick up your tickets at ʻIolani Barracks, located on the palace grounds. The palace is wheelchair-accessible; call ahead for any special requirements.

Other things to do nearby Lots! The Mission Houses Museum, Kamehameha Statue, Hawaii State Archives, Hawaii State Library, and State Capitol are all within easy walking distance from the palace.

Mission Houses Museum

Location: 553 S. King St.
Phone: (808) 531-0481

Web site: www.lava.net/~mhm/main.htm

Hours: Tuesday–Saturday, 9 a.m.–4 p.m.

Admission: $6 for adults; $5 for senior citizens and military personnel; $3 for youths ages 13–18 and college students; $2 for children ages 4–12

When to go: Anytime

How much time to allow: 1 hour

Author's rating: ★★★; Another good bet for history lovers, but a tad boring for kids.

Overall appeal by age group:

Pre-school	Grade School	Teens	Young Adults	Over 30	Senior Citizens
★	★½	★★	★★★	★★★	★★★

Description and comments　Of all the groups who made their way to Hawaii since the arrival of Captain Cook, it's safe to say that none made as much impact on the Islands as the 19th-century missionaries. Today, the triumphs and trials of these dedicated men and women are retold at this well-kept museum complex, which features three historic buildings and a visitor's center. This is where the first American Protestant missionaries established their headquarters in 1820. Built between 1821 and 1841, these structures—the oldest surviving Western-style buildings in all of Hawaii—house such original artifacts as furniture, books, quilts, and other household items belonging to missionary families. Visit the main white Frame House, which served as home to several of Hawaii's most prominent missionaries; the Chamberlain House, which was used as a storehouse and separate home; and the Coral House, where the first-ever printing in the Pacific was done. (The first printed sheet was produced on January 7, 1922; Chief Ke'eaumoku had the honor of pulling the lever of a creaky wooden press. It was through this printing press that the missionaries brought literacy to the Hawaiian nation.) The missionaries also introduced the art of quilting to Hawaiian women, and this museum has a sizable collection of some early Hawaiian quilts.

Touring tips　Guided tours are scheduled at 9:30, 10:30, and 11:30 a.m., and 1, 2, and 3 p.m.

Other things to do nearby　The museum sits next to historic Kawaiaha'o Church and is within a block or two of the Hawaii State Library, 'Iolani Palace, the State Capitol, the Kamehameha Statue, and State Archives.

National Memorial Cemetery of the Pacific

Location: 2177 Puowaina Dr.

Phone: (808) 566-1430

Hours: Daily. March 2–September 29, 8 a.m.–6:30 p.m.; September 30–March 1, 8 a.m.–5:30 p.m.; Memorial Day, 7 a.m.–7 p.m.

Admission: Free

When to go: Anytime

How much time to allow: 1 hour

Author's rating: ★★★; A poignant experience, especially for the older adults who know and understand the harrowing experience of a world war.

Overall appeal by age group:

Pre-school	Grade School	Teens	Young Adults	Over 30	Senior Citizens
½	★	★★	★★½	★★★½	★★★★

Description and comments   Also known as Punchbowl (the entire 112-acre site sits inside Punchbowl Crater), this national cemetery is the final resting place for more than 40,000 war veterans (and their family members) who served the United States in World War II, the Korean War, and the Vietnam War. It is a solemn sight, with small, flat, white headstones stretching far across the crater floor. Among those buried here is famed war correspondent Ernest Taylor "Ernie" Pyle. (While serving as a correspondent with the 77th Infantry Division, Pyle was killed on April 18, 1945, by Japanese gunfire on the small Pacific islet of Ie Shima.) Panoramic views of Waikiki, Honolulu, and Pearl Harbor add to the experience here. Each Easter morning, the cemetery is visited by thousands of Hawaii residents and visitors for the annual Easter Sunrise Service.

Pacific Aerospace Museum

Location: Central lobby, main terminal, Honolulu International Airport

Phone: (808) 839-0777

Hours: Daily, 9 a.m.–6 p.m.

Admission: $3 for adults; $2.50 for students; $1 for children ages 6–12

When to go: Simply put, this is a good place to kill some time while waiting for your return flight home.

How much time to allow: 40 minutes

Author's rating: ★★½; Insightful and fun for kids and adults alike.

Overall appeal by age group:

Pre-school	Grade School	Teens	Young Adults	Over 30	Senior Citizens
★★	★★★½	★★★½	★★★½	★★★	★★★

Description and comments A 27-minute multimedia presentation, "The Great Skyquest Theater," highlights this $3.8 million, 6,500-square-foot mini-museum, which opened in December 1991. The presentation—staged in three adjoining theaters—traces the history of aviation in Hawaii and the Pacific region and includes an account of the infamous Japanese attack on Pearl Harbor. Hands-on exhibits include a computerized globe that displays flight distances and lengths, a "Learn to Fly" lesson, a model of the moon, and (our favorite) a full-scale NASA space shuttle flight deck.

Queen Emma Summer Palace

Location: 2913 Pali Hwy.

Phone: (808) 595-3167

Hours: Daily, 9 a.m.–4 p.m.

Admission: $5 for adults; $1 for children under the age of 12

When to go: Anytime

How much time to allow: 1 hour

Author's rating: ★★★; A worthwhile visit for anyone with an appreciation of Hawaiian history.

Overall appeal by age group:

Pre-school	Grade School	Teens	Young Adults	Over 30	Senior Citizens
½	★★	★★½	★★★½	★★★½	★★★½

Description and comments Maintained and operated by the non-profit Daughters of Hawaii, this charming white-frame house served as a summer retreat for Queen Emma, consort to Alexander Liholiho (King Kamehameha IV). Many of the queen's possessions are on display here, including an opulent gold necklace and various wedding and baby gifts presented to Emma by England's Queen Victoria. This was among the first Hawaiian properties to be listed on the National Register of Historic Places.

Other things to do nearby Behind the palace, off Pu'iwa Road, is Nu'uanu Valley Park, a serene hideaway favored for its shady trees.

Royal Mausoleum

Location: 2261 Nu'uanu Ave.

Phone: (808) 587-2590

Hours: Monday–Friday, 8 a.m.–4:30 p.m.

Admission: Free

When to go: Anytime

How much time to allow: 45 minutes

Author's rating: ★★½; Not your typical visitor attraction.

Overall appeal by age group:

Pre-school	Grade School	Teens	Young Adults	Over 30	Senior Citizens
½	★½	★★	★★½	★★★	★★★

Description and comments   Considered the most sacred burial ground in the entire state, this three-acre site is the resting place for six of the eight Hawaiian monarchs: Kings Kamehameha II, III, IV, and V; King Kalakaua; and Queen Liliʻuokalani. (The bones of Kamehameha I were hidden at a secret location on the Kona Coast of the island of Hawaii, while William Lunalilo, or Kamehameha VI, per his wishes, was buried in a private tomb on the grounds of Kawaiahaʻo Church.) This current site was prepared in 1865 by Kamehameha V to replace the original royal burial tomb on the grounds of ʻIolani Palace.

Touring tips   Call ahead to arrange for guided tours.

ZONE 3: WINDWARD OAHU

Byodo-In Temple

Location: Valley of the Temples Memorial Park, 47-200 Kahekili Hwy.

Phone: (808) 239-8811

Hours: Daily, 8 a.m.–5 p.m.

Admission: $2 for adults; $1 for senior citizens and children ages 6–12

When to go: Anytime

How much time to allow: 45 minutes

Author's rating: ★★½; A nice visit that provides great photo opportunities.

Overall appeal by age group:

Pre-school	Grade School	Teens	Young Adults	Over 30	Senior Citizens
★★	★★	★★½	★★★	★★★	★★★½

Description and comments   Nestled at the foot of the scenic Koʻolau Mountains, the Byodo-In Temple is an exact duplicate of the famous 900-year-old temple in Japan. A stroll of the temple grounds leads you to an immaculate Oriental garden, a colorful carp pool, a nine-foot Buddha statue, and a stately teahouse. Peacocks, swans, ducks, and shimmering waterfalls add to the scenery.

Kualoa Ranch Activity Club and Secret Island

Location: 49-560 Kamehameha Hwy.

Phone: (808) 237-8515

Web site: www.kualoa.com

Hours: Daily, 9 a.m.–5 p.m.

Admission: Rates for individual activities begin at $14.

When to go: Anytime

How much time to allow: 2–6 hours

Author's rating: ★★★★; Offers myriad activities, with something for every age group. It could be argued, though, that this attraction tries to offer too much and, as a consequence, spreads itself a bit thin.

Overall appeal by age group:

Pre-school	Grade School	Teens	Young Adults	Over 30	Senior Citizens
★★½	★★★	★★★★	★★★★	★★★★	★★★

Description and comments   One of Oahu's lesser-known attractions is this 4,000-acre site, home to more than 15 (and probably still expanding) outdoor activities. You could spend your entire day here enjoying one or more of the following: all-terrain vehicles, snorkel tours, Jet-Skis, target shooting, canoe rides, volleyball, helicopter rides, tennis, a petting zoo, a garden tour, mini-golf, badminton, kayak rides, and even a narrated Ranch & Movie Set Tour (Kualoa Ranch was the setting for several major Hollywood films, including *Jurassic Park* and *Godzilla*). Our favorite activity here? Just relaxing at Secret Island, a pristine private beach where you can nap in a hammock, play volleyball, go snorkeling, play table tennis, and more.

Touring tips   Numerous tour packages are available, most including a buffet lunch and even transportation to and from your hotel. Many packages offer you a choice of one to three activities plus the Ranch & Movie Set Tour.

Sea Life Park

Location: 41-202 Kalaniana'ole Hwy.

Phone: (808) 259-7933

Web site: www.atlantisadventures.com/slp

Hours: Daily, 9:30 a.m.–5 p.m.

When to go: Anytime

How much time to allow: 3–4 hours

Author's rating: ★★★★½; Even if you have similar attractions back home, this is a thoroughly enjoyable visit for families.

Overall appeal by age group:

Pre-school	Grade School	Teens	Young Adults	Over 30	Senior Citizens
★★★★	★★★★★	★★★★½	★★★★	★★★★	★★★★

Description and comments   The first featured attraction you'll encounter upon entering the park is the marvelous 300,000-gallon Hawaiian Reef Tank, filled with more than 2,000 species of reef fish, rays, hammerhead sharks, and other colorful marine life. From there, head to the Rocky Shores exhibit, which provides above/below views of marine life in a tidal zone, and then the Sea Turtle Lagoon, where you'll get an up-close look at Hawaii's protected green sea turtles. Children especially will want to drop by the Discovery Pool, where they can hold tiny sea critters like sea cucumbers and spiny sea stars.

Other "don't-miss" exhibits include the Sea Lion Pool (you can purchase fish to feed the always-hungry sea lions), Sea Bird Sanctuary, and Penguin Habitat (home to a successful breeding colony of Humboldt Penguins). A special treat awaits at the *Essex* (a 70-foot replica of an old whaling ship) at Whaler's Cove, where you can view the park's dolphins, whales, and Kekaimalu, the world's only known "wholphin" (half false killer whale, half dolphin). The park offers three live shows: The Hawaii Ocean Theater, a 400-seat amphitheater, features bottle-nosed dolphins, sea lions, and penguins performing in a circular 220,000-gallon viewing tank. Whaler's Cove is the site of an entertaining show built around the amazing leaps and flips of the bottlenose dolphins. And the Kolohe Kai Sea Lion Show, in Maka-pu'u Meadow, spotlights a group of delightful sea lions and their trainers.

Also on the premises are two eateries (and you *will* build up an appetite): the Sea Lion Cafe and Rabbit Island Bar & Grill. Two gift shops—the Sea Life Park General Store and Little Treasures—offer a wide assortment of T-shirts, souvenirs, and other park-related merchandise.

Special programs   Offered three times daily, the park's Dolphin Adventures program lets you learn how the park's trainers use positive reinforcement to train the dolphins. Better yet, you'll have an opportunity to get in the water and interact with specially trained dolphins, including giving them your own "positive reinforcement" (in other words, you feed them fish!). The "tuition" is $99 per person, and participants must be at least 13 years of age. Dolphin Adventures is offered three times daily.

Splash University, meanwhile, also gives you an insider's look at how these friendly mammals are trained. You'll also learn a few signals that dolphins respond to and participate in training sessions during shallow-water interaction. The cost is $79 for adults and $67 for children ages 4–12 (children under age 12 must be accompanied by an adult). Splash University is held four times daily.

Both tuition costs include general admission into Sea Life Park. Each program lasts approximately one hour. Be sure to bring swimwear and a towel. Call (808) 259-2500 for more information or to place a reservation.

Touring tips "The Hawaiian Reef Show" begins at 9:45 a.m.; "Hawaii Ocean Theater" at 10 a.m.; "Whaler's Cove" at 11:15 a.m.; and "Kolohe Kai Sea Lion Show" at noon. The show rotation continues throughout the day, with the final set starting at 2:45 p.m. (*Note:* If you sit in the first few rows during the Hawaii Ocean Theater show, expect to get splashed!)

Other things to do nearby Sandy Beach and Makapu'u Beach are just a few minutes away by car.

Senator Fong's Plantation and Gardens

Location: 47-285 Pulama Rd.
Phone: (808) 239-6775
Web site: www.fonggarden.com/index.html
Hours: Daily, 9 a.m.–4 p.m.
Admission: $10 for adults; $8 for senior citizens; $6 for children ages 5–12
When to go: Anytime
How much time to allow: 90 minutes
Author's rating: ★★★; A refreshing visit with an ample dose of Hawaii's family-style aloha spirit.

Overall appeal by age group:

Pre-school	Grade School	Teens	Young Adults	Over 30	Senior Citizens
★★	★★½	★★★	★★★	★★★★	★★★★

Description and comments Hiram Fong was the first Asian American to serve in the U.S. Senate, retiring in 1977 after more than 30 years in politics. Today, Fong and his family run this 725-acre private estate, which boasts tropical flower gardens, more than 100 different fruits and nuts, and sweeping views of scenic windward Oahu. Hands-on activities here include lei-making lessons using flowers freshly picked from nearby gardens. A 50-

minute tram tour takes visitors through five valleys and plateaus, wending through forests of ti plants, *kukui* nut trees, and *lau hala*. A snack bar, fruit stand, and the obligatory gift shop are also located on the premises.

Touring tips   Narrated tram tours are scheduled daily at 10:30 and 11:30 a.m., and 1, 2, and 3 p.m. Reservations are not needed.

ZONE 4: THE NORTH SHORE

Polynesian Cultural Center

Location: 55-370 Kamehameha Hwy.

Phone: (808) 293-3333

Web site: www.polynesia.com

Hours: Monday–Saturday, 12:30–9 p.m.

Admission: General admission is $27 for adults and $16 for children ages 5–11 and includes admission to the center's 7 Polynesian villages, canoe rides, the Pageant of Long Canoes, and a tram tour. Special deluxe packages featuring an IMAX film, a buffet, and the evening show *Horizons* are as follows: Ambassador Package, $95 for adults and $63 for children; Lu'au Package, $64 for adults and $43 for children; and Buffet Package, $47 for adults and $30 for children.

When to go: Anytime. If you enjoy watching Samoan fire-knife dancers, however, be sure to come during the World Fire-Knife Dance Championships, which are held each year in April or May.

How much time to allow: Practically all day, including 2½ hours of drive time to and from Waikiki

Author's rating: ★★★★½; The most popular paid visitor's attraction in Hawaii.

Overall appeal by age group:

Pre-school	Grade School	Teens	Young Adults	Over 30	Senior Citizens
★★★	★★★★	★★★★½	★★★★½	★★★★½	★★★★½

Description and comments   Set on 42 acres in the sleepy seaside town of La'ie, the Polynesian Cultural Center delivers an all-out cultural experience that includes re-created villages representing seven Polynesian cultures: Samoa, Fiji, Tahiti, Tonga, New Zealand, the Marquesas, and, of course, Hawaii. Friendly natives, dressed in traditional attire, eagerly share their unique arts, crafts, songs, and dances. (Most of these Islanders are actually students at the neighboring Brigham Young University–Hawaii campus. They work a maximum of 20 hours a week at PCC in exchange for free tuition, room, board, and books. Among notable alumni is former Miss

Hawaii Elizabeth Lindsey, now a Hollywood actress who's appeared on television's *L.A. Law, Dynasty,* and *The Byrds of Paradise.*) Hands-on demonstrations include coconut husking, woodcarving, *lau hala* weaving, poi pounding, and tapa making. You'll even get to learn a Tahitian dance! One of our favorite performers was a delightfully humorous Samoan chief who showed us how to husk a coconut. Pristine waterways and lush gardens are among the eye candy here, and canoe rides, a tram tour, and a colorful pageant of canoes are just a few of the activities available. The seven-story-high IMAX Theater might seem out of place here, but it actually adds to the experience with a spectacular film tracing the history of Polynesia.

A variety of buffet/show packages are available, each culminating in a spectacular evening show featuring a cast of more than 150 dancers and musicians. Part of PCC's mission is to "demonstrate and radiate a spirit of love and service which will contribute to the betterment, uplifting, and blessing of all who visit this special place." That ambitious goal perhaps best explains why this attraction has virtually become an Island institution.

Waimea Valley Adventure Park

Location: 59-864 Kamehameha Hwy.

Phone: (808) 638-8511

Web site: www.atlantisadventures.com/wv

Hours: Daily, 10 a.m.–5:30 p.m.

Admission: $24 for adults; $12 for children ages 4–12

When to go: Anytime

How much time to allow: Between 2 and 6 hours, depending on the number of activities you want to participate in.

Author's rating: ★★★★; Spectacular scenery mixed with a variety of cultural demonstrations and outdoor activities.

Overall appeal by age group:

Pre-school	Grade School	Teens	Young Adults	Over 30	Senior Citizens
★★½	★★★	★★★★	★★★★	★★★★	★★★

Description and comments History abounds at this 1,800-acre park, the home of several important *heiau,* including one dedicated to Lono (the Hawaiian god of peace and agriculture). Waimea Valley is a prime photo op, featuring some 6,000 varieties of native and imported plants, trees, and flowers. Numerous cultural activities are offered for visitors: ancient Hawaiian games such as spear throwing, lawn bowling, and dart sliding; hula dancing and music; craft making; guided walking tours; and more. Not to be missed is a spectacular cliff-diving demonstration. You can also partake in several outdoor adventures, including horseback riding, all-terrain vehicles, mountain biking, and/or kayaking. (These activities cost extra, ranging from $15 to $45.) Paintball and archery are also available. The park's latest attraction is certainly unique: The "Butterfly Encounter" is an enclosed walk-through exhibit with hundreds of live Hawaiian butterflies. Educational displays and photographs offer scientific insights on the butterflies' life cycles. A trio of eateries—the Pikake Pavilion (offering a luncheon buffet), the Country Kitchen, and Wailele Café—are on the premises to satisfy hungry appetites.

ZONE 5: LEEWARD OAHU

Hawaiian Railway

Location: 91-1001 Renton Rd.

Phone: (808) 681-5461

Web site: www.members.aol.com/hawaiianrr

Hours: Sunday, 12:30 and 2:30 p.m. Charter groups may schedule weekday rides.

Admission: $8 for adults; $5 for senior citizens and children ages 2–12

When to go: Anytime

How much time to allow: 2 hours

Author's rating: ★★½; A nice way to get in some sight-seeing in the leeward area, but kids might get restless once the novelty of the ride wears off.

Overall appeal by age group:

Pre- school	Grade School	Teens	Young Adults	Over 30	Senior Citizens
★★	★★★	★★★	★★★	★★★	★★★

Description and comments   In the heyday of Hawaii's plantation era, more than 40 sugar plantations utilized private railway systems to transport their crops. (Trains ran on every populated island except Niihau.) Today, the Hawaiian Railway Society strives to preserve what's left of Hawaii's railroad history and has restored a 6.5-mile stretch of track. A trio of vintage diesel locomotives has been restored as well. The 90-minute ride begins at the 'Ewa station and travels at a leisurely pace of 15 miles per hour. Trained narrators tell of Hawaii's railway history, explain how the trains were used by the plantations, and point out intriguing sites along the way. The "end of the line," literally, is at scenic Kahe Point, and passengers can spend a few minutes enjoying magnificent, unspoiled views of the Pacific Ocean. Back at the 'Ewa station, you're free to browse around the train yard, enjoy a picnic lunch, and visit the gift shop, which offers a nice selection of books, shirts, photographs, postcards, maps, magnets, and other souvenirs.

Hawaiian Waters Adventure Park

Location: 400 Farrington Hwy.

Phone: (808) 945-3928

Web site: www.hawaiianwaters.com

Hours: Daily, 10:30 a.m.–6 p.m.

Admission: $29.99 for adults; $19.99 for children under 4 feet tall; $9.99 for senior citizens

When to go: Anytime

How much time to allow: Between 4 and 6 hours

Author's rating: ★★★½; This attraction scores high on the fun barometer.

Overall appeal by age group:

Pre-school	Grade School	Teens	Young Adults	Over 30	Senior Citizens
★★	★★★★½	★★★★½	★★★★½	★★★½	★★

Description and comments   Opened in May 1999, this is one of Oahu's newest attractions. The theme here, as you might expect, is having a splashy good time within the park's 25 acres. This is the *only* water park in the entire state. Highlights include the Kapolei Kooler, a leisurely tube cruise down an 800-foot-long river; Keiki Kove, a made-for-kids playground featuring mini-slides, water cannons, and waterfalls; Waterworld, a large, multi-level activity pool with seven different water slides; Hurricane Bay, a wave pool that lets visitors "surf" mini-waves; Wai'anae Coaster, a four-and-a-half-story ride featuring four separate double-tube slides; and The Cliffhanger, a seven-story free fall down two speed slides. There is also the Cutter's Island Bar & Spa, where adults can relax in a hot whirlpool. A food court serving everything from pizza to hot dogs is available, as are changing rooms and showers, a video arcade, a beach volleyball court, and a gift shop. A main stage in the center of the park presents local entertainment and special events.

Hawaii's Plantation Village

Location: 94-695 Waipahu St.

Phone: (808) 677-0110

Web site: www.openstudio.hawaii.edu/hpv

Hours: Monday–Friday, 9 a.m.–3 p.m.; Saturday, 10 a.m.–3 p.m.
   Guided tours begin at the top of every hour.

Admission: $7 for adults; $5 for military personnel; $4 for senior citizens; $3 for children ages 5–12

When to go: Anytime

How much time to allow: 90 minutes

Author's rating: ★★★; Our vote for the best place to learn about Hawaii's plantation history.

Overall appeal by age group:

Pre-school	Grade School	Teens	Young Adults	Over 30	Senior Citizens
★	★★	★★½	★★★	★★★★	★★★★

Description and comments Located in the former plantation town of Waipahu, this outdoor museum pays tribute to Hawaii's storied plantation era. Included here are artifacts, household items, photos, and documents representing the cultures and lifestyles of eight different ethnic groups that labored on the sugar plantations: the Japanese, Chinese, Okinawans, Filipinos, Koreans, Puerto Ricans, Portuguese, and Hawaiians. Nearly 30 re-created dwellings make up the village's three acres, including a Chinese cookhouse, a plantation store, and a community bath. The park also features a nice display of medicinal plants.

Zone 6: Central Oahu

Dole Plantation

Location: 64-1550 Kamehameha Hwy.

Phone: (808) 621-8408

Hours: Daily, 9 a.m.–6 p.m.

Admission: $4.50 for adults; $3.50 for military personnel; $2.50 for children ages 4–12

When to go: Anytime

How much time to allow: 90 minutes

Author's rating: ★★★½; The outdoor maze has breathed new life into this venerable attraction.

Overall appeal by age group:

Pre-school	Grade School	Teens	Young Adults	Over 30	Senior Citizens
★½	★★★★	★★★★	★★★★	★★★★	★★★★

Description and comments Situated just outside the small town of Wahiawa, the Dole Plantation features outdoor displays that share the history of

Hawaii's pineapple history as well as the life of the plantation founder, Jim Dole. Sample some pineapple juice and stroll through the unique Pineapple Garden, which features 21 different varieties of the prickly fruit that are grown around the world. Since its debut in 1998, the biggest attraction here (and the one the children will most want to see) is the Pineapple Garden Maze, an outdoor maze that covers nearly two acres and has a path length of 1.7 miles. The maze was built from 11,400 Hawaiian plants, including varieties of the official state flower, the hibiscus. Upon entering the maze, you search for six secret stations on the way to finding your way out. The maze was recognized in 1998 by the *Guinness Book of World Records* as the world's largest maze. A gift shop features a select line of pineapple-related merchandise.

Tropic Lightning Museum

Location: Schofield Barracks

Phone: (808) 655-0438

Hours: Tuesday–Saturday, 10 a.m.–4 p.m.

Admission: Free

When to go: Anytime

How much time to allow: 30 minutes

Author's rating: ★★½; Strictly for military buffs.

Overall appeal by age group:

Pre-school	Grade School	Teens	Young Adults	Over 30	Senior Citizens
★	★★	★★	★★½	★★★	★★★★

Description and comments This cozy museum documents the history of Schofield Barracks and the famed "Tropic Lightning" 25th Infantry Division, which fought in World War II, the Korean War, and the Vietnam War. The exhibits include artifacts, photographs, and other archival materials.

USS *Arizona* Memorial

Location: 1 Arizona Memorial Pl.

Phone: (808) 422-0561

Web site: www.nps.gov/usar

Hours: Daily, 7:30 a.m.–5 p.m. Program runs 8 a.m.–3 p.m. (weather permitting). Shuttle boats to the memorial leave every 15 minutes between 8 a.m. and 3 p.m.

Admission: Free

When to go: Anytime

How much time to allow: Between 2 and 4 hours. Due to the popularity of this attraction, waits in line between 1 and 2 hours often occur. The program itself lasts about 75 minutes.

Author's rating: ★★★★; The most popular free attraction in the state, with about 1.5 million visitors each year. A very solemn, moving experience.

Overall appeal by age group:

Pre-school	Grade School	Teens	Young Adults	Over 30	Senior Citizens
★½	★★★	★★★½	★★★½	★★★★½	★★★★★

Description and comments   The visitor center is the site of a bookstore and a museum that exhibits numerous historic photos, news clippings, and other memorabilia taken from December 7, 1941, the day Japanese war planes bombed Pearl Harbor. Visitors are shown a 23-minute film depicting the attack as well as events that led to that day of infamy. Then visitors are transported to the memorial via shuttle boat. The memorial itself is a distinctive white structure that sits over the sunken *Arizona,* where 1,102 men went down with the ship and remain entombed. A marble wall pays tribute to the 1,177 sailors and marines who perished during the surprise attack. Interestingly, the memorial, designed by a Honolulu architect, was made possible after a benefit concert staged in Honolulu in 1961 by an ex-G.I. by the name of Elvis Presley.

Touring tips   Tickets are issued on a first-come, first-served basis (no reservations are accepted). Each guest must pick up his/her own ticket in person at the ticket office.

Other things to do nearby   The USS Battleship *Missouri* and USS *Bowfin* Submarine and Park are both within the immediate vicinity.

USS Battleship *Missouri* Memorial

Location: Ford Island, Pier Fox Trot 5

Phone: (808) 423-2263 or (877) MIGHTY-MO

Web site: www.ussmissouri.com

Hours: Daily, 9 a.m.–5 p.m.

Admission: General admission: $10 for adults; $8 for military personnel; $6 for children ages 4–12 ($5 for children of military personnel)

When to go: Anytime

How much time to allow: 90 minutes–2 hours

Author's rating: ★★★★; Forms an appropriate "bookend" to the USS *Arizona* Memorial.

Overall appeal by age group:

Pre-school	Grade School	Teens	Young Adults	Over 30	Senior Citizens
★½	★★★	★★★½	★★★½	★★★★½	★★★★★

Description and comments   One of America's most decorated and storied battleships now calls Pearl Harbor home as an interactive museum and memorial. The 45,000-ton "Mighty Mo," as the *Missouri* is affectionately called, is the last of four Iowa-class battleships built during World War II. It was on the deck of the *Missouri* that Japan officially surrendered to the Allied Forces, marking the end of World War II. The *Missouri* earned three Battle Stars for missions in Iwo Jima, Okinawa, and Japan during that war, then garnered five more while serving in the Korean War. More recently, the *Missouri* served during the Persian Gulf War. Also, in 1986, it became the first battleship to circumnavigate the world. Buses transports visitors to Ford Island, where the ship is anchored. Touring "Mighty Mo," which is nearly three football fields long, you'll be able to view documents and photographs and hear a portion of a speech made by General Douglas MacArthur.

Touring tips   A Chief's Guided Tour, which includes head-of-the-line privileges and a tour led by a crew member, is available: $14 for adults; $12 for military personnel; $10 for children ages 4–12 ($9 for children of military personnel). All tickets must be purchased before 4 p.m. Another tour, the Missouri Signature Tour, is available for $29 and includes admission, a guided tour of an area of the ship not open to the public, and transportation to and from select Waikiki hotels.

Other things to do nearby   The USS *Arizona* Memorial and USS *Bowfin* Submarine Museum and Park.

USS *Bowfin* Submarine Museum and Park

Location: 11 Arizona Memorial Dr.

Phone: (808) 423-1341

Web site: www.aloha.net/~bowfin

Hours: Daily, 8 a.m.–5 p.m.

Admission: Entry to both museum and submarine: $8 for adults; $6 for senior citizens and military personnel; $3 for children ages 3–13.
  Entry to museum only: $4 for adults; $2 for children ages 3–13

When to go: Anytime

How much time to allow: 1 hour–90 minutes

Author's rating: ★★★½; Another good recommendation for military and history buffs.

Overall appeal by age group:

Pre-school	Grade School	Teens	Young Adults	Over 30	Senior Citizens
★½	★★★	★★★½	★★★½	★★★★	★★★★½

Description and comments   Nicknamed the "Pearl Harbor Avenger," the *Bowfin*—credited with 44 enemy ship sinkings on nine patrols—is one of only 14 U.S. submarines still in existence. Visitors can check out the interior of the vessel and even examine defused torpedoes. The park houses a museum filled with submarine history, featuring outdoor exhibits and a mini-theater.

Other things to do nearby   The USS *Arizona* Memorial and USS Battleship *Missouri* Memorial.

Maui

ZONE 7: CENTRAL MAUI

Alexander & Baldwin Sugar Museum

Location: 3957 Hansen Rd.

Phone: (808) 871-8058

Hours: Monday–Saturday, 9:30 a.m.–4:30 p.m.

Admission: $4 for adults; $2 for children ages 6–18

When to go: Anytime

How much time to allow: 45 minutes

Author's rating: ★★★; An insightful look at Maui's sugar plantation era.

Overall appeal by age group:

Pre-school	Grade School	Teens	Young Adults	Over 30	Senior Citizens
★½	★★	★★½	★★★	★★★½	★★★½

Description and comments   Formerly the residence of a factory superintendent, this history museum houses a number of artifacts, photographs, and a working scale model of sugar-processing machinery.

Bailey House Museum

Location: 2375-A Main St.

Phone: (808) 244-3326

Web site: www.mauimuseum.org

Hours: Monday–Saturday, 10 a.m.–4 p.m.

Admission: $4 for adults; $3.50 for senior citizens; $1 for children ages 7–12

When to go: Anytime

How much time to allow: 1 hour

Author's rating: ★★★; A worthwhile stop for students of Hawaii's history-filled missionary era.

Overall appeal by age group:

Pre-school	Grade School	Teens	Young Adults	Over 30	Senior Citizens
★½	★★	★★½	★★★	★★★½	★★★½

Description and comments   The Bailey mission home, built in 1833 out of lava rock and native woods, sits on land given to the missionaries by Hawaiian chiefs. It was originally used as the central Maui mission station, then became the Wailuku Female Seminary. Here, Hawaiians attended reading and writing classes, using Hawaiian language books printed on the island. Today the Bailey House displays intriguing Hawaiian artifacts, including tapa, weaving, featherwork, and native tools made out of stones, shells, and bones. A gallery of paintings—all circa the late 1800s—portrays the unfettered beauty of the Valley Isle, and a stroll through the outside gardens brings you face to face with rare native plants, a koa wood canoe, and a surfboard once used by the legendary surfer/swimming champion Duke Kahanamoku. A gift shop offers crafts, apparel, Hawaiian music, and books.

Other things to do nearby   The Hawaii Nature Center and Kepaniwai Park are a short drive away.

Hawaii Nature Center

Location: 875 'Iao Valley Rd.

Phone: (808) 244-6500

Web site: www.panworld.net/~hinature

Hours: Daily, 10 a.m.–4 p.m.

Admission: $6 for adults; $4 for children ages 4–12

When to go: Anytime

How much time to allow: 1 hour

Author's rating: ★★★★; Proves once and for all that learning can be fun.

Overall appeal by age group:

Pre-school	Grade School	Teens	Young Adults	Over 30	Senior Citizens
★★★	★★★★	★★★★	★★★★	★★★★	★★★★

Description and comments The Nature Center's Interactive Science Arcade features more than 30 interactive exhibits celebrating Maui's natural environment. The main exhibit hall features an amazing 10-foot-high, 30-foot-long, three-dimensional replication of four streams that feed into the 'Iao Stream. Aquariums, rain-forest explorations, arcade games, telescopes, and live insect and animal exhibits are among the other highlights. The Nature Center's gift shop features an extensive selection of nature-themed merchandise, from T-shirts to toys. All proceeds go to fund environmental education programs for Maui's elementary school children.

Touring tips Guided nature walks are offered daily. Call for reservations (required).

Other things to do nearby Kepaniwai Cultural Park and the Bailey House Museum

Kepaniwai Cultural Park

Location: 'Iao Valley Rd.

Phone: (808) 243-7389

Hours: 7 a.m.–7 p.m.

Admission: Free

When to go: Anytime

How much time to allow: 1 hour

Author's rating: ★★★; A pleasant stop if you're in the area, but not worth going out of your way to find.

Overall appeal by age group:

Pre-school	Grade School	Teens	Young Adults	Over 30	Senior Citizens
★★	★★½	★★★	★★★	★★★½	★★★½

Description and comments Picturesque gardens and pavilions representing Hawaii's different ethnic groups are featured here.

Other things to do nearby The Hawaii Nature Center and Bailey House Museum

Maui Tropical Plantation & Country Store

Location: 1670 Honoapi'ilani Hwy.

Phone: (808) 244-7643

Hours: Daily, 9 a.m.–5 p.m.

Admission: Free. Tram tours cost $8.50 for adults (plus tax) and $3.50 for children ages 5–12.

When to go: Anytime

How much time to allow: 75 minutes

Author's rating: ★★★; If you love tropical plants, this is highly recommended. Pick up some fruits and other goodies at the country store.

Overall appeal by age group:

Pre-school	Grade School	Teens	Young Adults	Over 30	Senior Citizens
★★	★★½	★★★	★★★½	★★★★	★★★★

Description and comments From the visitor center, head out to the plantation's 50-acre garden, which is filled with tropical plants including pineapple, sugarcane, papaya, guava, star fruit, anthuriums, and protea. A restaurant and plant nursery are also on the premises.

Touring tips Narrated tram tours of the garden are available. The rates are $8.50 for adults (plus tax) and $3.50 for children ages 5–12. The tour lasts about 40 minutes.

Other things to do nearby 'Iao Valley is a short drive away.

ZONE 8: SOUTH MAUI

Maui Ocean Center

Location: Ma'alaea Harbor Village, 192 Ma'alaea Rd.

Phone: (808) 270-7000

Web site: www.coralworld.com/moc

Hours: Daily, 9 a.m.–5 p.m.

Admission: $17.50 for adults; $12 for children ages 3–12. Senior citizens and military personnel receive 10% discount.

When to go: Anytime

How much time to allow: 2 hours

Author's rating: ★★★★; One of Maui's newest attractions is also one of its most unique. A visual treat, and a definite "must" for aquarium lovers.

Overall appeal by age group:

Pre-school	Grade School	Teens	Young Adults	Over 30	Senior Citizens
★★★★½	★★★★★	★★★★	★★★★	★★★★	★★★½

Description and comments   Exhibits here include a supervised "touch pool" for kids, allowing them to hold unique sea critters like sea stars and urchins. A whale exhibit showcases life-size models and a series of interactive displays about the humpback whale. By far, however, the star attraction at the Maui Ocean Center, which opened in 1998, is its 600,000-gallon ocean aquarium—the largest aquarium in the entire state. Inhabitants include sharks (including a six-foot tiger shark), spotted eagle rays, mahi-mahi, triggerfish, sea turtles, eels, and a dazzling number of colorful reef fish. The most popular section of the aquarium is a walk-through tunnel that provides 240° views (you can look up and see schools of fish gliding over your head!). Smaller aquariums offer an up-close look at eels, shrimp, coral, and other sea life. All exhibits have signs providing pertinent information about what you're viewing, adding an educational element to the visit. A couple of eateries—the Reef Cafe and Seascape Cafe and Bar—provide food and drinks; a large gift shop carries logo and ocean-themed goods.

ZONE 9: WEST MAUI

Baldwin Home Museum

Location: 120 Dickenson St.

Phone: (808) 661-3262

Hours: Daily, 10 a.m.–4 p.m.

Admission: $5 for families (any size); $3 for individuals; $2 for individual senior citizens

When to go: Anytime

How much time to allow: 1 hour

Author's rating: ★★★; Another insightful peek into Hawaii's missionary era.

Overall appeal by age group:

Pre-school	Grade School	Teens	Young Adults	Over 30	Senior Citizens
★½	★★	★★★	★★★	★★★½	★★★½

Description and comments   This two-story structure served as the home of Reverend Dwight Baldwin (a Protestant medical missionary) and his family from 1838 to 1871. The house was also the setting for Baldwin's medical practice and various missionary activities. Today, the home and its grounds, lovingly restored by the Lahaina Restoration Foundation, gives visitors a fascinating glimpse of what life was like for 19th-century missionary families in Lahaina. On display here are various household items and furniture, photographs, and other historic artifacts.

Other things to do nearby Located at the corner of Dickenson and Front Streets, the Baldwin Home is just one of several history-filled stops in Lahaina. The Brig *Carthaginian* and Wo Hing Temple are among those within easy walking distance.

Brig *Carthaginian*

Location: Lahaina Harbor

Phone: (808) 661-3262

Hours: Daily, 10 a.m.–4 p.m.

Admission: $5 for families (any size); $3 for individuals; $2 for individual senior citizens

When to go: Anytime

How much time to allow: 75 minutes

Author's rating: ★★★; A unique way to learn about the whaling era that defined Maui's economy in the mid-1800s.

Overall appeal by age group:

Pre-school	Grade School	Teens	Young Adults	Over 30	Senior Citizens
★★	★★½	★★★	★★★½	★★★½	★★★½

Description and comments This 93-foot ship is a replica of a 19th-century brig and serves as a unique maritime museum featuring whale exhibits, audiovisual displays, and an original whaleboat. The square-rigged ship is typical of the vessels that brought the first commerce to the Hawaiian Islands. A video about humpback whales is shown continuously.

Other things to do nearby The Wo Hing Temple and Baldwin Home Museum are just minutes away by foot.

Hawaii Experience Theater

Location: 824 Front St.

Phone: (808) 661-8314

Hours: Daily, 10 a.m.–10 p.m. Tickets go on sale beginning at 9:30 a.m.

Admission: $6.95 for adults; $3.95 for children ages 4–12. If you purchase $25 worth of merchandise at the gift shop, you receive a free ticket to the show.

When to go: Anytime

How much time to allow: 50 minutes

Author's rating: ★★★½; A nice diversion located in the heart of Lahaina.
   A sure treat for the senses.

Overall appeal by age group:

Pre-school	Grade School	Teens	Young Adults	Over 30	Senior Citizens
★★★	★★★½	★★★½	★★★½	★★★½	★★★½

Description and comments   A planetarium-like theater with a domed
screen more than three stories high, this attraction features a spectacular
40-minute film shown at the top of every hour. The film displays Hawaii
in all her scenic glory.

Other things to do nearby   Historical attractions including the Wo Hing
Temple and Baldwin Home Museum are within easy walking distance.

Lahaina-Ka'anapali & Pacific Railroad

Location: 975 Limahana Pl., Suite 203

Phone: (808) 661-0089 or (808) 661-0080

Hours: 12 rides scheduled daily, beginning at 9:45 a.m.

Admission: $14.50 for adults; $8 for children ages 3–12 (round-trip)

When to go: Anytime

How much time to allow: 90 minutes

Author's rating: ★★★; A pleasant ride offering pretty views (nothing dramatic, though) of the West Maui coastline.

Overall appeal by age group:

Pre-school	Grade School	Teens	Young Adults	Over 30	Senior Citizens
★★½	★★★	★★★	★★★	★★★	★★★½

Description and comments   All aboard! Better known as the "Sugar Cane
Train," this 1890s locomotive was used by the Pioneer Mill to transport
sugar crops until the early 1950s. Today, the train shuttles visitors between
Lahaina and the resort area of Ka'anapali. The six-mile route through a
cane field lasts about 40 minutes (each way). A friendly conductor shares
the history of Maui's sugarcane industry and even provides musical entertainment with his trusty ukulele.

Whalers Village Museum

Location: Whalers Village (3rd floor), 2435 Ka'anapali Pkwy.

Phone: (808) 661-5992

Web site: www.mauimapp.com/museums/whalersvillagemuseum.htm

Hours: Daily, 9:30 a.m.–10 p.m.

Admission: Free

When to go: Anytime

How much time to allow: 1 hour

Author's rating: ★★★½; Informative displays and historic artifacts add up to a "whale" of a good time.

Overall appeal by age group:

Pre-school	Grade School	Teens	Young Adults	Over 30	Senior Citizens
★★	★★★½	★★★½	★★★½	★★★½	★★★½

Description and comments This museum traces the history of Lahaina's colorful whaling era, roughly from 1825 to 1860. Among the more than 100 items on exhibit are a six-foot model of a whaling ship, harpoons, maps, logbooks, and an extensive collection of scrimshaw. In addition, a 30-minute video about whales is shown continuously.

Wo Hing Temple Museum

Location: Front Street

Phone: (808) 661-3262

Hours: Daily, 10 a.m.–4 p.m.

Admission: Donations accepted

When to go: Anytime

How much time to allow: 30 minutes

Author's rating: ★★½; Good for historians; young kids will likely be bored.

Overall appeal by age group:

Pre-school	Grade School	Teens	Young Adults	Over 30	Senior Citizens
★	★★	★★	★★½	★★½	★★★

Description and comments A Buddhist shrine is the centerpiece of this restored Chinese temple, which provides a revealing look at how early Chinese settlers to Hawaii lived. (The Chinese were among the first immigrants to arrive in Hawaii and held a prominent role in Lahaina's formative years.) Old photographs and artifacts are also on exhibit. A cookhouse (built separately from the main building to reduce the risk of a house fire) sits just to the right of the building. A unique highlight here is a pair of Hawaii films shot in 1898 and 1906 by famed inventor Thomas Edison.

The temple is affiliated with Chee Kung Tong, a Chinese fraternal society with branches throughout the world.

Other things to do nearby The Baldwin Home Museum and Brig *Carthaginian* are among the historic sites within the area.

Zone 10: Upcountry Maui and Beyond

Haleakala National Park

Location: The park extends from the 10,023-foot summit of Haleakala down to the southeast flank of the mountain and to the Kipahulu coastline near Hana. The summit area is accessible from Kahului via Rds. 37, 377, and 378. The park's Kipahulu area, at the east end of the island between Hana and Kaupo, can be reached via Hwy. 36. Driving times are about 3–4 hours each way.

Phone: (808) 572-9306

Web site: www.nps.gov/hale

Hours: Park Ranger Headquarters open daily, 7:30 a.m.–4 p.m. The visitor center is open daily, sunrise–3 p.m. (Overnight camping is permissible. The Hosmer Grove Campground in the summit area, located just inside the park's entrance, can be used without a permit; all other camping areas require permits.)

Admission: $10 per vehicle. The entrance fee is good for 7 days.

When to go: Anytime. Haleakala is renowned as a setting for dramatic sunrises and sunsets, although most people come for the sunrise. Be sure to arrive at least 30 minutes before either event.

How much time to allow: Up to half a day, depending on whether you plan to spend time hiking or taking part in one of the park's programs.

Author's rating: ★★★★; Simply one of the most awe-inspiring locales on Maui.

Overall appeal by age group:

Pre-school	Grade School	Teens	Young Adults	Over 30	Senior Citizens
★★	★★★	★★★½	★★★★	★★★★	★★★★

Description and comments Once considered part of Hawaii Volcanoes National Park, Haleakala ("House of the Sun")—a dormant volcano—was redesignated as a separate entity in 1961. The park consists of nearly 29,000 acres, most of it wilderness. This is a fabulous place for stargazing. In the summit area, begin at the park's headquarters and the Haleakala Visitor Center, which houses a variety of cultural and natural history exhibits.

Rangers are on duty to answer your questions and can be a tremendous help in making the most out of your visit. In the Kipahulu area, start at the Kipahulu Ranger Station/Visitor Center. Each facility has a nice selection of books, maps, postcards, and other souvenirs for sale. From the summit area are two hiking trails: The four-mile Sliding Sands Trail begins at the visitor center parking lot and descends 2,500 feet to the valley floor. (The return trip is much more difficult due to the steep grade; allow twice the time to hike out as you take to hike in.) The longer Halemau'u Trail, meanwhile, starts at the parking lot 3.5 miles above the park headquarters. At Kipahulu, all trails begin at the ranger station/visitor center.

Touring tips Check the park's bulletin board for a schedule of daily programs and guided hikes. Obey all posted warning signs. Because the weather at the summit of Haleakala is unpredictable—temperatures usually range from 40° to 65° Fahrenheit but can dip below freezing level at any time, with the wind chill factor—it's advisable to wear lightweight, layered clothing. Sturdy and comfortable shoes are a must. There are no restaurants or gas stations at the park. Due to the high elevation and reduced oxygen at the park, anyone with heart or respiratory conditions is advised to check with their doctor before visiting here.

Hana Cultural Center

Location: 4974 Uakea Rd.

Phone: (808) 248-8622

Web site: www.planet-hawaii.com/hana

Hours: Daily, 10 a.m.– 4 p.m.

Admission: Donations accepted

When to go: Anytime

How much time to allow: 1 hour

Author's rating: ★★★; A nice reward after the long journey to Hana.

Overall appeal by age group:

Pre-school	Grade School	Teens	Young Adults	Over 30	Senior Citizens
★★	★★½	★★½	★★★	★★★	★★★

Description and comments This cultural center is home to a quaint museum—Hale Wai Wai O Hana ("House of Treasures")—that features more than 500 artifacts, 600 books, 680 Hawaiian bottles, and 5,000 historic photographs of the Hana district. Opened in 1983, the non-profit museum houses Hawaiian quilts, poi boards, stones, *kapa,* ancient tools, fish hooks, gourd bowls, stone lamps, and a century-old fishing net. Also featured are tributes to some of Hana's most significant residents, including Samuel Kalalau, a former crew member on the historic double-hulled voyaging canoe *Hokule'a*. The cultural center also includes a series of old Hawaiian *hale* (houses), the historic Hana courthouse, and a jailhouse.

Hui No'eau Visual Arts Center

Location: 2841 Baldwin Ave.

Phone: (808) 572-6560

Web site: www.maui.net/~hui

Hours: Monday–Friday, 8 a.m.–4 p.m. Gallery hours are Saturday, 10 a.m.–4 p.m.

Admission: Donations accepted

When to go: Anytime

How much time to allow: 1 hour

Author's rating: ★★★; A haven for art lovers.

Overall appeal by age group:

Pre-school	Grade School	Teens	Young Adults	Over 30	Senior Citizens
★★	★★½	★★★	★★★	★★★½	★★★½

Description and comments Occupying a beautiful nine-acre estate in Makawao, this non-profit art center features stellar works by both local and international artists. The estate itself is a historic landmark (built in 1917 for Harry and Ethel Baldwin) dotted with pine and camphor trees and adorned with an immaculate European-style garden and reflecting pool. The arts center features classes and workshops for aspiring artisans, and exhibits are open to the public on Saturdays. The gift shop offers a nice selection of original artworks, note cards, books, and other gift items.

Kula Botanical Garden

Location: RR4 Box 288

Phone: (808) 878-1715

Hours: Daily, 9 a.m.–4 p.m.

Admission: $4 for adults; $1 for children ages 6–12

When to go: Anytime

How much time to allow: 90 minutes

Author's rating: ★★★; A botanist's dream come true.

Overall appeal by age group:

Pre-school	Grade School	Teens	Young Adults	Over 30	Senior Citizens
★★	★★½	★★½	★★½	★★★	★★★½

Description and comments   Kula, blessed with a mild climate and fertile soil, is the home of this five-acre wonderland originally owned by Princess Kinoiki Kekaulike. Opened in 1969, the garden today features more than 1,700 tropical plants, including exotic flora such as proteas, heliconias, orchids, anthurium, and gingers.

Tedeschi Winery

Location: 'Ulupalakua Ranch, about 10 miles past the junction of Hwys. 377 and 37

Phone: (808) 878-6058

Web site: www.maui.net/~winery

Hours: Daily, 9 a.m.–5 p.m. Guided tours are held on the half-hour every hour from 9:30 a.m. to 2:30 p.m.

Admission: Free

When to go: Anytime

How much time to allow: 1 hour

Author's rating: ★★★; Worth a look for wine lovers.

Overall appeal by age group:

Pre-school	Grade School	Teens	Young Adults	Over 30	Senior Citizens
★½	★★	★★½	★★★	★★★	★★★

Description and comments   Tedeschi Vineyards is renowned for its unique Island-accented wines, including the famous Maui Blanc Pineapple Wine. Wines are available for sampling and purchase at the tasting room, which is located in the King's Cottage, a historic building formerly used as a retreat by King David Kalakaua. A selection of Hawaii-made specialty goods, books, and gifts are also on sale.

Touring tips   Free tours of the grounds and the winery operation are offered free of charge from 9:30 a.m. to 2:30 p.m. The tour explains how the wines are processed and bottled.

The Big Island

ZONE 11: KONA

Ahu'ena Heiau

Location: Next to Kamakahonu Beach, fronting the King Kamehameha's Kona Beach Hotel

Phone: (808) 329-2911

Hours: No set hours

Admission: Free

When to go: Anytime

How much time to allow: Up to 1 hour

Author's rating: ★★½; One of Hawaii's most treasured *heiau.*

Overall appeal by age group:

Pre-school	Grade School	Teens	Young Adults	Over 30	Senior Citizens
★	★★	★★	★★½	★★★	★★★

Description and comments   Rebuilt by King Kamehameha I, this historic *heiau*—a temple of peace dedicated to Lono, the god of fertility—is part of a free walking tour offered at the King Kamehameha's Kona Beach Hotel. The *heiau* was used by ancient Hawaiians to pray for bountiful harvests, healthy children, and good weather, among other desires for good fortune. The four structures that make up the *heiau* were built from different indigenous materials. The temple grounds are only a third of their original size: The tallest structure is the *anu'u* (oracle tower), where the *kahuna* (priest or minister) received messages from the gods. Kamehameha himself spent the last seven years of his life in this area. Many Hawaiians still believe the *heiau* is a site of great spiritual significance, so access to the temple's platform is strictly forbidden. The grounds surrounding the platform, however, are open to the public.

Touring tips   Guided tours held Monday–Friday at 1:30 p.m. For self-guided tours, stop by the hotel's guest services desk to pick up a free brochure detailing the history and insights of the *heiau.*

Other things to do nearby   Hulihe'e Palace and the Kailua Candy Company are just minutes away by car.

Amy B. H. Greenwell Ethnobotanical Garden

Location: 82-6188 Mamalahoa Hwy., off Hwy. 11 in Captain Cook

Phone: (808) 323-3318

Web site: www.bishop.hawaii.org/bishop/greenwell

Hours: Monday–Friday, 8:30 a.m.–5 p.m.

Admission: A $4 donation is requested.

When to go: Anytime

How much time to allow: 1 hour

Author's rating: ★★★; A first-class garden with lots of photo ops.

Overall appeal by age group:

Pre-school	Grade School	Teens	Young Adults	Over 30	Senior Citizens
★★	★★	★★½	★★★	★★★	★★★★

Description and comments Owned by the Bishop Museum, this 12-acre ethnobotanical garden features more than 250 varieties of plants, including 10 rare native plants that are on the endangered species list. These plants were used by ancient-day Hawaiians for food, medicine, and other daily necessities. The garden's landscape layout highlights four vegetation zones used by the early Hawaiians in the Kona area: Coastal, Lowland Dry Forest, Food and Fiber Crops, and Upland Forest. Some of the crops on display include banana, breadfruit, sugarcane, and taro.

Touring tips A guided tour is offered at 10 a.m. on the second Saturday of every month. Helpful information for self-guided tours is provided in an outside rack.

Astronaut Ellison S. Onizuka Space Center

Location: Keahole-Kona International Airport

Phone: (808) 329-3441

Web site: www.planet-hawaii.com/astronautonizuka

Hours: Daily, 8:30 a.m.–4:30 p.m.

Admission: $3 for adults; $1 for children under the age of 12

When to go: The most practical time to visit is while waiting for your flight out of Kona. Arrive a half-hour early at the airport.

How much time to allow: 30 minutes

Author's rating: ★★★½; A hands-on attraction with equal parts fun and education.

Overall appeal by age group:

Pre-school	Grade School	Teens	Young Adults	Over 30	Senior Citizens
★★	★★★★	★★★½	★★★	★★★	★★★

Description and comments This space museum features ten interactive exhibits and more than a dozen audiovisual displays, including an authentic *Apollo 13* space suit and a Space Theater showing NASA videos. You can launch a miniature space shuttle, log in to the space shuttle's computer program and learn about the system's components, and even attempt a "rendezvous" with an object in outer space. Proceeds from the gift shop (featuring space-related merchandise) help maintain the center, which is named in honor of Hawaii's first astronaut, Ellison S. Onizuka. A local hero born and raised in the Kona area, Onizuka was among the shuttle crew members who perished in the tragic *Challenger* explosion as it launched into space on January 28, 1986.

Hulihe'e Palace

Location: 75-5718 Ali'i Dr.

Phone: (808) 329-1877

Hours: Monday–Friday, 9 a.m.– 4 p.m.; Saturday and Sunday, 10 a.m.– 4 p.m.

Admission: $5 for adults; $4 for senior citizens; $1 for children under the age of 18

When to go: Anytime

How much time to allow: 45 minutes

Author's rating: ★★★; A historic treasure right in the heart of Kailua-Kona.

Overall appeal by age group:

Pre-school	Grade School	Teens	Young Adults	Over 30	Senior Citizens
★★	★★½	★★★	★★★½	★★★★	★★★★

Description and comments Operated by the Daughters of Hawaii, this handsome Victorian structure—the only palace on the Big Island—was built in 1838 out of lava rock, coral, and koa and ohi'a wood for Governor John Adams Kuakini. It later served as a vacation retreat for Hawaiian royalty, including King Kalakaua and Princess Ruth Ke'elikolani. Among the treasures here are *kahili* (feathered staffs), stone tools, tapa, jewelry, and a collection of javelins that once belonged to Kamehameha I. *Note:* Photography and videotaping are not allowed inside the palace, as most of the furnishings are privately owned and the owners do not want them to be replicated.

Touring tips Tours are offered by staff members throughout the day.

Other things to do nearby Ahu'ena Heiau and the Kailua Candy Company are among the other notable stops located in Kailua-Kona. Also, a ten-minute drive from Kailua-Kona leads you to Holualoa, a trendy art town featuring several talented local artisans.

Kailua Candy Company

Location: 74-5563 Kaiwi St.

Phone: (808) 329-2522

Web site: www.kailua-candy.com

Hours: Daily, 8 a.m.– 6 p.m.

Admission: Free

When to go: Anytime

How much time to allow: 30 minutes

Author's rating: ★★★; Satisfies any sweet tooth.

Overall appeal by age group:

Pre-school	Grade School	Teens	Young Adults	Over 30	Senior Citizens
★★	★★★	★★★	★★★	★★★	★★★

Description and comments   Viewing windows provide an insightful look at how this candy company creates these chocolate confections made with Kona coffee, macadamia nuts, and fruit. Of course, you'll also be able to purchase these candies as well as other gift items. Everything else worthwhile about this attraction can be summed up in two words: free samples.

Other things to do nearby   The Ahu'ena Heiau and Hulihe'e Palace are a short drive away.

Kaloko-Honokohau National Historical Park

Location: Situated at the base of Hualalai Volcano, 3 miles north of Kailua-Kona and 3 miles south of the Keahole-Kona International Airport (along Hwy. 11)

Phone: (808) 329-6881

Web site: www.nps.gov/kaho

Hours: 8 a.m.–3:30 p.m.

Admission: Free

When to go: Anytime

How much time to allow: 1 hour

Author's rating: ★★★; A worthwhile stop for anyone interested in Hawaiian history.

Overall appeal by age group:

Pre-school	Grade School	Teens	Young Adults	Over 30	Senior Citizens
★★	★★½	★★½	★★★	★★★	★★★½

Description and comments This 1,300-acre park features more than 200 archaeological prizes, including *heiau*, petroglyphs, fishing shrines, *holua* (stone slides), and fishponds. Several species of endangered animals and plants also occupy the area (do not, however, disturb the wildlife). Picnicking, fishing, snorkeling, swimming, bird-watching, and hiking are among the activities you can enjoy here. Overnight camping is not permitted.

Kamuela Museum

Location: Situated at the intersection of Hwys. 25 and 19

Phone: (808) 885-4724

Hours: Daily, 8 a.m.–5 p.m.

Admission: $5 for adults; $2 for children under the age of 12

When to go: Anytime

How much time to allow: 1 hour

Author's rating: ★★½; Not worth going out of your way to see, but it's a nice enough visit with several intriguing exhibits.

Overall appeal by age group:

Pre-school	Grade School	Teens	Young Adults	Over 30	Senior Citizens
★½	★★½	★★½	★★★	★★★	★★★

Description and comments This cozy museum features an eclectic collection of Island artifacts, including some that were originally housed at 'Iolani Palace in Honolulu. Among the historical prizes here are antique American furniture, Chinese porcelains, and an ancient Hawaiian knuckle-duster.

Parker Ranch Visitor Center and Historic Homes

Location: Parker Ranch Shopping Center, 67-1185 Mamalahoa Hwy.

Phone: (808) 885-7655

Hours: Daily, 9 a.m.–5 p.m.

Admission: $5 for adults; $3.75 for children ages 4–11

When to go: Anytime

How much time to allow: 2 hours

Author's rating: ★★★½; A rip-snortin' good time, especially for visitors interested in the cowboy way of life.

Overall appeal by age group:

Pre-school	Grade School	Teens	Young Adults	Over 30	Senior Citizens
★★½	★★★½	★★★½	★★★½	★★★½	★★★½

Description and comments   One of the largest privately owned ranches in the United States, the 225,000-acre Parker Ranch is a major presence in Waimea (also known as Kamuela), known by many as "*paniolo* (cowboy) country." The Parker Ranch Visitor Center traces the storied history of the Parker family through a variety of displays, photographs, artifacts, and a 20-minute video. In 1809, a sailor from Massachusetts named John Palmer Parker arrived in the Islands, befriended King Kamehameha I, and married a Hawaiian princess. With Kamehameha's approval, Parker began domesticating the wild horses and cattle that roamed the fertile slopes of Mauna Kea. In the 1850s, Parker began purchasing land in the area, laying the foundation for Parker Ranch. Today, guided tours are provided to both Pu'u'opelu and a replica of Mana Hale, the Parker family homes (located about three-fourths of a mile from the visitor center). The Parker Ranch Store carries an assortment of *paniolo*-style apparel, hats, boots, buckles, music, artworks, greeting cards, and books.

Pu'uhonua O Honaunau National Historical Park

Location: Approximately 22 miles south of Kailua-Kona. From Hwy. 11, turn onto Hwy. 160 at the Honaunau Post Office near mile marker 103. Follow the road for about 3.5 miles to the park's entrance.

Phone: (808) 328-2326

Web site: www.nps.gov/puho

Hours: Visitor Center: daily, 8 a.m.–4:30 p.m. Picnic Area: Monday–Thursday, 6 a.m.–8 p.m.; Friday–Sunday, 6 a.m.–11 p.m.

Admission: $2 for adults; free for children under the age of 16

When to go: Anytime. If you visit during the weekend closest to July 1, you can take part in the park's annual cultural festival, featuring Hawaiian games, hula performances, and arts and crafts demonstrations.

How much time to allow: 1–2 hours

Author's rating: ★★½; One of Hawaii's premier and most sacred cultural attractions.

Overall appeal by age group:

Pre-school	Grade School	Teens	Young Adults	Over 30	Senior Citizens
★	★★	★★½	★★½	★★★	★★★★

Description and comments   In ancient Hawaii, this area served as a place of refuge, where offenders could seek safety and redemption. Drop by the park's visitor center and pick up a brochure to help you take a self-guided tour of this historic site. You can listen to an audio message along the center's mural wall or, better yet, sit in on an orientation discussion in the amphitheater. From there, explore Hale O Keawe Heiau, built in 1650, as well as wooden *ki'i* images, canoe sheds, and other ancient artifacts and structures. A self-guided tour takes about 30 minutes if you rush through it, but you'll likely want to stop and observe cultural demonstrators working at their crafts; they are friendly and eager to share their knowledge of Hawaiiana. Hikers can follow a mile-long trail that hugs the Kona coastline and is dotted with several archaeological sites, including *heiau.*

Touring tips   Orientation talks at the visitor center are scheduled at 10, 10:30, and 11 a.m., and 2:30, 3, and 3:30 p.m.

Other things to do nearby   Kealakekua Bay, where Captain Cook landed and met his untimely death, is a five-minute drive north. Historic Saint Benedicts Painted Church, off Highway 160, is about 2.5 miles from the park.

Pu'ukohola Heiau

Location: Situated in South Kohala on the northwestern shore of the
   island. From the intersection of Rt. 270 and Hwy. 19, drive a quarter-
   mile north of Rt. 270 to the park's access road.

Phone: (808) 882-7218

Web site: www.nps.gov/puhe

Hours: Daily, 7:30 a.m.–4 p.m.

Admission: Free

When to go: Anytime. In mid-August, the park stages a cultural festival
   featuring Hawaiian food and games, hula performances, a royal court
   procession, and arts and crafts demonstrations.

How much time to allow: 1 hour

Author's rating: ★★★; Another good bet for lovers of Island culture and
   history.

Overall appeal by age group:

Pre-school	Grade School	Teens	Young Adults	Over 30	Senior Citizens
★	★★	★★½	★★½	★★★	★★★★

Description and comments   Two historic *heiau*—Pu'ukohola and Maile-kini—are within a short walk from the visitor center. Pu'ukohola was originally constructed in 1550 and was rebuilt by Kamehameha I in 1790. (There is, in fact, a third *heiau,* Hale O Kapuni, which rests underwater and is not visible.) Hiking and tours of the park (both guided and self-guided) are among the activities available here.

Other things to do nearby   Spencer Beach County Park is within walking distance from the park.

Sadie Seymour Botanical Gardens

Location: 76-6280 Kuakini Hwy.

Phone: (808) 329-7286

Hours: Daily, 24 hours

Admission: Donations accepted

When to go: Anytime

How much time to allow: 1 hour

Author's rating: ★★★; A beautifully kept Eden for nature lovers.

Overall appeal by age group:

Pre-school	Grade School	Teens	Young Adults	Over 30	Senior Citizens
★★	★★½	★★½	★★★	★★★½	★★★★

Description and comments   Maintained and operated by the Kona Outdoor Circle, this international garden features beautiful landscapes and exotic flora representing areas from throughout the globe, including Hawaii, the Pacific region, Asia, Central America, South America, and Africa. Brochures for self-guided tours are available.

Wakefield Botanical Gardens

Location: City of Refuge Rd.

Phone: (808) 328-9930

Hours: Daily, 11:30 a.m.–3:30 p.m.

Admission: Free

When to go: Anytime

How much time to allow: 1 hour

Author's rating: ★★½; For botany lovers only.

Overall appeal by age group:

Pre-school	Grade School	Teens	Young Adults	Over 30	Senior Citizens
★★	★★½	★★½	★★★	★★★	★★★½

Description and comments   More than a thousand varieties of plants and flowers are available for viewing at this small (five-acre) botanical garden and macadamia nut orchard.

ZONE 12: HILO AND VOLCANO
Akatsuka Orchid Gardens

Location: Off Hwy. 11, just north of Volcano Village (on the way to Hawaii Volcanoes National Park)

Phone: (808) 967-8234

Hours: Daily, 8:30 a.m.–5 p.m.

Admission: Free. Self-guided tours.

When to go: Anytime

How much time to allow: 45 minutes

Author's rating: ★★★; The variety of orchids here is astounding.

Overall appeal by age group:

Pre-school	Grade School	Teens	Young Adults	Over 30	Senior Citizens
★	★★½	★★½	★★★	★★★	★★★½

Description and comments   This six-acre garden is recognized as a world leader in the hybridization of orchids, nurturing more than 400,000 such plants. Many of the latest varieties were developed by noted horticulturist Mori Akatsuka. A gift shop offers orchids (they can be shipped home) and other gift items for sale.

Other things to do nearby   Hawaii Volcanoes National Park is minutes away by car.

Big Island Candies

Location: 585 Hinano St. From the Hilo airport, drive straight onto Kekuanaoa St. and turn right on Hinano.

Phone: (808) 935-8890

Hours: Daily, 8:30 a.m.–5 p.m.

Admission: Free

When to go: Anytime

How much time to allow: 30 minutes

Author's rating: ★★★; A straightforward attraction recommended for chocoholics.

Overall appeal by age group:

Pre-school	Grade School	Teens	Young Adults	Over 30	Senior Citizens
★★	★★★½	★★★	★★★	★★★	★★★

Description and comments As soon as you enter the facility, a smiling hostess gives you a small paper cup with the day's free sampling of chocolates and cookies. From there, you're immediately drawn to the large viewing windows; from there you can see for yourself how the company's candies and cookies are made. Chances are, you'll be salivating over these delectable confections, and suddenly the free samples aren't enough. Conveniently (if not predictably), there's a retail shop on the premises offering Big Island Candies' entire line of products, including chocolate-covered macadamia nuts, cookies, and some rather unique items (chocolate-covered dried squid?). A snack bar offers refreshments and a free cup of Kona coffee.

Hawaii Tropical Botanical Garden

Location: RR 143A, 7 miles north of Hilo. Watch for a sign that says "Scenic Route 4 Miles Long," turn right, then drive to the garden's headquarters and registration area.

Phone: (808) 964-5233

Web site: www.htbg.com

Hours: Daily, 8:30 a.m.–4:30 p.m.

Admission: $15 for adults; $5 for children ages 6–16

When to go: Anytime

How much time to allow: 1 hour to 90 minutes

Author's rating: ★★★½; One of the most beautiful spots in the entire state.

Overall appeal by age group:

Pre-school	Grade School	Teens	Young Adults	Over 30	Senior Citizens
★★	★★½	★★½	★★★	★★★½	★★★★

Description and comments This 45-acre nature preserve, opened to the public in 1984, offers a unique tropical rain-forest experience. Visitors are provided with trail maps for self-guided tours. At the entrance gate, you're greeted by helpful volunteers who will answer any questions and even supply you with an umbrella in the event of rain. A 500-foot-long boardwalk leads you through a steep ravine filled with banana plants, bamboo, ferns, and other tropical growth. From there, other trails bring you to waterfalls, a lily pond, streams, an aviary, and more than 2,000 plant species, including palms, ferns, orchids, bromeliads, heliconia, and fruit trees collected from around the world. Upon your return, drop by the gift shop again (where you register upon your arrival) and browse through local arts and crafts, books, and other souvenir items. Proceeds go toward the preservation of the garden.

Hawaii Volcanoes National Park

Location: About 30 miles from Hilo, traveling down Hwy. 11. Follow the road signs and turn left into the park entrance.

Phone: (808) 985-6000

Web site: www.nps.gov/havo

Hours: Visitor center: daily, 7:45 a.m.–5 p.m. The park itself is open 24 hours a day year-round.

Admission: $10 per vehicle. Admission is good for 7 days.

When to go: Anytime. The best time of day to view eruption activity is after sunset.

How much time to allow: At least half a day.

Author's rating: ★★★★; One of Hawaii's premier attractions. Don't expect up-close views of fountaining lava, however.

Overall appeal by age group:

Pre-school	Grade School	Teens	Young Adults	Over 30	Senior Citizens
★	★★★½	★★★★	★★★★½	★★★★½	★★★½

Description and comments   The 377-acre Hawaii Volcanoes National Park, established in 1916 by the U.S. National Park Service, is certainly one of the world's most unique visitor attractions. What other park, after all, houses an active volcano? (Kilauea Volcano has been spewing lava continuously since New Year's Day 1983.) The starting point is the visitor center, which houses a gallery of volcano exhibits and a 200-seat mini-theater showing a terrific 23-minute film about the history of Hawaii's volcanoes and their significance to the Hawaiian culture. Park rangers are on hand to answer any questions and offer suggested itineraries at the park. Taking the time here to learn all you can about the park will help you make the most out of your experience.

Next door, the Volcano Art Center offers a wide range of works by some of Hawaii's top artists. A park ranger leads an optional introductory hike from the visitor center. If you're ready to venture out on your own, return to your car and head farther into the park, where you'll soon arrive at the

Thomas A. Jaggar Museum, which features exhibits spotlighting Hawaii's volcano eruption history, current seismic activity, land formations, and even a profile of Madame Pele, Hawaii's goddess of fire. Just outside the museum are stunning views of Halemaʻumaʻu Crater—measuring 2.5 miles wide and more than 400 feet deep—inside the Kilauea Caldera. (Translated, Halemaʻumaʻu means "House of Ferns." Centuries ago, two craters existed, one filled with ferns. A terrible eruption caused the two fire pits to merge.)

From the museum, you can drive to any and all public trails in the park. Devastation Trail is a short (less than a mile) hike on a paved path that shows the havoc caused by lava flows. Farther up Crater Rim Drive is the Thurston Lava Tube, a pleasant nature walk that includes a trek through a large lava tube. It's a half-hour drive (about 20 miles) to the end of Chain of Craters Road, which hugs the ocean coastline. At the end of the road, you'll see billowing steam clouds rising at a distance, the result of molten lava pouring into the sea. A short 300-yard hike on a rocky and uneven trail is marked by cones. A longer, more strenuous seven-mile hike is also available but is not recommended. Other notes: Overnight camping is available via free permit (stays are limited to seven days per year), but collecting lava rocks or plants from the park is strictly *kapu* (prohibited). Overall, be respectful of the surroundings, which native Hawaiians regard as sacred to their culture.

Other things to do nearby   The tranquil village of Volcano is just a mile from the park.

Lyman Mission House and Museum

Location: 276 Haili St., a few blocks up from Hilo Bay
Phone: (808) 935-5021
Hours: Monday–Saturday, 9 a.m.–4:30 p.m.
Admission: $7 for adults; $5 for senior citizens; $3 for children ages 6–18
When to go: Anytime
How much time to allow: 1 hour
Author's rating: ★★★; Another worthwhile stop for history lovers, particularly those interested in Hawaii's missionary era.
Overall appeal by age group:

Pre-school	Grade School	Teens	Young Adults	Over 30	Senior Citizens
★	★★	★★½	★★★	★★★	★★★★

Description and comments   The mission house was built in 1839 for David and Sarah Lyman, the first Christian missionaries to Hilo. This well-preserved New England–style home—the oldest standing wooden frame structure on the island—houses authentic missionary-era furnishings, clothing, photographs, and other artifacts. Guides provide detailed information throughout the 25-minute tour. The adjacent two-story museum, built in 1973, showcases Hawaii's natural and cultural histories. Exhibits here include mineral, rock, and shell collections, original documents, historic photographs, and period pieces paying tribute to the many people who have immigrated to the Islands (including a Chinese shrine, Japanese furnishings, and a Portuguese musical instrument). A gift shop is located on the ground floor.

Other things to do nearby   The Pacific Tsunami Museum is a few minutes away on Kamehameha Avenue.

Mauna Loa Macadamia Nut Visitor Center

Location: On Hwy. 11, 5 miles south of Hilo. Turn onto Macadamia Road and drive to the road's end (you'll pass through Mauna Loa's 2,500-acre orchard).

Phone: (808) 966-8612

Web site: www.maunaloa.com

Hours: Daily, 8:30 a.m.–5:30 p.m.

Admission: Free

When to go: Anytime

How much time to allow: 1 hour

Author's rating: ★★★½; Similar to the Kailua Candy Company and Big Island Candies experiences.

Overall appeal by age group:

Pre-school	Grade School	Teens	Young Adults	Over 30	Senior Citizens
★★	★★★½	★★★½	★★★½	★★★½	★★★½

Description and comments   Head to the visitor center first and enjoy a free sampling of Mauna Loa's macadamia nut products, then head outside and watch a brief video presentation about Mauna Loa and the macadamia nut industry. A mini-factory shows how macadamia nut chocolates are made. Adjacent to the visitor center is the company's nut-processing plant, where you can watch the proceedings through large viewing windows (helpful signs explain the process). Also on the premises is a pleasant nature walk through tropical foliage and a snack shop serving macadamia nut ice cream, soft drinks, Kona coffee, and other treats. All of the above offerings are centered around, not coincidentally, an extensive gift shop stocked with all types of Mauna Loa products and souvenirs.

Other things to do nearby   Both Nani Mau Gardens and Pana'ewa Rainforest Zoo are just minutes away by car.

Nani Mau Gardens

Location: 421 Makalika St. From Hilo, drive about 3 miles south on Hwy. 11. Look for the "Nani Mau Gardens" sign and turn left onto Makalika St.

Phone: (808) 959-3541

Web site: www.nanimau.com

Hours: Daily, 8 a.m.–5 p.m.

Admission: $10 for adults; $6 for children ages 6–18

When to go: Anytime

How much time to allow: 1 hour to 90 minutes

Author's rating: ★★★; The price is a little steep for our tastes, but Nani Mau certainly lives up to its name, which means "forever beautiful."

Overall appeal by age group:

Pre-school	Grade School	Teens	Young Adults	Over 30	Senior Citizens
★½	★★	★★★	★★★	★★★½	★★★½

Description and comments   This botanical garden, established in 1970, grows more than a hundred varieties of tropical fruit trees and some 2,000 varieties of tropical flowers, including anthuriums, orchids, and bromeliads. A handy map is provided upon entry into the garden, and you're free to walk throughout the 20-acre site. Highlights include the Orchid Walkway, Hibiscus Garden, Bromeliad Garden, Lily Pond, Polynesian Garden, European Garden, Fruit Orchard, and Annual Garden. Everything here is immaculately maintained, with the exception of the Japanese Garden, which was rather disappointing. A man-made lake and waterfall add to the scenery, and gazebos and pavilions provide good resting spots. A restaurant and gift shop are also on the premises.

Touring tips   A 35-minute tram tour is available for an additional $5.

Other things to do nearby   Attractions in the vicinity of Nani Mau Gardens include the Mauna Loa Macadamia Nut Visitor Center and Pana'ewa Rainforest Zoo.

Onizuka Center for International Astronomy and Mauna Kea Observatory

Location: Take Hwy. 200 to the visitor center, which is located at the 9,300-foot elevation level on Mauna Kea.

Phone: (808) 961-2180

Web site: www.ifa.hawaii.edu/info/vis

Hours: Visitor Information Station: Thursday, 5:30–10 p.m.; Friday, 9–noon, 1–4:30 p.m., and 6–10 p.m.; Saturday and Sunday, 9 a.m.–10 p.m.

Admission: Free

When to go: Anytime

How much time to allow: Half a day

Author's rating: ★★★½; An "out of this world" experience, especially for visitors who are able to ascend to Mauna Kea's summit.

Overall appeal by age group:

Pre-school	Grade School	Teens	Young Adults	Over 30	Senior Citizens
★	★★	★★★½	★★★½	★★★½	★★★½

Description and comments   The Onizuka Center offers several fascinating displays covering the observatory's history, programs, and accomplishments. The Visitor Information Station (VIS) offers free tours to the 13,796-foot summit of Mauna Kea every Saturday and Sunday from 1 to 5 p.m. (weather permitting). Visitors should arrive promptly at 1 p.m., as participants are required to spend an hour of acclimation time here before ascending to higher elevations. A video presentation and Q&A session help pass the time. At 2 p.m., participants return to their vehicles and are led to the summit, perhaps the finest spot on Earth for stargazing.

Touring tips   Children under the age of 16, pregnant women, and anyone with respiratory, heart, and severe overweight conditions are not allowed to travel to the summit. Be aware that the weather conditions at Mauna Kea can be quite severe and can include freezing temperatures, snow, and high winds. Warm clothing is a must. Also, scuba divers must wait at least 24 hours after their last dive before being allowed to ascend to the summit. The drive up to the summit requires a four-wheel-drive vehicle; consult your rental car agency before planning a visit to Mauna Kea.

Pacific Tsunami Museum

Location: 103 Kamehameha Ave. in downtown Hilo

Phone: (808) 935-0926

Web site: www.planet-hawaii.com/tsunami

Hours: Wednesday–Saturday, 10 a.m.–4 p.m.

Admission: Donations accepted

When to go: Anytime

How much time to allow: 1 hour

Author's rating: ★★★; A good visit for young and old alike, the museum is a sad but fitting reminder of an important chapter in Hilo's history.

Overall appeal by age group:

Pre-school	Grade School	Teens	Young Adults	Over 30	Senior Citizens
★★	★★★	★★★	★★★	★★★½	★★★½

Description and comments   One of the Big Island's newest attractions, the Pacific Tsunami Museum serves two purposes: It pays tribute to the hundreds of Hilo residents who perished during the horrific tsunamis that struck the city in 1946 and 1960, and it educates today's residents about what to do when the next tsunami hits. Exhibits include informative video presentations, photographs, and "Fire and Water," a thorough history of the devastation brought to the Big Island by volcanic eruptions and tsunamis. A touching exhibit is a quilt sewn by local high school and grade school students in honor of the children and teachers who died during the 1946 tsunami disaster. A gift shop offers souvenirs.

Other things to do nearby   The Lyman Mission House and Museum is a few blocks away.

Pana'ewa Rainforest Zoo

Location: Mamaki St., off Hwy. 11 south of Hilo

Phone: (808) 959-7224

Hours: Daily, 9 a.m.–4 p.m.

Admission: Free

When to go: Anytime

How much time to allow: 1 hour

Author's rating: ★★½; Not a large zoo, but the kids will love it.

Overall appeal by age group:

Pre-school	Grade School	Teens	Young Adults	Over 30	Senior Citizens
★★★	★★★½	★★★	★★★	★★½	★★½

Description and comments   This 12-acre zoo in the Pana'ewa Rainforest Reserve is the only tropical rain-forest zoo in the United States. Opened to the public in September 1977, the zoo spotlights the world's rain-forest animals, reptiles, and birds, including a Bengal tiger, water buffalo, pygmy hippos, spider monkeys, deer, iguanas, feral goats, tapirs, vultures, and some native birds (including the nene, Hawaii's official state bird). Picnic tables and rain shelters are provided for rest and relaxation. One not-so-minor quibble: Most of the exhibit cages are constructed in a way that makes taking clear photos of the animals almost impossible.

Other things to do nearby   The Mauna Loa Macadamia Nut Visitor Center and Nani Mau Gardens are minutes away by car.

Suisan Fish Market and Auction

Location: 85 Lihiwai St., at the corner of Banyan Dr. and Lihiwai St.

Phone: (808) 935-9349

Hours: Monday–Saturday, 7 a.m.

Admission: Free

When to go: Anytime

How much time to allow: 30 minutes

Author's rating: ★★½; For early risers with an appreciation of "fishy" business.

Overall appeal by age group:

Pre-school	Grade School	Teens	Young Adults	Over 30	Senior Citizens
★	★★★	★★★	★★½	★★★	★★★

Description and comments   The public is invited each morning to watch buyers representing restaurants and markets from around the state bid on the day's freshest catches, including 'ahi (tuna), mahi-mahi, snappers, marlin, swordfish, and even squid. Consumers may purchase fresh fish at the market next door.

Other things to do nearby   Downtown Hilo, home to attractions including the Pacific Tsunami Museum and the Lyman Mission House and Museum, is a few minutes away by car.

Volcano Winery

Location: Off Hwy. 11, 30 miles south of Hilo. Turn onto Pi'i Mauna Dr. and follow the road (also called Golf Course Rd. on some maps).

Phone: (808) 967-7479

Web site: www.volcanowinery.com

Hours: Daily, 10 a.m.–5:30 p.m.

Admission: Free

When to go: Anytime

How much time to allow: 1 hour

Author's rating: ★★½; A great stop for wine lovers on the way to (or from) Hawaii Volcanoes National Park.

Overall appeal by age group:

Pre-school	Grade School	Teens	Young Adults	Over 30	Senior Citizens
★	★★	★★	★★½	★★★	★★★

Description and comments   The southernmost winery in the United States, this 18-acre vineyard, resting at the 4,000-foot elevation mark, produces 100% tropical honey (no grapes) and tropical fruit blend (half-grape, half-fruit) wines. Visit the tasting room and sample unique flavors including Macadamia Nut Honey Wine, Lehua Blossom Honey Wine, Guava Chablis, Passion Chablis, and Volcano Blush. The gift shop offers wine and souvenirs for purchase.

Other things to do nearby   Winery borders Hawaii Volcanoes National Park.

Kauai: Zone 13

Grove Farm Homestead

Location: Just off Nawiliwili Rd. just outside Lihu'e.

Phone: (808) 245-3202

Hours: Monday, Wednesday, and Thursday, guided tours at 10 a.m. and 1 p.m. Reservations required.

Admission: Donations of $5 for adults and $2 for children ages 12 and under are requested.

When to go: Anytime

How much time to allow: 90 minutes

Author's rating: ★★½; A good visit if you're interested in the island's plantation history.

Overall appeal by age group:

Pre-school	Grade School	Teens	Young Adults	Over 30	Senior Citizens
★½	★★	★★½	★★★	★★★	★★★½

Description and comments This 80-acre homestead, owned by the prominent Wilcox family, provides a revealing glimpse of plantation life during the 19th century. The complex encompasses a museum, washhouse, teahouse, and other plantation memorabilia.

Other things to do nearby Kauai Museum is a short drive away on Rice Street in Lihu'e.

Guava Kai Plantation

Location: At the end of Kuawa Rd., off Hwy. 53 in Kilauea

Phone: (808) 828-6121

Hours: Daily, 9 a.m.–5 p.m.

Admission: Free

When to go: Anytime

How much time to allow: 45 minutes

Author's rating: ★★½; A pleasant stop near Kauai's scenic north shore.

Overall appeal by age group:

Pre-school	Grade School	Teens	Young Adults	Over 30	Senior Citizens
★½	★★½	★★½	★★★	★★★	★★★

Description and comments Visit the plantation's visitor center and enjoy free samples of guava juice. Here you can learn how the fruit is grown and processed. A leisurely stroll through the plantation's gardens is a pleasant activity, and the gift shop carries a good selection of guava products and souvenirs to bring home.

Other things to do nearby The Kilauea Point National Wildlife Refuge is just a few minutes away by car.

Kauai Museum

Location: 4428 Rice St.

Phone: (808) 245-6931

Hours: Monday–Friday, 9 a.m.–4 p.m.; Saturday, 10 a.m.–4 p.m.
    Guided tours are scheduled each Tuesday at 10 a.m.

Admission: $5 for adults; $4 for senior citizens; $3 for children ages
    14–17; $1 for children ages 6–12

When to go: Anytime

How much time to allow: 75 minutes

Author's rating: ★★★½; Kauai's best history museum.

Overall appeal by age group:

Pre-school	Grade School	Teens	Young Adults	Over 30	Senior Citizens
★★	★★★	★★★	★★★	★★★½	★★★★

Description and comments   The Garden Isle's history is brought to life through an extensive selection of displays and artifacts.

Other things to do nearby   Nearby is the Grove Farm Homestead, another attraction focusing on Kauai's history.

Kilauea Point National Wildlife Refuge

Location: Turn off Hwy. 56 near mile marker 23, then take Kolo Rd. down to Kilauea Rd.

Phone: (808) 828-1413

Hours: Daily, 10 a.m.–4 p.m.

Admission: $2 for adults; free for children age 16 and under

When to go: Anytime

How much time to allow: 75 minutes

Author's rating: ★★½; The views from Kilauea Point are breathtaking.

Overall appeal by age group:

Pre-school	Grade School	Teens	Young Adults	Over 30	Senior Citizens
★★	★★★	★★★½	★★★½	★★★★	★★★★

Description and comments   A variety of wildlife can be viewed from Kilauea Point, including more than a dozen species of seabirds, spinner dolphins, Hawaiian green sea turtles, Hawaiian monk seals, and, during the winter months, humpback whales. A 52-foot-high lighthouse, built in 1913, once boasted the largest lens of its kind in the world. It was deactivated in 1976 and is now listed on the National Register of Historic Places.

Other things to do nearby   The Guava Kai Plantation is minutes away by car.

Kilohana Plantation

Location: 3-2087 Kaumuali'i Hwy.

Phone: (808) 245-5608

Hours: Daily, 9:30 a.m.–9:30 p.m. A 20-minute carriage ride is available (no reservations required), and a 1-hour horse-drawn wagon tour of the cane fields is offered 11 a.m. and 2 p.m. Monday–Thursday.

Admission: Free. The carriage ride costs $8 for adults and $4 for children under the age of 12. The wagon tour costs $21 for adults and $10 for children.

When to go: Anytime

How much time to allow: 1–2 hours

Author's rating: ★★★; The *keiki* will enjoy the carriage ride.

Overall appeal by age group:

Pre-school	Grade School	Teens	Young Adults	Over 30	Senior Citizens
★★½	★★★	★★★	★★★½	★★★★	★★★★

Description and comments This 35-acre estate, owned by the *kama'aina* Wilcox family (see the Grove Farm Homestead above), was built in 1935 and today features a wealth of agricultural displays, antiques, and other treasures from Kauai's plantation era.

Koke'e National History Museum

Location: Koke'e State Park

Phone: (808) 335-9975

Web site: www.aloha.net/~kokee

Hours: Daily, 10 a.m.–4 p.m.

Admission: A $1 donation is requested.

When to go: Anytime

How much time to allow: 1 hour

Author's rating: ★★★; A surprisingly good museum that is well worth a visit if you're in the Koke'e area.

Overall appeal by age group:

Pre-school	Grade School	Teens	Young Adults	Over 30	Senior Citizens
★½	★★½	★★½	★★★	★★★½	★★★★

Description and comments This is an intimate museum focusing on the island's ecology, geology, and climatology. Featured here are stone artifacts, shells, hands-on samples of native Hawaiian woods, and an informative display about weather systems in the Pacific region (including information on Hurricane 'Iniki, which devastated Kauai in September 1992). The museum's gift shop has an impressive selection of Hawaiian books, maps, and hiking guides.

Lawai and Allerton Gardens

Location: Near the end of Lawai Rd. in Lawai

Phone: (808) 332-7361 for tour information; (808) 742-2623 for reservations

Web site: www.ntbg.org

Hours: The visitor center is open daily, 9 a.m.–5 p.m.

Admission: For guided tours: $25 for adults; $15 for children ages 13–18; $10 for children ages 6–12. (Not recommended for toddlers due to mosquitoes and toxic plants.)

When to go: Anytime

How much time to allow: About 2½ hours for guided tours

Author's rating: ★★½; The experience here is so serene, it borders on therapeutic.

Overall appeal by age group:

Pre-school	Grade School	Teens	Young Adults	Over 30	Senior Citizens
★	★½	★★	★★½	★★★	★★★

Description and comments   The National Tropical Botanical Garden in Lawai is a 186-acre Eden that boasts one of the world's largest collections of tropical flora, including palms, heliconia, orchids, and other plants that have been collected from tropical regions throughout the world. Neighboring Allerton Garden, meanwhile, features a large collection of flora and beautiful waterfalls, gazebos, and a bamboo jungle. A gift shop offers a charming collection of Island gift items.

Touring tips   Lawai Garden has guided tours every Monday at 9 a.m. and 1 p.m. Allerton Garden offers guided tours Tuesday–Saturday at 9 and 10 a.m., and at 1 and 2 p.m. Reservations are required.

Other things to do nearby   The Spouting Horn blowhole is across the road.

Limahuli Garden

Location: In Ha'ena, near Ha'ena State Park

Phone: (808) 826-1053

Web site: www.ntbg.org

Hours: Tuesday–Friday and Sunday, 9:30 a.m.–4 p.m.

Admission: Guided tours are $15 for adults (reservations required); self-guided tours are $10 (no reservations needed). Children under the age of 12 are admitted free.

When to go: Anytime

How much time to allow: 2 hours

Author's rating: ★★½; A photographer's paradise.

Overall appeal by age group:

Pre-school	Grade School	Teens	Young Adults	Over 30	Senior Citizens
★	★½	★★	★★½	★★★	★★★

Description and comments This award-winning 17-acre garden and 990-acre forest preserve—it was named America's "Natural Botanical Garden of the Year" in 1997 by the American Horticultural Society—features terraced gardens and a lush rain forest. Three distinct ecological zones are found within the garden.

Moir Gardens

Location: Kiahuna Plantation, 2253 Po'ipu Rd.

Phone: (808) 742-6411

Hours: Daily, 24 hours

Admission: Free

When to go: Anytime

How much time to allow: 1 hour

Author's rating: ★★★; A living symbol of why Kauai is the "Garden Isle."

Overall appeal by age group:

Pre-school	Grade School	Teens	Young Adults	Over 30	Senior Citizens
★★	★★½	★★½	★★★	★★★½	★★★½

Description and comments Nearly 4,000 varieties of plant life are featured in this pristine garden, which surrounds the former home of Koloa Plantation Company's last plantation manager. Lagoons, lily ponds, trees, and flowers provide great photo opportunities. A unique highlight here is one of the finest cactus gardens in the world.

Touring tips Free guided tours are held Tuesday at 9 a.m. and Thursday at 4 p.m.

Other things to do nearby Lawai and Allerton Gardens are a short drive away in Lawai.

Wai'oli Mission House Museum

Location: Grove Farm Homestead

Phone: (808) 245-3202

Hours: Tuesday, Thursday, and Saturday, 9 a.m.–3 p.m. Guided tours are available.

Admission: Donations of $5 for adults and $2 for children age 12 and under are requested.

When to go: Anytime

How much time to allow: 1 hour

Author's rating: ★★½; Recommended for anyone interested in Hawaii's storied missionary era.

Overall appeal by age group:

Pre-school	Grade School	Teens	Young Adults	Over 30	Senior Citizens
★½	★★	★★½	★★½	★★★	★★★½

Description and comments Built in 1837, this structure was the home of missionaries Lucy and Abner Wilcox. The New England–style Wai'oli Mission Hall and Wai'oli Hui'ia Church are located on adjoining grounds.

Molokai: Zone 14

Molokai Museum and Cultural Center

Location: On Kalae Hwy., just west of Kaunakakai

Phone: (808) 567-6436

Hours: Monday–Saturday, 10 a.m.–2 p.m.

Admission: $2.50 for adults; $1 for students ages 5–18

When to go: Anytime

How much time to allow: 1 hour

Author's rating: ★★½; Not terribly exciting, but filled with history.

Overall appeal by age group:

Pre-school	Grade School	Teens	Young Adults	Over 30	Senior Citizens
★½	★★	★★½	★★★	★★★	★★★½

Description and comments The museum is a converted sugar mill established in 1878 by Rudolph Wilhelm Meyer, an engineer and surveyor who arrived on Molokai in 1851 and married a Hawaiian princess. Now listed on the National Register of Historic Places, the mill houses original machinery and other artifacts from the island's sugar plantation days. Guided tours and Hawaiian cultural programs are offered.

Molokai Ranch

Location: 100 Maunaloa Hwy.

Phone: (808) 552-2791

Web site: www.molokai-ranch.com

Hours: Monday–Saturday, 7:30 a.m.–4:30 p.m.

Admission: Prices for activities range from $10 for target archery and $15 for outrigger canoe paddling to $55 for a *paniolo* roundup (rodeo).

When to go: Anytime

How much time to allow: Half a day

Author's rating: ★★★★; From unique camping packages to a deluxe menu of activities, Molokai's biggest attraction has something for the entire family.

Overall appeal by age group:

Pre-school	Grade School	Teens	Young Adults	Over 30	Senior Citizens
★★½	★★★★	★★★★½	★★★★½	★★★★	★★★½

Description and comments   Encompassing more than 54,000 acres (covering a third of the entire island of Molokai), Molokai Ranch is the starting point for many great outdoor activities on the island. At the ranch's Outfitters Center, you can sign up for a horseback ride or learn the basic cowboy skills—you can even compete in the day's Malihini Rodeo! Camping is one of the ranch's newer offerings; three camps—Paniolo, Kolo Cliffs, and Kaupoa Beach—are available, and meals and transportation are included. Other activities include mountain biking, snorkeling, hiking, kayaking, outrigger canoe paddling, archery, a ropes challenge course, and whale-watching (seasonal).

Part Eleven
Dining in Hawaii

Experiencing Hawaii's Multicultural Cuisine

THE NEW HAWAII REGIONAL CUISINE

Little more than a decade ago, food gurus planning a trip to Hawaii might have been advised to "forget the food unless you love cholesterol-laden plate lunches piled with two scoops of rice, potato salad, meat, and gravy." Ironically, today the Islands have become a destination with so many fine dining establishments and cutting-edge chefs that it is impossible to sample all of the best during a single ten-day vacation. Dozens of Island chefs have been guest chefs at the prestigious James Beard House in New York; some, like Sam Choy and Roy Yamaguchi, now have restaurants in several states and foreign countries, and they have gained international reputations through their own television shows. In less than ten years, Hawaii regional cuisine and its many incarnations—fusion, contemporary, Pacific Rim, Euro-Asian—has captured Island and visitor taste buds, replacing Continental cuisine in hotel dining rooms and restaurants across the state.

ETHNIC ELEMENTS

Today's flavorful and sophisticated Hawaii regional cuisine springs from humble beginnings. The earliest Polynesian voyagers brought taro, bread-fruit, coconuts, bananas, sugarcane, mountain apples, yams, and Polynesian sweet potatoes among the 27 plants they loaded for survival on their doubled-hulled outrigger canoes from the Marquesas Islands. Successive waves of immigrants from the 1800s on arrived to work the sugarcane fields, incorporating their own ingredients and styles of cooking. From community kitchens and plantation homes, Chinese, Japanese, Portuguese, Filipinos, and other laborers brought *bento* boxes for lunch in the fields, and at *pau hana* (quitting time), they shared platters of ethnic *pupus* (appetizers). Asian flavors—soy sauce, oyster sauce, sesame oil, mirin, homemade tofu—were adopted and combined, incorporating the individual cooking styles of home cooks.

The makings of a cuisine found nowhere else in the world thrived in Island gardens. Backyard plots nurtured exotics like bok choy, daikon, lemongrass, and Kaffir lime leaves, as well as indigenous ingredients—coconuts, bananas, papayas, mangos, star fruit, lychees, breadfruit. When European chefs were eventually imported to create hotel food for Hawaii's developing tourist business, they tasted what local chefs were doing in Island kitchens and stirred in elements based on their own classical training, and by the early 1990s, Hawaii regional cuisine had taken on intriguing flavors, plus an artistic appearance on the plate.

In 1992, the movement rose faster than a loaf of Portuguese sweet bread set out to proof when a dozen highly trained restaurant chefs formalized the term "Hawaii regional cuisine" by banding together to trade creative cooking secrets and to develop and promote locally grown produce, meat, and seafood. Today, many Island chefs consult with fishermen, farmers, and fruit growers in order to move exotic and varied homegrown ingredients from ground to gourmet restaurant in the shortest time possible. On the Big Island, fishermen, ranchers, and small specialty farmers who grow taro, hearts of palm, fern shoots, exotic fruit, and herbs are enjoying new popularity with chefs in resort hotels along the Big Island's Kohala Coast. These imaginative chefs delight diners with taro fritters, poi-based sauces, Puna goat cheese appetizers and salads, tropical fruit desserts, and the like. Some chef/owners (like Keo Sananikone of Keo's Thai Restaurants on Oahu) actually grow their own herbs and greens, or, like Jean Marie Josselin of A Pacific Café on Kauai, Maui, and Oahu, buy directly from a specific farmer who sets aside plots of produce grown to the chef's specifications.

Frequently, regional cuisine menus note the local origin of gourmet items in elaborate descriptions of entrées flavored with ginger and shoyu, cilantro and sesame oil. From the Big Island, for example, you'll find Puna goat cheese (a creamy white cheese produced from goats raised on a particular farm in the Puna district), Waimea strawberries (deliciously sweet and juicy vine-ripened berries grown near the upcountry town of Waimea), and Keahole lobster (a succulent big red or blue lobster raised in aquaculture ponds at Keahole near the Kona International Airport), as well as abalone and crunchy ogo, or seaweed. On Lanai, island venison is noted as favorite fare on hotel menus.

Gourmet items are not only available in fine dining rooms; they can also be taken home as gifts. In the last decade or so, gourmet coffee cultivation has spread from the island of Hawaii's Kona district, so now you can buy coffee as a souvenir grown on any island you visit except Lanai. In addition, the only chocolate grown in the United States blankets upcountry Kona on bushes laden with burnished ripe red pods, processed and marketed as Hawaiian Vintage Chocolate. The supply of this rich, high-quality dessert ingredient can't keep up with the demand from dessert chefs and individual buyers.

FISH FACTS

One of the most frequently voiced questions about Hawaii regional cuisine concerns a clear-cut definition, including the identity of signature ingredients and dishes. As the genre evolved, certain fresh fish emerged as ingredients unique to the Islands. In the past, mahi-mahi had always been the fish identified with Hawaii. Today, mahi, a mild white fish, remains a favorite in the overall scheme of things, but a vast array of other types of fish, which once were caught by fishermen only for their home tables, are now found on restaurant menus.

For the uninitiated, choosing a fish dish can be a challenge, as fish are known by any number of names—local, mainland, and scientific—and often are served in a multitude of preparations listed and described on menus. To allay some of the confusion and encourage the use of fish that are not so well known, the Department of Business, Economic Development, and Tourism promotes a statewide Seafood Festival during the month of July and has published a chart naming and describing various fishes. Following is an abbreviated guide that can help you in choosing a fish dish from an Island menu, though it's always best to ask your waiter for specific descriptions, particularly regarding preparations.

Aku, Skipjack tuna   Red, translucent flesh turns to firm ivory-colored meat when cooked. The high fat content makes this fish good sliced raw for sashimi.

Bigeye 'ahi, Bigeye tuna   Light red flesh cooks to creamy white. The high fat content makes this fish good sliced raw for sashimi.

Yellowfin 'ahi, Yellowfin tuna   Light red flesh cooks to creamy white. The high fat content makes this fish good sliced raw for sashimi.

Shutome, Broadbill swordfish   Firm, well-textured, mild-flavored pinkish meat cooks to white.

Mahi-mahi, Dolphinfish   Firm, light flesh cooks to delicate, sweet white meat.

Ono, Wahoo   Delicate pink meat changes to flaky, sweet meat when cooked.

Opah, Moonfish   Rich, large-grained flesh ranges from pink to orange to bright red throughout the fish.

Moi, Threadfish   Islanders like the moist, mild white meat of this fish steamed, though some chefs prepare it crisp-fried with the edible scales still on.

Monchong, Bigscale, or sickle pomfret   Delicately flavored, smooth, well-textured flesh cooks to moist white meat.

Onaga, Ruby, or long-tailed snapper   The onaga's pale pink flesh, which has a delicate flavor, is considered a good luck food when served raw. It's also delicious cooked.

'Opakapaka, Crimson snapper   A favorite fish in Hawaii restaurants, with pink flesh that has a mild flavor whether sautéed, grilled, or baked.

If there is a signature dish for Hawaii regional cuisine, it's 'ahi sashimi, served in fine dining rooms and local eateries, sushi bars, and Japanese restaurants—in short, in any number of restaurants of all ethnic persuasions. Sometimes a block of tuna is quickly seared on the outside, then thinly sliced for blackened 'ahi, or sometimes the buttery red fish is simply chilled, sliced, and laid on a bed of shredded cabbage and served with a hot soy-wasabi dipping sauce.

On the cooked scene, a second widely served fish that could symbolize Hawaii regional cuisine is often designated as "local-boy style." One popular restaurant uses ono, a white fish, for the preparation, which is flavored with nori (seaweed)-soy vinaigrette and sizzling hot peanut oil. This fish preparation could be classified as "local-style" regional cuisine, as opposed to "haute" regional cuisine. It's the kind of dish that might pop up at a backyard barbecue or a home luau, along with mounds of white rice.

LUAU LORE: TO GO OR NOT TO GO?

You'll probably hear complaints about commercial luaus that range from "Nobody, but nobody, could eat that gray wallpaper paste they call poi" to "The Mai Tai punch was so watered I couldn't even get a buzz on." Nonetheless, if you have never been to a luau, it's one of those things you really should experience. Bear in mind, you don't go to a luau for fine dining; it's most fun to go with friends; and finally, you've got to mentally put yourself in a "hang-loose mode"—wear your wildest print outfit, tuck a flower behind your ear, and be prepared to go barefoot during dinner.

Visitors can experience leisurely and romantic luaus in a garden or on the beach in front of their hotels, or at elaborate, rollicking affairs on a secluded shoreline programmed by professional outfits such as Paradise Cove or Germaine's on Oahu. Some commercial luaus include pageantry, with participants dressed like early Hawaiian royalty; all of them include a Polynesian show. Before dinner, guests might even have a chance to wade barefoot into the sun-warmed ocean to help pull in the *hukilau* net filled with flopping fish.

In old Hawaii, the most popular way of preparing food was to *kalua* the meat—chicken, dog, or fish—in an underground oven, and the heart and soul of any luau is still the preparation and unearthing of the *imu.* Though dog is no longer part of the menu, current luau food is reasonably authentic, except for such items as teriyaki steak, barbecued chicken, and macaroni and potato salads, added to suit all tastes along the buffet line. You'll still find pig roasted to moist tenderness in the *imu,* then shredded; poi, pounded into a pastelike consistency from the cooked taro corm; sweet potatoes; marinated lomi salmon, small pieces of fish with chopped tomatoes and onions; and sometimes 'opihi, a Hawaiian shellfish plucked from wave-washed rocky shorelines and eaten raw as a special delicacy. Chicken or squid luau serves as a vegetable dish made of the tender leaves of the taro plant cooked in coconut milk. Many Island feasts ladle out chicken long rice, a tasty dish of chicken cooked with slithery translucent noodles made of rice flour and garnished with green onions, and frequently you'll find lau lau, little green bundles of taro leaf, which tastes like spinach, containing pork and fish. Luau menus are light on vegetables, but usually fresh pineapple, bananas, and other fruits are found on every table. Relishes—Hawaiian salt, 'inamona made of ground kukui nuts, stalks of green onions, and individual bowls of poi—are also placed on every table. Dessert consists of a white cake with layers of haupia, a pudding of sweetened coconut milk thickened with cornstarch, all crowned with a fluffy white frosting and shredded coconut. Additional haupia cut into finger-sized rectangles always tops off a luau.

The entertainment at one of these feasts is like a mini-tour of Polynesia. Hawaii's contribution includes the haunting chants that perpetuate the legends of the past, as well as the graceful hula. And yes, someone in your party is likely to get dragged onto the stage, so take a camera and capture that Kodak moment, or maybe snap Mom digging into the poi bowl with two fingers, the traditional way to enjoy it.

Our final word about poi comes from an expert. Chef Sam Choy, a "local boy" if ever there was one, says, "It is very nutritious and good for you, and if you sample it often enough, you will eventually acquire a taste for it—maybe. If you're not used to it, it's best to eat it when it's very fresh, although some people like it better after it has sat around for a few days and become sour. You must have poi with your luau whether you like it or not. It just isn't a luau without it."

ISLAND DINING SCENES

Oahu, with the largest population and the highest visitor count (about 5 million annually), and as the center of commerce and transportation, naturally has more restaurants than any other island. In general, fine dining is concentrated in the Waikiki area; however, many former hotel chefs have opened freestanding restaurants of their own on the edges of Waikiki or in shopping centers near residential areas. Hotel restaurants tend to be more expensive, but often they enjoy special ocean-side settings and big-name chefs. The cost doesn't keep local residents away; we dine in high-profile restaurants for special celebrations, for business lunches, and with visiting guests.

On the Neighbor Islands, you'll find the best hotel restaurants on Maui at Wailea, Ka'anapali, Makena, and Kapalua Resorts; on the Big Island along the Kohala Coast; on Kauai at Po'ipu and Princeville; and on Lanai in the two major hotels, the Lodge at Ko'ele and Manele Bay Hotel.

Office workers in downtown Honolulu frequent nearby restaurants— perhaps an ethnic gem in Chinatown, an upbeat contemporary getaway in the Aloha Tower Marketplace, or a favorite hangout on Restaurant Row. A multitude of ethnic restaurants with reasonably priced menus can also be found on the Diamond Head edge of Waikiki along Kapahulu Avenue and a few miles away in Kaimuki.

In the tourist meccas of Lahaina on Maui and Kailua-Kona on the Big Island, many restaurants are of the casual open-air kind. Interestingly, the little upcountry residential town of Waimea on the Big Island has a growing reputation for good food prepared by good chefs in reputable restaurants—Merriman's, Edelweiss, Parker Ranch Grill, Koa House, and Daniel Thiebaut, to mention just a few.

TRENDS

When Hawaii regional cuisine became a recognized movement, chefs sometimes went overboard concocting dishes with a combination of flavors that confused the palate. One year, everything came with at least three sauces artistically spread on the plate like an overcomplicated yin-yang design. Another year, stacking was in, so entrées might come piled six inches high in layers that teetered when the plate was set on the table. As with any new movement trying to gain a foothold, sanity eventually returned. Dishes in today's upscale restaurants are still beautiful to behold, but the trend now is toward flavors that are balanced in courses that complement each other.

Most chefs are aiming toward simplicity and freshness, with the true flavor of meat, fish, and poultry enhanced by fresh herbs. Though the vogue continues to lean toward healthier preparations, with lighter sauces made of fruit coulis or puréed vegetables, meat is on the rebound. People do, however, like variety, and fish and seafood continue to be popular, as evidenced by a proliferation of new seafood bars and buffets.

Wine continues to increase in popularity as an important accompaniment. The best restaurants allow experimentation by making available many wines by the glass, so you can match each course to the wine best suited, rather than confine yourself to one bottle for multiple courses. More and more restaurants are listing suggested wines on the menu that have been matched to the entrées by in-house sommeliers or by Hawaii's best-known master sommelier, Chuck Furuya.

In addition, micro-breweries have finally come into their own in a number of Island restaurants on all major islands. Some are mainland imports; a few, such as Waimea Brew Pub on Kauai and Kona Brewing Company on the Big Island, are local endeavors. In all, you'll find beers made and named for their Island-grown ingredients and flavors, and you'll generally find that the brew pubs offer contemporary food attractively served at reasonable prices.

THE MELTING POT IS SIZZLING

On all islands, food festivals with Hawaiian entertainment, arts and crafts booths, and food samples showcase the diversity of Hawaii's exciting bounty. July is seafood month, featuring public celebrations that include tastings, cooking contests, and demonstrations at markets and restaurants. Spring and summer taro festivals are staged on Maui, Oahu, and Kauai. The Big Island boasts the Try-a-Papaya Festival, a Macadamia Nut Festival, a Kona Coffee Festival, Big Island Bounty, and the Winter Wine Escape. Maui jumps on the food wagon with a wacky Maui Onion Festival, the 'Ulupalakua Thing (agricultural fair), and the Kapalua Wine and Food Symposium. If you're lucky enough to be in the Islands during a food festival, loosen your belt and get set to sample some of the most exciting cuisine around.

The Restaurants

OUR FAVORITE ISLAND RESTAURANTS: EXPLAINING THE RATINGS

We have developed detailed profiles for the best restaurants and for those that offer some special reason to visit, be it decor, ethnic appeal, or bargain prices. Each profile features an easily scanned heading that allows you, in just a second, to check out the restaurant's name, cuisine, star rating, cost, quality rating, and value rating.

Cuisine In a locale where Hawaii regional cuisine has been seeking to define itself only since 1992, categorizing cuisine becomes a challenging endeavor. Hawaii regional cuisine, itself, is an olio of ethnic foods, so we've ended up with dishes that incorporate Asian flavors, Hawaiian flavors, Cajun flavors, Pacific Rim flavors, Mediterranean flavors, and more. Many chefs prefer not to be categorized at all, as they are afraid this will limit others' perception of their creativity. In most cases, we let restaurant owners or chefs name their own categories. In many cases, fusion cuisines are called simply "contemporary cuisine." Even restaurants that once served classic French cuisine now prepare sauces with a lighter hand and are innovative about using Island-grown ingredients, one of the prerequisites of Hawaii regional cuisine. You can get an idea of the type of food served from the heading, then glean a better understanding by reading the detailed descriptions of specialty items and other recommendations.

Star Rating The star rating is an overall rating that encompasses the entire dining experience, including style, service, and ambience, in addition to the taste, presentation, and quality of the food. Five stars is the highest rating possible and connotes the best of everything. Four-star restaurants are exceptional, three-star restaurants are well above average, and two-star restaurants are good. One star indicates an average restaurant that demonstrates an unusual capability in some area of specialization—for example, an otherwise unmemorable place that has great saimin (noodle soup).

Cost To the right of the cuisine is an expense description that provides a comparative sense of how much a complete meal will cost. A complete meal for our purposes consists of an entrée with a vegetable or side dish and a choice of soup or salad. Appetizers, desserts, drinks, and tips are excluded. Categories and related prices are listed below:

Inexpensive	$14 and less per person
Moderate	$15–30
Expensive	More than $30 per person

Quality Rating   On the far right of each heading appear a number and a letter. The number rates food quality on a scale of 0–100, where 100 is the best rating attainable. It is based expressly on the taste, freshness of ingredients, preparation, presentation, and creativity of the food served. There is no consideration of price. If you want the best food available, and cost is not an issue, you need look no further than the quality ratings.

Value Rating   If, on the other hand, you are looking for both quality and value, then you should check the value rating, expressed in letters. Remember, the perception of value can vary from state to state and country to country. Hawaii is a tourist destination, so restaurant prices in the state probably compare favorably with prices in New York, San Francisco, and other major tourist destinations, but not so favorably with smaller, residential towns. Because it is a common perception that hotel restaurants are universally overpriced (where else would you pay $4–6 for a glass of orange juice?), we have indicated restaurants of this sort with a C– rating rather than a discouraging D. The C– is meant to convey that yes, the restaurant charges perhaps more than you would pay for a similar entrée somewhere else, but because the setting, service, and preparation are exceptional, it's still worth the splurge. We wouldn't want to rate the restaurant a D, causing a reader to automatically forgo a special dining experience. The value ratings are defined as follows:

A	Exceptional value; a real bargain
B	Good value
C	Fair value; you get exactly what you pay for
D	Somewhat overpriced
F	Significantly overpriced

Locating the Restaurant   Just below the heading is a designation for geographic zone. This zone description will give you a general idea of where the restaurant described is located. We've divided the six major islands into the following 15 geographic zones.

Zone 1	Waikiki
Zone 2	Greater Honolulu
Zone 3	Windward Oahu
Zone 4	The North Shore
Zone 5	Leeward Oahu
Zone 6	Central Oahu
Zone 7	Central Maui
Zone 8	South Maui

Zone 9	West Maui
Zone 10	Upcountry Maui
Zone 11	Kona
Zone 12	Hilo and Volcano
Zone 13	Kauai
Zone 14	Molokai
Zone 15	Lanai

Payment   We've listed the type of payment accepted at each restaurant using the following codes:

AMEX	American Express
CB	Carte Blanche
D	Discover
DC	Diners Club
MC	MasterCard
VISA	VISA

Who's Included   Restaurants open and close frequently in Hawaii, so most of those we've included have a proven track record. However, some of the newest upscale restaurants owned and operated by chefs who have become local celebrities have been included to keep the guide as complete and up-to-date as possible. Local chains, such as Sam Choy's and Roy's, are included, as are a few franchises that have a distinctly Hawaiian look in food and decor, such as TS Incorporated. Also, the list is highly selective. Our leaving out a particular place does not necessarily indicate that the restaurant is not good, only that it was not ranked among the best in its genre. Detailed profiles of individual restaurants follow in alphabetical order at the end of this chapter. In the section titled "More Recommendations," we've named reputable restaurants that you might want to try for a specific reason—for pizzas, bagels, plate lunches—that don't otherwise merit a full description. These are listed according to their island location, but you might notice that every "best" category may not have a listing on each island. This is not an oversight; an omitted island simply may not have a good restaurant that fits the category.

The Best Hawaii Restaurants

Name	Star Rating	Price Rating	Quality Rating	Value Rating	Zone
Oahu					
Chinese					
The Golden Dragon	★★★★	Moderate	90	C	1
Contemporary American					
3660 on the Rise	★★★★	Moderate	92	C	2
Diamond Head Grill	★★★★	Mod/Exp	89	C	1
The Surf Room	★★★½	Mod/Exp	80	C	1
Duke's Restaurant	★★★	Inexp/Mod	75	B	1
Contemporary International					
Hoku's	★★★½	Mod/Exp	86	C	2
Continental/Pacific Rim					
Hau Tree Lanai	★★★	Moderate	76	C	1
Euro-Asian					
Indigo	★★★★	Inexp/Mod	90	B	2
Roy's Restaurant	★★★★	Moderate	90	C	2
Bali-by-the-Sea	★★★½	Mod/Exp	86	C	1
Euro-Japanese					
L'Uraku	★★★★	Moderate	87	C	2
French/Continental					
Michel's at the Colony Surf	★★★★½	Expensive	92	D	1
Hawaii Regional					
Alan Wong's Restaurant	★★★★★	Mod/Exp	99	B	1
Prince Court Restaurant	★★★★	Moderate	90	C	1
Sam Choy's BLC and Diamond Head	★★★★	Moderate	88	B	1,2
Don Ho's Island Grill	★★★	Inexpensive	80	B	2

The Best Hawaii Restaurants (continued)

Name	Star Rating	Price Rating	Quality Rating	Value Rating	Zone
Island Eclectic					
'Ahi's	★	Inexpensive	70	A	4
Italian					
Sarento's Top of the "I"	★★★½	Mod/Exp	86	C	1
Mediterranean/Island Flair					
Padovani's Bistro & Wine Bar	★★★★½	Mod/Exp	96	C	1
Cascada	★★★½	Moderate	86	C	1
Palomino Euro Bistro	★★★	Inexp/Mod	81	B	2
Neo-Classical (Contemporary)					
La Mer	★★★★★	Expensive	99	C–	1
Pacific Edge/Pacific Rim					
Chef Mavro Restaurant	★★★★★	Expensive	98	C	1
A Pacific Café	★★★★½	Moderate	92	C	2
Seafood					
Orchids	★★★★½	Mod/Exp	92	C	1
John Dominis	★★★½	Mod/Exp	85	D	1
Steak and Seafood					
Hy's Steak House	★★★	Mod/Exp	85	C	1
Buzz's Original Steakhouse	★★	Inexp/Mod	80	C	3
Thai					
Singha Thai Cuisine	★★★★	Inexp/Mod	90	B	1
Keo's in Waikiki	★★★★	Inexp/Mod	90	B	1
Maui					
Contemporary					
David Paul's Lahaina Grill	★★★★	Mod/Exp	91	C	9

The Best Hawaii Restaurants (continued)

Name	Star Rating	Price Rating	Quality Rating	Value Rating	Zone
Plantation House Restaurant	★★	Inexp/Mod	84	C	9
Contemporary Island/French					
Gerard's	★★★★	Mod/Exp	85	B	9
Continental					
Ma'alaea Waterfront Restaurant	★★★½	Moderate	90	C	7
Bay Club Restaurant	★★★	Mod/Exp	75	C–	9
Euro-Asian					
Roy's Kahana Bar & Grill and Nicolina	★★★½	Moderate	85	B	9
French					
Chez Paul's	★★★★	Mod/Exp	87	C	7
Hawaii Regional					
Seasons	★★★★½	Mod/Exp	93	C–	8
Pacific'O	★★★★½	Moderate	92	C	9
Hali'imaile General Store	★★★★	Mod/Exp	90	C	10
A Pacific Café	★★★½	Mod/Exp	90	C	8,9
Anuenue Room	★★★½	Mod/Exp	85	C–	9
Sam Choy's	★★★½	Inexp/Mod	82	A	7,9
Hula Grill	★★★	Inexp/Mod	83	B	9
Japanese/Pacific Rim					
Sansei	★★★★	Mod/Exp	90	B	9
Mediterranean/Italian					
Longhi's	★★★½	Moderate	84	B	9
Seafood					
Ma'alaea Waterfront Restaurant	★★★½	Moderate	90	C	7
Mama's Fish House	★★★½	Mod/Exp	90	C	7

	The Best Hawaii Restaurants (continued)				
Name	Star Rating	Price Rating	Quality Rating	Value Rating	Zone

Steak and Seafood

Kimo's	★★½	Inexp/Mod	70	B	9

Vietnamese

A Saigon Café	★★★	Inexpensive	85	A	7

The Big Island

American

Parker Ranch Grill	★★½	Moderate	81	C	11
Kona Ranch House	★★½	Inexp/Mod	71	B	11

Contemporary

The Grill and Lounge at the Orchid	★★★½	Expensive	86	C–	11
Café Pesto	★★★½	Inexpensive	84	B	11,12

Continental

Kilauea Lodge	★★★½	Moderate	84	C	12
Edelweiss	★★★½	Moderate	81	B	11

Euro-Asian

Roy's at the King's Shops	★★★★½	Moderate	91	B	11

Hawaii Fusion

Pahu iʻa at Four Seasons	★★★★½	Expensive	91	C–	11

Hawaii Regional

Merriman's	★★★★½	Mod/Exp	94	C	11
Batik Restaurant	★★★★½	Expensive	91	C–	11
CanoeHouse	★★★★½	Mod/Exp	91	C–	11
Coast Grille	★★★★½	Mod/Exp	91	C–	11
Sam Choy's Restaurant	★★★	Moderate	87	B	11

Italian

Donatoni's	★★★★½	Mod/Exp	91	C–	11

The Best Hawaii Restaurants (continued)

Name	Star Rating	Price Rating	Quality Rating	Value Rating	Zone
Pacific Rim/Mediterranean					
Huggo's	★★½	Moderate	81	C	11
Steak and Seafood					
Harrington's	★★	Moderate	76	B	12
Thai					
Royal Siam	★★★½	Inexpensive	86	A	12
Kauai					
American					
Shells	★★★½	Mod/Exp	80	C	13
Contemporary					
Postcards	★★★½	Moderate	85	B	13
Brennecke's Beach Broiler	★★★	Moderate	78	B	13
Tidepools	★★★	Mod/Exp	78	C–	13
Continental/Island Flair					
Café Hanalei and Terrace	★★★★	Expensive	91	C	13
Euro-Asian					
Roy's Po'ipu Bar & Grill	★★★★	Moderate	91	C	13
Island Eclectic					
Hamura Saimin	★	Inexpensive	75	A	13
Italian					
Piatti	★★★½	Moderate	85	C	13
Casa di Amici	★★½	Moderate	80	C	13
Pacific Rim					
A Pacific Café	★★★★½	Moderate	94	C	13
The Beach House	★★★	Moderate	85	C	13

	Star	Price	Quality	Value	
The Best Hawaii Restaurants (continued)					
Name	Star Rating	Price Rating	Quality Rating	Value Rating	Zone
Seafood					
Duke's Canoe Club	★★★	Inexp/Mod	81	B	13
Seafood and Steak					
Keoki's Paradise	★★★½	Moderate	85	B	13
Thai/Chinese					
Mema Thai Cuisine	★★	Inexp/Mod	80	A	13
Molokai					
American					
'Ohia Lodge	★★	Moderate	80	C	14
Contemporary					
Moanaloa Room	★★★★	Mod/Exp	87	C	14
Island Eclectic					
The Village Grill	★★	Moderate	80	C	14
Hotel Molokai Restaurant	★★	Inexpensive	70	A	14
Pizza and Sandwiches					
Molokai Pizza Cafe	★★	Inexpensive	75	B	14
Lanai					
American Country					
Henry Clay's Rotisserie	★★★	Moderate	80	B	15
Contemporary					
Formal Dining Room	★★★★½	Expensive	94	C–	15
Hawaii Regional					
'Ihilani	★★★★½	Expensive	91	C–	15
Island Eclectic					
Blue Ginger Café	★	Inexpensive	70	A	15

More Recommendations

BEST BAGELS

Oahu

Hawaiian Bagels (Bagel Bakers) 753B Halekauwila Street, Honolulu (808) 596-0638

Manoa Marketplace 2764-A Woodlawn Drive, Honolulu (808) 942-2243

Maui

Jack's Bagels 333 Dairy Road, Kahului (808) 871-5225; 2395 Kihei Road, Suite 115 (808) 891-2227; or 910 Honoapi'ilani Highway, Unit 16, Lahaina (808) 667-5225

BEST BAKERIES

Oahu

Mary Catherine's Bakery 2820 South King Street, Honolulu (808) 946-4333

Maui

Komoda Store & Bakery 3674 Baldwin Avenue, Makawao (808) 572-7261. For cream puffs and macadamia nut cookies.

Kauai

Kilauea Bakery and Pau Hana Pizza Kong Lung Center, Kilauea (808) 828-2020

Molokai

Kanemitsu Bakery 79 Ala Malama Street, Kaunakakai (808) 553-5855. For Molokai bread and lavosh.

BEST BREAKFASTS

Big Island

Pahu i'a Four Seasons Hualalai, 100 Ka'upulehu Drive, Ka'upulehu-Kona (808) 325-8000

Kauai

Eggberts 4-484 Kuhio Highway, Coconut Marketplace, Kapa'a (808) 822-3787

BEST BREW PUBS

Oahu
Brew Moon   1200 Ala Moana Boulevard, Honolulu (808) 589-1818

Maui
Maui Brews   900 Front Street, Lahaina (808) 667-7794

Big Island
Kona Brewing Company and Brew Pub   75-5629 Kuakini Highway, Kailua-Kona (808) 329-2739

Kauai
Whaler's Brewpub   3132 Ninini Point, Lihu'e (808) 245-2000

BEST DELI FOOD

Oahu
Strawberry Connections   1931 Kahai Street, Honolulu (808) 842-0278

Maui
Pauwela Café   375 West Kuiaha Road, Ha'iku (808) 575-9242

Big Island
A Piece of the Apple   75-5799 Ali'i Drive, Suite 2A, Kailua-Kona (808) 329-4668

Lanai
Pele's Other Garden   811 Hausten Street, Lanai City (808) 565-9628

BEST DOWN-HOME LOCAL ATMOSPHERE

Oahu
La Mariana Restaurant and Bar   50 Sand Island Access Road, Honolulu (808) 848-2800

Big Island
Bamboo Restaurant   'Akone Pule Highway, Hawi (808) 889-5555

Kauai
Green Garden   Highway 50, Hanapepe (808) 335-5422

Best Fresh Fish

Maui

Mama's Fish House   799 Poho Place, Ku'au (808) 579-84█

Big Island

Seaside Restaurant   1790 Kalaniana'ole Avenue, Hilo (808) 935-88█

Best Golf Course Restaurants

Oahu

Niblick Restaurant   Ko Olina Golf Club, 921220 Ali'i Nui Drive, Kapolei (808) 676-6703

Maui

Sea Watch   100 Wailea Golf Club Drive, Wailea (808) 875-8080

Big Island

The Club Grill   Hualalai Resort, 100 Ka'upulehu Drive, Ka'upulehu-Kona (808) 325-8525

Kauai

Princeville Restaurant and Bar   Prince Clubhouse, 5-3900 Kuhio Highway, Princeville (808) 826-5050

Lanai

The Challenge at Manele Bay Clubhouse   Manele, Lanai (808) 565-2230

Best Hamburgers

Oahu

Kua 'Aina Sandwich   66-214 Kamehameha Highway, Hale'iwa (808) 637-6067; 1116 'Auahi Street, Honolulu (808) 591-9133

Maui

Cheeseburger in Paradise   811 Front Street, Lahaina (808) 661-4855

Kauai

Bubba's Hawaii   4-1421 Kuhio Highway, Kapa'a (808) 823-0069; Hanalei (808) 826-7839

...ahulu Avenue, Kapahulu (808) 737-

...233 Helumoa Road, Waikiki (808) 931-
...ch buffet.

Maui

Pukalani Country Club ... ...urant   360 Pukalani, Pukalani (808) 572-1325

Big Island

Kuhio Grille   111 E. Puainako, Prince Kuhio Plaza, Suite A106, Hilo (808) 959-2336

Kauai

Aloha Diner   971F Kuhio Highway, Waipouli (808) 822-3851

BEST ICE CREAM (LOCALLY MADE)

Call listed numbers for other outlets.

Oahu

Bubbie's Homemade Ice Cream and Desserts   Kahala Mall Shopping Center, Kahala (808) 739-2822; 1010 University Avenue, Honolulu (808) 949-8984

Big Island

Tropical Dreams Ice Cream   Kress Building, Kamehameha Highway, Hilo (808) 935-9109; Kohala Coffee Mill, 'Akone Puli Highway, Hawi (808) 889-5577

Kauai

Lappert's Ice Cream   1-3555 Kaumuali'i Highway (808) 335-6121

BEST ITALIAN CUISINE

Oahu

Matteo's   364 Seaside Avenue, Waikiki (808) 922-5551

Maui
Carelli's 2980 South Kihei Road, Keawakapu, Kihei (808) 875-0001

Big Island
Donatoni's Hilton Waikoloa Village, 425 Waikoloa Beach Drive, Waikoloa (808) 886-1234

Kauai
La Cascata Princeville Hotel, Princeville Resort (808) 826-9644

BEST JAPANESE TEA HOUSES
Oahu
Natsunoya Tea House 1935 Makanani Drive, Honolulu (808) 595-4488. Minimum of ten diners.

Kauai
Hanama'ulu Restaurant, Tea House and Sushi Bar 1-4291 Kuhio Highway, Hanama'ulu (808) 245-2511

BEST LUAU
Oahu
Paradise Cove 92-1089 Ali'inui Drive, Kapolei (808) 973-5828 or (808) 945-3571

Maui
Old Lahaina Lu'au 1251 Front Street, Lahaina (808) 667-1998

Big Island
Kona Village Queen Ka'ahumanu Highway, Ka'upulehu-Kona (808) 325-5555

Kauai
Pa'ina o Hanalei Princeville Hotel, Princeville Resort (808) 826-9644

BEST MEXICAN CUISINE
Oahu
Rosie's Cantina Hale'iwa Shopping Plaza, Hale'iwa (808) 637-3538

Maui
Polli's 1202 Makawao Avenue, Makawao (808) 572-7808

Kauai

La Bamba   4261 Rice Street, Lihu'e (808) 245-5972

BEST PIZZA

Oahu

Pizza Bob's Hale'iwa   Shopping Plaza, Hale'iwa (808) 637-5095

Maui

Pizza Paradiso Express   Whalers Village, 2435 Ka'anapali Parkway, Ka'anapali (808) 667-0333

Pizza Paradiso Italian Caffe   Honokowai Marketplace (808) 665-0055

Big Island

Bianelli's Gourmet Pizza and Pasta   75-240 Nani Kailua Drive, Kailua-Kona (808) 326-4800

Kauai

Brick Oven Pizza   2-2555 Kaumualii Highway, Kalaheo (808) 332-8561

Molokai

Molokai Pizza Café   Kaunakakai Place on Wharf Road, Kaunakakai (808) 553-5655

BEST PLACES TO HANG OUT

Oahu

The Pier Bar   Aloha Tower Market Place, 1 Aloha Tower Drive, Honolulu (808) 536-2166

Maui

Hula Grill's Beach Bar   Whalers Village, 2435 Ka'anapali Parkway, Ka'anapali (808) 667-6636

Big Island

Kona Inn Restaurant   75-5744 Ali'i Drive, Kailua-Kona (808) 329-4455. Go at sunset.

BEST PLATE LUNCHES

Oahu

Kaka'ako Kitchen   1216 Waimanu Street, Honolulu (808) 594-3663

Maui

Sam Sato's in Wailuku Millyard   1750 Wili Pa Loop, 244-7124

Big Island

Island Grinds   Hilo Bay Front on the beach near Suisan Fish auctic Hilo (808) 895-0625. Lunch wagon.

Kauai

Mixed Plate   5-5190 Kuhio Highway, 3E4, Ching Young Village, Hanalei (808) 826-7888

BEST ROMANTIC RESTAURANTS

In all cases, ask for a table with an ocean view.

Oahu

Michel's   2895 Kalakaua Avenue, Waikiki (808) 923-6552

Maui

Carellis   2980 South Kihei Road, Kihei (808) 875-0001

Big Island

Pahu i'a Restaurant at Four Seasons Hualalai   100 Ka'upulehu Drive, Ka'upulehu-Kona (808) 325-8000

Kauai

Tidepools   Hyatt Regency Kauai, 1571 Po'ipu Road, Po'ipu (808) 742-1234

BEST SEAFOOD BUFFETS

Oahu

Orchids at Halekulani   2199 Kalia Road, Waikiki (808) 923-2311

Maui

The Terrace at the Ritz-Carlton   1 Ritz-Carlton Drive, Kapalua (808) 669-6200

Kauai

Café Hanalei and Terrace   Princeville Resort, Princeville (808) 826-2760. Friday night only.

Kamehameha Highway, Hale'iwa (808)

...:e   1913 South Kihei Road, Kihei (808)

Big Island
Oodles of Noodles   75-1027 Henry, Suite 102, Kailua-Kona (808) 329-9222

BEST STEAK HOUSES
Oahu
Ruth's Chris Steak House   Restaurant Row, Honolulu (808) 599-3860

Maui
Outback Steak House   4405 Honoapi'ilani Highway, Honoapi'ilani (808) 665-1822

Big Island
Big Island Steak House   King's Shops, Waikoloa Beach Drive, Waikoloa (808) 885-8805

Kauai
Kalaheo Steak House   4444 Papalina Road, Kalaheo (808) 332-9780

BEST SUNDAY BRUNCH
Oahu
Orchids   Halekulani, 2199 Kalia Road, Waikiki (808) 923-2311

Maui
Grand Wailea Hotel   3850 Wailea Alanui Drive, Wailea (808) 875-1234

Big Island
The Terrace   Mauna Kea Beach Hotel, 62-100 Mauna Kea Beach Drive (808) 882-7222

Kauai

Café Hanalei and Terrace   Princeville Resort, Princeville (808) 826-2760

BEST SUSHI BARS

Oahu

Kacho   Waikiki Parc Hotel, 2233 Helumoa Road, Waikiki (808) 924-3535

East Maui

Hakone   Maui Prince Hotel, 5400 Makena Alanui Road, Makena (808) 874-1111

West Maui

Sansei Restaurant and Sushi Bar   115 Bay Drive, Unit 115, Kapalua Shops, Kapalua (808) 669-6286

Big Island

Imari at Hilton Waikoloa Village   425 Waikoloa Beach Drive, Kohala Coast (808) 886-1234

BEST THAI CUISINE

Oahu

Singha Thai   1910 Ala Moana Boulevard, Honolulu (808) 941-2898

Big Island

Royal Siam   70 Malama Street, Hilo (808) 961-6100

Bangkok Houses   75-5626 Kuakini Highway, Building 5, Kailua-Kona (808) 329-7764

Kauai

Mema Thai Chinese Cuisine   Wailua Shopping Plaza, 4-361 Kuhio Highway, Kapaʻa (808) 823-0899

BEST THEME RESTAURANTS

Oahu

All Star Café   King Kalakaua Plaza, 2080 Kalakaua Avenue, Waikiki (808) 955-8326

Maui

Bubba Gump Shrimp Company   889 Front Street, Lahaina (808) 661-3111

Big Island

Hard Rock Café   75-5815 Aliʻi Drive, Kailua-Kona (808) 326-7655

BEST VEGETARIAN

Oahu

Down to Earth Deli   2525 South King Street, Honolulu (808) 947-7678

Maui

The Vegan   115 Baldwin Avenue, Paʻia (808) 579-9144

Big Island

Sibu Café   75-5695 Aliʻi Drive, Kailua-Kona (808) 329-1112. Also serves Asian food.

Kauai

Hanapepe Cafe & Espresso   3830 Hanapepe Road, Hanapepe (808) 335-5011

Molokai

Outpost Natural Foods   70 Makaʻena Street, Kaunakakai (808) 553-3377

BEST VIETNAMESE CUISINE

Oahu

A Little Bit of Saigon   2633 South King Street, Honolulu (808) 528-3663

Maui

A Saigon Café   1792 Main Street, Wailuku (808) 243-9560

BEST VIEWS

Oahu

John Dominis   43 ʻAhui Street, Honolulu (808) 523-0955

Maui

The Bay Club　Kapalua Bay Hotel, 1 Ba[...]
5656

Big Island

Pavilion　Mauna Kea Beach Hotel, 62-100 Maun[...]
Kohala Coast (808) 822-7222

Kauai

Café Hanalei and Terrace　Princeville Resort, Princeville [...]
2760

Lanai

Manele Bay Clubhouse　Manele Bay Resort, Manele (808) 565-223[...]

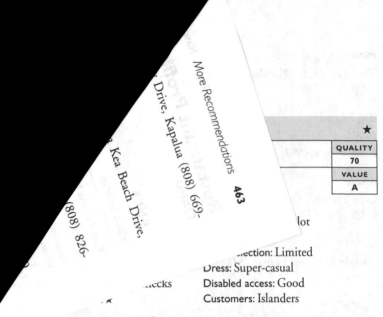

Drive, Kapalua (808) 669-

Kea Beach Drive,

(808) 826-

★

QUALITY
70
VALUE
A

...lot

...ection: Limited

...ecks

Dress: Super-casual
Disabled access: Good
Customers: Islanders

...⌐ and dinner: Every day, 11 a.m.–9 p.m.

Setting & atmosphere: When 'Ahi Logan's original restaurant in Kahuku burned to the ground in June 1996, he and his sons, Bula, Lance, and Byron, moved to what used to be the Paniolo Café, a country casual hangout surrounded by tangled tropical foliage about an hour's drive from Waikiki. The ambience here is authentic hang-loose Hawaii with good, inexpensive comfort food, mellow music, and plenty of aloha spirit. Inside, tables are on two levels, separated by stucco archways. Logan, who ambles around the restaurant barefoot, is a big man. He admits to six feet and close to 300 pounds, and the meals he serves correspond to his size.

House specialties: Dinners are a few steps above "plate lunch" in quality, but they boast some of the same ingredients. For example, entrées are skimpy on the vegetables, but they come with a choice of lots of rice, french fries, or mashed potatoes, *and* a scoop of macaroni salad. Add $2 and you get a tossed green salad, soft drink, and sherbet or ice cream. The fresh fish of the day (which might be ono, 'ahi, shutome, or mahi) and the shrimp plates—scampi, cocktail, tempura, deep-fried, or a combination of all four preparations—are among the best meals. A long-running special is 30 shrimps for about $10. Wine by the glass or bottle and domestic and imported beer, Mai Tais, and Blue Hawaiis can keep you hanging out until the wee hours.

Other recommendations: Hamburger steaks, grilled or teriyaki New York steaks, and chicken and mahi-mahi combination plates are all down-home good.

Entertainment & amenities: The Oahu Group, a guitarist and a bassist who both sing, plays Island-style tunes on Friday and Saturday nights.

Summary & comments: It's the local experience that makes 'Ahi's worth checking into. If you've got an explorer's spirit and happen to come across the North Shore eatery on a night when the music is in full swing and the crowd is lively, you'll have a great time; otherwise, it's a long drive to eat Mom-style cooking.

ALAN WONG'S RESTAURANT		★★★★★

Hawaii Regional	Moderate/Expensive	QUALITY
		99

1857 South King Street, 3rd floor, Waikiki/Honolulu; (808) 949-2526	VALUE
Zone 1 Waikiki	B

Reservations: Highly recommended
When to go: Anytime, but less crowded 5–6:30 p.m.
Entrée range: $15–30
Payment: VISA, MC, AMEX, DC, JCB
Service rating: ★★★★★
Parking: Valet or limited on-street parking
Bar: Full service
Wine selection: Extensive, mostly domestic, good selection by the glass
Dress: Dressy resort attire
Disabled access: Good, via elevator
Customers: Islanders and visitors

Dinner: Every day, 5–10 p.m.

Setting & atmosphere: Situated a short cab ride out of Waikiki, Alan Wong's is hard to spot if you're unfamiliar with South King Street, but the third-floor restaurant is worth the search. Local artwork decorates the walls, and sparkly lights hang overhead. An exhibition kitchen on one side of the comfortable restaurant showcases the action indoors, while outdoors, lanai diners look across part of the city to the Ko'olau Mountains.

House specialties: "Da Bag," an appetizer in a billowy foil pillow, is pierced at the table to yield aromatic kalua pig, steamed clams, spinach, and shiitake mushrooms. Pacific flavors continue throughout the meal in desserts such as "The Coconut," an eye-catching ball of Hawaiian Vintage Chocolate filled with haupia sorbet nestled in tropical fruits and liliko'i sauce.

Other recommendations: Even mashed potatoes take on new meaning when served as roasted garlic smashed potatoes to accompany shellfish, or flavored with wasabi and served with beef tenderloin and lobster-scallop medallion. Ginger-crusted onaga with miso sesame vinaigrette on a bed of sweet corn and shiitake mushrooms is the best-selling entrée.

Summary & comments: Wong's Hawaii regional cuisine is a work of art in flavor and appearance. Containers of soy sauce and chili-pepper water on the tables instead of salt and pepper supplement the local touch in this fine dining restaurant. Some specials, and a five-course tasting menu for $65, change frequently. Alan Wong's Restaurant was chosen "Restaurant of the Year" in the local Hale 'Aina (restaurant) Awards in 1996, 1997, and 1999. Wong was named best North West chef in the James Beard Awards in 1996. Many Islanders consider this their favorite restaurant, though with the opening of Padovani's Bistro and Wine Bar and Chef Mavro's late in 1998, Alan Wong's now faces stiff competition.

BALI-BY-THE-SEA		★★★½
Euro-Asian	Moderate/Expensive	**QUALITY** 86
		VALUE C

Hilton Hawaiian Village Hotel, 2005 Kalia Road, Waikiki
(808) 941-BALI (2254)
Zone 1   Waikiki

Reservations: Highly recommended
When to go: Sunsets are most
  pleasant
Entrée range: $25.50–30.95
Payment: VISA, MC, AMEX, D,
  DC, JCB
Service rating: ★★★★★
Parking: Valet or hotel lot
Bar: Full service
Wine selection: Exceptional; the
wine selection has been named
"The Best" in 1999 in the local
Hale 'Aina Awards—half a dozen
wines are available by the glass
Dress: Resort attire, collared shirts
  and slacks for gentlemen
Disabled access: Good
Customers: Hotel guests and
  Islanders for special occasions

Dinner: Monday–Saturday, 6–10 p.m.

Setting & atmosphere: White linens, candlelight, and fine china and crystal impart an elegance to this romantic, though large, open-air restaurant that overlooks ocean and lagoon vistas. Diamond Head looms beyond the window tables.

House specialties: The regular menu hints of Chef Jean-Luc Voegele's French background. Escargot in phyllo with warm ratatouille and roasted garlic beurre blanc followed by succulent rack of lamb crusted with macadamia nuts and herbs are two of Voegele's classic presentations. Complete dinners climax with a showy presentation of truffles in a miniature chocolate replica of Diamond Head swirling with dry ice.

Other recommendations: From half a dozen appetizers you might choose char siu and shiitake pot-stickers with port wine balsamic glaze or shrimp and scallop Provençales. Seafood lovers often go for Island bouillabaisse as a main course.

Summary & comments: It's not only the open-air dining with soft breezes and lapping waves carrying in from the ocean that make this prize-winning restaurant a favorite of those ready to pop the question, but also the knowledge that they'll receive impeccable service as well as good food to win a sweetheart's heart and hand.

BUZZ'S ORIGINAL STEAK HOUSE ★★

Steak and Seafood	Inexpensive/Moderate	QUALITY
		80

	VALUE
413 Kawailoa Road, Kailua; (808) 261-4661	C
Zone 3 Windward Oahu	

Reservations: Highly recommended
When to go: Anytime
Entrée range: $11–30
Payment: No credit cards
Service rating: ★★★
Parking: Free in adjacent lot
Bar: Full service

Wine selection: Adequate, many by
  the glass
Dress: Casual
Disabled access: Good
Customers: Islanders, tourists
  brought in by Islanders

Lunch: Every day, 11 a.m.–3 p.m.

Dinner: Every day, 5–10 p.m.

Setting & atmosphere: Across the street from Kailua Beach and bordered on one side by Kaʻelepulu Stream, Buzz's has the appeal of an old-fashioned beach house. The wait-help wears Polynesian prints and T-shirts to serve customers at wooden-topped tables and booths indoors and on an outdoor deck. Inside, the bar is a local gathering spot for beachgoers and the young people of this family-oriented small windward town a little less than 15 miles from Waikiki.

House specialties: Salad lovers invariably remember Buzz's bar because avocado is generally among the offerings of tossed greens, sprouts, olives, bacon bits, sesame seeds, and the like. This is a good place to choose fresh fish; thick, juicy steaks; prime rib; and rack of lamb accompanied by a baked potato. If you want good, straightforward food without all the fancy coulis, aïoli, and other sauces of today's trendy cuisine, Buzz's is the place.

Other recommendations: Share an artichoke surprise, a whole artichoke with a butter, herb, and garlic dipping sauce for an appetizer, before sampling fresh fish prepared Chinese-style. You'll catch whiffs of peanut oil, soy sauce, garlic, ginger, and cilantro when this dish is served.

Summary & comments: If you sit at the last table on the open-air deck, you'll notice a little plaque commemorating the fact that President and Mrs. Clinton dined at that table during a stopover in the Islands. Lunch at Buzz's is a pleasant way to take a break from a day spent windsurfing or sunning at the nearby beach.

CASCADA		★★★½
Mediterranean with Island Flair	Moderate	QUALITY 86
Royal Garden Hotel, 440 'Olohana Street, Waikiki; (808) 945-0270 Zone 1 Waikiki		VALUE C

Reservations: Recommended
When to go: Anytime
Entrée range: $18–26
Payment: VISA, MC, AMEX, D, DC, JCB
Service rating: ★★★★½
Parking: Complimentary valet or limited on-street

Bar: Full service
Wine selection: Adequate, 10 wines by the glass
Dress: Casual resort attire
Disabled access: Good
Customers: Tourists and Islanders for special occasions

Breakfast: Every day, 6:30–9:30 a.m.

Lunch: Every day, 11 a.m.–2 p.m.

Dinner: Every day, 6–10 p.m.

Setting & atmosphere: You'll feel as if you made your own special discovery when you wander up a Waikiki side street to this boutique hotel. The restaurant sports a handpainted trompe l'oeil ceiling that depicts trellises, birds, and flowers. Tables are set inside and out on a marble terrace beside a soothing waterfall that feeds into a swimming pool.

House specialties: Whatever you do, don't miss sampling the gnocchi with ricotta cheese and spinach, a delicious accompaniment to Mongolian lamb chops or pan-seared pork tenderloin.

Other recommendations: Salmon tartare, Thai spring rolls, and crab cakes with chipotle sour cream and avocado tomatillo sauces are tried-and-true favorites among the appetizers. Opt for entrées like seafood risotto or fresh Island fish for a lighter meal.

Summary & comments: *Gourmet* magazine named Cascada one of America's Top Tables. Dining here is like finding a peaceful Mediterranean oasis in the middle of frantic Waikiki. Cascada works equally well for a serious business meeting or a quiet tête-à-tête.

CHEF MAVRO RESTAURANT		★★★★★

Pacific Edge	Expensive	QUALITY
		98
1969 South King Street, Waikiki/Honolulu; (808) 944-4714		VALUE
Zone 1 Waikiki		C

Reservations: Highly recommended
When to go: Anytime
Entrée range: $27–38; prix fixe
   menus: $48–72 without wines,
   $66–96 with wines
Payment: VISA, MC, AMEX, DC,
   JCB

Service rating: ★★★★★
Parking: Valet only
Bar: Full service
Wine selection: Good
Dress: Dressy resort attire
Disabled access: Good
Customers: Islanders

Dinner: Every day, 6–9:30 p.m.

Setting & atmosphere: Gleaming pink marble at the entry foretells the simple elegance of the interior. A graceful arch divides the upper and lower portions of the dining area, with banquette seating beside two walls of etched glass windows. The intimate 68-seat restaurant is lit with pinpoint lights with tiny shades suspended like stars from the ceiling and decorated with sprays of orchids for a peaceful, refined atmosphere.

House specialties: Anyone who appreciates sashimi must try the 'ahi tartare topped with Sevruga caviar, which comes in a colorful little mound in the center of a big white dinner plate. The menu changes monthly, but chef/owner George Mavrothalassitis lets the natural flavors of fresh Island ingredients shine through in perfectly balanced dishes, such as crispy fried moi, a moist fish prepared with the edible scales left on and gently flavored with curry and bacon, then presented on a bed of julienned snow peas. The chef is also famous for his onaga baked in a Hawaiian salt crust, which arrives at the table like a little aromatic gift package wafting tarragon and chervil, which the waiter carefully opens, to extract a perfect boneless filet of fish for the serving plate. One of Hawaii's master sommeliers, Brian Geiser, has paired all entrées on the restaurant's menu with a suggested wine. You might start with a flute of French Champagne, then sip a light Alsatian Pinot Blanc, continue with a California Chardonnay, and finish the menu with a Loire Valley Vouvray, all in perfect harmony with your courses.

Other recommendations: Start with warm lobster salad with Molokai sweet potatoes and you may just want to order seconds. Chicken, rotisseried in a glaze of huli huli (soy) sauce, is served with sweet cream corn. Portions are neither huge nor overly rich, so even after multi-course dinners, the chocolate dome with Kona coffee crème brûlée can be fully appreciated for dessert. Tarte tropezienne is another sumptuous dessert: pineapple custard, coconut ice cream, and sorbet.

Summary & comments: Chef George Mavrothalassitis is a true culinary artist with a longtime reputation for award-winning food in Hawaii. He was executive chef of Halekulani when it was first awarded five diamonds by AAA and of Four Seasons Resorts before opening Chef Mavro's Restaurant late in 1998. Dedicated to using fresh Island ingredients, he says his philosophy is not "I have a recipe and I'm going to find an ingredient. I say, I have an ingredient and I'm going to find a recipe." Billed as "affordable fine dining," the tab is still dear, but this is serious gourmet dining for those who appreciate the best.

DIAMOND HEAD GRILL		★★★★
Contemporary American	Moderate/Expensive	QUALITY 89
W Hotel, 2885 Kalakaua Avenue, Waikiki; (808) 922-3734 Zone 1 Waikiki		VALUE C

Reservations: Highly recommended, but not required	Parking: Valet or on-street meters
When to go: Anytime	Bar: Full service
Entrée range: Lunch $13–22, dinner $18–32	Wine selection: Extensive, nearly 2 dozen wines by the glass, including Champagne
Payment: VISA, MC, AMEX, DC, D, JCB	Dress: Resort attire, no beach wear
Service rating: ★★★★½	Disabled access: Good, via elevator
	Customers: Islanders and tourists

Lunch: Monday–Friday, 11:30 a.m.–2:30 p.m.

Dinner: Every day, 5:30–10 p.m.; a lighter bistro menu is also available Thursday–Saturday, 10–11:30 p.m.

Setting & atmosphere: The second-floor location of this restaurant, opened in 1998, is a winner, thanks to Los Angeles architect Steve Jones, who incidentally designed Wolfgang Puck's outlets. It's light and airy in atmosphere, with tables nicely spaced, and the view of Diamond Head right outside a huge picture window seems bigger than life. Jan Kasprzycki's vivid paintings throughout the restaurant and a 7' × 13' mural beside the entry staircase add a sophisticated touch. The main dining area seats 226, with a serpentine martini and appetizer bar on one side; a separate banquet room holds 125. And a glass-enclosed "Chef's Table" is perfect for ten guests.

House specialties: A delicately flavored white snapper called 'opaka-paka—a longtime Islander favorite—is fire-roasted with Kahuku corn ragout and served with creamy basil potatoes and truffled Manila clam nage. The spicy peanut-crusted opah (moonfish) served with a coconut-and-roasted-red-pepper coulis and a little crisp Asian slaw with jasmine rice is also a memorable fish entree. For non–fish lovers, the guava-and-mustard-crusted rack of lamb with goat cheese and roasted garlic gratin is full flavored. Chocolate decadence cake is another memory maker, especially if you add a dollop of tropical fruit-flavored sorbet, pehaps lychee or mango.

Other recommendations: It's hard to pass up appetizers like kalua pork lumpia with mango guacamole and spicy mustard sauce and a lighter grilled portobello mushroom with grilled asparagus, Gorgonzola, and polenta. But if you push on to selections from the stone oven, you'll find an even more imaginative rotisserie pork panini with smoky mozzarella, sun-dried tomato aïoli, and arugula on a rustic flat bread.

Entertainment & amenities: Tuesday through Saturday you'll find a pianist and sometimes another musician rippling out strains of jazz in the evening.

Summary & comments: When this restaurant opened, it was an immediate success and quickly won several dining awards. A new, well-respected chef, David Reardon, took the helm and introduced a complex new menu for the new millennium.

DON HO'S ISLAND GRILL ★★★

Hawaii Regional Comfort Food	Inexpensive	QUALITY
		80

		VALUE
Aloha Tower Marketplace, 1 Aloha Tower Drive, Honolulu		B

(808) 528-0807
Zone 2   Greater Honolulu

Reservations: Recommended
When to go: Sunset for best views of
  a working harbor
Entrée range: $5.95–16.95
Payment: VISA, MC, AMEX, DC,
  JCB
Service rating: ★★★★

Parking: Valet or in adjacent pay lot
Bar: Full service, good selection of
  tropical drinks
Wine selection: Adequate
Dress: Casual
Disabled access: Good if using valet
Customers: Islanders and tourists

Lunch & dinner: Every day, 11 a.m.–11 p.m.

Setting & atmosphere: This restaurant is a Polynesian nostalgia trip right back to the Hawaii depicted by Hollywood in the 1940s and 1950s. Walls are covered with surfboards, paddles, rattan, and Don Ho memorabilia and pictures. The salad bar is nestled in an outrigger canoe. The restaurant opens to views of busy Honolulu Harbor on one side, and a thatched roof bar just outside the confines of the restaurant also overlooks the harbor. Pillars decorated like palm trees and a bamboo-lined bar with stools covered in colorful Polynesian prints are all part of the yesteryear atmosphere.

House specialties: Most fun for sharing is the surfboard pizza with a variety of toppings presented at the table on a miniature surfboard resting on two big pineapple cans. You can get a cheeseburger anytime, but the chop chop salad with rotisserie roast pork and crispy Oriental vegetables is only one of many more interesting choices.

Other recommendations: Stir-fry dishes—teriyaki beef with broccoli, Phoenix and Dragon with shrimp and chicken, Chinatown noodles, etc.— come in big portions, but the fresh Island fish is better. It comes macadamia nut–and-pesto-crusted, or luau-roasted with Hawaiian salt, or local-style with ginger, shoyu, sesame oil, and chives.

Entertainment & amenities: Seven days a week musicians grace the stage during afternoon happy hour, while bigger-name entertainers often appear on weekends and for special events.

Summary & comments: People say they haven't seen anything like this place in 30 years, since Don Ho's heyday. The atmosphere receives bigger raves than the food, however. Ho tends to show up several nights a week, generally after 10 p.m.

DUKE'S RESTAURANT ★★★

Contemporary	Inexpensive/Moderate	QUALITY
		75

Outrigger Waikiki Hotel, 2335 Kalakaua Avenue, Waikiki
(808) 922-2268
Zone 1   Waikiki

		VALUE
		B

Reservations: Accepted
When to go: Anytime
Entrée range: $7.95–23.95
Payment: VISA, MC AMEX, D, DC
Service rating: ★★★
Parking: Valet or hotel lot
Bar: Full service

Wine selection: Good
Dress: Daytime, off-the-beach casual; at night, it's still casual
Disabled access: Good if using valet
Customers: Islanders, beach boys, tourists

Breakfast: Every day, 7–11 a.m.

Lunch: Every day, 11 a.m.–5 p.m.

Dinner: Every day, 5–10 p.m.—a simpler menu is served in the Barefoot Bar 5 p.m.–midnight

Setting & atmosphere: *Pau hana* (after work) surfers, paddlers, and tourists hang out at the big wooden bar watching the sunset over Waikiki Beach in this casual, oceanfront eatery. Historic photos, surfboards, and saltwater aquariums bring back memories of the days when Duke Kahanamoku was an Olympic swimmer and surfer extraordinaire.

House specialties: At dinner try a huge slab of prime rib or awesome fresh fish—'ahi, mahi-mahi, ono, or 'opakapaka—available in five preparations: baked, firecracker, Parmesan- and herb-crusted, hibachi-style teriyaki, or simply grilled. At lunch this is a convenient spot for anything from a burger to huli huli chicken to Thai-style seafood coconut curry.

Other recommendations: Breakfast and lunch buffets and a salad bar at dinner boast value "grinds," or if you prefer table service you might order burgers, fries, pasta, and salads.

Entertainment & amenities: From 4 to 6 p.m. thoroughly modern musicians play Island sounds. On Friday, Saturday, and Sunday, dance bands keep the lower lanai jumping.

Summary & comments: Duke's is one of the most popular places to hang out after a day on Waikiki Beach for both Islanders and tourists, partly because it opens right onto the sand, but also because local surfers are rightly proud of the great Hawaiian swimmer this restaurant commemorates.

THE GOLDEN DRAGON ★★★★

Chinese	Moderate	QUALITY
		90

	VALUE
	C

Hilton Hawaiian Village Hotel, 2005 Kalia Road, Waikiki
(808) 946-5336
Zone 1   Waikiki

Reservations: Highly recommended
When to go: Anytime except
  Monday
Entrée range: $9–30
Payment: VISA, MC, AMEX, D,
  DC, JCB
Service rating: ★★★★½
Parking: Valet or validated self-park

in hotel's garage
Bar: Full service
Wine selection: Good
Dress: Resort attire
Disabled access: Good if using valet
Customers: Hotel guests, Waikiki
  tourists, Islanders

Dinner: Tuesday–Sunday, 6–9:30 p.m.

Setting & atmosphere: Ask to sit on one of the open-air lanais that extends out from the restaurant, for the most romantic views over the Hilton Hawaiian Village lagoon and the little coconut-clad island that rests in its center. The dining room itself has the imperial grandeur of a modern Oriental palace. Golden dragon statues greet you at the entrance, and one wall is lined with lacquer screens decorated with Oriental figures. Tempting aromas float from a circular, glass-enclosed "smoke room" that displays plump juicy roasted ducks. At the back of the restaurant, a private room secluded by a glass partition etched in a lily design is available for groups.

House specialties: A few signature items on the Cantonese menu are a legacy to Chef Dai Hoy Chang, who opened this first Chinese restaurant in Hawaii. Imperial beggar's chicken has to be ordered 24 hours in advance, then, when the waiter presents the dish, he shares the legend with you. A beggar who stole a chicken had only lotus leaves to wrap it in. He improvised a pan by covering the leaves with mud from the lily pond and cooking the whole thing in a campfire. At the Golden Dragon, beggar's chicken arrives at the table in its clay encasement, and the diner is given a beribboned "good luck hammer" to crack it, after which the waiter peels away the clay and the lotus leaves and carves the juicy chicken.

You can see the Peking duck, another traditional dish, hanging in the glass house in the restaurant's center before you eat it. It's carved at the table and served with plum sauce rolled in Mandarin pancakes by your waiter, an easy, non-messy way to eat a dish that could otherwise have you licking your fingers all through the meal.

Other recommendations: Islanders traditionally love the succulent chunks of cold ginger chicken and a tangy lemon chicken dish, but personally, we would opt for the shelled lobster meat with a delicate curry sauce and haupia (coconut pudding). Two chef's signature dinners for $32 and $39 per person feature enough food that you can tuck leftovers in your hotel mini-fridge for dinner the next night.

Summary & comments: Don't say no when the tea lady offers to tell your fortune (at no extra cost), though you must reveal your birth year so she can determine which animal sign you are in the Chinese zodiac. You'll be amazed at how often the fortune fits your personality. *Gourmet* magazine named the Golden Dragon one of America's Top Tables in 1997 and 1998.

HAU TREE LANAI		★★★
Continental/Pacific Rim Moderate		**QUALITY** 76
New Otani Kaimana Beach Hotel, 2863 Kalakaua Avenue, Waikiki		**VALUE** C

New Otani Kaimana Beach Hotel, 2863 Kalakaua Avenue, Waikiki
(808) 921-7066
Zone 1   Waikiki

Reservations: Recommended, especially for dinner	**Parking:** Valet or on-street meters
When to go: Anytime; at dinner sunset is preferred	**Bar:** Full service
Entrée range: Breakfast $9.50–12.95, lunch $7.95–14.95, dinner $17.50–35	**Wine selection:** Good, some selections by the glass
Payment: VISA, MC, AMEX, DC, D, JCB	**Dress:** Casual for breakfast and lunch, resort attire at dinner
Service rating: ★★★★	**Disabled access:** Good, with ramp to the beach-level terrace
	Customers: Waikiki visitors, hotel guests, Islanders

Breakfast: Monday–Saturday, 7–11 a.m.; Sunday, 7–11:30 a.m.

Lunch: Monday–Saturday, 11:30 a.m.–2 p.m.; Sunday, noon–2 p.m.

Dinner: Every day, 5:30–9 p.m.

Setting & atmosphere: A favorite, unpretentious place for Islanders to take out-of-town guests, the Hau Tree Lanai's linen-draped tables are snuggled under a spreading hau tree on the beach at the Diamond Head end of Waikiki. If you want a beach-edge table, go early, about 5:30 p.m., and be sure to make reservations noting your request.

House specialties: Hau Tree Lanai's signature dish is fresh 'opakapaka (snapper) Oriental-style, steamed and garnished with hot peanut oil, soy sauce, cilantro, and green onions. Other favorites among the main courses include filet mignon teamed with the day's fresh catch, seafood penne pasta, shrimp scampi, or, on the wilder side, Thai pesto black tiger prawns and scallops with garlic chili-pepper fried rice. Complete dinners can be made of any entrée item for $6 extra, which adds soup or salad, dessert, and coffee or tea.

Other recommendations: The manager recommends filet Madagascar, sautéed and served with a creamy green peppercorn sauce, potatoes, and vegetables. Appetizers encompass and combine international flavors ranging from Cajun blackened 'ahi sashimi, to chicken and vegetable lumpia, to hoisin duck quesadilla.

Summary & comments: Dawdle over dessert at sundown and eventually you'll see someone you know heading home from paddling or surfing. The Hau Tree Lanai is often named Oahu's best outdoor dining location in local competitions.

HOKU'S ★★★½

Contemporary International	Moderate/Expensive	QUALITY
		86
		VALUE
		C

Kahala Mandarin Hotel, 500 Kahala Avenue, Honolulu
(808) 739-8777 or (808) 739-8888
Zone 2   Greater Honolulu

Reservations: Highly recommended
When to go: Anytime
Entrée range: Lunch $14.95–29.95, dinner $26.50–32.50, vegetarian entrée at $21.95
Payment: VISA, MC, AMEX, D, DC, JCB
Service rating: ★★★★★

Parking: Valet or validated in hotel garage
Bar: Full service
Wine selection: Extensive, including half a dozen ports
Dress: Resort attire
Disabled access: Good
Customers: Hotel guests, repeat local diners

Lunch: Monday–Friday, 11:30 a.m.–2:30 p.m.

Dinner: Monday–Sunday, 5:30–10 p.m.

Setting & atmosphere: Hoku's is a stylish restaurant where every table has a panoramic vista of the Pacific, thanks to a multi-level layout. An open kitchen at one end of the dining room showcases a kiawe wood grill, woks, a tandoori oven, and a wood-burning pizza oven. An oyster and sushi bar offers additional tidbits.

House specialties: Hoku's satisfies international appetites in a single appetizer: Indian naan bread with an Island-style 'ahi poke dip. Slip back to India by sampling tandoori chicken salad, try all-American braised short ribs of beef with a little French truffle sauce, or enjoy a tasty trip to Asia in an Island hot pot of poached seafood (scallops, prawns, clams, lobster, fish) and vegetables (daikon, carrots) in miso broth, served with naan bread, great for sopping up every last drop.

Other recommendations: The chef's tasting menu, which changes frequently, tops out at $65 for five courses, but it allows you to sample a bit of the best of everything. A similar business lunch special includes a salad, the chef's special entrée of the day, and tiramisu for dessert. You can go light and refreshing for dessert with a Möet & Chandon White Star Champagne Granita made with fresh fruit, or order Hoku's dessert sampler for two if you prefer sweet and decadent.

Entertainment & amenities: The restaurant is adjacent to a lobby lounge where live music is featured nightly.

Summary & comments: Hoku's was a big winner in 1998, as it was named Top Restaurant in Hawaii by *Honolulu Magazine*'s Hale 'Aina Awards, Favorite Hotel Restaurant on Oahu in the 'Ilima Awards by the *Honolulu Advertiser,* and America's Top Table by *Gourmet* magazine.

HY'S STEAK HOUSE ★★★

Steak and Seafood	Moderate/Expensive	QUALITY
		85

	VALUE
Waikiki Park Heights Condominium, 2444 Kuhio Avenue (808) 922-5555 Zone 1 Waikiki	C

Reservations: Recommended	**Bar:** Full service
When to go: Anytime	**Wine selection:** Hy's has a wine list
Entrée range: $19.95–47.95, market price may be slightly higher	that never ends!
	Dress: From dressy attire to resort casual
Payment: VISA, MC, AMEX, D, DC, JCB	**Disabled access:** No ramp for stairs, but staff will help
Service rating: ★★★★½	
Parking: Valet in garage	**Customers:** Islanders and tourists

Dinner: Sunday–Thursday, 6–10 p.m.; Friday and Saturday, 6–11 p.m.

Setting & atmosphere: Meat lovers revel in the traditional formal candlelit ambience found beyond the massive carved doors to this elegant, Old

World club-like room. Rich, warm wooden wall paneling with heavy carved filigree accenting ceiling moldings, gleaming brass chandeliers, and a huge beveled mirror reflect tables dressed in pretty pink cloths.

House specialties: Start with a grand, garlicky Caesar salad and proceed to your favorite steaks: The Only, a tender New York Strip broiled over kiawe and served with the restaurant's secret sauce; or T-bone, prime rib, or filet of beef Wellington topped with foie gras (in season) and mushroom druxelles, baked in a light pastry and served with Cabernet truffle sauce. Chateaubriand is also a popular choice not always found in other restaurants. Hy's signature dessert is bananas Foster, a French-Creole version of fresh bananas, orange juice, liqueurs, butter, brown sugar, cinnamon, and rum, flambéed table-side and served over ice cream.

Other recommendations: Seafood combos, lamb, scallops, and scampi can also be ordered with twice-baked potatoes (whipped with sour cream and butter) or with pan-fired O'brien potatoes, steak fries, steamed rice, or rice pilaf, all accompanied by Hy's famous cheese bread.

Entertainment & amenities: Audy Kimura, winner of eight Na Hoku Hanohano Awards, strums the guitar and sings Wednesday through Saturday evenings.

Summary & comments: Even though it's in the heart of Waikiki, Hy's has a loyal *kama'aina* (longtime resident) following.

INDIGO		★★★★
Euro-Asian	Inexpensive/Moderate	**QUALITY** 90
		VALUE B

1121 Nu'uanu Avenue, Honolulu; (808) 521-2900
Zone 2   Greater Honolulu

Reservations: Recommended
When to go: Anytime
Entrée range: $8.25–16.95, vegetarian $7.25
Payment: VISA, MC, D, DC, JCB
Service rating: ★★★★
Parking: Valet, street, or nearby Gateway Plaza lot
Bar: Full service

Wine selection: Good, many by the glass
Dress: Casual
Disabled access: Good if using valet
Customers: Islanders and their out-of-town guests, businesspeople at lunch, pre– and post–Hawaii Theatre attendees

Lunch: Tuesday–Friday, 11:30 a.m.–2 p.m.

Dinner: Tuesday–Friday, 5:30–10 p.m.

Setting & atmosphere: Great care has been taken to create a tropical-Eurasian retreat in the heart of old Honolulu by chef/owner Glenn Chu. The indoor part of the restaurant is set in a historic building erected in 1903. With a high ceiling, suspended fans circling lazily overhead, antique carved panels from Indonesia, and big paintings of Chinese goddesses by local artist Pegge Hopper, you get the feeling you've traveled back in time to some exotic foreign locale for lunch. The back of the building opens onto Chinatown Gateway Park. Diners on the lanai are surrounded by lush greenery, with paper lanterns hung overhead and Balinese umbrellas placed here and there. A bar at the edge of the lanai is roofed with ironwood shingles brought from Indonesia.

House specialties: Appetizers here give diners a chance to taste a variety of textures and flavors, from little steamed, filled dumplings, to spring rolls, to deep-fried wonton and shrimp lumpia served with chipotle aïoli and tangerine sauce. Miso salmon, breast of chicken with peanut sauce, and steamed fish with a soy-oyster-sesame dressing are flavorful entrées.

Other recommendations: Regulars won't let Chef Chu take the crab, tomato, and garlic soup off the menu. And the pizzettas—duck or chicken—are also good for a light meal, especially if you want to try the signature dessert: Madame Pele's chocolate volcano, a cone-shaped mound of mousse spouting raspberry coulis and crème anglaise, arrives at the table amid a cloud of dry-ice smoke announced by a resonating gong.

Summary & comments: Located across the park from the historic Hawaii Theatre, Indigo is a perfect spot for a preperformance dinner. Romantics might like to mention any special occasions when making a reservation, as one table is screened by greenery and set near a bubbling waterfall. Chu has bottled a line of his special sauces, such as raspberry-hoisin sauce, which can be purchased at the restaurant.

JOHN DOMINIS ★★★½

		QUALITY
Seafood	Moderate/Expensive	85
		VALUE
43 'Ahui Street, Honolulu; (808) 523-0955		D
Zone I Waikiki		

Reservations: Recommended
When to go: Sunset brings out gorgeous colors over Diamond Head, even though you don't see the setting sun itself
Entrée range: $19.95 – 68.95
Payment: VISA, MC, AMEX, DC, JCB
Service rating: ★★★½

Parking: Valet
Bar: Full service
Wine selection: Good, 8 wines by the glass
Dress: Resort attire
Disabled access: Good
Customers: Tourists and Islanders for special occasions

Brunch: Sunday seafood buffet, 9 a.m.–1 p.m.

Dinner: Sunday–Thursday, 6–9:30 p.m.; Friday and Saturday, 5:30–9:30 p.m.

Setting & atmosphere: On the lower level of this split-level restaurant, a saltwater fishpond is filled with Island fish, stingrays, and lobsters, so you get an effect of water all around, from the ocean outside to the pool inside. A moss-rock wall, koa furnishings, orchids throughout the restaurant, and green pothos vines hanging from the ceiling create the effect of a cool tropical oasis. Near the entry a large, comfortable lounge and 20-seat bar is a fine place to drop by with friends for an appetizer and a glass of wine.

House specialties: Island fish served in half a dozen different preparations are John Dominis's area of expertise. Everyone loves the 'opakapaka (snapper) en papillote (in a parchment bag), served with freshly made pasta and sautéed vegetables du jour. Mild, moist moi steamed with lemon, shoyu, and ginger delights local diners, though tiger prawns, sautéed scampi-style or stir-fried with black bean sauce, are also high on the list of favorites. Abalone with white wine and capers, though costly, is another delicacy seldom seen on standard menus. The restaurant is known for live lobster fresh from the tank, which can be Hawaiian spinies or live Maine lobster.

Other recommendations: You can order good things to preclude dinner, like stuffed mushrooms with crab and hollandaise, or, for an Island flair, 'ahi poke (made with raw fish). Then, if you haven't gotten your fill of good things, John Dominis's Bailey's mud pie in an Oreo cookie crust filled with ice cream and dressed in Bailey's liqueur sauce is a perfect way to end a meal.

Entertainment & amenities: A four-piece band, including a vocalist, renders contemporary pop music on Friday and Saturday nights.

Summary & comments: John Dominis is a five-time 'Ilima winner for fine dining, an award offered annually by Hawaii Newspaper Agency and Diamond Head Theater. We hear that service tends to be inconsistent.

KEO'S IN WAIKIKI ★★★★

Thai/Island	Inexpensive/Moderate	QUALITY
		90

		VALUE
Ambassador Hotel, 2028 Kuhio Avenue, Waikiki; (808) 951-9355		**B**
Zone 1 Waikiki		

Reservations: Recommended, but not required	Parking: Valet
	Bar: Full service
When to go: Anytime	Wine selection: Adequate
Entrée range: $8.95–16.95	Dress: Resort attire
Payment: VISA, MC, AMEX, D, DC, JCB	Disabled access: Good
	Customers: Tourists and Islanders
Service rating: ★★★★½	

Breakfast: Every day, 7–11 a.m.

Lunch: Every day, 11 a.m.–2 p.m.

Dinner: Every day, 5–10:30 p.m.

Setting & atmosphere: Creative chef/owner Keo Sananekone designed and decorated this newest of his five Keo's restaurants with teak furnishings, Thai carvings, and Hawaiian artwork. In the heart of Waikiki, the restaurant still has the ambience of a quiet refuge, with indoor and outdoor seating at linen-draped tables surrounded by blooming orchids.

House specialties: Locally grown filet of catfish, deep-fried with a tapioca crust, and evil jungle prince (a delicious concoction of shrimp, chicken, or beef in a spicy coconut milk sauce) are favorites.

Other recommendations: You can feel free to try any dishes that sound good, as the chef adapts his Thai recipes to suit Western tastes using coconut milk with no preservatives, prime meat, seafood, poultry, and fresh herbs and produce grown on his own four-acre farm.

Summary & comments: At the grand opening celebration in January 1999, celebrities, whose pictures line the walls, showed up, just as they used to at the old Keo's on Kapahulu Avenue, now closed. It's fun to try family-style dining here, with each person choosing a different dish and sharing. Keo's has received numerous awards from local and national publications.

LA MER		★★★★★
Neo-Classical (Contemporary)	Expensive	**QUALITY** 99
		VALUE C–

Halekulani Hotel, 2199 Kalia Road, Waikiki; (808) 923-2311
Zone 1   Waikiki

Reservations: Highly recommended	**Parking:** Valet
When to go: Sunset for most roman-	**Bar:** Full service
tic atmosphere	**Wine selection:** Extensive
Entrée range: $36–43	**Dress:** Dressy attire
Payment: VISA, MC, AMEX, DC,	**Disabled access:** Good, via elevator
JCB	**Customers:** Hotel guests, Islanders
Service rating: ★★★★★	for special occasions

Dinner: Every day, 6–10 p.m.

Setting & atmosphere: Serene, understated elegance focuses your attention on spectacular views of Diamond Head and glowing sunsets over the ocean, interrupted only by the gracious service of haute cuisine prepared by the French chef. Soft sand colors, reflecting mirrors, waiters in white dinner jackets, and the best of all beachfront views at this second-level fine restaurant can keep you dallying over dinner for more than three hours, despite the fact that the service is the best in the Islands. There's a big bar situated near the restaurant's entry, but it doesn't seem to attract much of a bar crowd.

House specialties: Try frog legs sautéed with shallots and parsley coulis and snails in potato skins with hazelnut butter, before an outstanding seafood entrée such as filet of kumu in a rosemary salt crust with mushrooms, vegetables, and herb butter. Two complete dinners of four and six courses are also offered nightly for $85–105. La Mer's soufflé with liliko'i sauce has gained regional fame for dessert.

Other recommendations: Avoid the most expensive appetizers, such as fois gras of duck for $34, or Beluga caviar for $105, unless, of course, price is no object. Sample medallions of fresh Scottish salmon with golden gnocchi and caviar sauce, or veal chop sautéed with chanterelles. A sip of port with a selection of French cheeses and walnut bread can be a perfect finish to the meal, though the symphony of La Mer desserts, a selection that includes a crêpe suzette with passion fruit, cappuccino cream, crème brûlée with mango, and Island dream with coconut sorbet is perfect for more than one sweet tooth.

Entertainment & amenities: Music drifts up from atrium below during dinner hour.

Summary & comments: This is one of the few restaurants where jackets are suggested (but no longer required) for men, and on breezy winter nights when the windows are open, women might also want to bring a light wrap. At press time, La Mer was Hawaii's only AAA Five Diamond Award restaurant.

L'URAKU		★★★★

Euro-Japanese	Moderate	QUALITY
		87

1341 Kapi'olani Boulevard, Honolulu; (808) 955-0552	VALUE
Zone 2 Greater Honolulu	C

Reservations: Recommended
When to go: Anytime; for value you might try a weekender lunch menu, 4 courses including appetizer, salad entrée, and dessert, for $15–18
Entrée range: Lunch $8.95–17.50, dinner $15.75–27.50, vegetarian $17.50
Payment: VISA, MC, AMEX, DC, JCB

Service rating: ★★★★
Parking: Complimentary self-parking in garage
Bar: Full service
Wine selection: Good, 20 wines by the glass
Dress: Dressy casual
Disabled access: Good, via elevator from parking building
Customers: Islanders and a few tourists

Lunch: Every day, 11 a.m.–2 p.m.

Dinner: Every day, 5:30–10 p.m.

Setting & atmosphere: L'Uraku has a festive, contemporary setting that comes alive in vibrant colors and multi-colored napkins on snowy white linen–covered tables. Kiyoshi, an artist whose pictures are displayed on the walls, hand-painted table vases, menu covers, and cheerful umbrellas that hang suspended from the ceiling. A big marble-topped black bar near the entrance to the dining room is a good place to relax if you forgot to make reservations.

House specialties: The chef's presentations of finely flavored dishes are as artistic as the restaurant's surroundings. The catch of the day comes with a delicate miso cream sauce and pan-seared scallops served with steamed vegetables and rice. Lobster tomalloy is marinated in its own juices and a bit of soy sauce and mirin, then quickly deep-fried. Natural flavors are not obliterated with too much spice or overpowering sauces. At lunch, salads such as the spinach with grilled pepper shrimp with mustard-sesame vinaigrette can be ordered as an entrée or to precede pasta or other dishes.

Other recommendations: Crab cake with Japanese pickled mustard greens crusted with corn flakes and served with roasted bell pepper aïoli, or baked oyster stuffed with crab meat and avocado, are tasty appetizers, while liliko'i mousse cake is a light and tangy dessert.

Summary & comments: The *l* in L'Uraku symbolizes the French influence in food preparation, while "Uraku" is from the Japanese word for pleasure, *yuraku,* a fitting description of dining at the restaurant. The chef had training in the *kaiseki* tradition, preparation of traditional Japanese cuisine that focuses on artistically presented dishes prepared to match the seasons of the year. In 1997, L'Uraku won *Honolulu Magazine's* Hale 'Aina Award for one of three best new restaurants; in 1998, it was named a restaurant of distinction; and in 1999, it was named one of the top 15 restaurants on Oahu.

MICHEL'S AT THE COLONY SURF		★★★★½
French/Continental	Expensive	QUALITY **92**
		VALUE **D**

Colony Surf Condominium, 2895 Kalakaua Avenue, Waikiki
(808) 923-6552
Zone 1   Waikiki

Reservations: Highly recommended	Bar: Full service
When to go: Sunset	Wine selection: Extensive, a dozen wines by the glass
Entrée range: $26–68.95	
Payment: VISA, MC, AMEX, DC, JCB	Dress: Dressy
	Disabled access: Good
Service rating: ★★★★★	Customers: Tourists, hotel guests, Islanders for special occasions
Parking: Valet	

Dinner: Every day, 5:30–8:30 p.m.

Setting & atmosphere: For the romantically inclined, a seat at the ocean's edge, with flickering lights from torches casting shadows on surfers headed home in the setting sun, plus the lights of hotels twinkling all along Waikiki's crescent of white sand, are languid mood setters. This is a fine restaurant and one of the few where table-side service from carts is still the norm.

House specialties: Michel's food has traditional roots, but it's beautifully presented in updated versions, so you may want to sip a perfectly iced cocktail while you peruse the menu. Then choose the chef's Hudson Valley foie gras, sautéed and served with a sweet-and-sour poha berry sauce, or steak tartare. Michel's is probably the only restaurant left in Hawaii that prepares steak tartare table-side, where the waiters mix in crushed capers and onions, Tabasco, ground pepper, and Worcestershire sauce with flair and serve the dish on toast points. Take your time: There's lobster bisque or Caesar salad to come, unless you go straight to an entrée of beef Wellington.

Other recommendations: Escargot are a good garlicky introduction to Chateaubriand or a lighter crab capellini, sautéed scallops, or 'opakapaka with oyster mushrooms. Don't miss ordering a flambéed dessert to experience the waiter's artistry one last time. Crêpes suzettes, crème brûlée, or strawberries Romanoff (with vanilla cream Grand Marnier and kirsch sauce) are heavenly finales.

Summary & comments: Plan on an extended dining experience; you may even want to finish dinner with a snifter of Hennessy X.O. Michel's is that kind of place—dreamy, traditional, and lethargy-inducing. And the sunset can't be beat—on a good evening you may even see the infamous green flash as the sun sets on the ocean's horizon.

ORCHIDS ★★★★½

Seafood/International	Moderate/Expensive	QUALITY
		92

		VALUE
Halekulani Hotel, 2199 Kalia Road, Waikiki; (808) 923-2311		C
Zone 1 Waikiki		

Reservations: Highly recommended
When to go: Anytime, but sunset is best, particularly if you sit outside
Entrée range: $27–38
Payment: VISA, MC, AMEX, DC, JCB
Service rating: ★★★★

Parking: Valet
Bar: Full service
Wine selection: Extensive
Dress: Resort attire
Disabled access: Good
Customers: Tourists and Islanders

Breakfast: Every day, 7–11 a.m.

Lunch: Every day, 11:30 a.m.–2 p.m.

Dinner: Every day, 6–10 p.m.

Setting & atmosphere: This lovely, light, and airy room is decorated with orchids and has a peaceful feeling even when crowded. Ask to sit outdoors, where the view of Diamond Head seems bigger than life, and Waikiki Beach is just beyond the green lawn.

House specialties: A well-stocked seafood bar set smack in the middle of the room is only one highlight of Orchids. As a full dinner, it's priced at entrée rates, but as an appetizer course with an entrée it's priced at a remarkable bargain (if you can eat that much), particularly considering that the buffet carries lobster thermidor (rich lobster meat prepared with a brandy cream sauce), as well as 'opakapaka with cucumber slices and wasabi mashed potatoes, garnished with fresh ginger and a citrus-mirin-sake sauce. Oysters on the shell, shrimp, 'ahi poke, smoked ono, seafood salads, and house-cured gravlax are just part of this bountiful buffet.

Other recommendations: Baked Australian prawns stuffed with king crab and served with freshly made fettuccini, or aromatic five-spice chicken roasted in the tandoori oven, are a few of the interesting treats on a menu that ranges from imaginative to traditional—rack of lamb, filet, and lobster, for example. Lemon curd tart or Halekulani's own tropical sorbets in pineapple, guava, liliko'i, and lychee flavors are light, refreshing desserts.

Entertainment & amenities: Sunday and Monday, 8:30–10:15 p.m., a pianist plays classical music in the restaurant's atrium; during the rest of the week, it's light jazz and contemporary tunes for diners' listening pleasure.

Summary & comments: A perfect evening might begin with a cocktail outside at sunset at House without a Key next door, then dinner on the covered patio at Orchids.

A PACIFIC CAFÉ		★★★★½
		QUALITY
Pacific Rim	Moderate	92
		VALUE
Ward Centre, 1200 Ala Moana Boulevard, Honolulu		C
(808) 593-0035		
Zone 2 Greater Honolulu		

Reservations: Recommended	Parking: Valet or free self-parking in
When to go: Anytime	Ward Centre garage
Entrée range: Lunch $9–16, dinner	Bar: Full service
$16.50–23.95	Wine selection: Extensive
Payment: VISA, MC, AMEX, D,	Dress: Casual
DC, JCB	Disabled access: Good, via elevator
Service rating: ★★★★½	Customers: Islanders and a few
	tourists

Lunch: Every day, 11:30 a.m.–2 p.m.

Dinner: Sunday–Thursday, 5:30–9 p.m.; Friday and Saturday, 5:30–9:30 p.m.

Setting & atmosphere: Floor-to-ceiling windows looking down on Ala Moana Boulevard give this pretty-in-pastel restaurant designed by Sophronia Josselin, the chef/owner's wife, a chic, contemporary feeling. A bar near the entrance adds to the convivial atmosphere. The restaurant is in an upscale two-story mall, convenient for pre- or post-lunch window shopping.

House specialties: Besides lamb and local fish from the kiawe wood–burning grill, the chef presents a prix-fixe, four-course Hawaii regional cuisine sampler nightly. In addition to an appetizer such as firecracker salmon, it comes with two demi-entrées and dessert. The best bargain has got to be the early-bird special between 5:30 and 6:30 p.m., Sunday through Thursday, when you can order a set four-course dinner for only $20.

Other recommendations: Light diners can choose tasty morsels—kalua pork pot-stickers, seared sea scallops, handmade crab cakes, crispy char-siu chicken lumpia, or angel hair pasta with shrimps, scallops, and pancetta—from an appetizer bar, while serious diners go for the ever-changing menu with a regional cuisine slant. Even the wood-fired pizzas are special, topped with kalamata olives, goat cheese, grilled eggplant, and other goodies.

Summary & comments: Chef/owner Jean Marie Josselin oversees a total of five restaurants on Maui, Kauai, and Oahu. One of the original founders of Hawaii Regional Cuisine, Inc., he always uses fresh Island ingredients or the finest of imported ingredients such as extra virgin olive oil, and he has an eye to healthy preparations.

PADOVANI'S BISTRO & WINE BAR ★★★★½

	QUALITY
Mediterranean/Island Flair Moderate/Expensive	96
	VALUE
	C

Doubletree Alana Hotel, 1956 Ala Moana Boulevard, Honolulu
(808) 946-3456
Zone 1   Waikiki

Reservations: Recommended
When to go: Anytime
Entrée range: Breakfast $9–22,
  lunch $14–19 (prix fixe, $28),
  dinner $20–34, multi-course
  degustation menus $48–75
Payment: VISA, MC, AMEX, DC,
  JCB
Service rating: ★★★★★

Parking: Valet
Bar: Full service
Wine selection: Excellent, 16 wines
  by the glass in the restaurant, 48
  in the Wine Bar
Dress: Resort attire
Disabled access: Good
Customers: Hotel guests, tourists,
  Islanders

Breakfast: Every day, 6–10 a.m.

Lunch: Every day, 11:30 a.m.–2 p.m.

Dinner: Every day, 6–10 p.m.

Setting & atmosphere: Attention has been paid to every detail to create an elegant, gracious setting that reflects Island-inspired touches used in fine estate homes in Hawaii. A *maile* lei painted on the wooden floor at the entry leads to the carpeted interior past a polished cherry-wood wine cru-vinet. It dispenses 16 wines by the glass. Nothing but the best—Riedel crystal, Frette linens, Bernardaud china, and Christofle flatware—comple-ments the Old World cart service. Rich golds, jade greens, and cherry-wood furnishings under a low ceiling add a warm, intimate touch. Light fixtures held by geometric chevrons have the look of 1930s Ossipoff-designed homes and were actually taken from a Hawaii *kama'aina* home. Artwork by tropical-impressionist painter Zhou Ling also adds a touch of the Orient found so often in the decor of local residences.

House specialties: Padovani's dishes rely on herbs and natural seasonings to bring out the peak flavors of ingredients. Hearts-of-palm and prosciutto salad provides a crispy, clean-flavored opening to a meal that might pro-ceed with filet of kumu (Island fish) and nage of lobster, or pan-fried sea scallops with gnocchi, leeks, and sun-dried tomatoes.

The chef is a master at desserts—15 are listed on the menu. The best way to experience as many as possible is to order a dessert sampler, which might include Vintage Chocolate mousse, tropical fruit with chocolate sabayon,

Golden Delicious apple tart with kiawe honey ice cream, crème brûlée with essence of star anise, and more. The fresh sorbets and ice creams are made from fresh Island fruits and other ingredients almost as you order.

Other recommendations: A degustation menu offers two matched and balanced choices, one with three courses for $48, the other with five courses for $75. It's worth ordering the degustation menu for the fresh Maine lobster in a tomato tarragon jus with light-as-air gnocchi alone. Wines are extra. Padovani has crafted a line of truffles made with Island-grown Hawaiian Vintage Chocolate and filled with nougat, amaretto, red raspberry, and liqueurs. Gift boxes are available at the restaurant.

Summary & comments: Chef/owner Philippe Padovani has a distinguished culinary background in Hawaii as one of the founding chefs of the Hawaii regional cuisine movement. On his arrival from France, he first served as executive chef of La Mer at the Halekulani Hotel; then he went to the Ritz-Carlton, Mauna Lani, where he launched the Big Island Bounty food festival; and finally he was executive chef at Manele Bay Hotel on Lanai. Padovani's Bistro & Wine Bar is a family venture with his wife, Pierrette, managing restaurant service, and his brother, Pierre, serving as pastry chef. The Wine Bar, a separate venue upstairs, is a great place for sampling up to 50 wines by the glass from the cruvinet system. Here you can pick and choose dim sum tidbits from a rosewood cart for a casual meal or afternoon appetizers.

PALOMINO EURO BISTRO ★★★

Mediterranean	Inexpensive/Moderate	QUALITY 81
Harbor Court, 55 Merchant Street, Honolulu; (808) 528-2400 Zone 2 Greater Honolulu		VALUE B

Reservations: Recommended
When to go: Anytime
Entrée range: Lunch $5.95–18.95, dinner $6.95–22.95
Payment: VISA, MC, AMEX, DC, D
Service rating: ★★★½
Parking: Valet or self-park in Harbor Court garage
Bar: The full-service bar has one of the largest selections of scotch in town, plus a good selection of

Champagnes, a dozen beers on tap, and grappa (Italian brandy)
Wine selection: Good, many by the glass
Dress: Casual
Disabled access: Via an elevator and ramps in the restaurant
Customers: Downtown office workers during lunch, Islanders and some tourists at dinner

Lunch: Monday–Friday, 11 a.m.–2:30 p.m.; lunch is served until 3:30 p.m. in the lounge

Dinner: Sunday–Thursday, 5–10 p.m.; Friday and Saturday, 5–11 p.m.

Setting & atmosphere: Palomino seems very cosmopolitan in a glamorous way, with its extraordinary views of Honolulu Harbor through soaring windows and an interior that shines with rose marble–topped tables and counters, highlighted with African woods and art deco hand-blown glass ceiling fixtures.

House specialties: Palomino's food is rustic Mediterranean-style in approach, well-seasoned with fresh herbs and spices and smoke-infused flavors. A 60-foot exhibition kitchen turns out spit-roasted tenderloins, and cracker-thin crusted pizzas come from a wood-burning oven.

Other recommendations: Palomino is surprisingly affordable—maybe that's why Islanders can't stay away. The most expensive dinner entrée is whole-roasted Island snapper with Israeli couscous and Moroccan spices for less than $30. Pasta dishes are among the most reasonable, starting at less than $10 and topping out under $20, with spit-roasted seafood ravioli made with prawns, scallops, salmon, and Dungeness crab mascarpone and rosemary-lemon beurre blanc.

Summary & comments: A curved marble bar that seats 70 is a fun place to meet friends, but be sure to use the valet parking; otherwise you'll get dizzy circling to the top of the parking building past floors of reserved stalls.

PRINCE COURT RESTAURANT	★★★★		
		QUALITY	
Hawaii Regional	Moderate	90	
		VALUE	
Hawaii Prince Hotel, 100 Holomoana Street; (808) 944-4494		C	
Zone 1 Waikiki			

Reservations: Highly recommended; required for Chef's Studio

When to go: Anytime, though sunset provides the loveliest view

Entrée range: $19–28

Payment: VISA, MC, AMEX, DC

Service rating: ★★★★

Parking: Valet or self-parking in hotel garage ($1 with validation)

Bar: Full service

Wine selection: Extensive, many domestic and imported Bordeaux and Burgundies, 20 wines by the glass

Dress: Resort attire

Disabled access: Good, via elevator

Customers: Islanders, hotel guests, tourists

Breakfast: Every day, 6–10:30 a.m.

Brunch: Sunday, 11:15 a.m.–1 p.m.

Lunch: Every day, 11:30 a.m.–2 p.m.

Dinner: Monday–Thursday, 6–9:30 p.m.; Friday–Sunday, 5:30–9:30 p.m.

Setting & atmosphere: Views of boats bobbing lazily at the Ala Wai Yacht Harbor and sometimes a rainbow over nearby Magic Island through floor-to-ceiling windows give this spacious restaurant nearly as much appeal for lunch or Sunday brunch as for an evening repast. Tropical flowers on the tables add a Hawaiian touch.

House specialties: The most popular item on the menu is a seafood extravaganza that includes Kona lobster, Island shrimp, and sea scallops with coconut saffron sauce, but the lemongrass crab-crusted 'opakapaka (red snapper) on seasoned crab with a Thai curry sauce comes in a close second. All dishes are artistically presented, but the best time to schedule dinner might be on Tuesday or Wednesday, for a Chef's Studio dinner, which includes a "flight" of wines (three matched to four courses). Three courses are prepared in front of guests in the restaurant, and then guests get a mini-tour of the kitchen while the chef completes the dessert course.

Other recommendations: Monday, Tuesday, and Wednesday evenings, an appetizer shellfish bar featuring poke, sashimi, smoked fish, oysters, California hand rolls, and more, followed by a demi-entrée of the diner's choice, is a great way to sample a variety of Hawaii's seafood specialties. Friday and Saturday nights, an abundant seafood buffet is a highlight.

The menu at Prince Court changes monthly, but a dessert standby is chocolate soufflé with vanilla ice cream and crème anglaise.

Summary & comments: Prince Court offers spectacular buffets. Make it easy on yourself and use valet parking, as it's a tiresome drive up many levels to find an empty space in the parking garage.

ROY'S RESTAURANT ★★★★

			QUALITY
Euro-Asian		Moderate	90

	VALUE
	C

Hawaii Kai Corporate Plaza, 6600 Kalaniana'ole Highway
(808) 396-7697
Zone 2   Greater Honolulu

Reservations: Highly recommended
When to go: Anytime, though sunsets over Maunalua Bay are especially mood-inducing
Entrée range: $16–33
Payment: VISA, MC, AMEX, D, DC, JCB
Service rating: ★★★★½

Parking: Free in adjacent lot
Bar: Full service
Wine selection: Extensive, 10 wines by the glass
Dress: Casual
Disabled access: Good, via elevator
Customers: Islanders and tourists

Dinner: Monday–Thursday, 5:30–9:30 p.m.; Friday, 5:30–10 p.m.; Saturday, 5–10 p.m.; Sunday, 5–9:30 p.m.

Setting & atmosphere: The lounge downstairs is fine in the evening for drinks and *pupus,* but upstairs is where the dining action is. The best tables, arranged around an exhibition kitchen, are those that are farthest from it and closest to the floor-to-ceiling windows, which look out over Maunalua Bay. This high-ceilinged restaurant is generally a full and vibrant (translate: noisy) place, a sign, says Chef Roy Yamaguchi, that people are having a good time. Soft pink walls decorated with artwork by Island artists, white tablecloths, and fresh flowers on the table complete the picture.

House specialties: An extensive menu of special items, up to 20, which change every night, is where Roy's Restaurant shines. In addition, eight to ten different fresh fish in a myriad of preparations are available nightly. Tops on the list is steamed fish of the day drizzled with sizzling hot peanut oil and served with rice and Chinese vegetables. Crispy Thai chicken stuffed with Chinese noodles and an exotic mushroom-fungus served with chutney and macadamia nut curry sauce is a poultry favorite.

Other recommendations: Some dainty eaters like to confine themselves to two appetizers, perhaps blackened 'ahi and Szechuan baby-back ribs, so they'll have room for a dessert of hot cobbler (the fruit fillings change according to what's in season), or a hot chocolate soufflé, or other desserts that change on a nightly basis.

Entertainment & amenities: Various musical entertainers perform in the downstairs lounge on weekends.

Summary & comments: This is the original of 15 Roy's Restaurants, established by chef/owner Roy Yamaguchi, so this is where you'll most often catch him cooking in the exhibition kitchen when he's not on the road.

SAM CHOY'S BREAKFAST, LUNCH, AND CRAB AND SAM CHOY'S DIAMOND HEAD ★★★★

Hawaii Regional	Moderate	QUALITY
		88

		VALUE
580 North Nimitz Highway, Honolulu; (808) 545-7979		B
Zone 2 Greater Honolulu		

449 Kapahulu Avenue, 2nd level, Waikiki; (808) 732-8645
Zone 1   Waikiki

Reservations: Recommended for dinner
When to go: Anytime
Entrée range: Lunch $6.50 and up, dinner $26.95
Payment: VISA, MC, AMEX
Service rating: ★★★½
Parking: Valet or nearby lot
Bar: Full service. A brewmaster at Choy's Big Aloha Brewery within the spacious BLC turns out 8 varieties of beer. His latest is Hibiscus White, infused with Island ingredients like Ka'u orange peel, hibiscus, and coriander.
Wine selection: Good
Dress: Casual
Disabled access: Good
Customers: Islanders, businesspeople at lunch, large family groups and others at dinner

Brunch: *Sam Choy's Diamond Head:* Sunday, 9:30 a.m.–2 p.m.

Breakfast: *Breakfast, Lunch, and Crab:* Monday–Friday, 6:30–10:30 a.m.; Saturday and Sunday, 6:30–11 a.m.

Lunch: *Breakfast, Lunch, and Crab:* Every day, 11 a.m.–4 p.m.

Dinner: *Breakfast, Lunch, and Crab:* Every day, 5–10 p.m.; *Sam Choy's Diamond Head:* Monday–Thursday, 5:30–9:30 p.m.; Friday–Sunday, 5–10 p.m.

Setting & atmosphere: Breakfast, Lunch, and Crab has a lively atmosphere, with an exhibition kitchen, showcases full of fresh seafood, and table seating in more than one room for true old salts and junior sailors. It's a big restaurant with fun touches, like a fishing sampan with tables in it, and a fountain or two in the middle of the dining room so you can rinse your hands conveniently after ripping into cracked crab legs.

Sam Choy's Diamond Head Restaurant is less casual, with views of Diamond Head through an open window and an exhibition kitchen with counter seating, as well as linen-draped tables. It is no less popular, however.

House specialties: Menus vary from restaurant to restaurant, but the top-ten menu items are served in all Sam Choy's restaurants. Entrées like local-style osso bucco with shiitake mushrooms, or marinated 'ahi salad layered with fresh greens, somen noodles, and crispy tostada shells, shock diners with their sheer size. Sam Choy's fried poke in three preparations—on a bed of Kula cabbage with furikake rice, wrapped in a tortilla, or in a salad with creamy Oriental dressing—is perhaps one of his most famous local dishes.

Other recommendations: People go for the beef stew and moi-moi saimin at both restaurants. At Breakfast, Lunch, and Crab, crab is served in cakes, dip, Louis, claws, burgers, or roasted with garlic, but you'll find shrimp, oysters, calamari, and fresh fish on the menu, too. At Sam Choy's Diamond Head, Sunday brunch is the answer to a glutton's prayer, with local foods included even at the omelet station, where you can get two-egg omelets made to order with fillings of kalua pig, Spam, char-siu, and all the regular meats, cheeses, and vegetables as well.

Summary & comments: In 1998, BLC was chosen Hawaii's favorite restaurant for lunch by readers of the *Honolulu Advertiser* because of its big portions and great local food.

SARENTO'S TOP OF THE "I"	★★★½

Italian	Moderate/Expensive	QUALITY 86
		VALUE C

'Ilikai Hotel, 1777 Ala Moana Boulevard, Waikiki; (808) 955-5559
Zone 1   Waikiki

Reservations: Recommended	Parking: Discounted with validation in hotel garage
When to go: Sunset is most romantic if sitting at window tables	Bar: Full service
Entrée range: $15.95–42.95	Wine selection: Extensive
Payment: VISA, MC, AMEX, DC, D, JCB	Dress: Resort attire
	Disabled access: Adequate, via elevator
Service rating: ★★★★½	Customers: Tourists and Islanders

Dinner: Every day, 5:30–10 p.m.

Setting & atmosphere: The ride in the glass-sided elevator to Sarento's, perched high atop the 'Ilikai Hotel, sets a fantasy mood for this top-notch Italian restaurant. Waiters in dark jackets help adjust your lighting, individually controlled at booths that enjoy panoramic views of the Ala Wai Yacht Harbor, Waikiki's bright lights, and the beach or Diamond Head. The decor in this restaurant is as beautifully Italian (with graceful archways and a green-and-white tiled exhibition pizza and dessert kitchen) as the food. Frescoes on the walls of two cozy private dining rooms and in the main restaurant show scenes typical of the Mediterranean area—a mother cooking, grapes being crushed, gardens. One scene of a large family at the dining table depicts one of the restaurant's three owners, Aaron Placuorakis, his wife, two children, grandfather Sarento, grandmother, uncles, and aunts.

House specialties: The risotto here has got to be among the best in Honolulu, and at a moment's notice, the chef can stir together any of dozens of variations. Homemade pastas, pizza from a wood-burning oven, osso bucco, filet wrapped with pancetta and topped with fontina cheese, and crisp Jerusalem artichoke chips are superb choices.

Other recommendations: Lobster ravioli with mushroom cream sauce is a soul-satisfying entrée. Top dinner off with cool tiramisu made of lady fingers, espresso, mascarpone cheese, and liqueurs. *Hint:* One way to keep the dinner cost down here is to go from 5:30 to 6:30 p.m. for an early evening special that includes soup or salad, a choice of several entrées, and dessert. Pizzas are also a value if chosen as an entrée, ranging from $12.95 to $16.95.

Summary & comments: By request, guests can take a gander at the restaurant's wine cellar and view a bottle of $9,500 Chateau Cheval Blanc stored with some 3,000 other wines.

SINGHA THAI CUISINE	★★★★

		QUALITY
Thai	Inexpensive/Moderate	**90**
		VALUE
		B

Canterbury Place, 1910 Ala Moana Boulevard, Waikiki
(808) 941-2898
Zone 1   Waikiki

Reservations: Highly recommended for dinner, accepted for lunch
When to go: Anytime
Entrée range: $11.95–31.95
Payment: VISA, MC, AMEX, DC, JCB
Service rating: ★★★★½

Parking: Free with validation in Canterbury Place lot
Bar: Full service
Wine selection: Extensive
Dress: Casual
Disabled access: Good
Customers: Tourists

Lunch: Monday–Friday, 11 a.m.–4 p.m.

Dinner: Every day, 4–11 p.m.

Setting & atmosphere: After dark Singha's exotic magic emerges, though it's not so evident during the lunch hour. During dinner, lights twinkle on the restaurant's mirrors and golden Buddha, and a fountain tinkles in the open-air patio dotted with orchids. Outdoor patio seating at umbrella tables is right next to the street but set at a lower level and surrounded by a wall so it feels like a private garden.

House specialties: Blackened 'ahi summer rolls with a soy-ginger-sesame dipping sauce and shredded green mango, and boneless breast of duck with Panang curry sauce, successfully combine Hawaii regional and Thai cuisine. Seafood lovers go for the grilled jumbo black tiger prawns with Thai peanut sauce, or lobster tail with Singha's signature Thai chili, ginger, and light black bean sauce.

Other recommendations: If you have qualms about choosing a balanced number of dishes from the a la carte menu, sampling menus for two, three, four, or five people are composed of an appetizer sampler plus an ample variety of entrées and rice, plus dessert, for just under $30 per person.

Entertainment & amenities: Thai dancers in extravagant headdresses and colorful silk costumes perform on a tiny stage, while rose petals float through the air.

Summary & comments: Named Honolulu's best Thai restaurant by Gayot's *The Best of Hawaii Guide, Zagat Survey, Honolulu Advertiser*'s 'Ilima Awards, and *Honolulu Magazine*'s Hale 'Aina Awards. Chef/owner Chai Chaowasaree's food is a work of art (melons might be carved into flower shapes, for example) that balances fresh Island ingredients and flavors with Thai spices, fresh herbs, and reduced sauces.

THE SURF ROOM   ★★★½

Contemporary	Moderate/Expensive	QUALITY
		80

		VALUE
		C

Royal Hawaiian Hotel, 2259 Kalakaua Avenue, Waikiki
(808) 923-7311
Zone 1 Waikiki

Reservations: Highly recommended
When to go: Sunset
Entrée range: Breakfast $10–21,
lunch $10–20, dinner $25–40
Payment: VISA, MC, AMEX, DC,
D, JCB
Service rating: ★★★★
Parking: Valet or validated self-
parking in hotel garage
Bar: Full service
Wine selection: Good
Dress: Resort attire
Disabled access: Good
Customers: Hotel guests, other
tourists, and Islanders for special
occasions

Breakfast: Every day, 7–11 a.m.

Lunch: Every day, 11:30 a.m.–2:30 p.m.

Dinner: Every day, 6–10 p.m.

Setting & atmosphere: Near the entry to the Surf Room at the Mai Tai Bar, a hula dancer performs old favorites, such as "Lovely Hula Hands" or "The Hawaiian Wedding Song," to live Hawaiian music, while rustling palm trees and lapping ocean waves furnish a dreamy backdrop. The best seating is right beside the sands of Waikiki Beach, where you can watch couples stroll by in the moonlight.

House specialties: Though Cajun-spiced crab pot-stickers might not sound Hawaiian, the plump little Chinese dumplings with a mustard cream sauce are a great way to dive into this menu, which claims to focus on the flavors of Hawaii. Pan-fried Pacific salmon in a balsamic vinegar glaze with shiitake-garlic mashed potatoes, or togarashi-peppered 'ahi with Maui onion, Ka'u orange relish, and lime-soy vinaigrette, are two Island favorites.

Other recommendations: A three-course dinner selection dubbed the Art of Food and Wine includes two glasses of wine for $39.95. Friday seafood buffets and Sunday brunches draw repeat visitors. If you've got a big appetite, the breakfast buffet is lovely to dawdle over.

Summary & comments: The open-air atmosphere beside Waikiki Beach makes The Surf Room special, so for its fullest impact, request a table as close as possible to the sand. After dining, wander through the elegant old hotel and take a moment to enjoy what is left of the big trees and green lawns at the front entrance. This is the Waikiki from a more gracious era.

3660 ON THE RISE ★★★★

Contemporary	Moderate	QUALITY
		92
		VALUE
		C

3660 Wai'alae Avenue, Kaimuki; (808) 737-1177
Zone 2   Greater Honolulu

Reservations: Highly recommended
When to go: Anytime
Entrée range: $19–25
Payment: VISA, AMEX, MC, DC, D, JCB
Service rating: ★★★½
Parking: Free in garage
Bar: Full service

Wine selection: Well-rounded; primarily California wines; many great matches for Chef Siu's Euro-Asian-Island flavors
Dress: Resort attire
Disabled access: Good
Customers: Islanders and their visiting guests

Dinner: Sunday, Tuesday–Thursday, 5:30–9 p.m.; Friday and Saturday, 5:30– 10 p.m.; closed Monday

Setting & atmosphere: Jade green marble floors, a black marble bar, frosted glass panels, and light wood accents are a cool background for this busy restaurant, where repeat clientele are likely to table-hop, saying hello to friends. Indoor tables seat 88, while a street-side lanai surrounded by plants holds another 25.

House specialties: Appetizers of 'ahi katsu, duck confit ravioli, potato-crusted crab cake; entrées of flaky tempura catfish with ponzu sauce, Chinese steamed 'opakapaka (red snapper), or Angus New York steak 'alaea. Dessert lovers rave about the pastry chef's bread puddings.

Other recommendations: Desserts are so good that it makes sense to order a sampler of three appetizers to share. Dine lightly on seared scallops with 'ahi taro cake and allow yourself to go crazy on desserts of warm chocolate soufflé cake with mocha sauce and ice cream or mile-high Wai'alae pie, which combines vanilla and coffee ice cream, macadamia brittle, and caramel and chocolate sauces for a sweet treat. For lunch, hale ice tea is a cooling limeade/tea blend, while French-press coffeepots make rich coffee to go with your favorite after-dinner cognacs.

Summary & comments: Chef Russell Siu's chic restaurant has won countless awards and always places near the top overall in the Hale 'Aina Awards, but for the last two years the restaurant has won first place for its desserts. 3660 has the feel of a favorite neighborhood restaurant because it's outside Waikiki and is not a showy place, but the service and food make it worth the cab fare from your hotel.

MAUI

ANUENUE ROOM ★★★½

Hawaii Regional	Moderate/Expensive	QUALITY
		85

		VALUE
		C–

Ritz-Carlton Hotel, 1 Ritz-Carlton Drive, Kapalua
(808) 669-1665
Zone 9   West Maui

Reservations: Highly recommended
When to go: Anytime except Sunday
and Monday
Entrée range: $27–42
Payment: VISA, MC, AMEX, DC,
D, JCB
Service rating: ★★★★★
Parking: Valet or free self-parking in
hotel lot
Bar: Full service
Wine selection: Extensive, 20 wines
by the glass
Dress: Dressy resort attire
Disabled access: Good
Customers: Resort guests and
Islanders on special occasions

Dinner: Tuesday–Saturday, 6–9:30 p.m.

Lounge: Every day, 5:30–11 p.m.

Setting & atmosphere: This elegant room is dressed in rich koa wood, brocade draperies, and chandeliers, giving it an Old World, club-like atmosphere. The walls are decorated with landscapes of the Kapalua area by local artists, and impressive formal arrangements of flowers highlight the entry and the dining areas. A separate dining room with wall sconces carved in the shape of pineapples holds private parties of a dozen.

House specialties: Start with the seared duck foie gras, a duck confit highlighted with pineapple and vintage port. For an entrée, barbecued rack of lamb with a *paniolo* (cowboy) glaze of poha berry and Zinfandel has a reputation as the best lamb on Maui, though lighter appetites might prefer orange-shoyu caramelized salmon served with gingered jasmine rice and Ka'u lime.

Other recommendations: For big splurges, grilled Keahole lobsters are fresh from aquaculture tanks on the Big Island, or you can sample the succulent warm lobster in a hearts-of-palm salad dressed with fresh mango and black truffle vinaigrette. To complete what's sure to be a truly special evening, plan ahead and order the rich and light-as-air Grand Marnier or chocolate soufflé when you order your entrée, so it will be ready when you are.

Entertainment & amenities: The Anuenue Lounge, next to the dining room, features live entertainment Tuesday–Saturday, 8–11 p.m.

Summary & comments: To make a night of it, you might plan on coffee and cognac in the lounge after dinner. People do get out on the dance floor to cut the light fantastic. *Anuenue,* by the way, is the Hawaiian word for "rainbow"; the restaurant is so designated because rainbows are sometimes visible over the ocean from the Anuenue Room's windows.

THE BAY CLUB RESTAURANT		★★★
		QUALITY
Continental	Moderate/Expensive	75
		VALUE
		C–

1 Bay Drive, Kapalua; (808) 669-5656
Zone 9   West Maui

Reservations: Highly recommended	Parking: In adjacent lot
When to go: Sunset	Bar: Full service
Entrée range: Lunch $9.75–14, dinner $25–38 (vegetarian $21)	Wine selection: Good
	Dress: Resort attire
Payment: VISA, MC, AMEX, DC, JCB	Disabled access: Good
	Customers: Islanders and tourists
Service rating: ★★★★	

Lunch: Every day, 11:30 a.m.–2 p.m.

Dinner: Every day, 6–9 p.m.

Setting & atmosphere: Considered one of the loveliest oceanfront settings on Maui. Tables on the open-air deck fill up quickly, so it's best to make reservations and go early for the full romantic effect of sunset. Inside the restaurant resembles a gracious *kama'aina* beach home, with a fireplace near the entry, a piano surrounded by comfortable linen-draped tables, and low lighting.

House specialties: From the moment you sit down to dinner, you can munch on crispy lavosh lavished with salmon mousse. At lunch, the Monte Cristo sandwich filled with ham, turkey, and Swiss cheese and sautéed in an egg batter is one of the most reasonable items on the menu. Caesar salad prepared table-side precedes main courses such as scallops and prawns with white truffle risotto and a veal demi-glacé, or a half roasted duck with butternut squash, or a more traditional filet mignon with chanterelles and foie gras sauce.

Other recommendations: Hawaiian fish are caught fresh daily and can be ordered Mediterranean-style (with tomato concasse, lemon, capers, parsley, garlic, and anchovies, in white wine butter sauce) or Oriental-style (with shiitake mushrooms, scallions, cilantro, and soy and sesame oil sauce).

Summary & comments: Shuttles run from Kapalua Bay and the Ritz-Carlton Kapalua, so resort guests do not need a rental car. However, for those staying at Kapalua Bay Hotel, a palm-shaded path along the ocean's edge is pleasant for a pre- or post-dinner stroll. Diners may charge checks to their rooms in either hotel.

CHEZ PAUL'S		★★★★
French	Moderate/Expensive	**QUALITY** 87
		VALUE C

Highway 30 (4 miles south of Lahaina), Olowalu Village
(808) 661-3843
Zone 7   Central Maui

Reservations: Highly recommended	Bar: Full service
When to go: Anytime	Wine selection: Good; wine cellar in
Entrée range: $22–36	restaurant
Payment: VISA, MC, AMEX, D	Dress: Resort attire
Service rating: ★★★★	Disabled access: Good
Parking: Free in adjacent lot	Customers: Islanders, a few tourists

Dinner: Every day, seatings at 6:30 p.m. and 8:30 p.m.

Setting & atmosphere: You might smell the garlic wafting in through your open car window if you drive past this little blink-and-you'll-miss-it roadside restaurant at Olowalu. Classical French Provençal cuisine is served at 14 linen-covered, candlelit tables. Two mirror-lined walls make the place look bigger, and banquette seating upholstered in green splashed with pink roses adds an Old World touch. A private dining room seats 22.

House specialties: Repeat customers often order poisson des iles (fresh fish) with beurre-blanc sauce, or medallions of veal simmered in chardonnay, lemon, and orange jus, while the dessert to die for is profiteroles, puff pastry with ice cream in a warm chocolate sauce.

Other recommendations: Regulars regard as "très bien" an appetizer of escargot de Bourgogne presented in their shells in garlic butter. We favored the 'opakapaka Provençal (snapper with fennel and artichokes). Another recommended entrée is the Tahitian, duck à l'orange presented with a variety of tangy fruits.

Summary & comments: It's a nice surprise to learn that here, unlike on many contemporary French menus, soup or salad and vegetables are included with entrée items. Chez Paul is owned by Belgium-born Lucien Charbounier, who joined with chef Patric Callares in 1999 to update the menu. Chez Paul was named Maui's best French restaurant by the readers of *Maui News* in 1998 and has been recommended in *Travel/Holiday* magazine.

DAVID PAUL'S LAHAINA GRILL		★★★★	
Contemporary American	Moderate/Expensive	**QUALITY**	
		91	
127 Lahainaluna Road, Lahaina; (808) 667-5117		**VALUE**	
Zone 9 West Maui		C	

Reservations: Highly recommended
When to go: Early or late to avoid the 7 p.m. crowd
Entrée range: $24–37
Payment: VISA, MC, AMEX, DC
Service rating: ★★★★★
Parking: On-street or in adjacent lot

Bar: Full service
Wine selection: Extensive, many by the glass
Dress: Resort wear
Disabled access: Good, separate wheelchair access
Customers: Islanders and tourists

Dinner: Every day, 6–10 p.m.

Setting & atmosphere: This lively bistro, composed of two dining rooms plus the Chef's Table (which provides an exceptional, personalized dining experience for up to eight guests), is located next door to the old restored Lahaina Inn. The restaurant has a Victorian ceiling of pressed-tin panels embossed with an abstract design. Soft peach, blue, and sand tones in the decor are set off by simple black chairs at candlelit tables set with white linens, Mikasa china, and fresh flowers. In addition, the full menu is available for those seated at the bar.

House specialties: David Paul's signature dish of tequila shrimp with fire-cracker rice competes with the kalua duck with reduced plum wine sauce, seasonal vegetables, and Lundberg rice for first place on the dinner menu. Kona coffee–roasted rack of lamb boasts a full-flavored Kona coffee Cabernet demi-glaze served with garlic mashed potatoes.

Other recommendations: The vegetarian eggplant Napoleon and the Maui onion-crusted seared 'ahi (tuna) with vanilla bean rice and an apple cider soy-butter vinaigrette are light enough to reserve room for dessert— a luscious triple berry pie of raspberries, blueberries, and black currants topped with crème fraîche, or the Hawaiian Vintage Chocolate decadence, a flourless torte served with chantilly cream and raspberry port sauce. "Flights" of wine are offered nightly. Generally these consist of a tasting of three wines, either whites or reds.

Entertainment & amenities: Thursday through Saturday evenings, a jazz pianist plays and sings.

Summary & comments: If you'd like a quiet little table in the corner for a romantic dinner, ask for Table #28, #29, or #34. These tables for two are tucked into an out-of-the-way corner of the restaurant, where you can check out the action in the dining room, but the action can't check you out! A few of David Paul's most recent awards include *Honolulu Magazine*'s Hale 'Aina Award, received six years in a row for Best Maui Restaurant, as well as the 1998 Legendary Service Award, as voted by the readers of *Maui News*.

GERARD'S		★★★★
Contemporary Island/French	Moderate/Expensive	QUALITY 85
Plantation Inn, 174 Lahainaluna Road, Lahaina; (808) 661-8939 Zone 9 West Maui		VALUE B

Reservations: Recommended
When to go: Anytime
Entrée range: $26.50–32.50
Payment: VISA, MC, AMEX, DC, D, JCB
Service rating: ★★★★★
Parking: In nearby lot
Bar: Full service

Wine selection: Excellent, 10 wines by the glass
Dress: Casual resort attire
Disabled access: Good for garden-level dining, adequate via a back entry for in-house dining
Customers: Tourists and Islanders for special occasions

Dinner: Every day, 6–9 p.m.

Setting & atmosphere: Seated in this plantation-style inn, diners in Gerard's might feel as if they are eating in someone's gracious old-fashioned home dining room. Walls are papered in a pink-and-beige floral design, windows are stained glass, and tables are lit with candle lamps. You can also sit outside on a porch screened with plantings.

House specialties: Starting with the appetizers, people rave about the calamari sautéed with lime and ginger and the shiitake and oyster mushrooms in puff pastry. Though the menu changes annually, chef/owner Gerard Reversade's confit of duck and his roasted Hawaiian snapper, served with vegetables and potato purée or rice pilaf, are a constant.

Other recommendations: Islanders go for 'ahi tartare with taro chips; mainlanders love the fresh Kona lobster and avocado salad. Rack of lamb with mint crust is filling, but most people find room to share spoons over crème brûlée or flourless chocolate cake.

Summary & comments: Reversade opened this special restaurant in 1982, and over the years his traditional French cuisine has been adapted to Island tastes, so sauces are lighter and hints of Island flavors and ingredients show up. He has been featured on PBS's *Country Cooking* and the Discovery Channel's *Great Chefs of America*. The wine list repeatedly receives *Wine Spectator*'s award of excellence.

HALI'IMAILE GENERAL STORE		★★★★	
Hawaii Regional	Moderate/Expensive	**QUALITY**	90
		VALUE	C

900 Hali'imaile Road, Hali'imaile; (808) 572-2666
Zone 10   Upcountry Maui and Beyond

Reservations: Highly recommended for dinner	Parking: In adjacent lot
When to go: Anytime Monday– Friday	Bar: Full service
	Wine selection: Good, many by the glass
Entrée range: $17–32	Dress: Casual
Payment: VISA, MC, DC, D, JCB	Disabled access: Adequate, via ramp
Service rating: ★★★★½	Customers: Islanders and tourists

Brunch: Sunday, 10 a.m.–2:30 p.m.

Lunch: Monday–Friday, 11 a.m.–2:30 p.m.

Dinner: Monday–Friday, 5:30–9:30 p.m.

Setting & atmosphere: Chef/owner Bev Gannon's Hawaii regional cuisine is famous throughout the Islands, but you'll still feel as if you've made a discovery when you search out the restaurant, located in a restored 1920s plantation store in the middle of nowhere surrounded by sugarcane and pineapple fields. The only drawback is that the noise level inside can be irritating if you like peace while dining.

House specialties: The crab boboli is legendary for lunch, while for dinner it's a good idea to check the fish preparations, as they vary every night. As an appetizer, sashimi Napoleon, a crispy wonton layered with smoked salmon, 'ahi tartare, and sashimi and served with a spicy wasabi vinaigrette, is always in demand. Rack of lamb Hunan-style keeps Islanders coming back for more.

Other recommendations: *Paniolo* ribs done with a secret lime barbecue sauce and coconut seafood curry also have local enthusiasts. As pastry chef, Gannon's daughter Theresa whips up chocolate macadamia nut caramel pies, liliko'i cheese torte (a sweet-tart tart), gingerbread with caramelized pears, a variety of crème brûlées, and piña colada cheesecake.

Summary & comments: Chef Bev Gannon was one of the founding members of the Hawaii regional cuisine movement and has been featured many times in national publications such as *Bon Appetit*. Locally the restaurant has won the Best Maui Restaurant title and is a favorite stomping ground for upcountry residents. *Hint:* It's a treat to see the store after dark during the Christmas season, when it's dressed in full holiday regalia.

HULA GRILL ★★★

		QUALITY
Hawaii Regional	Inexpensive/Moderate	83

	VALUE
Whalers Village, 2435 Ka'anapali Parkway, Ka'anapali; (808) 667-6636	B
Zone 9 West Maui	

Reservations: Recommended for dinner

When to go: Anytime, but it's best to sit on the open lanai at sunset

Entrée range: Lunch $6.95–10.95, dinner $14.95–24

Payment: VISA, MC, AMEX, D, DC

Service rating: ★★★★

Parking: Validated, in shopping center garage

Bar: Full service

Wine selection: Good, 10 wines by the glass

Dress: Casual

Disabled access: Good

Customers: Tourists and Islanders

Lunch: Every day, 11 a.m.–10:30 p.m. (pizzas, salads, sandwiches served through the dinner hour in the casual Barefoot Bar area)

Dinner: Every day, 5–9:30 p.m.

Setting & atmosphere: Hula Grill is set in a re-created Hawaiian plantation home, with the main dining room an open-air lanai at the ocean's edge. During the day you'll see beachgoers sunning and walking along Ka'anapali's golden sands; at night flickering torches light the path along the beach. Near the entry, koa walls and shelves in a library area are decorated with Hawaiian collectibles, while an exhibition kitchen allows you to watch the chefs if there's a wait for a table. Smokers can relax in a stepped-down waterfall room or a designated section of the Barefoot Bar.

House specialties: Even the appetizers are special at Hula Grill. As a starter you can order Asian-style dim sum, such as scallop and lobster potstickers served in bamboo baskets, or Hawaiian-style *pupus,* like wok-charred 'ahi seared on the outside, sashimi-style on the inside, and served with a dipping sauce of wasabi and shoyu.

Hula Grill's signature entrée is macadamia-nut-roasted fresh Island 'opakapaka, garnished with a sauce made of Hana rum and mango and served with bamboo rice. Some diners swear by the Hawaiian seafood gumbo, a linguini dish with fresh shrimp, fish, clams, and scallops that can be ordered from mild to spicy hot.

Other recommendations: At lunch this is a great place to pop by for a casual bite to eat, maybe a warm focaccia chicken sandwich with Monterey Jack cheese, roasted poblano pepper, avocado, and tomato–chili pepper aïoli. Pizzas topped with Puna goat cheese, fresh spinach, tomato, and mushrooms come crispy hot from the kiawe wood–fired oven. You might want to share Hula Grill's famous dessert—a homemade ice cream sandwich, made with two chocolate macadamia nut brownies, vanilla ice cream, and raspberry purée and whipped cream.

Entertainment & amenities: It's easy to slip off the beach for a Lava Flow, a piña colada–like drink made with fresh coconut, pineapple juice, and rum and topped with a strawberry "eruption," during happy hour, when a guitarist and vocalist entertain from 3 to 5 p.m. Hawaiian musicians return during dinner hours from 6:30 to 9 p.m., and hula dancers sway at table-side around 7 p.m. every night.

Summary & comments: Chef Peter Merriman is the same Big Island chef who was instrumental in officially founding the Hawaii regional cuisine movement. Merriman's other restaurant on the Big Island offers a completely different dining experience than Hula Grill, though both are true to fresh Island ingredients. Hula Grill has won the Restaurant of Distinction Award and been named as the Maui restaurant with the best ambience for three years in a row by the readers of *Maui News*.

KIMO'S   ★★½

Steak and Seafood	Inexpensive/Moderate	QUALITY 70

845 Front Street, Lahaina; (808) 661-4811

| | | VALUE B |

Zone 9   West Maui

Reservations: Recommended for dinner

When to go: Anytime; to sit outside in the upstairs dining room, go early—it's first-come, first-seated

Entrée range: Lunch $6.95–10.95, dinner $6.95–23.95

Payment: VISA, MC, AMEX, DC, D, JCB

Service rating: ★★★½

Parking: Limited on-street or use Lahaina Center lot and walk a couple of blocks

Bar: Full service

Wine selection: Good, 8 wines by the glass

Dress: Casual

Disabled access: Access to the main dining room upstairs is inadequate for wheelchairs, but seating is available downstairs in a secondary dining area near the bar

Customers: Tourists, some Islanders

Lunch: Every day, 11 a.m.–3 p.m.

Pupus: Every day, 3–5 p.m.

Dinner: Every day, 5–10:30 p.m.

Bar: Every day, open until 1:30 a.m.

Setting & atmosphere: This two-level restaurant is a casual place where it's easy to drop by for lunch or a cocktail downstairs at sunset, then find your way upstairs for dinner. Kimo's takes full advantage of its ocean's-edge setting, with an open lanai perched one story above the rocks and lapping waves. Signal flags promote the sailing motif, and tropical foliage adds an Island touch. At night, flaming torches cast flickering shadows on the spreading limbs of a rustling monkeypod tree. You can order from the full menu or a lighter menu at the bar, which seats 22 downstairs.

House specialties: Kimo's fresh fish might be ono, 'ahi, onaga, a'u, mahi, opah, 'opakapaka, or lehi, depending on what comes in on any given day. Of four preparations, Kimo's Style, baked in garlic, lemon, and sweet basil glaze, has widespread approval.

Other recommendations: Meat eaters swear by the prime rib, but fence-sitters are likely to choose the top sirloin and Tahitian shrimp (touched up with a bit of garlic and cheese) combination. Try a lighter, healthier lunch, such as the veggie sandwich that boasts Maui onions, fresh tomatoes, sprouts, cheese, and avocado, and then you can afford to top it off with the dessert that sailors swim to shore for—the original hula pie, a wedge of vanilla macadamia nut ice cream nestled in an Oreo cookie crust.

Entertainment & amenities: Kimo's is the place to be Friday and Saturday nights from 10 p.m. to midnight, when live rock-and-roll music livens the night. Monday–Friday, 7–8 p.m., there's live Hawaiian music.

Summary & comments: Interestingly, local people voted Kimo's, in the heart of touristy Lahaina, Maui's best restaurant in the *Honolulu Advertiser's* 'Ilima Awards. The restaurant has neither a "big-name" chef nor a nationwide reputation, but Kimo's entrées come with Caesar salad, carrot muffins, sour cream rolls, and steamed herb rice, so you don't go broke ordering a la carte. Generous portions and fairly priced food of a consistent quality probably had a lot to do with the vote, too. It's one of the nicest Lahaina bars to sit in and have a drink at sunset.

LONGHI'S		★★★½
Mediterranean/Italian	Moderate	**QUALITY** 84
888 Front Street, Lahaina; (808) 667-2288 Zone 9 West Maui		**VALUE** B

Reservations: Recommended for dinner

When to go: Anytime

Entrée range: Breakfast $2.50–12.50, lunch $8–16, dinner $17–27, except for lobster at $55

Payment: AMEX, VISA, MC, DC, D, JCB

Service rating: ★★★

Parking: Free valet at dinner, free self-parking in adjacent lot

Bar: Full service

Wine selection: Extensive, many Italian wines and 3 house wines, 20 by the glass

Dress: Casual

Disabled access: Good for downstairs dining

Customers: Tourists and Islanders

Breakfast: Every day, 7:30–11 a.m.

Lunch: Every day, 11:45 a.m.–4:45 p.m.

Dinner: Every day, 5–10 p.m.

Setting & atmosphere: This sleek, cosmopolitan, open-air restaurant has a fun and casual ambience. Big black-and-white tiles cover the floor downstairs, interrupted only by a wide staircase that leads upstairs to additional koa-topped tables open to the trade winds.

House specialties: Here, nobody wants to stop at just one appetizer, even if it's as good as the grilled portobello mushrooms with goat cheese pesto.

Follow it with shrimp Longhi, a classic first, served on opening night more than 20 years ago. Plump white shrimp are sautéed in butter, lemon juice, and white wine, then fresh Maui basil and tomatoes are simmered before it's all served on garlic toast. Fresh white fish, often onaga, prepared with white wine and garnished with grapes, is another longtime specialty.

Other recommendations: The in-house bakery prepares oven-fresh cinnamon buns, macadamia nut rolls, coffee cakes, quiches, and cheesy jalapeño and pizza bread. Pastas, freshly made on the premises, and salads, all composed of fresh vegetables, are available both at lunch and dinner. Desserts are presented on a tray and served to you even as you point your finger at macadamia nut pie, cheesecake, or strawberry mousse cake, though you may want to order a special chocolate or Grand Marnier soufflé in advance.

Entertainment & amenities: Longhi's is the place to be on Friday nights from 9:30 p.m. to closing, when various live bands play music to swing to on the upstairs dance floor.

Summary & comments: Created in 1976 by "a man who loves to eat," Bob Longhi, the restaurant has remained a family affair, with son Peter the general manager and daughter Carol O'Leary an executive chef. It's a winning combination, as the restaurant won best overall restaurant in the *Maui News* readers poll in 1998 and has repeatedly received *Wine Spectator's* Best Award of Excellence since 1988. Longhi's has an all-verbal menu, which can prove irritating or exciting, depending on your mood. On the plus side, it gets diners to interact with the waiter, new menu items can be introduced easily, and you can get a true description of the food that you order. On the other hand, it can be difficult to remember all the choices (especially if you've had a libation or two), and it's easy to lose track of what you're spending.

MA'ALAEA WATERFRONT RESTAURANT ★★★½

Seafood/Continental	Moderate	QUALITY
		90
		VALUE
		C

50 Haouli Street, Ma'alaea; (808) 244-9028
Zone 7   Central Maui

Reservations: Highly recommended
When to go: Sunset for outside
Entrée range: $17.95–54
Payment: VISA, MC, AMEX, DC, D, JCB
Service rating: ★★★½
Parking: Free in upper level of adjacent condominium garage
Bar: Full service
Wine selection: Extensive, 30 by the glass
Dress: Resort attire
Disabled access: Adequate, via elevator
Customers: Islanders and tourists

Dinner: Every day, 5 p.m.–closing

Setting & atmosphere: Remodeled in 1998, this elegant oceanfront restaurant has pretty textured pale green walls, white tablecloths decorated with candles and tropical flowers, and scenic Island paintings on the walls. Outdoor dining on the deck is lovely on a balmy night, but bring a sweater if the trade winds are up.

House specialties: Depending on what the fishermen bring in, seven or eight different kinds of Island fish are served daily in your choice of nine preparation styles. This means there are always 50 or more choices to make while you nibble on homemade bread slathered with the house's special beer-cheese spread or watch the table-side preparation of your Caesar salad.

Other recommendations: Besides the rack of lamb, Ma'alaea Waterfront specializes in game meats, so you might find venison, red deer, pheasant, or ostrich, on a rotating basis. For dessert, the white chocolate blueberry cheesecake will satisfy every cheesecake aficionado.

Summary & comments: Ma'alaea Waterfront Restaurant is a family endeavor, opened in 1990 by the Smiths: mom, Donna; and brothers Ron, the chef; Gary, the manager; and Rick, the detail man. Their success is evidenced by the fact that the restaurant has repeatedly been named by the readership of *Maui News* as the restaurant with the best seafood and best service. Local voters repeatedly mention the warmth of the proprietors and the intimate ambience of the room.

MAMA'S FISH HOUSE		★★★½
Seafood	Moderate/Expensive	**QUALITY** 90
799 Poho Place, Ku'au; (808) 579-8488 Zone 7 Central Maui		**VALUE** C

Reservations: Highly recommended	Parking: Valet or adjacent lot
When to go: Anytime, but sunset is most romantic	Bar: Full service
Entrée range: Lunch $14–28, dinner $27–36	Wine selection: Excellent, half a dozen by the glass
Payment: VISA, MC, AMEX, DC, D, JCB	Dress: Casual resort wear
Service rating: ★★★★	Disabled access: Good, but it's some distance from the lot
	Customers: Tourists and Islanders

Lunch: Every day, 11 a.m.–2:30 p.m.

Pupus: Every day, 2:30–5 p.m.

Dinner: Every day, 5–9:30 p.m.; closed Christmas Day

Setting & atmosphere: You'll find Mama's reminiscent of a rambling, open-air beach house, at the end of a gecko-patterned walkway beside the ocean, with cool green lawns and shady coconut palms out front. A wooden bar and wooden paneling inside are made of tropical almond, monkeypod, and mango wood. It's a perfect place to while away an afternoon over a Mai Tai Roa Ae—the same kind of fresh fruit and rum concoction originated by Trader Vic's years ago—or to sample other retro drinks: Singapore Slings of Raffles hotel fame, Zombies, and Scorpions.

House specialties: Fishermen get written credit for catching the fresh fish on this menu, so the fish is always top-notch, whether you have ono, 'ahi, uku, or opah. Preparations include sautéed with garlic butter, white wine, and capers; grilled with Thai red curry; fried with Maui onion, chili pepper, and avocado; or served with honey-roasted macadamia-nut-lemon sauce. A signature dish, Pua me hua Hana, features sautéed fish with fresh coconut milk and lime juice served surrounded by fresh tropical fruit and accompanied by Molokai sweet potatoes.

Other recommendations: To sample Island-style cooking, try a lau lau, a bundle of mahi-mahi baked in ti leaves and served with tender, moist kalua pig. Another imaginative entrée with local flair is crispy kalua duck with mango-mui glaze served with baby bok choy and wild rice. Traditionalists can always get Black Angus New York steak or veal shank roasted with Asian spices served with portobello mushrooms, wasabi mashed potatoes, and Kula vegetables.

Summary & comments: In 1999, the Fish House added rattan tables and chairs and decorated an open-air area near the entrance to look like old Hawaii—they dubbed it "Grandma's Living Room." The room has become a popular spot for locals, who come to hang out, listen to the strains of vintage music, and nibble on *pupus* rather than order a full-blown meal from a menu that most Islanders consider "higher end." In contrast to the windsurfers who show up from nearby Ho'okipa Beach, there are occasional celebs—Jason Alexander for one—who have discovered the charms of Mama's Fish House and Grandma's Living Room. For five consecutive years, Mama's has won a five-diamond award from *Hospitality Sciences*. Locally, *Maui News* readers have named it as serving the best seafood, and it has been named a restaurant of distinction in *Honolulu Magazine*'s Hale 'Aina Awards.

A PACIFIC CAFÉ   ★★★½

Hawaii Regional	Moderate/Expensive	QUALITY
		90

	VALUE
Azeka II Shopping Center, 1279 Kihei Road, Kihei; (808) 879-0069	C

Zone 8   South Maui

Honokowai Market Place, 3350 Lower Hono-a-Pi'ilani Road, Honokowai
(808) 667-2800 or (808) 669-2724
Zone 9   West Maui

Reservations: Recommended
When to go: Anytime
Entrée range: $19–30
Payment: VISA, MC, AMEX, DC
Service rating: ★★★★½
Parking: Free in adjacent shopping
  center lot

Bar: Full service
Wine selection: Extensive, but few in
  lower price range
Dress: Resort wear
Disabled access: Good
Customers: Tourists and Islanders

Dinner: Every day, 5:30–9:30 p.m.

Setting & atmosphere: The newest of Jean Marie Josselin's excellent restaurants, the Honokowai location, with 2,600 square feet, is spacious enough that diners don't rub elbows with people at adjacent tables. The peach walls and golden decorative touches, including a copper air duct in the high-ceilinged restaurant, add warmth and a modern look. Unfortunately, the high ceiling makes this a noisy restaurant when full. Rattan fish traps, nets, and wall hangings are highlighted with gleaming brass cutouts of fish. Wooden tables have pounded brass inlays, as does a long counter for sushi or light meals that borders the exhibition kitchen.

House specialties: Beautifully presented Hawaii regional cuisine has interesting influences from the Mediterranean in seafood and from India in tandoori (clay) oven specialties. But it's the pan-seared "Local-Boy Ono" (white fish) served Hawaiian-style, with soba noodles on baby bok choy drizzled with nori-soy vinaigrette and sizzling hot peanut oil, that Islanders favor most of all. For a cosmopolitan experience, the Mongolian lamb with toasted Israeli couscous, Chinese roasted duck, or lemon-marinated tandoori pork with saffron-cashew rice can take you out of this world. Meals are accompanied by a variety of fresh breads: tiny Asian scones, walnut-olive bread, and sourdough French bread from the in-house bakery.

Other recommendations: Tiger eye sushi tempura, crispy on the outside, sushi on the inside, with a Chinese mustard dipping sauce, or the salmon firecracker roll with green papaya salad are tangy, tasty starters.

Also, in appetizers, seafood lovers go for the Hood Canal oysters wrapped in 'ahi tartare with a passion fruit mignonette, while meat-and-potato folks are more apt to enjoy barbecued pork ribs with charred Maui onion–hoisin glaze, or house-made beef pipikaula with sweet-potato butter. On a budget? For a main course, try the pizzas—with tandoori chicken or smoked salmon—from the kiawe-fired pizza oven. No matter how full you are, don't skip dessert: perhaps a chocolate-filled warm malassada, homemade sorbets, or a Toasted Hawaiian, made with layers of white chocolate cake, haupia (coconut) pudding, and white chocolate mousse.

Summary & comments: Food is an exciting flavor adventure at Jean Marie Josselin's restaurants. At A Pacific Café Honokowai, check to see if early-bird specials are still offered for dinner. At press time, an early dinner of three courses was being offered from 5:30 to 6:30 p.m. for the price of an entrée alone later in the evening.

PACIFIC'O		★★★★½
Hawaii Regional	Moderate	QUALITY 92
		VALUE C

505 Front Street, Lahaina; (808) 667-4341
Zone 9   West Maui

Reservations: Recommended
When to go: Sunset for best ocean views
Entrée range: Lunch $8.50–14.50, dinner $19–25
Payment: VISA, MC, AMEX, DC, JCB
Service rating: ★★★★

Parking: Free in lot across the street
Bar: Full service
Wine selection: Excellent
Dress: Casual
Disabled access: Adequate, but it's a long way from the parking lot
Customers: Tourists and Islanders

Lunch: Every day, 11 a.m.–4 p.m.

Dinner: Every day, 5:30–10 p.m.

Setting & atmosphere: This is a pleasant spot for indoor or outdoor dining at tables shaded by umbrellas and set right at the edge of the ocean. Inside, ceiling fans suspended above the checked marble floor lazily stir the air. A long bar is bordered by tables beside windows wide open to the ocean breezes and to views of three islands.

House specialties: You'll see why Chef James McDonald has won Taste of Lahaina competitions ever since 1993 when you try his appetizer of prawns and basil wontons served with a spicy sweet-and-sour sauce and

Hawaiian salsa. Another Taste of Lahaina winner is Asian Gravlax, slices of house-cured salmon on a warm sweet-potato applejack with wasabi chive sour cream, radish sprouts, and caviar.

Other recommendations: Artistic presentations include fresh fish, prepared seared in sesame with Kula lettuce and wasabi, or tandoori-flavored with Indonesian spices and caramelized Maui pineapple, or crispy deep-fried in a seaweed wrapper, or steamed in shiitake-sake bouillon in an old-fashioned Chinese bamboo steamer. A melt-in-your-mouth dessert of pineapple lumpia and macadamia nut ice cream is a beautiful blend of texture and taste.

Entertainment & amenities: Thursday–Saturday nights 9 p.m.–midnight, the indoor/outdoor restaurant at ocean's edge attracts jazz aficionados with live jazz performances.

Summary & comments: The same chef/owner, James McDonald, also owns I'o, a black-and-white metallic modern restaurant next door.

PLANTATION HOUSE RESTAURANT		★★
Contemporary	Inexpensive/Moderate	QUALITY 84
		VALUE C

Plantation Course Clubhouse, 2000 Plantation Club Drive,
Kapalua Resort; (808) 669-6299
Zone 9   West Maui

Reservations: Recommended for
  dinner
When to go: Anytime
Entrée range: Lunch $6.50–13,
  dinner $21–25
Payment: VISA, AMEX, MC, DC
Service rating: ★★★
Parking: In adjacent lot

Bar: Full service
Wine selection: Extensive
Dress: Casual
Disabled access: Good, drop off at
  front door
Customers: Golfers, tourists, and
  Islanders

Breakfast & lunch: Every day, 8 a.m.–3 p.m.

Dinner: Every day, 5:30–9 p.m.

Setting & atmosphere: Cool mountain breezes and views of velvety green fairways and distant blue ocean are a calming backdrop seen through paned windows that open to catch the breeze. Natural light woods, comfortable rattan chairs, and lazy overhead fans add to the relaxing atmosphere. A double-sided fireplace creates a warm glow in the evening, and by the bar, a big mural of workers in the pineapple fields depicts Kapalua's plantation past.

House specialties: Plantation House is known for Australian double-cut lamb chops with rosemary-bordelaise sauce and for fresh Island fish—try the Taste of the Rich Forest preparation, done with a mushroom crust on a bed of tot soi (Chinese spinach) with garlic mashed potatoes.

Other recommendations: A wide variety of appealing choices exists: smoked salmon Benedict dotted with capers for breakfast; chicken Caesar salad, burgers, or pasta at lunch; and desserts that range from old-fashioned Molokai sweet bread pudding to flashy bananas Foster, or da kine brownie with vanilla ice cream, chocolate sauce, whipped cream, and macadamia nuts.

Summary & comments: The Plantation House is a good alternative to the restaurants of the two Kapalua Resort hotels. Guests of both hotels can charge meals to their rooms and ride the free shuttle to get to this hillside golf course restaurant.

ROY'S KAHANA BAR & GRILL AND ROY'S NICOLINA ★★★½

Euro-Asian/Hawaii Regional	Moderate	QUALITY 85
Kahana Gateway Shopping Center, 4405 Honoapi'ilani Highway, Kahana; (808) 669-6999 Zone 9 West Maui		VALUE B

Reservations: Highly recommended	Bar: Full service
When to go: Anytime	Wine selection: Excellent, 10–15 by the glass
Entrée range: $13–26	
Payment: VISA, MC, AMEX, DC, D, JCB	Dress: Casual
Service rating: ★★★★½	Disabled access: Good, via elevator to upstairs restaurants
Parking: Free in shopping center lot	Customers: Tourists and Islanders

Dinner: *Nicolina:* every day, 5:30–9:30 p.m.; *Roy's Kahana Bar & Grill:* every day, 5:30–10 p.m.

Setting & atmosphere: Even owner Roy Yamaguchi admits there's not a lot of difference between these two restaurants that sit side by side on an upstairs level of a West Maui shopping center. Originally, he opened them with differing concepts in mind, but found that people liked his original ideas, so both restaurants are guided by the same corporate chef, and both offer 20 to 25 specials nightly. Roy's Kahana has a long bar near the entry and a centrally located open kitchen, so the high noise level seems to make it more suited to a lively, younger crowd, while Nicolina has a quieter appeal. Nicolina's kitchen is enclosed, but diners can enjoy lanai seating. Both have wooden-topped tables and local artwork that changes every six weeks; the art is available for sale.

House specialties: Since items change so rapidly, you never know what you'll find, but everything is made with the freshest local ingredients and has Euro-Asian and international flavorings. Appetizers like Szechuan baby-back ribs or Roy's shrimp and pork spring rolls with hot sweet mustard and black bean sauce set a spicy scene for perhaps a lighter entrée. Lemongrass-crusted shutome (swordfish) reflects a touch of Thailand, with sticky rice and basil peanut sauce. Hibachi-style salmon and blackened 'ahi entrées are signature items in both restaurants.

Other recommendations: If you pass up seared poke-style 'ahi, you might want to pay attention to the nightly fish specials. In any case, Roy's original dark chocolate soufflé with raspberry purée, which can always be ordered a la mode, is a must.

Entertainment & amenities: At Nicolina, you can hear live music Friday nights by a soloist who plays and sings.

Summary & comments: Roy Yamaguchi has won so many awards that it's difficult to credit them to his specific restaurants. *Gourmet* magazine's Top Tables, *Honolulu* magazine's top 20, *Maui News*'s best overall Maui restaurant, the James Beard Foundation, and many others applaud this imaginative and energetic chef, whose name was attached to 15 Roy's restaurants (with plans for more) throughout the country in 1999.

A SAIGON CAFÉ   ★★★

Vietnamese	Inexpensive	QUALITY
		85

1792 Main Street, Wailuku; (808) 243-9560
Zone 7   Central Maui

	VALUE
	A

Reservations: Recommended, especially for dinner	**Parking:** In adjacent lot
When to go: Anytime	**Bar:** Full service
Entrée range: $6.75–17.95	**Wine selection:** Limited
Payment: VISA, MC, AMEX, DC, D, JCB	**Dress:** Casual
Service rating: ★★★★	**Disabled access:** Good
	Customers: Islanders and a few tourists

Lunch & dinner: Every day, 10 a.m.– 8:30 p.m.

Setting & atmosphere: Sit at the low wooden bar with roll-around chairs, or choose a Formica-topped table or booth for lunch and dinner in this basic, white-walled restaurant minimally decorated with Vietnamese carved and lacquered art. A gold statue of Buddha greets guests at the door, ceiling fans whir overhead, and the TV might be on at the bar. It's a low-key place that can be difficult to find because there is no sign.

House specialties: It's almost de rigueur to start with cha gio (fried spring rolls)—little deep-fried bundles of ground pork, long rice, carrot, and onion wrapped in rice paper; the waiter will show you how to roll them in romaine lettuce with mint leaves and vermicelli noodles, then dip them in sweet-sour garlic sauce before enjoying them. Among any number of in-demand Vietnamese entrées, garden party shrimp dipped in a light batter, deep-fried, and served with sautéed ginger and green onions on bean sprouts and lettuce (with rice on the side) is one of the most delicious.

Other recommendations: With 92 items on the menu, it's hard to make a choice, let alone describe the best. Green papaya salad is a much-loved starter. For lunch, any of the noodle soups—with seafood and chicken, calamari and shrimp, or wonton, and others—provide a big bowl of steaming goodness. There are several rice-in-a-clay-pot variations done with chicken, catfish, shrimp, or pork.

Summary & comments: Everybody loves A Saigon Café, and regulars love the proprietor, Jennifer Nguyen, as well. Nguyen opened the restaurant in January 1996, but the identifying sign is still stored in a box somewhere. The sprightly, hard-working proprietor says, "We've been so busy, we've never gotten around to putting it up!"

SAM CHOY'S		★★★½

Hawaii Regional	Inexpensive/Moderate	QUALITY 82
		VALUE A

Ka'ahumanu Center, Kahului; (808) 893-0366
Zone 7   Central Maui

900 Front Street, Lahaina; (808) 661-3800
Zone 9   West Maui

Reservations: Recommended for dinner
When to go: Anytime
Entrée range: Breakfast $3.50–7.95, lunch $6.75–12.95, dinner $17.95–27.95
Payment: VISA, MC, AMEX
Service rating: ★★★½

Parking: In shopping center lot
Bar: Full service, including micro-brewery beers
Wine selection: Adequate
Dress: Casual
Disabled access: Good
Customers: Islanders and a few tourists

Breakfast: Every day, 7–10:15 a.m.

Lunch: Every day, 10:30 a.m.–3 p.m.

Dinner: Every day, 5–9 p.m.

Setting & atmosphere: In 1998, Hawaii's ambassador of "ono grinds" opened his Kahului breakfast, lunch, and dinner place with a big exhibition kitchen that has counter seating all along one side. It's a shopping center restaurant that draws shoppers during the day and is equally appealing to visitors and locals at night.

Somewhat newer, Sam Choy's Lahaina restaurant has an unobstructed view of the ocean and is decorated in contemporary shades of blue and green. On the walls, mosaic tiles depict fish and shellfish. Diners have a choice of sitting on the trellis-shaded garden terrace or at the Chef's Table, looking into the open kitchen.

House specialties: Choy is sticking to his tried and true formula—entrée portions with Island flavors that are often big enough to satisfy two people. A super dinner appetizer is shrimp Christopher, stuffed with crab meat, wrapped in bacon, and served with creamed shrimp and corn sauce. The seafood lau lau (fish, shrimp, scallops, and fresh vegetables wrapped and steamed in ti leaves) is a famed dinner entrée. The Asian veal osso bucco served over Oriental stir-fried noodles is enough for two.

Other recommendations: Beef stew and fried poke omelets and "awesome fried rice" are breakfast specialties. "Bento on a plate," with chicken katsu, or teri beef, fish, Spam, eggs, and rice, or Papa Choy's beef stew, satisfy any cravings for a plate lunch.

Entertainment & amenities: Live music on occasional weekends.

Summary & comments: Micro-brewed beers tout the local touch (Bumbucha Stout, Ehu Ale, Bruddah's Cream Ale), making this a great place just to "hang loose." Souvenir T-shirts, recipe books, and other memorabilia are for sale—shades of Hard Rock Café.

SANSEI SEAFOOD RESTAURANT AND SUSHI BAR ★★★★

Japanese/Pacific Rim	Moderate/Expensive	QUALITY
		90

The Shops at Kapalua, 115 Bay Drive, Kapalua; (808) 669-6286	VALUE
Zone 9 West Maui	B

Reservations: Highly recommended	Parking: In shopping village lot
When to go: Anytime	Bar: Full service
Entrée range: $12.95–37.95	Wine selection: Extensive
Payment: VISA, MC, AMEX, D, JCB	Dress: Resort attire
	Disabled access: Adequate
Service rating: ★★★★	Customers: Islanders and tourists

Dinner: Every day, 5:30–10 p.m.; laser karaoke Thursday and Friday from 10 p.m.

Setting & atmosphere: Booths and tables fill up fast in the intimate 120-seat restaurant, which includes a sushi bar and cocktail lounge area, so reservations are wise. Restaurant decor blends a bit of Japan with a Maui plantation look. The glass panel of the entry door is etched with a pineapple, and a window beyond the bar showcases a garden of tropical plants. There are samurai pictures on the walls, and the sushi bar, with its scalloped awning, could have come straight from Tokyo (as some of the sushi chefs did).

House specialties: At the 12-stool sushi bar, sushi chefs roll out tidbits ranging from crab and mango salad hand roll; to spider rolls with soft-shell crab; to bagel rolls with smoked salmon, Maui onion, and cream cheese. You can make a meal of several small appetizers tossed down with sake, or enjoy a full-scale dinner of the house's special black tea duck with two sauces. Other favored menu items include Asian rock shrimp cake, panko-crusted 'ahi sashimi, and nori ravioli of shrimp and salmon.

Other recommendations: Pay attention when the waiter describes nightly specials like asparagus tempura and fresh fish preparations, or try shrimp tempura deep-fried in a light-as-air batter, or a healthy preparation of grilled fresh mahi-mahi on Kula greens. Granny Smith baked apple tart is a pure American finish to any meal.

Entertainment & amenities: Sansei's karaoke after 10 p.m. on Thursday and Friday draws a happy crowd.

Summary & comments: Even big-name Maui chefs gather at this casual restaurant set unobtrusively in the Kapalua Shops center. Chef/owner D. K. Kodama says his menu reflects the way he likes to eat, with playful flavors and bits of this and that. In 1999, Sansei was named Best Maui Restaurant by *Honolulu Magazine*'s Hale 'Aina Awards, and in 1998 *Maui News* readers called it the best sushi bar on Maui.

SEASONS		★★★★½
		QUALITY
Hawaii Regional	Moderate/Expensive	93
		VALUE
Four Seasons Resort, 3900 Wailea Alanui, Wailea		C–
(808) 874-8000		
Zone 8 South Maui		

Reservations: Highly recommended

When to go: Sunset is spectacular from the panoramic seating on the lower level

Entrée range: $36–42; multi-course tasting menus, $78–145

Payment: AMEX, VISA, MC, DC, D, JCB

Service rating: ★★★★★

Parking: Complimentary valet or self-parking in covered hotel lot

Bar: Full service

Wine selection: Extensive; tops on the list is a 1994 Silver Oak Alexander Valley for $160; a dozen wines by the glass

Dress: Resort attire, jackets optional

Disabled access: Good, via elevator

Customers: Hotel guests and Islanders for special occasions

Dinner: Tuesday–Saturday, 6–9:30 p.m.

Setting & atmosphere: Seasons enjoys a spectacular setting, with sweeping ocean vistas the entire length of Wailea's coastline offering glimpses of the island of Kahoolawe through the tops of swaying coconut palms. Superbly executed service complements the understated decor of crisp white linen tablecloths, oversized hurricane lamps, and unassuming French china. Natural materials accent the decor with caramel-colored marble side tables, slate tile floors on the lower lanai, and heavy rattan and leather chairs throughout.

House specialties: One of Hawaii's most popular fish, onaga, is seared crispy on top with julienned endives and puréed snow peas, or you might want to try an updated version of an old favorite, roasted rack of lamb in a Cabernet sauce paired with Camembert potato soufflé and confit tomato.

Other recommendations: Salad of charbroiled Keahole (Big Island) lobster and Molokai sweet-potato purée; for dessert, the Hawaiian Vintage Chocolate Surprise is made of chocolate grown on the Big Island over Tahitian vanilla ice cream.

Entertainment & amenities: A Hawaiian trio serenades diners with traditional sounds of Hawaii from 7 to 10 p.m. nightly, and a dance floor beckons romantics. In the adjacent lobby lounge, a guitarist strums contemporary tunes from 8:30 to 11 p.m.

Summary & comments: This is the only restaurant on Maui with a master sommelier. Repeat diners say Seasons is what a hotel restaurant should be. It has a gracious elegance that makes an Absolut martini straight up with a twist, stirred not shaken, just right as a predinner cocktail. Free shuttles operate between all Wailea hotels, so if a postdinner snifter of Remy Martin XO also seems just right, you need not worry about driving your car.

THE BIG ISLAND

BATIK RESTAURANT		★★★★½
Hawaii Regional	Expensive	**QUALITY** 91
62-100 Mauna Kea Beach Drive, Mauna Kea Beach Hotel, Kohala Coast; (808) 882-7222 Zone 11 Kona		**VALUE** C−

Reservations: Highly recommended	Bar: Full service
When to go: Anytime	Wine selection: Extensive
Entrée range: $29–48, vegetarian $24, prix fixe menus $65–85	Dress: Evening resort wear
Payment: VISA, MC, AMEX, DC, JCB	Disabled access: Adequate, via elevator
Service rating: ★★★★★	Customers: Tourists and Islanders celebrating special occasions
Parking: Valet or hotel parking lot	

Dinner: Monday, Wednesday, Thursday, Friday, and Sunday, 6–9 p.m.; closed Tuesday and Saturday for house luau and clambake/seafood buffet

Setting & atmosphere: This is Mauna Kea Beach Hotel's premier restaurant, and care has been taken to do everything right. Batik panels decorating one wall are authentic, there are candles and tropical flowers on the tables, and a bronze charger rests under fine china plates for a look of burnished elegance. Patio tables overlooking Kauna'oa Bay were added in 1999 for those who prefer outdoor dining.

House specialties: Thai-style curries are the house specialty and the most often ordered entrée on the menu, though some people prefer to choose traditional items like beef Wellington, crispy salmon with saffron pepper jus, or lobster tail with saffron risotto. Meals are accompanied by tandoori oven–baked naan bread. Starters, such as langostinos sautéed in garlic and served with angel hair pasta with lobster sauce, or scallop ravioli with ginger-lime sauce, are as satisfying as the entrées.

Other recommendations: The number-one choice from the decadent dessert menu is a Grand Marnier soufflé, but the warm Valrhona chocolate cake comes a close second.

Entertainment & amenities: A classical solo guitarist strums tunes every evening. After dinner in the Batik Lounge, a jazz duo performs from 9 to 11 p.m. nightly.

Summary & comments: This place was once on the stuffy side, but today jackets are only recommended, and the food and decor have been finely honed to provide a high-quality dining experience.

CAFÉ PESTO		★★★½
Contemporary	Inexpensive	**QUALITY** 84
		VALUE B

Wharf Road and Mahukona Highway, Kawaihae Center, Kawaihae
(808) 882-1071
Zone 11   Kona

308 Kamehameha Avenue, Hilo; (808) 969-6640
Zone 12   Hilo and Volcano

Reservations: Accepted	Bar: Full service
When to go: Anytime	Wine selection: Limited, some by
Entrée range: $13–28	glass
Payment: VISA, MC, AMEX, D,	Dress: Casual
DC, JCB	Disabled access: Good
Service rating: ★★★	Customers: Islanders and tourists
Parking: Adjacent parking lot	

Lunch: Every day, 11 a.m.–4:30 p.m.

Dinner: Every day, 4:30–9 p.m.

Setting & atmosphere: Café Pesto in Hilo and at Kawaihae Harbor both have a bright, cheerful outlook, with black-and-white flooring and big windows reflecting a contemporary art deco theme. Kawaihae has a more intimate feeling, with a low ceiling, while the Hilo restaurant is in the historic S. Hata Building, which retained the high ceiling of turn-of-the-century architecture when it was restored.

House specialties: Café Pesto is known for its use of fresh Island ingredients and simple healthy preparations, particularly its Island fish, served sautéed or grilled. A wood-burning pizza oven fired on kiawe or ohia produces ten different pizzas, including one where you compile as many ingredients as you like. The Marguerite cheese pizza is most popular, but the Oriental al pesto pizza is a top vegetarian choice, with eggplant, sun-dried tomatoes, and roasted garlic.

Other recommendations: Pastas are great; risottos are creamy and good, particularly the seafood risotto made with Keahole lobster, prawns, scallops, and grilled local fish. A beef tenderloin of Kamuela Pride beef comes with lobster tempura and garlic prawns served with mozzarella mashed potatoes. The macadamia-crusted apple pie and the chocolate ganache torte are desserts to diet for.

Summary & comments: Café Pesto won the local Hale 'Aina Award for Best Big Island Restaurant in 1999. Diners pen comments such as "Move the restaurant to where we live," or "You cook better than my wife, but don't tell her." Both restaurants have a smoke-free policy.

CANOEHOUSE ★★★★½

Hawaii Regional	Moderate/Expensive	QUALITY
		91
		VALUE
		C–

68-1400 Mauna Lani Drive, Mauna Lani Bay Hotel & Bungalows, Kohala Coast; (808) 885-6622
Zone 11   Kona

Reservations: Highly recommended
When to go: Sunset
Entrée range: $23–50
Payment: VISA, MC, AMEX, D, DC, JCB
Service rating: ★★★★
Parking: Valet or hotel lot

Bar: Full service
Wine selection: Good
Dress: Resort attire
Disabled access: Adequate, but it's some distance from the parking
Customers: Resort and hotel guests and Islanders

Dinner: Every day, 6–9 p.m.

Setting & atmosphere: A torchlit path with a little bridge over a koi-filled stream and the ocean waves lapping on the beach a few steps away set the scene for a romantic evening. Inside, a huge koa canoe is the focal point. You can choose semi-privacy by sitting in a raised booth, choose to be in the middle of things at a table, or join the conviviality at a central bar.

House specialties: Imaginative entrées include miso-sake marinated mahi-mahi with stir-fried soba noodles, and grilled lemon-pepper scallops with wild mushroom mashed potatoes.

Other recommendations: It's tempting to try two appetizers, perhaps kalua pork spring rolls or baby-back ribs grilled with guava hoisin sauce, instead of an entrée, just so you can try the intriguing preparations. If you still have room for a decadent dessert, try the CanoeHouse Chocolate Pillar, a rich torte with vanilla sauce and fresh berries.

Summary & comments: The food is innovative, the setting lovely, and wines suggested for each entrée are available by the glass. It almost makes paying the hefty bill worth it.

COAST GRILLE		★★★★½
		QUALITY
Contemporary/Hawaii Regional	Moderate/Expensive	91
		VALUE
62-100 Kauna'oa Drive, Hapuna Beach Prince Hotel, Kohala Coast		C–
(808) 880-1111		
Zone 11 Kona		

Reservations: Recommended
When to go: Sunset under the stars if you sit outside overlooking the ocean
Entrée range: $20–36
Payment: VISA, MC, AMEX, DC, JCB
Service rating: ★★★★

Parking: Valet or hotel lot
Bar: Full service
Wine selection: Extensive
Dress: Resort wear
Disabled access: Adequate, via elevator and curving ramp walkway
Customers: Hotel and resort guests and Islanders for special occasions

Dinner: Every day, 6–9:30 p.m.

Setting & atmosphere: This is a big, spacious restaurant where you can sit at interior tables (which is a waste of an exhilarating view), out on the deck, or at banquettes that face the ocean when the breeze is a little too nippy for comfort. Tables inside the multi-level, circular building seem dwarfed under a high ceiling but give you a nice feeling of privacy from neighboring diners. Natural woods and soft lighting tone down the empty effect.

House specialties: The oyster bar is a rare find in Island restaurants, while Kona lobster, raised just down the coast, comes in a steamer basket with shrimp, Manila clams, and Waipi'o taro ravioli. The hotel is the home of the Sam Choy Poke Contest, a blessing for seafood lovers, as many types of poke, generally made of raw fish, seaweed, and spices, are available.

Other recommendations: For non–seafood lovers, there's peppercorn-crusted lamb rack with star anise sauce, or grilled smoked veal chop. The dessert sampler eases the pain of making a decision, but you might want to order the warm chocolate pudding with fresh nutmeg ice cream in advance so this creamy rich treat will be ready when you are.

Summary & comments: Sit outside at sunset on warm summer and fall evenings to fully appreciate the inspiring view of turquoise ocean and white sand.

DONATONI'S	★★★★½
Italian Moderate/Expensive	**QUALITY** 91
Hilton Waikoloa Village, 425 Waikoloa Beach Drive, Waikoloa (808) 886-1234 Zone 11 Kona	**VALUE** C–

Reservations: Highly recommended	Bar: Full service
When to go: Anytime	Wine selection: Extensive wine and champagne list
Entrée range: $19.25–45	
Payment: VISA, MC, AMEX, D, DC, JCB	Dress: Resort attire
Service rating: ★★★★½	Disabled access: Adequate, at some distance from the parking lot
Parking: Valet or complimentary hotel parking lot	Customers: Hotel and resort guests, some Islanders

Dinner: Every day, 6–10 p.m.

Setting & atmosphere: This is an intimate, romantic restaurant reminiscent of old Italy, and it seems even more dreamy if you have the chance to sit outdoors next to a saltwater canal where boats drift by in the moonlight—almost like being in Venice.

House specialties: With a name like Sascia Marchesi, is it any wonder the Milanese-born chef is an expert in preparing the northern Italian cuisine served at Donatoni's? Among his best dishes are Torre Di Granseola e Vitello (king crab and veal scaloppini with lemon sauce) and a daily fresh catch of fish served with risotto and fresh asparagus.

Other recommendations: Delectable pastas may be ordered as appetizers or entrées. Traditional tiramisu and exquisite crème brûlée take top dessert honors at this restaurant.

Entertainment & amenities: A violinist strolls from table to table in the evenings.

Summary & comments: More than one publication has lauded Donatoni's for its Italian food and romantic atmosphere. Oddly, the romantic ambience is nearly as heady inside (with opulent chandeliers and pretty upholstered booths and chairs) as it is outside beside the waterway.

EDELWEISS		★★★½
Continental	Moderate	QUALITY 81
Highway 19, Waimea; (808) 885-6800 Zone 11 Kona		VALUE B

Reservations: Recommended	Parking: In adjacent lot

When to go: Anytime for dinner
  except Sunday and Monday;
  go early on weekends to avoid
  waiting
	Bar: Full service
	Wine selection: Average
	Dress: Casual
	Disabled access: Good

Entrée range: $18.50–24.50	Customers: Islanders and some
Payment: VISA, MC, AMEX	tourists
Service rating: ★★★★	

Lunch: Tuesday–Saturday, 11:30 a.m.–1:30 p.m.

Dinner: Tuesday–Saturday, 5–8:30 p.m.

Setting & atmosphere: You feel as if you're back in Bavaria in this charming chalet-restaurant with rustic redwood furnishings, traditional blue-and-white curtains, and rich aromas of robust food wafting from the kitchen over the room's 15 tables.

House specialties: You'll always find a delicious rack of lamb on the menu. Complete dinners include everything but dessert, for which you can choose the three-layer raspberry, vanilla, and chocolate Edelweiss torte, or rice pudding.

Other recommendations: More than a dozen specials might be served nightly—Texas wild boar, venison ragout, Black Forest chicken, veal chalet Emily—so you never get tired of the menu. A word of warning: Sometimes the chef gets a little heavy on the salt.

Summary & comments: Edelweiss has been a Big Island favorite for years, steadily withstanding competition from new, trendy restaurants that have come and, in many cases, gone from the Big Island dining scene.

THE GRILL AND LOUNGE AT THE ORCHID	★★★½	
Contemporary	Expensive	**QUALITY** 86
1 North Kaniku Drive, The Orchid Hotel, Kohala Coast (808) 885-2000 Zone 11 Kona		**VALUE** C–

Reservations: Highly recommended
When to go: Anytime
Entrée range: $28–50
Payment: VISA, MC, AMEX, D, DC, JCB
Service rating: ★★★★½
Parking: Valet or free self-parking in hotel lot

Bar: Full service
Wine selection: Extensive
Dress: Dressy resort attire
Disabled access: Good, via elevator
Customers: Hotel and resort guests, Islanders for special occasions

Dinner: Every day, 6:30–9:30 p.m.

Setting & atmosphere: Comfortable club-like atmosphere, with richly polished koa wood bar and wall paneling, enhances relaxed dining. Tables are covered in beige Frette linens and softly lit with candle lamps. Chairs are upholstered in rich tapestry, while the walls are hung with scenes by local artists.

House specialties: The Grill and Lounge is especially good for the grilled meat items on the menu. Rack of lamb is crusted with pesto accompanied by apple-smoked bacon, sweet potato, and wild mushrooms, and garnished with tropical fruit chutney. Veal chops are similarly crusted with Parmesan and served with a sweet corn risotto and Waimea tomato fondue. To start, Maui onion soup topped with imported Gruyère and Reggiano cheeses, or warm baby spinach salad garnished with fresh buffalo mozzarella, sets the taste buds tingling.

Other recommendations: The oven-roasted breast of organic chicken (mainlanders might call it "free-range") oozes melted Puna goat cheese and is served with baby bok choy and roasted garlic potatoes. Dessert lovers have to ask which selections of soufflés are available nightly, though for a lighter conclusion, you might opt for the apple Florentine served in a crust of crisp macadamia nut butter snaps.

Entertainment & amenities: Classical guitarist Charles Brotman, whose instrumental CDs can be found in Island music outlets, strums contemporary tunes most evenings. Couples often linger a while to take advantage of the restaurant's dance floor.

Summary & comments: The Grill and Lounge has been recognized by *Gayot's The Best of Hawaii* for fine dining.

HARRINGTON'S   ★★

		QUALITY
Steak and Seafood	Moderate	**76**

		VALUE
135 Kalaniana'ole Street, Hilo; (808) 961-4966		**B**

Zone 12   Hilo and Volcano

Reservations: Recommended
When to go: Anytime for dinner except Wednesday
Entrée range: $14.75–27.95
Payment: VISA, MC
Service rating: ★★★★
Parking: In adjacent lot

Bar: Full service
Wine selection: Adequate, about 30 wines
Dress: Casual dress, no tank tops, no swimwear for women
Disabled access: Good
Customers: Tourists and Islanders

Lunch: Monday–Friday, 11 a.m.–2 p.m.

Dinner: Monday, Tuesday, and Thursday–Saturday, 5–9:30 p.m.; Sunday, 5–9 p.m.; closed Wednesday

Setting & atmosphere: Harrington's is in an old brown freestanding building on the edge of the Ice Pond in Hilo; it's best viewed in kinder lighting after dark. Inside, hanging plants and other greenery, blue tablecloths, and tropical flowers on the tables create an intimate atmosphere.

House specialties: Among reliable choices like prime rib, New York steak, and teriyaki steak offerings, the Slavic steak is a tasty chilled mainland sirloin sliced thin and topped with a savory garlic butter sauce.

Other recommendations: Dinners, including seafood selections—fresh fish, lobster, prawns, calamari, scallops—come with a choice of starch and salad. If you're a vegetarian in a world of steak eaters, opt for the eggplant parmigiana. Waiters tempt you by presenting desserts on a tray. If you can't say no, try the house cheesecake with strawberries or liliko'i.

Entertainment & amenities: On Friday and Saturday nights a musician livens up the lounge with contemporary Hawaiian music.

Summary & comments: The menu in this old standby may have been updated by new ownership several years ago, but basically if you liked steak and seafood restaurants 20 years ago, you'll find this pleasant restaurant comforting in a world of nouvelle cuisine.

HUGGO'S		★★½

Pacific Rim/Mediterranean	Moderate	QUALITY
		81
75-5828 Kahakai Road, Kailua-Kona; (808) 329-1493		VALUE
Zone 11 Kona		C

Reservations: Recommended
When to go: Sunset for most roman-
   tic lighting
Entrée range: $16.95–37
Payment: VISA, MC, D, DC, JCB
Service rating: ★★★
Parking: Adjacent lot

Bar: Full service
Wine selection: Adequate, a dozen
   by the glass
Dress: Casual
Disabled access: Good
Customers: Islanders and tourists

Lunch: Every day, 11:30 a.m.–2:30 p.m.

Dinner: Every day, 5:30–10 p.m.

Setting & atmosphere: With tables in an open-air restaurant set just above water's edge, Huggo's proved such a popular place for sunset watchers that the owners opened an adjacent waterfront lounge with a similar view next door called Huggo's on the Rocks. The new bar, which serves lunch and *pupus* at dinner, is also a popular hangout for longtime Huggo's loyalists. The established restaurant is decorated with marine memorabilia, big anchors, lamps that must have come from some oceangoing vessel at one time, rope lines, and natural wood. One open-to-the-elements deck has half a dozen tables shaded by big umbrellas.

House specialties: The fresh local seafood is the reason Huggo's has earned a dedicated following. Try sesame-crusted mahi-mahi or coconut-kiwi ono, both delicately flavored white fish adeptly seasoned.

Other recommendations: A number of vegetarian choices and a juicy cut of certified Angus prime rib gives non–seafood lovers a chance to enjoy Huggo's casual atmosphere and fine food.

Entertainment & amenities: Performers render live contemporary music nightly at the adjacent bar, for diners who want to hang out before or after the meal.

Summary & comments: Ask for a table by the window to fully appreciate Huggo's oceanfront appeal.

KILAUEA LODGE		★★★½

		QUALITY
Continental	Moderate	84
		VALUE
		C

19-4055 Old Volcano Road, Volcano Village; (808) 967-7366
Zone 12   Hilo and Volcano

Reservations: Highly recommended
When to go: Anytime, but post–nighttime lava viewing is always fun
Entrée range: $15.50–33
Payment: VISA, MC
Service rating: ★★★½
Parking: Adjacent lot

Bar: Full service
Wine selection: Good, some wines by the glass
Dress: Casual. Bring a sweater; Volcano nights can be cool
Disabled access: Adequate, via lift
Customers: Islanders and tourists

Dinner: Every day, 5:30–9 p.m.

Setting & atmosphere: This mountain lodge, surrounded by tree ferns in the cool, secluded Volcano area, dates from 1938, when the property was a scouting retreat. A stone fireplace glows in the dining room, which has a vaulted cedar ceiling, hardwood floors, local artwork, and a rustic, remote appeal.

House specialties: The cool climate is great for duck l'orange with red cabbage and potatoes du jour or a rich seafood Mauna Kea, pasta made with bay shrimp, prawns, fresh 'ahi, scallops, mushrooms, capers, and basil-wine sauce. Lighter appetites go for the fresh Island fish. The Lodge's signature dessert is Portuguese sweet bread pudding garnished with a variety of fruit sauces.

Other recommendations: This is a cozy place to sip a full-bodied red wine and nibble away on an appetizer, such as Brie cheese deep-fried in coconut batter and served with brandied apples and bread.

Summary & comments: Kilauea Lodge has long been considered *the* place to eat in Volcano, and people from Hilo often drive the half-hour from town to enjoy the "getting-away-from-it-all" feeling the lodge provides.

KONA RANCH HOUSE ★★½

American	Inexpensive/Moderate	QUALITY
		71

		VALUE
75-5653 Ololi Street; (808) 329-7061		B
Zone 11 Kona		

Reservations: Recommended
When to go: Anytime
Entrée range: Breakfast $4.75–9.25,
   lunch $5.95–9.95, dinner
   $10.95–22.95
Payment: VISA, MC, AMEX, DC,
   D, JCB

Service rating: ★★★
Parking: In adjacent lot
Bar: Full service
Wine selection: Limited, all by glass
Dress: Casual
Disabled access: Good
Customers: Islanders and tourists

Breakfast: Every day, 6:30 a.m.–2 p.m.

Lunch: Every day, 6:30 a.m.–2 p.m.

Dinner: Every day, 4–8 p.m.

Setting & atmosphere: This family-style restaurant is divided into two sections. The Paniolo Room has booths handy for a quick lunch; the Plantation Lanai is nicer for dinner or Sunday brunch, with white wicker chairs, flowers, and candles in the evening.

House specialties: Known for good breakfasts of omelets, eggs Benedict, and pancakes, this place is especially busy on Sunday mornings. At dinner, big barbecue platters are the draw, but the menu is so varied you'll find Tex-Mex and vegetarian items as well.

Other recommendations: You can choose fresh local fish—'ahi, mahi-mahi, and ono—prepared broiled, Cajun, sautéed, and fried. Meals come with salad, vegetables, and starch.

Summary & comments: Ample food, reasonable prices, and pleasant surroundings are the reason this family restaurant has been an Island favorite since 1981.

MERRIMAN'S		★★★★½
		QUALITY
Hawaii Regional	Moderate/Expensive	94
		VALUE
'Opelo Plaza II, Highway 19 and 'Opelo Road, Waimea		C
(808) 885-6822		
Zone 11 Kona		

Reservations: Highly recommended
When to go: Anytime for dinner
Entrée range: $12.95–25.95
Payment: VISA, MC, AMEX, JCB
Service rating: ★★★★★
Parking: In adjacent lot

Bar: Full service
Wine selection: Extensive
Dress: Casual
Disabled access: Good
Customers: Tourists and Islanders

Lunch: Monday–Friday, 11:30 a.m.–1:30 p.m.

Dinner: Every day, 5:30–9 p.m.

Setting & atmosphere: Set in the heart of Big Island cowboy country, Merriman's is a classy, understated restaurant with an exhibition kitchen. Artwork by local artists is ever-changing and available for purchase. Light colors and potted palm plants add to the pleasant contemporary ranch country feel.

House specialties: Chef/owner Peter Merriman serves fresh, locally raised meat and produce, available in dishes that reflect the cooking styles of Hawaii's various cultures. The restaurant's signature dish is original wok-charred 'ahi, seared on the outside, sashimi-rare on the inside, available as an appetizer or an entrée. New York steaks are from nearby Parker Ranch, while the lamb, raised at Kahua Ranch, is prepared differently each day. You might find herb-roasted leg of lamb served with mango port wine jus, or a rack of lamb. Lokelani Farms grows special tomatoes just for Merriman's, while Honopua Farms raises an organic spinach that turns up on plates tossed with hot balsamic vinegar and garnished with pipikaula (spicy dried beef) and crumbled bacon.

Other recommendations: Fresh Island fish is served sautéed with shellfish and vegetable nabemono, herb-grilled on mango chutney, or sesame-crusted with spicy liliko'i sauce and tomato papaya relish. Vegetarians will appreciate pan-fried Asian cake noodle served with a medley of vegetables: broccoli, snow peas, cauliflower, and carrots, with a spicy black bean sauce. Dessert lovers say the coconut crème brûlée is the best they've had, though some prefer the liliko'i passion fruit mousse.

Summary & comments: This is probably the Big Island's favorite restaurant. The chef/owner's reputation for the best food on the island is so widely known that visitors (including celebrities like Robert Redford and Kevin Costner) drive from miles away to Merriman's for special occasions. *Hint:* Take a sweater, as the restaurant can get cool in the chilly Waimea night.

PAHU I'A AT FOUR SEASONS		★★★★½

Hawaii Fusion	Expensive	QUALITY
		91
		VALUE
		C–

Four Seasons Resort Hualalai, 100 Ka'upulehu Drive,
Ka'upulehu-Kona; (808) 325-8000
Zone 11 Kona

Reservations: Recommended
When to go: Sunset is most
  romantic
Entrée range: $25–43; 4-course
  chef's tasting menu plus dessert,
  $65; with wine pairings, add $20
Payment: VISA, MC, AMEX, D,
  JCB
Service rating: ★★★★★
Parking: Complimentary valet or
hotel lot
Bar: Full service
Wine selection: Extensive
Dress: Resort wear
Disabled access: Adequate, via paved
  pathways
Customers: Hotel and resort guests
  and Islanders celebrating special
  occasions

Breakfast: Every day, 6–11:30 a.m.

Dinner: Every day, 5:30–10 p.m.

Setting & atmosphere: Outdoor deck seating features candlelit tables, with spotlights illuminating the rhythmic surf, and is romantic even for hand-holding at breakfast. Cross a wooden bridge suspended across a natural fishpond to reach the polished mahogany and teak interior, where a four-foot rectangular aquarium that stands nine feet tall holds colorful reef fish. Candles in black sand in hurricane lamps light individual tables. Check out three original hand-colored woodcuts by Charles Bartlett (circa 1921–1922)—"Duke Kahanamoku," "Surfing at Waikiki," and "Hawaiian Fisherman"—displayed on restaurant walls.

House specialties: There's a mind-boggling daily breakfast buffet that's even more extensive on Sundays for brunch. At dinner, an 'Ahi, 'Ahi, 'Ahi appetizer features the popular tuna in a trio of preparations: sashimi, seared, and poke. Steamed 'opakapaka Oriental-style with shiitake mushrooms, Chinese parsley, and ginger-shoyu is both good and good for you.

Other recommendations: As with most top-notch hotel restaurants, you'll find a plethora of fresh Island fish on the menu, which may save enough on calories that you'll feel no guilt at plunging into the kope pukolu (coffee trio), a tower of classic tiramisu and cappuccino crème brûlée on a cinnamon sugar puff pastry, and homemade espresso ice cream wrapped in a coconut wave cookie. On the other hand, Vintage Chocolate soufflé, a melt-in-your-mouth warm delight made of chocolate from locally grown cocoa beans, is also a pretty spectacular finish to a meal.

Entertainment & amenities: A slack key guitarist plays nightly from 6:30 to 9:30 p.m.

Summary & comments: This is the closest to the beach you could possibly sit without spreading a towel in the sand for a picnic, but the price may reduce you to opting for a real picnic next time.

PARKER RANCH GRILL		★★½
American	Moderate	**QUALITY** 81
Parker Ranch Shopping Center, 67-1185 Mamalahoa Highway, Waimea; (808) 887-2624 Zone 11 Kona		**VALUE** C

Reservations: Recommended
When to go: Anytime
Entrée range: Lunch $6 – 8.50, dinner $13–23
Payment: VISA, MC, AMEX, D, DC, JCB
Service rating: ★★★½

Parking: Free in adjacent lot
Bar: Full service
Wine selection: Adequate
Dress: Casual
Disabled access: Fully accessible
Customers: Islanders and tourists

Lunch: Every day, 11:30 a.m.–2:30 p.m.

Dinner: Every day, 5:30–9:30 p.m.

Setting & atmosphere: Recently renovated by partners who have a good reputation in the restaurant business as the owners of Huggo's in Kailua-Kona, this old favorite seems destined to become a new favorite in Waimea. Picture windows frame the lofty peak of Mauna Kea, while inside are pictures of horses hung on the curly koa paneling, as well as saddles, boots, and spurs on display. Rich ruby reds, deep forest greens, and polished koa tables and paneling are the perfect setting for hearty *paniolo* cuisine.

House specialties: Savory liliko'i barbecued spareribs or Parker Ranch prime beef are hearty entrées, but a more unusual and most delectable entrée is lobster pot pie. Warm, caramelized mango tart is marvelous with or without a dip of ice cream.

Other recommendations: For a down-home taste of *paniolo* cooking, the roasted chicken is enough to take home to snack on the next day.

Entertainment & amenities: A comfortable lounge with a glowing fire in the fireplace has board games that are great for killing time if you've got to wait a few moments, but it's the live entertainment that makes this a hopping place every weekend.

Summary & comments: An iron-gated wine cellar provides seating for private parties up to 10, and Colonel Sam's Library can handle parties of 35 or 40.

ROYAL SIAM		★★★½
Thai	Inexpensive	**QUALITY** 86
70 Mamo Street, Hilo; (808) 961-6100 Zone 12 Hilo and Volcano		**VALUE** A

Reservations: Accepted
When to go: Anytime except Sunday
Entrée range: $6.95–8.95, vegetarian dishes start at $4.95
Payment: VISA, MC, AMEX, DC, D
Service rating: ★★★

Parking: On-street
Bar: Full service
Wine selection: Very limited
Dress: Casual
Disabled access: Adequate
Customers: Islanders and some tourists

Lunch: Monday–Saturday, 11 a.m.–2 p.m.

Dinner: Every day, 5–8:30 p.m.

Setting & atmosphere: This small restaurant seats about 50 at booths that line the walls and central tables covered with pink-and-white striped tablecloths. Pictures of the Thai king and queen, Buddha, and Thai dancers hang on the walls. Sprays of orchids and potted trees add a colorful touch.

House specialties: Diners always love the deep-fried spring rolls made with either vegetables only or pork and vegetables and served in the traditional way, with mint and lettuce leaves to roll them in and a sweet-sour sauce for dipping. The most popular entrée on the menu is Buddrama, chicken prepared with spinach and peanut sauce, though curries, which can be ordered mild, medium, or hot, are also favored. Choose yellow or green curry with chicken, beef, or shrimp, or a healthy vegetarian curry with basil, green peas, and eggplant.

Other recommendations: The chef's favorites are Thai garlic shrimp and cashew chicken with orders of sticky rice. Thai jasmine rice and brown rice are other starchy choices.

Entertainment & amenities: The sound system plays subdued Thai music to set the mood.

Summary & comments: Quality- and value-wise, though it's certainly not fancy, this is sometimes called the best food in Hilo. In 1999 the restaurant expanded, adding a second room that can seat about 25 people. It can be booked for private parties, though it's normally used for dinner seating.

ROY'S AT THE KING'S SHOPS   ★★★★½

Euro-Asian	Moderate	QUALITY
		91
		VALUE
		B

King's Shops, 250 Waikoloa Beach Drive, Waikoloa
(808) 886-4321
Zone 11   Kona

Reservations: Highly recommended	Bar: Full bar
When to go: Early to avoid crowds	Wine selection: Very good, some by
Entrée range: $14–27	the glass
Payment: VISA, MC, AMEX, D,	Dress: Casual, no tank tops for
DC, JCB	men, no swimwear
Service rating: ★★★★	Disabled access: Good
Parking: Shopping center lot	Customers: Islanders and tourists

Lunch: Every day, 11:30 a.m.–2 p.m.

Dinner: Every day, 5:30–9:30 p.m.

Setting & atmosphere: This Roy's, with green carpets, a green marble bar, an exhibition kitchen, and window tables that overlook a golf course lake, is the nicest yet of Roy Yamaguchi's popular restaurants in Hawaii.

House specialties: Sample grilled Szechuan-style baby-back ribs or Thai noodle peanut chicken salad at dinner, or choose among entrées like imu-roasted pork lau lau, pizza, or sweet sake-glazed shrimp. Blackened Island 'ahi, served in spicy hot soy mustard butter sauce, is a Roy's standby. More than half a dozen fish and their preparations change nightly, as do appetizers, pizzas, pastas, salads, and soups.

Other recommendations: Salads and sandwiches at lunch are complete meals, such as the teriyaki Big Island beef sandwich or fresh Island fish of the day with panzu sprout salad, as are the pastas, like penne pasta with Neapolitan sauce and chicken, shrimp, or beef.

Summary & comments: It's no problem matching a wine to any of the Euro-Asian flavors, given the extensive wine list. Youngsters are welcome; Roy's offers a children's menu and crayons. According to the chef's mood and the ingredients available, often more than 30 menu items change nightly, so you will never get bored with the food no matter how many times you return.

SAM CHOY'S RESTAURANT		★★★	
Hawaii Regional	Moderate	**QUALITY**	
		87	
73-5576 Kauhola Street, Bay 1, Kaloko Light Industrial Park		**VALUE**	
(808) 326-1545		B	
Zone 11 Kona			

Reservations: Highly recommended
  for dinner
When to go: Anytime
Entrée range: $16.95–24.95, daily
  specials can top out at $31.95
Payment: VISA, MC, D
Service rating: ★★★★

Parking: In adjacent lot
Bar: None
Wine selection: Bring your own
Dress: Casual
Disabled access: Good
Customers: Islanders and tourists

Breakfast and Lunch: Every day, 6 a.m.–2 p.m.

Dinner: Tuesday–Saturday, 5–9 p.m.

Setting & atmosphere: During the day, Sam Choy's is a casual, local-style restaurant frequented not only by workers from the surrounding area but also by visitors looking for real local food. In the evening, the room undergoes a transformation with white cloths and colored napkins added to the tables, but you can still watch the cooks zip around the open kitchen.

House specialties: Islanders love the seafood lau lau, an assortment of fresh fish, vegetables, and spinach steamed in a luau leaf. Equally famous is Sam's seafood trio, three types of local fresh fish, one served seared, one ogo-crusted in crispy tempura, and one macadamia-nut-crusted. All meals come with soup or salad and a choice of rice or potato.

Other recommendations: Duck, lamb chops, macadamia-nut-crusted pork loin, and teriyaki steak round out a dinner menu that's sure to round out an average person's body. Big hearty breakfasts of stew omelets or fried poke (barely seared seafood and seaweed) are filling, and omelets come with rice, home fries, or hash browns, and toast and jelly. At lunch, specials change daily, but a big steaming bowl of saimin (Island-style noodle soup) is always on the menu.

Summary & comments: Sam Choy is Hawaii's most famous native Hawaiian/Chinese chef, and his restaurants are known almost as much for their *big* portions as for the high-quality food with a real local touch and robust flavors. Expect to take home enough food for the next day's lunch.

KAUAI

THE BEACH HOUSE		★★★
Pacific Rim	Moderate	QUALITY 85
5022 Lawaʻi Road, Poʻipu; (808) 742-1424 Zone 13 Kauai		VALUE C

Reservations: Highly recommended	Bar: Full service
When to go: Sunset	Wine selection: Extensive
Entrée range: $18.95–32.50	Dress: Resort wear
Payment: VISA, MC, AMEX, DC, JCB	Disabled access: Good; valet parking is free for disabled
Service rating: ★★★★	Customers: Tourists and Islanders
Parking: Valet or street	

Dinner: *May 2–October 1:* every day, 6–9:30 p.m.; *October 2–May 1:* every day, 5:30–9:30 p.m.

Setting & atmosphere: Artwork by local artists can be purchased right off the walls, if you have time to tear your eyes away from floor-to-ceiling windows that showcase Poʻipu's best ocean view. It's most romantic at sunset, when surfers and frolicking whales might still be spotted.

House specialties: A kiawe wood–burning grill adds a flavorful touch to kal-bi-style lamb rack or Jawaiian pork tenderloin with jerk spices.

Other recommendations: The on-property chef, under the guiding wing of Kauai's well-known chef/owner Jean Marie Josselin, prepares such delicacies as wok-charred mahi-mahi in a ginger-sesame crust and lime ginger sauce, or seared sea scallops with a polenta herb crust and papaya-avocado guacamole. Save calories on a short stack of portobello mushrooms with spring vegetables, then splurge on Toasted Hawaiian, a white chocolate cake layered with haupia (coconut pudding), white chocolate mousse, macadamia nuts, and caramel sauce.

Summary & comments: Make reservations early and request a seat by the window for the full effect of this beach area's stunning views. In 1998, The Beach House won honors as the top restaurant on Kauai in the local Hale 'Aina Awards.

BRENNECKE'S BEACH BROILER		★★★

		QUALITY
Contemporary	Moderate	78

	VALUE
2100 Ho'one Road, Po'ipu Beach; (808) 742-7588	B
Zone 13 Kauai	

Reservations: Recommended	Bar: Full service
When to go: Sunset	Wine selection: Limited
Entrée range: $6.95–29.50	Dress: Casual
Payment: VISA, MC, AMEX, D, DC, JCB	Disabled access: Poor, but staff will carry wheelchairs up the stairs
Service rating: ★★★	Customers: Tourists and Islanders
Parking: In 2 adjacent lots	

Lunch: Every day, 11 a.m.–4 p.m.

Dinner: Every day, 4–10 p.m.

Setting & atmosphere: Climb the stairs to this restaurant situated across from Po'ipu Beach Park in a freestanding blue building. Then sit by an open window so you can see surfers, palms, blue ocean, and golden sands just beyond the petunia-filled window boxes.

House specialties: After a trip to the salad bar, specialties called *makai* (from the ocean) and *mauka* (from the land) arrive sizzling from the kiawe charcoal broiler. Fresh Island fish, Hawaiian spiny lobster, or Brennecke's signature scampi with choice of barbecue, teriyaki, or garlic sauce will satisfy most diners.

Other recommendations: Sea breezes through the open windows and a varied menu of Kauai *pupus,* including fresh sashimi caught by local fishermen, New York steak and mushrooms, and nachos with peppers, make this a great spot for a glass of wine or one of Brennecke's world-famous Mai Tais.

Entertainment & amenities: The restaurant sound system usually carries 1960s tunes.

Summary & comments: Brennecke's is handy if you've had enough sun and sand but still want a peaceful beach-side ambience while you eat a big burger for lunch. The open-air view makes this place an old favorite. For quick and casual snacks, Brennecke's Deli downstairs serves cool shave ice and sandwiches with your choice of fillings.

CAFÉ HANALEI AND TERRACE		★★★★
Continental (with Island ingredients)	Expensive	QUALITY 91
Princeville Hotel, Princeville; (808) 826-2760 Zone 13 Kauai		VALUE C

Reservations: Recommended
When to go: Anytime, though sunsets are best
Entrée range: $26.95–31.95, $21.95 (vegetarian dish); 3-course dinner $43.95
Payment: VISA, MC, AMEX, D, DC, JCB

Service rating: ★★★★★
Parking: Valet or hotel lot
Bar: Full service
Wine selection: Good
Dress: Resort wear
Disabled access: Good, via elevator
Customers: Resort and hotel guests, Islanders for special events

Breakfast: Every day, 6:30–11 a.m. includes buffet

Lunch: Every day, 11 a.m.–2:30 p.m.

Dinner: Every day, 5:30–9:30 p.m.

Setting & atmosphere: Cafe Hanalei and Terrace enjoys the most stunning view of any restaurant on Kauai; it overlooks Hanalei Bay and Makana Peak (the jutting spire of land that gained fame as Bali Hai in the movie *South Pacific*). A placid reflecting pool is on one side of the covered terrace seating, and when rain sprinkles over the bay, it becomes an artist's extravagant scene; sometimes a vivid rainbow arches across the misty sun-streaked sky. Inside, you have a feeling of soaring space, as the restaurant is surrounded by towering windows and the ceiling is two floors above the lobby level.

House specialties: The restaurant's Sunday brunch buffet is both a gourmand's and a glutton's dream come true, with made-to-order omelets, seafood, salads, and a dessert spread that requires at least two trips. Breakfast buffets the rest of the week are well stocked with Island fruit. At dinner the most popular entrée is steamed Hawaiian snapper, a sweet, white fish prepared with fresh ginger, cilantro, and shiitake mushrooms. Such a low-calorie meal calls for a decadent dessert—chocolate macadamia nut pie or Kona coffee crème brûlée.

Other recommendations: Sushi addicts are lucky if they come by on Saturday, Sunday, Tuesday, or Wednesday: On those nights, sushi chefs handcraft these little balls of rice and seafood to order in the restaurant.

Entertainment & amenities: The lilting music of a pianist and a vocalist filters down from an upstairs lobby bar to diners who eat inside.

Summary & comments: The view is what people remember, but the food and service also make dining a pleasure.

CASA DI AMICI		★★½

Italian/Contemporary	Moderate	QUALITY
		80
		VALUE
		C

2301 Nalo Road, Po'ipu; (808) 742-1555
Zone 13   Kauai

Reservations: Requested	Parking: In adjacent lot
When to go: Thursday–Saturday if you like piano music	Bar: Full service
	Wine selection: Excellent
Entrée range: $13–27	Dress: Casual
Payment: VISA, AMEX	Disabled access: Good
Service rating: ★★★★	Customers: Islanders and tourists

Lunch: Tuesday–Friday, 11:30 a.m.–2:30 p.m.

Dinner: Every day, 6–9 p.m.

Setting & atmosphere: Windows open to the balmy air around this comfortable Po'ipu restaurant. Casa di Amici means "house of friends," and with rattan furnishings under ceiling fans inside and sweeping views to the ocean on the deck outside, it feels like the kama'aina home the building once was. If you must wait for a table, a small open-air bar is near the entry, where a big fish tank is filled with colorful reef fish for your diversion.

House specialties: The Italian menu is translated into English, so you can figure out what you're getting when you mix and match your favorite pasta with perhaps a salsa arrabiatta—spicy tomato with sautéed pancetta and chilis. The most popular item on the menu is a porcini-crusted chicken breast in a sun-dried cherry, port wine, and mushroom sauce.

If you like bold flavors, try Japanese mahogany-glazed salmon served on frijole chorittos and black beans, or salmon steak painted with heavy soy sauce, sprinkled with furukake, baked and garnished with jalapeño-tequila aïole, and served on a corn husk.

Other recommendations: Picatta (as in veal picatta) and marsala sauces are particularly flavorful and rich. The chef loves Mexican/southwestern food, so he's proud of his chili verde risotto. He has fun with risotto, creating classic four-cheese risotto, Indian curried lamb, kalua (usually pork), and other variations. Besides the bananas Foster, a dessert with a tropical appeal is Sugarloaf—upside-down cake topped with liliko'i cream.

Summary & comments: Some entrées are available in light portions, but once you taste the house scampi with a good red wine, you may want more. Because of the variety of ethnic flavors in his preparations, the French-trained chef/owner describes his restaurant as "the most un-Italian Italian restaurant you'll ever be in." It has been given high marks by *Zagat*, the *Los Angeles Times*, *Gourmet*, the *Chicago Tribune*, and other food writers.

DUKE'S CANOE CLUB ★★★

		QUALITY
Seafood	Inexpensive/Moderate	81
		VALUE
Kauai Marriott Hotel, Kalapaki Beach, Lihu'e; (808) 246-9599		B
Zone 13 Kauai		

Reservations: Recommended	Service rating: ★★★½
When to go: Anytime; for cocktails at the Barefoot Bar, show up from 4–6 p.m. for reasonable prices and live entertainment	Parking: In adjacent lot
	Bar: Full service
	Wine selection: Adequate
	Dress: Casual
Entrée range: $10.99–24.99, market price for lobster	Disabled access: Adequate
	Customers: Tourists and Islanders
Payment: VISA, MC, AMEX, D	

Lunch: Every day, 11:30 a.m.–11:30 p.m. downstairs

Dinner: Every day, 5–10 p.m.

Setting & atmosphere: At this Polynesian-style restaurant with open-air views onto Kalapaki Beach, diners can sit downstairs at the Barefoot Bar for lunch, snacks, afternoon cocktails, and people-watching, or amble upstairs for dinner. A tinkling stream and waterfall, edged by lush plantings, creates an outdoor garden effect even in the building's cool, shady interior.

House specialties: Fresh fish is the name of the game after a trip to Duke's "all-you-care-to-eat" salad bar. Entrées come with salad, herbed rice, muffins, and sourdough bread. Best of the five preparations for fish is "Duke's Style," baked in garlic, lemon, and sweet basil glaze, although if you want to spice things up a bit, you might go for the "Firecracker Fresh Fish" preparation with tomato-chili-cumin aïoli, served with black bean, Maui onion, and avocado relish.

Other recommendations: Macadamia nut and crab wontons are such delicious little deep-fried pockets of Dungeness crab, cream cheese, and macadamia nuts served with a mustard plum sauce, you might be tempted to limit dinner to these appetizers and a trip to the salad bar.

Entertainment & amenities: A strolling trio of guitar and ukulele players presents Hawaiian-style dinner music in the restaurant upstairs. Downstairs, a band plays nightly from 8:30 to 10:30 p.m., and on Thursday and "Tropical Friday" afternoons, a band entertains, and tropical drinks are a special happy hour price.

Summary & comments: This is an easy, casual place to grab a hamburger as you come off Kalapaki Beach for lunch or enjoy a Mai Tai at sunset, and then climb the stairs for a pleasant dinner. Unfortunately, service isn't always as attentive as it should be. *Keiki* (children's) dinner items, which also include the salad bar, make this a reasonably "nice" place to take kids, a welcome change from fast-food dinners.

HAMURA SAIMIN ★

Island Eclectic	Inexpensive	QUALITY 75
		VALUE A

2956 Kress Street, Lihu'e; (808) 245-3271
Zone 13   Kauai

Reservations: Not accepted
When to go: This little café is always busy, especially on rainy days, but right after opening there might be a lull.
Entrée range: $3–6
Payment: Cash or traveler's checks
Service rating: ★★
Parking: Limited in lot and on-street

Bar: None, diners can bring libations
Wine selection: None
Dress: Casual
Disabled access: Accessible, but there is no ramp over an entry step
Customers: Islanders and adventuresome tourists

Lunch & dinner: Monday–Thursday, 10 a.m.–11 p.m.; Friday and Saturday, 10 a.m.–1 a.m.; Sunday, 10 a.m.–9 p.m.

Setting & atmosphere: This is down-home Hawaii on a dusty side street in Lihu'e. The restaurant is in a single-board, plantation-style building, with louvered windows that let in a breath of air that is never enough on a muggy summer day. Counter space fills the center of the restaurant, there are a few tables, and you'll note good-luck porcelain cat statues and other Island touches.

House specialties: Everybody ends up at Hamura's at one time or another for a big steaming bowl of saimin that's especially good on a wet, windy, Kauai winter day. The saimin special bowl has a little bit of everything: noodles garnished with vegetables, wonton, fish cake, chopped boiled egg, sliced pork, green onion, and sliced luncheon meat.

Other recommendations: Soup is the ticket at Hamura's, but carnivores will love the grilled chicken skewers and beef sticks. Manapua, big bread-like buns with a savory filling, are also favored, while liliko'i chiffon pie is a don't-miss dessert.

Summary & comments: Hamura Saimin has been a Lihu'e standby for so long it's an institution. Go for a steaming bowl of soup, but don't expect to be blown away by fancy food or service; just enjoy the fun of having a unique local experience.

KEOKI'S PARADISE		★★★½
Seafood and Steak	Moderate	QUALITY
		85
Po'ipu Shopping Village, Po'ipu; (808) 742-7535		VALUE
Zone 13 Kauai		B

Reservations: Recommended	Parking: In adjacent lot
When to go: Anytime	Bar: Full service
Entrée range: $8.95–23.95, or	Wine selection: Good
market price	Dress: Casual
Payment: VISA, MC, AMEX	Disabled access: Good
Service rating: ★★★	Customers: Tourists and Islanders

Lunch: Every day, 11 a.m.–11:30 p.m.

Dinner: Every day, 5:30–10 p.m.

Setting & atmosphere: From outside in the generally crowded parking lot of this centrally located resort shopping center, you wouldn't expect to find a pleasant, cool boathouse-style restaurant set on a peaceful lagoon with tropical foliage and a thatched-roof bar. It takes you back to the Hawaii depicted on movie screens in the 1950s.

House specialties: Fresh seafood, from starters of sashimi or chowder to a fresh-catch entrée served in your choice of five preparations and sauces, is most popular. Types of fish served depend on what is delivered that day and could range from 'ahi (tuna) to ulua (pompano) to opah (Hawaiian moonfish). For dessert, the hula pie with an Oreo cookie crust filled with ice cream is made for sharing.

Other recommendations: For a taste of local flavor, order Koloa pork ribs glazed with plum sauce or Balinese chicken marinated in lemongrass and served with a lemon shoyu sauce, or try both in a combination plate. A variety of steaks are served with garlic mashed potatoes.

Summary & comments: You can get just about any down-to-earth food you're in the mood for. You feel as if you are getting your money's worth, as healthy-sized entrées all include Keoki's Caesar-style salad, fresh-baked bread, and herbed rice, all served in a pleasant Polynesian setting.

MEMA THAI CHINESE CUISINE ★★

Thai/Chinese	Inexpensive/Moderate	QUALITY
		80

		VALUE
4-361 Kuhio Highway, Wailua Shopping Center, Kapa'a		A

(808) 823-0899
Zone 13   Kauai

Reservations: Accepted	Parking: In adjacent lot
When to go: Anytime	Bar: Full bar
Entrée range: $7.95–16.95	Wine selection: Limited
Payment: VISA, MC, AMEX, D, DC	Dress: Casual
	Disabled access: Good
Service rating: ★★★	Customers: Islanders and tourists

Lunch: Monday–Friday, 11 a.m.–2 p.m.

Dinner: Every day, 5–9:30 p.m.

Setting & atmosphere: Set in a tiresome little strip mall, Mema Thai Chinese is surprisingly attractive, with pretty pink linen tablecloths and lovely Oriental rosewood chairs. Orchid sprays add to the gracious atmosphere.

House specialties: Curries come in colors of the rainbow—red, green, and yellow—made with your choice of vegetables, chicken, pork or beef, shrimp, or fish, and other seafood. A local dish named evil jungle prince, a savory blending of coconut milk, basil, and red chili, can also be ordered with seafood (including calamari), poultry, or meat.

Other recommendations: There's plenty to satisfy vegetarians here; many dishes can be ordered with tofu instead of meat, such as rice noodles with cabbage, mushrooms, and carrots, or stir-fried broccoli with oyster sauce.

Summary & comments: *Thai Scene* magazine once named Mema "one of the ten best Thai restaurants outside Thailand." You may want to sit toward the back of the semi-divided room, away from the bar and the entrance to the kitchen, for the most peaceful dining experience.

A PACIFIC CAFÉ		★★★★½

		QUALITY
Pacific Rim	Moderate	94
		VALUE
4-831 Kuhio Highway, Suite 220, Kauai Village Shopping Center,		C
Kapa'a; (808) 822-0013		
Zone 13 Kauai		

Reservations: Highly recommended
When to go: Anytime, but it's less
  crowded 5:30–6:30 p.m.
Entrée range: $22–26
Payment: VISA, MC, AMEX, D,
  DC
Service rating: ★★★★★

Parking: Shopping center lot
Bar: Full service
Wine selection: Extensive, several by
  the glass
Dress: Casual
Disabled access: Good
Customers: Islanders and tourists

Dinner: Every day, 5:30–9 p.m.

Setting & atmosphere: The pretty-in-pastel restaurant has light-colored wooden tables, a few colorful tropical floral arrangements, and paintings from nearby Wyland Art Galleries decorating the walls.

House specialties: The wok-charred mahi-mahi served with julienned vegetables and lime-ginger sauce is an award winner that never fails to please. Another popular standby on what is otherwise a most inventive menu is the certified Black Angus New York steak.

Two desserts have a loyal following: Crème brûlée is pure ambrosia enveloped in a crispy pastry crust. Or you can order a hot Vintage Chocolate tart made of Big Island–grown chocolate. Prepared individually, the chocolate tart takes 15 minutes, so order while you're still eating, or be prepared to relax over coffee while you wait.

Other recommendations: Almost too pretty to eat, the tiger eye sushi is sliced into thin, melt-in-the mouth slices that resemble tiger eyes, because the 'ahi (tuna) that it's made of encases green asparagus and tobiko roe. The 'ahi is dipped in tempura, then flash-fried on the outside, so the inside slices remain sushi rare.

Summary & comments: For years this classy Kapa'a community restaurant has been *the* place to go for beautifully presented dishes with complex flavors made with homegrown ingredients. Chef/owner Jean Marie Josselin works with an Island farmer who grows herbs, lettuces, fruit, and vegetables to meet the restaurant's specific requirements.

PIATTI		★★★½

Italian	Moderate	QUALITY
		85

		VALUE
2253 Po'ipu Road, Kiahuna Plantation; (808) 742-2216		C
Zone 13 Kauai		

Reservations: Recommended
When to go: Anytime after 5:30 p.m. for dinner; for cocktails and pizza, drop by between 4 and 5:30 p.m.
Entrée range: $13.95–27.95
Payment: VISA, MC, AMEX, DC

Service rating: ★★★★
Parking: In adjacent lots
Bar: Full service
Wine selection: Excellent
Dress: Kauai casual
Disabled access: Good
Customers: Tourists and Islanders

Dinner: Every day, 5:30–10 p.m.

Setting & atmosphere: Gardens with torchlit paths, rock work, a rich wood interior, and veranda dining offer a lovely setting for Italian food served in a historic Polynesian home, which once belonged to an early sugar baron.

House specialties: Many items on the menu change monthly, but Piatti is known for its fresh fish and house-made pastas. The signature pasta dish, pappardelle fantasia, is a wide saffron pasta sautéed in white wine, herbs, and spices and tossed with fresh garden vegetables and shrimp. Fish of the day varies depending on what the fishermen bring to the door. If you hang out around the display kitchen, you can watch your pizza with portobello mushrooms, pancetta, and fontina cheese emerge sizzling from the wood-burning oven. A kiawe broiler gives steaks and fish that special smoky flavor.

Other recommendations: Currently on the menu, manzo brasato is slow-roasted pot roast served with mascarpone mashed potatoes (whipped with sweet Italian cream cheese), served with gravy and fresh veggies of day, which might be bok choy and Koloa asparagus when in season.

The restaurant is famous for a classic tiramisu, but the banana liliko'i cream cheesecake with cream cheese frosting is equally decadent.

Entertainment & amenities: If you're lucky, you may hit a weekend summer night when a rising Kauai group might drop by to play.

Summary & comments: Fresh herbs are plucked from the garden out back, and Island fish might have been picked or caught only hours before reaching your table.

POSTCARDS		★★★½
		QUALITY
Contemporary	Moderate	85
		VALUE
5-5075 A Kuhio Highway, Hanalei; (808) 826-1191		B
Zone 13 Kauai		

Reservations: Highly recommended
When to go: Anytime for dinner
Entrée range: $14–22, fish are market price
Payment: VISA, MC, AMEX
Service rating: ★★

Parking: In adjacent lot
Bar: None
Wine selection: Bring your own
Dress: Casual
Disabled access: Adequate
Customers: Islanders and tourists

Brunch: Sunday, 8 a.m.–noon

Breakfast: Every day, 8–11 a.m.

Dinner: Every day, 5:30–9:30 p.m.

Setting & atmosphere: Set in a small restored single-board plantation-style house with a front porch, the restaurant has the charm of an earlier era.

House specialties: Gourmet vegetarian cuisine and savory seafood dishes draw repeat visitors. Start with an organic salad, or Thai summer rolls with spicy peanut sauce, then plunge into fresh fish or shrimp tacos or sample the taj triangles, crusty phyllo pastry filled with potatoes, peas, carrots, and Indian spices served with tropical chutney. Youngsters love the fresh fruit smoothies and cheese quesadillas.

Other recommendations: If you're tired of hotel food, this is possibly Hanalei's next best bet for breakfast. Sunrise Scramble features sautéed tofu with onions, garlic, and herbs mixed into the eggs. Other highlights include a full espresso bar, Irish red-roasted potatoes, homemade muffins, fresh orange juice, and Hanalei hotcakes.

Summary & comments: Guests sign the guest book with notes like "We ate here three nights in a row" and "The best seafood in the Islands."

ROY'S PO'IPU BAR & GRILL ★★★★

		QUALITY
Euro-Asian	Moderate	**91**

	VALUE
Po'ipu Shopping Village, 2360 Kiahuna Plantation Drive, Po'ipu Beach	**C**
(808) 742-5000	

Zone 13 Kauai

Reservations: Highly recommended
When to go: Early for a quieter dinner, later for a livelier crowd
Entrée range: $17–32
Payment: VISA, MC, AMEX, DC, D
Service rating: ★★★★

Parking: In shopping center lot
Bar: Full bar
Wine selection: Excellent, many wines by the glass
Dress: Casual
Disabled access: Good
Customers: Tourists and Islanders

Dinner: Every day, 5:30–9:30 p.m.

Setting & atmosphere: Chef/owner Roy Yamaguchi's sleek shopping center restaurant is a mecca for fans of what he dubs Euro-Asian Pacific cuisine—Asian seasonings mixed with French techniques. The restaurant has a very airy feeling, with windows that let in the night air. The exhibition kitchen is enclosed by glass, so the noise level is kept down. A newer expansion and lounge area across a public walkway brings shoppers seemingly through the middle of the restaurant.

House specialties: Hibachi-style salmon and oven-roasted pot roast have emerged from a long list of specials as steady favorites. Seafood lovers might choose fresh seared 'opakapaka (snapper) with orange shrimp butter and Chinese black bean sauce. Dark chocolate soufflé and volcanic puffed pastry filled with caramelized apple are dessert winners.

Other recommendations: It's fun to go for dim sum and appetizers followed by a pizza from the wood-fired oven, so you have a chance to sample a number the culinary creations available. Or, couples might share appetizers like lemongrass shrimp sticks with Thai chili cocktail sauce, or pot-stickers with spicy peanut satay sauce, or escargot cassoulet with caramelized onions and creamy polenta.

Summary & comments: Diners return again and again to this most popular restaurant in Po'ipu, so Roy's chefs make sure they will never get bored with the menu by offering 25 or more specials nightly.

SHELLS, AT THE SHERATON KAUAI HOTEL ★★★½

American	Moderate/Expensive	QUALITY
		80

		VALUE
Sheraton Kauai Hotel, 2440 Ho'onani Road, Po'ipu Beach		C

(808) 742-1661

Zone 13   Kauai

Reservations: Recommended
When to go: 6 – 7 p.m. for sunset
  ocean view
Entrée range: $15.50–36
Payment: VISA, MC, AMEX, DC,
  D, JCB
Service rating: ★★★★

Parking: Valet or hotel lot
Bar: Full service
Wine selection: Good
Dress: Resort wear
Disabled access: Good
Customers: Tourists

Breakfast: Every day, 6:30–11 a.m.

Dinner: Every day, 5:30–9:30 p.m.

Setting & atmosphere: Floor-to-ceiling windows let the trade winds and the sound of the waves drift off the ocean to diners on the lanai and inside this high-ceilinged restaurant. The airy, tropical room has rattan furnishings set under elaborate shell chandeliers that remained intact through Hurricane 'Iniki, which destroyed the hotel in 1992.

House specialties: Baby rack of lamb prepared with herb and hoisin sauce is 'ono (delicious), though non–meat lovers might prefer the fresh fish and prawns served with spicy pineapple, baked sweet potato, Kauai slaw, and steamed rice, for a touch of Island flavor.

Other recommendations: Appetizer crab cakes are a perennial favorite, but the restaurant is really known for a dessert called Mount Wai'ale'ale, a mountain of chocolate mousse cake piled with sorbet and fresh Island fruit.

Summary & comments: This big, pretty hotel dining room is located adjacent to The Point, a great spot for predinner cocktails indoors or out-, where the ocean view is even more encompassing.

TIDEPOOLS ★★★

Contemporary	Moderate/Expensive	QUALITY
		78

1571 Po'ipu Road, Hyatt Regency Kauai, Po'ipu Beach
(808) 742-6260
Zone 13   Kauai

	VALUE
	C–

Reservations: Highly recommended
When to go: Anytime
Entrée range: $22–34
Payment: VISA, MC, AMEX
Service rating: ★★★★
Parking: Valet or hotel lot
Bar: Full service
Wine selection: Adequate

Dress: Resort attire
Disabled access: Make prearrangements; it's quite a distance from the parking lot via an elevator and a service tunnel
Customers: Tourists, hotel guests, a few Islanders for special events

Dinner: Every day, 6–10 p.m.

Setting & atmosphere: Romantic tropical atmosphere makes this restaurant special for honeymooners and longtime lovers. Torchlit paths lead to the restaurant, which floats on a fish-filled lagoon; some thatched dining huts hold single candlelit tables for total privacy under Kauai's starry skies.

House specialties: Tidepools serves interesting grilled entrées seasoned with Hawaiian 'alaea sea salt, such as chicken breast filled with Puna goat cheese and a lemongrass butter sauce, or pork chops topped with Asian pear marmalade, but fish and seafood are truly most appropriate for this watery restaurant. Macadamia-nut-crusted Island fish with Kahlua, lime-ginger butter sauce, and jasmine fried rice is the signature dish. A selection from ten kinds of Island fish is offered nightly, and the server can describe each fish in detail. You can order four different preparations: sautéed with liliko'i butter, grilled with papaya and mango relish, steamed with sweet chili and lime sauce, or blackened with Hana Bay rum pineapple sauce.

Other recommendations: Combination plates are the most expensive, but by ordering from a menu of ten combination items you can sample meat *and* seafood. Don't miss banana chocolate silk, a heavenly combination of bittersweet chocolate silk with bananas and cream, crème anglaise, and caramelized macadamia nuts.

Summary & comments: You don't need to be afraid to take the kids to eat at Tidepools, as the restaurant actually offers a children's menu, with most items from $5 to $11—pasta, hamburger, chicken nuggets—and they will be enchanted by the lagoons all around.

MOLOKAI

HOTEL MOLOKAI RESTAURANT		★★

Island Eclectic	Inexpensive	QUALITY 70
		VALUE A

Box 1020 Kamehameha Highway; (808) 553-5347
Zone 14   Molokai

Reservations: Accepted	Bar: Full service
When to go: Anytime	Wine selection: Adequate
Entrée range: $10–19	Dress: Casual
Payment: VISA, MC	Disabled access: Good
Service rating: ★★★	Customers: Tourists and Islanders
Parking: Free in hotel lot	are split about 50-50

Lunch: Every day, 11 a.m.–2 p.m.

Dinner: Every day, 5–9 p.m.

Setting & atmosphere: Being right on the beach in this open-air restaurant enhances the feeling of old Polynesia imparted by decorative tiki carved pillars and outrigger canoes pulled up on the nearby shore. You can sit under the roof at candlelit tables, or at plastic tables arranged on the adjacent pool deck.

House specialties: Cockeyed Molokai coconut shrimp, dipped in batter, rolled in coconut, and deep-fried may not be good *for* you, but it's good. Soups and specialties change daily, so one night the theme might be Oriental, with Chinese food, another it might be country-and-western, featuring barbecued back ribs and chicken, while Friday and Saturday, prime rib is the featured dinner.

Other recommendations: This is truly a menu with something for everyone. There's Chinese chicken salad or taco salad, and mahi-mahi comes with your choice of caper sauce, papaya-pineapple relish, or pepper sauce. If you've been hanging loose at the bar, down a big bowl of mana'uele (taro) boy chili or Molokai stew before heading out into the night.

Entertainment & amenities: Island-style musicians make this one of the few places to hang out after dark on Molokai on Friday and Saturday nights.

Summary & comments: For a hotel restaurant, prices are surprisingly reasonable, and the management's goal is to keep them low in hopes of building a clientele of loyal Molokai residents.

MOANALOA ROOM ★★★★

Molokai Regional	Moderate/Expensive	QUALITY
		87

The Lodge at Molokai Ranch, #8, Moanaloa; (808) 660-2725

	VALUE
	C

Zone 14 Molokai

Reservations: Recommended	Bar: Full service
When to go: Anytime	Wine selection: Good
Entrée range: $19–39	Dress: Resort wear
Payment: AMEX, MC, VISA	Disabled access: Excellent
Service rating: ★★★★	Customers: Tourists, Islanders for a
Parking: Free in hotel lot	very special occasion

Breakfast: Monday–Saturday, 6:30–10 a.m.

Brunch: Sunday, 11 a.m.–1 p.m.

Lunch: Sunday–Monday, 11 a.m.–1:30 p.m.

Dinner: Sunday–Monday, 6–9 p.m.

Setting & atmosphere: Inside the decor follows a ranch theme with wooden tables, chairs with pineapple print seats, and chandeliers with electric candles in a wagon wheel shape. Views from an open-air deck stretch three miles to the ocean. Deck chairs are metal with woven lau hala seats and backs that sport the Molokai Ranch logo, the profile of a cow.

House specialties: Chef Paul Heerlein describes his menu as Molokai Regional because he buys as many ingredients locally as possible and blends flavors originating with the various ethnic groups that populate Molokai. He also mixes his own spices and grows many of his herbs just outside the Lodge. This is one of the few menus that feature Molokai opihi (a crunchy limpet that is an island delicacy) as an appetizer or pan-seared venison as an entrée. Corn and crab bisque, followed by macadamia nut–crusted catch of the day on spinach surrounded by lobster-coconut curry sauce and garnished with pineapple-ginger relish are two of the menu's stars.

Other recommendations: Big, tender, crispy coconut shrimp come with an orange-ginger sauce for a tasty appetizer. A truly island-style entrée is panko-crusted 'ahi (tuna) wrapped around a fern shoot, packaged in nori (seaweed), and seared crisp on the outside and rare on the inside. Cut into slices, it's served with rice and a fern shoot salad. A carving station at Sunday brunch might feature prime rib, lamb, or other succulent meats. Brunch will run you $22.95, or $27.95 with champagne.

Summary & comments: Bar none, the Moanaloa Room serves the finest haute cuisine on the island. It's also the priciest restaurant on Molokai, but dining here is a splurge you should enjoy at least once during an island visit. After dinner, it's a pleasure to relax in the Great Room with its enormous stone fireplace and listen to acoustic Hawaiian music strummed and sung by a ranch *paniolo* (cowboy). Often, a hula dancer joins him—either a pretty Molokai wahine (lady) or, when the bar next door is slow, the bartender might render a dance or two.

MOLOKAI PIZZA CAFÉ		★★
Pizza and Sandwiches	Inexpensive	QUALITY 75
15 Kaunakakai Place, on Wharf Road; (808) 553-3288 Zone 14 Molokai		VALUE B

Reservations: Not accepted	Bar: None
When to go: Anytime	Wine selection: None
Entrée range: $4.50–12.99	Dress: Casual
Payment: Cash only	Disabled access: Good
Service rating: ★★	Customers: Locals and tourists
Parking: Adjacent lot	

Breakfast: Every day, 8–11 a.m.

Lunch & dinner: Monday–Thursday, Sunday, 11 a.m.–10 p.m.; Friday and Saturday, 11 a.m.–11 p.m.

Setting & atmosphere: This is a clean, air-conditioned cafe with booths and tables in a spacious room. It's a Molokai family kind of place, often decorated with artwork and thank-you cards by schoolkids. Some of the Formica-topped tables are set in a smaller, quieter area at the front of the restaurant away from kids, and there is also outside lanai dining, where guests are welcome to bring their own wine or beer to enjoy with dinner.

House specialties: Fresh fish is served at market price whenever available. Wednesday nights a Mexican menu featuring burritos, fajitas, tacos, and nachos is added for variety, and Sunday nights prime rib is the big draw.

Other recommendations: You can order pizza by the piece, or a Molokini pizza for a single person, or get a big one to go or to eat in. Chicken dinners come with rice or french fries and hot veggies. Sandwiches, pasta, salads, and frozen yogurt are also on the menu.

Entertainment & amenities: Strolling musicians are hired for big private parties and sometimes for special holidays.

Summary & comments: Eventually everyone stops by the Pizza Café. Kids hang out here after school, and tourists stop by for a slice of pizza, as it's one of the few places that serves until 10 p.m. nightly.

'OHIA LODGE AT THE KALUAKO'I HOTEL		★★

		QUALITY
American	Moderate	**80**
		VALUE
Kaluako'i Hotel and Golf Club, Kepuhi Beach; (808) 552-2555		**C**
Zone 14 Molokai		

Reservations: Highly recommended
When to go: Friday and Saturday
  evenings to hear live music
Entrée range: $15–24.95
Payment: VISA, MC, AMEX, D,
  DC, JCB
Service rating: ★★★

Parking: Hotel lot
Bar: Full service
Wine selection: Limited to about 30
  wines
Dress: Casual
Disabled access: Good
Customers: Tourists and Islanders

Breakfast: Every day, 6:30–10:30 a.m.

Dinner: Every day, 6–9 p.m.

Setting & atmosphere: High pink ceilings lighten stained wooden walls, as do pretty ocean vistas through windows along one wall. Ask for a table on the lower level, close to the picture windows.

House specialties: An Islander favorite is the Molokai baby-back ribs. The menu is American with Island overtones—kalua pork, pot-stickers, tempura, and Portuguese white bean soup with Molokai bread. Fresh fish of the day is either sautéed with soy sauce and butter or broiled with lemon and tartar sauce.

Other recommendations: Pastas are among the most reasonable items on the menu. Grilled chicken pasta, chicken marinara, seafood linguini, and angel hair pesto are among the choices. If you just go for the weekend music, *pupu* platters with tempura prawns, pot-stickers, and the like go well with libations in the lounge.

Entertainment & amenities: Live contemporary Hawaiian music in the lounge on Friday and Saturday evenings.

Summary & comments: Food preparation here can be inconsistent, but the view, friendly waitresses, and the scarcity of places to eat on Molokai make 'Ohia Lodge worth a visit. For special events and holidays the hotel features occasional buffets with prime rib or seafood.

THE VILLAGE GRILL   ★★

Island Eclectic	Moderate	QUALITY
		80

		VALUE
Maunaloa Highway, Maunaloa Town; (808) 552-0012		C
Zone 14 Molokai		

Reservations: Recommended
When to go: Anytime; 5–6 p.m. for
   the early-bird special; it gets
   busier later
Entrée range: $17–24.50
Payment: VISA, MC, AMEX, DC
Service rating: ★★★
Parking: Adjacent lot

Bar: Full service
Wine selection: Adequate, with sev-
   eral wines in a reasonable price
   range
Dress: Casual
Disabled access: Good
Customers: More tourists than
   Islanders, but a good mix

Lunch: Monday–Friday, 11:30 a.m.–2:30 p.m.

Dinner: Every day, 5–9 p.m.

Setting & atmosphere: Remodeled in 1998 by Molokai Ranch, the former
Jojo's Cafe still sports a historic bar that once graced Oahu's Pearl City Tavern, but it now has a bronze countertop with a lariat design. The restaurant
has a Western feeling, with light fixtures sporting Western-designed shades,
and saddles and cowboy pictures on the wall, but most people prefer to sit
outside on the screened deck to enjoy the stars above this quiet little town.

House specialties: Good, filling entrées, like prime rib, New York steak,
and pizza are flavored with locally grown herbs. There's always a fresh catch
of the day that can be ordered sautéed, broiled, or Cajun-style, plus lobster
and king crab. Try a "sky high pie" for dessert, a mound of vanilla,
macadamia, and coffee-flavored ice cream in a graham cracker crust with
custard, strawberry, and chocolate sauces.

Other recommendations: Wok-seared Asian stir-fry, with veggies,
shrimp, and scallops, and baby-back ribs impart a Molokai flavor. A local
favorite for dessert is liliko'i-coconut cream pie, a coconut–passion fruit
cream pie on a macadamia cookie crust made with a layer of haupia
(coconut pudding), glazed with passion fruit, and topped with whipped
cream and toasted coconut flakes.

Summary & comments: Much of the fun here comes from cooking your
own entrée on a stone grill brought to your table. Dinner in this small-
town restaurant makes you feel as if you're rubbing elbows with the local
folks, even though tourists are likely to be sitting at the next table.

LANAI

BLUE GINGER CAFÉ		★

Island Eclectic	Inexpensive	QUALITY
		70

409 7th Avenue, Lanai City; (808) 565-6363	VALUE
Zone 15 Lanai	**A**

Reservations: Accepted, but
  requested only for large parties
When to go: Anytime
Entrée range: $5.50–13.95
Payment: VISA, MC
Service rating: ★★★
Parking: Street

Bar: Full service
Wine selection: Limited
Dress: Casual
Disabled access: Good
Customers: Islanders, *kama'aina*
  travelers

Breakfast: Every day, 6–11 a.m.

Lunch & dinner: Every day, 11 a.m.–9 p.m.

Setting & atmosphere: Set in a little single-board plantation building in Lanai City's main square. Diners order and pick up food at the counter and eat at tables draped with plastic cloths in this old, somewhat grubby-looking restaurant. An inexpensive alternative to Lanai's costly hotel dining rooms.

House specialties: Try the tasty vegetarian breakfast omelet that comes with rice, or order fresh-baked apple turnovers or cinnamon rolls to carry back to your hotel, as this is Lanai's only bakery outside the hotel bake shops. For lunch, the bacon-cheddar cheeseburgers are better than Big Macs, but you might want to try the local soup called saimin, a generous steaming bowl of noodle soup garnished with sliced fish cake, green onions, and shredded egg. At dinner, sautéed mahi-mahi with capers, onions, and mushrooms is the signature dish. Top it off with an ice cream dessert. Blue Ginger serves Dave's ice cream, made in the Islands with local ingredients.

Other recommendations: Banana or blueberry pancakes accompanied by cappuccino for breakfast. For dinner, if an Island-style plate with a choice of teriyaki beef, katsu chicken, hamburger steak with gravy, plus rice and macaroni salad, sounds like too much cholesterol for one meal, there's also New York steak with a baked potato or shrimp scampi.

Summary & comments: This has been a Lanai hangout owned by the same family for years. Blue Ginger and the little deli called Pele's Other

Garden, located across the park, are the best independent restaurants around the square in central Lanai City.

THE FORMAL DINING ROOM, THE LODGE AT KO'ELE   ★★★★½

Contemporary	Expensive	QUALITY
		94

		VALUE
Lodge at Ko'ele, Keomuku Drive, Lanai City; (808) 565-7300		C–
Zone 15 Lanai		

Reservations: Highly recommended
When to go: Anytime, but sunset is generally more peaceful; the restaurant can get crowded by 7 p.m.
Entrée range: $34–42
Payment: VISA, MC, AMEX, DC, JCB
Service rating: ★★★★★

Parking: Valet, hotel lot
Bar: Full service
Wine selection: Excellent
Dress: Jacket required
Disabled access: Adequate
Customers: Hotel guests, other tourists, and visiting Neighbor Islanders

Dinner: Every day, 6–9:15 p.m.

Setting & atmosphere: Relaxed elegance sums up the ambience of this refined restaurant overlooking the fountain, a man-made lake, and the croquet lawn of Ko'ele Lodge. With fine silver and sparkling crystal, twinkling lights in the chandelier, and a fire in the dining room's own fireplace, this is a peaceful place for a romantic dinner.

House specialties: The chef makes flavorful soups with Lanai-grown fresh herbs and produce and creates food that fits the cool lodge atmosphere: grilled quail with a fava bean, sweet pea risotto, smoked ham, and quail juice, or roasted Lanai venison loin rolled in cracked black pepper with layered sweet potatoes and pineapple cider sauce.

Other recommendations: Grilled tenderloin of beef with buttered lobster tail and succotash vegetable sauce; a lighter option is seared Hawaiian 'ahi (tuna) with foie gras, summer vegetable hash, and Cabernet butter.

Entertainment & amenities: Dinner music, often traditional Hawaiian melodies, piano, or classical musical scores, drifts in from the adjoining lobby. You can extend what is sure to be an expensive evening by relaxing in the Lodge's lobby after dinner with a snifter of brandy in front of a crackling fire in either of two massive fireplaces.

Summary & comments: This could be the perfect place to pop the question, as lovers enjoy an intimate feeling of isolation in this quiet dining room. Tables are far enough apart to whisper sweet nothings, and the food is delicious. No wonder The Formal Dining Room keeps winning awards.

HENRY CLAY'S ROTISSERIE ★★★

American Country	Moderate	QUALITY
		80

	VALUE
828 Lanai Avenue, Lanai City; (808) 565-7211	B

Zone 15   Lanai

Reservations: Highly recommended
When to go: Anytime
Entrée range: $12–28
Payment: VISA, MC; guests of all 3 island hotels have signing privileges to their rooms
Service rating: ★★★
Parking: Hotel lot; many people ride a shuttle from Lanai's other 2 hotels
Bar: Full service
Wine selection: Good, especially California wines, many of which are available by the glass
Dress: Casual
Disabled access: Adequate
Customers: Tourists and Islanders

Dinner: Every day, 5:30–9 p.m.

Setting & atmosphere: Two fireplaces create a warm glow on knotty pine walls, oak floors, and a granite-topped bar. Rich floral tapestries in mauve, green, and gold, Island scenes by Lanai artists, and outdoor lanai seating add to the old Hawaii country charm. Diners can watch the chefs and rotisserie action through a display window into the kitchen.

House specialties: The chef/owner, Henry Clay, has ties to the South, so his ragin' Cajun shrimp is only one example of some of the Louisiana-style menu items. The restaurant is recognized for rotisserie chicken and wild game, including venison, quail, rabbit, and duckling, as well as fresh-caught Hawaiian fish. Salads—Caesar or Hawaiian greens with Roma tomatoes, feta cheese, and Maui onions—are a la carte, but meals come with fresh vegetables, rice or potatoes, and French bread.

Other recommendations: For a bit more of the southern flavor, try seafood jalapeño pasta or eggplant Creole. Everything is made from scratch, so you can't miss by sampling the pâté, clam chowder, or pecan pie.

Summary & comments: Lanai visitors often say this is the best dinner value on the island, considering the cost in comparison with the major hotel restaurants.

'IHILANI	★★★★½

Hawaii Regional/Mediterranean	Expensive	QUALITY
		91

	VALUE
Manele Bay Hotel, I Manele Road; (808) 565-7700	C−
Zone 15 Lanai	

Reservations: Highly recommended
When to go: Anytime
Entrée range: $32–40; vegetarian menu, $28–32
Payment: VISA, MC, AMEX, DC, JCB
Service rating: ★★★★★

Parking: Valet
Bar: Full service
Wine selection: Extensive
Dress: Jacket required
Disabled access: Good
Customers: Tourists and visiting Neighbor Islanders

Dinner: Every day, 6–9:30 p.m.

Setting & atmosphere: Fine china, silver, and lace-bedecked tables under hand-blown Italian crystal chandeliers are a lovely backdrop for dining in this formal dining room, which boasts a soothing view of pool and ocean from tables on an upper and lower bank.

House specialties: The chef presents picture-perfect food in entrées such as roasted pheasant breast with foie gras and Madeira truffle sauce, pan-fried veal loin, or sautéed 'opakapaka (snapper) served with ragout of white beans, pancetta, and fresh thyme. Many of the more than a dozen desserts include sweets and truffles made of Big Island–grown Hawaiian Vintage Chocolate. Diners can order an extensive selection of gourmet cheeses from the a la carte menu.

Other recommendations: A nightly degustation menu of six or seven courses can be ordered paired with wines for $95 or sans wines for $65 per person. Prices may change according to what is featured. You might begin with oysters, then sample Maine lobster with shiitake mushrooms, proceed to pan-fried 'ahi, and savor a main course of roasted muscovy duck breast in red wine port sauce with Molokai sweet-potato purée and sautéed endive. Next, a selection of cheeses and walnut bread is served, plus a dessert selection followed by Hawaiian Vintage chocolates and mignardises.

Entertainment & amenities: Classical background music is set at a pleasant listening level.

Summary & comments: This is the kind of dining experience that is more than just grabbing a bite to eat. Expect to take several leisurely hours to do all the courses justice.

Index

Unofficial Guide **Reader Survey**

If you would like to express your opinion about Hawaii or this guide-book, complete the following survey and mail it to:

> *Unofficial Guide* Reader Survey
> P.O. Box 43673
> Birmingham AL 35243

Inclusive dates of your visit: _____

Members of your party:	Person 1	Person 2	Person 3	Person 4	Person 5
Gender:	M F	M F	M F	M F	M F
Age:					

How many times have you been to Hawaii?   _____
On your most recent trip, where did you stay?   _____

Concerning your accommodations, on a scale of 100 as best and 0 as worst, how would you rate:

The quality of your room? _____   The value of your room?   ___
The quietness of your room? _____   Check-in/check-out efficiency?___
Swimming pool facilities?   _____

Did you rent a car? _____ From whom? _____

Concerning your rental car, on a scale of 100 as best and 0 as worst, how would you rate:

Pick-up processing efficiency? ____   Return processing efficiency? ____
Condition of the car?   ____   Cleanliness of the car?   ____
Airport shuttle efficiency?   ____

Concerning your dining experiences:

Including fast food, estimate your meals in restaurants per day: _____
Approximately how much did your party spend on meals per day?_____
Favorite restaurants in Hawaii: _____

_____

Did you buy this guide before leaving? ☐   while on your trip? ☐

How did you hear about this guide? (check all that apply)

Loaned or recommended by a friend ☐   Radio or TV ☐
Newspaper or magazine ☐   Bookstore salesperson ☐
Just picked it out on my own ☐   Library ☐
Internet ☐

Unofficial Guide **Reader Survey (continued)**

What other guidebooks did you use on this trip? _____

_____

_____

_____

On a scale of 100 as best and 0 as worst, how would you rate them?

_____

_____

_____

Using the same scale, how would you rate *The Unofficial Guide(s)?*

_____

Are *Unofficial Guides* readily available at bookstores in your area? _____

Have you used other *Unofficial Guides?* _____

Which one(s)? _____

_____

_____

_____

_____

Comments about your Hawaii trip or *The Unofficial Guide(s):*

_____

_____

_____

_____

_____

_____

_____

_____

_____

_____

_____

_____

_____

✂